U.S. Arms Exports: Policies and Contractors

Paul L. Ferrari
Raúl L. Madrid
Jeff Knopf
IRRC

U.S. Arms Exports:
Policies and Contractors

by

Paul L. Ferrari, Raúl L. Madrid and Jeff Knopf

A book by the
Investor Responsibility Research Center

BALLINGER PUBLISHING COMPANY
Cambridge, Massachusetts
A Subsidiary of Harper & Row, Publishers, Inc.

The Investor Responsibility Research Center compiles and impartially analyzes information on the activities of business in society, on activities of institutional investors, on efforts to influence such activities, and on related public policies. IRRC's work is financed primarily by annual subscription fees paid by some 350 investing institutions for the Social Issues Service, the Corporate Governance Service and the South Africa Review Service. This study is a publication of the Social Issues Service. The Center was founded in 1972 as an independent, not-for-profit corporation. It is governed by a 21-member board of directors who represent subscribing institutions.

This study was prepared by the Investor Responsibility Research Center for educational purposes. While IRRC exercised due care in compiling the information in this study, from time to time errors do occur. IRRC makes no warranty, express or implied, as to the accuracy, completeness or usefulness of this information, nor does it assume any liability with respect to the consequences of the use of this information. Changing circumstances may cause the information to be obsolete.

International Standard Book Number: 0-88730-282-3

Library of Congress Catalog Card Number: 88-24131

Printed in the United States of America

Library of Congress Cataloging-in-Publication Data

Ferrari, Paul L.
  U.S. arms exports.

  "A book by the Investor Responsibility Research Center."
  Bibliography
  Includes index.
  1. Munitions—Government policy—United States. I. Madrid, Raul L.
II. Knopf, Jeff . III. Investor Responsibility Research Center. IV. Title.
HD9743.U6F47   1988   382'.456234'0973   88-24131
ISBN 0-88730-282-3

About the Authors

This report was written by Paul L. Ferrari, a senior analyst, Raúl L. Madrid, a research analyst with the Investor Responsibility Research Center, and Jeff Knopf, a former IRRC research analyst, now a Ph.D. candidate at Stanford University.

Table of Contents

PART III: Orders for U.S. Arms by Region and Country

LIST OF FIGURES

LIST OF TABLES

Acknowledgements

This study would not have been possible without the assistance of a cast of dozens that provided the support of many times its actual number. Stephen Goose and Leslie Parks provided invaluable direction in the early stages of the effort. Kevin Downey, Alex Meerovich, Ann Schonfield and Renee Hill amassed, synthesized and reconciled a tremendous body of data. The authors thank Nell Booth for her contribution to Chapter 6, Hillel Gray for his statistical work throughout, Ken Bertsch for his insightful review of chapter drafts, and Joel Johnson of the American League for Exports and Security Assistance for his thoughtful comments. A note of appreciation goes to Charine Adams; were it not for her patience and stamina, this book would still be swirling about randomly in a sea of electronically coded symbols.

The authors extend a special thanks to Margaret Carroll, the executive director of the Investor Responsibility Research Center, and Carolyn Mathiasen, the director of IRRC's Social Issues Service, for their unwavering support and guidance and invaluable editing. Finally, we thank Carol Franco and Carolyn Casagrande for the Ballinger Publishing Company's commitment to this project.

Needless to say, the interpretation of the data and conclusions contained in this study are those of the authors, as is responsibility for any errors.

Introduction

The subject of the exportation of weapons of war percolates to the surface periodically, indicating that although calm waters might prevail most of the time, heated and active currents move below. In the 1970s, it was the replacement of American troops abroad—primarily in Southeast Asia—with increasingly large shipments of war materiel, and revelations of kickbacks involving U.S. defense contractors and officials of foreign governments, that brought the business of arms exports to the fore. In the 1980s, pitched battles between Congress and the Executive Branch over transfers to certain Arab nations and to insurgent movements fighting against Communist-backed governments and most recently revelations that the Reagan administration covertly sold weapons to Iran and funneled the profits to the Nicaraguan contras, have done the trick.

These recent events, combined with mounting global economic pressures, have set the stage for an impending domestic debate that will touch upon the value of arms exports as an implement of achieving foreign and economic policy objectives, the role of congressional and public oversight and control of weapons transfers, and the U.S. industry's involvement in and dependence on the trade.

Although in most people's eyes the issues connected to the exportation of conventional weapons pale in urgency in comparison with matters of national security such as the superpowers' reliance on weapons of mass destruction, arms export issues by their very nature permeate a larger universe of interrelated questions. Broad foreign policy debates frequently rage around more narrow decisions as to whether the United States should sell military equipment to this or that country. The merits of weapons sales are discussed both for their symbolic and for their actual value. Proponents of selling military equipment to Saudi Arabia and other moderate Arab states, for example, argue that sales are necessary because they confer upon the recipient a military capability to defend itself from hostile adversaries, such as Iran, and display the resolve of the United States to stand by its friends for all to see. They also argue that it is better for the United States rather than someone else to act as supplier because the act of selling military equipment confers a measure of leverage that can be used to restrict or otherwise influence the manner in which the recipient uses the equipment. Finally, the economic benefit to be derived by the suppliers of weapons to these countries is not lost on many domestic audiences, which are quick to point to increased revenues to be had and levels of employment to be sustained. Critics of sales to moderate Arab nations, conversely, worry about the symbolic gesture of support embodied in an arms sale and do not believe the sale is warranted because the countries in question have not gone far enough in the direction of achieving an agreement with

Israel, and they fear that the American equipment being sold now might one day be used against Israel in an armed conflict.

The Investor Responsibility Research Center undertook this study with the realization that the reevaluation of policies that govern actions such as the exportation of armaments reoccur naturally in a democratic political system, largely because the issues involved are complex, they will not disappear with time, and they involve political choices that are somewhat constrained because of the nature of international competition. This volume was designed to illuminate the debate over the exportation of military equipment, and it was prepared to help readers form intelligent judgments. The study's purpose is two-fold. One purpose, covered in Part I, is to provide an overview of the global trade in arms and to look at the range of issues involved in U.S. arms export policy-making. Part I, which includes 11 chapters, is designed to acquaint the reader with the current dimensions of the world arms trade and the most important trends in global military export practices, drawing from existing literature and schools of thought. Chapters 1 and 2 look at the changing face of the arms trade. Chapters 3 and 4 describe the evolution and mechanics of U.S. policy on conventional arms transfers, and Chapters 5 and 7 explore the debates over the positive benefits and negative consequences that different observers attribute to arms sales. Chapters 6 and 8 through 11 examine the current status of global and U.S. arms exports to the different regions of the world.

Part II of this study accomplishes its second purpose, which is to provide a glimpse into the often overlooked dimension of U.S. corporate involvement in the exportation of military equipment and the effects of the trade on the American defense industry. Much has happened to the defense industry since weapons exporters were last scrutinized publicly more than a decade ago amid revelations of bribes and other unethical business practices. The exportation of military equipment now accounts for less of most U.S. defense contractors' business today than it did during the 1970s, but not by choice. Shifting economic and political climates have accounted for the decline. The two variables, however, have not reinforced each other. During the late 1970s, the global demand for arms ran high, as did the funds available to buyers. The receptivity of the U.S. government to requests for the export of military equipment, however, was one characterized by restriction. Conversely, the 1980s have been marked by the loosening of governmental restrictions at the same time that the competitive nature of the market has increased because fewer buyers now possess the funds necessary for purchasing weapons, and more suppliers have emerged. The apparent decline in the importance of arms exports to the U.S. defense industry might well be illusory, however. The early part of the 1980s saw record demands for weapons worldwide and a substantial U.S. military buildup that increased the level of government orders from U.S. defense contractors to a point where they might have overshadowed any absolute increase in orders from abroad.

Nevertheless, U.S. arms exporters will continue to be caught between conflicting influences. The domestic arms buildup of the 1980s has peaked, and the defense industry will be squeezed during the end of the decade by the mounting federal deficit and the Department of Defense's need to pay for the weapons it ordered during the early days of the buildup. This squeeze, in turn, will add to the pressure to market abroad. Current indicators, however, suggest that the international arms market over the short term will continue to be one that favors the purchaser: Low demand and the continued shortage of available capital will accentuate existing competition and give buyers a significant degree of influence over the terms of weapon sales. Domestic political considerations will heighten the dilemma of U.S. arms exporters. At the same time that U.S. arms contractors have begun to cite economic imperatives to support their wish to export military goods more freely, Congress has expressed a desire for closer scrutiny of and control over U.S. arms export policy.

The domestic side of arms exports—as opposed to their implications for American foreign policy—will be scrutinized more closely in the years ahead as the global economic environment continues to worsen and as the United States faces ever-growing economic challenges from its industrialized allies. With this consideration in mind, Part II of the book details for 19 of the largest American arms exporters the military products they sell, the recipients of their goods, and the portion of their business accounted for by military sales abroad. The section also separately profiles eight of these companies' recently acquired subsidiaries. Part III presents a geographically arranged list of orders placed with the 19 companies listed in Part II by foreign governments for military equipment in recent years.

A Note on Methodology

The difficulties involved in getting a firm grasp on the global arms trade and the role the United States plays in it are compounded by problems of evidence and data. Confusion springs from numerous quarters. The publicly available sources of information employ different methodologies for defining and counting military equipment and for tabulating the total size of the worldwide trade in weapons. Sources, for example, define geographic regions differently, and do not agree on which is the more accurate method of compiling the dollar value of weapons exports—constant or current dollars. The sources that prefer presenting constant dollar figures also frequently use different base-line years, compounding the task of comparing data. Nor do all sources agree on what precisely constitutes military equipment. Some studies include "dual-use" equipment—hardware that in most cases are commercially configured but can also have military applications. For these reasons, understanding the methodologies employed by an arms transfer study is important.

Even the most methodologically rigorous of studies is fraught with pitfalls. All sources present data for other nations' arms imports and exports that in many instances are only rough estimates based on scarce and ambiguous material. This is a particular problem with estimates of communist bloc exports and of the imports of some Third World nations, where information is tightly controlled or records kept in an unsystematic or uncomprehensive manner. Readers, therefore, must pay particularly close attention to the methodologies used in any study of the world arms trade and U.S. weapons exports.

IRRC used a variety of publicly available studies for this book, and in every instance it identifies the studies from which the data presented were drawn. The major sources of information on arms transfers are the U.S. Congressional Research Service, the Arms Control and Disarmament Agency of the State Department, the Stockholm International Peace Research Institute—a research center established and funded by the Swedish government—and the Defense Department's Defense Security Assistance Agency, the arm of the Pentagon that oversees and keeps records on U.S. weapons export activities. A brief description of each follows. The order in which the sources are listed in no way suggests that some are inherently more reliable than others.

The Arms Control and Disarmament Agency (ACDA) compendium on arms exports examines all transfers of conventional weapons (i.e., everything except nuclear, chemical or biological weapons), and estimates the "equivalent U.S. dollar value" of actual deliveries on an annual basis. The ACDA publication is the only publicly available document that provides a comprehensive tabulation of total arms imports and exports for every nation. For the United States, ACDA includes commercial weapons sales (direct American company-to-foreign government transactions), but excludes all military services—such as construction, training and technical support—from its count of U.S. arms transfers. This exclusion is significant. For 1982, ACDA reported that such excluded services had a value "of $3.1 billion, an amount equal to 33 percent of the value of counted arms transfers."[1] ACDA, however, included other countries' services, which it said "are of a much smaller magnitude."[2] Many scholars of arms exports, in the words of one, "view this practice as peculiar." The point is made that "an F-15 fighter, for example, is lethal only if it has proper runways, if the pilots have proper training, and if the ground crews have been trained and provided with major technical services."[3] This omission is particularly glaring because ACDA does include military-related training, services and construction equipment in its arms transfer totals for all countries other than the United States. ACDA also differs from other sources in classifying some nations as developed or developing, most notably by counting Greece, Spain, Turkey, Yugoslavia and Bulgaria as developing.

The Congressional Research Service (CRS) bases its findings on data collected by other government agencies, and examines only arms sales to the Third World, which it defines as all countries except NATO and other Western European nations, Warsaw Pact nations, Japan, Australia and New Zealand. In calculating U.S. arms sales, CRS includes grants of military equipment and services and all agreements under the government-to-government Foreign Military Sales (FMS) program, including FMS construction sales. CRS does not include arms sales made through commercial channels, which in the 1980s have accounted for approximately 20 percent of all U.S. arms exports. CRS presents its data in three forms: the value of annual arms agreements, the value of actual arms deliveries per year, and the total number of weapons systems in particular categories that were delivered. CRS appears to use the same register and valuation system for transfers of weapons systems that ACDA employs.

The Stockholm International Peace Research Institute (SIPRI) believes the methods used by U.S. government agencies to calculate transfers may overstate Soviet exports relative to American ones. SIPRI bases its estimates on a slightly narrower set of types of equipment, which it calls "major weapons." These are aircraft, armored vehicles, missiles and warships. Items such as military trucks, unguided rockets and small arms are not included. (The four types of weapons that SIPRI looks at include all the "big ticket" defense items that account for most of the dollar value of arms purchases. Thus, in SIPRI's estimation, the exclusion of "lesser" items is not likely to cause significant divergence of its estimates from other calculations that include these items.) Like ACDA, SIPRI bases its calculations on actual deliveries during the year in reference.

SIPRI seeks to minimize its reliance on data from the U.S. government and, instead, bases its estimates on reports of arms transfers found in about 200 trade journals, daily newspapers, military reference books, and official national and international documents. Once a transfer has been reported in several independent sources, it is entered into SIPRI's data base. This technique means that estimates for a given year are not complete until two to three years later. Following the same practice as ACDA and CRS, SIPRI assigns an estimated value to the equipment transferred rather than using the actual price paid. ACDA and CRS may sometimes use the actual contract amount for Western sales, however. In SIPRI's accounting, the assigned value is based on the system's performance characteristics and similarity to other equipment for which a value was set according to either actual price at the time SIPRI initiated its data base or "ex factory unit cost." U.S. government agencies do not make their accounting technique public, but they appear to estimate what it would cost the Pentagon in U.S. dollars to produce the equipment involved in each transfer.

Data available from the Defense Security Assistance Agency cover Foreign Military Sales, FMS construction and commercial sales agreements, deliveries and the many forms of military assistance extended by the United States to recipients of American arms. The data are for U.S. government fiscal years (which end Sept. 30) and not calendar years. IRRC has used both current and constant dollar figures available from the DSAA, and used the compendium of DSAA data that covers the period through Sept. 30, 1986.

Wherever possible, IRRC presents data and trends from each of these sources. The authors have relied primarily on military deliveries—as opposed to agreements—throughout Part I as the ultimate measure of arms exports. Agreements are used in those instances where future delivery patterns are of direct interest, but readers should realize that because some agreements are never consummated, they constitute a measure of intention and not actual action and should be used only as a rough gauge of arms export activity. IRRC uses the terms "agreements" and "orders" interchangeably. Sections of Part II and all of Part III present data on agreements entered into during the period 1982 through 1986. IRRC has tried to identify and delete from these listings any orders that were placed during this period but were subsequently canceled. Because data on commercial sales are difficult to come by and are not recorded in a systematic manner, the sections of Part II that address U.S. corporations' arms export activities rely primarily on contracts awarded under the auspices of the Foreign Military Sales program. Sales executed under that program currently account for nearly 80 percent of all U.S. military exports.

Because this volume covers issues of U.S. industry's involvement in the exportation of military goods as well as government policies governing the trade of arms, IRRC focuses principally on military hardware and services provided by U.S. contractors, giving less attention to training and other services provided to the recipients of U.S. military assistance and weapons directly by the Department of Defense or other arms of the federal government. Therefore, the charts and figures of U.S. military deliveries presented in this study include deliveries conducted through the Foreign Military Sales (FMS) and Foreign Military Construction Sales (FMCS) programs, the Military Assistance Program (MAP), commercial sales channels, the Military Service Assistance Fund (MASF) and the Excess Military Articles Program. Services provided through the International Military Education and Training (IMET) program have been excluded.

Throughout this volume, IRRC employs definitions of geographic regions that are slightly different from those used in other studies. "Latin America" includes Mexico, Central America, South America and the Caribbean. "Africa" includes the nations of North Africa except for Egypt, which is considered part of the "Middle East." The authors refer to a single "Asia" that includes the nations of East Asia and South Asia. A listing of the exact countries assigned to each of these regions appears at the beginning of each of the Chapters 6 through 9.

IRRC used very specific methodologies in compiling the data presented in Sections II and III of this book, which are described in full in the Notes on Methodology that precede each of the sections.

Footnotes

1. U.S. Department of State, Arms Control and Disarmament Agency (ACDA), *World Military Expenditures and Arms Transfers 1984* (Washington: ACDA, 1984), pp. 82–83.
2. U.S. Department of State, Arms Control and Disarmament Agency (ACDA), *World Military Expenditures and Arms Transfers 1985* (Washington: ACDA, 1985), p. 143.
3. Paul Hammond, David L. Louscher, Michael D. Salomone and Norman A. Graham, *The Reluctant Supplier: U.S. Decisionmaking for Arms Sales* (Cambridge, Mass.: Oelgeschlager, Gunn & Hain, Publishers Inc., 1983), p. 29.

Part I
Arms Exports:
An Overview

Chapter 1
Recent Trends in the Export of Arms

American arms export policy, once influenced principally by moral or political battles, is increasingly dominated by economic pressures. Economic factors abroad began to obstruct U.S. arms exports in the mid-1980s when declining oil revenues among oil exporting nations and the debt crisis significantly reduced the demand for arms in the Third World, and the trend appears to be accelerating.

While the worldwide demand for arms has lessened, competition among suppliers has intensified, creating a tight world arms market dominated by commercial considerations. Both the traditional Western European exporters and emerging Third World suppliers have stepped up their arms export efforts in the 1980s, seeking to gain foreign exchange and reduce the cost of domestic weapons production by achieving economies of scale. These factors should continue to hinder U.S. sales abroad, at least in the short-term.

While economic conditions abroad will inhibit U.S. arms exports, economic pressures at home should encourage them. Growing domestic defense budget constraints will make the Defense Department and the American defense industry even more eager to sell abroad, while concern about the mounting trade deficit will bolster the arguments of proponents of U.S. arms exports within both Congress and the administration.

These conflicting currents will vie to determine the extent of U.S. arms exports in the years ahead. The outcome is crucial not solely to the American defense industry, but, as considered in the ensuing chapters, to the direction of American foreign policy as a whole.

A Declining World Arms Market

Worldwide arms sales have declined considerably in recent years. This trend is unmistakable, whether measured in deliveries or agreements, by government or non-government sources. Reduced arms imports by the Third World are responsible for the decline; arms imports by the industrialized countries have remained steady, or even increased. The U.S. State Department's Arms Control and Disarmament Agency records the value of arms deliveries to the Third World as falling to $21.7 billion in 1985, the lowest total in real terms since 1978. The Stockholm International Peace Research Institute (SIPRI), an independent institute for research sponsored by the Swedish

Parliament, and the Congressional Research Service (CRS), the research arm of the U.S. Congress, similarly report the lowest Third World arms import totals in recent years in both 1985 and 1986. Moreover, the current low level of arms agreements—in 1986, agreements by developing nations to purchase arms fell to $29.2 billion, the lowest total in real terms since the early 1970s—means that the actual deliveries of arms will continue to be low for several years.[1]

While a decline in worldwide arms transfers cannot be denied, the extent of this decline cannot be documented with precision. Structural changes in the arms market have made cataloguing and counting weapons transactions more difficult, which in turn obscures the full value of a trade. Traditionally, arms transactions involved exchanging finished end products, such as fighter aircraft or tanks for cash or credit. Weapons deals, however, increasingly involve technology transfer or some type of offset arrangement that complicate efforts to determine the value of any transaction (offsets are sale arrangements whereby the seller agrees to compensate the buyer by making reciprocal purchases, often of components used in the weapon system that is being sold—see box on pp. 144–145). SIPRI also points out that there is an "increasing flow to recipient countries of weapons-related items, such as spare parts, components,upgrading and modification kits, and so on . . . which are omitted from SIPRI's and most other estimates of the size of the global arms trade."[2] Some analysts also cite the growth in the black market arms trade, now estimated as high as $9 billion per year, the majority of which is not recorded by the primary sources for arms trade statistics.[3]

In spite of these mitigating factors, a significant decline in arms transfers to the Third World has taken place. The reasons for this downturn are not in general to be found in international political developments. No international agreements for limiting the conventional arms trade have been signed, nor have tensions in any of the world's regional hot spots been defused by new political developments. Instead, the decline in Third World arms transactions has its primary causes in economic factors. Heavy debt burdens, continued low prices for raw materials and the recent oil glut have prevented many Third World countries from buying arms abroad. As a representative of an American arms exporting company put it, "We're all down now to nibbling crumbs . . . The damn oil boom has gone, and there's not much money around anymore. The world in general is bankrupt."[4]

By most accounts, the debt crisis has worsened since 1982, when Mexico first announced that it could no longer service its debt. Total Third World debt now exceeds $1 trillion, and commercial banks have set aside huge loan-loss reserves, expecting that much of the debt will never be repaid. Third World debtor countries have been forced to reduce formerly extravagant arms imports and pursue policies of fiscal austerity. Thus, arms imports by the Third World's 10 largest debtor nations declined 15 percent from the period 1980–82 to the period 1983–85.[5] Peru, for example, canceled part of its order for French Mirage aircraft, while Argentina canceled the remainder of its German submarine orders and asked for permission to resell the submarines it had already purchased. Other debtor countries have honored existing arms agreements but have reduced their involvement in new ones. In Latin America, where most of the large debtors are located, arms agreements with Western countries declined from $6.3 billion between 1979 and 1982 to $3.8 billion between 1983 and 1986.[6] Although arms agreements with the Soviet Union increased during this period, these consisted principally of subsidized arms transfer agreements.

A more important economic factor in the decline of Third World arms imports is the drop in the price of oil. From 1973 on, OPEC nations have accounted for a large portion of Third World arms imports (approximately 40 percent in the 1980s), as their oil wealth has enabled them to afford costly weapons. The decline in the price of oil that occurred in the mid-1980s, however, caused oil revenues among OPEC nations to drop from $280 billion in 1981 to $80 billion in 1986, creating widespread recession among oil-exporters. Forced to tighten their budgets, they slashed their arms imports. OPEC nations were responsible for $8.5 billion of the $11.6 billion drop in Third World arms imports between 1984 and 1985, according to the Arms Control and Disarmament Agency.[7] Financial constraints also have forced the oil exporters to postpone purchases temporarily or lengthen the terms of their payments. Saudi Arabia, for example, renegotiated the terms of its enormous Tornado/Hawk/PC-9 aircraft purchase from Great Britain in 1986.[8]

The oil glut also has affected arms imports by countries dependent on OPEC nations—especially Saudi Arabia—for financial assistance. In 1986, financial considerations led Oman to postpone the receipt of eight British Tornado fighters that were on order.[9] Similarly, Jordan's search for an advanced fighter to replace its French Mirage F-1s is reportedly on hold because "Saudi Arabia has not responded to a Jordanian request to finance such a deal," according to one diplomat.[10] Partly for financial reasons, Saudi Arabia is reportedly reluctant to continue assisting Syria in its tremendous weapons buildup as well.

Finally, the decline of oil prices has affected arms imports by all nations because of the resultant tightening of credit. In the late 1970s, loans were much more easily available to developing nations, partly because of the need to recycle enormous oil revenues. Developing nations used the credit to finance arms imports (among other purchases) during the massive borrowing spree of the 1970s. With the credit available to the Third World now sharply curtailed, the ability of developing nations to import arms has been constrained.[11]

Another factor in the decline of the world arms trade has been the growth in indigenous Third World arms industries. Many Third World countries are now fulfilling much of their defense needs through domestic production. SIPRI reports that the ratio of Third World arms production to Third World arms imports rose steadily in the 1980s after a brief decline in the late 1970s, and currently stands at approximately .12.[12]

In 1986, 54 developing nations manufactured some type of military equipment, according to SIPRI. Most Third World arms production consists of the manufacture of relatively simple ammunition, small arms or boats. However, a growing number of nations—19 as of 1984—have reached the point where they can produce advanced weapon systems such as aircraft, armored vehicles or missiles and can therefore satisfy much of their weaponry needs without imports. The value of major weapon systems production in the Third World increased 37 percent from the late 1970s to the early 1980s, according to SIPRI figures.[13] This number will no doubt grow as developing nations build their industrial bases and seek to reduce their external dependence and drains on foreign exchange.

Some analysts furthermore maintain that Third World arms imports were destined to decline after the massive purchasing binge that took place during the late 1970s and early 1980s. Michael Klare, who studied arms transfers for 10 years at the Institute for Policy Studies, describes this phenomenon:

> As the large quantities of sophisticated weapons ordered in the 1977–82 period began arriving in these nations' arsenals, their military forces have had to be retrained in order

to operate, maintain and repair all of these new (and largely unfamiliar) systems. This process can take several years—especially in those LDCs [less-developed countries] which have not previously had much experience with high-tech military gear—and thus temporarily inhibit the demand for new arms.[14]

The problem of absorption may be secondary to the problem of saturation, however. As two long term followers of the arms trade succinctly put it, "military arsenals in many countries are full."[15] Most developing nations that could afford to fulfilled their primary military needs—namely, high-profile fighter aircraft—during the peak years of the arms trade. One defense industry executive maintains that "this binge that we went through in '60s and '70s has equipped most of the world with modern airplanes."[16] Recent orders for American combat aircraft bear this out—in both 1985 and 1986, agreements for the sale of U.S. combat aircraft totaled less than $700 million, whereas they had exceeded $4 billion in each of the three previous years. The drop in orders for combat aircraft accounted for much of the total decrease in U.S. arms agreements in these years.[17]

The question of saturation has a greater long term implication for the world arms trade than the question of absorption. Whereas Third World militaries would be expected to absorb the new military equipment within the next couple of years, many Third World nations may not see the need to modernize their air forces again for at least a decade.

Increased Competition Between Suppliers

While the worldwide demand for arms has been shrinking in recent years, the worldwide supply has been rising. New Third World suppliers have entered the international marketplace, and many of the existing industrialized country suppliers have loosened their export controls and stepped up their marketing efforts. The result has been an increasingly competitive international arms market, and a phenomenon that analysts identify as the "commercialization" of the arms trade. In order to win contracts, nearly all suppliers have been offering some of their most sophisticated equipment along with extensive technology sharing and logistics support, cut-rate financing, and offset arrangements that sometimes exceed the purchase price. Suppliers also have been increasingly willing to sell to any nation, with the result that nations widely censored for human rights violations or engaged in protracted wars have had relatively little trouble obtaining sophisticated weaponry. Similarly, political or ideological differences among sovereign nations have not prevented arms transactions between them.

New suppliers: Both the quantity of military equipment exported by the developing nations and the number of Third World countries exporting arms increased dramatically in the 1970s and 1980s. Major suppliers such as Israel and Brazil have emerged from the ranks of the developing nations and now compete with industrialized countries for sales of all but the most sophisticated weapon systems. Meanwhile, a host of minor suppliers are beginning to compete with more established ones in the world market for small arms and other low-technology equipment. According to ACDA figures, arms exports by developing nations (excluding the People's Republic of China) exceeded $200 million for the first time in 1975, when they reached $500 million (in 1983 constant dollars). They then soared to $1.2 billion in 1979 and have averaged approximately $2 billion in the 1980s. SIPRI reports that Third World arms exports quadrupled from 1975 to 1979, before leveling off at a 20 percent higher level in the 1980s.[18]

Third World arms have been widely purchased for a number of reasons. The low labor costs associated with Third World arms production and the relative simplicity of much of the equipment produced have enabled the Third World arms exporters to underbid the industrialized countries in many instances. Moreover, many nations have preferred to purchase arms from developing nations in order to avoid dependence or the appearance of dependence on the superpowers. These nations also have been glad to avoid the quid-pro-quo requests for access to military facilities or prohibitions on the use or resale of the equipment that frequently accompany arms transactions with the superpowers. Arms produced by Third World industries are also often more geared to the needs and conditions of the developing nations. The low maintenance requirements of Brazilian armored vehicles and their suitability for dusty terrain have been among their principal selling points. Finally, Third World exporters have found markets by selling to countries with which other nations are reluctant to do business.

The Third World arms export industry, outside of the People's Republic of China, did not begin to develop until the early 1970s. Although Third World arms exports had occurred earlier, these were for the most part re-transfers of equipment that had been imported previously from industrialized nations. With the growth of indigenous arms industries in many developing countries, weapons exports became possible. The movement on the part of Third World countries to export arms was based largely on economic considerations. Developing nations sought to gain precious foreign exchange and recoup or spread out research and development and production costs. Rarely were political motives, such as the desire to gain influence in the recipient nations, a significant factor in the decision-making. Political considerations, however, had played a large part in the earlier decisions to develop indigenous arms industries.

Israel and Brazil are the developing nations that have gained the largest slice of the world arms market in recent years, and both have followed the traditional path of a Third World arms exporter. They developed their arms export industries in the late 1970s and substantially increased their exports in the 1980s. They also export military equipment for economic reasons and have sold arms abroad largely without restrictions.

Israel, which exports ships, aircraft, combat vehicles and missile systems, often has had difficulties finding purchasers for its weapons because of its poor relations with most of the developing world. As a result, its exports frequently have gone to other pariah nations such as South Africa, Taiwan, Guatemala and Iran. Israel, more than most Third World countries, has sought to build allies on its own periphery and to reduce its isolation in the international community through the exportation of military equipment. Nevertheless, economic considerations are paramount, and Israel has sought to gain foreign exchange and to reduce military expenditures by lowering the unit costs of its production for domestic needs. The latter need is inordinately strong in Israel because of the large scale of Israel's domestic arms production and the country's tremendous military burden, which is estimated at more than 25 percent of its gross national product. The ACDA estimates that the value of Israel's military exports grew by nearly 570 percent from the mid 1970s to the mid 1980s; they totaled $240 million for the period 1973 to 1977 and $1.36 billion from 1981 through 1985.

In the space of 10 years, Brazil has become one of the world's leading arms exporters. Its arms industry now employs some 100,000 workers dispersed among 350 companies. More than half of the companies are privately owned, and all are regulated and coordinated by a state research and planning agency known as Industria de Material Belico de Brasil (Imbel).

Before 1977, Brazil enjoyed an orthodox relationship with the United States with regard to arms purchases but also received military equipment from European suppliers. In 1977 Brazil abrogated a 25-year-old military assistance treaty with the United States to protest President Carter's criticism of Brazilian human rights violations and rejected further American military credits. The need to replace aging weapons, combined with the rising price of oil in the late 1970s, gave Brazil a powerful incentive to build up its own arms industry in order to gain revenue through sales abroad and to prevent future dependence on foreign arms suppliers. Brazil accomplished this largely by securing licensed production agreements, which gave it the necessary production technology and know how.

Eighty percent of the Brazilian military's needs today are filled by indigenous production, and the ACDA estimates the average annual value of foreign sales for the 1980s at $220 million, although one estimate that most likely included the value of agreements entered into that year placed Brazil's 1984 exports as high as $2.4 billion.[19] Brazil exports at least 80 percent of its arms production. The strategy of mass export has contributed to the country's continuing trade surpluses.

Imbel's active pursuit of contracts and its indiscriminate sales policy have made Brazil popular with Third World customers. Like Israel, Brazil is willing to sell military equipment to almost anyone wishing to buy it. For the Brazilians, the arms trade is a matter of business: Arms sales are unencumbered by preconditions and other political strings. Brazil eschews control over resale of its equipment by not requiring buyers to sign an "end users certificate" stipulating that recipients of arms cannot resell the weapons without the supplier nation's prior consent. Brazil sees this certificate, which is always required by the United States, as representing unwarranted interference in the affairs of other states.

Brazil's most widely exported military products have been the armored personnel carriers and armored trucks. It has also sold light tanks, rockets, missiles and flight trainers to African, Asian and Latin American clients, and it is working on a subsonic jet fighter with Italy. Brazil's products have caught the attention of developed nations as well: France and Britain have bought its turbojet trainers, and the United States reportedly is considering the Urutu and Cascavel for its Middle East-based Central Command forces, formerly the Rapid Deployment Force.

The success Israel and Brazil have had exporting arms has encouraged other Third World nations to develop arms export industries. (See Table 1–1.) A number of small exporters such as Chile, Peru, Nigeria and Malaysia have recently emerged in the international arms market, while other countries such as Egypt are renewing earlier efforts to gain export earnings. One exception to this general trend is India. Although it is the largest Third World arms producer next to China, India exports relatively few weapons because of such factors as its own weapon demands, restrictions on its licensed production programs, and New Delhi's desire to maintain a non-aligned diplomatic position.

The largest Third World arms exporter, the People's Republic of China, has followed a somewhat separate path from other Third World exporters. China's arms industries developed many years before those of other developing nations, and its arms exports began in the early 1960s. Between 1964 and 1973, Chinese arms exports totaled more than $1.6 billion while those of other developing nations were negligible.[20] During the 1960s and early 1970s, specific political motives fueled China's arms sales—the desire to support like-minded Third World liberation movements, gain influence in fledgling nations and bolster allies against a shared adversary.

Table 1–1

Leading Third World Arms Exporters, FY 1982–1985
(in millions)

	ACDA (current dollars)			SIPRI (constant 1985 dollars)	
1.	China (Mainland)	$4,950	1.	China (Mainland)	$3,695
2.	South Korea#	$1,895	2.	Israel	$1,105
3.	North Korea#	$1,530	3.	Brazil	$1,087
4.	Israel	$1,010	4.	Egypt#	$ 618
5.	Brazil	$1,010	5.	Jordan*	$ 384
6.	Pakistan**	$ 650	6.	Libya*	$ 372
7.	Egypt#	$ 620	7.	South Korea#	$ 275
8.	Libya*	$ 430	8.	Syria*	$ 158
9.	Syria*	$ 160	9.	Singapore	$ 96
10.	Cuba*	$ 70	10.	North Korea#	$ 92

*	These arms exports consist almost entirely of re-transfers of military equipment originally imported from industrialized nations.
#	These arms exports consist mostly of re-transfers of military equipment originally imported from industrialized nations.
**	Pakistan's arms exports consist almost entirely of exported military manpower.
Source:	U.S. Arms Control and Disarmament Agency (ACDA), *World Military Expenditures and Arms Transfers* 1986 edition (Washington: ACDA, 1986), and Stockholm International Peace Research Institute (SIPRI), *World Armaments and Disarmament Yearbook* 1987 edition (New York: Oxford University Press, 1987)

In recent years, Chinese arms export policy and practice have more closely paralleled those of other developing nations. Political motives for arms sales appear to have been subordinated gradually to economic considerations. China has shown a willingness to sell arms to almost any country, as exemplified by its massive arms transfers to both Iran and Iraq. The PRC has used this open policy, along with the other advantages Third World arms suppliers enjoy, to boost its weapon sales dramatically in the 1980s. The U.S. Arms Control and Disarmament Agency reports that China's arms exports quadrupled from 1976–80 to 1981–85, and SIPRI also records a large increase in China's exports during this period.[21]

Intensified competition: In recent years, the increased commercialization of the arms trade has been apparent in Europe as well, creating even stiffer competition for American arms exporters. European governments have on the whole loosened their restrictions governing arms exports in the 1980s, permitting sales to previously embargoed countries and allowing the transfer of some of the most advanced weapon systems and technology in their arsenals. European companies have stepped up their international marketing efforts, offering favorable financial packages and extensive technology transfer arrangements in order to win orders. As a result of these efforts, the three largest European suppliers significantly increased their total arms exports and their share of the worldwide arms market in the 1980s. The U.S. Arms Control and Disarmament Agency reports that arms exports by France, Great Britain and West Germany accounted for 19.1 percent of worldwide arms transfers between 1980 and 1985, as opposed to only 15.2 percent between 1974 and 1979. (See Figure 1–1.) The recent decline in the worldwide demand for arms has caused European exports to fall, but the European suppliers have tenaciously held onto their market share.[22]

European defense industries always have had more incentive to export than their American counterparts. The small size of European defense budgets as compared with that of the United States has encouraged exports as a means of reducing unit costs. European countries producing military aircraft exclusively for domestic use were likely to limit production to several hundred planes at most, whereas the United States air forces would frequently require 1,000 aircraft. While the difference in unit cost is relatively small if 2,000 planes are manufactured instead of 1,000, the unit cost difference is substantial if 1,000 aircraft are produced instead of 200. Thus, by spreading out production costs and recouping research and development expenditures, European defense companies and defense ministries benefit significantly. (Defense ministries are allowed to make downward contract adjustments based on cost savings gained through exports). The French claim that without export orders maintaining aircraft production at Dassault-Breguet would be impossible.

Because exports are so crucial to European arms industries, European defense companies traditionally have pursued international sales more vigorously than their American counterparts. European companies have aggressively marketed their equipment in foreign nations through advertising, exhibitions and employment of foreign representatives, and have been willing to offer numerous concessions in order to win contracts. European governments have supported these efforts through defense marketing organizations, diplomatic pressure and financing programs, and also have facilitated exports by adopting relatively permissive arms transfer policies. As a result, European countries have been able to export a much larger portion of their weapons production than the United States. SIPRI estimated that in 1984 the four largest European suppliers were able to export approximately 45 percent of their total weapons production.[23] This compares with estimates of between 5 and 20 percent for the United States. Major European defense companies such as Thomson-Simtra and Aerospatiale of France annually export more than 70 percent of their total weapons production, an unheard of export-dependence for an American defense corporation.[24]

France: In the 1980s, French arms export policy has been characterized on the whole by a further relaxation of restraints, despite initial indications that Socialist French President Francois Mitterand might clamp down on sales to many countries. This relaxation has combined with France's traditionally active arms sales lobby and loose restrictions to enable France to make a large dent into the world arms market. According to the Arms Control and Disarmament Agency, France has captured more than 10 percent of the international arms market in the 1980s, up from less than 7 percent in the late 1970s. SIPRI similarly reports that France's share of the world arms trade has risen considerably in the 1980s, reaching a 14.9 share from 10.8 percent in the late 1970s.[25]

From the beginning, French arms exports have been driven by economic considerations. Since World War II, successive French governments have agreed on the necessity of maintaining an autonomous French arms industry capable of manufacturing almost all types of military equipment. This plan, however, clashed with the realities of French military requirements and economic

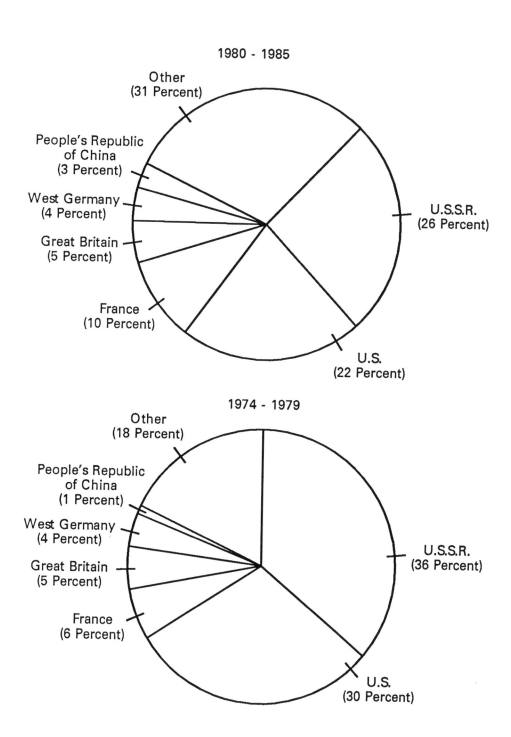

Figure 1–1. Suppliers' Share of Worldwide Arms Deliveries

resources. In his detailed study of French arms exports, Edward Kolodziej of the University of Illinois explains the nature of this dilemma:

> The decision to maintain a military-industrial complex to meet France's security needs implies a major commitment of economic resources which is not easily shouldered by a middle-range power. The ability of the French economy to maintain such a complex industrial system at full employment is limited. On the other hand, for many weapons and weapon systems France's productive capacity exceeds the military requirements of its armed services.[26]

Arms exports have been viewed as the logical way out of this dilemma. Through the production of weapons for export, France has been able to recoup research and development costs and pass on some of its capital expenditures.

But French arms exports have gradually come to represent more than simply a means to sustain a large domestic arms industry. As export revenues rose and companies and labor forces became dependent on the French arms trade, military exports came to be viewed as essential to the economic well-being of France. This perspective began to take shape under the Pompidou administration and was encouraged by the quadrupling of oil prices during the Yom Kippur war. Before Pompidou the French government had undertaken arms sales with some restraint—arms sales to many Middle Eastern nations, for example, were largely banned shortly before the 1967 Six-Day War. But beginning in 1969 the new economic imperatives led to an increasingly laissez-faire policy. Pompidou's defense minister, Michael Debre, actually undertook a major campaign to increase arms sales that led French arms exports to triple between 1969 and 1972.[27]

This drive accelerated under President Valery Giscard d'Estaing as France sought to counter the financial burden of drastically increased oil prices.[28] Under Giscard France exhibited an increased willingness to sell to any nation, exemplified by its August 1974 decision to end the arms embargo to Middle Eastern nations. At the same time, Giscard increased French promotion of armament exhibitions and created an office to provide logistic support to purchasers of French weapon systems.[29]

French arms sales almost doubled in real terms under Giscard's administration as the French industry shifted its focus from the industrialized to the developing world. French arms proved popular with many developing nations, because buying them freed them from the stigma associated with arms transfer relationships with the superpowers. The lifting of the Middle East embargo also opened up an enormous market in the Middle East, where many nations were beginning to embark upon large military buildups. France also found a natural market for its arms in many of its former colonies, with which it had retained close military and economic relationships.

The 1981 election to the presidency of the socialist candidate, Francois Mitterand, created considerable fear within the French arms industry that arms sales would be curtailed. In its statement of principles, Mitterand's coalition government had declared that sales to "colonialist, racist or fascist" governments would be stopped, a declaration that Mitterand's original Defense Minister, Charles Hernu, echoed when he assumed office.[30] Mitterand's Foreign Minister, Claude Cheysson, went somewhat further, stating that the embargo would include repressive and militarily aggressive governments as well as nations currently at war, while Socialist Prime Minister Pierre Mauroy stated only that "French policy aims for peace and detente. Our country will, therefore, try worldwide to curtail and moralize arms exports."[31]

Any fears that French arms sales would be reined in were quickly dispelled by Mitterand's actions in the months following his accession to power. Mitterand's government immediately announced that all existing arms contracts would be honored, the most important of which were $4 billion in orders from Saudi Arabia.[32] Although Chile's order of armored vehicles was canceled on the grounds that they could be used to repress the population, other controversial sales such as the transfer of patrol boats to Argentina and missile-launching ships to Iran went forward as planned.[33]

In many ways, French arms export policy loosened in the following years. Mitterand lifted a ban on the delivery of Mirage fighters, helicopters and patrol boats to Libya that Giscard had imposed because of Qadaffi's intervention in Chad.[34] Mitterand also reinstated arms sales to Argentina shortly after the Falklands/Malvinas war despite British protests, and sold 7,000 air-to-surface missiles to Nicaragua over U.S. objections.[35] Most significant, however, have been the Mitterand government's sales of military equipment to Iraq. Despite earlier pledges to ban arms exports to nations involved in conflicts, France's arms sales to Iraq skyrocketed from $430 million between 1974 and 1978 to $5.3 billion between 1981 and 1985.[36]

This shift has been accompanied by a number of steps Mitterand's government has taken to promote the sale of military equipment abroad. In order to win sales, it has cleared for release the most advanced arms technology it possesses. Indonesia was offered unprecedented design and engineering support and technology on a par with that being used in France's planned Rafale fighter in an attempt to secure a cooperation agreement for development of an indigenous Indonesian fighter.[37] The Mitterand government's sensitivity to the export market is such that export potential is affecting the development of French weapon systems to an unparalleled extent. The current French Defense Minister has said that "the defense ministry should not be forcing industry to make a product that does not interest other countries or is not competitive—unless there is a specific reason for it. Therefore, I plan to examine each program to see whether it is well-suited for export in face of the competition."[38] Joint arms production efforts with European neighbors are also being increasingly pursued, partially with the intention of increasing export potential and securing natural export markets among the other participants.

Great Britain: Great Britain has similarly increased its arms export efforts in the 1980s, but until recently, with few results. SIPRI figures show a slight decline in Great Britain's share of the worldwide arms market between the 1970s and the 1980s. While the U.S. Arms Control and Disarmament Agency records a small increase in Great Britain's share from the period 1974–79 to the period 1980–85, ACDA figures show that its share declined steadily beginning in 1982.[39]

In 1985 and 1986, however, British arms transfer agreements rose dramatically, which will translate into elevated levels of arms deliveries in the coming years. Fiscal 1985 in particular was a record year for Britain, as it surpassed both France and the United States in exports to the Third World largely because of the Tornado sale to Saudi Arabia. (See box p. 21.) British arms transfer agreements should be high in 1987 as well, because of a $1 billion agreement to provide three naval frigates to Pakistan. This new-found success is largely the result of a concerted effort on the part of the British government and defense companies to push arms sales.[40]

In the immediate post World War II era, the British were the second largest arms exporters in the world after the United States. As Great Britain ceased to be a world power, however, so too did it decline as a leading arms exporter. In the 1970s, it ceased even to be the leading European supplier as French arms exports eclipsed those of the British. Although British arms exports had increased steadily during the 1960s and 1970s, the country lacked France's determination to maintain an independent arms industry. Great Britain was and continues to be more willing to purchase American weapons than France, and less willing to invest enormous amounts of money in its own arms industry. The British also have tended to be more restrained about arms sales than the French, and they have failed to maintain the close military and economic relationships with former colonies that have facilitated French arms exports in many instances.

Nevertheless, British companies and the Ministry of Defence have aggressively pursued the sale of arms abroad. In the last decade and a half, this has been done principally for the same economic reasons that characterize exports of other European nations. Political considerations were important in the 1940s, 1950s and early 1960s as the British sought to maintain influence in their former colonies. More recently, political considerations have figured in arms exports to the People's Republic of China as the British sought to solidify ties and trade relationships there, but this has been the exception rather than the rule.[41] The British have relatively few restrictions governing arms exports, and, according to one scholar, "the government has tended to permit sales unless adequate justification for disallowing the sale is provided."[42] Moreover, British arms transfers and arms transfer policy have been traditionally cloaked in secrecy, which has inhibited calls for restraint.

The British government does have an official policy of not selling weapons to countries engaged in wars, however. Restrictions also have been placed on a few countries such as Chile and South Africa because of human rights considerations, although in both of these instances some arms sales have continued to these nations with or without government knowledge. Further restrictions have varied from administration to administration, with Labor governments tending to be slightly more restrictive than Conservative administrations, but in no instances have restraints been far-reaching.

Upon the ascendance of Prime Minister Margaret Thatcher's Conservative government in 1979, the British initiated a comprehensive program to boost their arms exports. According to one British analyst, Thatcher's former Minister of Defense, Michael Heseltine, had "a whole new view for the United Kingdom. He's really wanting the United Kingdom to be a world-beater" in the production and export of arms.[43] These policies have continued under the current Defense Minister, George Younger, and restraints on sales to certain countries have been relaxed. Approximately $270 million in military equipment was sold to Iran and Iraq between 1981 and 1985, despite prohibitions on weapons sales to nations embroiled in conflict. Recently, the British government approved sales that included air-defense radar systems to Iran and a naval destroyer to Chile.

The British also have made efforts to reduce arms purchases from the United States and to increase cooperation among European countries in arms production in order to build military equipment that is available for export. The Tornado fighter, for example, is a joint production effort by Britain, West Germany and Italy, and a similar consortium that includes Spain has been created to develop an advanced fighter for the 1990s. The British also have tried to adapt weapon systems to suit Third World conditions—such as the RO-2000 series armored vehicle, which was designed to be made and ovehauled by an underdeveloped country.[44]

In addition, the British government has become more involved in facilitating sales. In 1986, it established a Defence Export Services Organization office in Malaysia, adding to the ones opened earlier in India, Saudi Arabia and the United States.[45] These offices provide a variety of services in support of British arms sales to the host nation. The British government also has increased its efforts to export arms through advertising and personal lobbying by government figures. According to one analyst, "In the last year or so, [Prime Minister Thatcher] has been lobbying for everything she can get, and that hasn't been the case before." Prime Minister Thatcher's lobbying reportedly played a key role in the massive Tornado sale to Saudi Arabia from which British companies stand to gain $3.8 billion. Similarly, the British government has begun to finance more arms deals, such as the recent sale of helicopters to India and aircraft parts to Brazil.[46] To complete the helicopter sale, Great Britain is lending India $94 million, 95 percent of the cost of the 21 Westland helicopters.[47]

West Germany: In recent years, West Germany also has relaxed its arms export policy significantly, which has led to an expansion of German arms exports. The Stockholm Peace Research Institute records a doubling in West Germany's share of the Third World arms market, from 1.7 percent between 1977 and 1981 to 3.9 percent for the period 1982–1986, while the Arms Control and Disarmament Agency shows a somewhat smaller increase during roughly the same period.

West Germany's arms export policy remains considerably more restrictive than those of most other Western European countries. As a result of controversy provoked by revelation of secret German military assistance to Israel and the illegal re-transfer of German combat aircraft to India and Pakistan, West Germany established strict "political principles" in 1971 that governed military transfers. These principles required end-user certificates to prevent the re-transfer of German equipment without Bonn's approval, banned arms sales to "areas of international tension," and expressed strong opposition to arms sales to non-Western countries. The government resisted passing specific laws on arms transfers, however, and documents later revealed that the German government had secretly signed a treaty with France, giving it "free rein over exports of jointly produced weapons."[48] Moreover, Bonn consistently interpreted the "political principles" in a loose fashion with regard to exports of equipment it had produced alone. Between 1973 and 1982, approximately 70 percent of West Germany's $8 billion in arms exports were made to non-Western countries, including countries such as Pakistan, Argentina and Egypt that were embroiled in regional conflicts.

While the "political principles" failed to halt a great deal of West German arms traffic, they did inhibit arms exports somewhat. In 1982, however, Bonn took steps to eliminate these restrictions formally. Chancellor Helmut Schmidt's government redrafted the principles, omitting the stipulation that arms would not be exported to areas of international tension and stating instead that arms exports were to be contingent on the "vital interests" of the Federal Republic of Germany. This new policy has been retained under Chancellor Herbert Kohl.

Under the new policy, West Germany has subordinated foreign policy concerns to economic interests even further.[49] Chancellor Kohl's government, for example, reversed earlier denials of licenses to export military equipment to Malaysia and Egypt.[50] Despite the relaxation of restraints, West Germany's arms transfer policy remains considerably more restrictive than those of the other major European suppliers. Although no formal policy has been invoked to bar a huge proposed sale of Leopard II tanks and electronic surveillance systems to Saudi Arabia, bureaucratic impediments and widespread opposition to the sale amidst the German government have effectively canceled the deal. These continued restrictions are a significant factor in the low level of arms transfer agreements made by West Germany in recent years.

Other European suppliers: A number of smaller European suppliers also have intensified the competition in the world arms market in recent years. Italian arms exports account for the majority of exports of the smaller European suppliers, and some sources believe Italy has now surpassed West Germany as the third largest European arms supplier. Italian exports approximately doubled between the 1970s and the 1980s, although they have subsided in recent years. Arms exports by the smaller NATO nations also registered dramatic increases throughout the late 1970s and early 1980s. These jumped from $1.9 billion between 1974 and 1977 to $3.1 billion between 1978 and 1981, before reaching $4.6 billion for the period 1982–1985, according to ACDA figures. Arms exports by Spain have led this upward push. They totaled more than $2.2 billion between 1982 and 1985, as opposed to only $270 million between 1978 and 1981, according to the ACDA.[51] Spain's largest deal to date was a $1 billion agreement in 1982 to supply Egypt with trucks and combat vehicles.[52]

The arms export policies of these smaller European countries are almost entirely governed by economic considerations, and therefore, their arms exports for the most part are relatively unrestrained. This has been a key factor in the growth of their arms exports, as they have made inroads into markets that the United States and some other larger suppliers have been reluctant to approach. In addition, the smaller European suppliers, like their Third World counterparts, have achieved success because their equipment is inexpensive, easy to operate and requires little maintenance, and because they do not restrict re-sale of the equipment or demand political or military privileges. The overwhelming majority of these countries' exports go to the Third World, as most of their equipment is not sophisticated enough to be of value to the industrialized countries.

Competing Pressures on American Arms Exports

The decline in Third World demand for arms alongside the rise in competition has created a tight international arms market where suppliers battle fiercely simply to maintain sales levels. In this sense, the United States has acted very much like the other suppliers in the 1980s. For both ideological and commercial reasons, the Reagan administration and American arms-exporting companies have increased their own efforts to sell arms abroad. The U.S. government has loosened its arms export regulations, and U.S. companies have sweetened their contract offers. Both have taken steps to improve the infrastructure that supports U.S. arms sales and have increased their promotion of American arms worldwide.

In the coming years, additional factors such as a declining domestic defense budget and a growing trade deficit should add considerable impetus to efforts to sell abroad. At the same time, however, other pressures such as a growing congressional drive to control arms transfers and a movement to reduce military assistance in the wake of mounting American budget deficits will magnify the difficulties of attempting to expand U.S. military exports in a tight international market. These conflicting pressures will vie to determine the nature and extent of American arms exports in the years to come.

Reagan administration policy: The Reagan administration has brought an increased permissiveness to the conduct of U.S. arms transfers, making it clear from the outset that it views arms transfers in an entirely different light than its predecessor. It sees them as an "essential tool" rather than an "exceptional instrument" of foreign policy. The Reagan administration has deemphasized the potential of arms transfers to threaten regional stability in favor of an emphasis on their ability to "foster regional and internal stability." It has largely abandoned the use of arms transfer restrictions to censor human rights violators, and now ostensibly uses arms transfers to repressive governments as a means to retain the leverage necessary to promote human rights through quiet diplomacy.

This reorientation in viewpoint has been noticeable in the conduct of arms transfers to specific nations such as Taiwan, South Korea, Guatemala and Iran. The reorientation has had its effect on more general policy initiatives as well. Upon assuming office, the Reagan administration immediately eliminated many of the restraints the Carter administration had placed on arms transfers. A ceiling on major U.S. arms transfers to Third World nations and the ban on new coproduction agreements were rescinded, although the Carter administration had already undermined the significance of these two measures by exempting numerous nations from them. The Reagan administration also rescinded Carter's ban on the development of weapons solely for export, although here again the Carter administration had made exceptions to the ban, encouraging the development of the F-20 export fighter. (See box, p. 51.) The Carter administration's pledge not to be "the first nation to introduce into a region newly developed, advanced weapons systems which would create a new or significantly higher combat capability" was also repealed, as was its ban on arms sales promotion by U.S. embassy and military officials. This last action was reinforced in early 1987 by Secretary of State George Shultz, who sent a cable to all U.S. embassies and consulates advising them to become personally involved in promoting arms sales. The cable states that:

> If the chief of mission believes that a potential acquisition by the host country could significantly advance USG [U.S. government] foreign policy and/or national security objectives, he/she should expeditiously bring this to the attention of the department and, upon specific authorization from the department, become personally involved in furthering that acquisition.[53]

The Reagan administration also has bolstered U.S. arms exports by building up grant and loan military assistance. Security assistance, which includes the Economic Support Fund, jumped from $4.4 billion in fiscal 1980 to $7 billion in 1982 (Reagan's first budget year) and then peaked at $13.7 billion in 1985. Foreign Military Sales credits mirrored the general increase, rising from $2.1 billion in 1980 to $6.6 billion in 1985. The Military Assistance Program also rose sharply, from $110 million in 1980 to $805 million in 1985. The Reagan administration established lower interest rates for FMS loans and enlarged the number of nations eligible for concessional repayment periods. As a result, concessional or grant military assistance grew from 20 percent of all military aid in 1981 to 75 percent in 1986.[54]

These measures helped fuel the early Reagan administration boom in American arms transfers worldwide. Deliveries of all types of U.S. military-related equipment and services rose in this period from $13.3 million in 1980 to a record high of $19.2 million (in constant 1986 dollars) in 1983. The Americans share of all worldwide arms transfer agreements was also at a high point during the early Reagan years, but both indicators have since declined considerably.[55]

Movement to loosen technology export controls: The one area of arms export policy that has not been loosened under the Reagan administration is the domain of advanced technology export controls. Rather, the Department of Defense, led by former Assistant Secretary of Defense Richard

Perle, has succeeded in tightening advanced technology export controls with the intention of preventing the Soviet bloc from gaining access to Western technology.

A growing movement both inside and outside the administration, however, is convinced that the United States has gone too far with the export controls, and is seeking to loosen them considerably. They argue that much of the restricted technology is easily available from other Western European countries and that the United States only hurts its own industries by so tightly restricting exports. A 1987 National Academy of Sciences study estimated that strict export controls had cost the U.S. economy $9.3 billion and 188,000 jobs in 1985. A French defense manufacturer, echoing this viewpoint, remarked that France should erect a statue to Assistant Secretary Perle to thank him for the military contracts French companies had won because of the absence of American competition.[56]

The National Academy of Sciences panel and other experts have recommended that the Department of Commerce be put in control of technology export licensing. Perle and others in the Department of Defense have countered that the DoD is playing a valuable role in export licensing and that the controls have prevented much technology from reaching the Soviet Union. They cite a 1986 study conducted by Deputy Under Secretary of Defense Stephen Bryen which concluded that the Soviet Union defense production costs will be between $4.6 and $12 billion higher over the next 10 years because of the export controls.

The movement to loosen technology export controls has received added impetus from concern about the mounting U.S. trade deficit, which has reached record levels. Because of the sophistication of its products, trade in advanced technology, much of which has military applications, is one area in which the United States enjoys a considerable market advantage. It is also a line of business that has had a traditionally large positive exports/imports balance, which has helped reduce the trade deficit. Because of the export controls, however, the trade surplus in high technology had been steadily deteriorating, to the point that the National Academy of Sciences projected the United States would run its first deficit in that area in 1986.

In the administration, the Commerce Department has taken the lead in the battle to loosen export controls. In February 1987, then Secretary of Commerce Malcolm Baldrige announced 10 proposals for loosening export controls. One proposal was to speed up the export licensing process by waiving export-license requirements for reliable end-users. This would include government entities and government-controlled entities among the 16 Western nations that belong to the Coordinating Committee for Multilateral Export Controls (COCOM) as well as non-COCOM free-world countries with sufficient export control restrictions. The Commerce Department planned to extend the license waiver to private firms in these countries as well. The export-license waiver, dubbed the "Gold Card," has foundered at least temporarily, however, as the Defense Department and Commerce experienced difficulties cooperating on the joint initiative. Other proposals by Baldrige included allowing re-exports between COCOM countries and eliminating license requirements for non-COCOM free-world nations for exports of technology freely available elsewhere. Baldrige's successor at the Department of Commerce, C. William Verity, indicated a commitment to continue Baldrige's efforts to loosen export controls.

Trade pressure led Congress in 1987 to pass legislation aimed at facilitating military exports. A continuing appropriations resolution encouraged the Department of Defense to compensate American arms exporters for costs incurred in air shows and other military equipment exhibitions.[57]

The movement toward export liberalization was slowed somewhat by the March 1987 revelation that Toshiba Machine Company of Japan and Kongsberg Vaapenfabrikk of Norway exported milling machines to the Soviet Union. These machines allowed the Soviets to manufacture quieter propellor blades for their submarines. Although congressional advocates of loosened export controls are determined not to let the fierce public and congressional sentiment against Toshiba and Kongsberg Vaapenfabrikk interfere with their plans, defenders of the current export control regime used the episode to dramatize their concerns.

Declining defense budgets: Declining domestic defense budgets should also encourage increased American arms exports in the coming years. The enormous rise in defense spending that characterized the early years of the Reagan administration came to an end in the second term. In 1985, movements to reduce federal spending brought on by record budget deficits combined with sentiment that the American defense buildup had served its purpose to turn the tide against further increases in the defense budget. While the defense budget rose an average of 11 percent above inflation annually between 1980 and 1985, it declined by 4.2 percent in 1986 and 2.5 percent in 1987 in real terms. The fiscal 1988 national defense budget is expected to be approved at between $289 and $297 billion, which even at the higher level would represent no increase in real terms for 1987. While the Reagan administration hopes to boost sharply the national defense budget in 1989 and beyond, it is unlikely that it will succeed given the current budget constraints and the success of the Democrats in the 1986 elections.

The declines in the defense budget will mean fewer domestic purchases of weapon systems in the years to come. American defense contractors will therefore seek to sell their equipment abroad in order to sustain their high sales levels, as they did during the period of the post-Vietnam War domestic defense spending cuts. This pressure should lead to increased international marketing efforts and, possibly, the development of weapons principally for export. Budget constraints will also give the Department of Defense considerable incentive to encourage sales overseas. By passing along research and development and production costs to foreign buyers, the Department of Defense might be able to save monies that will allow it to extend or preserve its preferred programs.

Trend toward commercial sales: The trend toward conducting arms transfers through direct company-to-government commercial sales rather than through the government-arranged foreign military sales program could also facilitate American arms exports in the years ahead. Analysts say that direct commercial sales are quicker and at times cheaper, and allow more flexibility in arranging offset packages, all of which make U.S. military products more competitive on the international market. While purchasing through the foreign military sales program offers certain advantages as well, industry officials believe that it facilitates sales to have either option available to American companies and foreign governments.

In the early 1980s, the number of commerical sales increased considerably. Sales through the Commercial Sales program averaged 21 percent of total military exports in the 1980s, up from 12 percent in the 1970s, partly because the $100 million ceiling on industrial sales made through this program was eliminated early in 1981. While the rise in the proportion of arms sales going through commercial channels leveled off in the mid-1980s, the U.S. Defense Security Assistance Agency estimated that it will increase again in 1987 and 1988. Defense contractors have been complaining, however, that the Department of Defense is discouraging commercial sales. (See box, p. 75.) If the defense industry wins its battle to increase the use of commercial sales channels, U.S. arms exports might well be bolstered further in the coming years.

Factors obstructing U.S. arms exports: While the aforementioned factors should support increased U.S. arms exports in the years ahead, a number of other domestic pressures should hinder them. Congress has had increasing success restricting arms transfers in recent years, and the Iran-Contra scandal has added impetus to these efforts. Although the budget and trade deficits could fuel arms exports, they could just as easily obstruct them by leading to drastically reduced military assistance and a worldwide spirit of protectionism. These pressures along with the abnormally tight worldwide arms market will be a restraining force on American arms transfers in the coming years.

Growing movement to stop Arab arms sales: In the 1980s Congress has had unprecedented success blocking arms sales to Arab nations proposed by the administration. The first major success for pro-Israel lobbying groups and congressmen came in 1985 when, rather than fight a potentially losing battle in Congress for approval of a sale of McDonnell Douglas F-15 fighters to Saudi Arabia, the Reagan administration had the Saudis purchase Western European aircraft. (See box, p. 21.) In 1986, pro-Israel congressmen also forced the administration to postpone indefinitely plans to sell fighter aircraft and missiles to Jordan, and required the administration to scale down a missile sale to Saudi Arabia. This was followed by shocking success in early 1987, when the pro-Israel lobby forced the Reagan administration to remove 1,600 Maverick missiles—whose sale had been approved in 1984 but never executed—from a proposed $1 billion arms deal with Saudi Arabia.

There has been increasing talk of legislation strengthening congressional oversight of arms transfers in recent years. A possible model is the Arms Export Reform Act, first introduced by Sens. Joseph Biden (D-Del.) and Claiborne Pell (D-R.I.) and Rep. Mel Levine (D-Calif.) in September 1986. Reintroduced in January 1987, the legislation engendered considerable controversy. The bill was to create a pool of favored nations consisting of NATO countries, Japan, Australia, Israel, Egypt and any other future signatories to the Camp David accords for whom arms sales would be subject to the current regulations. Sales of "sensitive weaponry" worth more than $14 million to other nations would have to be approved by both houses of Congress, however. This contrasts sharply with the existing law, under which sales of more than $14 million to any nation can be blocked only by the passage of a joint resolution of disapproval. A joint resolution of disapproval requires a majority of both houses and is subject to presidential veto, effectively requiring Congress to win votes from two-thirds of both houses to block a sale.

Industry executives fear that this approach would drastically curtail U.S. arms exports, since Congress could more easily block arms sales, particularly those to Arab nations. According to one study, restrictions on arms sales to the Middle East could cost the United States between $8.5 and $28.3 billion by the year 2000.[58] Industry officials also argue that a bureaucratic logjam would result if every sale required approval by Congress. Harry Gray, the former chairman of United Technologies, testified that the legislation "would add to the burden of American firms in the marketplace" and would cause a "rapid deterioration" of American arms exports.[59]

Supporters of the legislation, however, contend that arms sales should not be undertaken unless there is significant support in Congress. Sen. Biden argued that passage of the 1986 Saudi missile sale which "survived on the basis of support from one-sixth of the House of Representatives and one-third plus one in the Senate . . . was most extraordinary and disturbing," and expressed the opinion that "the major foreign policy business of the United States must be conducted on the basis of far stronger support from the Congress."[60] Supporters of the Arms Export Reform Act denied that it would necessarily create a bureaucratic logjam while Congress debated whether to approve

Congressional Concern Gives Saudi Fighter Deal to the British

In 1983, the Kingdom of Saudi Arabia decided to purchase combat aircraft in in response to heightened tension in the Middle East brought on by Iranian militarism, the Iran-Iraq war and the resurgence of Islamic fundamentalism. The Saudi government settled on the McDonnell Douglas F-15, and sought to purchase 48 fighters from the United States to supplement some 60 F-15s already in its arsenal. The Reagan administration was committed to the sale from the start but chose to wait until after the 1984 election to close it. Early in 1985, however, strong lobbying by pro-Israeli groups, coupled with a wave of international violence involving Arab terrorists, moved Congress to oppose the sale. Remembering the difficult passage of F-15 and Awacs aircraft sales to Saudi Arabia in 1978 and 1981, the administration grew reluctant to face another congressional battle.

In an attempt to overcome opposition at home, the administration then tried to link the sale to a Saudi commitment to a peace initiative launched by Jordan's King Hussein— a tactic that the Saudis rejected. From the Saudis' perspective, the military and political pressures on their eastern border were of primary and immediate importance and were reason enough to justify the sale. The Royal Family believed that as a key ally of the United States in the region, Saudi Arabia, deserved American aid as much as Israel and Egypt, which receive it without preconditions. Finally, the Saudis also feared that formal adherence to Hussein's initiative would antagonize radical Arab factions at home and abroad.

The absence of a U.S. commitment to sell the aircraft and concern with pressing defense needs prompted the Saudis to request official U.S. authorization for buying the aircraft from European suppliers. Washington reassured the Saudis that purchasing fighters elsewhere would be acceptable, and the Kingdom decided to purchase 72 British-built Tornado interdiction and air defense aircraft and 60 trainers, all to be delivered by the end of 1988 at an estimated cost of nearly $6 billion. Experts estimate that when the costs of training personnel and providing replacement parts and maintenance services are included, the value of the deal could exceed $10 billion. Britain's willingness to accept payment in oil and its special relationship with the Americans were major factors in the Saudi decision.

Congressional opinion was sharply divided over whether arms sales to moderate Arab states help the peace process—by giving the moderates sufficient security to pursue agreements—or do little more than fuel the Middle East arms race. There was a greater consensus on the impact of the Saudis' European purchase on the United States. In addition to commercial losses—$3.5 billion and 75,000 jobs for 48 F-15s, according to *Aviation Week & Space Technology*—many observers felt that America's credibility had been damaged. Administration officials and others saw the reliability of the United States as an arms supplier questioned by moderate Arabs. More importantly, they felt that Washington's longstanding role as regional peacemaker had been vitiated because moderate Arab states might now doubt its willingness to support them in the future. The administration and other observers argued that U.S. political influence in the Middle East is largely predicated on arms transfers and, therefore, if the United States cannot sell its weapons to its allies, it may well lose a large share of the market to other suppliers, and its influence could be reduced as moderate Arab states look elsewhere for supply and support.

sales. Rep. Levine claimed that the majority of cases could be considered and approved "en masse in the same manner that military promotions or diplomatic lists are considered."[61]

Efforts to regulate commercial sales: The Iran-Contra scandal strengthened a number of other efforts to restrict U.S. arms transfers. In February 1987, Sen. David Pryor (D-Ark.) conducted a wide-ranging hearing into U.S. arms exports at which he sharply criticized the administration's regulation of arms transfers. Pryor particularly criticized the State Department's Office of Munitions Control, which regulates commercial sales of military equipment, stating that "commercial sales appear to be almost entirely uncontrolled."[62] Pryor's request to the Senate Governmental Affairs Committee to conduct a "broad, government-wide review" of arms transfer policy was turned down, however.[63] Sen. Pryor has since stated that he is contemplating legislation to reform the Office of Munitions Control, including possibly moving it out of the State Department. Pryor asked the Department of Defense for its comments on the possibility of taking control of the office from the State Department, to which the Pentagon initially responded with indifference. Industry officials oppose the proposed move because of fear that Pentagon officials, led by Under Secretary of Defense Stephen Bryan, "would impose much more stringent controls than at present."[64]

Rep. George Miller (D-Calif.) also tried to restrict licensing by the Office of Munitions Control. He is introducing legislation that would require the office to conduct background checks on applicants for export licenses, report on all fees paid as a result of the arms transactions and verify the deliveries of the military equipment to the approved destination. Miller asserted that "if a violent felon applies for a government license to export U.S. weapons, it is virtually certain that the license will be granted."[65] In September 1987, the General Accounting Office issued a report backing up some of these claims. The GAO cited one instance where the OMC issued 322 licenses for the export of $15 million worth of military equipment to a firm that had been barred by the Commerce Department from receiving export licenses because of its past practices.[66] Amidst this and other criticism of the ineffectiveness of the Office of Munitions Control, the agency is working on efforts to automate its licensing system and make other organizational improvements.

Declining U.S. military assistance: The decline in U.S. security assistance may also hinder U.S. arms exports. The budget constraints brought on by record budget deficits have hit security assistance particularly hard in recent years. Because most security assistance programs have no natural constituency in Congress, they are often the first programs cut if the overall budget needs to be reduced. Security assistance overall dropped from $13.7 billion in 1985 to $9.5 billion in 1986, and then even further to $8.5 billion in 1987. The director of the Defense Security Assistance Agency, Lt. Gen. Philip Gast, has warned that further cuts might result in the loss of overseas arms markets and domestic jobs.[67] Both he and Secretary of Defense Caspar Weinberger have also warned that the cuts might lead allies to purchase arms from the Soviet Union.

The foreign military sales financing program has been the hardest hit. It was cut from $6.6 billion in 1985 to $4.9 billion in 1986 and then to $4.2 billion in 1987. It is expected to come in at approximately $4.4 billion in 1988, with only six countries now eligible for foreign military sales financing. The foreign military sales financing program is particularly unpopular in Congress because of the consistent financial problems it has experienced. Many nations are far behind on payments, partly because of the high interest rates assessed during the 1970s. In fiscal 1984, for example, the United States was obliged to make payments of $613 million because of missed repayments by FMS borrowers.[68]

Protectionism threatens arms exports: Defense industry officials also fear that proposed protectionist measures may hinder U.S. military exports in the coming years. They claim that protectionist measures in the United States would lead to similar actions abroad, which would imperil U.S. arms sales. For this reason, the U.S. aerospace industry and many other defense contractors lobbied intensely to defeat the 1987 trade bill. Similarly, U.S. arms exporters vigorously oppose protectionist measures that would restrict offset arrangements, including a 1987 bill that would require the Commerce Department to monitor offsets and would have the President initiate international efforts to regulate offsets. While U.S. defense companies do not like offsets, they view them as necessary to win many foreign defense orders. If they were not able to provide offsets, they contend, many defense customers would instead purchase arms from European nations and other suppliers who have no such prohibitions.

Looking Ahead: Competition among suppliers appears likely to intensify. New suppliers among the developing nations will emerge, while existing ones will develop further—although their burgeoning arms exports industries will continue to rely on industrialized nations such as the United States for key components and technology, which should offset somewhat the markets American exporters will lose to the Third World suppliers. The European suppliers will most likely become even tougher competitors as their defense industries also begin to experience declining domestic arms budgets.

Domestic factors are harder to predict. The uncertain political future of the United States could bring on various winds of change. For example, any of several Democratic presidential candidates who have voiced a determination to curb American arms exports to the Middle East could be elected in 1988—although it is highly uncertain whether any of these candidates would translate such a platform into an actual policy if elected. Even given some kind of stability in the ideology of the Executive branch, the various opposing pressures confronting policymakers of all stripes at this time make any long-term forecast of U.S. arms exports exceedingly tenuous.

Footnotes

1. U.S. Arms Control and Disarmament Agency (ACDA), *World Military Expenditures and Arms Transfers* 1986 edition (Washington: ACDA, 1986), and Stockholm International Peace Research Institute (SIPRI), *World Armaments and Disarmament Yearbook* 1987 edition (New York: Oxford University Press, 1987) and Richard Grimmett, *Trends in Conventional Arms Transfers to the Third World by Major Supplier, 1979–1986* (Washington: Congressional Research Service, 1987).
2. SIPRI, *Yearbook 1985*, p. 345.
3. Michael T. Klare, "The State of the Trade," *Journal of International Affairs*, Summer 1986 (vol. 40/ no. 1), p. 13.
4. *The Washington Post*, June 23, 1985, p. A8.
5. ACDA, *op. cit.* 1986 edition.
6. CRS, *op. cit.* 1987 edition.
7. ACDA, *op. cit.* 1986 edition.
8. SIPRI, *op. cit.* 1987 edition.
9. SIPRI, *op. cit.* 1987 edition.
10. *Washington Times*, Aug. 10, 1987, p. C-10.
11. SIPRI, *op. cit.* 1986 edition, p. 323.
12. Michael Brzoska and Thomas Ohlson, *Arms Production in the Third World* (Philadelphia: Taylor & Francis, 1986), p. 27.
13. Ibid, p. 8.
14. Michael T. Klare, "The State of the Trade," *Journal of International Affairs*, Summer 1968 (vol. 40/ no. 1), p. 4.
15. SIPRI, *op. cit.* 1986 edition, p. 323.
16. *The Washington Post*, June 23, 1985, p. A8.
17. Defense Security Assistance Agency (DSAA), *Weapons Acquisition Report (WAR)* 1987 edition.
18. ACDA, *op. cit.* 1986 edition and Brzoska and Ohlson eds., *op. cit.*, p. 30.
19. H.M.F. Howarth, "Brazil's Industry," *International Defense Review*, vol. 9, 1985.
20. ACDA, *op. cit.* 1975 edition.
21. ACDA, *op. cit.* 1986 edition and SIPRI, *op. cit.* 1987 edition.
22. ACDA, *op. cit.* 1986 edition, SIPRI, *op. cit.* 1987 edition, and CRS *op. cit.* 1987 edition.
23. SIPRI, *op. cit.* 1986 edition, p. 336.
24. Shawn Tully, "Europe's Arms Exporters Challenge the Superpowers," *Fortune* Aug. 5, 1985, p. 93.
25. ACDA, *op. cit.* 1986 edition and SIPRI, *op. cit.* 1987 edition.
26. Edward A. Kolodziej "French Arms Trade: The Economic Determinants" in SIPRI, *op. cit.* 1983 edition, pp. 372–73.
27. ACDA, *op. cit.* 1978 edition and SIPRI, *op. cit.* 1987 edition.
28. Paul Hammond, David J. Louscher, Michael D. Salomone and Norman A. Graham, *The Reluctant Supplier: U.S. Decisionmaking for Arms Sales* (Cambridge, Mass.: Oelgeschlager, Gunn & Hain, Publishers Inc., 1983), p. 220.
29. Hammond et al, *op. cit.*, p. 221.
30. Andrew Pierre, *The Global Politics of Arms Sales* (Princeton, N.J.: Princeton University Press, 1982), pp. 93–95.
31. Pierre, *op. cit.*, p. 95, and Edward A. Kolodziej "French Arms Trade: The Economic Determinants" in SIPRI, *op. cit.* 1983 edition, p. 382.
32. Pierre, *op. cit.*, p. 95.
33. Pierre, *op. cit.*, p. 95.
34. Pierre, *op. cit.*, p. 95.
35. Hammond et al, *op. cit.*, p. 225.
36. ACDA, *op. cit.* 1979 and 1986 editions.
37. SIPRI, *op. cit.* 1987 edition.

38. Jeffrey M. Lenorovitz, "French Seek Competitive Edge Through International Efforts" *Aviation Week & Space Technology*, June 15, 1987, p. 140.
39. ACDA, *op. cit.* 1986 edition and SIPRI *op. cit.* 1987 edition.
40. ACDA, *op. cit.* 1986 edition, SIPRI *op. cit.* 1987 edition, and CRS *op. cit.* 1987 edition.
41. Hammond et al., *op. cit.*, p. 238.
42. Hammond et al., *op. cit.*, p. 237.
43. *The Wall Street Journal*, Oct. 4, 1985, p. 25.
44. SIPRI, *op. cit.* 1987 edition.
45. SIPRI, *op. cit.* 1987 edition.
46. SIPRI, *op. cit.* 1986 edition, p. 335.
47. *Aviation Week & Space Technology*, March 24, 1987, p. 27.
48. Ulrich Albrecht, "The Federal Republic of Germany and Italy: New Strategies of Mid-Sized Weapons Exporters?" *Journal of International Affairs*, Summer 1986 (vol. 40/No. 1), p. 130.
49. Albrecht, *op. cit.*, p. 130.
50. Frederic S. Pearson, "Of Leopards and Cheetahs: West Germany's Role as a Mid-Sized Arms Supplier" *Orbis*, Spring 1985, p. 194.
51. ACDA, *op. cit.* 1986 edition and SIPRI, *op. cit.* 1987 edition.
52. Evamaria Loose-Weintraub, "Spain's new defence policy: arms production and exports" in SIPRI, *op. cit.*, 1984 edition, p. 146.
53. "Shultz Cable Urges Embassies to Assist U.S. Arms Exporters," *Defense News*, March 23, 1987, p. 25.
54. William Hartung, "The Reagan revival of arms deals," *Bulletin of Atomic Scientists*, July/Aug. 1987, p. 20.
55. ACDA, *op. cit.* 1986 edition, and DSAA, *Fiscal Year Series* 1987 edition.
56. Ann Reilly Dowd, "How U.S. Arms Dealers are Making a Killing" *Fortune*, Feb. 16, 1987, p. 68.
57. "Provision Gives Boost to U.S. Participation in Exhibitions," *Defense News*, Oct. 27, 1986, p. 11.
58. "Report: Mideast Arms Sales Restrictions Could Cost $28 Billion" *Defense News*, Aug. 31, 1987, p. 3.
59. "Reagan Advised to Veto Arms Export Reform Bill" *Defense News*, March 9, 1987, p. 7.
60. *The Congressional Record*, January 29, 1987, p. S1398.
61. "Reagan Advised to Veto Arms Export Reform Bill" *Defense News*, March 9, 1987, p. 7.
62. "Arms Sale Process Assault is a Step Closer to Reality" *Defense News*, Feb. 23, 1987, p. 24.
63. "Senate Panel Turns Down Request for a Review of Arms Sale Process" Jan. 12, 1987.
64. "Pentagon May Absorb State Department's Export Licensing Office of Munitions Control," *Defense News*, June 15, 1987.
65. "House Legislation Would Tighten State Department's Arms Export Controls" *Defense News*, June 22, 1987, p. 10.
66. *The Washington Post*, Sept. 11, 1987, p. 23.
67. *Jane's Defence Weekly*, July 25, 1987, p. 125.
68. General Accounting Office, *Military Loans: Repayment Problems Mount as Debt Increases*, Oct. 1985, p. 14.

Chapter 2
The Evolution of the
World Arms Trade

Arms exports are by no means a new phenomenon. From the beginnings of the modern arms industry during the Industrial Revolution of the mid-nineteenth century, the sale of weapons abroad has been an integral part of its business. Arms merchants such as Alfred Krupp of Prussia and Lord Armstrong of England survived in their early years only because of foreign orders.[1] Krupp found at first that French, Russian and Austrian concerns were more interested in his weapons than was his native Prussia, which he said forced him "to seek the means for the employment and nourishment of [his] people for the most part abroad among the natural enemies of [his] industry."[2]

Even though today weapons manufacturers in general are less dependent on foreign customers for survival, marketing arms abroad remains an important part of doing business, and the international trading of weapons is brisk. Until quite recently, in fact, the exportation of arms around the globe was a steadily growing business. International sales and other transfers expanded rapidly during the 1960s and 1970s from a few billion dollars a year to the current annual level of more than $30 billion. According to the U.S. government, the total value of weapons deliveries measured in constant 1983 dollars peaked at more than $42 billion in 1981 and 1982 before declining to the $30 billion range in 1985.[3]

The character of the arms trade has changed since its inception in the mid-nineteenth century—in some cases dramatically. While sales in the early days were the work of individuals, unrestrained by their governments, in the post-war era they have become instruments of nations' foreign policies. The market for arms has been shifting since the years immediately following World War II from Europe to the Third World. The kinds of weapons involved in sales have evolved from surplus stocks, often technologically inferior, to very sophisticated, state-of-the-art equipment. Transfers of equipment now generally are accompanied by transfers of production technology and technical advisers as well. The United States and the Soviet Union are no longer the dominant arms traders they once were, as European and developing nations have begun to build their own armaments industries.

Arms transfers as an instrument of foreign policy: The original weapons manufacturers and brokers of the modern age were without exception individuals—such as Alfred Krupp, Lord Armstrong and Sir Basil Zaharoff—who made deals directly with foreign nations unfettered by their own governments. Thus, frequently an arms manufacturer's marketing practices ran at cross purposes with its government's foreign policies. The British journalist Anthony Sampson singles out one such instance in his book, *The Arms Bazaar*: "In April 1866 Krupp insisted, against the express request of [the Prussian Chancellor] Bismarck, on exporting a consignment of guns to Austria, and Krupp's guns fired on both sides in the Austro-Prussian war."[5] Sir Basil Zaharoff was unexcelled at putting profits before national interests. As he candidly told the London *Sunday Chronicle* in 1936: "'I sold armaments to anyone who would buy them. I was a Russian when in Russia, a Greek in Greece, a Frenchman in Paris.'"[6]

The experience of World War I produced a backlash in the United States and abroad that led to close scrutiny of the behavior of these "merchants of death," as the arms manufacturers came to be called. Critics increasingly were inclined to view arms manufacturers as supranational entities whose activities verged on the conspiratorial and increased the likelihood of armed conflict. Criticism came from soldiers and politicians as well as civilians who were horrified by the carnage wrought by the war. The commander of Britain's war-time naval forces wrote:

> The interrelation between foreign and home trade in armaments is one of the most subtle and dangerous features of the present private system of production. The evil is intensified by the existence of international armaments rings, the members of which notoriously play into each other's hands.[7]

The Covenant of the ill-fated League of Nations stated more generally that "The Members of the League agree that the manufacture by private enterprise of munitions and implements of war is open to grave objections."[8]

From the critics grew calls for the nationalization of weapons production. Few of the western arms manufacturers were nationalized, but many nations did tighten regulation of the industry's conduct in selling weapons abroad, and the typical arms sale is no longer negotiated independently by private firms free from government control. Instead, over the last 40 years a nation's government has become an important arbitrator overseeing where the nation's defense industry markets its wares, and nations have come to view arms transfers and sales as a diplomatic instrument for attaining broader political goals. As Anthony Sampson has observed:

> The important arms salesmen of today . . . are government servants, honoured or knighted for their services to exports: The major arms exports . . . are achieved not by gun-running or quick bargains in Manchester or Paris, but by long drawn-out negotiations between civil servants in Washington or London, endorsed by presidents and cabinets. The setting for a modern arms deal is not an old hulk unloading crates at night at a deserted wharf, but an Arab prince [or other foreign leader] being welcomed in London or Paris by a guard of honour and by the Minister of Defence.[9]

Governments became even more involved in the weapons-exporting business with the rise of fascism in Europe and the war against Hitler and his allies. The fascist governments of Germany and Italy sent military equipment to aid Franco in Spain (as well as troops, the more traditional form of aid), while Soviet Russia sent arms to his opponents. When war broke out over the whole continent, the United States began transferring military equipment through the Lend-Lease Act to the United Kingdom and, later, to the Soviet Union.

With the onset of the Cold War, governments became more deeply involved in coordinating the exportation of weapons. In the years immediately following World War II, the United States and Russia sought to strengthen their respective European allies through grants of military equipment. The United States came to believe that the economic rebirth of western Europe would occur only if freedom from fear of external aggression and internal agitation could be guaranteed. Later, the focus of weapons exportation shifted away from Europe toward other regions of the globe, but belief in the efficacy of arms transfers as a legitimate instrument of foreign policy continued to grow.

Starting in the 1960s, arms transfers began to skyrocket, the result of both economic stability in Europe and growing Third World interest in creating military establishments. According to the U.S. State Department's Arms Control and Disarmament Agency (ACDA), world arms transfers (measured in the current dollar value of deliveries) grew from $3 to $4 billion a year in the early 1960s to more than $40 billion in 1982, the peak year. Growth in Third World arms imports accounted for a significant portion of the increase. Developing nations, according to ACDA, increased their arms purchases from $1 to $2 billion a year to an annual average of nearly $30 billion over this 20 year period.[10] The Stockholm International Peace Research Institute found a similar increase in Third World arms buying. SIPRI found that arms transfers to developing nations increased in value from about $5 billion (in constant 1985 dollars) a year in the early 1960s to more than $20 billion a year by the end of the 1970s.[11]

The Changing Face of the Global Arms Trade

Some observers of the international arms trade suggest that the quantitative increase in arms transfers may be of less import than several qualitative changes in the world arms trade. One has been alluded to already: The principal recipients of weapons have changed over time. In the immediate post-war years, the United States and the Soviet Union poured weapons into Europe. As the European nations rebuilt their economies and armaments industries throughout the 1950s and into the 1960s, the flow of American arms into European arsenals slackened. At about the same time, the nations of the developing world were gaining their independence from colonial rulers and developing military establishments of their own. The Third World rapidly emerged as an important market for weapons sales, and the proportion of arms transactions involving developing nations climbed. The Stockholm International Peace Research Institute calculates that arms imports by the Third World annually accounted for between 65 and 70 percent of all weapons delivered around the world between 1977 and 1986.[19] ACDA also attributes most of the growth in global arms transfers to increased imports by the Third World. It estimates that the value of arms transfers to developed countries, when measured in constant 1982 dollars, grew only slightly, from $6.7 billion in 1973 to $7.6 billion in 1983. The value of arms transfers to developing nations, in comparison, increased from $20.1 billion in 1973 to $27.5 billion in 1983, a 37 percent increase. The disparity between the two growth rates is greater when more than single years are compared. ACDA places the Third World's share of the total arms trade even higher than does SIPRI, at 80 percent between 1977 and 1985.[20]

As the focus of arms transfers moved from the developed to the developing world—and largely because of this shift—the number of nations buying arms increased dramatically. The United States engaged in arms transfers with 115 countries in fiscal 1980, twice the number of clients it had two decades before.[21]

Not only has the usual destination of exported weapons been altered, but the types of weapons being exported have also changed. Andrew Pierre, in a study of the arms trade for the Council on Foreign Relations, noted:

In the past, most arms transferred to less developed countries were the obsolete weapons of the major powers which they wanted to eliminate from their inventories to make room for new, more advanced ones. Often they were gifts from surplus stocks of overage, technologically inferior equipment. . . . In contrast, today many of the arms being sold are among the most sophisticated in the inventories of the supplier states.[22]

In some cases, Third World nations have been able to obtain technologically sophisticated, top-of-the-line equipment that has only recently become available for the armed forces of the exporting nation itself.

Another factor in the changing dimensions of the arms transfer picture is the increasing transfer of the production technology and know-how along with the finished products. Many industrialized nations want to learn the advanced manufacturing techniques employed in producing sophisticated weapons, while a number of less-developed countries desire assistance in establishing more basic high technology industrial capabilities. In addition, many arms buyers seek to reduce their net outlays for military items through "offset" arrangements such as a guaranteed share of the production. The resulting demands by recipients for technology transfers have led the main supplier countries to enter into ever greater numbers of co-production agreements with other nations. These agreements allow the recipients to assemble all or part of the exported arms, and require the supplier to pass along the blueprints and necessary manufacturing know-how.

The arrangements frequently require the exporting nation to send technical advisers abroad to service the agreements. This is especially common in the case of agreements with Third World nations, where few among the population have the training to oversee high technology operations. Before the overthrow of the Shah, estimates were that up to 60,000 U.S. contract personnel would be needed in Iran by 1980. The General Accounting Office reports that the acquisition of the F-5 by Saudi Arabia required more than 1,600 U.S. personnel alone and that more sophisticated aircraft would need more.[23]

To date, European exporters have entered into more co-production agreements with Third World countries than has the United States, which has sought to limit agreements to NATO countries and other close allies such as Japan. However, Michael Klare, currently the Five College Associate Professor of Peace and World Security Studies in Massachusetts, contends that:

> as competition among the major arms suppliers increases—thereby enhancing the bargaining position of potential buyers—U.S. producers have come to regard technology transfers as an inescapable 'fact of life' of the arms business. While U.S. officials may prefer to inhibit the export of U.S. arms technology, the CRS reported in 1977, when faced with adamant clients they will usually 'agree to coproduce the item rather than lose the entire sale to another country.'[24]

The Western Europeans are also more willing to modify and refurbish arms that were originally produced by manufacturers other than themselves. The high cost of new, technologically sophisticated weapons increasingly has led many Third World nations to opt for upgrading older equipment in lieu of purchasing new systems. As a result, arms companies in several countries have found a considerable market for modernizing Soviet-built weapons owned by countries outside the Soviet bloc. So far, British firms have been the most active in refurbishing Soviet-made weapons. Though not so deeply involved as other nations, interest in this sort of activity is increasing among

U.S. policymakers, and some American companies have landed contracts to retrofit Russian-built arms for countries that have ended close ties with the Soviets. A program—formally named "Project Mogul, " but referred to in Pentagon circles as "Bear's Spares"—was launched in 1984 to promote the upgrading of Soviet-made weapons by American firms. A total of $200 million was allocated to the program in 1984, and the U.S. government and private concerns have worked on Soviet equipment or established programs in Egypt, Botswana and Pakistan.[25]

As Chapter 1 points out, arms exports by developing nations are also rapidly increasing. According to the ACDA, the annual average of arms transfers by Third World nations was three times higher in the early 1980s than it was in the late 1970s. While arms exports by developing nations are growing, they are not by most estimates responsible for a large percentage of total arms transfers. According to ACDA statistics, the Third World (excluding the People's Republic of China) accounted for 5.6 percent of all arms exports between 1981 and 1985. SIPRI's accounting method yields a much lower percentage, showing developing nations other than the PRC as responsible for 3.1 percent of the arms trade in 1982–86.[26] Stephanie Neuman, director of the Comparative Defense Studies Program at Columbia University, argues on the basis of "available evidence . . . that defense production in the Third World will remain a small fraction of the world's arms production and trade."[27]

Indeed, perhaps the one aspect of world arms transfers that has not changed significantly over time is the relatively small number of suppliers that account for most transfers. Historically, six supplier nations have dominated the world arms market. These countries—the United States, the Soviet Union, France, Great Britain, West Germany and Italy—accounted for 82.1 percent of arms deliveries to the Third World in 1985, according to CRS, and 79.5 percent of new agreements in 1985.[28]

As noted earlier, the Western European suppliers significantly increased their share of the world arms market in the 1980s. This trend was evident in the late 1960s and early 1970s as well. From 1964 to 1973 France, Great Britain and West Germany accounted for 9.2 percent of the world arms market, which grew to 15.2 percent between 1974 and 1979, and 19.1 percent between 1980 and 1985. These increases occurred at the expense of the superpowers. The decline in the superpowers' dominance of arms transfers is most pronounced for the Third World. According to SIPRI, the U.S. share of the Third World arms market dropped from 36.6 percent between 1973 and 1979 to 26.3 percent between 1980 and 1986, while the USSR's share dropped from 36.6 percent to 34.6 percent during these same periods. The Congressional Research Service also shows the superpowers' overall share dropping from 70.6 percent between 1973 and 1979 to 61.3 percent between 1980 and 1986. But, according to CRS, the decline was entirely due to a shrinking American portion because the Soviet share rose from 36.3 percent to 42.8 percent during this period.

Nevertheless, all sources of data on arms transfers agree on identifying the Soviets and the Americans as the world's leading suppliers during the last 10 to 15 years. Sources do not always agree, however, on which of the two superpowers is the larger. Different organizations use different methodologies that sometimes result in contrasting conclusions. Moreover, even within a single source the leading supplier tends to vary from year to year.

The U.S. Arms Control and Disarmament Agency reports that the Soviets had $43.7 billion to the United States' $40.7 billion in worldwide arms transfers between 1982 and 1985. For the period 1978–81, ACDA shows an even more marked domination, with Soviet exports totaling $45.7

billion and American exports totaling $27.6 billion. SIPRI, on the other hand, ranks the United States slightly ahead between 1978 and 1981 and strongly in front for 1982–85.

There is somewhat more agreement between sources on arms transfers to the Third World. SIPRI, ACDA and the Congressional Research Service show the U.S. trailing the Soviet Union in deliveries of arms to the Third World in almost every year since 1978, whereas before 1978 the United States leads in most years. CRS records Soviet arms deliveries to developing nations as more than twice the level of those of the United States between 1978 and 1986. SIPRI calculates a slightly less marked Soviet lead during this period, with Soviet exports to the Third World totaling about 40 percent higher than those of the United States. CRS' calculations of recent arms agreements would indicate that the Soviet lead in arms transfers to the Third World will continue in the near future. According to CRS, between 1984 and 1986, the Soviets made $45.5 billion in arms transfer agreements with Third World nations, while the United States entered into $15.8 billion worth.

The U.S. State Department prefers a totally different technique for comparing American and Soviet arms transfers. In a 1982 report covering the years 1972–81, the State Department said Soviet deliveries of major weapons systems to Third World nations greatly exceeded American deliveries. During the decade, according to the department, the Soviets transferred 74,000 major weapons systems to nations in Asia, Africa, the Middle East and Latin America, compared with 44,000 U.S. transfers.[29]

The State Department report divided major conventional weapons into 12 categories, ranging from tanks and self-propelled guns to guided-missile patrol boats. (The remaining 10 categories are light armor, artillery over 100mm, major surface warships, minor surface warships, submarines, supersonic combat aircraft, subsonic combat aircraft, helicopters, other military aircraft and surface-to-air missiles.) In each category, it reported "best minimum" estimates of the number of systems transferred by the United States, the Soviet Union, the Warsaw Pact nations, the major Western European suppliers, the minor Western European suppliers, and the rest of the world. For the decade covered by the report, the United States led all suppliers in five categories and the Soviet Union in four. In the remaining three categories, America transferred more weapons than Russia in two. For the last five years, however, the Soviet Union led the world in seven categories, and the United States in only one, and the Soviets were ahead of America in three of the remaining four categories.[30]

When he released the report for the State Department, Under Secretary of State for Security Assistance James Buckley claimed that State's form of accounting gives a more accurate picture of comparative Russian and American exports than data based on price. Buckley argued that dollar estimates of arms transfers, which he said place the United States ahead of the Soviet Union, are distorted because the Soviets make sales at discount prices and because "over 60 percent" of U.S. arms deals include spending for construction and training.[31] The analysis section of the State Department report itself hedges somewhat on this claim. The report says that each of the two main measures of arms transfers "has shortcomings and neither is a true measure of military capability." It does add, however, that "prices vary with the terms and conditions of other transactions," and it asserts that estimates of numbers and types of weapons delivered are a "more concrete measure of military capability transferred."[32]

The most recent CRS report also contains updated data on the numbers of weapons delivered by major suppliers to the Third World. CRS reported on essentially the same 12 categories of weapons. For 1979–86, CRS figures show a larger number of weapons systems transferred by the Soviet Union than by the United States in all 12 categories, and for just 1983–86, the Soviets delivered more weapons than the Americans in 11 of the 12 categories. (The only category in which the United States delivered more systems was subsonic combat aircraft.) CRS data place the Soviet Union in the lead in such categories as tanks and self-propelled guns, helicopters, supersonic combat aircraft, and surface-to-air missiles.[33] (See Table 2–1.)

CRS argues for somewhat more caution in interpreting data on aggregate numbers of weapons delivered. Pointing out that "quality and/or sophistication of weapons can offset a *quantitative* disadvantage," CRS says:

> The fact that the United States, for example, may not "lead" in *quantities* of weapons delivered to a region does not necessarily mean that the weaponry it has transferred cannot compensate, to an important degree, for larger quantities of *less capable* weapons systems delivered by the Soviet Union or others.

Table 2–1

Weapon Systems Delivered to the Third World, 1979–1986
(in units)

Weapon System	U.S.	U.S.S.R.	Major West European*
Tanks and self-propelled guns	3,595	9,210	860
Artillery	3,253	11,320	1,355
APCs and Armored Cars	8,077	13,355	4,785
Major Surface Combatants	13	52	80
Minor Surface Combatants	49	199	214
Submarines	0	13	12
Supersonic Combat Aircraft	518	2,770	448
Subsonic Combat Aircraft	195	280	189
Other Aircraft	316	600	540
Helicopters	319	1,565	825
Guided Missile Boats	0	50	34
Surface-to-Air Missiles	5,568	26,425	3,310

*   Major West European category includes France, the United Kingdom, West Germany and Italy.

Source: Richard Grimmett, *Trends in Conventional Arms Transfers to the Third World By Major Supplier, 1979–1986* (Washington: Congressional Research Service, 1987).

CRS adds:

> Further, these data do not provide an indication of the capabilities of the recipient nations to use effectively the weapons actually delivered to them. Superior training—coupled with quality equipment—may, in the last analysis, be a more important factor in a nation's ability to engage successfully in conventional warfare than the size of its weapons inventory.[34]

Indeed, some question the utility of comparing U.S. and Soviet transfers by any measure. To the extent that comparisons are valuable, they say, it would be more accurate to compare Western-bloc and Eastern-bloc transfers. Because the major West European suppliers export much more than European communist countries, such comparisons would put the West in the lead by all measures used. In contrast, Reagan administration officials believe that Western Europe follows arms export policies that are too independent of the United States to make this larger comparison valid. The State Department report on arms transfers argued that "The USSR . . . to a far greater degree than any Western [nation] can orchestrate the arms exports of its allies," implying that U.S.-Soviet comparisons if anything understate the Soviet lead.[35]

An even stronger criticism of such comparisons is sometimes offered. It suggests that they make superpower competition the most important factor in assessing foreign military sales, when it is really more important to examine how particular transfers are affecting regional military balances and the promotion of economic development and human rights. In a 1983 critique of Reagan administration arms transfer policy, the Democratic Policy Committee argued:

> [The administration] has inflicted its bipolar view of global politics on the facts of increased arms sales and declared another arena for U.S./Soviet competition. By viewing regional problems through an East/West optic, there is a likelihood that the administration has misread and misrepresented the potential dangers of unbridled trade in sophisticated weapons.[36]

Administration officials have said, however, that publishing their estimates of Soviet and U.S. arms transfers was necessary to dispel a "myth" that the United States is the leading supplier of weapons to the Third World and to prevent complacency in the face of increased Soviet use of arms sales as a policy tool.[37]

A final judgment of the importance of U.S.-Soviet arms transfer comparisons cannot be made until one has reached some conclusions about what advantages and disadvantages such transfers confer. These questions will be taken up elsewhere in this study.

Footnotes

1. Anthony Sampson, *The Arms Bazaar* (New York: The Viking Press, 1977), p. 45.
2. Berdrow, William, ed., *The Letters of Alfred Krupp 1826–1887* (London: Gollancz Press, 1930), p. 164.
3. U.S. Department of State, Arms Control and Disarmament Agency (ACDA), *World Military Expenditures and Arms Transfers 1986*, (*WMEAT 1986*) (Washington: ACDA, 1986), p. 6.
4. *Ibid.*, p. 42.
5. Sampson, *op. cit.*, p. 41.
6. *Ibid.*, pp. 49–50.
7. *Ibid.*, p. 68.
8. *Ibid.*, p. 69.
9. *Ibid.*, p. 31.
10. ACDA, *op. cit.* and earlier editions.
11. Stockholm International Peace Research Institute, (SIPRI) *World Armaments and Disarmament Yearbook 1987* (New York: Oxford University Press, 1987) and earlier editions.
12. *Ibid.*, p. 346.
13. SIPRI *Yearbook 1984*, (Philadelphia: Taylor & Francis, 1984), pp. 175–177.
14. Richard Grimmett, *Trends in Conventional Arms Transfers to the Third World By Major Supplier, 1978–1985* (Washington: Congressional Research Service, May 9, 1986), p. 31.
15. *Ibid.*, p. 37.
16. *The Washington Post*, June 23, 1985, p. A8.
17. SIPRI *Yearbook 1985*, p. 345.
18. *The New York Times*, Sept. 29, 1985, p. E–5.
19. SIPRI, *Yearbook 1987*.
20. ACDA, *op. cit.* 1986 edition, p. 101, 1985 edition p. 89.
21. U.S. Department of Defense, Defense Security Assistance Agency, *Foreign Military Sales, Foreign Military Construction Sales and Military Assistance Facts 1981* and earlier editions.
22. Andrew Pierre, *The Global Politics of Arms Sales* (Princeton, N.J.: Princeton University Press, 1982), p. 10.
23. U.S. General Accounting Office, *Opportunities to Improve Decisionmaking and Oversight of Arms Sales* (Washington: U.S. Government Printing Office, May 1979), p. 69.
24. Michael Klare, *American Arms Supermarket* (Austin, Tex.: University of Texas Press, 1984), p. 166.
25. *Technology Review*, April 1985, pp. 32–33; *Business Week*, March 4, 1985, pp. 117–118; *Defense News*, Nov. 11, 1986, p. 1.
26. SIPRI database and ACDA, *op. cit.* 1986 edition. Figures cited reflect IRRC definition of Third World with the exclusion of the People's Republic of China, as noted.
27. Stephanie Neumann and Robert G. Harkavy, eds., *Arms Transfers in the Modern World*, (New York: Praeger Books, 1979), p. 169.
28. Grimmett, *op. cit.*, pp. 31, 37.
29. U.S. Department of State, *Conventional Arms Transfers in the Third World, 1972–1981*, Special Report No. 102 (Washington: U.S. Government Printing Office, Aug. 1982), pp. 12–13.
30. *Ibid.* pp. 12–13.
31. *The Washington Post*, Aug. 3, 1982.
32. U.S. Department of State, *op. cit.*, p. 7.
33. Grimmett, *op. cit.*, p. 42.
34. Grimmett, *op. cit.*, pp. 28–29.
35. U.S. Department of State, *op. cit.*, p. 8.
36. U.S. Senate Democratic Policy Committee, *An Unconventional Arms Policy: Selling Ourselves Short, Promotion of Foreign Military Sales to the Developing World Under the Reagan Administration* (Washington: U.S. Government Printing Office, 1983), p. 11.
37. *The Washington Post*, Aug. 3, 1982.

Chapter 3
A Historical Perspective on U.S. Arms Transfer Policy

Although the U.S. government did not become extensively involved in the peace-time transfer of arms until after World War II, American companies had long been in the business of selling arms. In the first part of the nineteenth century, according to Anthony Sampson, Du Pont was the most active American arms exporter. Du Pont sold gunpowder to both Spain and the nascent Latin American nations fighting for their independence, and it also supplied Russia and Britain in the Crimean War. Later in the century, Carnegie Steel received orders for armor-plate from the Russian navy, and in 1900, Electric Boat licensed the British company Vickers to build its submarines in Europe.[1]

These and nearly all other arms exports conducted before the twentieth century were not regulated by the government. The prevailing view was that U.S. citizens should be free to sell and export arms at any time. Starting in 1905, however, the United States began restricting arms shipments to certain Latin American countries that were experiencing civil strife that could threaten U.S. interests. In 1919 the government placed similar restrictions on military exports to China.[2]

Orders placed with U.S. firms for military wares fell off sharply after World War I. The U.S. government, in particular, reduced its purchasing. American companies, therefore, actively sought out the few available foreign orders, and some of the new aviation companies that sprang up in the 1920s and 1930s established themselves through foreign military sales.[3] Throughout this period, however, Britain and France had a greater volume of arms exports than America.[4]

A sort of delayed revulsion to World War I at this time also led to the first attempts at exerting extensive government controls over arms exports. The Nye Committee hearings in Congress, initiated in 1934, focused attention on the sometimes unsavory techniques used by American companies to sell arms and portrayed a desire by U.S. firms and banks to reap excessive war profits as the primary cause of American involvement in the war. Arms manufacturers such as Henry Carse, president of Electric Boat, argued that their business "is no different than any other business."[5] But Congress (and much of the American public) viewed their activities as much more pernicious, and sought to prevent arms companies from—as they saw it—ever dragging America into war again. The 1935 Neutrality Act required an automatic arms embargo against any foreign nations that went to war and established a Munitions Control Board to supervise U.S. arms exports.

Arms transfers and World War II: The U.S. desire to remain above international frays, however, gradually crumbled in the face of Mussolini's invasion of Ethiopia, Hitler's annexation of the Rhineland, and the general resurgence of German military power and aggressiveness. Hence, Congress repealed the arms embargo in November 1939. By that time, the Lockheed aircraft company was already delivering bombers to the British Royal Air Force under the largest order an American aviation firm had ever received.[6] President Roosevelt also made a deal to send 50 destroyers to Britain in 1940, after Germany had invaded France, in return for leases on British bases in the Western Hemisphere.

World War II brought about the most significant change yet in U.S. arms export policy. The Lend-Lease Act, passed in March 1941, created a channel for the American government to funnel military aid to its allies. "Starting with arms transferred pursuant to this act," a report by the U.S. General Accounting Office noted, "the U.S. government converted arms transfers from predominantly private to predominantly public channels."[7] From this time onward, arms transfers remained an important instrument of U.S. foreign and national security policy.

Arms Transfers in the Post-War World

During the war, President Roosevelt had hoped that America's sometimes strained wartime alliance with the Soviet Union would make a transition to friendly and cooperative peacetime relations. The reality, however, soon turned out to be an increasingly antagonistic relationship between the world's new "superpowers." U.S. foreign policy grew more and more dominated by fears that Soviet communism stood poised to sweep over a Europe that had been shattered by the war.

Policymakers in the United States believed that America's pre-war isolationism and the failure of England and France to take an early stand against Hitler had contributed to the rise of fascism, and they endeavored to avoid repeating these mistakes in dealing with the Soviet Union, a nation that they perceived as being, like Nazi Germany, an expansionist totalitarian regime. "Collective security" became America's strategy for defending what came to be called the Free World. In practice, this doctrine took the form of regional alliances for mutual defense against Soviet expansion and communist-supported insurrection. In Europe, where Americans perceived the greatest immediate threat and had the strongest historical ties, the United States sought to bolster collective security with military aid and a massive infusion of economic assistance.

Historians point to a speech made by President Truman on March 12, 1947, as the formal dedication of the United States to the prevention of communist expansion via military and economic assistance to threatened nations around the globe. This policy of "containment," unveiled in the Truman Doctrine, was precipitated by Great Britain's announcement that it no longer possessed the means with which to aid the government of Greece in a battle against an internal communist guerrilla movement. Arguing that "it must be the policy of the United States to support free peoples who are resisting attempted subjugation by armed minorities or by outside pressures," President Truman asked Congress for $400 million in economic and military aid for Greece and also Turkey, which the Soviet Union was pressuring in the hope of gaining joint control over the Dardanelles straits.

The Marshall Plan followed hard on the heels of the Greek-Turkish aid package. Congress voted for the massive infusion of economic assistance into Western Europe in the wake of a February 1948 communist coup in Czechoslovakia. A year later, 10 European nations joined the United States and Canada in a formal military alliance, the North Atlantic Treaty. Congress put teeth in the new collective security arrangement in the fall of 1949 when it passed the Mutual Defense Assistance Act, which led to the creation of programs that collectively came to be known as "security assistance." These included programs to grant, lend and sell military equipment and provide training in its use. (Security assistance programs and their relation to foreign military sales are discussed in detail in the next chapter.)

In the early years of pursuing containment through collective security, sales of weapons were generally low; deliveries of weapons through the foreign military sales channel did not reach $1 billion a year until the early 1960s.[8] Instead, most military equipment that was transferred took the form of grants under the Military Assistance Program. Initially, most of these grants came from war surplus stockpiles.

During the first decade of security assistance programs, the 1950s, by far the greatest portion of military aid went to the nations of Europe. The outbreak of the Korean War and an American commitment to help Taiwan defend itself against the threat from its communist mainland neighbor led to a significant commitment of resources to East Asia as well. Finally, the 1956 Arab-Israeli war led America to renew its commitment to friendly nations in the Middle East. (See Table 3–1) President Nasser of Egypt strengthened his country's ties with the Soviet Union after the resolution of the Suez Canal crisis. In response, and with the memory of the strong threats it had had to make to get Soviet troops out of Iran 10 years earlier, the United States sought to bolster pro-Western regimes in Iran, Jordan and Lebanon.

Until the late 1950s, these security assistance efforts enjoyed widespread support and generated little controversy. In the closing years of the decade, though, Congress began expressing some dissatisfaction with the program in its existing form. Cases of waste, fraud and poor administration aroused concern; other critics labeled the grant military aid program a "giveaway" that the United States could not fully afford. As a result, opponents in Congress who belonged to the committees responsible for security assistance succeeded in cutting the programs back and shifting some of the grant military aid to loans.[9]

Changes in the world political situation during the decade, as well as the inclinations of the new Kennedy administration, provided a more powerful impetus for shifts in the military assistance effort in the early 1960s. The first decade of the Cold War had focused on the "forward defense" nations that were either on or near the borders of communist-controlled countries. By the early 1960s, the political map in these areas had become more stable. Security assistance had helped the United States achieve many of its chief national security objectives, most notably the economic and military rebuilding of Western Europe and the defense of South Korea against communist aggression.

With much of the initial mission of military aid fulfilled, and with the United States able to ride out such tense moments as the erection of the Berlin Wall and the Cuban missile crisis without military conflict, the sense of urgency that had motivated strong support for security assistance efforts diminished substantially. At the same time, the Kennedy administration came into office espousing a belief, which had become prevalent among Democrats, that U.S. policy overemphasized military aid. President Kennedy believed that security assistance should emphasize long-term commitments rather than short-term emergency aid, and that promoting the economic development of the less-developed world would be a more effective counter to communist expansion than excessive military assistance. As a result, Kennedy reduced grant military aid and placed greater emphasis on economic assistance.

Table 3–1

U.S. Military Deliveries by Region, FY 1950–1986
(In thousands of FY 1986 Constant Dollars)

	Asia	Middle East	Africa	Latin America	Third World	Developed World
1950	$ 29,464	—	—	$ 685	$ 30,149	$ 470,602
1951	595,635	$ 60,072	—	5,734	661,441	5,326,963
1952	893,990	29,057	$ 87	74,529	997,663	7,346,782
1953	3,056,661	154,721	421	435,472	3,647,275	16,273,252
1954	3,032,265	216,608	23,798	279,393	3,552,064	14,898,963
1955	2,484,932	156,382	6,226	277,556	2,925,096	10,174,537
1956	3,993,758	208,335	23,088	168,121	4,393,302	11,270,220
1957	4,332,368	297,880	24,980	240,455	4,895,683	8,527,484
1958	3,733,535	753,647	49,927	387,663	4,924,772	7,637,423
1959	3,394,132	494,313	30,708	196,989	4,116,142	5,561,743
1960	2,951,858	444,022	45,753	314,407	3,756,040	5,523,899
1961	2,617,552	280,023	66,675	270,982	3,235,232	3,677,054
1962	2,557,250	161,973	80,825	228,381	3,028,429	3,669,945
1963	3,172,407	324,323	116,707	308,431	3,921,868	5,901,675
1964	2,504,978	182,180	126,485	250,483	3,064,126	3,657,424
1965	3,120,943	383,804	74,799	253,790	3,833,336	4,869,335
1966	4,079,397	502,772	107,440	291,189	4,980,798	3,706,185
1967	3,664,442	491,932	169,901	277,194	4,603,469	3,544,510
1968	6,144,754	610,949	119,450	387,871	7,263,024	3,558,691
1969	6,239,175	913,038	77,731	219,060	7,449,004	4,116,236
1970	7,584,072	1,358,755	114,735	179,408	9,236,970	3,365,952
1971	8,058,859	1,774,641	100,320	177,330	10,111,150	4,186,378
1972	8,667,043	1,952,544	158,379	242,258	11,020,224	3,454,067
1973	12,130,836	1,856,018	44,077	223,338	14,254,269	3,159,755
1974	4,522,894	4,807,194	68,298	224,946	9,623,332	3,775,329
1975	4,303,430	4,583,328	67,316	303,468	9,257,542	3,314,403
1976	1,516,404	8,107,613	169,909	428,596	10,222,522	4,692,635
1977	1,399,579	10,017,667	290,623	380,947	12,088,816	3,781,207
1978	1,787,743	9,927,813	353,968	206,285	12,275,809	3,630,088
1979	1,647,153	8,543,042	346,928	180,975	10,718,098	4,115,674
1980	1,662,938	5,677,650	182,300	188,498	7,711,386	5,657,559
1981	1,910,152	6,012,502	276,279	124,131	8,323,064	6,554,667
1982	1,531,807	7,285,994	246,019	265,612	9,329,432	5,511,298
1983	2,141,057	9,561,282	432,199	318,365	12,452,903	6,956,248
1984	1,869,106	5,699,062	443,517	392,351	8,404,036	6,338,474
1985	1,457,868	4,210,010	308,877	512,085	6,488,840	4,776,806
1986	1,589,559	3,745,826	212,356	400,018	5,947,759	3,831,451
Total	126,379,996	101,786,972	4,961,101	9,616,996	242,745,065	206,814,914

Kennedy did not seek to cut military aid too greatly, however. He saw military assistance as a highly cost-effective way to enhance U.S. national security. But a majority in Congress had begun to feel that America was overcommitted abroad. Accordingly, they made significant cuts in Kennedy's aid requests in his second and third years in office.[10]

The shift from military grants to military sales: Pressure to reduce grant military assistance came from another source as well: Concern about America's balance of payments deficit, then about $3 billion—a figure that seemed alarmingly large at the time.[11] The Eisenhower and the Kennedy administrations shared this concern, and both tried to persuade the once again prosperous nations of Europe to shoulder more of the cost of foreign economic aid. President Kennedy, for example, asked West Germany to bear the entire cost of aid to Turkey, which at the time cost the United States roughly $150 million.[12] Kennedy also sought to persuade the Western Europeans to spend more on U.S. arms. In a speech before Congress in February 1961, the President counseled that "the government must play a more vigorous part in helping to enlarge foreign markets for American goods and services." He therefore ordered Secretary of Defense Robert McNamara to "urge the purchase of new weapons and weapon systems by those of our allies who are financially capable of doing so."[13] Here too, Kennedy was following in the footsteps of his predecessors who during the late 1950s began trying to boost sales and reduce grants to Europe.

Concern over the American balance of trade deficit in part prompted McNamara to establish in 1962 a new agency in the Defense Department called the International Logistics Negotiations (ILN) group. The move away from grant military aid, coupled with the rebirth of the Western European armaments industry, caused unforeseen logistical problems. Once the United States stopped giving weapons to its European allies, American policymakers could no longer know with certainty what weapons the Europeans had stocked in their arsenals or what condition they were in. As one high ranking Pentagon official put it: "The cooperative logistics problem actually developed from the gap that resulted from congressional pressure to reduce grant assistance. When it was reduced, then we didn't know what our allies had."[14] Thus, the International Logistics Negotiations group was charged with the twin—but not entirely separate—duties of increasing logistical cooperation among the Allies and promoting the sale of American weapons to Western Europe. The creation of the ILN group was a watershed, for—in the words of one scholar—"the concept of military exports as government activity was institutionalized through [its] creation."[15]

To facilitate the sales effort, the United States offered credit arrangements to some arms purchasers, and the Defense Department developed logistics systems to provide substantial follow-on support for recipients of American military equipment. The change in emphasis had lasting effects on U.S. military aid figures. Under the auspices of the ILN office, U.S. foreign military sales in 1963 topped the $1 billion mark for the first time, with almost the entire increase coming from sales to the industrialized world.[16] In fiscal year 1961, grant aid totaled twice as much as sales. By 1966, however, foreign military sales totals were double those of grant assistance (excluding aid to South Vietnam).[17] (See Table 3–2.)

This first escalation of arms sales initially caused little reaction. Anthony Sampson has suggested as the reason that "the new involvement of governments helped to muffle any public concern about arms sales. For governments not only conferred a new respectability on the business; they also appeared to take over the moral responsibilities."[18] By the end of the decade, however, various factors would lead to the first widespread questioning of American arms export practices.

Table 3–2

U.S. Military Deliveries by Program, FY 1950–1986
(In Thousands of FY 1986 Constant Dollars)

FY	FMS & FMCS	CS	MAP	MASF	Excess MAP	Total
1950	$ 12,570	—	$ 310,228	—	$ 176,426	$ 499,224
1951	100,235	—	4,680,321	—	1,470,391	6,250,947
1952	374,648	—	7,318,924	—	958,726	8,652,298
1953	334,583	—	20,009,006	—	741,834	21,085,423
1954	698,257	—	17,458,187	—	509,440	18,665,884
1955	639,993	—	12,120,732	—	478,392	13,239,117
1956	600,965	—	14,792,293	—	475,344	15,868,602
1957	520,246	—	12,903,989	—	358,306	13,782,541
1958	1,570,500	—	10,808,971	—	990,311	13,369,782
1959	930,048	—	9,503,020	—	812,969	11,246,037
1960	1,466,771	—	7,729,153	—	978,813	10,174,737
1961	1,291,555	—	5,558,820	—	1,015,618	7,865,993
1962	1,462,539	—	4,714,482	—	1,054,197	7,231,218
1963	3,374,471	—	6,593,364	—	906,871	10,874,706
1964	1,993,904	—	4,886,863	—	584,203	7,464,970
1965	2,820,568	—	5,459,540	—	702,181	8,982,289
1966	2,784,653	—	3,791,586	$ 1,750,735	709,501	9,036,475
1967	2,854,156	—	3,342,808	2,264,877	1,360,000	9,821,841
1968	3,377,492	—	2,467,813	3,706,077	1,514,025	11,065,407
1969	4,157,320	—	1,969,108	3,879,251	1,725,692	11,731,371
1970	4,083,195	—	1,518,751	5,541,614	1,555,941	12,699,501
1971	4,027,859	$ 1,221,070	1,422,760	6,346,044	1,353,149	14,370,882
1972	3,851,688	1,266,447	1,379,469	7,027,159	975,022	14,499,785
1973	3,679,479	881,292	1,253,901	10,529,018	917,555	17,261,245
1974	7,195,891	1,135,396	1,572,450	2,620,462	690,611	13,214,810
1975	7,265,087	1,134,640	1,433,783	2,336,505	205,091	12,375,106
1976	11,197,245	2,726,889	708,001	—	086,987	14,719,122
1977	12,706,036	2,752,789	195,663	—	113,838	15,768,326
1978	12,637,051	2,805,636	367,412	—	9,126	15,819,225
1979	12,164,402	2,353,094	244,029	16,327	4,263	14,782,115
1980	9,955,707	2,716,291	418,530	181,470	23,650	13,295,648
1981	11,351,308	2,732,498	259,787	123,902	21,855	14,489,350
1982	12,273,734	2,097,235	333,172	151,480	6,716	14,862,337
1983	14,565,369	4,487,372	193,244	—	—	19,245,985
1984	10,472,953	4,136,029	139,413	—	—	14,748,395
1985	8,988,960	2,368,857	24,151	—	—	11,381,968
1986	7,739,352	2,013,275	28,040	—	—	9,780,667
Total	$185,520,790	$36,828,810	$167,911,764	$46,474,921	$23,487,044	$460,223,329

Table 3–2. Continued

Legend: FMS—Foreign Military Sales.
FMCS—Foreign Military Construction Sales.
CS—Commercial Sales
MASF—Military Assistance Service Fund
Excess MAP—Excess Military Articles Program

Source: Department of Defense Security Assistance Agency (DSAA), 1986 Fiscal
Year Series, (Washington: DSAA, 1987).

Congress further formalized the distinction between sales and grants in 1968 with passage of the Foreign Military Sales Act. This legislation removed cash and credit arms sales from the Military Assistance Program, which previously had included them, and gave the Foreign Military Sales program separate legislative authority. The act also expressed some of Congress's growing concerns about arms exports. For example, it urged the President to refrain from arms sales to countries ruled by dictators or lacking sufficient funds for both arms purchases and social development.[19]

Perhaps the most significant trend of the 1960s, however, saw a shift in the focus of U.S. security assistance efforts from the industrialized to the developing world. (See Figure 3–1.) The deepening U.S. involvement in Vietnam gave particular impetus to this development. In 1965, Congress established a separate grant aid program, the Military Assistance Service Fund (MASF), specifically earmarked for South Vietnam and the other Southeast Asian countries involved in the conflict. As public opinion in the United States turned against American military actions in Vietnam, new pressures developed to restrict and redirect U.S. military aid programs. Members of Congress grew to resent what they viewed as insufficient consultation with them by President Johnson on foreign policy matters. Members also expressed concern that the high costs of military aid would substantially increase levels of inflation.[20]

The negative assessment of the Vietnam experience among Americans translated into an aversion to military aid, a practice that seemed likely to lead to other undesirable entanglements abroad. In addition, the OPEC price shocks of 1973–74 changed the economic environment within which military assistance decisions were made. As a result, significant shifts occurred in American arms transfer practices in the early 1970s.

The Nixon doctrine: Some of the changes resulted from initiatives of President Nixon. In reaction to the Vietnam experience, Nixon decided that the United States should reduce its presence abroad and—while maintaining treaty commitments and a willingness to provide security assistance—shift more of the burden for defense of other nations onto those countries themselves. In 1969, the President unveiled the Nixon Doctrine, under which the United States would "look to the nation directly threatened to assume the primary responsibility of providing the manpower for its defense."[21] Nixon also believed that more of the costs of military assistance needed to be shifted abroad, leading to further efforts to replace grant aid with credits and sales.

The oil price rise after 1973 and its attendant effects on nations' trade balances created additional pressures to export arms. The United States began to sell modern, sophisticated weaponry to nations other than its traditional treaty allies. In particular, the United States sought to offset the rising costs of oil imports by increasing its sales of weapons—especially expensive top-of-the-line equipment—to the oil-producing nations of the Middle East. Indeed, the Nixon administration's largesse in

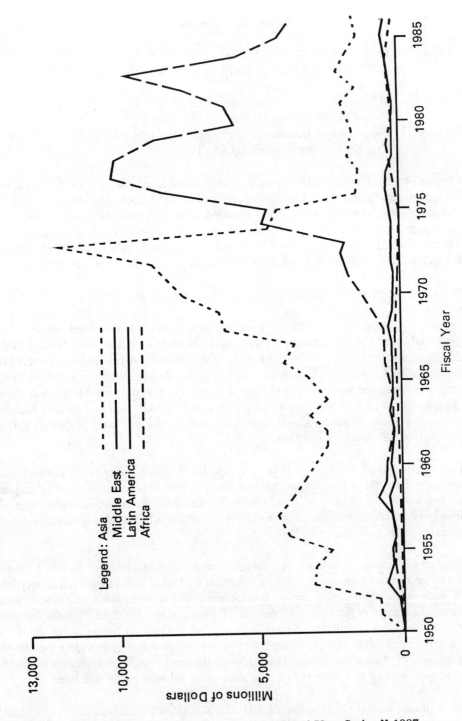

Source: Defense Security Assistance Agency "Fiscal Year Series," 1987.

Figure 3–1.   U.S. Military Deliveries to the Third World
(in millions of constant 1986 dollars)

offering American arms to other nations soon began to generate controversy. At one point, Secretary of State Henry Kissinger offered to sell Pershing intermediate-range ballistic missiles, which can carry a nuclear warhead, to Israel. The Pentagon, which had not been consulted, later dissuaded him. An offer made by President Nixon, with no staff consultation, to the Shah of Iran caused even greater disquiet. Nixon told the Shah that the United States would sell him any weapons he desired short of nuclear arms. Agreements to sell F-14 fighters and advanced Spruance class destroyers to Iran were made in a manner that bypassed the usual government review process.[22]

Episodes such as these left many observers with the impression that the administration had a cavalier attitude towards arms transfers. At the same time, the volume of weapons sales was climbing dramatically. In the first five years of the 1970s, U.S. foreign military sales increased by a factor of 14, to more than $16 billion in new agreements in 1975, measured in current dollars.[23] A large percentage of this increase reflected inflation, and another portion was offset by declining levels of grant aid. Still, the Arms Control and Disarmament Agency reported a 150 percent real increase in the value of annual U.S. arms deliveries over the 1968–77 decade.[24]

One additional factor prompted concern about foreign military sales in the mid-1970s. During 1974–76, as a result of information uncovered during the Watergate investigation, the public learned that a number of aerospace companies had been spending large sums of money to bribe foreign officials to buy their arms. Northrop was the first company forced to admit that it had given money to foreign officials. In June 1975, the Senate Subcommittee on Multinational Corporations began public hearings on Northrop's foreign payments. Company officials admitted paying $30 million to foreign consultants and sales agents between 1971 and 1973, including $450,000 earmarked to bribe two Saudi Arabian generals.[25]

After Northrop, attention turned to Lockheed. The Senate subcommittee accumulated evidence of major Lockheed payments to high officials in a number of countries. In all, Lockheed paid what it called "kickbacks" of at least $22 million to officials and political organizations in 15 countries to promote foreign sales between 1970 and 1975. Revelations of some of the payments had repercussions abroad. In the Netherlands the monarchy was nearly toppled when Lockheed admitted paying $1 million to the Dutch prince, the husband of Queen Juliana. Even larger bribes of Japanese officials became a factor in elections in Japan. While the Northrop and Lockheed scandals were the most visible, other arms firms such as Boeing and McDonnell Douglas also ended up admitting questionable payments.[26]

The combination of certain specific Nixon arms sales decisions (particularly a 1973 proposal to sell jet fighters to several Arab and Latin countries), rapid growth in the total amount of weapons sales, and corporate bribery scandals led to a perception among much of the press, the public and Congress that U.S. arms sales had gotten out of control. Sen. Gaylord Nelson's (D-Wis.) sentiments were typical: "Despite the serious policy issues raised by this tremendous increase in government arms sales, these transactions are made with little regard for congressional or public opinion. The Department of Defense is consulted. The manufacturers of weapons and providers of military services are consulted. The foreign purchasers are involved. But Congress is hardly informed of these transactions, much less consulted as to their propriety. As it stands now, the Executive Branch simply presents Congress and the public with accomplished facts."[27] In the mid-1970s, therefore, Congress took steps to try to increase its oversight of military exports.

A 1974 amendment to the Foreign Assistance Act sponsored by Nelson gave Congress a limited legislative veto over arms sales. The Nelson Amendment required that the Executive Branch give

20 days advance notice of any foreign military sale to any single country of more than $25 million, during which time Congress could block the sale if both houses passed a concurrent resolution of disapproval. Congress, therefore, could block an arms sale with a majority vote in both houses, and since concurrent resolutions need not be signed by the President in order to take effect, the legislative measure could not be vetoed by the Executive Branch.

Also by the mid-1970s, the political context in which policymakers discussed military assistance efforts had changed, and the rationale for transfers of arms shifted somewhat. According to Steven Hildreth, a fellow at the Georgetown Center for Strategic and International Studies, there was "a change from the explicit emphasis on anticommunism and the consequent benefits to the United States derived from reliance upon anticommunist regional powers. The thrust now became one of enhancing U.S. ability to influence others and pursue U.S. foreign policy objectives."[28] At the same time, however, questions about the effectiveness of arms transfers in achieving these goals were increasing, as were concerns about potentially adverse effects of some transfers. The post-Vietnam war feeling that arms relationships often served only to draw America into unwanted conflicts persisted. Members of Congress and sections of the public, though, also expressed greater concern about the human rights consequences of sales to regimes with records of abuse, and they questioned whether certain sales might be fueling arms races and adding to instability in regions such as the Middle East.

Even before the 1974 Nelson Amendment, Congress had been showing signs of becoming more assertive—and more critical—with regard to arms sales. A 1971 resolution expressed the sense of Congress that the President should institute a comprehensive review of military assistance and sales programs and initiate efforts to control the world arms trade. Sen. William Fulbright (D-Ark.) also led an unsuccessful attempt to shift a greater portion of sales back to commercial channels and reduce government involvement. However, commercial sales remained relatively steady while government-to-government sales continued to climb.[29]

Congress also began to take actions focused on specific countries. After the Turkish invasion of Cyprus in 1974, the legislature imposed an arms embargo against Turkey. (Congress passed a de facto repeal of the embargo in 1978, having been convinced that Turkey's strategic location in the eastern Mediterranean and its common border with Russia necessitated maintaining American aid.) In the winter of 1975–76, Congress also approved an amendment sponsored by Sen. Dick Clark (D-Iowa) to prohibit the use of funds to support anticommunist rebels in Angola. (With the encouragement of the Reagan administration, which argued that the President should not have his hands tied, Congress voted to lift this ban in 1985. Opponents of repeal argued that it would be seen as "further evidence of America entering into cooperation with the apartheid government of South Africa.")[30]

Congress's growing desire to be involved in arms sale decisionmaking culminated in the passage of the Arms Export Control Act of 1976. Through this legislation, Congress sought to change the emphasis in U.S. policy from selling weapons to controlling their sale. The act's opening paragraphs directed: "It shall be the policy of the United States to exert leadership in the world community to bring about arrangements for reducing the international trade in implements of war. . . ."[31] Although President Ford vetoed a slightly stronger version of the bill, the version enacted still expanded the oversight function that Congress had voted for itself with the Nelson Amendment and it lengthened the time during which Congress could pass a concurrent resolution to block a sale from 20 to 30 days. In addition, the Pentagon in February 1976 agreed to provide Congress with "preliminary notification" of imminent arms sales 20 days in advance of submitting a formal notice, leaving the Legislative Branch with close to two months instead of one in which to review proposed sales. The informal notice, according to the Congressional Research Service:

> would give additional time to both Congress and the Executive Branch to explore aspects of the particular sale that might need clarification or which might be especially controversial. It was also hoped that through this approach, potential misunderstandings could be resolved before formal submission of an arms sale case.[32]

In a reversal of the unsuccessful initiative of a few years earlier, the act also mandated that any non-NATO arms sale of more than $25 million be handled through government-to-government rather than commercial channels. Congress viewed this requirement as a way to cut down on dealings between U.S. companies and foreign governments of the sort revealed in the Senate subcommittee hearings. The legislation also contained a restriction on the activities of U.S. military assistance advisory groups in foreign countries.

In addition, Congress required the President to submit quarterly reports on arms transfers, and also amended earlier legislation to prohibit security assistance, except in extraordinary circumstances, to any country "engaged in consistent patterns of gross violations of internationally recognized human rights."[33] Finally, the act required the President to phase out the grant Military Assistance Program, and it created a separate International Military Education and Training program, a step that sought to cement a trend already underway for more than a decade. Grants under the Military Assistance Program aid had fallen to $1 billion for fiscal 1975, while sales agreements through the Foreign Military Sales program totaled $16 billion that year.[34]

The Carter Policy: An Exercise in Restraint

Also in 1976, a presidential candidate, Jimmy Carter, raised the issue of arms sales in an election campaign for the first time. Upon assuming the presidency Jimmy Carter directed Secretary of State Cyrus Vance to develop a new set of guidelines for U.S. arms export policy. After review by the National Security Council, Carter incorporated Vance's recommendations in a Presidential Directive, PD-13. The Congressional Research Service has described the policy set out in this document as, "in important ways, a continuation and further development of congressional initiatives of the early 1970s."[35]

The President announced PD-13 with the release, on May 19, 1977, of a statement on the arms trade. "The virtually unrestrained spread of conventional weaponry threatens stability in every region of the world," Carter's statement began. After a brief review of recent trends in global arms sales, the President added: "Because of the threat to world peace embodied in this spiraling arms traffic, and because of the special responsibilities we bear as the largest arms seller, I believe the United States must take steps to restrain its arms transfers."[36]

Carter announced that henceforth Washington would view arms transfers as "an exceptional foreign policy implement, to be used only in instances where it can be clearly demonstrated that the transfer contributes to our national security interests." He added that, "in the future, the burden of persuasion will be on those who favor a particular sale, rather than those who oppose it." To implement this policy, the President specified several controls that would be applied to all arms transfers except those to NATO nations, Japan, Australia and New Zealand. The presidential statement also made reference to "our historic responsibilities to . . . the state of Israel." And the statement reserved to the President the right to make other exceptions under "extraordinary circumstances."[37]

The controls that were to guide U.S. policy were:

1. A ceiling on arms sales. The President pledged to hold new arms sales agreements, excluding services and commercial sales, to less than their fiscal 1977 total.

2. Limits on sophistication. The United States would "not be the first supplier to introduce into a region newly developed, advanced weapons systems which would create a new or significantly higher combat capability." Export or coproduction agreements regarding such weapons would be prohibited until they had been operationally deployed by U.S. armed forces, in order to remove incentives to promote foreign sales as a way to lower unit costs for the Pentagon.

3. A ban on export-only weapons and coproduction. "Development or significant modification of advanced weapons systems solely for export" would be prohibited, as would new coproduction agreements for major weapons with non-exempt nations.

4. A ban on retransfers. No U.S. weapons or components could be sold to third parties without American consent.

5. Restrictions on promotion. Embassy and military representatives would not promote arms sales, and arms manufacturers would have to obtain State Department authorization to do so.

In addition, the document made mention of the need to "promote and advance respect for human rights" and to "assess the economic impact of arms transfers" to developing nations. Finally, the Carter statement committed the United States to initiate negotiations with other suppliers in the understanding that "actual reductions in the worldwide traffic in arms will require multilateral cooperation."[38]

The Carter policy in action—mixed results: The effort to implement these controls had mixed results. According to government officials, the Carter administration turned down 614 requests from 92 countries totaling more than $1 billion in the first 15 months of the new policy. The administration denied requests from Iran for F-4G Wild Weasel electronic warfare aircraft, from Taiwan for F-4 Phantom fighters, from Guatemala for F-5 fighters, from Pakistan for A-7 fighter-bombers (although the administration did let Pakistan know that it would look favorably upon requests for the less capable A-4 or F-5 aircraft), and from Turkey and Greece for F-16 fighters. In each of these cases, the country involved did not turn to other suppliers to make equivalent purchases. But in other instances, countries denied arms by the Carter administration did acquire comparable weapons from alternate suppliers. Ecuador, for example, purchased French Mirage fighters after the United States prevented it from obtaining F-5s or Israeli Kfir fighters (which contain American components). India bought British Jaguar fighters after its effort to buy Swedish Viggen fighters was blocked because the Swedish aircraft contained an American engine. Argentina secured jets from Israel, submarines from Germany and helicopters from France because it was barred by legislation from obtaining American military equipment.[39]

The attempt to apply human rights criteria to security assistance programs also led to some reductions in transfers of military equipment. During consideration of the foreign aid bill in 1977, Congress earmarked several countries, including Brazil, Argentina, Uruguay, El Salvador, Guatemala and Ethiopia, for reductions in aid. Carter, while vocal about human rights concerns, sought to maintain flexibility in making actual responses. Thus, the degree of aid cuts varied from country to country. This angered some members of Congress who believed that Carter's policy needed to be more consistent.[40] Aid reductions also resulted in lower levels of arms sales for indirect reasons. Latin American countries such as Brazil were angered by the restrictions on military assistance, and responded by reducing their purchases of American arms.[41] (A more detailed discussion of human rights and arms transfers is contained in Chapter 5.)

Although the Carter administration decided against some arms sales that other administrations might have approved, it still agreed to a large number of sales, including some that were quite controversial. A 1978 agreement to provide a $4.8 billion plane package to three Middle Eastern countries proved to be Carter's most controversial decision. The package consisted of 60 F-15 fighters, America's most advanced, for Saudi Arabia; 50 F-5 fighters for Egypt; and 15 F-15s plus 75 F-16s for Israel. (The administration later gave Egypt permission to ask for the more advanced F-15 or F-16 as well.) Only assurances that the Saudi F-15s would not be equipped with offensive capabilities and would be based beyond striking distance of Israel prevented congressional veto of the sale. An earlier decision to sell Iran seven Airborne Warning and Control System (Awacs) planes also generated controversy. Congressional opposition delayed, but did not prevent, reaching an agreement on this sale (which was canceled when the Shah fell). Other significant arms export decisions of Carter's term included an agreement to extend $1.8 billion in grants and credit to South Korea for a variety of major weapons and another to sell OV-10 counterinsurgency aircraft to Morocco.[42]

With decisions such as these, the announced ceiling on arms transfers turned out in practice to be relatively ineffective. Carter did reduce sales to the nonexempt nations, from their $9.3 billion level in fiscal 1977 to $8.55 billion in fiscal 1978 and $8.43 billion the following year (making two annual reductions of 8 percent after inflation had been factored out). But overall U.S. arms exports did not drop during this time. Sales to the 18 exempt nations as well as commercial exports and sales of military services and construction, which were also not counted in the ceiling, increased more than enough to offset the decline in arms transfers to the nonexempt nations. In fact, total U.S. arms exports (including both government-to-government and commercial sales) climbed from $12.8 billion in 1977 to $17.1 billion in 1980. Moreover, when he announced the second 8 percent reduction in December 1978, Carter added that any further reductions would depend "on the degree of cooperation we receive in the coming year from other nations" in limiting their own exports. In March 1980, the President decided against any further reductions in arms exports to the nonexempt nations.[43]

Concerns about the behavior of nations receiving military assistance, though, continued to influence administration and congressional policy throughout the Carter presidency. In 1979, Congress reduced aid to several nations, including South Korea, the Philippines, Panama and the Sudan, because of their human rights records. Reports that Pakistan was engaged in efforts to develop a nuclear weapons capability also led the Carter administration to suspend all aid to that nation in 1979.[44]

The Carter administration also initiated international discussions aimed at limiting the world arms trade. Preliminary quiet discussions with America's allies in Europe revealed that these countries believed the Soviet Union needed to be included in any talks. As a result, the Carter administration focused most of its subsequent efforts on discussions with the Soviet Union. American and Russian delegations met four times between December 1977 and December 1978 to discuss multilateral restraint of weapons transfers. These delegations to the Conventional Arms Transfer Talks made some progress, but reached no final agreements. This was in large part because of the general deterioration of U.S.-Soviet relations that followed on the heels of the Soviet invasion of Afghanistan. Other contributing factors included internal disagreements within the Carter administration about the American approach, failure to involve the Europeans, and the unilateral commitment to restraint that the United States had made before the talks even began.[45]

With regard to the qualitative controls set out in PD-13, President Carter made a number of exceptions. The Congressional Research Service reported that the President waived major guidelines of his policy in 17 instances, 13 of them involving agreements for the coproduction of weapons abroad.[46] One of the other exceptions led to considerable controversy and a dispute between Congress and the Air Force. Contrary to the order he had given three years earlier, in 1980 Carter called upon U.S. aerospace firms to develop fighters specifically for the export market. The fighters, initially designated FX, were to be less sophisticated versions of America's most advanced modern fighters, which Carter was unwilling to sell to any but a handful of nations, but more advanced than older export planes such as the F-5, which many nations were no longer interested in buying. Two American firms developed FX planes. General Dynamics developed a less-capable version of its F-16, while Northrop devised a plane that eventually was designated the F-20 Tigershark. However, the two companies found themselves without a market for their FX aircraft when the Reagan administration proved willing to sell front-line fighters to a number of countries that had been denied such planes by its predecessor. Northrop eventually decided that it would have to sell F-20s to the U.S. armed forces in order to recoup the money it had invested in developing the aircraft, and launched an ill fated but intensive campaign to persuade the government to purchase F-20s for American use. (See box, p. 51.)

Assessing the Carter initiative: On balance, most observers found a great deal to criticize about Carter's arms export policies. Those who had reacted favorably to Carter's early pronouncements on the need to reduce arms transfers were disappointed when arms exports continued to be a widely used foreign policy tool. And those who supported arms sales as such a tool were critical of Carter's inconsistencies in applying his controls, feeling that the President succeeded only in alienating valuable friends without limiting the global arms trade. In a 1981 critique of both the Carter policy and the earlier congressional initiatives, the conservative Heritage Foundation wrote: "Policy initiatives taken first by the Congress and then by the Carter administration to restrict security assistance have seriously eroded the cohesion and military capabilities of the non-Communist world." The limitations of introducing new weapon systems into a region, developing export-only weapons, coproduction agreements and retransfers "effectively precluded all but the sale of aging or obsolete equipment and drove other nations to purchase Soviet or Western European equipment," Heritage argued. "Perhaps most importantly," the Heritage report added, "the range of restrictions imposed by the U.S. only reinforced the growing belief that the U.S. was no longer a reliable supplier of military equipment."[47]

Other observers, however, assert that the Carter policy also had important positive aspects. Leslie Gelb, who served in the State Department under Carter and represented the United States at some of the Conventional Arms Transfer Talks, testified that "The existence of the ceiling made

The Death of The Northrop F-20

The F-20, born out of President Carter's decision that the United States would "not be the first supplier to introduce into a region newly developed, advanced weapons systems which would create a new or significantly higher combat capability," conflicted with many Third World allies' desire to update their 1960s vintage fighters. The FX (fighter for export) program was unveiled as the solution: It called for the private development of a fighter with "intermediate capabilities designed exclusively for export." The FX would be cheaper and not as technologically advanced as the top-of-the-line U.S. warplanes, but it still would be an improvement over the older fighters then flown by recipients of American arms. Carter assured the defense industry that he would create a market for the new fighter by refusing to issue export licenses for more advanced planes.

Northrop and General Dynamics were the only contractors to respond to the FX call. General Dynamics offered a downgraded version of its F-16, while Northrop designed an essentially new fighter, the F-20 Tigershark. Northrop spent $1.4 billion of its own money developing the aircraft, an unusual decision on its part; most defense contractors do not embark on a weapons program unless they have government contracts in hand.

When President Reagan abandoned the Carter policy of restraint and began supplying friendly nations with top-of-the-line F-16 fighters, foreign customers lost interest in the less capable F-20. As a result, Northrop was not able to conclude a single Tigershark sale, although some Middle Eastern and Southeast Asian nations expressed an interest in acquiring the fighter at various points. Early in his tenure, President Reagan denied a request from Taiwan for F-20s on the grounds that the plane's offensive potential would alarm the People's Republic of China.

Frustrated abroad, Northrop decided in 1984 to market the F-20 at home and lobbied the Pentagon aggressively. The company embarked on this course of action in the belief that even a small-scale sale of F-20s to the U.S. military would help recoup some of the development costs that it had incurred. More importantly, the company hoped that acceptance of the F-20 into the American arsenal would boost the plane's image overseas and perhaps lead to foreign military sales. Foreign customers are more comfortable with weapons already used by the U.S. military because they are then guaranteed the continued availability of spare parts and maintenance.

With interest in reforming the military procurement process running high, some members of Congress supported the F-20 as a way of injecting competition into the Pentagon's procurement process. In September 1985, Congress instructed the Pentagon to conduct a fly-off between the downgraded F-16 and the F-20 and allocated funds for the projected purchase of 270 of whichever aircraft prevailed. The Department of Defense settled on an alternative path when in November 1986 it elected to remove 270 early model F-16s from active Air Force units and reassign them to the National Guard. The Air Force fighters, in turn, will be replaced with newer, more sophisticated F-16s, and the aircraft reassigned to National Guard duty will be upgraded with modern radar, communications and weapons systems, for which General Dynamics will receive a $633 million contract. Two weeks after the announcement of the Pentagon decision, Northrop closed its books on the F-20.

a real difference in giving the State Department some real authority, for the first time, in the general management of the sales program."[48] Andrew Pierre elaborates on this point in an assessment of the Carter policy:

> The Carter policy as implemented, in spite of its shortcomings, made the internal decisionmaking process on arms sales more rigorous and systematic. By shifting the burden of persuasion from those who opposed a sale to those who favored it, the policy added requirements for analysis and long-range planning.[49]

Some observers attribute the Carter administration's arms export policy's shortcomings to less than perfect execution. Paul Hammond of the University of Pittsburgh, David Louscher of the University of Akron, Michael Salomone of Carnegie Mellon University and Norman Graham of the Futures Group in a 1983 study of U.S. arms export policy point to the administration's inability to "follow through with its implementation with single-minded determination."[50] In their view, the many exceptions made to the rules resulted in a gradual erosion of the Carter administration's credibility and overall efforts at restraint. Hammond and his colleagues explain the myriad exceptions made to the Carter policy guidelines this way:

> Despite his desire for restraint and his public and diplomatic support for restraint, President Carter learned that because of the limited number of instruments available to him for dealing with international problems, arms transfers were simply too useful for too many purposes to be extensively curtailed.[51]

In the analysis of Hammond and his colleagues, the erosion of the administration's unilateral effort, combined with the fact that President Carter relegated the Conventional Arms Transfer Talks to backseat status, drastically lessened the likelihood that the initiative could succeed. This last point figures prominently in the analysis of the Carter approach offered by Hammond and his colleagues. In their view, because "CATT became a secondary issue, a stepchild among the seven arms control initiatives given birth to or nurtured by the Carter administration," enormous bureaucratic splits that developed within the U.S. government were never settled or reconciled, which precluded the projection of a focused and firm American position and made it difficult to attract the attention and cooperation of other weapons suppliers.[52] To a certain extent, Pierre agrees: "Ultimately . . . [the Carter administration's] success depended upon the ability of the United States to enlist other nations in a multilateral strategy for restraining arms sales . . . [and] only minimal advances were made in this direction."[53]

Nevertheless, all experts—irrespective of their political or ideological sympathies—at heart agree in their assessment of the Carter policy: It was ambitious in its aspirations because of the complicated interplay between arms and exports and larger foreign policy objectives, the mechanics of international relations, domestic politics and economic imperatives. Analysis of the myriad inter-connected issues clustered around the practice of exporting arms suggest that any attempts to curb the international sale of arms must overcome formidable political and economic barriers before they can be successful.[54]

The Reagan Reversal

The approach of the Reagan administration to arms transfer policy has been nearly a polar opposite to that of the Carter White House. In his first months in office, the new President ended most of the Carter control initiatives and instituted reforms of his own intended to facilitate the use of arms transfers as a policy tool. The Reagan administration quickly dropped the annual ceiling on arms sale levels, for example. It also rescinded the so-called "leprosy letter" of Aug. 31, 1977, that had directed personnel in U.S. embassies and military missions abroad to refrain from activities that would help promote foreign arms sales. In addition, the President instructed the State Department to devise an alternative policy to Carter's PD-13.

The first announcement of the new policy came on May 21, 1981, in a speech to the Aerospace Industries Association by the new Under Secretary of State for Security Assistance, James Buckley (a former Republican Senator). Buckley argued that the Soviet Union had greatly improved its military position vis-à-vis the United States in recent years. In the face of this Soviet challenge, he said, the Carter administration had shirked responsibility with a policy on arms transfers "that substituted theology for a healthy sense of self-preservation." Buckley also criticized congressional limitations placed on arms transfers for reasons such as human rights violations or nuclear proliferation intentions. "While these well-intentioned efforts have had little detectable impact on such behavior or intentions," he said, "they did lead at times to the awkward result of undercutting the capabilities of strategically located nations in whose ability to defend themselves we have the most immediate and urgent self-interest." Buckley said the Reagan administration believed that "arms transfers, judiciously applied, can complement and supplement our own defense efforts and serve as a vital and constructive instrument of American foreign policy."[55]

Formal announcement of the new policy came on July 8, with the issuing of a directive to supersede PD-13. Where Carter's directive had begun by decrying the effect of an "unrestrained" arms trade on regional stability, the Reagan statement focused immediately on "challenges and hostility toward fundamental U.S. interests . . . (that) have grown significantly in recent years." It said, "The United States must, in today's world, not only strengthen its own military capabilities, but be prepared to help its friends and allies to strengthen theirs through the transfer of conventional arms and other forms of security assistance." The new directive listed several advantages that the administration believed would derive from judiciously applied arms transfers. It said weapons transfers can "help deter aggression," improve the effectiveness of U.S. armed forces, increase the ability of American forces to operate with those of friends and allies, demonstrate American commitment to the security of friends and allies, "foster regional and internal stability," and "help enhance United States defense production capabilities and efficiency."[56]

In place of the specific guidelines, designed to constrain U.S. arms exports, contained in PD-13, the Reagan directive emphasized that requests for arms would be reviewed on a case-by-case basis and suggested only generally the criteria that policymakers would use to evaluate such requests. Washington would look at potential arms transfers "primarily in terms of their net contribution to enhanced deterrence and defense," it said. The directive listed seven more specific factors on which decision-makers would base such evaluations. These were:

- the degree to which the transfer responds appropriately to the military threats confronting the recipient;

- whether the transfer will enhance the recipient's capability to participate in collective security efforts with the United States;

- whether the transfer will promote mutual interests in countering externally supported aggression;

- whether the transfer is consistent with U.S. interests in maintaining stability within regions where friends of the United States may have differing objectives;

- whether the transfer is compatible with the needs of U.S. forces, recognizing that occasions will arise when other nations may require scarce items on an emergency basis;

- whether the proposed equipment transfer can be absorbed by the recipient without overburdening its military support system or financial resources; and

- whether any detrimental effects of the transfer are more than counter-balanced by positive contributions to U.S. interests and objectives.

The directive also explicitly countermanded two other elements of the Carter policy. It said that proposals to develop intermediate-capability weapons solely for export would be given "careful consideration," and also that overseas government officials "will be expected to provide the same courtesies and assistance to firms that have obtained licenses to market items on the United States Munitions List as they would to those marketing other American products." Finally, the Reagan statement addressed the question of multilateral restraints. It said the United States "retains a genuine interest in arms transfer restraint" and would entertain any proposals made toward that end. But it did not commit the United States to take any initiatives, saying: "There has been . . . little or no interest in arms transfer limitations manifested by the Soviet Union, or the majority of other arms-producing nations. In the absence of such interest, the United States will not jeopardize its own security needs through a program of unilateral restraint."[57]

The Reagan directive made no specific mention of human rights as a concern. Under Secretary Buckley described administration policy in this area in Senate testimony later in the month. The administration would seek to encourage human rights, Buckley said. However, such concerns would not be foremost. Rather, "our primary purpose in transferring arms to another country is not to help a particular regime but to buttress our own security and serve our own interests," he cautioned the senators.[58]

The contrast between these Reagan administration pronouncements and the rhetoric of the Carter era caused concern among some observers. Congressional Quarterly described the Reagan policy as one that "contains no guidelines."[59] Even some of those who greatly preferred Reagan's defense policies to Carter's expressed some doubt about the new arms transfer policy. Aviation Week & Space Technology editorialized that "the Reagan guidelines are more a repeal of Carter human rights doctrinarism than the adoption of a new policy."[60]

Certainly, the initial signs pointed to a boom in U.S. arms exports. Even before the new policy had been given its final formulation, the Reagan administration had granted approval to several arms sales that had been delayed by Carter. Indeed, Reagan offered foreign countries military equipment and services worth $15 billion in his first three months in office.[61] Reagan dropped the Carter ban on aid to Pakistan, and agreed to sell it F-16 fighters. The administration also gave Venezuela permission to buy F-16s, reversing a longstanding U.S. policy of restraint in selling supersonic combat aircraft to nations in Latin America. In addition, the United States sold Cobra helicopters with anti-tank missiles to Jordan and tanks and planes to Morocco, and dropped its objections to Israeli exports of the Kfir fighter, which contains an American engine.

With the more open policy of the new administration, agreements under the Foreign Military Sales and Foreign Military Construction Sales programs grew from $7.6 billion in fiscal year 1981 to $20.3 billion in fiscal 1982.[62] Measured in constant 1985 dollars, arms agreements with the Third World rose from $7.9 billion to $14.1 billion between 1981 and 1982.[63] Yet, some observers felt that the contrasting rhetoric of the Carter and Reagan administrations exaggerated the actual level of difference in their policies. A report by the Congressional Research Service in fall 1981 suggested: "In practice the Reagan arms transfer policy may prove to be less distinct from the Carter policy than the two policy statements would indicate. The Carter administration did not drastically reduce U.S. transfers, and the Reagan administration has stated it does not expect to increase transfers drastically."[64] In fact, after the record levels of fiscal 1982, the volume of U.S. arms sale agreements has declined. However, as Chapter 1 discusses, the reasons appear to lie more in the faltering economies of most Third World nations and the time required to absorb earlier purchases of American weapons than in any disinclination of the Reagan administration to export more arms.

An arms sale decision made during Reagan's first few months in office proved to be one of the most controversial sales ever approved. In February 1980, Saudi Arabia asked the United States for E-3A Awacs planes. The Carter administration had pledged not to provide Saudi Arabia with sophisticated air surveillance aircraft of this nature or other equipment that would enhance the capabilities of the F-15 fighters it sold the Saudis in 1978, in order to get congressional approval of this earlier controversial sale. Carter decided to delay a decision on the new Saudi request until after the 1980 election.

The new administration announced shortly after Reagan took office, however, that it had decided to approve an Awacs package for Saudi Arabia that also included Sidewinder missiles and long-range fuel tanks for the F-15s plus aerial tankers. Many congressional leaders, as well as the government of Israel and U.S. Jewish groups, expressed opposition almost immediately. After the administration gave Congress formal notification of the sale on Oct. 1, 1981, the House voted overwhelmingly to block the transaction. An intense lobbying campaign focused on the Senate followed. The Reagan administration put a great deal of pressure on wavering senators and was supported in this effort by large numbers of American corporations, including both the main contractors for the Awacs and many firms that would not be directly affected by the sale. On Oct. 28, the Senate voted to uphold the sale in a 48–52 vote against the resolution of disapproval.

The Awacs sale led to a followup program that generated little controversy. In February 1985, Boeing was selected to be the prime contractor for an advanced air defense system for Saudi Arabia designed by the U.S. Air Force. The computerized system, called Peace Shield, is supposed to link the Saudis' Awacs planes with five underground command centers and 17 long-range radars and reportedly will be worth $4 billion.

The public attention focused on arms sales dropped off considerably after the Awacs debate, but was revived in the mid-1980s within the context of sales to moderate Arab nations. The rate of foreign orders for weapons also subsided somewhat, but the Reagan administration has continued to make significant arms transfer decisions. Several Southeast Asian nations will be receiving F-16s with full-powered engines, the first to be sent to this region. In 1985, Thailand and Singapore reached agreements with the United States for F-16s, and in 1986 South Korea received the first of the 36 F-16s it had ordered to date. In June 1986, Indonesia chose the F-16 over the French Mirage-2000 fighter. In addition, the early part of 1985 also saw American offers to sell OV-10 counterinsurgency aircraft to South Korea and Harpoon anti-ship missiles to Singapore. Other nations given approval by the Reagan administration to buy F-16s have included Turkey and Greece, and Pakistan has been promised Sidewinder missiles for the F-16s it had purchased earlier.

The Reagan administration has also sought to initiate new arms relationships. The President in 1985 told Algeria's leader that his nation would be permitted to buy U.S. arms for the first time. The United States also signed an agreement with India that is expected to lead to large-scale arms sales to that nation. (American military exports to India have been negligible since that country's 1965 war with Pakistan, in which both sides used American weapons.)

Perhaps the most significant development along these lines, however, is the encouragement that Washington has given to the People's Republic of China to buy U.S. military equipment. In 1984, China reached agreement to purchase 24 Sikorsky S-70 civilian helicopters for its army, and one year later it agreed to buy five General Electric gas turbine engines for use in its naval modernization program. Also in 1985, the Reagan administration announced plans for a government-to-government deal with China—reportedly worth more than $100 million—that involves providing the Chinese with the means for modernizing their large-caliber munitions production facilities. In May 1986, President Reagan notified Congress of his plans to sell advanced avionics kits that will be used to upgrade the Chinese air force's fleet of F-8 combat aircraft. The transaction is worth $500 million and is being routed through the U.S. Foreign Military Sales program. (See Chapter 9.)

The Reagan administration, though, has also turned down some requests. Taiwan was rebuffed when it expressed interest in the Northrop F-20 and was encouraged to accept the less capable F-5 instead. In 1984 Honduras unsuccessfully requested F-5 fighters. Late in 1986, however, the Reagan administration indicated that it might consider favorably the resale of F-5s possessed by foreign armed forces or the transfer of Israeli Kfir fighters—which contain U.S. parts and, therefore, cannot be sold by Israel without the permission of the United States—to Honduras. The administration also intimated that it might allow the aircraft to be purchased with U.S. grants and credits.

The Reagan policy and structural reform: The Reagan administration has done more than simply apply a more liberal set of criteria to arms export decisions than did its predecessor: It has also promulgated several initiatives designed to make transferring weapons easier. "This is the currency in which foreign policy now deals," a senior State Department official told *Newsweek* in 1981. "We can't sign treaties any more, we can't deploy forces abroad—so how the hell else do you do it?"[65]

One important initiative of the Reagan administration sought to offer easier credit terms to selected countries. The administration argued, and Congress agreed, that mounting Third World debt problems required establishing a way for other countries to buy U.S. arms without taking on as heavy an economic burden as that imposed by loans at full Treasury rates of interest. As a result, the administration reformed FMS financing procedures in order to be able to offer "direct" FMS credits at below-market interest rates. The administration also expanded the list of nations eligible for "concessional" repayment arrangements. The United States offered concessional financing to such nations as Egypt, Sudan, Somalia, Greece and Turkey for the first time (previously only Israel had received these repayment terms). Under the terms of this arrangement, these countries are entitled to a 10-year grace period on their loans followed by a 20-year repayment period. Normally, nations are given a grace period of one to three years followed by a nine to 12-year period for repayment. For reasons similar to those behind its expanded use of concessional credits, the Reagan White House also reversed the trend toward elimination of grant aid. Military assistance grants increased from

$250 million to $700 million in the first four years of the Reagan presidency, with most of the increase coming from aid to countries in Central America.[66]

The administration and Congress also agreed to create a Special Defense Acquisition Fund to enable the Defense Department to purchase military equipment in anticipation of future arms sale agreements. With the SDAF, the United States hoped to reduce the time-lags between order and delivery that frequently occur in foreign military sales, and to ensure that sales agreements did not lead to the diversion to foreign governments of equipment being manufactured for the U.S. armed forces. The SDAF was originally designed to be a revolving fund, but that has not turned out to be the case, and the Department of Defense must seek congressional approval for the fund's program level annually. Congress established a $300 million maximum capitalization level for fiscal 1982, which subsequently increased to $600 million in 1983, $900 million by 1985 and $1 billion by 1986. From fiscal 1982 through 1984, the Special Defense Acquisition Fund's appropriations totaled $475 million. Congress set the fund's appropriation authority at $325 million for each of the years 1985 and 1986, but the Department of Defense would like to increase the SDAF's annual appropriations level to $400 million and says a capitalization level of $1.5 billion would be needed to support annual outlays of this magnitude. The administration says these increases would allow it to make larger purchases of materiel at more economical rates.[67]

In addition to accepting FMS financing reforms, Congress agreed to amendments proposed early in its first term by the Reagan administration to reduce Legislative Branch oversight of arms sales. These amendments focused on the reporting requirements in the Arms Export Control Act. Congress loosened the reporting requirements for sales to NATO and its member countries, Australia, New Zealand and Japan. Under the new rules, the requirement for advance notice to Congress for arms sales to these countries dropped from 30 to 15 days. This provision resulted from a compromise with the administration, which had sought to eliminate all opportunities for congressional review and veto of weapons sales to close allies. The new 15 day-notification measure also applied to sales of U.S.-made arms among those countries and to transfers from them to the rest of the world. Perhaps most significantly, Congress also agreed in 1981 to raise the threshold for required notification of any single sale from $7 million to $14 million for major defense equipment and from $25 million to $50 million for entire packages of defense articles or services, and set $200 million as the threshold at which defense construction projects and services would have to be reported to Congress.[68]

Finally, the 1981 Foreign Aid Authorization bill repealed the provision built into the 1976 Arms Export Control Act (AECA) that set a cap on the size of commercial arms sales that involved major defense equipment. Commercial contracts that initially exceeded $25 million and later—as a result of a late 1970s amendment to the AECA—$100 million had to be channeled through the government-to-government Foreign Military Sales program. Since 1982, however, the administration has allowed the sale of weapon systems through direct commercial channels irrespective of the size of the transaction.

Congress proved more reluctant to remove restrictions it had imposed for human rights reasons, however. The administration requested the lifting of bans on arms sales to Chile and Argentina imposed because of human rights abuses in these countries. Congress has declined so far to do so for Chile. The conditions of the ban no longer apply to Argentina, which in 1984 returned to democratic rule. The administration also asked for repeal of the Clark Amendment barring aid to anti-government forces in Angola. After demurring for several years, Congress agreed to this step in 1985. Congress, in fact, through the early 1980s appeared to grow more willing in general to approve certain forms of aid (usually "non-lethal") for anticommunist insurgent movements. Aid to rebels fighting the governments of Afghanistan, Nicaragua and Cambodia received congressional approval in 1985.

Congressional control weakened by Supreme Court decision: Not all of the recent structural changes in U.S. arms export policy, though, have been born out of political compromises. Congressional control over arms exports was severely curtailed by a 1983 Supreme Court decision that judged the legislative veto unconstitutional. The Court's verdict brought to an end Congress's ability to block an arms sale by passing a concurrent resolution, which entails a straightforward majority vote in each house and does not require the President's signature to be effective and, therefore, cannot be vetoed by the Executive Branch. Instead, congressional rejection of an arms sale now requires the passage of a joint resolution, which must be signed by the President. The decision, therefore, conferred upon the Executive Branch the power to veto actions Congress might take to block a weapons sale, and forces Congress to muster two-thirds of the votes in both the House and Senate if it is to override the veto and prevent the sale from occurring. The Executive Branch, on the other hand, would need only to rally one-third of the votes plus one in either of the houses in order to sustain its veto.

The new system was put to the test in 1986 during a White House–Capitol Hill showdown over a weapons package that the President proposed selling to Saudi Arabia. Although congressional pressure forced the administration to reduce the size of the transaction greatly before submitting it for congressional review, both chambers voted to block the sale. President Reagan vetoed the joint resolution and managed to sustain it by cornering 34 votes in the Senate.

Many members of Congress find the new system unacceptable because they believe that the it has radically weakened the legislature's ability to influence arms export policymaking. This belief, compounded by other factors, led some in Congress to back proposed legislation introduced by Sen. Biden (D. Del.), Sen. Claiborne Pell (D-R.I.) and Rep. Melvin Levine (D-Calif.), designed to give Congress a more active role in arms export decisionmaking process. (See Chapter 1.)

Clandestine weapons shipments to Iran force executive–legislative showdown: Congress's willingness to compromise with the Reagan administration over aid to anticommunist guerrilla movements such as the Nicaraguan contras may be waning. The administration's arms export policy—as well as its credibility in general—came under intense scrutiny as a result of revelations made late in 1986 of secret dealings masterminded by the President's National Security Council and the Central Intelligence Agency that sent weapons to Iran and funneled profits from the sales to the Nicaraguan contra forces challenging the Sandinista regime of Nicaragua. According to Israeli and American government sources, 2,008 TOW (tube launched, optically sighted, wire-guided) anti-tank missiles and parts for 235 Hawk anti-aircraft missile batteries were secretly transferred either from Israeli stocks or through Israel to Iran in 1985 and 1986.

Press reports and some members of Congress alleged that the arms shipments to Iran were part of a plan designed to free a handful of American hostages that are being held by pro-Iranian fundamentalist Arabs, but the Reagan administration initially denied emphatically that the arms were meant as ransom. Instead, the President insisted that the clandestine sales were made as a sign of good faith and part of a larger plan for cultivating contacts with moderate elements in the Iranian government in the hope that American support would assist these elements in their bid for power. However, following the Feb. 26 publication of the President's Sepcial Review Board ("The Tower Commission"), which Reagan had appointed after the Iran-Contra disclosures to investigate the workings of the National Security Council, the President acknowledged that arms for hostages had been one element of the deal.

The revelations moved members of Congress from both sides of the aisle and many U.S. allies in the Middle East and Europe to criticize President Reagan's policy and conduct. Allies of the United States expressed surprise because the shipments to Iran conflict sharply with the administration's rhetoric, which in very strong terms denounced Iran as a nation that sponsored international terrorism and sought to persuade the international community to eschew any and all dealings with the Persian state. Congress bristled over having been circumvented in the case of the shipments to Iran, and over the perception that direct Executive Branch involvement in the clandestine delivery of funds to the contras violated congressionally imposed limits on U.S. assistance to the contras. The revelations of the secret deals may well lead to increased pressure for closer congressional oversight of U.S. arms export policy and practice.

Congress responded to news of the clandestine transfers of weapons and monies by launching investigations in five committees: the Senate Select Committee on Intelligence, the House Permanent Select Committee on Intelligence, the House Foreign Affairs Committee and one special select committee in each chamber patterned after the congressional committees that investigated the Watergate affair. The Justice Department also initiated a full criminal investigation and appointed an independent counsel to look into allegations of misconduct by high-ranking Executive Branch officials. Investigators were to determine whether any one of a series of laws that involve executive-legislative consultations were broken by the covert shipment of arms to Iran and funds to the Nicaraguan contras. (See Chapter 8.)

Criticism of the Reagan policy: Although Congress had proved willing to support many Reagan security assistance reforms before the Iranian-contra crisis surfaced, a significant body of opinion among its members even then felt that Congress's role in arms export decisionmaking is too limited. A report on Reagan administration arms sale policy by the Democratic Policy Committee asserted, "Despite better information, it is apparent that Congress has not become a full partner to the process."[69] Congress therefore continues to consider various initiatives to improve its oversight role. For example, an amendment to the fiscal year 1985 foreign aid bill sponsored by Sen. John Glenn (D-Ohio) requires the administration to notify Congress if it makes significant upgrades in the technology or mission capability of military equipment whose sale has already been approved by Congress.

While Reagan's arms transfer policies have not been reversed by Congress, they definitely have encountered strong criticism. Sen. Christopher Dodd (D-Conn.) wrote in 1982, "The Reagan administration seems willing to sell more highly sophisticated weapons to a wider variety of countries than any previous administration." He added that the administration's policy of reviewing requests on a case-by-case basis "really amounts to no policy at all."[70] Other observers also saw flaws in Reagan's arms export practices. In his study for the Council on Foreign Relations, Andrew Pierre expressed the belief that the Reagan administration had overestimated the political utility of arms transfers, a conclusion echoed in the report of the Democratic Policy Committee. Pierre wrote:

Nations pursue their interests; their friendship or foreign policies cannot long be "bought" with weapons. Many problems, especially in the Third World, could best be addressed by a greater attention to other means, such as economic assistance or traditional diplomacy to deal with political conflicts.[71]

More recently, Congress in general has become more vocal in its opposition to specific sales, and it has effectively forced the administration to scale back or cancel a series of planned deals with nations of the Middle East. In 1985, stiff congressional resistance forced the President to abort a planned sale of 48 F-15s to Saudi Arabia. (See box, p. 21.) Similarly, a proposed deal that would have sent $2 billion worth of fighters and missiles to Jordan was postponed indefinitely in February 1986 for the same reason. Most recently, congressional pressure prompted the Reagan administration to cut out 800 Stinger missiles from a $354 million arms package destined for Saudi Arabia. Even with the deletion of the Stingers, the Senate came within one vote of killing the downscaled $265 million package. (These arms deals are discussed in greater detail in Chapter 8.)

While the Reagan administration certainly emphasizes arms sales in its foreign policy more than the Carter administration did, some observers argue that overall the thrust of U.S. military assistance efforts has changed little. Steven Hildreth of the Center for Strategic and International Studies concluded after a survey of the post-war years that "there has been remarkable continuity in Executive Branch rationale for the security assistance program" since the mid-1950s. He writes:

> First and foremost among the dominant themes is that anticommunism, whether explicit or implicit, has been a driving force for security assistance. . . . Security assistance is [also] seen by the Executive Branch as a shield behind which political, economic and social development could occur throughout the world. The rationale is that a community of independent and prosperous nations is the best long-term guarantee of a secure United States in a peaceful world. . . . In addition, this military aid is perceived to be more efficient and less costly than regular defense expenditures for U.S. security.[72]

Hildreth acknowledges that there have been changes in emphasis, such as those in the relative balance between grant aid and loans. He also notes that Congress grew more skeptical and assertive in the 1970s. But, he adds, "there has always been a consensus" in Congress that security assistance programs are "important to U.S. interests and necessary to the conduct of foreign policy." Hildreth argues that congressional limitations either have been directed only to specific requests that the legislature views as misguided, or have attempted to make up for Congress's minimal role in formulating the program in its early years. Congress, he says, has never shown a complete lack of support for the idea of military assistance. Thus, while criticisms of Reagan's arms sale policy as excessive may lead to future curbs on U.S. military exports, it appears unlikely that the practice of using arms transfers as a policy tool will be terminated or significantly reduced in the foreseeable future.

Some observers believe that despite the restrictions imposed by Third World debt, the United States will be faced with growing economic pressures to export arms in the future. Rick Atkinson and Fred Hiatt, staff writers for *The Washington Post*, have argued that: "Arms makers in the West, building ever more expensive weapons, must find customers abroad to subsidize their costs at home." They point to various trends that confront the Pentagon—rising costs, fewer weapons purchased for more money, fewer types of new planes being developed—and suggest the result will be "a growing impulse to export."[73] Others speculate that defense contractors increasingly will look abroad as the U.S. arms buildup of the 1980s levels off.

The tight control exercised over arms exports by the government—a legacy of the evolution of arms transfers into a major policy tool—may mean that an administration and Congress determined to curb the arms trade could resist the economic pressures speculated on by Atkinson and Hiatt. But many observers believe the existing machinery to manage arms transfers is geared more toward exports than toward control. The next chapter examines the mechanics of arms transfer decisionmaking in the United States.

Footnotes

1. Anthony Sampson, *The Arms Bazaar* (New York: The Viking Press, 1977), pp. 56–61.
2. U.S. General Accounting Office, *Opportunities to Improve Decisionmaking and Oversight of Arms Sales* (Washington: U.S. Government Printing Office, May 1979), p. 64.
3. Sampson, *op. cit.*, pp. 90–94.
4. Roger P. Labrie, John G. Hutchins, and Edwin W.A. Peura, *U.S. Arms Sales Policy: Background and Issues* (Washington: American Enterprise Institute for Public Policy Research, 1982), p. 6.
5. Quoted in Sampson, *op. cit.*, p. 78.
6. *Ibid.*
7. GAO, *op. cit.*, p. 64.
8. Paul Hammond, David J. Louscher, Michael D. Salomone and Norman A. Graham, *The Reluctant Supplier: U.S. Decisionmaking for Arms Sales* (Cambridge, Mass.: Oelgeschlager, Gunn & Hain, Publishers Inc., 1983), p. 161.
9. Ernest Graves and Steven A. Hildreth, Eds., *U.S. Security Assistance: The Political Process* (Lexington, Mass.: D.C. Heath and Co., 1985), pp. 44–50.
10. *Ibid.* pp. 51–5.
11. Sampson, *op. cit.*, p. 116.
12. Hammond *et al.*, *op. cit.*, p. 66.
13. U.S. House of Representatives, 87th Congress, 1st Session, Document 84, (Washington: U.S. Government Printing Office, Feb. 6, 1961).
14. Quoted in Hammond *et al.*, *op. cit.*, p. 73.
15. *Ibid.*, p. 60.
16. *Ibid.*, p. 161.
17. Labrie *et al.*, *op. cit.*, p. 10.
18. Sampson, *op. cit.*, p. 117.
19. U.S. Senate Democratic Policy Committee, *An Unconventional Arms Policy: Selling Ourselves Short, Promotion of Foreign Military Sales to the Developing World Under the Reagan Administration* (Washington: U.S. Government Printing Office, 1983), p. 7.
20. Graves *et al.*, *op. cit.*, pp. 61–2.
21. Quoted in Congressional Research Service (CRS), *Changing Perspectives on U.S. Arms Transfer Policy*, (Washington: U.S. Government Printing Office, Sept. 25, 1981, pp. 3–4. (Hereafter cited as CRS, *Changing Perspectives*.)
22. Andrew Pierre, *The Global Politics of Arms Sales* (Princeton, N.J.: Princeton University Press, 1982), p. 46–48.
23. Hammond *et al.*, *op. cit.*, p. 129.
24. Pierre, *op. cit.*, p. 46.
25. Sampson, *op. cit.*, pp. 271–274.
26. *Ibid.*, pp. 274–284.
27. U.S. Congress, House of Representatives, Committee on Foreign Affairs, 93rd Congress, 2nd Session, House Report 93–1471, *Foreign Assistance Act of 1974* (Washington: Government Printing Office, 1974), pp. 48–49.
28. Graves *et al.*, *op. cit.*, p. 58.
29. CRS, *Changing Perspectives*, pp. 4–7; GAO, *op. cit.*, p. 67.
30. Rep. Howard Wolpe, in the *Wall Street Journal*, July 11, 1985, p. 29.
31. Quoted in U.S. Senate Democratic Policy Committee, *op. cit.*, p. 7.
32. *Ibid.*, p. 16.
33. U.S. Department of Defense, Defense Security Assistance Agency (DSAA), *Foreign Military Sales and Military Assistance Facts, 1985 (FMS and MAP FACTS)* (and earlier editions) (Washington: Data Management Division, Comptroller, DSAA, 1985).

34. Congressional Research Service, *Executive-Legislative Consultation on U.S. Arms Sales* (Washington: U.S. Government Printing Office, 1982), pp. 6–7. (Hereafter cited as CRS, *Executive-Legislative Consultation*.)

35. CRS, *Changing Perspectives*, p. 10.

36. Jimmy Carter, *Statement By the President on Conventional Arms Transfer Policy* (Washington: Office of the White House Press Secretary, May 19, 1977). (A copy can be found in CRS, *Changing Perspectives*, pp. 122–123.)

37. *Ibid.*

38. *Ibid.*

39. Pierre, *op. cit.*, p.55; CRS, *Changing Perspectives*, p. 30.

40. Graves *et al.*, *op. cit.*, pp. 75–76.

41. Pierre, *op. cit.*, p. 55.

42. *Ibid.*, p. 56; *Congressional Quarterly*, April 10, 1982, p. 799.

43. *Ibid.*, p. 57; Michael Klare, *American Arms Supermarket* (Austin, Tex.: University of Texas Press, 1984), pp. 45–46.

44. Graves *et al.*, op. cit., p. 78.

45. Pierre, *op. cit.*, pp. 285–290; Labrie *et. al*, *op. cit.*, pp. 12–14.

46. CRS, *Changing Perspectives*, p. 25.

47. Heritage Foundation, "New Directions in Security Assistance," (Washington: High Frontier, May 1981).

48. Testimony of Leslie Gelb before the Senate Committee on Foreign Relations, March 4, 1980, U.S. Senate, *The Conventional Arms Transfer Policy of the United States* (Washington: U.S. Government Printing Office, 1980), p. 6.

49. Pierre, *op. cit.*, pp. 61–62.

50. Hammond *et al.*, *op. cit.*, p. 171.

51. *Ibid.*, p. 194.

52. *Ibid.*, p. 171.

53. Pierre, *op. cit.*, pp. 61–62.

54. Klare, *op. cit.*, pp. 46–47.

55. James Buckley, "Arms Transfers and the National Interest," (Washington: U.S. Department of State, Bureau of Public Affairs, May 21, 1981), Current Policy No. 279. (A copy can be found in CRS, *Changing Perspectives*, pp. 124–126.)

56. Ronald Reagan, *Text of President Ronald Reagan's July 8, 1981, Arms Transfer Policy Directive*, (Washington: Office of the White House Press Secretary, July 9, 1981.) (A copy can be found in CRS, *Changing Perspectives*, pp. 127–128.)

57. *Ibid.*

58. CRS, *Changing Perspectives*, p. 131.

59. *Congressional Quarterly*, April 10, 1982, p. 797.

60. William H. Gregory, "Controlling Military Sales," *Aviation Week and Space Technology*, June 29, 1981, p. 11.

61. Pierre, *op. cit.*, p. 65.

62. DSAA, *FMS and MAP Facts 1984*.

63. Richard Grimmett, *Trends in Conventional Arms Transfers to the Third World By Major Supplier, 1978–1985* (Washington: Congressional Research Service, May 9, 1986), p. 31.

64. CRS, *Changing Perspectives*, p. 95.

65. "Arming America's Friends," *Newsweek*, March 23, 1981, p. 33.

66. DSAA, *FMS and MAP Facts 1985*.

67. Department of Defense, *Congressional Presentation for Security Assistance Programs*, Fiscal Year 1987, Volume 1, (Washington: U.S. Government Printing Office, 1986), p. 108; GAO, *op. cit.*, p. 41; Congressional Quarterly, *Weekly Report*, Dec. 19, 1981, p. 2500.

68. ''Major defense equipment'' is defined as ''any item of significant combat equipment on the United States Munitions List having a nonrecurring research cost of more than $50,000,000 or a total production cost of more than $200,000,000 million.'' Arms Export Control Act, Section 47, (22 U.S.C. 2794 note).

69. U.S. Senate Democratic Policy Committee, *op. cit.*, p. 27.

70. Christopher Dodd, ''Arms Sales Non-Policy,'' *New York Times*, April 9, 1982.

71. Pierre, *op. cit.*, p. 68.

72. Graves *et al.*, *op. cit.*, pp. 83–84.

73. Rick Atkinson and Fred Hiatt, ''Arms Merchants' Shrinking Market,'' *The Washington Post*, June 23, 1985.

Chapter 4
The Mechanics of the
Arms Sale Process

The channels through which U.S. arms sales are made evolved out of security assistance programs established in the years immediately following World War II. Changes in the security assistance budget still have an impact on arms sales, even though the two are now somewhat independent of one another. This chapter thus begins with a brief summary of the way the security assistance budget is set and then examines the overall mechanics of arms sales as they move through the government approval process.

The Security Assistance Budget Process

Four major programs: Funds for security assistance programs must be authorized and appropriated by Congress (in most cases annually) as part of the process of setting the federal budget. The security assistance budget has four major elements. The largest, and the one with the most impact on overall arms exports, is the Foreign Military Sales credit program. This program helps to finance weapons acquisitions by foreign governments that are unable to pay the full purchase price at the time of agreement or are considered deserving of financial assistance for other reasons.

Until recently, the FMS credit program, which is also referred to as the FMS financing program, mostly comprised market-rate loans guaranteed by the U.S. Treasury, coupled with waivers of a portion of loans to Israel and Egypt. The Reagan administration, however, has decided to emphasize direct government loans over Treasury guarantees. Because loan guarantees do not come from appropriated funds, guaranteed loans were not included in the budget, and the changeover to direct loans has thus allowed the entire FMS financing program to be brought "on budget." In addition, direct loans permit the use of "concessional financing" arrangements that involve below-market interest rates and lenient repayment schedules. Concessional financing has so far been made available only to a small number of countries, including Israel, Egypt, Turkey and Greece, but the Reagan administration has been gradually expanding the list.

A second major element of security assistance is the Military Assistance Program (MAP), which makes grants to foreign governments for use in obtaining military equipment and services. As discussed in Chapter 3, grant levels declined steadily throughout the 1970s as a result of the shift to greater emphasis on loans. MAP appropriations have risen in each year since fiscal 1982, however.

A third security assistance program, the Economic Support Fund (ESF), is intended to aid in financing non-military projects. According to the government, the ESF program "provides loans and grants for general budget and balance of payments support to friendly governments. It also finances individual development projects where doing so would enhance our ability to achieve important national security objectives."[1] The Defense Department does not regard ESF as a form of military assistance because the funds distributed through the program cannot be used to purchase military equipment. Nevertheless, there is clearly a military connection. A former official of the Defense Department's International Security Affairs division has described the purpose of ESF as being to "provide budget support for countries pressed by the burden of maintaining their military."[2] Others contend that this program should be considered straight military aid since ESF funds granted to support development expenses in a country with heavy military expenditures free up an equal amount of money in the recipient government's budget to spend on arms.

The final major element of the security assistance budget is the International Military Education and Training (IMET) program. The IMET program provides grants to pay for the training of foreign military personnel by members of the U.S. armed forces.

In addition to these major programs, the security assistance budget includes relatively small amounts for peacekeeping and anti-terrorism operations. In some years, the security assistance budget also includes an appropriation for the Guarantee Reserve Fund. Monies are withdrawn from this fund when recipients of FMS loans default, in order to make payments to the lenders. Another element of the international affairs function in the federal budget, outside of security assistance, also supports arms sales. This is the Special Defense Acquisition Fund, established in 1981 so the Defense Department could order, in anticipation of foreign sales, military items that require a long lead time for procurement.

Other FMS financing arrangements: Other FMS financing arrangements do not appear in the budget but nevertheless affect the level of foreign arms sales. In certain circumstances, the Defense Department will grant an FMS waiver that exempts a purchasing country from paying for development and administrative costs associated with the production and sale of an export item. Of more significance, Israel and Egypt have been allowed to use a "cash flow" method of financing in which they are exempt from the usual requirement that a purchasing nation reserve, or set aside, the full cost of the purchased equipment at the time the order is placed. Instead, these nations are required only to reserve an amount of money sufficient to cover the payments they will have to make in the current fiscal year. Some 78 countries have been authorized for "dependable undertakings" in which they can arrange to make periodic payments to the U.S. government rather than paying the full amount of a purchase up front. Because both the cash flow and dependable undertakings arrangements reduce the amount of cash a foreign government must have in hand before it can purchase U.S. arms, the General Accounting Office (GAO) has noted that their effect may be to "commit countries and the United States to larger programs than would normally be undertaken." Finally, some countries default on their FMS loans (though rarely for more than one year), and are sometimes allowed to reschedule their debt. As of June 30, 1985, 22 countries had failed to make loan payments when due, totaling $595 million.[3]

Cash transactions: While the security assistance budget and distribution of funds among its various elements affect total U.S. arms sales, they do not determine the ultimate level of such sales. A significant portion of U.S. arms transfers are straight cash transactions, made either through the Foreign Military Sales cash program or through commercial channels. Data in a 1985 GAO report indicate that government arms sales involving cash or a mixture of cash and credit totaled twice as much as the FMS financing program budget in fiscal years 1982–84.[4] Because cash sales require no outlay of U.S. government funds, they do not form a part of the federal budget. Nevertheless, an examination of the procedure followed in setting the security assistance budget is important to understanding the factors that influence the overall level of American arms exports, in part because changes in the budget can affect other aspects of U.S. arms sales. Thus, increases in MAP grant aid or FMS credits can reduce cash foreign military sales, while reductions in grant assistance have been used to stimulate greater cash payments for arms transfers. In addition, the policy issues that arise in making security assistance decisions are often the same as those that come into play in decisions about whether to promote or restrict arms sales to a given region or country.

Establishing funding levels: The formal process followed in establishing funding levels for security assistance is similar to that used in setting most other parts of the federal budget. Security assistance must be approved by Congress as part of a foreign aid bill. This bill also includes economic and financial programs such as development assistance and food and refugee aid. Because the State Department holds the formal responsibility for managing security assistance efforts, State is the agency with the greatest initiative is setting the security assistance budget. State has the dual role of receiving requests from its embassies and regional bureaus, and trying to stay within the bounds of a budget "mark," or overall target figure, set by the Office of Management and Budget (OMB). After an interagency review by State, the Defense Department, OMB and the National Security Council, a security assistance budget figure is presented to the President, who, after a last review, includes it in his annual budget request to Congress.

The congressional committees responsible for authorizing security assistance programs are Foreign Relations in the Senate and Foreign Affairs in the House. These committees generally give preliminary approval to the budget figure requested by the President so that the Budget Committees in each chamber can use this total in passing a first budget resolution. This measure sets targets for Congress to aim for in its subsequent authorizations and appropriations for the year. The authorizing committees then subject the foreign aid bill to more thorough scrutiny. Countries receiving the largest portion of security assistance funds or for which the requested aid is significantly different from the previous year's total are scrutinized the most carefully. Grant aid and some FMS credits are approved on a country-by-country basis, while remaining authorizations are generally lump sums which the Executive Branch may distribute as it sees fit. Action on the security assistance budget is completed when the Appropriations Committees, followed by the full houses, vote to provide funds for the programs that have been authorized by Foreign Relations and Foreign Affairs.

The Broader Picture

As discussed above, while the security assistance budget can affect some dimensions of the arms trade, it does not set any total for U.S. arms exports. Arms sales are handled through various channels that were established by Congress, and are, in most instances, subject to congressional oversight. However, most of the responsibility for managing arms transactions lies with the Executive Branch, and there is also room for arms manufacturers to play a significant role.

Foreign military sales programs had the same legislative origins as other security assistance efforts. The Mutual Defense Assistance Act of 1949 established the basis for grants of military aid and training as well as for sales of military equipment. Authority for the FMS cash and credit programs came from this act, as amended, until 1968, when Congress passed the Foreign Military Sales Act. The Foreign Military Sales Act established separate authority for foreign military sales and made some procedural reforms, but Congress did not formulate a comprehensive approach to foreign arms sales until the 1976 International Security Assistance and Arms Export Control Act. It is the Arms Export Control Act (AECA) portion of this bill, as amended, that governs American sales of weapons today.

The AECA gave to the President authority "to control the import and export of defense articles and defense services" and instructed the Executive Branch to develop a list of the military equipment and services that fall under its control. The list, known as the U.S. Munitions List, is found in the International Traffic in Arms Regulations, which is a part of the U.S. Code of Federal Regulations. The list is revised periodically by the State Department.

The AECA also established two channels for the sale of weapons—Foreign Military Sales (FMS) and direct commercial sales. The FMS program, in both the cash and credit versions, involves government-to-government agreements. The U.S. government either contracts with arms manufacturers to supply the goods sold under an FMS agreement or, less frequently, provides them out of existing stocks of the U.S. armed forces. In order to cover the administrative costs associated with FMS exports, the Department of Defense charges the buyer a fee—currently 3 percent of the value of the sale—and a 1.5 percent surcharge.

Under the commercial sales program, foreign governments purchase goods directly from private manufacturers rather than the U.S. government. Before 1982, the AECA mandated that any sale of "major defense equipment" in excess of $100 million, except to NATO countries or as part of a previously approved coproduction agreement, be handled through FMS, government-to-government channels. The ceiling on commercial sales—which originally had been set at $25 million, but later raised to $100 million—was revoked in 1981, thereby allowing all U.S. government approved arms exports to be arranged directly between U.S. corporations and foreign governments. In some cases, foreign governments may buy equipment for their military that is not on the Munitions List. Such transactions are then bound only by Commerce Department regulations that apply to all international trade.

In practice, the FMS program is the channel used for most sales of major combat equipment (See Table 4–1), particularly weapons originally developed for the U.S. armed forces. Approximately 80 percent of all U.S. arms exports travel through the FMS route. In part, this reflects Congress's efforts to bring a greater portion of arms sales under its oversight by making the government rather than private firms the usual contractor that foreign purchasers deal with. In addition, though, many foreign nations prefer to deal with the U.S. government rather than directly with private firms. The total value of FMS sales is thus much greater than that of commercial sales. In recent years, arms transfers through the FMS program (including military construction) have run at $8 billion to $15 billion annually (in constant 1986 dollars). Commercial sales, in contrast, have generally totaled between $2 billion and $5 billion a year.[5] Because most exports of major defense equipment take place through FMS channels, a relatively small number of companies, most of which also are among the Pentagon's leading contractors, account for the bulk of FMS sales. Sales through the commercial sales program are diffused among a larger number of companies, many of which are small firms that specialize in only a few lines of military hardware. While commercial sales were originally comprised of relatively unsophisticated equipment such as small arms, jeeps or radios, they increasingly consist of larger weapon systems. Greece's purchase of F-16 aircraft, for example,

Table 4–1

**Value of U.S. Foreign Military Sale and Grant Aid Agreements
By Type of Article or Service for Fiscal Years 1983–1986**
(current year dollars)

Category	1983	1984	1985	1986
Combat Aircraft	$ 4,550,550	$ 4,381,913	$ 640,512	$ 564,056
Combat Ships	6,446	2,031	1,560	8,247
Combat Vehicles	312,077	418,913	152,324	326,838
Weapons	226,869	136,415	173,695	489,268
Ammunition	343,028	272,270	428,920	268,437
Missiles	2,658,998	1,164,747	2,264,096	754,417
Total Weapons and Ammunition	8,097,967	6,376,291	3,661,107	2,411,264
Percent of Total	50%	45%	30%	33%
Other Aircraft	412,310	500,929	262,914	79,837
Other Ships	1,444	262	7,472	19,464
Support Vehicles	104,791	38,330	38,083	43,711
Communications Equipment	309,712	1,255,483	1,314,523	241,147
Other Equipment	358,686	257,881	324,041	341,825
Total Support Equipment	1,186,944	2,052,886	1,947,034	725,984
Percent of Total	7%	14%	16%	10%
Aircraft Parts*	2,564,112	1,655,845	1,423,736	1,219,688
Ship Parts*	108,293	340,217	247,195	109,125
Weapon Parts*	165,811	187,716	168,997	150,089
Auto Supplies and Parts*	272,890	312,844	291,800	124,842
Missile Parts*	152,084	157,369	247,477	87,602
Communications Equipment Parts*	7,964	106,057	248,564	70,320
Total Spare Parts*	3,342,832	2,760,049	2,627,769	1,761,666
Percent of Total	21%	19%	21%	24%
Construction	722,896	304,902	754,304	69,323
Repair & Rehabilitation	305,156	148,839	207,461	244,319
Supply Operations	750,555	678,302	666,025	415,224
Training	619,381	560,941	477,003	392,584
Other Services	1,153,450	1,423,930	1,975,040	1,187,058
Total Support Services	3,551,438	3,116,914	4,079,833	2,308,509
Percent of Total	22%	22%	33%	32%
Worldwide Total	16,179,182	14,306,140	12,315,742	7,207,422

Figures include FMS, MAP, IMET and MASF programs.

*   Category includes spares, modifications and upgrades to systems.

Source: Department of Defense, DSAA, *Weapons Analysis Report.*

has been handled through the commercial sales program. This trend means that the larger defense corporations should come to dominate arms sales made through this channel as well.

Approving an Arms Deal

Regardless of the channel through which arms transfers take place, they are subject to review and approval by the government. The process of completing a deal involves several steps and many actors. The formal process is initiated by a request for military equipment, which may arise from any of several procedures. A foreign country may decide on its own, for whatever reasons (some of which will be discussed below), that it desires to purchase certain American weapons. In some cases, a country considering making a purchase will first request data on the weapons' cost, availability and capabilities and background information on how to submit a formal request for the equipment. These requests must be approved by the State Department before the data can be released. The American Enterprise Institute notes that: "The decision to release the data is given careful consideration because turning down a request for arms is easier at this point in the process than later when the request becomes formal. . . . The issuance of the data is [therefore] often perceived by potential recipients as an indication that the United States is prepared to sell."[6] In situations where a country has not developed an interest in buying particular arms on its own, the United States may take the initiative. This occurs when the Military Assistance Advisory Group, or the U.S. embassy in the country, or a multi-agency evaluation, determines that the country needs a certain item to meet its mutual defense obligations with the United States. In these cases, the American government urges the nation to request the hardware in question.

While a request for arms, once formulated, may be transmitted through any of several channels, formal responsibility for arms export decisions rests with the State Department. Within State, most of the work relating to such decisions is done by the Bureau of Politico-Military Affairs. Potential transactions that would be Foreign Military Sales are handled by the bureau's Office of Security Assistance and Sales, while commercial sales requests are routed to the Office of Munitions Control. Because the procurement of arms for export is handled in the same way as domestic weapons procurement, the Department of Defense also has a significant say in arms sales decisions and has taken over much of the day-to-day management of the FMS program. Most policy decisions in DoD are made by the Office of the Assistant Secretary for International Security Affairs, which is divided into regional and functional desks along the same lines as the State Department. The functions of coordinating information exchange within DoD, providing analysis, and supervising day-to-day management of Foreign Military Sales and security assistance programs are handled by the Defense Security Assistance Agency (DSAA), with the assistance of Military Assistance Advisory Groups and military missions in about 50 foreign countries. Each of the individual military services also has a sales and assistance division. The Arms Control and Disarmament Agency (ACDA) is another agency with regular involvement in policy decisions. Other agencies, including the Treasury, the Central Intelligence Agency and the Agency for International Development, are asked for their analysis of proposed sales when relevant. In addition, both the Carter and the Reagan administrations have established interagency groups in attempts to coordinate arms transfer decisions overall. Finally, when proposed sales are controversial, the President and the National Security Council will also often enter into the deliberations.

As indicated above, submission by another government of a formal request to buy arms represents only an intermediate step in a process that really begins even earlier. According to Michael

Klare, "most major transactions have an elaborate 'prehistory' involving informal discussions between U.S. and foreign military officials, as well as promotional activities conducted by U.S. arms firms."[7] Discussions and negotiations between U.S. and foreign government officials of the type described above are often replicated by the country in question and representatives of arms manufacturers. Arms companies engage in sometimes fierce competition with one another to try to get foreign governments to request their version of a particular weapon system specifically, so that the Pentagon will not select a rival's product to sell to the country instead. The best known promotional activity is the display of weapons at various trade shows, ranging from the famous Paris and Farnborough Air Shows to smaller events often sponsored by the individual military services. Defense firms also promote their wares by taking military products on world tours, inviting foreign officials to visit U.S. production facilities, and advertising in trade journals such as *Aviation Week & Space Technology*.

Assessing the process, the U.S. General Accounting Office, in a study of arms export decisionmaking, reported that:

> The incremental nature of the process . . . tends to continuously reinforce expectations that requests will be approved. Various verbal and written pronouncements to the effect that such actions do not constitute a U.S. commitment to sell appear to be lost, if ever considered seriously, in the momentum that builds with each successive step taken on a major case. It is the actions and judgments which normally precede consideration of the formal request which strongly influence the outcome of the formal decision.[8]

Despite the pressures that may have built up behind a possible sale before the formal request, there is no certainty that the government agencies involved will be unanimous in their position on a given sale. The different agencies generally have institutional functions that strongly influence their position. Thus, the Arms Control and Disarmament Agency will focus mainly on the possible effect of a proposed transfer on regional stability, while the office of the Under Secretary of Defense for Research and Engineering will be most concerned with how quickly industry could respond to a particular request and whether the transfer might involve sensitive technology.

Nevertheless, most requests do not precipitate major review. The extent of review and the agencies involved vary according to both the type of request and the nation making the request. The first distinction, as noted earlier, is between Foreign Military Sales and commercial sales. In addition, the Carter administration made a distinction in FMS cases between "Category A" and "Category B" nations which, although abolished by the Reagan administration, is carried on in practice. Category A transfers include all sales to NATO nations (except Turkey, Greece, Portugal and Iceland), other west European countries (except Spain), Australia, New Zealand and Japan, and sales of non-combat gear to a larger list of countries. Approval of such requests is generally automatic, especially when the transfer in question falls below the thresholds established for advance notification of Congress. Requests that are made by Category B countries, or that raise important policy issues, receive a more substantial review. This review is managed by the Office of Security Assistance and Sales in the Bureau of Politico-Military Affairs, and generally involves most or all of the actors identified above as well as relevant regional bureaus in the State and Defense Departments.

If all the agencies involved in the review reach the same recommendation, the transaction is normally processed accordingly. If there is disagreement, the various agencies involved may form coalitions to press their position and attempt to recruit other agencies to their point of view or take their case to higher authorities. According to the GAO, "Decisions on major requests are made through the process of building a consensus, which is sought within organizational units, within agencies, and between departments."[9] Michael Klare adds that if, as a result of this process, a particular position becomes prevalent throughout the bureaucracy, the remaining opponents will either concede the issue or propose a compromise that retains a portion of their original position.[10] Once a consensus is reached, the Secretary of State, who by law is responsibile for making arms sale decisions, will generally step in and approve the prevailing view. On occasions where no agreement can be reached, the Secretary of State may decide to refer the dispute to the National Security Council. The NSC's recommendations will be given to the President, who, in consultation with the National Security Adviser, makes the final decision. Thus, the decisionmaking process in most controversial proposed arms sales involves a wide array of government agencies.

The review process for commercial arms sales is somewhat different. Primary responsibility in this case is with the Office of Munitions Control in the Bureau of Politico-Military Affairs. OMC generally solicits the views of the relevant regional bureaus in the State Department and the Defense Department's Office of Internal Security Affairs and of the Arms Control and Disarmament Agency, and it may ask other agencies or divisions for comments where relevant. The Defense Security Assistance Agency has also tightened its review of commercial sales in recent years, following several cases of apparent fraud or impropriety. When a commercial export is approved, OMC grants a license to export the equipment in question to the company that has lined up the sale. While sales through the commercial program are small in comparison with FMS transfers, they can be significant when they involve paramilitary and counterinsurgency equipment that can have an important impact on human rights. (This aspect of commercial sales is discussed further in Chapter 7.) Moreover, the rescinding of the ceiling on the size of commercial sales in 1982 means that exports that otherwise would have gone through the FMS program can be routed through commercial channels. Greece, for example, elected to purchase its fleet of F-16 fighters directly from General Dynamics rather than work through the U.S. government's FMS program.

Congressional Involvement

The negotiations within the bureaucracy on whether to approve a potential sale, regardless of the channel, take place before the point at which Congress formally enters the fray. Any commercial sale of more than $1 million must be reported to Congress, but Congress has veto power only over those that exceed $14 million. If the Executive decides to approve an FMS transaction, the Defense Security Assistance Agency prepares a Letter of Offer and Acceptance, which specifies the terms that have been agreed upon in discussions with the foreign government in question. Any proposed sale involving more than $14 million of major combat equipment or more than $50 million of other defense equipment and services must by law be reported in the Congressional Record. From that date, Congress has 30 days in which it can veto a sale by passing a joint resolution of disapproval. (By informal arrangement, the Executive Branch provides Congress with an additional 20 days' notice before it inserts the Letter of Offer in the Record.)

To date, Congress has never killed an arms sale, but it has come close on two occasions, and in several others congressional opposition forced the Executive Branch to postpone closure on deals. Both close calls involved Saudi Arabia. The first, in 1981, entailed the sale of Awacs planes, which the Senate approved by just four votes. In 1986, both chambers voted down a White House plan to sell a $265 million weapons package to the Saudis, and the Senate upheld President Reagan's veto of the resolution by the narrowest of margins, 34–66—one-third plus one of the Senate's 100 members.

The threat of a congressional veto has also caused the Executive Branch to cancel or scale down sales it had approved. President Reagan was forced to delete 200 Stinger launchers and 600 reloads from the 1986 Saudi arms package in order to win the veto override, a move that Sen. Alan Cranston (D-Calif.) contended left the President with a "10 percent victory." Earlier, congressional pressure had led President Ford to alter a proposal to sell mobile Hawk anti-aircraft missiles to Jordan to one involving only immobile missiles, and to reduce by almost 60 percent the number of Maverick air-to-ground missiles he had proposed to sell to Saudi Arabia.[11] In 1985, in the face of congressional opposition, the Reagan administration decided not to press forward with the sale of F-15 combat aircraft to Saudi Arabia, which opened the door to a major sale by the British. (See box, p. 39.) In February 1986, the administration officially threw in the towel on an effort, formally proposed in October 1985, to sell $2 billion worth of advanced warplanes and missiles to Jordan. Earlier, the Senate had voted 97-1 in favor of a resolution to bar the sale pending meaningful peace talks between Jordan and Israel, and the House, although it had gone on record in favor of an even tougher measure, went along with the Senate because it was the only proposal that had a chance of passage within the 30-day review period.

Those who wish to see greater control exercised over U.S. arms exports view as a significant problem the lack of earlier or more extensive congressional (or public) participation in the decisionmaking process. This concern is amplified by the widespread impression that the predisposition of the relevant Executive Branch agencies is to approve proposed sales. In 1979, even before the more permissive Reagan administration took office, the GAO offered the following assessment: "From the moment of first interest through the step-by-step process of informal discussions, briefings, surveys, studies, official visits, test-rides or firings, and negotiations, the process is geared toward seriously responding to a buyer's perceived needs."[12]

Other observers disagree sharply with this evaluation. In a study of U.S. arms export decisionmaking, University of Pittsburgh Professor Paul Hammond and three colleagues draw a contrasting conclusion from their review of the number of agencies involved in decisions on controversial cases and congressional reporting requirements. They argue that "the U.S. security assistance system operates domestically in an environment that accentuates the pressures for restraint."[13]

Hammond and his colleagues do agree with the GAO that responsibility for arms transfer decisions is currently centered in the Executive. In part, this is a reflection of inherent limitations imposed by the fact that arms exports are part of America's relations with foreign governments and such relations are traditionally the province of the Executive. But many of those who argue for reform of the arms export process believe that more substantial public and congressional participation in this process would improve decisionmaking.

It is not clear, however, that increased congressional oversight alone will prove to be the panacea that arms sales critics claim. Leslie Gelb, currently a senior correspondent with *The New York Times*, has observed that "the performance of Congress with regard to arms transfers has been mixed, at best." Gelb's knowledge of conventional arms transfer and foreign policy issues and extensive government experience—which has included stints with the Pentagon, the State Department, and

Senate staffs—prompted the Senate Committee on Foreign Relations to request him to testify in March 1980. Gelb told the committee that "the Executive Branch needs watching, and Congress has been at its best in challenging specific administration decisions and pressing for policy explanations." Nevertheless, he offered the opinion that "most of the time . . . Congress has been a disruptive force, following new fashions without careful examination, and imposing the latest fashions on the Executive Branch."

Gelb told the assembled senators:

> The fashion parade is long, so let me mention only the following: The phasing out of grant military aid and phasing down of credit sales and a phasing in of cash sales; then a phasing out of government-to-government cash sales and a phasing in of commercial sales; then back to government-to-government sales; then a phasing down of all arms transfers; and now it's difficult to tell what next. This roller coaster has caused the Executive Branch to be even more quixotic in dealing with other countries than normal.

Gelb concluded, "It is virtually impossible for any administration to conduct a serious arms transfer policy, assuming that Congress is going to impose another new wrenching change every few years." Finally, he criticized past congressional reforms of the arms transfer process for being "based on slogans like 'Military aid got us involved in Vietnam,' or 'The presence of U.S. military advisers creates a commitment' or 'If we don't sell, others will.'" analyses which, in his view, are "too simplistic to bear scrutiny," despite the fact that "each had a powerful impact" on Congress."[14]

Gelb's arguments, however, may be overstated. A 1982 study by the Congressional Research Service (CRS) on executive-legislative consultations on U.S. arms exports decisions concluded that "the Executive Branch has made it very difficult for the Congress to influence the final shape of a prospective arms sale." The study's principal findings state:

> Negotiations with Congress—the essential feature of the consultative process—are generally viewed by the Executive Branch as "damage limitation". . . . When an arms sale proposal is presented to Congress the Executive Branch has concluded by then that the sale is appropriate and is primarily concerned with getting it implemented in the least contentious and most expeditious way possible.[15]

The study adds:

> Although Congress has continued since the early 1970s to strengthen its oversight authority in the arms sale area, most recently it has had increasing difficulty in compelling the Executive Branch in determining the outcome of controversial arms sales cases. . . . The President and the Executive Branch appear, at this time, to have regained the upper hand in the continuing struggle over the process of making arms sales.[16]

The President's hand was strengthened even more in 1983 when the Supreme Court ruled that the legislative veto—the process by which the Congress can irrefutably stop a proposed arms sale by passing a concurrent resolution by a simple majority in both chambers—is unconstitutional. The decision made it significantly more difficult for the Legislative Branch to block a sale because

Foreign Military Sales versus Direct Commercial Sales

Once the U.S. government approves a weapons sale, the buyer must decide how to follow through. Whether a recipient nation should purchase U.S. military equipment through the government-to-government Foreign Military Sales program or through the company-to-government direct commercial sales avenue has become controversial. Before 1982, the choice was limited by a dollar value ceiling on commercial sales under the Arms Export Control Act of 1976, which decreed that equipment worth more than $25 million had to be sold through the FMS program. The ceiling—later raised to $100 million—was abolished early in 1981, thereby allowing U.S. defense contractors to sell "big ticket" items directly to foreign governments.

A recipient's decision on which of the vehicles best meets its needs depends on its estimate of the relative advantages and disadvantages of each, and the variables are numerous. Some customers find the FMS program desirable because the Department of Defense acts as the purchasing agent and negotiates with American companies on their behalf. Others, confident of their negotiating abilities, choose instead to deal directly with U.S. manufacturers. Each approach has potential benefits and drawbacks.

Critics of the FMS approach object that working through an additional layer of bureaucracy lengthens the period between the time an order is placed and the goods are delivered. They also complain that because the final prices and delivery schedules of FMS sales are estimates, buyers do not know exactly when the equipment will be delivered or how much it will cost. Companies selling directly to foreign countries, on the other hand, are able to offer fixed prices and delivery dates up front. Others, however, find the Pentagon's presence helpful in the event of disputes with contractors and its established negotiating skills useful in securing the best deal possible.

Recently, the FMS program has come under attack from both U.S. companies involved in the arms trade and recipients of American arms. The director of foreign military procurement for Saudi Arabia—the largest FMS customer—and a vice president of Rockwell publicly criticized the program at an industry sponsored symposium late in 1986. The Saudi official complained that government-to-government sales allow for the intrusion of disruptive "political factors" into the transactions and introduce provisions that are "very one-sided to the United States." Industry officials, on their part, maintain that the total 4.5 percent of all sales' value assessed by the Pentagon as fees and surcharges to cover its administrative costs makes it difficult for U.S. firms to compete with foreign suppliers. Some in the industry claim that the DoD deliberately steers sales through the FMS program in order to secure the fees, which are used to fund the Defense Security Assistance Agency (DSAA). The DSAA budget is not appropriated by Congress, and the agency, therefore, relies on the fees from FMS sales for its livelihood. Industry representatives maintain that declining global arms sales are serving as an impetus for the DSAA to shunt arms sales through FMS channels in order to preserve its bureaucratic integrity and status.

A shift from FMS to commercial sales would make it more difficult for those interested in following corporate involvement in the arms trade. FMS sales are easier to track because the Pentagon keeps detailed records of contracts and awards. Commercial sales records are less comprehensive and harder to come by.

Congress now must pass a joint resolution of disapproval, which requires the President's signature in order to hold. The new system effectively gives the Executive Branch the ability to veto Congress's joint resolution (by not signing it) and places the burden of the veto override requirements—two-thirds of the votes in both houses—squarely on the shoulders of Congress.

Although Congress can still prevent an arms sale from occurring, mustering the requisite number of votes will be more difficult, given what the Congressional Research Service terms "the institutional difficulty Congress has in achieving consensus on the proper course to take when confronted with a controversial sale."[17] The CRS emphasized the importance of the legislative veto in its 1982 study:

> Most in the Executive and Legislative Branches agree that were it not for the existence of the legislative veto . . . consultations or negotiations regarding controversial arms sales would almost never occur to the extent that they do today. The primary incentive would be missing for the Executive Branch to do so.[18]

The loss of the legislative veto, in part, has led to calls for reforming the laws that govern U.S. arms export policy and practice in such a way as to strengthen congressional participation in the process. The Biden-Pell-Levine legislation discussed in Chapter 1 is one such effort.

A final assessment of the reform plea is not possible, however, without taking into consideration the relative benefits and drawbacks of arms exports. The next two chapters examine this question.

Footnotes

1. Office of Management and Budget, *Budget of the United States Government, Fiscal Year 1986* (Washington: U.S. Government Printing Office, 1985), pp. 5–17.

2. Ernest Graves and Steven A. Hildreth, Eds., *U.S. Security Assistance: The Political Process* (Lexington, Mass.: D.C. Heath and Co., 1985), p. 102.

3. U.S. General Accounting Office, *U.S. Security and Military Assistance: Programs and Related Activities—An Update* (Washington: General Accounting Office, 1985), p. 15.

4. *Ibid.*, pp. 4, 37.

5. Department of Defense Security Assistance Agency (DSAA), 1986 Fiscal Year Series, (Washington: DSAA, 1987).

6. Roger P. Labrie, John G. Hutchins, and Edwin W.A. Peura, *U.S. Arms Sales Policy: Background and Issues* (Washington: American Enterprise Institute for Public Policy Research, 1982), p. 29.

7. Klare, *op. cit.*, p. 63.

8. U.S. General Accounting Office, *Opportunities to Improve Decisionmaking and Oversight of Arms Sales* (Washington: U.S. Government Printing Office, May 1979), pp. 31–2. (Hereafter cited as GAO, *Opportunities.*)

9. *Ibid.*, p. 26.

10. Klare, *op. cit.*, pp. 69–70.

11. *Congressional Quarterly Weekly Report*, April 10, 1982, p. 799.

12. GAO, *Opportunities*, p. 31.

13. Paul Hammond, David J. Louscher, Michael D. Salomone and Norman A. Graham, *The Reluctant Supplier: U.S. Decisionmaking for Arms Sales* (Cambridge, Mass.: Oelgeschlager, Gunn & Hain, Publishers Inc., 1983), p. 84.

14. Testimony of Leslie Gelb before the Senate Committee on Foreign Relations, March 4, 1980, U.S. Senate, *The Conventional Arms Transfer Policy of the United States* (Washington: U.S. Government Printing Office, 1980), pp. 7–8.

15. Congressional Research Service, *Executive-Legislative Consultation on U.S. Arms Sales* (Washington: Congressional Research Service, Dec. 1982), p. 3.

16. *Ibid.*, p. 4.

17. *Ibid.*

18. *Ibid.*, p. 3.

Chapter 5
The Domestic Rationale For Arms Sales

The prevailing view on the sale of arms in the United States until the early part of this century held that the arms trade is strictly a commercial activity no different from any other form of commerce. Sympathy for this view continues in some quarters. Early in its first term, the Reagan administration directed that "U.S. government representatives overseas will be expected to provide the same courtesies and support to firms that have obtained licenses to market items on the U.S. munitions list as they would to those marketing other American products," thereby reversing a policy of the Carter administration.[1]

Another common view holds nearly the opposite—that the arms trade is an unsavory business that rarely brings good results. In the days when private firms were free to pursue arms exports with little governmental regulation, critics of the exporters labeled them "merchants of death." In the modern era, in which governments play the central role in making arms sales, critics contend that arms exports contribute to ever-spiraling regional arms races and make conflicts more likely, as well as more violent when they do occur. From this perspective, the arms trade is quite different from other forms of international commerce. Sen. Dick Clark (D-Iowa) articulated this view in 1978: "The export of such enormous military potential cannot be controlled in the same way we manage the export of refrigerators or automobiles."[2]

Even the Reagan administration, with its laissez-faire bent, views arms exports as an area in which exercise of governmental control is essential. Its reasoning is not primarily that arms exports generally have deleterious effects, however, but rather that arms transfers are a vital foreign policy tool—"the currency in which foreign policy now deals," in the words of one official.[3] Thus, the administration has maintained the framework built during the previous three decades under which most arms sales are negotiated by the government, not private firms, and under which agreements independently reached by companies can be disallowed if the government believes they would undermine important U.S. foreign policy interests.

Political Dimensions of Arms Sales

No administration would advocate returning arms exports to their earlier unregulated status. This is true not only because transfers are deliberately used as a policy instrument but also because arms transfers affect the world's political geography. They have consequences for the competition between the Eastern and Western blocs, and they also have led to a diffusion of power to the developing nations of the world. The importance of arms sales as a commercial activity is dwarfed nowadays by these political dimensions.

The political importance of arms transfers is a relatively recent phenomenon, and it has grown as a result of other trends in the United States and the world. Ideology has become less of a motivating force in international politics; nations are less inclined to explain their actions in such terms as desire to make the world safe for democracy or to extend the communist revolution. Economic assistance through bilateral channels has decreased. The expressions of military power that nations traditionally employed to advance their interests have become less important, particularly for the United States. As these changes have occurred, America has come to rely on arms transfers—and on arms sales in particular, with the deep reductions in grant aid—as a principal tool for promoting its security interests.

To say that arms transfers are a political tool does not indicate what political goals they are supposed to achieve, whether they are effective in achieving these goals, or whether, as some critics maintain, other consequences of arms sales more than negate any political advantages they confer. Indeed, the question of whether arms sales merely fuel arms races and regional conflicts or are instead an effective policy instrument that can promote regional stability (among other goals) can be assessed only by first examining the specific objectives that policymakers believe arms sales used as a policy tool can help them to achieve, and then looking at actual cases.

Official documents advance as reasons for arms transfers both the relatively altruistic goal of helping forge a world order that better reflects American democratic ideals and the more self-interested goal of solidifying U.S. national security. The fiscal 1986 edition of the Congressional Presentation Document, an annual report in which the administration describes and justifies its security assistance programs for the year, calls security assistance "an important instrument for pursuing a just and lasting peace."[4] The document closely links U.S. national security with such goals as global stability and development. It claims that "the Soviets and their allies have presented challenges to critical U.S. security interests in Southwest and Southeast Asia, Africa and Central America. In order to maintain a stable international order, it is essential that threatened countries, allied or friendly to the U.S., be able to defend themselves, thereby making economic growth and social development possible."[5] Other presentations are less idealistic in tone, emphasizing instead the role of military assistance in U.S. national defense. In the first official statement from the Reagan administration on arms transfer policy, Under Secretary of State Buckley argued in 1981:

> Arms transfers . . . serve as an important adjunct to our own security by helping deter acts of aggression, by enhancing the self-defense capabilities of nations with which we share close security ties, and by facilitating access by American forces to military facilities abroad.[6]

In some cases, government documents have spelled out quite specifically the various rationales for arms transfer agreements. In their report on the United States Military Posture for fiscal 1984, the Joint Chiefs of Staff said:

> In support of U.S. interests, the strategic objectives of the [security assistance] program are as follows: (1) to assist countries vital to U.S. national interests in preserving their independence and regional security, (2) to help secure access, overflight, transit and

forward basing rights [for U.S. military forces], (3) to promote standardization and interoperability of military forces, (4) to ensure continued access to critical raw materials, and (5) to provide a vehicle for maximizing U.S. influence abroad while minimizing that of the Soviets. Secondarily, the U.S. security assistance program also contributes to U.S. domestic goals by helping to expand the industrial base, lower unit costs of equipment production, maintain U.S. employment in key industries, and improve the U.S. balance of payments through revenue generated by foreign military sales.[7]

The specific rationales given by the Reagan administration in the President's July 1981 directive on arms transfers largely mirror those reported by the Joint Chiefs. But the directive does include two other, slightly different reasons for arms exports. The document states that transfers can "demonstrate that the United States has an enduring interest in the security of its friends and partners," and also can "foster regional and internal stability, thus encouraging peaceful resolution of disputes and evolutionary change."[8]

These rationales are not unique. Even the Carter administration, with its many differences in emphasis from those of its successor, evaluated the positive contribution to U.S. national interests made by arms transfers in a similar fashion. In his 1977 report to Congress, Secretary of State Cyrus Vance listed 10 uses of arms transfers:

To support diplomatic efforts to resolve major regional conflicts . . . ;

To influence the political orientation of nations which control strategic resources; To help maintain regional balances . . . ;

To enhance the quality and commonality of the capabilities of major allies participating with us in joint defense arrangements; To promote self-sufficiency in deterrence and defense . . . ;

To strengthen the internal security and stability of recipients; To limit Soviet influence . . . ;

To enhance our general access to and influence with government and military elites . . . ;

To provide leverage and influence with individual governments on specific issues of immediate concern to us; and To secure base rights, overseas facilities, and transit rights. . . .[9]

A final argument advanced in support of arms exports and other forms of security assistance is that they are cost effective. "Without the direct and indirect benefits we gain [from security assistance]," the Annual Report to Congress of the Secretary of Defense for fiscal 1986 states, "the projected demands of the defense budget would be far greater."[10] Under Secretary of State Buckley explained the logic of this argument in congressional testimony in 1981. "The marginal U.S. dollar loaned under FMS to the Turkish Army or the Thai or Pakistani Air Force is a dollar that we would otherwise have to spend outright on our own forces to do a job that the Turks and Thais and Pakistanis can do better and at less cost," Buckley told the Senate Foreign Relations Committee.[11]

Michael Klare, a critic of current arms transfer policy, calls the specific rationales spelled out above the "primal motives" behind weapons transfers. He writes that "it is the *clustering* of these motives behind any given transaction that most accounts for its success in winning government approval.''[12] Klare believes that ''clustering'' of primal motives is also closely related to aggregate trends in U.S. arms exports. He adds, however, that these rationales ''represent a set of beliefs or expectations about the efficacy of arms transfers, not a record of demonstrated performance.''[13]

Three Sets of Expectations

Policymakers' expectations about the utility of arms transfers can be grouped into three general categories. One set of expectations holds that military assistance also aids U.S. national security by strengthening allies and friends and deterring unwanted conflict. Another set of expectations sees security assistance as a way to advance other U.S. political interests because in exchange for aid the country gains influence over foreign political and military leaders and rights of access to facilities. The third set of expectations sees economic benefits in arms transfers; they assure the health of the U.S. defense industry, and they lower the costs of procurement for U.S. armed forces.

National security benefits: Policymakers believe judicious use of arms transfers benefits U.S. national security by enhancing the security of nations that America has an interest in preserving and by promoting stability in regions where changes in the balance of power or the outbreak of conflict could have adverse consequences for the United States. More specifically, military assistance is supposed to improve the self-defense capabilities of allied and friendly governments, in some cases enabling them to take over some or most of a military burden previously assumed by the United States; it is believed to deter aggression by external enemies, or aid in suppression of internal revolt; and it is believed useful in promoting regional stability when used to maintain a balance of power.

Security assistance undoubtedly has been an important factor in some cases, in helping nations defend themselves, particularly when the recipient is a politically isolated nation with one or more hostile states on its borders. Military aid has been a key factor in South Korea's ability to maintain its independence since the conflict of the early 1950s, and it also has been vital to the survival of Taiwan and Israel. However, boosting a nation's military capabilities does not by itself appear to make that nation's defense secure. Michael Klare writes, for instance, that ''the morale and fighting ability of the forces involved and the perceived determination of the population to resist conquest'' can be equally important.[14] Thus, America's policy of selling massive amounts of arms to Iran to make that nation a bulwark against possible Soviet aggression in the Persian Gulf and a counterweight to the more ''radical'' Arab states became a disastrous failure when lack of popular support for the Shah's policies led to the overthrow of his regime.

Indeed, many observers agree with Klare's observation that ''the U.S. arms program exacerbated, and in some cases created, the problems that led to the monarchy's collapse.''[15] These problems included the opportunity costs involved in massive expenditures on arms and the strains created by a sizable influx of foreign technicians. To make matters worse, as the Shah's regime began to collapse, he increasingly used American arms to suppress dissent, a purpose for which they had not primarily been intended. In the end, the United States lost an arsenal of sophisticated U.S. military equipment to forces unfriendly to America, as well as Iran as an ally.

To argue that arms transfers deter aggression is essentially to say they help friendly nations defend themselves, but with the added implication that the value of the weapons on the battlefield should never need to be tested. Many of the same examples can be used in assessing the validity of this argument. An additional case that supports this perception of military aid's utility is U.S.

security assistance to Western Europe after World War II, which arguably helped to prevent the Soviets from attempting to extend their sphere of influence further westward in these years (although the actual extent to which the Soviets held expansionist intentions at this time is still a subject of historical debate and the United States' possession of nuclear weapons played a significant role). In another example, aid to Israel has certainly been vital in enabling that country to maintain its territorial integrity, but just how far military assistance has gone in deterring aggression, given the history of Middle East conflict, is an open question. Finally, in the case of South Vietnam, where the regime had limited support among its people, American aid proved incapable of sustaining the existing order.

While in certain instances bolstering the military capabilities of other nations has clearly helped them defend themselves and deter potential enemies, there also are instances in which arms transfers undercut U.S. interests. One set of examples makes clear that recipients of U.S. security assistance have not always used that aid for purely defensive purposes. Turkey used U.S. equipment in its invasion of Cyprus in 1974, and Israel employed American arms in Lebanon in 1982. Once the arms have been transferred, the United States cannot expect to control how they will be used. The weapons also may be illegally transferred to a third country, which in some cases undercuts U.S. foreign policy or compromises U.S. technology. The latter reportedly occurred after the fall of the Shah when Iran sold a state-of-the-art Phoenix missile to the Soviet Union. Another set of examples shows that, particularly when emergency requests for aid are made, if the arms sought from abroad are also being procured by U.S. forces, agreeing to export the equipment in question can reduce the readiness of American combat forces. A 1981 Democratic Policy Commission study, for example, showed that the numerous F-16 exports hurt U.S. military readiness.

When the primary military concerns of a recipient of American arms involve regional rivals rather than the Soviet bloc, the effectiveness of arms transfers in promoting U.S. national security depends on their impact on another goal listed above—regional stability. The Reagan administration believes that, if military exports are properly managed, their impact in this regard is positive. Under Secretary Buckley asserted that, "given the growing disorder that we confront today," arms transfers can "help to reestablish some sense of equilibrium."[16] Other observers are less sanguine. Michael Klare argues that " 'equilibrium' is inherently unattainable in a world of multiple suppliers, and that every major delivery of sophisticated weaponry to one side in a rivalry will almost always provoke comparable (or larger) deliveries to the other side, leading to fresh arms requests by the original party, and so on."[17]

Klare adds that the range and destructive power of modern arms also make any conflict between two well-equipped adversaries a threat to all of their neighbors. "Under these circumstances," he writes, "it is not hard to imagine a chain reaction of violence as one country after another joins the conflict in an effort to confine the fighting to the others' territory."[18]

The obvious example by which to measure the efficacy of arms transfers in promoting regional stability is the Middle East. On the face of it, the record does not support a very positive assessment. There has been a steady upward spiral in the sophistication of the equipment supplied to the region, and new wars erupt about once a decade. Still, it can also be argued that arms transfers have played a constructive role in promoting peace in the region. Agreements to supply sizable arms packages to Egypt and Israel were an important factor in getting these nations to agree to the Camp David accords. The U.S. government expects military assistance will continue to be important in the Middle East peace process. The 1986 Congressional Presentation Document justifies aid to Israel in part by asserting:

Further progress toward peace depends in part on Israel having sufficient confidence not only in its ability to withstand external threats but also in the fundamental underpinning of U.S. support and assistance which help to maintain Israel's strength. Without such confidence, Israel will not be prepared to take the perceived risks necessary to pursue meaningful peace negotiations with its neighbors."[19]

Similar justifications are given for aid to the moderate Arab states.

Political benefits: Even when transferal of arms to another nation is perceived as not directly bolstering U.S. national security, or sometimes even if it is, as an additional benefit, military assistance agreements are thought to be valuable because they will help advance U.S. interests in other ways. The primary political benefit that is supposed to accrue from arms transfers is influence over the policymakers of the recipient nation. Military deals are seen as a tangible demonstration of commitment by the supplier to the recipient state, leading to the expectation that the recipient will support the policies of the supplier in return. In addition to their symbolism as a sign of friendship, arms deals give rise to expectations of leverage in another way. The nation that purchases weapons, especially sophisticated modern systems, often remains dependent on the supplier for spare parts, ammunition and various technical services and training. Desire not to jeopardize this supply relationship puts pressure on the recipient country to support the supplier's political initiatives in the recipient's region.

In some cases, it is not measurable influence that is sought, but simply access to the political and military elites in a nation to which arms are sent. The long process of negotiating an arms deal, and the subsequent need for training the recipient's armed forces in the use of the weapons systems provided, result in close contact between American political and military officials and their counterparts in the recipient country. When the nation in question is one that has not previously had close ties with the United States, arms agreements can provide the entree that leads to closer ties.

Superpower competition also figures into the political calculations behind arms agreements. In cases where the United States might not seek for intrinsic geopolitical reasons to improve ties with a relatively non-aligned nation, it might feel impelled to provide arms to the country in order to prevent the Soviet Union or another supplier from stepping in and thereby gaining the presumed influence over that country's policies.

Finally, in a number of cases the United States does not seek influence across the board from arms transfers, but rather a specific quid pro quo. Most frequently, this is the right to maintain a military base on the recipient's soil. It also could be overflight rights or docking privileges, or the opportunity to gather or share intelligence.

In assessing the efficacy of arms transfers in delivering leverage, it is easier to locate the cases where the expected influence did not develop than those in which it did, simply because it generally is not possible to determine whether a country that supports U.S. policies would still do so in the absence of military aid. Examples can be found of nations supporting a specific U.S. policy initiative at least in part because of the promise of U.S. arms. Egypt's decision to recognize the state of Israel and agree to the Camp David accords was aided by the promise of $1.5 billion in American arms. On the other hand, similar American largesse in providing military equipment to Saudi Arabia has not resulted in an endorsement by that nation of the Camp David process. In terms of more general support for American policies over a long period, Michael Klare cites the Philippines and South

Korea as countries that arguably have been influenced in this direction by the steady supply of U.S. arms they have received.[20] Yet other countries that have received large amounts of American arms have followed policies directly contrary to key American desires. Andrew Pierre asserts that Iran under the Shah consistently played a leading role in pushing for higher oil prices in OPEC (in part to pay for its extensive arms purchases) and declined to make internal reforms that Washington thought were necessary for the stability of the regime.[21] Likewise, extensive military aid to Turkey did not provide the United States with power to dissuade that country from invading Cyprus in 1974.

Review of these and other examples led Klare to conclude that "arms sales provide only a limited degree of influence over recipient governments, and whatever influence is acquired tends to vanish whenever fundamental issues are at stake."[22] Pierre even suggests that the implied commitment of an arms supply relationship can provide leverage in the opposite direction, and that "the transfer of arms can go so far as to make the supplier hostage to the recipient."[23] Pierre cites the case of Iran in the mid-1970s, where the United States could not have closed off its arms pipeline without risking a serious worsening of the oil crisis. In addition, American arms transfers often require the presence of American military and civilian personnel in the recipient country to train recipient country nationals to use and maintain the weapon systems. The presence of these individuals—there were 24,000 of them in Iran—risks entangling the United States in any military conflict that the recipient country fights.

Some critics similarly maintain that because arms transfers have become the currency in which foreign policy deals, the United States has become powerless to refuse the arms demands of friendly countries. Nations initiating or improving relations with the United States frequently ask for arms transfers as a pre-condition to the rapprochement. Despite misgivings the United States may have about transferring arms to some of these countries, the United States meets these demands because refusal would mean sacrificing a potentially valuable ally. The recently discovered covert arms transfers to Iran are a classic example of the United States viewing arms sales as its only means to achieve a diplomatic foothold. To improve relations the United States also has sold arms to moderate Arab states and the People's Republic of China despite qualms it has had about the possibility of these arms being used against other allies.

Arms transfers as a means of gaining access to elites are employed most explicitly by the United States in Latin America. The military threats to most of these nations are minimal, but Washington has sought to maintain contact between U.S. and Latin American armed forces because of the frequent periods of military rule and the military influence on civilian governments that prevail south of the American border. The U.S. government believes that the training of Latin American officers by their U.S. colleagues, both in Latin countries and at U.S. military schools, affords an opportunity to teach greater respect for democratic institutions in addition to counterinsurgency techniques. For example, with respect to Brazil, the Congressional Presentation Document for fiscal 1986 states:

> Although the Brazilian military establishment [relinquished] control of the government to a civilian president in March 1985, it will continue to exercise a major influence on numerous political and, especially, security issues. For this reason, positive, productive relations between U.S. and Brazilian armed forces will remain highly important to the advancement of bilateral interests and objectives."[24]

A similar argument is made with respect to aid to Guatemala. "A security assistance program designed to assist the Guatemalan government in overcoming its insurgency and to continue its civic action program will permit the government to redirect more of its limited resources to the socio-economic root causes of dissatisfaction," the Congressional Presentation states.[25] "Such a program offers an important means by which the United States can increase its influence with the Guatemalan military, and promote increased understanding and sharing of mutual concerns."[26]

The influence the United States has gained from access to military elites in Latin America is questionable. If the United States has had influence over the internal policies of these elites, such as their human rights practices and respect for democratic institutions, it does not appear to have achieved positive results. (The human rights question is examined in greater detail in the following chapter.) Indeed, the number of military coups in Latin America increased as U.S. arms transfers to Latin America and the International Military Education and Training program were stepped up in the 1960s. In their foreign and economic policies, however, Latin American militaries and military governments have seemed on the whole more attentive to U.S. demands and interests than their civilian counterparts (one notable exception is the reform-minded officers that came to power in Peru in 1968). But whether this is a result of greater U.S. access to the military or simply a product of the military's conservatism is open to debate.

The preemptive aspect of arms agreements, in which one supplier strikes a deal primarily to prevent another supplier from gaining the influence expected to accompany the deal, is of questionable effectiveness in at least some cases. The ties developed, however solid they appear, often prove transitory, as in the case of Ethiopia, which quickly turned to the Soviet Union instead of America for aid after the ouster of Haile Selassie.[27] Perhaps the most spectacular example of the collapse of an arms relationship involves the Soviet Union. The Soviets began supplying weapons to Egypt in 1955, and soon it became the leading Third World recipient of Soviet arms. In the early 1970s, however, President Sadat expelled Soviet advisers from Egypt and turned to the United States for aid instead. In some cases, as Pierre notes: "If arms sales have the effect of closely associating the supplier with a certain regime in a country, and that regime is overturned, the former association can have serious negative consequences."[28] The United States' support of the Shah earned it the animosity of the current Iranian government and its supporters throughout the Arab world.

A decision to deny a particular weapon to a country that is seeking it, though, does not always lead that country to turn to another supplier. A study by the American Enterprise Institute suggests several reasons why this might be especially true of some U.S. clients:

> If the potential buyer has equipped most of its forces with American arms, turning to another supplier could require costly retraining of personnel to operate and maintain the new system. Moreover, other major suppliers are often seen as less reliable than the United States when it comes to training and providing spare parts. Another problem the potential buyer may face is system incompatibility. Mixing arms from several countries can result in noncomplementary systems that could degrade the military effectiveness of the weapons on hand. Last, the potential buyer may invite strained relations with the United States should it turn to another country for arms.[29]

Thus, as Chapter 3 noted, requests that the Carter administration turned down from Iran, Taiwan, Guatemala, Pakistan, Greece and Turkey were not filled by alternate suppliers. On the other hand, Ecuador, India, Argentina and, most recently, Saudi Arabia, did receive equivalent weapons from European sources. In another case, the Nixon administration's refusal to sell F-5 fighters to

Peru led that country to purchase Soviet SU-22 fighter-bombers instead, although Soviet leverage over Peru does not appear to have increased as a result of its provision of arms to that country.[30] Still, whether or not the superpowers are aware of these limitations on arms sales as a source of influence, neither can predict with certainty whether a given denial of arms to a particular country will or will not enable the other to step in and gain political influence. This fact makes it hard for either to pull out of the competition and show unilateral restraint in its arms exports.

A final political use of arms transfers has an underlying military motive. Some American arms relationships are primarily reciprocal arrangements in which the United States is granted base rights or similar privileges. In such cases, arms transfers are implicitly understood to be a form of "rent" on the facilities in question. Countries that receive U.S. security assistance primarily in return for base rights include Spain, Portugal, Greece and the Philippines. The decision in the Carter administration to develop the Rapid Deployment Force led to new requirements for rights of access and overflight that have been factors in agreements with nations such as Oman and Kenya.

Since World War II, the United States has been able to maintain a number of bases considered vital to monitoring Soviet activity and enabling America to respond quickly to military maneuvers in return for the "rent" paid in military equipment. But the overall value of arms transfers in providing indirect benefits to U.S. national security through quid pro quo arrangements is again open to question. Some critics of U.S. foreign policy above all charge that the practice of maintaining a military presence in far-flung locations around the world, which is made possible by arms transfers, only exacerbates East-West tensions. Others who support the need for bases as part of a policy of containment still acknowledge that the United States cannot always be certain that the arrangements will last indefinitely. America lost base rights in Ethiopia after the coup there (although it gained corresponding rights in Somalia as a result), and modern naval facilities that the United States constructed at Cam Ranh Bay in Vietnam now provide the Soviet Union with an important Pacific port. In addition, American expressions of dissatisfaction with the behavior of a recipient state can lead to a loss of the quid pro quo rights. After the United States imposed an arms embargo on Turkey following the invasion of Cyprus, Turkey responded by restricting U.S. intelligence activities on Turkish soil. Sometimes a concern over loss of base rights can lead to conflicts with other U.S. policy goals. Desire to maintain access to military bases in the Philippines, for example, is widely believed to have resulted for many years in a muting of U.S. criticism of the human rights practices and the overall corruption of the Marcos regime. Even in cases where ties with an ally appear fairly sturdy, continued access to bases in return for arms may not be assured. Both Greece and Spain in recent years have placed restrictions on U.S. base rights, the result of a combination of growing anti-American feelings among their populations and the rise of new leaders determined to steer a more independent path from the United States than their predecessors did.

Economic benefits: Among the rationales that policymakers give for arms transfers, security and political factors clearly are emphasized more than economic factors. Yet many observers also believe that military exports generate important economic benefits, and critics sometimes assert that these perceived economic advantages are the hidden motor that really drives arms sales. Benefits from arms sales are seen as arising at three levels of the economy. For the economy as a whole, arms sales are valued as a source of foreign exchange that improves America's balance of payments, as a source of employment, and as a tool to ensure access to raw materials. For the Defense Department, arms transfers can reduce the outlays necessary both for research and development and for purchasing some weapons systems. Some R&D costs can be passed on to foreign purchasers, and larger production runs generally reduce unit costs. Finally, arms transfers can result in economic benefits to the manufacturers themselves, over and above the income they provide, by offering a way to keep production lines busy at times when domestic demand is slack.

While most of these economic factors can be measured empirically, there still is disagreement about how to interpret the statistics and, in some cases, about the statistics themselves. Observers do agree that arms exports do not constitute an especially high percentage of American trade. Data compiled by the U.S. Arms Control and Disarmament Agency indicate that the export of military equipment by the United States from 1973 to 1983 accounted for 4.5 percent of total U.S. exports for the period.[31] Similarly, Andrew Pierre estimates that arms exports accounted for about 4 to 5 percent of total U.S. exports in 1980, while Michael Klare and the American Enterprise Institute, using data different from Pierre's, place the figure at closer to 3 percent.[32] For evidence on the importance of military exports for the trade deficit, Pierre cites a study by the Treasury Department of the likely effect of cuts of up to 40 percent on the balance of payments as well as on employment. Its conclusion, he says, is that "the impact . . . of any plausible policy curtailing arms exports is likely to be modest."[33] Hammond and his colleagues, on the other hand, find the significance of arms sales for the balance of payments to be greater. They contend: "The nearly $17 billion in foreign military sales and commercial sales abroad of defense equipment represents one of the largest industrial sector contributions to balancing the U.S. international payments deficit."[34]

The importance of arms exports for employment also is in dispute. One government study, by the Bureau of Labor Statistics in 1975, estimated that arms exports provided 277,000 jobs at that time, or 0.3 percent of national employment.[35] Other officials have estimated that military exports support about 400,000 jobs.[36] And calculations by the Defense Security Assistance Agency indicate that about 1 million jobs are related to arms sales. Pierre contends that "even this figure, which is surely inflated, does not make a convincing case against greater restraints [on exports] because . . . limited and tempered reductions would have relatively minor consequences."[37] Pierre notes that the Treasury Department study suggested that a 40 percent decline in military export orders would result in a 0.1 percent decline in national employment.[38] But Hammond and his associates argue that it is misleading to draw conclusions from the percentage of total employment accounted for by arms sales. "Many key electronics, communications and transportation industries depend upon military exports a great deal," they claim.[39] They cite a 1977 study by the Electronic Industries Association which predicted that President Carter's proposed arms ceiling would result in the loss of 100,000 jobs in the communications, electronics and transportation equipment industries.

The other benefit for the U.S. economy attributed to arms exports is their value as "barter" for raw materials, especially oil. The American Enterprise Institute contends that the Shah of Iran broke the 1973 OPEC oil embargo "in part because of his special arms relationship with the United States," a relationship America had not yet established with other Arab states (although it soon did).[40] Yet, as indicated earlier, the provision of arms by America did not prevent the Shah from being a leader in the push for higher oil prices.

As far as the U.S. military budget is concerned, some observers believe that arms exports yield significant savings for the Pentagon. Savings are expected because foreign purchasers can be made to share R&D and overhead costs and because larger production runs that result from adding foreign sales generally reduce unit costs because of economies of scale and learning curves. Data on the actual extent of savings come from a 1976 Congressional Budget Office study.[41] The CBO found that the Defense Department realized savings of $560 million in fiscal 1976 on $8 billion in foreign military sales. However, the CBO noted that not all programs generate savings. The money recouped on training and repair services or export of ships, for example, is negligible. But exports of aircraft, missiles, vehicles and communication equipment do generate savings. In particular, sales of modern, high technology equipment such as advanced fighters and missiles result in substantial savings. In these cases, CBO found the savings from exports average 14 cents on the dollar, although they still never total more than 8 percent of R&D costs. Interpretations of these data vary. Pierre says they suggest "that large savings do not generally result from U.S. foreign military sales," while AEI claims that "These figures translate into many hundreds of millions of dollars in today's vibrant market."[42]

While the overall benefits of arms exports for the U.S. economy and the federal budget are open to conflicting interpretations, it is clear that the impact for an individual firms may be quite significant. A particular sale may mean the difference between profit and loss for a manufacturer, and it could prevent the loss of dozens or hundreds of jobs on a production line. One example is Grumman's F-14 Tomcat fighter, one of the Navy's most advanced planes. Because of skyrocketing F-14 development costs in the early 1970s and the loss of other military orders, Grumman came to the conclusion that it might not be able to continue with the project on the basis of Navy funding alone. The company mounted an intensive campaign to market the plane to Iran, and the Shah's 1974 decision to buy 80 F-14s for $2 billion apparently saved the program from termination.[43]

Few major American defense contractors rely wholly or primarily on the export market, however. One study of the Pentagon's 10 largest contractors in 1977 found that for only one did foreign military sales account for more than 25 percent of total sales, while the remaining nine received an average of about 12 percent of their revenues from arms exports.[44] IRRC's own analysis of the leading arms exporters between 1982 and 1986 found that the importance of foreign military sales to leading defense contractors had declined. As Table 5–1 illustrates, foreign military sales constituted only 5.2 percent of the total sales of the top 10 arms-exporting companies during this period.

Table 5–1

Ratio of FMS Awards to Total Sales of the Leading U.S. FMS Contractors, 1982–1986

Contractor	1982	1983	1984	1985	1986	1982–86 Average
Boeing	.043	.081	.045	.095	.012	.054
General Dynamics	.126	.065	.129	.151	.154	.129
General Electric	.009	.006	.011	.018	.017	.011
Hughes Aircraft	.069	.035	.035	.016	NA	.037
Lockheed	.062	.026	.028	.031	.005	.027
McDonnell Douglas	.141	.062	.103	.141	.045	.095
Northrop	.362	.056	.044	.059	.018	.081
Raytheon	.033	.081	.085	.037	.086	.049
United Technologies	.054	.021	.012	.020	.014	.023
Westinghouse	.015	.020	.023	.008	.019	.017
Company Average	.091	.045	.052	.058	.041	.052

Some observers have also speculated as to whether the economic benefits accrued from arms sales may not be counteracted by other economic effects of promoting arms business. Seymour Melman, professor of industrial engineering at Columbia University, and Robert DeGrasse, formerly of the Center on Economic Priorities, argue that a sizable military sector in the U.S. economy has deleterious effects because it diverts capital and skilled technical personnel from the civilian sector and promotes an inefficient style of management (because of the relative unimportance of minimizing costs in the defense industry).[45] If this perspective is correct, then, to the extent that they bolster the defense industry, arms exports may be harming economic growth in the United States. Evidence for this conclusion, however, is at least as tentative and open to dispute as the other data presented here on the question of economic benefits from arms sales.

Footnotes

1. Congressional Research Service (CRS), *Changing Perspectives on U.S. Arms Transfer Policy* (Washington: U.S. Government Printing Office, Sept 25, 1981), p. 126.
2. Cited in Michael Klare, *American Arms Supermarket* (Austin, Tex: University of Texas Press, 1984), p. 16.
3. Pierre, Andrew, *The Global Politics of Arms Sales* (Princeton, N.J.: Princeton, 1982), p. 65.
4. Defense Security Assistance Agency (DSAA), *Congressional Presentation for Security Assistance Programs, FY 1986*, p. 1.
5. *Ibid.*, p. 1.
6. CRS, *op. cit.*, p. 125.
7. Joint Chiefs of Staff, *United States Military Posture, FY 1984*, p. 51.
8. CRS, *op. cit.*, p. 127.
9. Paul Hammond, David Louscher, Michael D. Salomone and Norman A. Graham, *The Reluctant Supplier: U.S. Decisionmaking for Arms Sales* (Cambridge, Mass: Oelgeschlager, Gunn & Hain, Inc., 1983), pp. 32–3.
10. Secretary of Defense Caspar Weinberger, *Annual Report to Congress, Fiscal Year 1986*, p. 271.
11. CRS, *op. cit.*, p. 132.
12. Klare, *op. cit.*, p. 35.
13. *Ibid.*, p. 37.
14. *Ibid.*, pp. 239–40.
15. *Ibid.*, p. 125.
16. CRS, *op. cit.*, p. 125.
17. Klare, *op. cit.*, p. 241.
18. *Ibid.*, p. 242.
19. Defense Security Assistance Agency, *op. cit.*, p. 135.
20. Klare, *op. cit.*, p. 243.
21. Pierre, *op. cit.*, p. 151.
22. Klare, *op. cit.*, p. 243.
23. Pierre, *op. cit.*, p. 18.
24. Defense Security Assistance Agency, *op. cit.*, p. 361.
25. *Ibid.*, p. 391.
26. *Ibid.*, p. 391.
27. Klare, *op. cit.*, p. 243.
28. Pierre, *op. cit.*, p. 17.
29. Roger P. Labrie, John G. Hutchins, and Edwin Peura, *U.S. Arms Sales Policy: Background and Issues* (Washington: American Enterprise Institute, 1982), p. 50.
30. Pierre, *op. cit.*, p. 241.
31. U.S. Department of State, Arms Control and Disarmament Agency, *World Military Expenditures and Arms Transfers*, 1985 edition, p. 127.
32. Pierre, *op. cit.*, p. 26; Labrie et al, *op. cit.*, p. 70; and Klare *op. cit.*, p. 245.
33. Pierre, *op. cit.*, p. 69.
34. Hammond et al., *op. cit.*, p. 36.
35. Bureau of Labor Statistics, 1975.
36. Hammond et al., *op. cit.*, p. 35.
37. Pierre, *op. cit.*, p. 69.
38. *Ibid.*, p. 69.
39. Hammond et al., *op. cit.*, p. 36.
40. Labrie et al., *op. cit.*, p. 71.
41. Congressional Budget Office, *Foreign Military Sales and U.S. Weapons Cost*, May 5, 1976.
42. Pierre, *op. cit.*, p. 70 and Labrie et al., *op. cit.*, p. 72.
43. Anthony Sampson, *The Arms Bazaar* (New York: The Viking Press, 1977), pp. 249–56.

44.   Pierre, *op. cit.*, p. 71.
45.   Robert W. DeGrasse, *Military Expansion and Economic Decline* (New York: Council on Economic Priorities, 1983); Seymour Melman, *The Permanent War Economy* (New York: Simon and Schuster, 1974).

Chapter 6
Arms Exports and the Developed World

The policies that govern the transfer of military equipment from the United States to developed nations have been shaped by close and fundamentally stable postwar ties, as evidenced by the series of formal military alliances that bind the industrialized allies. The 1949 North Atlantic Treaty links the United States with most of western Europe, Iceland and Canada. Through the 1951 ANZUS pact, Washington has pledged its military support to Australia and, until recently, New Zealand. Two additional security treaties provide for a broad range of military cooperation between the United States and Japan.

Arms transfers to industrialized allies raise issues quite different from those involving Third World recipients. U.S. national security interests are interlocked with those of its closest allies, and defense strategies are designed and executed in unison. Although the economically developed allies sometimes adopt policies that diverge from those preferred by Washington, these differences pale in comparison with those that are brought about by the radical internal political shifts that frequently occur in the Third World. The developed nations also have displayed far less inclination to engage in armed conflict in the postwar era, so that the United States has reason to assume that military equipment acquired by its closest allies will not be used in ways that run counter to its own security objectives. In making arms transfers to developed allies, the United States for the most part can also feel that it runs less risk of having its technology fall into the hands of unintended or unfriendly parties, and generally need not debate how transfers might affect the recipient countries' human rights practices. Finally, because developed nations have the purchasing power to stock their arsenals without adversely affecting their economies and have the infrastructure and skilled personnel needed to maintain and use military equipment effectively, the economic impact of major arms sales on the recipient nations is not an issue.

As is the case in any alliance, though, conflicting concerns born out of each partner's assessment of its economic and political self-interest invariably produces a degree of strife. And in relations between the United States and its industrialized allies, economic disagreements predominate as the largest single source of friction. While Americans have been concerned that they were bearing too much of the common defense, Europeans in particular have sought to strengthen their own defense industries and have felt that the United States has been stingy in its purchases of their locally made arms.

U.S. Arms Exports to the Developed World: An Overview

The United States transferred $429 million worth of military equipment to Japan and $615 million worth to Australia and New Zealand during 1986, a year in which arms imports by the developed world accounted for 39 percent of the total value of U.S. arms deliveries. Deliveries to Japan are on the rise. During the first seven years of the 1980s, the annual average value of U.S. military deliveries equaled $727 million (constant 1986 dollars), compared with $220 million during the 1970s, $256 million during the 1960s and $549 million during the latter half of the 1950s. U.S. deliveries to Australia and New Zealand, similarly measured to take the effects of inflation into account, have risen steadily. They grew from an annual average of $28 million during the 1950s, to $196 million in the 1960s, to $217 million in the 1970s, to $512 million for the period 1980 to 1986. The Arms Control and Disarmament Agency reports that transfers from the United States accounted for 92 percent of Australia's arms imports ($2.2 billion out of $2.4 billion) and 71 percent of New Zealand's ($120 million out of $170 million) during the period 1981 to 1985.

The United States delivered $2.8 billion worth of military equipment to Europe and Canada in 1986, according to the Pentagon's Defense Security Assistance Agency, which accounted for 28 percent of the value of American deliveries worldwide. Taking into account the effects of inflation, annual U.S. arms deliveries to NATO have consistently fallen into the $2.6 to $5.4 billion (constant 1986 dollars) range. Deliveries have exceeded the $6 billion per year mark only seven times in the postwar period, all during the 1950s when the United States was embarked on a program of assisting Europe to rearm. (See Table 6–1 and Figure 6–1.)

Of the 1986 total, 76 percent was carried out through the FMS program, and approximately 23 percent through direct, company-to-government channels, while less than one-half of 1 percent was financed through the Military Assistance Program. These proportions represent a tremendous shift from the 1950s, when the preponderance of American military deliveries to Euorpe took the form of MAP grants. U.S. arms deliveries to Europe are made primarily to NATO allies. The value of deliveries to the European nations that are not members of the alliance exceeded 10 percent of total deliveries to Europe in only one of the last 36 years, and constituted 6 percent of U.S. arms sent from 1980 to 1986. The ACDA reports that the United States' NATO allies and NATO itself imported $19.7 billion worth of military equipment during the period 1981 to 1985, of which $15.9 billion or 81 percent came from the United States. American arms accounted for a smaller portion— 51 percent of $3.8 billion—of the value of military imports by those European nations that are not parties to either NATO or the Warsaw Pact.

France, Great Britain and Germany are major arms producers in their own right, with advanced defense industries that supply weapons for domestic and export markets. Italy occupies an intermediate position below the big three in its production capacity, ahead of countries such as the Netherlands, Belgium and the neutral nations of Sweden and Switzerland, which in turn have more developed weapons industries than the rest of Western Europe. According to the ACDA, the European nations of NATO exported an annual average of $8.7 billion worth of military goods between 1981 and 1985, while the rest of Europe excluding those nations that belong to the Warsaw Pact exported an annual average of $1.6 billion. The comparable figure for the United States was an annual average of $9.7 billion.

The European nations' desires to sustain defense production capacities are inseparably wedded to issues of national sovereignty and autonomy: All want to minimize their reliance on an external

Table 6–1

U.S. Military Deliveries to the Industrialized World, 1950–1986
(in thousands of 1986 constant dollars)

Fiscal Year	NATO	Non-NATO Europe*	Japan	Australia and New Zealand	Total
1950	$ 470,602	—	—	—	$ 470,602
1951	5,326,963	—	—	—	5,326,963
1952	6,934,724	$ 400,955	—	$ 11,103	7,346,782
1953	15,316,117	898,555	—	58,580	16,273,252
1954	13,532,406	1,357,003	—	9,554	14,898,963
1955	9,133,364	765,083	$ 265,803	10,287	10,174,537
1956	10,327,070	353,878	549,698	39,574	11,270,220
1957	7,873,933	90,518	551,779	11,254	8,527,484
1958	6,589,474	306,332	735,312	6,305	7,637,423
1959	4,657,500	123,162	641,675	139,406	5,561,743
1960	4,822,043	125,480	544,516	31,860	5,523,899
1961	3,083,550	103,733	455,132	34,639	3,677,054
1962	3,035,576	23,029	577,500	33,346	3,669,451
1963	5,471,253	86,484	183,659	160,279	5,901,675
1964	3,355,656	64,134	143,393	94,241	3,657,424
1965	4,339,999	175,770	218,028	135,538	4,869,335
1966	3,223,398	49,021	152,882	280,884	3,706,185
1967	3,107,317	25,616	70,409	341,168	3,544,510
1968	2,935,784	28,117	152,477	442,313	3,558,691
1969	3,609,560	36,663	65,341	404,672	4,116,236
1970	3,015,446	105,028	58,963	186,515	3,365,952
1971	3,547,266	115,452	249,924	273,736	4,186,378
1972	2,998,645	58,894	241,590	154,938	3,454,067
1973	2,703,125	40,925	144,298	271,407	3,159,755
1974	3,046,303	57,937	190,177	480,912	3,775,329
1975	3,078,105	57,944	119,799	58,555	3,314,403
1976	4,116,096	181,763	341,651	53,125	4,692,635
1977	3,223,945	240,639	232,670	83,953	3,781,207
1978	2,896,038	153,096	265,873	315,081	3,630,088
1979	3,012,416	466,799	349,093	287,366	4,115,674
1980	4,729,304	150,918	480,942	296,395	5,657,559
1981	4,788,152	289,481	806,228	670,806	6,554,667
1982	4,402,962	163,812	733,438	211,086	5,551,298
1983	5,149,682	438,994	922,042	445,530	6,956,248
1984	4,407,353	328,213	959,740	643,168	6,338,474
1985	3,182,593	138,824	755,394	699,995	4,776,806
1986	2,646,624	140,080	429,368	615,379	3,831,451
Total	$166,390,344	$8,142,332	$12,588,794	$7,992,950	$195,114,420

*   Non-NATO Europe = Andorra, Austria, Bulgaria, Cyprus, Finland, Gibraltar, Ireland, Liechtenstein, Malta, Monaco, Romania, San Marino, Svalbard & Jan Mayen, Sweden, Switzerland, U.S.S.R., Yugoslavia

Source: IRRC calculations from DSAA Fiscal Year Series.

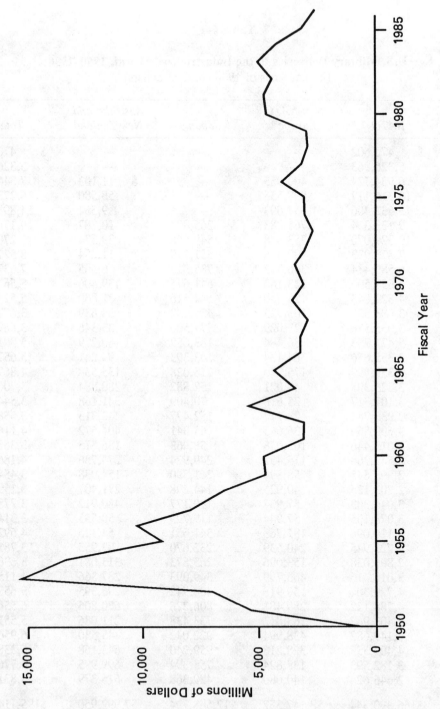

Source: Defense Security Assistance Agency "Fiscal Year Series," 1987

Figure 6–1.   U.S. Military Deliveries to NATO Nations
(in millions of constant 1986 dollars)

military supplier, and they view the maintenance of an arms industry both as crucial to their national security and as an important element of national prestige. The export market is essential to the survival of European arms industries because domestic markets are not large enough to make the production of major weapons cost-effective. Industry's dependence on exports has influenced the types of weapons developed in Europe, since the small scale production of equipment that lacks real export value would rarely be feasible economically. The enormous size of the U.S. defense budget and domestic procurement demands, on the other hand, have enabled U.S. manufacturers to produce weapons on a larger, more economical scale than their European counterparts could manage without exporting.

Reliable measures of any national defense industry's dependence on arms exports are hard to come by, and estimates conflict. IRRC found that the proportion of FMS awards to total sales for the 10 U.S. contractors with the highest proportion of FMS exports, which exclude direct commercial sales, averaged between 5 and 6 percent from 1982 to 1986, and reached a high of 9 percent in 1982. Using a different measure, that of FMS awards to total Defense Department awards—which in effect compares funding accrued because of arms exports with that earned from domestic procurement—reveals a higher percentage of 11 percent for the top 10 U.S. FMS contractors during the period 1982 to 1986. Both figures are conservative; they do not take into account the funds that changed hands during this period for transactions carried out through direct, company-to-government commercial sales channels, and they take into account only the 10 historically largest American exporters and not the industry as a whole. Moreover, defense contractors have accrued less of their sales overseas in the 1980s than they did in the previous decade. A 1980 study conducted by the private General Research Corp., for example, estimated that the value of total U.S. arms exports as a percentage of total U.S. arms production for the 1970s ranged from 20 to 25 percent.[1] By contrast, a 1979 report by the Senate Committee on Foreign Relations estimated that between 55 and 60 percent of military equipment produced in France and 25 to 30 percent of equipment made in Britain is exported. It also found that Belgium, though not a major European arms producer, exports up to 90 percent of the small arms that its industry manufactures.[2]

A more recent SIPRI study placed the annual average level of French arms exports for the period 1977 through 1980 at 38 percent, and the General Research Corp. concurred, estimating that France exported betweeen 35 and 45 percent of its arms production and Britain between 25 and 35 percent.[3] These lower figures still are higher than those that apply to the American industry. A 1978 summary of the British arms control policy by the Foreign and Commonwealth Office stated frankly: "Overseas orders make an important contribution to the maintenance of a viable defence industry in the UK, which is necessary to fulfill the equipment needs of our own forces and reduces unit costs to our forces."[4]

A Historical Perspective on Modern Problems

Many of the difficulties that the United States now encounters in its policies and practices governing arms exports to the developed nations of Europe spring from the successes of the policies it adopted toward the war ravaged continent in the years immediately after World War II. As Washington planned for the postwar era, the uneasy wartime alliance between the USSR and the other major allies quickly degenerated into mutual mistrust and fear. American policy increasingly became driven by apprehension over the possibility of expanding Soviet influence in Europe, and with the enactment of the Truman Doctrine and the Marshall Plan, and the signing of the North

Atlantic Treaty, the United States was well on its way to implementing its new strategy of "collective security" and its plans to assist in rebuilding western Europe. The transfer of military equipment to the physically and economically decimated nations of western Europe became an integral part of that strategy.

Initial arms transfers to Europe were made almost exclusively as grants under the Military Assistance Program, and most of the equipment used to restock the depleted European arsenals came from U.S. war surpluses. This aid was not considered to be the beginning of a long term program, but rather the response to an acute temporary need. Secretary of Defense Louis Johnson, in testimony before the Senate Foreign Relations Committee, estimated that the United States would need to provide military aid to its allies for about four or five years, and that the amount of aid would diminish in each successive year.[5] Military aid to Europe complemented economic assistance. Grants of military equipment, combined with the nuclear umbrella extended by the United States, gave allies suffering from the devastating effects of the war a measure of security that allowed them to concentrate their limited resources on economic recovery. The economic assistance embodied in the Marshall Plan quickened the pace of economic recovery and enabled European countries to become healthy trading partners and significant contributors to the military requirements of collective NATO security.

Despite initial assurances that military assistance to Europe was to be a short-term proposition, the level of U.S. MAP funds earmarked for delivery to Europe increased in the 1950s. The outbreak of the Korean war in 1950 intensified fears of communist expansionism around the globe, and U.S. arms transfers to NATO countries in 1953 reached a record high of $15.2 billion (in constant 1986 dollars) worth of deliveries, which were funded almost exclusively through MAP. In contrast to the early postwar transfers, little of this came out of U.S. surpluses. This type of commitment demonstrated the importance of a strong Europe in the eyes of U.S. policymakers; it also made demands on the nation's budget that aroused recurring domestic criticism and eventually contributed to a shift in the way NATO collective security was maintained.

At the same time that the United States was rearming Europe, it was becoming increasingly involved in other regions of the world. The Korean war heightened U.S. concern over the possibility of expanding Soviet and Chinese influence in Asia, and Washington moved to assist in providing for the security of South Korea and Taiwan. Communist influence in the Middle East began to attract U.S. concern and counteractive aid to the region, particularly after Egypt allied itself with the Soviet Union in 1955. At the beginning of the decade, Europe and Canada received roughly 90 percent of all U.S. arms transfers. By 1953, that portion of deliveries had fallen to 77 percent of the total, despite its huge increase in absolute terms, and had decreased further by the end of the decade, to 42 percent, of which about 90 percent was funded through MAP grants. These commitments to provide security assistance around the globe began to put noticeable strains on the American balance of payments.

Several other factors contributed to the payment deficit woes of the United States, whose foreign money payments exceeded receipts by $10 billion during 1958–60. U.S. businesses were investing dollars overseas, and foreign concerns were retaining the U.S. currency. U.S. export sectors were becoming less dynamic at the same time, and were not generating as much revenue from foreign sources as they had in the past. But as one scholar notes, "by far the greatest contribution to the deficit came from increased military expenditures abroad. Foreign military expenditures had climbed from $576 million in 1950 to an average of $3 billion per year after 1958."[6]

A significant part of these expenditures went toward the support of American troops in Europe, particularly in Germany. At the height of their deployment, in 1953, U.S. troops there numbered around 427,000.[7] By the late 1950s, U.S. officials were pushing for the withdrawal of some of these forces to reduce the flow of dollars from the United States, and to indicate to Europe that the United States could no longer afford to shoulder the existing proportion of the common defense burden. This drastic action was avoided, however, when West Germany agreed to purchase $600 million worth of advanced American military equipment as a kind of indirect offset to cover the cost of stationing U.S. troops on German soil. Gradually the sale of weapons became accepted in American and European decisionmaking circles as a means of sharing the economic burden of providing for the collective defense.

The European allies' interest in purchasing U.S. arms complemented the new strategic theory of flexible response developed under President Kennedy. The strategy of flexible response required a strong conventional capacity in Europe under NATO in order to give the alliance a variety of credible options below the nuclear threshhold. In 1961, President Kennedy encouraged U.S. government officials to facilitate the sale of U.S. arms abroad and urged allies who considered themselves financially able to purchase their weapons from the United States to do so. Arms sales promised to achieve a number of goals at that time; they would increase NATO strength collectively, promote the variety of conventional options demanded by the new flexible response strategy, and redistribute the burden of defense costs in a way that would satisfy European countries' desire to acquire strong defense capabilities of their own. Thus, arms sales rather than grants became the principal vehicle for U.S. military transfers to NATO. MAP deliveries to all but five European nations petered out during the 1960s, and MAP deliveries to Norway stopped after 1971.

Economic Issues Hindering U.S. Exports to the Allies

Given the importance of military exports to the health of the indigenous arms industries of the industrialized U.S. allies, it is not surprising that the issues that arise in negotiating U.S. arms transfers to NATO and the developed allies are primarily economic. Issues such as the maturity of the recipient's own defense industry or levels of domestic employment are not significant considerations in sales to most of the developing world, where buying technologically advanced weapons necessarily means buying abroad. When a country with a domestic arms industry purchases foreign weapons, on the other hand, it must take into account the effect of its decision on domestic manufacturers and its national economy.

Industrialized allies import weapons from the United States because they want a specific type of weapon or technology that is not made domestically, because it offers the best deal, or because they have entered into formal reciprocal purchasing arrangements with the United States. Although in some cases allies with highly developed economies find straightforward, off-the-shelf purchases of American equipment to be the financially cost-effective or convenient method of proceeding, more frequently they demand concessions of one sort or another. These include seeking licensing or coproduction arrangements that will allow their own manufacturers to take part in a venture; direct offsets, which require the U.S. contractor to subcontract a certain percentage of the sale to companies in the purchasing country; or indirect offsets, commercial packages unrelated to the weapons sale that guarantee that the U.S. contractor will assist the recipient in some economically beneficial venture or otherwise funnel capital back into the recipient's economy. When Great Britain, for example, realized that it could neither overcome technological hurdles in its Nimrod airborne early warning system development program nor afford to build the aircraft, it decided to buy Boeing Awacs instead, and demanded an offset package worth 130 percent of the cost of the Awacs purchase.

The nations of Europe have responded to the pressures created by large imports of American military equipment on their defense industries in a number of ways. First, they have taken steps to expand the level of their exports to the developing world. As earlier chapters have noted, the larger European exporters to a certain degree appear to be succeeding in this respect, and have gained ground in recent years on both the United States and the Soviet Union by increasing their market shares at the superpowers' expense. At the heart of this phenomenon is the fundamental manner in which the Europeans approach arms transfers: Unlike the United States, the Europeans, within certain limits, subordinate the foreign policy implications or perceived uses of foreign military sales to the domestic economic and industrial objectives to be derived from them.[8] This has occurred at the same time that the U.S. Congress has become increasingly willing to make its voice heard on U.S. foreign policy toward the Middle East—a large arms market—by restricting sales to certain Arab states.

The desire to expand markets for their defense wares has also led the European suppliers to explore the possibilities of selling more to each other, in effect to create or expand upon the European market. This course has gained momentum because of a longstanding and overriding alliance objective, that of maximizing the military capabilities of NATO as a whole by standardizing the equipment used by the different armed forces of NATO. The desirability of guaranteeing the rationalization, standardization and interoperability (a concept labeled RSI) of allied forces is obvious: A multinational army fighting in the field has a better chance of operating effectively and flexibly for prolonged periods if it is able to receive ammunition, spare parts, fuel, replacement equipment and repair services from any one of a number of stockpiles instead of having to seek out particular ones. At present, the armed forces of NATO are far from standardized. In 1983, one observer wrote:

> Along the Central Front [of Europe] alone, NATO allies are currently equipped with seven different types of main battle tanks and 22 different types of anti-tank weapons. In the fleets of NATO's navies cruise about 100 types of destroyers and other large ships, and these are equipped with 36 different radar systems, eight types of air-defense missiles, six different ship-to ship missiles, and more than 40 different artillery calibers above 30 millimeters. Additionally, there are 23 different types of fighter aircraft in operation. Neither ammunition nor spare parts are interchangeable, everything has to be procured and stored in duplicate or triplicate if combat effectiveness is to be assured.[9]

The imperatives of RSI and the urge to explore methods of increasing the size of the European market have led the European defense industries to cross national boundaries and collaborate more among themselves. They have favored pooling their research and development expertise, dividing up the production tasks, and marketing military goods to each other and to the Third World, on the theory that the economies of scale make this approach more profitable than pursuing independent paths or buying most systems from the United States.

Thus far, efforts have been limited in that they have involved cooperative ventures between a small number of countries and have concentrated primarily on aircraft and other aerospace systems. Britain and France pooled their resources starting in 1966 to develop and produce the Jaguar attack aircraft, which has since been bought by the Ecuadorian, Indian and Omani air forces in addition to those of Britain and France. West Germany and France agreed to develop jointly a trainer/light attack aircraft in 1969, and production models were delivered to the two nations at the end of the 1970s, by which time Belgium had placed orders for a small number of trainer versions of the aircraft. France also entered into agreements with West Germany in the mid-1960s for the development and manufacture of the Milan and HOT antitank and Roland anti-aircraft missile systems, and with Britain in the late 1960s for the joint development of the Puma, Super Puma, Gazelle and Lynx combat helicopters.

Perhaps most significant to date, Britain, West Germany and Italy formed the Panavia consortium in 1969 to produce what eventually emerged as the Tornado multi-role combat aircraft. The first Tornado production models were introduced into the participating countries' arsenals in the late 1970s and early 1980s, and Saudi Arabia became the first customer from outside the consortium when it ordered 72 of the aircraft in 1985 after its request for McDonnell Douglas F-15 fighters was rebuffed by the United States. Success with these multinational programs has led the Europeans to continue to explore possible collaborative programs. Britain, West Germany, Italy and Spain are currently examining the feasibility of producing an advanced fighter—the European Fighter Aircraft—for the 1990s, and France and West Germany are negotiating for the joint development and production of a new combat helicopter. The member nations of NATO have also collaborated in development of armored vehicles, communications systems, specialized aircraft and naval defense systems.[10]

These cooperative efforts have occurred against a larger backdrop of political consultations and initiatives that stretch back to the mid-1950s.[11] Discussions on the prospects for greater cooperation among the national European arms industries were conducted under the auspices of the Western European Union, which was founded in 1954, the European Community (founded in 1957) and the Eurogroup (founded in 1968). The Eurogroup formed a special subgroup, the Council of National Armaments Directors (CNAD), to consider issues of weapons production collaboration. With the exception of the specialized CNAD, these bodies, however, were mandated to consider a broad array of issues that affect European security, and it was not until 1976 that the Europeans created an organization—the Independent European Program Group—whose sole purpose would be to advance the cause of cooperation in the realm of military production. Because the IEPG operated independently of the NATO structure, it was the first European organization of its kind that France agreed to join. (Although France is a member of NATO, it removed its armed forces from the NATO military command structure so as to retain the right to use its armed forces independently, and it resisted participating in any organizations that might compromise its independence. The absence of France, one of the three largest European arms producers, from previous initiatives had been detrimental to their effectiveness.)

The IEPG set out to "bring about a more effective use of funds for the production of military equipment; to increase the standardization and interoperability of military equipment with the aim of inspiring cooperation in use; strengthen the European factor in relation to North America; maintain a European defense industry as a valid technological base, in order to place Europe in a valid position with the United States."[12]

Thus, the IEPG was viewed as a vehicle through which European producers would strive not only to cooperate among themselves and achieve the goals of rationalization, standardization and interoperability, but also to present a unified front in their dealings with the United States.

Some of the IEPG's pronouncements have been sweeping. In 1987, for example, a group appointed by the IEPG issued a set of recommendations that called for the creation of a common European arms market by opening up national markets and allowing the natural forces of competition to reign. Among other things, the study suggested that the governments agree to purchase in every instance equipment from the lowest priced European bidder regardless of which of the European nations produces it, and to eschew procuring comparable arms from non-European suppliers even if the prices are lower abroad. The study concluded that "any premium involved in purchasing within Europe rather than elsewhere during the years of transition will . . . be greatly outweighed by the long-term benefits."[13]

Many European observers, though, are critical of this view, pointing out that a wide chasm separates recommendations and pronouncements of this sort from actual implementation, and asserting that tangible signs of meaningful and sustained progress are hard to find. Some interpret the fact that an IEPG meeting was not held at the defense minister level until 1984 as an indication of the little regard that the participating parties held for the organization and its goals during its early years. Herbert Wulf of the University of Hamburg more generally argues that:

> Competition, not cooperation; protectionist initiatives, not trade liberalization; exor-
> bitant cost over-runs in joint production projects, not a two-way street with equal traffic
> in both directions across the Atlantic; destandardization, not standardization; national
> industrial overcapacities, arising in part from fierce competition; and unilateralism, not
> cooperative multilateralism, are the prominent characteristics of West European
> weapons procurement.[14]

Wulf echoes the sentiments of another scholar, who in 1984 found "11 firms in seven different countries working on anti-tank weapons; 18 firms in seven countries producing surface-to-air weapons; eight firms in six countries producing air-to-air weapons; 16 firms in seven countries working on air-to-ground weapons; and 10 firms in seven countries working on ship-to-ship missiles."[15]

Arms Relationships in a Maturing Alliance

U.S. sales to NATO Europe and Canada remained relatively stable during the 1970s despite the 1973 oil crisis, the unprecedented combination of economic recession and inflation, the U.S.-Soviet detente, and the maturation of European arms industries capable of supplying much of the continent's military needs. The nature of the transfers, though, began to change during the 1960s and 1970s. The European recipients increasingly entered into coproduction and licensed production agreements with the United States, instead of purchasing finished products. At least one country—Italy—used the skills and technologies gained through such transfers to build its own postwar defense industry. By the 1960s, the majority of western European nations were back on their feet economically and their defense industries began competing with that of the United States.

The most significant U.S. sale to Europe in this period was the 1975 agreement to sell F-16s to Belgium, Denmark, Norway and the Netherlands in what is widely referred to as the "deal of the century." General Dynamics' plane beat out the French Mirage F-1 and a Northrop entry in a very tense competition. (Sweden's Viggen and the Anglo-French Jaguar dropped out before the final decision was made.) The triumph of an American aircraft over those submitted by European manufacturers was one of the factors that prompted interest on the continent in European arms collaboration, and opened the way for the Independent European Programme Group.

As the alliance matured and as western Europe moved from being a dependent of the United States to being its equal, competition and friction between the two became inevitable. The Americans became attentive to the division of the economic burden of providing for the alliance's mutual security. Many persons within American governing circles began to feel that the United States was unfairly underwriting a disproportionately large share of the allies' military needs. As Europe and Japan began to prosper economically, Washington began to push them to spend more on defense, amid accusations from some quarters that they were getting a free ride at U.S. expense. In 1978, the NATO allies agreed to increase their defense budgets by approximately 3 percent per year above inflation on average over a five year period to bolster conventional forces in Europe, but this commitment has not been met consistently because of other strains on European economies. Japan only recently increased its level of defense expenditures above a 1976 ceiling of 1 percent of the country's GNP.

Differences of opinion persist among alliance partners over how much each country can and should contribute toward a common defense. As a testament to the frustration that many U.S. decisionmakers feel over what they perceive to be a continuing imbalance in the defense burden-sharing, Congress has periodically threatened to reduce significantly the number of American troops based in Europe. As recently as 1984, a group of senators led by Sam Nunn (D-Ga.) advocated withdrawing troops unless the Europeans contributed more to the defense of NATO. Although the Senate rejected the proposal by nine votes, both the House and the Senate agreed to place a cap on the number of U.S. troops in Europe, barring tangible signs of an increased European commitment to the collective defense.

Conversely, the Europeans have become most concerned that, until quite recently, the United States sold much more in the line of military equipment to the nations of western Europe than it bought from them, and they have sought to remedy the situation by opening a two-way street or flow of defense goods. During the 1970s, the United States often sold 10 times as much to individual European nations in a given year as it purchased in return. The idea of a two-way street for a more equitable flow of arms in both directions across the Atlantic was widely endorsed from about 1975 onward but did not come to fruition until recently, largely because of legal obstacles. The U.S. laws in question prevented foreign companies from bidding on certain kinds of contracts with the Department of Defense. The Buy American Act of 1933, which can now be waived, required that items for public use be purchased in the United States. Regulations in the same spirit designed to preserve the national industrial and mobilization base and prevent the United States from becoming dependent on outside suppliers effectively barred foreign companies from many contracts. Institutional and psychological hurdles had to be cleared as well. The U.S. military complex proved resistant at times to purchasing equipment that it did not have a hand in developing, and exhibited a general preference for soliciting bids from familiar sources.

Progress in this area has been hampered by a lack of agreement over what to count in evaluating the flow of traffic on the two-way street. On the one hand, the United States prefers to include what it spends on maintaining American troops in Europe in the count. The Europeans, on the other hand, are predominantly concerned with the ratio of imports to exports of hardware, a much more narrowly defined measure of the two-way street in which the balance generally has tilted in favor of the United States. The two sides also disagree on how the two-way street can be best advanced. Washington sees the rationalization and standardization of NATO military equipment as a necessary precursor, whereas European nations tend to argue that a successful two-way street will create the optimal environment in which rationalization and standardization will occur naturally.

The competitiveness of European versus U.S. products in both price and quality has been a problem from time to time, although this is no longer the case in many areas. Robert Komer, who was an under secretary of Defense in the Carter administration, has stated that, "in some ground systems, the Europeans have better stuff than we do."[16] Collaboration among defense companies from several European nations has also produced some weapons that are very price competitive. The Pentagon has an added incentive to buy off-the-shelf from European suppliers when it would otherwise have to subsidize the research and development costs of an American alternative to existing European systems. The U.S. Navy, for example, estimates that the $4.5 billion purchase of trainer models of the British Aerospace-developed AV-8B aircraft saved it $600 million that it would have had to spend on development of an American alternative.[17]

One recent arms transaction occurred largely because U.S. suppliers could not offer the Department of Defense a capable system in a timely fashion, but also underscored the partially deceptive nature of many trans-Atlantic military deals that on the surface appear to signal an increased equitable flow along the two-way street. In 1984, the U.S. Army requested bids for a communication system that would allow it to link all of its battlefield forces directly. Whereas European firms had already built suitable systems, American manufacturers would have had to start from scratch and invest considerable time and research and development funding. Two companies emerged as the frontrunners in the competition for the Mobile Subscriber Equipment system: Plessey, a private British concern, and Thomson CSF, France's government-owned electronics company. Both European systems were comparable in their capabilities, but a $3.1 billion price differential prompted the Pentagon to choose the $4.3 billion French bid in what may be the largest defense contract ever to be given to a foreign contractor. According to James R. Ambrose, the under secretary of the Army who was closely involved in the Mobile Subscriber Equipment decision, the selection of the existing French system will save the Pentagon $500 million in research and development expenditures, $1.5 billion in acquisition costs and between $8 billion and $10 billion in operating costs over the course of 20 years.[18]

Both companies, however, teamed up with American defense contractors—Plessey with Rockwell and Thomson with GTE—in order to increase their chances of being selected. Thomson offered to allow GTE to build the bulk of its RITA system with GTE-manufactured components and, had Plessey won, it would have transferred its technology to Rockwell, which would have built most of the system. By one account, the Thomson-GTE agreement called for the transfer to the American partner of approximately three-fourths of the money and work on the Thomson RITA system. Moreover, James R. Ambrose has said that the awarding of such a large contract to the French is an anomaly. "You won't find many opportunities [open to foreigners] for these large, complicated programs," he says.[19]

Despite the obstacles, the ratio of arms sales between the United States and its European allies appears to have evened out in recent years. Some analysts have suggested that within a decade the United States may even be buying more weapons from NATO countries than it sells to them. Heino Kopietz of London's International Institute for Strategic Studies told *The Wall Street Journal* that "U.S. arms dealers are going to find it harder and harder to sell to Europe, and the Europeans, more efficient in certain sectors, will sell more to the U.S. I can see the possibility of Europe selling more to the U.S. than it buys from it."[20] Others, though, like Francois Heisbourg, an executive with Thomson-CSF, warn that the balance of trade might well favor the United States more heavily again within a decade if Europe does not compensate for the increased American expenditure on research and development and procurement that occurred during the Reagan years. He says Europe is currently benefiting from research that it did during the Vietnam war, when the United States was focused on the conflict and did not devote much time or money to weapons research.[21]

According to the Department of Defense's International Acquisitions Department, which uses agreements as a measure of two-way street traffic, the ratio of U.S. sales to purchases from NATO Europe dropped from 7:1 in fiscal 1984 to 2.9:1 in 1985 to 1.6:1 in 1986, resulting from both reduced sales and an increase in purchases. (See Tables 6–2 and 6–3.) When trade with Canada is included, the ratios change slightly. The United States sold $9.8 billion worth of military equipment to all of NATO in 1984, $5.7 billion in 1985 and $4.5 billion in 1986, while it purchased $2.1 billion, $2.8 billion and $2.9 billion worth from NATO members.[22]

U.S. sales to France and West Germany dropped from 1985 to 1986, while its purchases from those countries increased, mirroring the overall trends. The ratio of U.S. sales to and purchases from its largest European arms trading partner, Great Britain, leveled off as well, although the volume of sales and purchases both increased during this period. Figures for 1986 show that the United States purchased $861 million worth of arms from Great Britain and sold it $1,051 million worth. The British assessment of the situation—like those of most western European nations—differs from that

Table 6–2

Two Way Street Trade Ratios

Country	FY 1983 Ratio	FY 1984 Ratio	FY 1985 Ratio	FY 1986 Ratio
Belgium	8.9:1	0.1:1	0.2:1	0.5:1
Denmark	1.1:1	1.4:1	13.0:1	1.0:1
France	6.0:1	3.8:1	1.5:1	0.3:1
Germany	1.7:1	1.0:1	5.7:1	1.2:1
Gr. Britain	4.9:1	3.1:1	1.4:1	1.2:1
Italy	3.7:1	1.5:1	1.3:1	1.3:1
Luxembourg	6.0:1	1.1:1	0.6:1	1.6:1
Netherlands	11.3:1	37.3:1	1.4:1	1.4:1
Norway	2.9:1	0.8:1	1.3:1	4.5:1
Portugal	1,470.0:1	14.4:1	1.2:1	6.9:1
Spain	67.9:1	3.1:1	11.0:1	3.6:1
Turkey	663.6:1	2,133.5:1	246.2:1	229.0:1
Europe	7.3:1	7.0:1	2.9:1	1.6:1
Canada	1.2:1	1.7:1	0.9:1	1.5:1
Total	4.3:1	4.8:1	2.0:1	1.6:1

Source: Office of the Undersecretary of Defense (Research and Engineering) Internal Acquisitions Section.

of the United States. According to British Defense Minister George Younger, an alternative measure reveals an imbalance. The United States spends 2 percent of its equipment budget abroad and Great Britain spends 7 percent of its budget in the United States alone.

Canada is still the largest U.S. arms trading partner overall; in 1986 it sold $810 million of arms to its southern neighbor and purchased $1,226 million in return.[23] Canada and the United States have had a unique defense trading relationship for a number of years, partly because of the high degree of integration between the Canadian and American arms industries. The relationship has been consciously fostered under a 1963 agreement providing for a roughly equal defense trade. The Canadian Commercial Corp. facilitates sales to the United States by acting as a guarantor of price and quality to the Pentagon and by helping Canadian contractors work through DoD requirements.[24]

Table 6–3

Arms Sales Agreements on the Two Way Street
(in millions of current year dollars)

Country	FY 1983 Sold by US	FY 1983 Bought by US	FY 1984 Sold by US	FY 1984 Bought by US	FY 1985 Sold by US	FY 1985 Bought by US	FY 1986 Sold by US	FY 1986 Bought by US
Belgium	$1,008.0	$ 113.0	$ 14.5	$ 114.1	$ 37.6	$ 156.2	$ 44.5	$ 85.0
Denmark	48.6	44.1	71.4	49.3	215.0	16.5	27.3	27.8
France	202.2	33.5	179.9	47.6	126.1	82.7	65.6	257.0
Germany	426.9	248.0	313.2	307.6	1,957.4	345.7	574.6	460.1
G. Brit.	2,212.0	450.8	1,543.5	492.9	863.6	596.8	1,050.6	860.6
Italy	168.3	45.4	98.4	65.0	237.5	183.7	117.5	89.5
Lux.	2.4	0.4	1.7	1.5	1.3	2.1	5.1	3.1
Neth.	375.1	33.2	1,454.7	39.0	144.7	101.1	224.2	155.1
Norway	106.6	37.0	35.5	43.7	51.3	40.8	206.3	46.3
Port.	147.0	0.1	18.7	1.3	19.6	15.7	241.0	34.9
Spain	2,255.7	33.2	78.0	25.0	445.6	40.5	209.6	58.8
Turkey	585.9	0.9	4,480.4	2.1	467.7	1.9	481.0	2.1
Europe	7,538.7	1,039.6	8,289.9	1,189.0	4,567.2	1,583.6	3,247.3	2,080.3
Canada	1,224.9	995.8	1,523.0	875.4	1,143.7	1,230.7	1,226.3	810.3
Total	$8,763.6	$2,035.4	$9,812.8	$2,064.4	$5,710.9	$2,814.2	$4,473.6	$2,890.6

Notes: U.S. sales figures include FMS and commercial sales agreements. U.S. purchases figures are based on prime and subcontract information and do not include subsistence, petroleum, construction and support services contracts, except in the case of Portugal.

Source: Office of the Undersecretary of Defense (Research and Engineering) Internal Acquisitions Section.

Residual Military Assistance within NATO

The United States still provides military assistance to the southern flank countries of Greece, Portugal, Spain and Turkey, the less developed of the NATO nations, whose military establishments are not as deeply integrated into the NATO command structure as those of other members, and U.S. exports to those nations raise somewhat different issues from those to the more industrialized allies. American military assistance to these nations serves two purposes: It helps them strengthen their own military forces so as to become stronger members in the alliance, and it is viewed as a form of compensation for allowing the United States to establish military bases in these countries, to use their national military facilities and to pass over or through their territories. These reciprocal arrangements have not always worked smoothly. Spain refused Washington's request to use its territory during the 1973 Arab-Israeli war, and both Spain and Greece would like to reduce the U.S. presence in their countries. Turkey feels that the amount of aid it receives does not adequately acknowledge or advance its contribution to NATO's defense.

Relations between Greece and Turkey pose a special dilemma for the United States because of the animosity toward one another that far transcends their common membership in NATO. In 1974, Turkey occupied part of the ethnically divided island of Cyprus after a military coup that was reported to be supported by the ruling military junta in Greece had deposed the reigning leader of Cyprus and replaced him with a Greek president. The occupation was strenuously protested by Greece and caused great consternation in Washington because Turkey used American-supplied weapons in its military invervention, despite the existence of specific agreements that the weapons were to be used only for mutual security purposes and general U.S. laws prohibiting the use of the materiel in acts of aggression. The Turkish occupation prompted the United States to restrict military transfers to Turkey from 1975 to 1978. Congress instituted a total arms embargo on deliveries of military equipment effective in February 1975, but loosened its restrictions in October to allow the transfer of weapons deemed necessary for NATO's common defense. Under pressure from the Carter administration, which maintained that even a partial ban was more counterproductive than constructive, Congress repealed the embargo in September 1978. Despite the various restrictions, American arms continued to flow into Turkey's arsenal: Turkey took delivery of $356 million in U.S. military equipment in 1975, $226 million in 1976, $89 million in 1977 and $292 million in 1978.

The northern section of Cyprus remains under Turkish control, and the rest of the island is governed by the Republic of Cyprus, which looks to Greece for support. Greece and Turkey now maintain a delicate balance of military forces on the island. Turkey reinforced its troops there early in 1987, and in the summer of that year the Republic of Cyprus ordered $250 million worth of French arms for its national guard.[25] The unusually large size of the purchase for Cyprus, whose defense budget in recent years has fallen into the $60 to $70 million range, led to speculation that the Greek government had supported the transaction as a way to counter Turkey's action indirectly and avoid further escalations.

Both Greece and Turkey are strategically important to the alliance because of their proximity to the Soviet Union. The United States demonstrated its determination to maintain a democratic, western allied Greece in 1947, when it helped to put down an indigenous Communist insurrection. At about the same time, the United States initiated economic and military assistance programs to Turkey and Greece to counter Soviet pressures in the region. Since then, Washington has continued to provide military assistance to both countries and to sell them additional arms through foreign military and commercial sales channels. The United States now allots security assistance, which includes FMS loans, MAP grants and Economic Support Funds, to Greece and Turkey in a seven to ten ratio. This policy is supported by a strong Greek lobby in Congress and is regarded as a slight by the Turks, who note that Turkey's armed forces are the second largest in NATO behind those of the United States and are responsible for the defense of one-third of the East-West border, despite the fact that Turkey is the poorest nation in the alliance. Much of its arsenal is stocked with inadequate and obsolete equipment: The U.S. Defense Department estimates that an expenditure of "at least $13 billion would be required over the next decade to bring Turkey's military up to NATO minimum standards."[26] The Reagan administration proposed security assistance allocations in 1984 through 1987 that diverged from the seven to ten formula further in Turkey's favor, but Congress chose to preserve the ratio.

From the Greek and Turkish perspectives, American military assistance has grown in importance during the postwar period with the decline of outright U.S. military grants. More than 98 percent of deliveries to the two nations during the 1950s and 1960s were made in the form of Military Assistance Program or Excess Military Articles Program grants. (Greece received $4.4 billion—measured in constant 1986 dollars—worth of American military equipment during the 1950s and $3.1 billion during the 1960s, while Turkey received $7.8 billion in the 1950s and $5.5 billion in the 1960s.) The percentage of deliveries accounted for by grants, however, dropped to 30 percent for Greece (out of total deliveries of $3.8 billion) and 58 percent for Turkey (out of $2.6 billion) during the 1970s, and even further, to 10 percent (out of $1.4 billion) for Greece and 6 percent (out of $1.9 billion) for Turkey, during the first seven years of the 1980s.

In recent years, the United States has viewed Greece as a less predictable and reliable ally than Turkey. Greece's prime minister, Andreas Papandreou, was elected on a campaign platform that included promises to pull his country out of NATO and to expel American armed forces from four major and between 12 and 20 minor Greek bases and installations. Once elected, he reversed his position, however, and said that he sees membership in the alliance as necessary for Greece's current national security. Greece also signed a five year military agreement with Washington in 1983 that allowed the American bases to operate until the end of 1988. Negotiations over the future of the bases beyond 1988 proved acrimonious. Papandreou has linked the issue of the bases to U.S. support for Turkey, and called for a national referendum to decide the fate of the facilities.

Despite Greece's quarrels with the United States, it has continued to buy American arms. Its most recent major order was for 40 F-16 aircraft, which it financed in part with FMS aid, although it made the purchase through direct, company-to-government channels. The United States and Greece have also recently undertaken to increase their collaboration on defense production under the terms of a 1986 Defense Industrial Cooperation Agreement. Several joint production projects are anticipated, and might include an arrangement for a Greek firm to provide maintenance for U.S. ships there.

Turkey negotiated an agreement to renew contracts for the American bases on its territory, but refused to ratify it until the U.S. Congress agrees to stop cutting the level of Turkish assistance sought by the White House—something that the legislature has done annually since 1984—and removes the restrictions that prohibit Turkey from using the military aid it receives in Cyprus. The Reagan administration requested $975 million in military assistance for Turkey in 1987, but received only $590 million from Congress. President Reagan pledged to do all he could to persuade Congress not to reduce the $913 million in assistance that he asked for Turkey for fiscal 1988, but was up against a budget cutting body concerned with the mounting national deficit.

The issue of military assistance and bases has also marred U.S. relations with Spain and Portugal in recent years. Like Turkey, both of these nations are struggling economically, and Portugal in particular is laboring under a large foreign debt load that restricts its military spending. Spain's military forces are somewhat less modern than the rest of NATO's. The U.S. Department of Defense says that assistance to Spain, "by promoting major Spanish purchases of U.S. equipment, will help bring Spanish forces closer to NATO standards."[27] Included among Spain's purchase of American military equipment are top-of-the-line McDonnell Douglas F/A-18 and AV-8B aircraft.

Modernization is also a goal of security assistance to Portugal, which, among other systems, has received American made A-7 attack aircraft. The United States and Portugal signed a seven year pact in 1982 in which Washington pledged to provide $1.32 billion in military and economic aid in return for use of Portuguese military bases on the mainland and the islands of the Azores. The United States and NATO recently embarked on an expansion of the military facilities in the Azores and the archipelago of Madeira, both of which are Portuguese possessions. The Azores project is reported to cost $100 million.[28] American access to these facilities, though, could be increasingly in jeopardy. In 1987, Portuguese Prime Minister Anibal Cavaco Silva raised the possibility of canceling the basing rights treaty because of growing irritation at the shrinking size of U.S. assistance allotments to Portugal. The Reagan administration asked for $225 million in aid for Portugal for fiscal 1987, but received substantially less—$147 million—from Congress. It was the second year in a row in which Portugal received less than the $205 million that it had been receiving during the early 1980s.

Using the value of deliveries made through the Military Assistance Program (MAP) and the Excess Military Articles Program (EXMAP) compared with those made through the Foreign Military Sales and commercial sales channels as a rough measure of U.S. military aid, Portugal remains more dependent on grants for the importation of American military equipment than do Greece, Turkey and Spain, even though Lisbon receives substantially fewer weapons. A full 90 percent of the $239 million (constant 1986 dollars) worth of U.S. military equipment delivered to Portugal during the 1960s was provided through the MAP and EXMAP programs. The percentage decreased to only 61 percent (of $107 million in deliveries) in the 1970s and 48 percent (of $432 million) during the first seven years of the 1980s.

Spain hosts four U.S. military bases under contracts that expire in 1988. In the course of renegotiating the lease for the facilities, the Spanish government has urged the United States to reduce substantially the number of troops at the bases—which now stands at 12,500—and to remove the wing of F-16 fighters at the Torrejon air base near Madrid. Spain's desire for a scaling back of troops has little to do with dissatisfaction with levels of American assistance. Instead, it is influenced by a growing desire to forge a more independent Spanish path in the realm of European security and by lingering resentment over U.S. support for the Franco regime, under which the basing rights agreements were originally negotiated.

Washington has agreed to the troop reductions, provided that Spanish forces are able to perform the NATO-related roles of the departing American personnel—a provision that the Spanish government is reluctant to embrace. Perhaps more significantly, the United States believes that its fighters are essential to NATO defense in the region, and has offered to move them to another base further from the Spanish capital, but Spain prefers that they be removed from its soil altogether. Despite recent disagreements, military deliveries to Spain remain strong. The United States registered weapons deliveries to Spain valued at $1.2 billion (constant 1986 dollars) during the first seven years of the 1980s—of which 8 percent took the form of grants, compared with $1.8 billion during the 1970s (16 percent in grants), $1.4 billion during the 1960s (85 percent in grants) and $1.5 billion during the 1950s (virtually all in grants).

The ANZUS Allies: Australia and New Zealand

The United States' arms export relationships with the Pacific allies Australia, New Zealand and Japan share many of the characteristics of those with the industralized allies of western Europe. At the same time, though, unique historical differences and developments have led to different sets of policy decisions and inter-alliance tensions.

A 1985 debate between the United States and New Zealand about the morality and utility of nuclear weapons fundamentally altered the traditionally solid, 30 year old ANZUS (Australia-New Zealand-United States) military alliance. The controversy was triggered by New Zealand's decision to reject reliance on nuclear weapons for its defense, which moved it to deny port access to any warships that carry nuclear weapons or are nuclear-powered. As a security matter, the United States does not reveal which of its ships are armed with nuclear weapons and which are not. Hence, when the United States requested port privileges for the U.S.S. Buchanan, in March 1985, New Zealand declined on the grounds that it could not obtain assurances that the ship was nuclear-free. The action strained relations between the two allies to the point that American Secretary of State George Shultz declared that the ANZUS Treaty "no longer applies."

Opposition to nuclear weapons in New Zealand had solidified with the election of the New Zealand Labour Party (NZLP) in July 1984. Led by David Lange, a vigorously anti-nuclear prime minister, the NZLP declared its belief that the security of the South Pacific need not depend on the use of nuclear weapons. It won a 17 seat majority in the 95 seat New Zealand Parliament. Lange kept his campaign promise and declared New Zealand to be nuclear-free. The exchange that led to the barring of the Buchanan provoked retaliation; Washington officially suspended its obligations to New Zealand as stipulated under the ANZUS pact and later refused to assist in the country's purchase of American military equipment.

Australia and New Zealand are the only two nations that fought with the United States in all four of its wars during this century. Until New Zealand's assumption of an anti-nuclear stance, mutual indebtedness and gratitude had characterized the tripartite alliance, and that harmony had been reflected in a steady and predictable arms trade pattern. Bonds with Australia remain strong, and historical ties may ultimately preserve some semblance of alliance with New Zealand.

The strength of those ties dates to World War II, when the United States filled the so-called power vacuum in the Pacific, protecting the two British Commonwealth members from Japan when Britain was unable to do so. Statements by Australian and New Zealand officials during and after the war revealed a deep feeling of appreciation towards the United States for its wartime role. Although New Zealand and Australia hoped for more recognition of their own wartime roles and, unlike the United States, believed that the 1945 peace treaty with Japan should have emphasized punishment instead of rehabilitation, both countries agreed to the settlement in hopes that it would promote permanent peace and security. The immediate postwar era, however, brought a variety of new concerns about security in the South Pacific and fostered the notion that New Zealand and Australia needed the United States to replace Great Britain as their major power ally in a more formal arrangement. The most immediate concern was the West's perennial fear of the possibility of Communist incursions into Asia, which was intensified by the fall of China to Communists in 1949, increasing fears that New Zealand and Australia were vulnerable to invasion.

Thus, support for a tripartite arrangement between the culturally similar nations emerged, and the ANZUS Treaty was signed in September 1951. Unlike the NATO treaty, the ANZUS agreement does not stipulate that an attack on one of the signatories would necessarily be considered an attack on all. Instead, ANZUS mandates that each of the three countries will meet the common danger "in accordance with its constitutional processes." While few believe that the United States would hesitate to defend the two countries in the event of a communist attack, many analysts have questioned U.S. willingness to intervene in a regional conflict. Nevertheless, despite the ambiguous wording of the treaty and occasional minor disagreements throughout the first three decades of the alliance, all three nations continued to think of each other as reliable allies.

Shortly after ANZUS was created, for example, both New Zealand and Australia, despite domestic reservations, supported the United States in its efforts to block UN recognition of China and provided troops for the United Nations contingent that fought in the Korean War. Both countries similarly supported Washington during the early years of the war in Vietnam. Although differences sometimes surfaced, as in the case of Australian condemnation of Indonesia's efforts to control Dutch New Guinea while America wavered, the allies generally agreed about matters relating to the South Pacific through the early 1970s. Thereafter, more independent-minded governments came to power in New Zealand and Australia. The two governments' increasingly vocal concern about nuclear testing in the South Pacific highlighted the reality that Australia and New Zealand have developed their own foreign policies and ideas on a number of issues and are no longer willing to follow fully Washington or London's lead. The culmination of this independence was Prime Minister Lange's defiant and definitive 1985 decision to declare New Zealand nuclear-free.

The impact that the end of ANZUS will have on arms trade between New Zealand, Australia and the United States is still unclear. In February 1987, the United States dropped New Zealand from the list of nations that it assists in purchasing military equipment and spare parts. Instead of continuing to view New Zealand as an ally, the Reagan administration now categorizes it as a friend, no longer entitled to special privileges accorded to strong military partners. Simply put, New Zealand lost its status as a preferred customer. In practical terms, this meant that New Zealand no longer had access to all weapons, and could no longer purchase weapons at special rates and at expeditious delivery schedules. The action was taken in order to discourage other governments that were under pressure from anti-nuclear movements from also barring American military forces from use of their facilities.

Nevertheless, the Defense Department in 1987 said that the United States "continues to have an interest in helping New Zealand to maintain its existing military equipment, continue its air and naval surveillance capabilities, and retain the capability to play a role in Southeast Asian and South Pacific security."[29] To achieve these goals, the United States has continued its plans to supply weapons to New Zealand on a Foreign Military Sale cash basis. Some analysts have suggested that the alteration in the manner by which arms are purchased may have the unintentional effect of harming American weapons manufacturers as well as making purchases more costly to New Zealand. Without the Department of Defense as a purchasing agent, the New Zealanders will be forced to pay full market rates for weapons and may move to strike better deals with alternate foreign suppliers. Others believe that the flow of American military equipment to New Zealand is likely to continue unimpeded. The United States has officially stated its intention to continue providing parts and services for New Zealand's fleet of McDonnell Douglas A-4 attack aircraft and Lockheed C-130 transport and P-3 maritime patrol aircraft, as well as ship support and communications equipment. Indeed, in fiscal year 1986, one year after the initial action to bar American ships, the United States entered into $25 million worth of FMS agreements with New Zealand—a 17 year high.

Nor has the rift seriously impaired economic relations between the two nations. Despite calls for economic sanctions against New Zealand by some high-ranking U.S. officials, including then-Secretary of the Navy John Lehman, agricultural imports from New Zealand have continued unabated. Washington's official position has been that the economic and military relationships between New Zealand and the United States should remain separate and that an alteration of the military relationship need not carry over into the realm of economic relations. Critics of this policy suggest that failure to respond with economic sanctions will encourage other anti-nuclear governments to ban U.S. ships. Additional, but peripheral, criticism of trade with New Zealand has been lodged by those who argue that the purchase of agricultural products from New Zealand merely adds insult to injury because it also unfairly harms American farmers.

While the shelving of the ANZUS agreement has certainly chilled relations between the United States and New Zealand, ties between America and Australia remain strong. The ruling Australian Labour Party (ALP) continued to welcome American ships in the country's ports unimpeded, and Prime Minister Bob Hawke has declared that it would be "an act of mutual insanity" if ANZUS's power were to be diminished in the South Pacific. Domestic public opinion in Australia accepts the notion that nuclear weapons are necessary to deter of Soviet aggression, in part because Australia is closer to the Asian mainland, and presumably a more likely target of attack.

Australia's displeasure with New Zealand's anti-nuclear stance was underlined by Prime Minister Hawke's refusal to meet with Prime Minister Lange for Lange's first three years in office. Not until Lange won a commanding re-election victory in August 1987 did Hawke decide that a meeting of the leaders of these traditionally staunch allies was appropriate. The attitude of Hawke's government has generally been that New Zealand's move to block the United States was foolish, if well-intentioned, and that Australia will take every step to preserve its relationship with the United States.

Like New Zealand, Australia has enjoyed a steady flow of arms from the United States. Because of the maturity of its indigenous arms industry, many of the weapons that Australia purchases from the United States complement domestically produced equipment. Recent major Australian purchases of American military equipment include the McDonnell Douglas F/A-18 aircraft, FFG-7 naval frigates, General Dynamics F-111 aircraft, Sikorsky Blackhawk helicopters, Lockheed P-3 maritime patrol aircraft, Harpoon anti-ship and Standard and Sidewinder anti-aircraft missiles, Mk-48 torpedoes, howitzers and equipment for submarine construction and other naval craft upgrades. Measured in constant 1986 dollars, U.S. military deliveries to Australia rose from an annual average of $196 million during the 1970s to $485 million during the first half of the following decade.

Japan: A Complex Relationship

The growing overall trade imbalance between Japan and the United States has emerged as the greatest single source of friction in relations between the two allies. The imbalance, which has increasingly tilted in Tokyo's favor since the mid-1960s—with exceptions during the oil crises of the 1970s—widened rapidly during the first half of the 1980s. By 1986, trade with Japan accounted for one-third of the $170 billion U.S. trade deficit, and U.S. imports of Japanese goods exceeded American exports to Japan by approximately 300 percent.[30] Concern over this imbalance has spilled into the realm of national security and has affected the bilateral military relationship, despite the fact that Japan relies almost exclusively on American industry for defense needs that it cannot satisfy indigenously and exports little military equipment to the United States. The ACDA estimates that 99 percent of the some $3.75 billion worth of military equipment imported by Japan between 1981 and 1985 came from the United States.[31] As Table 6–4 illustrates, Japan was the largest industrialized recipient of U.S. military deliveries (when measured in monetary value) in fiscal 1985 and the third largest in 1986.

The imbalance in defense trade and the dominance of American over other military suppliers are rooted in the predominant role that the United States played as victor over vanquished during the early postwar period. The United States moved quickly after the war from emphasizing punishment to regarding rehabilitation as its overriding objective in its dealings with Japan, and the importance of establishing Japan as a stable, democratic nation capable of providing for its defense took on an urgent significance in American eyes because of rising concern over the spread of communism and the outbreak of the Korean war.

Table 6–4

Leading Industrialized Country Recipients of U.S. Military Deliveries
Fiscal Years 1985 and 1986
(in thousands of current dollars)

Fiscal 1986		Fiscal 1985	
1. Australia	$588,505	1. Japan	$749,999
2. Great Britain	$565,239	2. West Germany	$743,285
3. Japan	$429,368	3. Australia	$674,582
4. Netherlands	$404,538	4. Great Britain	$513,166
5. West Germany	$331,043	5. Netherlands	$426,996
6. Turkey	$299,737	6. Turkey	$408,399
7. Spain	$190,549	7. Greece	$192,509
8. France	$169,736	8. Belgium	$156,466
9. Italy	$141,874	9. Spain	$125,886
10. Canada	$122,422	10. Italy	$121,048
11. Greece	$105,076	11. Portugal	$111,058
12. Belgium	$ 62,719	12. Switzerland	$ 92,622

Source: Department of Defense, Defense Security Assistance Agency, *Foreign Military Sales, Foreign Military Construction Sales and Military Assistance Facts*, Sept. 30, 1986.

Washington in 1952 returned to Japan 859 installations, including almost 500 weapons research and production centers, that it had seized as reparations payments, and placed the first postwar orders for military equipment with Japanese industry.[32] The Mutual Defense Assistance Agreement of 1954 paved the way for U.S. military deliveries to Japan. Between 1955 and 1965, deliveries totaled $4.9 billion worth of defense equipment (measured in constant 1986 dollars), 92 percent of which was routed through the Military Assistance Program and the Excess MAP/Military Assistance Service Fund. American deliveries dipped to $1.8 billion between 1966 and 1976—only 7 percent of which took the form of grant aid. They then rocketed up to $5.9 billion for the period 1977 to 1986, when all exports traveled through the Foreign Military Sales and commercial sales programs. (See Figure 6–2.)

In addition to making outright transfers of finished products, the United States began entering into licensed production agreements with Tokyo, which quickly satisfied Japan's growing aspirations for self-sufficiency in weapons production, and came to provide for the indigenous manufacture of technologically sophisticated top-of-the-line systems such as F-104, F-4 and F-15 fighter aircraft and Patriot, Hawk and I-Hawk anti-aircraft missiles. Between January 1976 and June 1980 alone, Japan concluded 110 licensing and coproduction agreements with the United States.[33] As a result, licensed production agreements have been the principal channel of U.S. military technology transfers that have assisted Japan in developing its own armaments industry.[34] An estimated 30 to 40 percent of the cost of systems built in Japan under license is snared by U.S. companies that participate in the manufacturing arrangements, and Japan devotes roughly 20 percent of its military hardware budget to American defense equipment.

A tradition that emphasizes self-reliance and the transfer of technological equipment and know-how from the United States has left Japan in the position of being able to fulfill much of its defense needs through indigenous manufacture. Figures from the Japan Ordnance Association, for example, show that the Self-Defense Forces obtain 99 percent of their ships, 89 percent of their aircraft and related equipment, 87 percent of their ammunition and 83 percent of their firearms via domestic production either of Japanese designed goods or those manufactured under coproduction and licensing agreements.[35]

In addition to providing traditional military assistance and arms transfers, the United States entered into a formal military pact with Japan in 1960. The Treaty of Mutual Cooperation and Security obligates the United States to defend Japan against attack. Tokyo in turn is obligated to develop its ability to resist attack, to provide facilities for U.S. bases in Japan free of charge and to defend itself and any U.S. forces on Japanese territory. The standing interpretation of this last commitment is that Japan will protect its own territory, the air and sea environs and the sea lanes extending from Tokyo and Osaka out to a range of 1,000 nautical miles. Japan is not required to pay for any of the expenses incurred in maintaining U.S. forces there, but it has been supplementing U.S. outlays in areas such as construction of housing and aircraft facilities and in certain types of local labor costs.

The order that emerged out of World War II in large measure has made Japan's defense establishment and industry unique in the industrialized world. Japan's postwar constitution eschews the use of military force in all circumstances except for self-defense, and has generally been interpreted by successive Japanese governments as allowing Japan only the minimum military potential necessary for its national defense. The line between defensive and offensive capabilities, though, has shifted over the years. At one time, all jet aircraft were considered off limits, but this

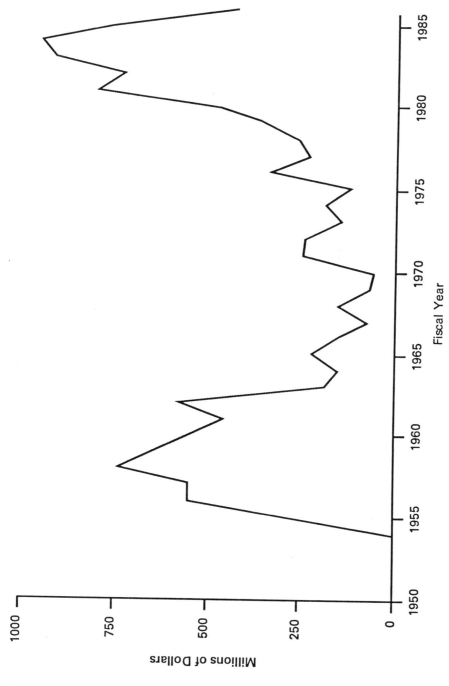

Source: Defense Security Assistance Agency, "Fiscal Year Series," 1986

Figure 6–2. U.S. Military Deliveries to Japan
(in millions of constant 1986 dollars)

is no longer the case. When Japan first purchased American F-4s as interceptors, it removed their air refueling and air-to-ground attack systems to ensure that they would have strictly defensive capabilities; it did not feel a need to do the same when it later purchased F-15s. The Japanese Self-Defense Forces still do not possess long-range bomber aircraft or missiles on the grounds that they are inherently offensive in nature.[36]

Japan also committed itself in 1976 to a self-imposed ceiling on defense spending by pledging that its annual defense expenditures would not exceed 1 percent of its gross national product, a figure well below the ratios sustained by its industrialized counterparts in the West. (Tokyo, however, broke through this political limit in 1986 when it approved defense outlays that equaled 1.004 percent of GNP, a figure whose psychological and symbolic significance dwarfs the real term increase in expenditures that it represents.) The Japanese government also elects to spend a much smaller portion of its defense budget on military research and development than major NATO nations do. Whereas the United States spent 47.3 percent of its government sponsored R&D expenditures in 1980 on defense, Japan emphasized civilian research, spending more than half of its R&D funds that year for energy and agriculture and only 4.9 percent on defense.[37]

Critics of the policies that govern how Japan allocates funds for purposes of national and collective defense point to these ratios, which are low relative to those sustained by the industrialized nations of the West. They claim that Japan has exhibited a tendency to rely on the West, particularly the United States, to provide for its defense—despite the fact that it has the world's second largest free market economy—which in turn has allowed it to devote the lion's share of its resources to commercial economic expansion. Those who see Japan as enjoying a free ride at U.S. expense argue that the security relationship between the two should be revised to take account of the fact that they are now much more evenly matched economically and that Japan needs to be pushed to do more.

This criticism of Japan is not universally shared, and some argue that too much stock is put into Japan's military policies as a cause of its ascendance to the higher reaches of economic power. Proponents of this position argue that in gauging a nation's contribution to defense, absolute measures matter more than those that are relative. They note that even though Japan dedicates only 1 percent of its gross national product to defense, the magnitude of its GNP puts Japan among the ranks of the top 10 nations for total defense expenditure.[38] They also maintain that although a small proportion of Japan's research and development funds are applied directly to defense, the nation's defense establishment does benefit indirectly from much of its non-defense R&D work because of the nature of the Japanese R&D infrastructure and general approach. One scholar argues that, unlike the United States, the Japanese economy is marked by "considerable interchange and permeability between civilian and military sectors. . . . Civilian companies in Japan can work together in the research and development phase for the mutual benefit of both sides; this cooperation is in stark contrast to the United States where the two sectors, even in one company, are strictly separated, a separation enhanced by very stringent regulations on military secrecy."[39]

Still others maintain that to condemn Japan for low defense expenditure-to-GNP ratios is to elevate unfairly the importance of "the bottom line" above an understanding of the historical, cultural and domestic political determinants of Japanese policy, and to ignore the incipient signs of change. They acknowledge that, from a Westerner's perspective, an increase in defense expenditure from 1 percent of gross national product to 1.004 percent hardly would appear to be a noteworthy event. Yet they argue that from the perspective of Japan—a nation that has taken a pacifistic path for the last four decades and has had to contend with a militaristic past and lingering international concern over the prospect of a resurgence in Japanese military power—exceeding a decade-old limitation governing military expenditure is no small feat, irrespective of the size of the increase. By one account, Japan now ranks seventh in the world according to defense allocations, and spends more on defense than all but one of the nations that do not possess nuclear weapons. Its per capita defense spending is reported to have reached $187, compared with the NATO average for the year of $242, and by some estimates will pass the $200 mark by the close of the decade.[40] According to the Defense Department, "Japan's defense budget . . . is the fourth largest (after the U.K., FRG and France) among [the U.S.] allies."[41] Both the Pentagon and those who do not subscribe to the "free ride" theory of U.S.-Japanese military relations point out that Tokyo contributes much to the relationship that is not highly visible. Although the terms of the Treaty of Mutual Cooperation and Security do not require Japan to provide funds for the stationing of American troops on its territories, each year it provides funds to the support and maintenance of these forces, funding that exceeded $1 billion in 1984 and $1.5 billion in 1987.[42]

Finally, analysts who believe that emanations of displeasure with Japanese military policies stem largely from irritation over the relations in general contend that signs of changes in Japan's defense policies are now emerging. The United States and Japan increased cooperative measures to allow for the enhanced ability to secure Japanese sea lanes beginning in 1981, and Japan has embarked on a program to increase its anti-submarine detection and airborne surveillance abilities. Finally, Tokyo agreed in 1986 to participate in the Reagan administration's controversial Strategic Defense Initiative. Although Japan was motivated in part by the prospects of commercial gain from research that might well have commercial applications, and although its role in the program, like that of all the U.S. allies, will probably be limited, the decision is significant given Japan's historical proclivity to shun all things related to nuclear weapons.

The U.S. security relationship with Japan is unique among those shared with Washington's industrialized international partners in two additional ways. First, inter-allied competition in the realm of arms exports has not yet surfaced as an issue. To its constitutional rejection of force as an acceptable method for settling disputes between nations, Japan added strong strictures limiting the export of military equipment. In 1967, Prime Minister Eisaku Sato unveiled the Three Principles, which state that "arms exports to the following countries shall not be permitted: (1) Communist bloc countries, (2) countries to which the export of arms is prohibited under United Nations resolutions, and (3) countries which are actually involved or likely to become involved in international conflicts."[43] The Japanese government reaffirmed its support for the Three Principles in 1976 and said further that it would use restraint in considering all other arms exports and that it would treat the export of unfinished products and industrial equipment or know-how that might have weapons production applications in the same way as it treated actual weapons systems. (Companies in other countries have sometimes negated export restrictions by selling entire weapons factories instead of finished products to their clients.)

Nevertheless, the laws restricting the export of military equipment are loosely worded and have been interpreted differently by various Japanese governments. In addition, the laws are not precise when it comes to those dual-use goods that can have either civilian or military applications, depending on the end to which the recipient chooses to put them. According to the definitions of military equipment used by the U.S. Arms Control and Disarmament Agency, the value of Japanese arms exports totaled $310 million for the period 1975 to 1980 and $1.07 billion for 1981 to 1985.[44] It is not clear, however, that in the near term Japan will become a major weapons exporter. Reinhard Drifte of the London-based International Institute for Strategic Studies points to numerous disincentives for Japanese leaders contemplating expanded arms exports. According to Drifte, a push for increased arms sales would be vigorously opposed by most quarters of society; would increase pressure on Japan actually to take sides, or to be perceived as taking sides in confrontations, which would negate its traditional desire to remain above international frays; and would exacerbate existing trade tensions and perhaps force a reevaluation of the existing technology transfer agreements with Japan by its industrialized allies.[45] Nevertheless, the pressure to export will be considerable if only because many of the products and technologies that Japan excels in—such as electronics—fall into the dual-use category of commodities.

The second way in which the U.S.-Japanese relationship is unlike any other is also one that might in the long run serve as a source of increased pressure for Japanese arms exports: Washington has taken the initiative and willingly seeks to import from Japan military-related goods and technologies. Discussions on the opening of a two-way street were initiated in 1979, and after the Department of Defense resorted to threatening to review the U.S. policy of allowing the licensed production of American weapons in Japan, the two governments signed an agreement that waived the provisions laid out in the Three Principles on arms exports in the case of the export of military equipment to the United States and provided for the promotion of trade in dual-use technology.

Japan's Defense Agency said that the waiver is necessary to ensure effective operation of U.S.-Japanese security arrangements and that it will apply only to arms-related technology and any sample weapons that would be necessary to make the technology meaningful.[46] Secretary of Defense Weinberger hailed the agreement in a 1986 speech in Japan by saying that "there are few opportunities for deterring Soviet power more promising than combining Japanese and U.S. technological capabilities."[47] In 1985, the United States made its first request for Japanese-produced military equipment, a homing device for missiles made by Toshiba, and in 1986 presented Japan with a pared down list of seven technologies in which the United States is interested.[48] Precisely how far the initiative will proceed in opening a flow of Japanese military equipment and technology into the United States remains to be seen, however, because suspicions and institutional hesitation to share too openly exist on both sides.

U.S.-Japanese relations took a sharp turn for the worse in 1987 when it was revealed that Toshiba Machine, a majority-held subsidiary of Toshiba Corp., in concert with Kongsberg Vaaperfabrikk, a state-owned Norwegian firm, had illegally sold four advanced computerized milling machines to the Soviet Union between December 1982 and June 1984. The machinery, whose export to Communist bloc nations is disallowed under COCOM rules, has given the Soviets the ability to produce submarine propellers that are quieter than those now available to their navy, which in turn makes the task of detecting and tracking Soviet submarines much more difficult for the western powers.

The immediate effect of the sale on the security of the West is widely disputed. Some analysts in U.S. defense circles were quick to link the sale directly to a growing body of evidence that the Soviet Union is fielding quieter submarines. Others noted conversely that the Soviets already had been making strides in this direction before the sale was executed, and that the milling machines probably were not installed at the Leningrad shipyard until 1983 and 1984, not long enough ago for the Soviets to have produced new propellers and to have integrated them into their submarine fleet. Nevertheless, the milling machinery will enhance the Soviets' ability to field quieter submarines in the near future. A classified Department of Defense study predicted that the United States would have to spend between $8 billion and $60 billion on new detection and tracking technologies over the next 10 years in order to counter the development of a quieter Soviet submarine. Most analysts both inside and out of U.S. government circles believe the higher number to be unreliable, and some believe that even $8 billion might be too high an estimate.

The American reaction was swift and severe. Members of Congress responded by proposing legislation designed to punish Toshiba and Kongsberg Vaaperfabrikk in particular, and future violators of COCOM regulations in general, for similar breaches. The Senate passed an amendment that would have banned all Toshiba products not vital for American manufacture or national security from the U.S. market for up to five years by a margin of 92–5. The Pentagon signaled its displeasure by restricting the contracts that it would award to Toshiba and Kongsberg Vaaperfabrikk.

Japan's reaction to the revelation was equally swift, but conciliatory. It, along with Norway, launched extensive investigations and vowed to institute bureaucratic changes to strengthen the existing national export regulatory regimes. Tokyo also moved to stiffen its criminal penalties governing the transgression of export laws and launched a massive lobbying campaign in the United States to head off punitive legislation.

The Toshiba affair and the criticism it generated from American quarters came to the fore at a critical point in U.S.-Japan military relations, when Japan was in the process of completing plans for a major arms procurement decision that placed the two allies at loggerheads. Japan had initiated a project during the late 1970s to field an indigenously designed and manufactured fighter aircraft—dubbed the FSX—to replace its aging fleet of American F-4s and the domestically developed F-1 aircraft, and characterized the venture as being vital to the health of its aerospace industry. American and European manufacturers counter-bid on the $7 billion FSX program, which envisioned a purchase of more than 100 aircraft, and offered fighters that they claimed were equally capable but less expensive. The European Panavia consortium's Toronado dropped out early in the competition, as General Dynamics' F-16 did later. As Tokyo entered the final phase of its decision-making process, it was faced with increased cries of unfair competition. American manufacturers claimed that Japan's insistence on developing the FSX on its own was an example of the way Tokyo preferred to create and protect a market out of self-interest rather than to weigh its aspirations against those of its economic and military partners. The heightened tension created by the growing trade imbalance with the United States was only exacerbated by the news of the illegal Toshiba sale, and the two combined to push Japan to agreeing either to develop the FSX in cooperation with the United States or to decide to acquire and modify the McDonnell Douglas F-18 or General Dynamics F-16 to its particular specifications.

Toward a Resolution: Initiatives and Prospects

Although the Toshiba affair above all highlighted the importance of export restraints in the modern age, it also underscored the generic difficulties inherent in the transfers of defense materiel among industrial allies—difficulties that affect U.S. arms relations with Europe as well as with Japan. The armaments trade invariably is played out against the larger issues of national sovereignty and self-interest. Progress toward easing some of the existing friction in the area of arms transfers must combat the deep rooted urge of a nation to retain as much sovereignty and independence as is possible, and is an unnatural act at best. All parties involved acknowledge the benefits of cooperation, but thus far most have proved reluctant to make the necessary sacrifices.

While cooperative ventures have led to full scale production of some defense equipment by consortia of European nations that sometimes have included the United States, they have been limited in both scope and number of participants. Most involve only two or three nations. The continent's largest defense producers—Great Britain, West Germany and France—have yet to cooperate on a major program, and, as already mentioned, the goals of rationalization, standardization and interoperability have not been met in a meaningful or far reaching way.

Nevertheless, proponents of closer inter-alliance cooperation see signs of progress. The United States, led by Secretary of Defense Weinberger, has issued repeated statements of support for and commitment to the goal of increased allied cooperation, and it cites the falling ratios of American military exports to imports as a sign of the growing U.S. resolve to increase the flow of traffic along the two-way street in its direction. In 1985, Weinberger issued a memorandum to his subordinates at the Pentagon that, in part, maintained that "We must convince our NATO allies, the U.S. Congress and Executive agencies, that collective security depends upon greater integration of military requirements with alliance-wide defense-industrial cooperation." Among other steps that the Secretary of Defense ordered to attain this goal was one stating that "in establishing operational and design requirements for future major weapons systems, the services *will* consult with their European counterparts" (emphasis added).[49]

As a testament to increased interest on the part of the United States in expanding the volume of its purchases of defense equipment manufactured by allied nations, the International Defense Equipment Exhibitors Association (IDEEA) in October 1987 sponsored a trade show in Washington whose exhibit space was open only to foreign manufacturers of military materiel. The sponsors of ComDef '87 (Common Defense '87) called it "the largest exhibition of foreign defense equipment ever held in the United States." More than 200 companies from 17 allied nations that have signed a Memorandum of Understanding (MOU) establishing a formal reciprocal military procurement relationship with the United States displayed their wares to officials from the Pentagon and the American defense industry and engaged in what the brochure called "frank discussions of the 'two way street,' its benefits, opportunities and problems." Among other things, ComDef '87 afforded foreign manufacturers who were unfamiliar with the U.S. weapons procurement system an opportunity to become acquainted with it.

The Department of Defense again signaled its commitment to broadening the two-way street in October 1987 when it launched an unprecedented, comprehensive review of the U.S. military trade relations with the nations with which it has entered into a Memorandum of Understanding. The evaluation will consider the trade issues from the angle of the United States as both importer and exporter. It will look into whether the MOU signatories are living up to the terms of the agreements and will explore any avenues for changing the existing export regime in a manner that might compensate for the facts that American military exporters face a more harshly competitive international environment and that the exportation of off-the-shelf, finished products has waned in the face of growing demands from allies for license and coproduction arrangements. More significantly, current indicators suggest that those charged with conducting the survey will subordinate these issues to the task of opposing the rising protectionist sentiment in Congress. The Pentagon believes that when it comes to the defense sector, protectionism is harmful to American industry, and it maintains that the United States would lose far more than it would gain if foreign governments were to retaliate against the protection of the American defense industry by erecting barriers of their own. In October 1987, the Department of Defense identified at least 10 pieces of pending legislation, some of which had been attached to the proposed Defense Authorization bill, that it judged to be protectionist measures.

Congress, though, has not turned a deaf ear to the calls for the importance of increased cooperation of the industrialized allies in the production of military goods, and in one notable instance it has launched an intiative designed to advance the cause of cooperation. In 1985, it passed a provision sponsored by Sen. Sam Nunn (D-Ga.), the chairman of the Senate Armed Services Committee, that earmarked funds exclusively for the purpose of entering into joint research and development programs with the NATO allies. The legislation authorized $100 million for the program for fiscal year 1986 and set aside $140 million for fiscal 1987, $100 million of which supported programs initiated in 1986. Nunn's committee recommended that $200 million be set aside for the program for fiscal years 1988 and 1989. Under the terms of the legislation, U.S. funds must be spent on research and development in the United States, and NATO allies are expected to fund work performed by their industries. Rather than duplicating research and development projects in their respective laboratories, however, participating nations coordinate their work in order to reduce costs and increase the amount of technological expertise that is applied to the project.

Several Nunn initiative projects have run into difficulties because some of the countries that initially expressed an interest in them have not provided their share of the funding. In other cases, allies have withdrawn from certain projects because the monetary outlay proved to be too large or because of a lack of interest on the part of their defense industries. Projects that received U.S. funds in 1986 and 1987 include an airborne radar demonstrator, an advanced anti-submarine mine, 155 mm autonomous precision guided munition, a common NATO aircraft identification system, enhanced fighter maneuverability research, a modular stand-off weapons program (MSOW) to develop new air-to-surface weapons for NATO tactical aircraft, and a naval frigate program.[50] The levels of participation vary from program to program. Whereas two nations are collaborating on the advanced sea mine and in the fighter manueverability program and three on the airborne radar demonstrator, a full eight are participating in the naval frigate program and seven in the MSOW work. The joint frigate program is the largest in NATO's history; it involves building 50 ships for the participating navies, who believe that the cooperative approach will reduce the procurement costs by 15 to 20 percent below what it would have cost had the individual nations elected to pursue independent programs.

In addition to funding the joint R&D program, the Nunn legislation allocated money for the comparative or "side-by-side" testing of American and foreign weapons. Congress set aside $25 million in fiscal 1986 funding for the project, and as of June 1987 49 testing projects had qualified for funding. Most of the projects involve Great Britain, which, according to one involved Pentagon official, has invested more time and energy than other countries in using the program effectively and "understand[s] the system."[51] Appropriations for comparative testing have risen steadily, to $39 million in fiscal 1987 and to $49 million in 1988.

Increased calls for and initiatives designed to foster cooperation in the production of weapons for the purpose of achieving a standardized allied arsenal must surmount numerous obstacles, however. The allied industrial nations must reconcile military requirements, procurement schedules and budgetary priorities and devise mutually acceptable plans for distributing the research and development and production contracts equitably. Some cooperative ventures have been stymied because one or more of the participants has been unable to come forth with the required funding. Others have foundered because the disparate military establishments are unable to agree over the requirements of the military equipment that they strive cooperatively to research and develop. The NATO frigate program, for example, has been held up because some of the militaries involved believe it should be configured for anti-submarine warfare, while others believe it should be designed primarily for anti-aircraft and fleet defense duties.

At root, accomplishing the task of increased cooperation requires of the participants a sustained willingness to make compromises in order to reach agreements across a broad spectrum of foreign, domestic and economic policy objectives, and the allied nations thus far have have been willing and able to proceed only so far in subordinating individual national priorities and aspirations to a more internationally integrated effort. Nations are reluctant to surrender the ability to produce a wide array of weapons in the name of national autonomy and the necessity of being able to provide independently for the national defense. One proposed solution, which involves a "family of weapons" approach, has not gotten far for this reason. (The concept calls for the specialized production of different models of the same type of weapon. The United States, for example, is working on a medium-range air-to-air missile, while European nations are concentrating on a short-range air-to-air missile.)

Progress in the direction of expanded cooperation also has been hampered by U.S. insistence on instituting strict export regulations on equipment that contains a significant proportion of American-supplied components. European nations that are interested in cooperating with the United States decline to do so out of concern that the more stringent American export regulations would hamper their ability to export the military equipment that their industries produce. France is developing its own high speed, integrated circuit technology, known as CITGV (circuits integres a tres grande vitesse), with applications in advanced fighter plane radars, communications equipment and electronic warfare systems. The CITGV program will eliminate French industry's current dependence on U.S. circuitry. French experts cite U.S. restrictions on exports to third parties as a principal reason for developing CITGV.[52] Concerns over potential American export regulations make U.S. participation in Europe's next major aircraft program, the European Fighter Aircraft project, unlikely.

The industrialized allies also view cooperation in the field of defense production as but a part of the larger and pressing issue of international trade and economic competition. In the eyes of western Europe and Japan in particular, research and development in the defense sector is crucial for the maintenance of a vibrant high-technology industrial base, and not pursuing independent military R&D and production is viewed as a move that would eradicate any potential for spill-over into the commercial industrial sectors of the national economies. Nor is the importance of retaining trade secrets lost on those within the decisionmaking circles of the United States. Although eight nations are formally involved in projects initiated under the Reagan administration's multi-billion dollar Strategic Defense Initiative, as of September 1987 the Pentagon had issued only 76 contracts worth $97 million to foreign firms, and the U.S. Senate that year contemplated legislation that would severely restrict foreign contractors' ability to participate any further.

This situation points to yet another barrier that must be cleared before a sustained and meaningful regime of cooperative defense programs can be erected: Before the allied nations can be expected to cooperate internationally, they individually must arrive at a national consensus. The United States, for example, suffers from deep internal divisions. The Department of Defense, which simultaneously must concern itself with the health and competitiveness of the American defense industy while working for greater burden-sharing and cooperation among the industrialized allies, faces an increasingly protectionist Congress and public. It must also reconcile the need for sustaining exports and expanding cooperation with its deep concern over restricting the flow of sensitive technology to unintended Soviet bloc recipients. This latter issue has forced the Pentagon into a head to head conflict with the Commerce Department and the U.S. industry at large, which advocate less stringent regulations for the sake of increased exports and domestic employment and enhanced competition. A report by the National Academy of Sciences that was released early in 1987, for example, estimated that strict export controls had cost the U.S. economy $9.3 billion and 188,000 jobs in 1985.[53] These figures, though, were criticized as unsubstantiated by then Assistant Defense Secretary Richard N. Perle, the architect of the Department of Defense's push for stricter controls. Until divisions such as these are patched up, and a national consensus in the United States and abroad emerge, the goals of increased cooperation and coordination among the industrial allies will remain elusive.

Footnotes

1. Catherine M. Kelleher and Gale A. Mattox, eds., *Evolving European Defense Policies* (Lexington, MA: Lexington Books, 1987), p. 29.
2. Senate Committee on Foreign Relations, *Prospects for Multilateral Arms Export Restraint* (Washington: Government Printing Office, 1979), pp. 27–28.
3. Stockholm International Peace Research Institute, "French Arms Trade: The Economic Determinants," *World Armaments and Disarmament Yearbook 1983* (New York: Taylor & Francis, Inc., 1983), p. 386.; Senate Committee on Foreign Relations, *op. cit.*
4. Paul Hammond, David Louscher, Michael D. Salomone and Norman A. Graham, *The Reluctant Supplier: U.S. Decisionmaking for Arms Sales* (Cambridge, Mass: Oelgeschlager, Gunn & Hain, Inc., 1983), p. 239.
5. Philip J. Farley, Stephen S. Kaplan and William H. Lewis, *Arms Across the Sea* (Washington: The Brookings Institution, 1978), p. 20.
6. Hammond et al., *op. cit.*, p. 66.
7. Phil Williams, *U.S. Troops in Europe* (London: Routledge & Kegan Paul, 1984, p. 19.
8. For arguments to this end, see Hammond et al., *The Reluctant Supplier*, pp. 33–35, Kelleher et al., *Evolving European Defense Policies*, pp. 28–30, and SIPRI, "The French Arms Trade: The Economic Determinants," *World Armaments and Disarmament Yearbook 1983*, p. 382.
9. Herbert Wulf, "West European Cooperation and Competition in Arms Procurement: Experiments, Problems, Prospects," *Arms Control: Journal of Arms Control and Disarmament*, September 1986, p. 181.
10. For a more complete list of weapons and equipment that have been jointly developed or produced, see Alexander H. Cornell, "Collaboration in Weapons and Equipment," *NATO Review*, October 1980.
11. For detailed chronologies and descriptions of these initiatives, see Herbert Wulf, *op. cit.*, pp. 177–178, and Lawrence S. Hagan, *Twisting Arms: Political, Military and Economic Aspects of Arms Cooperation in the Atlantic Alliance* (Kingston, Canada: Centre for International Relations, 1980), pp. 136–138.
12. Hagan, *op. cit.*, p. 18.
13. "NATO Group Recommends Forming Common European Arms Market," *Aviation Week and Space Technology*, Feb. 23, 1987, p. 18.
14. Wulf, *op. cit.*, p. 180.
15. *Ibid.*
16. "Pentagon Turns More to European Arms," *The Wall Street Journal*, Feb. 10, 1987, p. 42.
17. *Ibid.*, p. 42.
18. "C³ Heralds Future of Cooperation," *Defense News*, Sept. 28, 1987, p. 16.
19. John Newhouse, "Politics and Weapons Sales," *The New Yorker*, June 9, 1986, p. 69.
20. *The Wall Street Journal*, Nov. 8, 1985, p. 1.
21. *The Wall Street Journal*, Feb. 10, 1987, p. 42.
22. "Nunn Initiative Gains Momentum as Two-Way Street Becomes More Equitable," *Armed Forces Journal*, June 1987, p. 36.
23. *Ibid.*, p. 36.
24. Hagan, *op. cit.*, pp. 96–97.
25. "Cyprus Buys $250 Million Worth of French Weapons," *Defense News*, July 6, 1987, p. 1.
26. Defense Security Assistance Agency, *Congressional Presentation for Security Assistance Programs, Fiscal Year 1988*, p. 249.
27. Defense Security Assistance Agency, *Congressional Presentation for Security Assistance Programs, Fiscal Year 1987*, Vol. II, p.122.
28. "U.S., NATO Build Up Bases in Azores, Madeira," *The Washington Post*, April 30, 1987, p. 33.
29. Defense Security Assistance Agency, *Congressional Presentation for Security Assistance Programs, Fiscal Year 1988*, p. 298.
30. Ellen Frost, *For Richer, For Poorer: The New U.S.-Japan Relationship* (New York: Council on Foreign Relations, 1987), p. 14.

31. U.S. Arms Control and Disarmament Agency (ACDA), *World Military Expenditures and Arms Transfers*, 1986 edition (Washington: ACDA, 1986), p. 144.

32. Reinhard Drifte, *Arms Production in Japan: The Military Applications of Civilian Technology* (Boulder, Colo.: Westview Press, 1986), p. 9.

33. Office of the Under Secretary of Defense for Research and Engineering, *Report of Defense Science Board Task Force on Industry-to-Industry International Armaments Cooperation Phase III-Japan* (Washington: Government Printing Office, June 1984), p. 27.

34. Drifte, *op. cit.*, p. 12.

35. Drifte, *op. cit.*, p. 13.

36. Hisahiko Okazaki, *A Grand Strategy for Japanese Defense*, (Lanham, Md.: Abt Books, 1986), p. 81.

37. Office of the Under secretary of Defense for Research and Engineering, *op. cit.*, p. 31.

38. Yasuhisa Nakada, "Japan's Security Perceptions and Military Needs," in *Military Power and Policy in Asian States*, edited by O. Marwah and J.D. Pollack, p. 172.

39. Drifte, *op. cit.*, p. 90.

40. Frost, *op. cit.*, p. 132.

41. Defense Security Assistance Agency, *Congressional Presentation for Security Assistance Programs, Fiscal Year 1988*, p. 285

42. Defense Security Assistance Agency, *Ibid.*; U.S. Japan Advisory Commission, *Challenges and Opportunities in United States-Japan Relations*, September 1984, p. 27.

43. Defense Agency of Japan, *Defense of Japan* (Tokyo: Japan Times Ltd., 1986), p. 181.

44. ACDA, *op. cit.*, p. 122.

45. Drifte, *op. cit.*, pp. 78–79.

46. Defense Agency of Japan, *op. cit.*, p. 181.

47. *Japan Times*, April 6, 1986, p. 4.

48. Drifte, *op. cit.*, p. 81.

49. *Aviation Week & Space Technology*, Oct. 5, 1987, p. 58.

50. For a more complete list of cooperative NATO R&D programs, see "Nunn Initiative Gains Momentum as Two Way Street Becomes More Equitable," *Armed Forces Journal*, June 1987, pp. 36–38, and "Nunn Amendment Projects," *Aviation Week & Space Technology*, June 15, 1987, p. 315.

51. "Nunn Initiative Gains Momentum as Two Way Street Becomes More Equitable," *Armed Forces Journal*, June 1987, p. 38.

52. "France Seeks to Avoid Buying U.S. Chips Through CITGV," *Defense News*, March 30, 1987, p. 9.

53. *Aviation Week and Space Technology*, June 15, 1987, p. 316.

Chapter 7
The Impact of
Arms Sales on the
Third World

As chapter 5 suggests, critics of the arms trade dispute the effectiveness of arms transfers in achieving U.S. national security objectives, extending political influence abroad and bolstering the U.S. economy. Reformers, though, oppose weapon sales on other grounds as well. These additional criticisms are directed not at the utility of arms transfers for the industrialized supplier nations, but at their effect on the Third World recipients. The critics assert that military exports help fuel regional arms races, making conflict both more likely and more destructive. They also contend that arms sales abet human rights abuses in the recipient countries and lead Third World nations struggling with poverty to divert funds from needed economic development projects.

Supporters of arms sales respond to these criticisms in two ways. One group of supporters maintain that the effects of arms sales on Third World countries should not be a concern of the supplier nations. This response comes primarily from leaders of developing nations, who assert that the ways they allocate their resources and deal with regional conflicts or domestic dissent are internal matters. They contend that they, like their counterparts in industrialized countries, have the right to ensure their own national security through the purchase of foreign arms, regardless of the economic consequences, and that they are best positioned to determine what is and is not in their own best interest. These leaders also assert that they have the right to sacrifice certain human or political rights if necessary to ensure internal security or economic progress, and they reject as paternalistic intervention attempts to impose upon them Western morality or Western perceptions of their security needs through arms sales restrictions.

The other group of supporters of arms sales, those from industrialized countries, does not take this approach. Rather, these supporters believe that the effects of arms sales on Third World nations should be a concern of the supplier nations. They deny, however, the contention of arms transfer critics that arms sales contribute to regional conflicts or human rights violations and impede the economic development of the Third World recipient nations. This chapter examines these differing claims as to the effect that arms transfers have on the Third World.

The Arms Trade and Regional Conflict

That foreign military sales breed regional arms races—which, in turn, heighten the potential for conflict—is a concern frequently advanced by critics of arms transfers. These critics contend that, instead of promoting regional stability, arms transfers intensify fear and mistrust. They assert that the uncertainties and apprehensions caused by purchases of new, technologically advanced weapons lead to counter-purchases by regional adversaries. Arms sales critics contend that once this action-reaction dynamic is set in motion, it is difficult to short-circuit. Moreover, they warn that arms races bring those locked into them one step closer to war. Israel, in 1967, became so fearful of growing Arab air strength that it used its French and American warplanes to launch a pre-emptive strike on Egypt, and subsequently Syria and Jordan. These attacks started the 1967 Arab-Israeli war, which ended with 75,000 dead and the Israeli occupation of the Golan Heights, the West Bank and the Sinai Peninsula.

This point of view is countered by other policymakers and pundits who believe that arming allies and friends is essential for maintaining regional military balances and deterring aggression. This line of argument maintains that weapons transfers preserve the peace by eliminating the prospect of an easy and fruitful victory for either side. American arms sales to Taiwan and South Korea in particular have been justified in this way.

Recent administrations have championed both of these perspectives. President Reagan has been outspoken in his support of the latter view. Shortly after he took office, he issued a new directive on arms transfer policy which stated that arms transfers "foster regional and internal stability, thus encouraging peaceful resolution of disputes and evolutionary change."[1] The Carter administration had taken the opposite view, emphasizing the dangers of arms transfers, although as time wore on, the Carter administration also justified its arms transfers in the traditional ways. The presidential directive that spelled out the Carter arms transfer policy began with the statement: "The virtually unrestrained spread of conventional weaponry threatens stability in every region of the world."[2] Underlying its desire to avoid instigating regional arms races, the Carter White House declared that "the United States will not be the first supplier to introduce into a region newly developed, advanced weapon systems which would create a new or significantly higher combat capability."[3]

The debate over arms sales is complicated by the difficulties involved in obtaining information and in quantifying military strength, which lead rival nations to assess each other's military needs and strengths very differently. A purchase that one nation may regard as establishing a military balance may be seen by its regional rival as solidifying its opponent's strategic advantage. Similarly, one nation may feel the need to match the military strength of all of its regional rivals combined, while each of those rivals understandably views this buildup quite differently.[4] The Shah of Iran, for example, felt that he not only had to counter regional rivals in Saudi Arabia and Iraq, but also had to defend his country against a possible Soviet invasion. The resulting Iranian military buildup spurred similar buildups by the nervous Iraqi and Saudi governments.

Arms buildups can also be spurred by factors entirely unrelated to military threats. Nations, at times, want arms more for reasons of prestige or influence than for fear of their regional rivals. Some view India's development and explosion of a nuclear device in 1975 as one example of non-strategic considerations that help to drive a military program. Similarly, the series of arms buildups in Argentina and Brazil were geared more toward gaining prestige domestically and influence externally than toward posing a threat to each other. Nevertheless, in both instances, one buildup provoked another, causing arms imports to spiral upward.

The arms race syndrome is also complicated by secrecy and the long lead time needed to complete all arms transfer agreements. Soviet weapons transactions in particular are often conducted in secret, which frequently impels nations to initiate their own purchases on the mere inkling of a similar purchase by a rival. The long lag-time between initial request and acquisition of the weapons makes this buy-on-warning policy even more essential. In this way, critics argue, nations purchase arms in anticipation of rivals' purchases, causing adversaries to react similarly and so fueling the arms race. Leslie Gelb, who served as a high ranking appointee in the Carter State Department and who dealt extensively with arms transfers issues, acknowledged this "problem of timing." Gelb testified before the Senate Foreign Relations Committee in 1980: "If the Soviet Union introduces a new kind of capability, the first we would know of it would be when we spotted the actual deliveries. It would then take us several years to match it." Gelb intimated that eradicating a buy-on-warning mentality would involve figuring out "how to close this time gap to negate our putting ourselves at a unilateral disadvantage."[5]

Gelb also pointed to another complicating factor: the legitimate desire of nations to modernize their forces. According to Gelb, "at some point, it becomes reasonable for a nation to argue that its existing forces are relatively old and inefficient. These forces cannot simply be replaced by the same or similar models. In most cases, the older models are not even being produced any longer."[6]

Generalizing about the effect of arms transfers on regional stability is difficult. Nevertheless, a few observations seem evident. Recent history indicates that arms transfers have not maintained regional balances in certain areas. Rather, each superpower has frequently allowed, if not intended, certain clients to achieve regional superiority. This has been the case with Israel, Cuba and Nicaragua, and it was the case with Iran in the 1970s. Yet regional imbalance would exist in the absence of arms transfers because populous, semi-industrialized nations could field armies far superior to those of smaller, less-industrialized neighbors. Furthermore, regional imbalance does not necessarily mean that regional stability has decreased. Since their independence, Mexico and Nigeria, for example, have been at peace with their weaker neighbors.

It is difficult to say that large quantities of imported weapons play any role in inciting most conflicts. Certainly, arms imports beget further arms imports, but large arsenals do not mean that nations will go to war. Although many of the largest recipients of foreign military assistance, Iran-Iraq, Somalia-Ethiopia, Egypt-Israel-Syria, and India-Pakistan, have ultimately gone to war, the major causes of these conflicts were historical grievances and territorial ambitions, not excessive militarization.

Rather, the effect of arms transfers on regional stability varies with the circumstances. Bolstering nations such as Israel, Taiwan, South Korea, Cuba and Nicaragua through arms transfers may have in part deterred foreign invasions. On the other hand, arms transfers to Argentina enabled it to invade the Falklands/Malvinas, and Libya used foreign-made weapons to invade Chad. Similarly, arms transfers to Syria and Israel allowed them on separate occasions to invade Lebanon with comparatively little risk. Although arms sales supporters maintain that through arms transfers the industrialized nations gain leverage to prevent wars, this leverage seems evanescent. Indonesia's invasion of East Timor, Iraq's invasion of Iran, and Pakistan's invasion of India are among the numerous examples of wars begun despite the disapproval of the arms suppliers. It is evident, however, that it is within the power of the supplier countries to ensure that arms transfers at least do not heighten the potential for conflict. Any supplier can choose to refrain from shipping arms to adversarial nations where the additional equipment would tip the balance of power, but this is not always done. Argentina and Libya are only two of the many nations that have been shipped military equipment seemingly in excess of their legitimate self-defense needs and were thus permitted to undertake otherwise implausible military invasions. Chapters 8 through 11 scrutinize the Third World on a regional basis on closer detail to examine further the role played by foreign military sales in various conflicts.

Arms Sales and Human Rights

Critics of U.S. arms transfer policy also contend that arms sales to Third World countries foster and facilitate human rights violations. They maintain that when the United States provides weapons to repressive governments, it both signals its approval of the regimes and supplies them with the tools of repression. Because the United States has supplied arms to a large number of governments with poor human rights records (see Tables 7-1 and 7-2), these critics have denounced U.S. arms transfer policy frequently and vociferously.

Many observers, however, believe that concern for the effect of arms transfers on human rights should not or cannot be used to determine the policy governing the sale of American weapons abroad. Joseph Karth, formerly the president of the American League for Exports and Security Assistance, an industry lobbying group, expressed this sentiment when he testified before the Senate Foreign Relations Committee in 1980. According to Karth:

> human rights are subject to interpretation and definition. Not all nations have the same concept concerning 'internationally recognized human rights.' Our concept of individual rights is not generally held in the world. Other nations in different stages of development have different concepts—freedom from economic want or freedom from terror and lawlessness may be their most cherished right.[7]

Karth offered the opinion that for this reason, "attempts to export our own morality may be doomed to failure."[8] He concluded that "we certainly want to shine as a beacon to other nations of the world, encouraging them to aspire to our standard, helping—indeed pushing—them in this direction. But if we limit our trade and relationships only to countries who meet that standard, we will have few trading partners, friends or allies."[9]

Arms sales and human rights—U.S. initiatives: Nevertheless, beginning with John F. Kennedy, each American president has acknowledged, if not satisfied, the grievances of human rights advocates. As far back as 1964, for example, South Africa was barred from receiving American arms because of its human rights practices, although loopholes in this ban allowed South Africa to purchase $35 million worth of U.S. arms between 1964 and 1978.[10] Sanctions of this type were few and far between until the early 1970s, however. It was not until 1973 that a true congressional campaign to link arms transfers to human rights was launched. In that year, Rep. Don Fraser (D-Minn.), then the chairman of the House Subcommittee on International Organizations, began hearings on human rights violations in various countries, providing an impetus for congressional action.

Congress declared in Section 32 of the 1973 Foreign Assistance Act: "It is the sense of the Congress that the President should deny any . . . military assistance to the government of any foreign country which practices the internment or imprisonment of that country's citizens for political purposes."[11] The following year Congress reduced military aid to South Korea and Chile because of human rights abuses. In many instances, however, Congress was unable to force the

Table 7–1

U.S. Military Transfers and Human Rights:
The Carter Years
U.S. Arms Export Agreements
(excluding commercial sales)
(thousands of current dollars)

	1977	1978	1979	1980
Indonesia	$ 20,741	$113,793	$ 39,141	$ 21,234
Morocco	27,466	6,898	2,792	265,995
South Korea	555,356	328,238	239,969	457,407
Pakistan	128,327	42,260	20,798	28,310
Philippines	79,703	45,581	34,137	36,246
Turkey	118,825	157,235	144,786	66,484
Zaire	10,117	16,417	5,295	8,134
El Salvador	146	18	3	2,295
Guatemala	5,733	3,379	1,919	10
Paraguay	523	72	18	90
Argentina	18,450	5,064	0	0
N. Yemen	1,928	1,317	169,551	1,521
Uruguay	625	44	2	650
Chile	235	0	0	0

U.S. Commercial Sales Deliveries
(thousands of current dollars)

	1977	1978	1979	1980
Indonesia	$ 5,295	$ 3,011	$17,011	$ 6,221
Morocco	21,616	11,996	8,912	17,385
S. Korea	77,169	74,714	60,864	41,459
Pakistan	4,877	8,521	4,334	4,670
Philippines	14,082	7,184	5,589	7,954
Turkey	13,970	9,077	993	1,127
Zaire	1,733	937	424	5
El Salvador	0	0	0	0
Guatemala	1,020	550	868	417
Paraguay	435	212	277	640
Argentina	6,314	13,258	29,496	7,323
N. Yemen	1	2	35	14
Uruguay	395	67	114	259
Chile	1,357	0	0	0

Source: Defense Security Assistance Agency, *Foreign Military Sales, Foreign Military Construction Sales and Military Assistance Facts, 1985.*

Table 7–2

U.S. Military Transfers and Human Rights:
The Reagan Years
U.S. Arms Export Agreements
(excluding commercial sales)
(thousands of current dollars)

	1981	1982	1983	1984	1985
Indonesia	$ 43,461	$ 51,499	$ 35,904	$ 12,095	$ 20,365
Morocco	28,693	12,751	68,291	33,896	69,093
South Korea	384,777	1,188,692	369,708	191,460	262,707
Pakistan	53,063	1,431,906	148,067	207,849	251,116
Philippines	31,418	17,591	18,638	13,398	39,175
Turkey	289,462	473,402	555,381	4,442,495	456,243
Zaire	6,870	6,078	8,625	16,012	12,870
El Salvador	24,627	61,879	66,582	130,761	146,002
Guatemala	4	0	71	2,824	1,785
Paraguay	23	123	7	0	0
Argentina	0	0	0	75	5,724
N. Yemen	19,355	16,383	9,212	1,248	7,974
Uruguay	627	1,441	583	342	122
Chile	0	0	0	0	0

U.S. Commercial Sales Deliveries
(thousands of current dollars)

	1981	1982	1983	1984	1985
Indonesia	$ 6,673	$10,000	$ 25,083	$ 27,197	$23,088
Morocco	3,143	5,000	13,975	10,252	1,915
S. Korea	28,710	25,000	123,513	122,299	36,041
Pakistan	11,108	5,000	36,100	35,153	6,386
Philippines	967	1,000	5,859	4,018	9,098
Turkey	2,707	10,000	18,051	19,485	11,448
Zaire	45	100	39	25	0
El Salvador	17	300	4,056	1,692	2,196
Guatemala	7	750	3	37	135
Paraguay	177	300	195	63	60
Argentina	4,553	5,000	2,910	7,842	3,992
N. Yemen	4	100	663	276	1,315
Uruguay	591	250	444	159	338
Chile	0	0	0	11	964

Source: Defense Security Assistance Agency, *Foreign Military Sales, Foreign Military Construction Sales and Military Assistance Facts, 1985*.

administration to deny military assistance on human rights grounds, and it therefore passed legislation intended to make such a policy legally binding. When President Ford vetoed the legislation, Congress adopted the following compromise language in Section 502B of the Arms Export Control Act of that year:

> It is further the policy of the United States that, except under circumstances specified in this section, no security assistance may be provided to any country the government of which engages in a consistent pattern of gross violations of internationally recognized human rights.[12]

By the term security assistance, Congress meant not just military assistance, but:

> (B) Sales of defense articles or services, extensions of credits (including participation in credits and guarantees of loans under the Arms Export Control Act); or (C) Any license in effect with respect to the export of defense articles or defense services to or for the armed forces, police, intelligence, or other internal security forces of a foreign country under section 38 of the Arms Export Control Act.[13]

Throughout the late 1960s and early 1970s, actions against nations that violated human rights resulted largely from congressional pressure on the Executive Branch. With the election of President Carter in 1976, however, the Executive Branch took the initiative. During his campaign, candidate Carter repeatedly emphasized the importance of human rights considerations in foreign policy decisionmaking, and after his victory he declared that, henceforth, human rights would be the "soul of foreign policy," and that "our commitment to human rights must be absolute."[14]

The practical application of this policy proved more difficult. As one of the top staff members of Carter's United Nations ambassador, Andrew Young, observed: "Those of us who had been outside came in with lots of ideas about what was wrong and about what ought to be, but not many ideas of how to go about it."[15]

Competing foreign policy imperatives prevented the Carter administration from pursuing human rights goals singlemindedly, resulting in a foreign policy that was incomprehensible from a strictly human rights standpoint. Many governments with abysmal human rights records escaped censure, and even where sanctions were imposed they often were not comprehensive.

The approach the Reagan administration has taken toward the issue of human rights has only further frustrated human rights advocates. From the beginning, it emphasized that human rights criteria would not play as large a role in Reagan's arms transfer policy. As one Defense Department official put it, in the Reagan administration there would be "less hand wringing about the moral consequences of arms sales."[16] The Reagan administration has consistently argued that it can bring about change in human rights practices more effectively by maintaining its influence with repressive governments than by undermining it through arms embargoes or sanctions. Disappointed human rights advocates claim that this rationale has given the Reagan administration license to turn its back on human rights violations. They argue that without the threat of sanctions, repressive governments will not refrain from violence and persecution.

Foreign-supplied military equipment and repression: Perhaps the most outspoken critic of the effect of U.S. arms transfer policy on human rights is Michael Klare. In countless books and articles he has set forth the basis for his argument that U.S. arms transfers have aided and abetted repression in the Third World.

The American-made military equipment that he cites as being used in repression is supplied mainly through the commercial sales program. These sales are made directly from the American producer to the Third World government. Although the seller must obtain an export license from the State Department's Office of Munition Control (OMC), the vast quantity of applications received by this office each year has led to almost routine approval of sales to friendly governments.[17] The Congressional Research Service found that, "in 1984, OMC received about 46,000 license applications and other requests for approval. Most cases are routine and are approved or denied within two weeks."[18] Congress is not in a position to block most of these sales since it is notified of them beforehand only if they exceed $14 million for major defense equipment or $50 million for defense articles and services. Congress receives after the fact notification of commercial sales of more than $1 million, although most sales of the type of police equipment generally used in repression do not even reach this total.[19] Thus, Klare argues, even those commercial sales agreements that are likely to facilitate human rights abuses are seldom refused unless the recipient is a nation to which Congress or the President has formally restricted sales.[20]

Commercial sales products include a variety of equipment ranging from police helicopters and vehicles to automatic rifles and tear gas. Although the dollar value of commercial sales is low ($2-$4.5 billion per year) when compared with Foreign Military Sales, the quantity of weapons exported is substantial. Michael Klare's study of export licenses shows that between September 1976 and May 1979, Third World police forces alone received 615,000 gas grenades, 126,000 revolvers, 52,000 rifles and submachine guns, 12,000 canisters of Mace and 56 million rounds of ammunition. This does not include the even larger quantities of these weapons that are shipped to military and paramilitary organizations.[21] According to Klare's study, the leading exporter of weapons to Third World police forces was Smith & Wesson of Springfield, Mass., followed by Federal Laboratories of Saltsburg, Pa.[22] Other leading exporters to Third World police were Colt Industries (through Colt Firearms), Du Pont (through Remington Arms), and Olin Corp. (through Winchester International).[23] Table 7–3 reproduces the General Accounting Office's more comprehensive list of the leading exporters of arms to all destinations under the commercial sales program between 1977 and 1981, the last years for which data are available.

Because of the alleged loose supervision and large quantities of weapons exported under the commercial sales program, Klare contends that many of them end up in the hands of police and military organizations known for their use of violence and torture. According to Klare's study of export licenses, between September 1976 and May 1979 DINA (the Chilean secret police), the Carabineros (the Chilean uniformed police), SAVAK (the Iranian secret police under the Shah), the Haitian Palace Guard and the Thailand Border Patrol Police all received clearance from the OMC to receive arms through commercial sales.[24] Amnesty International condemned each of these organizations for human rights violations during this period.

Military equipment supplied through the Foreign Military Sales program is more closely regulated. The Foreign Assistance Act of 1974, for instance, forbids the use of Foreign Military Sales channels for sales to internal security organizations. Klare maintains, however, that in some instances this law has been ignored or circumvented, and repressive organizations with an

Commercial Sales: Leading Companies
1977-1981
(thousands of current dollars)

Company	1977 Total	1977 Rank	1978 Total	1978 Rank	1979 Total	1979 Rank	1980 Total	1980 Rank	1981 Total	1981 Rank
Lockheed	$102,394	1	$190,503	1	$49,369	6	$133,525	1	$198,662	1
Hughes Aircraft	29,925	8	78,577	4	23,489	11	52,261	6	121,372	2
Nissho-Iwai American*	19,960	15	32,406	11	44,177	8	64,300	4	79,857	3
Raytheon Corp.	19,204	17	81,360	3	187,049	1	47,702	7	79,857	3
Boeing Corp.	47,489	3	41,536	8	80,496	2	25,406	12	75,551	4
Teledyne Inc.	NA	NA	NA	NA	17,882	17	60,931	5	67,658	5
Texas Instruments	NA	NA	NA	NA	16,970	19	26,504	11	61,639	6
Olin Mathieson	23,869	11	38,026	10	47,589	7	25,109	13	47,007	7
Singer	10,615	23	30,868	12	21,426	12	39,689	8	45,482	8
Bendix Corp.	NA	NA	NA	NA	NA	NA	NA	NA	39,768	9
Nittler Forwarder	NA	NA	NA	NA	NA	NA	27,856	10	36,401	10
Avco	23,049	13	38,338	9	27,290	10	NA	NA	35,894	11
Electric Memories	NA	NA	13,223	21	15,592	21	NA	NA	29,897	12
Luigi Serra Inc.*	NA	NA	16,934	17	16,854	20	15,143	21	26,717	13
Colt's Inc.	21,617	14	NA	NA	20,891	13	14,845	22	25,888	14
Emery Air Freight	NA	NA	NA	NA	NA	NA	19,299	17	24,090	15
NAPCO Industry	NA	NA	NA	NA	NA	NA	NA	NA	21,929	16
FMC Corp.	NA	NA	NA	NA	NA	NA	17,112	20	21,510	17
Smith & Wesson	10,336	24	NA	NA	NA	NA	NA	NA	20,897	18
Sperry Rand Corp.	NA	NA	NA	NA	NA	NA	NA	NA	20,455	19
Sumitomo Shoji*	NA	NA	NA	NA	NA	NA	13,487	25	19,916	20
Thiokol Chemical	NA	NA	NA	NA	13,783	23	14,161	23	19,892	21
Northrop Corp.	41,005	5	53,341	6	NA	NA	NA	NA	19,353	22
Litton Industries	NA	NA	NA	NA	30,643	9	NA	NA	19,171	23
United Technologies	40,015	6	65,772	5	52,688	4	86,059	2	17,181	24
Other top 25 companies	322,088	NA	333,262	NA	233,862	NA	226,862	NA	17,110	25
Total commercial sales of the top 25 companies	$711,566		$1,014,146		$900,050		$910,251		0	NA
									$1,113,298	

Source: General Accounting Office

NA   Denotes "Not Available"
*   Non-U.S. companies

The ranking of the GAO's top 25 commercial sales military equipment exporters fluctuates from year to year. The GAO listed the annual totals only for those companies that were among the 25 largest in 1981. The entry "Other top 25 companies," provides the annual aggregate for 1977 through 1980 for those companies that were not among the top 25 in 1981, but were in previous years. The symbol "NA," therefore, denotes that the company was not among the largest 25 for that given year, and not that the company did not export military equipment through commercial sales channels that year.

exclusively internal mission, such as the Imperial Iranian Gendarmerie, the Philippine Constabulary and the Saudi Arabian National Guard, have received major American defense equipment that they can use in silencing domestic dissent.[25]

Human rights advocates maintain that, in any case, this law is ineffective since the military in the Third World is often as involved in repression as are police and internal security forces. Amnesty International in its 1984 report on El Salvador described the "continued involvement of all branches of the security and military forces in a systematic and widespread program of torture, mutilation, 'disappearance' and the individual and mass extrajudicial execution of men, women and children from all sectors of Salvadoran society."[26] In many Third World nations the military exercises internal police functions, often being called out to end strikes or demonstrations, seal off troubled areas or enforce curfews.

The presence of guerrilla movements in some countries, such as El Salvador, magnifies the military's internal role. U.S. policy since Kennedy has encouraged this enlarged role, pushing Third World militaries, sometimes at their reluctance, to take a more aggressive position in combatting insurgency. To this end the United States has used the Foreign Military Sales program to supply Third World militaries, especially in Latin America, with large quantities of counter-insurgency equipment. According to critics of this policy, the military in many of these countries, such as Peru, El Salvador, the Philippines, Indonesia and Morocco, has used this equipment to conduct counterinsurgency campaigns with little or no regard for human rights.

Foreign arms sales and the support of repressive regimes: In addition to their actual use in repression, critics believe arms transferred to Third World regimes through the Foreign Military Sales and, to a lesser extent, the commercial sales programs, affect human rights by bolstering and conferring legitimacy upon the recipient governments. They maintain that the arms enable the government to project an image of strength and stability that helps defuse potential challenges, and that when challenges do materialize, the arms often assist the government in crushing them. Perhaps most importantly, arms sales critics assert that the arms transfers indicate American backing of regimes, which is crucial to the survival of many Third World governments. When a repressive regime is sold American weapons, arms transfer critics contend, it receives not only instruments with which it can violate human rights, but also assistance it needs to stay in power. Thus, it remains free to continue its abuses.

As Tables 7–1 and 7–2 indicate, the United States has supplied military equipment to a number of Third World governments with poor human rights records. A study of political rights and civil liberties by the conservative Freedom House judged all of the countries listed in the table to be among the least free nations in the world. The governments of these nations were also condemned as being among the worst abusers of human rights by an independent study that ranked human rights in different countries according to State Department and Amnesty International reports.[27] (The State Department and Amnesty International do not themselves rank or compare human rights situations.)

It should be recognized, however, that arms transfers are only part, and usually not the most important part, of U.S. support for foreign governments. Diplomatic relations, trade and economic assistance—all of which may continue after termination of arms sales—can also play a significant role in conferring legitimacy upon or bolstering foreign governments.

Arms transfer policy as a means of preserving human rights—an assessment: Although American leaders to varying degrees have recognized and had serious qualms about the relationship between arms sales and human rights, they have faced many difficulties in attempting to alter the situation. As the Carter administration's efforts reflect, the formulation and execution of foreign policy is buffeted by conflicting imperatives. Many Third World countries strongly object to linking arms shipments to human rights policies on the grounds that their human rights policies are internal matters not to be subject to external review or interference. The Carter administration policy on this matter met with intense opposition, particularly in Latin America. When confronted with reduced military aid because of human rights violations, El Salvador, Guatemala, Brazil, Argentina and Uruguay all rejected any further U.S. military assistance instead of making concerted efforts to improve their records in order to avoid arms cutoffs.[28]

The problems of such a linkage are also illustrated by the inconsistency that befell the Carter administration arms transfer policy as a result of tying it to human rights. Although the Carter administration used the human rights records of Third World governments to help determine whether they were eligible for military sales and assistance, it was not willing to make them the sole determinant. National security considerations, for example, played a key role as well, and the administration was extremely reluctant to face the consequences of banning military aid and sales to friendly governments that were threatened by internal or external forces or that provided the United States with military bases. While the Carter administration imposed stiff sanctions against Guatemala and Argentina, it took almost no steps against countries with similar human rights records such as South Korea, Zaire, the Philippines and Iran under the Shah. Iran, in fact, was the largest purchaser of American arms during the first year of Carter's tenure. This inconsistent policy not only caused resentment among Third World governments singled out for censure, but gave strategically positioned nations little incentive to curtail their human rights abuses.

Beyond these problems lies the question of whether arms transfer restrictions or embargoes are an effective way to change human rights practices. The Reagan administration argues that they are not, contending that it can more easily influence human rights practices in Third World regimes by maintaining its relationship as an arms supplier. By rejecting restrictions, it believes it both retains leverage and avoids provoking nationalistic responses. It claims that this method has achieved positive results in countries such as El Salvador and South Korea. Most human rights advocates, however, deny that the human rights situation has improved in these countries, and many of them blame the Reagan administration's lenient policies in part for this lack of progress.

Questions also arise about the effectiveness of the more aggressive Carter administration posture in the areas where it was willing to pursue it. The Latin American nations against which Carter applied sanctions did not immediately respond by improving their human rights practices. Some claim that this is because Carter's sanctions were not comprehensive enough. Nations that were banned from foreign military sales were able to obtain American arms through commercial sales or dual-use (civilian and military) items through sales approved by the Commerce Department. More crucial, however, was the absence of accompanying economic sanctions such as loan and trade restrictions, which critics contend would have exerted considerably more pressure on these nations to improve their human rights records.

The effectiveness of sanctions in general, however, is open to question. Certainly, there are many more examples of sanctions that fell short of their goals than of sanctions that achieved them. A major study on the efficacy of sanctions, by the Institute for International Economics, *Economic Sanctions Reconsidered*, concludes that in order to be effective, sanctions must have limited goals, must impose the maximum cost on the targeted nation, and must be enacted firmly and decisively.[29] It maintains furthermore that sanctions are far more likely to succeed if they are imposed against comparatively weak and dependent nations. Many of the sanctions during the Carter administration were not imposed under these conditions, and this may account in part for their uncertain results.

Other human rights advocates contend that the Carter administration policy was effective. A last minute Carter administration ban on arms sales is generally credited with hastening the departure of Somoza, whose Nicaraguan government was reportedly one of the worst violators of human rights. And in Bolivia, Uruguay, and especially Brazil, some improvements in human rights practices did take place in the late 1970s. Some observers credit Carter administration policy with encouraging these improvements, which were important to the gradual evolution toward democracy that a number of Latin American nations have undergone.[30]

Regardless of the ability of arms transfer sanctions to improve human rights practices, imposing arms embargoes on governments that violate human rights may have other advantages. Ending U.S. support to repressive regimes might do much to improve the United States' reputation internationally, thus furthering American foreign policy initiatives. Disassociation with repressive governments might also avoid a repeat of the Iranian situation after the fall of the Shah when its close relationship with the Shah made the United States the subject of damaging attacks.

Arms Transfers and Third World Economic Development

The final major focus of criticism of arms transfers is directed at their impact on economic development. A number of scholars and organizations, including the United Nations, have linked lack of economic progress in Third World nations to their continued arms purchases. Critics claim that arms sales to Third World nations impede their development, tying up badly needed resources and foreign exchange, and that the weapons contribute little to Third World economies, producing no goods and employing comparatively few people.

Arms imports and Third World debt: One of the major economic problems of arms transfers cited by critics is their effect on the developing nations' balance of payments. According to this line of argument, arms imports exhaust badly needed foreign currency, aggravating the debt crisis that has afflicted many Third World countries. The ramifications of this debt crisis are serious. Some debtor nations have seen their real incomes plunge by as much as two-thirds since 1980, and the creditor nations are beginning to feel the effects as well. Many nations have fallen behind on their repayments, and banks worry that some Third World nations will repudiate their massive debts, triggering a worldwide financial crisis.

Critics maintain that by selling arms to many of the developing nations, Western countries, particularly the United States, are endangering their own economies as well as destroying those of the Third World. According to the U.S. Arms Control and Disarmament Agency, developing nations currently spend between $20 to $30 billion on arms imports each year, a significant drain on foreign exchange. The arms imports are not made only by oil-rich nations with a large balance of payments surplus, however. Five of the 10 largest debtor nations—Argentina, Venezuela, Nigeria, Morocco and Peru—have been among the leading arms importing countries during the last decade.[31] The 10 largest Third World debtor nations as a whole imported more than $9 billion worth of arms between 1978 and 1982, according to the ACDA.[32] A study by one leading critic, Michael Brzoska of SIPRI, reported that "one-fourth of the debt accumulated in Latin America is due to arms imports."[33] While many of these countries have reduced their arms imports in recent years, they continue to import a sizable quantity of arms. The ten largest debtor nations alone imported more than $6 billion worth of arms between 1983 and 1985.

Supporters of arms sales, however, maintain that the increasing number of offset agreements have helped to reduce the foreign exchange problems created by arms imports. Offsets are trade arrangements whereby the seller nation agrees to compensate the buyer nation at least partially by purchasing a certain quantity of products from it, thereby reducing the burden on the balance of payments of the buyer nation. A 1986 OMB study showed that offset agreements constituted $12 billion between 1980 and 1984 while total U.S. foreign military sales agreements were only $22 billion during this period.[34] Stephanie Neuman of Columbia University claims that in addition to reducing the balance of payments burden on the recipient nations, offsets may to a certain extent stimulate production in the recipient nations by creating an automatic foreign market for their goods. (See box, pp. 144–145.)

Offsets notwithstanding, arms transfer critics are correct in asserting that the overall burden of arms sales on the balance of payments of developing nations is serious. While offsets have great potential to alleviate this burden, at this point the vast majority are made with industrialized countries rather than developing nations. According to a 1984 Treasury Department study, Canada alone accounts for almost half of U.S. offset agreements, while Third World nations account for less than 4 percent of them, although offset agreements with Third World nations are likely to increase.[35] The role of arms imports in the Third World debt crisis should not be exaggerated, however. Arms imports are only a contributor to this serious problem, not its principal source.

The spinoff benefits of arms imports: Proponents of arms transfers maintain that for a variety of reasons arms imports are beneficial to Third World economies. A 1973 study by Emile Benoit for the Arms Control and Disarmament Agency laid the foundation for this school of thought. This study, which examined military spending in 44 Third World countries from 1950 to 1965 and from 1960 to 1965, found that for 1940 to 1965 period, growth in GNP was associated with growth in military spending. Benoit dismisses the argument that a high growth rate might cause military spending to increase. He argues that although "rapidly rising national income might generate an even more rapidly rising level of tax revenues of which the powerful defense lobby might be expected to secure a proportional (or rising) share," in his study, "no significant correlation was found between income per capita and defense burdens."[36] Thus, Benoit contends that it must be the defense expenditures that cause gross national product to rise rather than the reverse.

Benoit suggests several reasons why Third World military spending might be conductive to economic growth. First, military spending by developing countries tends to encourage foreign aid and, to a lesser extent, foreign investment, both of which, he says, fuel economic growth. More important, according to Benoit, are the direct growth-stimulating effects of military spending such as the creation of infrastructure and the dispersal of training and technology.

One of the most outspoken advocates of the spinoff benefits of arms sales is Stephanie Neuman. According to Neuman, 60 to 65 percent of the total eventual costs of arms imports are expenditures for support, training and construction, which she believes build nations' infrastructure and technological base and teach valuable skills to their citizens.[37] Her study of the military buildup in Iran illustrates the magnitude of the training. Between 1964 and 1978, "21,500 (Iranian nationals) passed through U.S. military training centers, and thousands more were trained in Iran."[38] The Iranians learned not only high-level electronics and management skills that are transferrable to the civilian economy, but also lower-level "transferrable skills such as driving, mechanics, the English language and medical aid," Neuman says.[39]

The infrastructure that Third World militaries create includes roads, airports, hospitals and power lines, which are often used by civilians as much as the military, according to Neuman. Benoit found that in many countries the military is also engaged in "hydographic studies, mapping, aerial surveys, dredging, meteorology, soil conservation, and forestry projects as well as certain quasi-civilian activities such as coast guard (and) lighthouse operation."[40] Although most of the military's constructive work in these countries appears unrelated to its purchases of foreign weapon systems, arms sales supporters argue that such work is part of a general military expansion and modernization that usually accompanies the arms transfers. Many of these projects conducted by recipients of U.S. military equipment and services are conducted under the auspices of the Foreign Military Construction Sales program.

Arms imports also play an important role in helping Third World countries develop arms factories which many supporters of arms sales believe help to spur economic growth and industrial development. In this line of reasoning, through arms imports Third World engineers and technicians learn how to maintain and repair sophisticated military equipment so that coproduction and eventually indigenous design and production become possible. The development of indigenous arms industries or, at least, coproduction abilities is worthwhile, arms transfer supporters claim, because they provide employment and stimulate internal demand and because they also give Third World nations industrial experience and can be a first step toward other industrial projects.

Coproduction is by far the more common of the two possibilities for developing nations, and the number of coproduction agreements with developing nations has been rising steadily. Turkey, for example, recently concluded a major coproduction agreement with General Dynamics whereby 152 of the 160 F-16 fighter aircraft purchased will be assembled in a new facility in Turkey, 51 percent of which will be owned by the Turkish government. Supporters of arms sales contend that the development of an entirely indigenous arms industry has even greater benefits for Third World economies. In addition to providing wider industrial experience and steadier employment for Third World nationals than coproduction ventures, in some instances indigenous Third World arms industries also bring in foreign exchange through arms exports. Supporters of arms sales point to the example of Brazil to illustrate their argument, for Brazil, once South America's largest importer of weapons, now supplies 80 percent of its military needs with indigenously produced goods, and by some accounts is the world's fifth largest exporter of weapons. The Brazilian arms industry produces everything from small arms to tanks, employs more than 100,000 workers and exports more than 80 percent of all that it manufactures, so that its arms export business has fast become an important source of foreign exchange.

Arms transfer critics, in contrast, view arms as largely unproductive imports with few beneficial effects for the economy. They complain that Benoit's study, whose findings are used as the basis for many pro-sales arguments, is skewed by inappropriate methodology and that his findings change radically, depending on which time frame and whose estimates of military spending are used. One critic, Prof. Steven Chan of the University of Colorado, maintains further that the numerous studies that "attempt to verify Benoit's results . . . have not supported his conclusion."[41] Another critic, Nicole Ball, formerly of the Swedish Institute for International Affairs cautions that: "Even if one could accept Benoit's conclusion, it still remains that the attainment of high economic growth rates in no way guarantees that socioeconomic development has occurred. Perhaps the greatest contribution to development research in the 1970s was the documentation of the fact that high rates of economic growth (i.e. rising GNP) can and do coexist with a high incidence of poverty."[42]

United Nations reports regularly criticize arms transfers. One UN report maintains that the spinoff benefits of arms imports are "grossly exaggerated and/or highly misplaced."[43] Critics claim that most of the infrastructure that the military creates makes no contribution to the civilian economy of an underdeveloped nation. According to these critics, civilians are prohibited from using many of the airports, hospitals and communication systems that militaries build, and the roads are often in remote, infrequently traveled areas.[44] Other military-run projects, such as topographical studies and conservation programs, are performed too infrequently in the Third World to be of much significance, critics say.

Critics of arms sales similarly dispute the value of the technology and training transferred in foreign military sales programs. Most military technology, critics contend, is too specialized to have civilian applications, and the manner in which military technology is closely guarded inhibits its dispersal to civilian industries. Although they acknowledge that basic skills imparted in such programs such as languages, driving and fundamental engineering are of some value in the civilian economy, they point out that many of the trainees never have the opportunity to use these skills outside of the military. Since many Third World countries maintain career armies, a large portion of the trained soldiers never return to work in their native cities and villages.

Arms sales critics also contest the value of developing indigenous arms industries. Arms production, they assert, almost always employs a capital-intensive manufacturing process that is ill-suited for the labor surplus economies of most Third World countries. Moreover, because the manufacturing process is capital-intensive it requires a degree of technology that developing nations lack. Thus, the countries must import much of the assembly process, as well as some of the key components. Domestically designed fighter aircraft in India and Israel, for example, still rely on the industrialized countries for major components such as engines. Peter Lock and Herbert Wulf of Hamburg University claim that the rapid innovation and the most advanced technology required in this industry mean that Third World nations will always be at a disadvantage.[45] Even when the domestic arms industries are developed, they contend, in most cases they still must rely on costly protectionist policies in order to compete with their more efficient and experienced counterparts in the industrialized world.

Critics also doubt that using arms imports to develop arms industries is a possibility for most Third World nations in the near future. While most Third World countries have been importing arms for decades, SIPRI reports that as of 1984 only eight nations could produce missiles, only eleven could produce armored vehicles, and only 33 could produce anything beyond simple firearms and ammunition.[46] For at least the next decade, SIPRI argues, the majority of Third World nations will continue to lack the technological base to establish domestic arms industries, regardless of the quantity of arms the nations import.

In the final analysis, many of the spinoff benefits ascribed to arms imports seem dubious. Although the creation of infrastructure and the training of individuals by the military has significant benefits, the percentage that reach the civilian economy is low. Moreover, the role of arms imports, in particular, in creating these benefits does not seem fundamental. Most spinoff benefits are attributable to Third World military spending that is largely unrelated to the acquisition of foreign weapon systems. While there is, no doubt, a correlation between arms purchases and other types of military spending, the correlation seems less causal than supporters of arms sales imply. Although the import of arms is often part of a general military expansion, there is no evidence to suggest that it causes it. Even if foreign weapon systems became unavailable, it is likely that Third World countries would expand or improve their military capabilities. It is therefore inaccurate to cite all the benefits of military spending as economic benefits of arms imports.

Other supposed benefits of arms transfers are more difficult to assess. Arms imports certainly are an essential first step toward the creation of Third World arms industries, but whether these industries have helped or hindered Third World economies cannot be established here. Yet, as arms transfer critics have pointed out, to most Third World countries it is a moot question because the possibility of creating a domestic arms industry remains remote.

In addition to the arguments presented here, supporters of arms sales offer numerous other examples of the spinoff benefits of arms imports. Some of these merit brief mention here. One such example revolves around the role of arms imports in creating inflation, and the expansionary effect this inflation has on Third World economies. Supporters of arms sales have claimed that arms imports cause inflation in the developing nations because they make heavy demands upon Third World industrial, agricultural and extractive sectors in order to gain the necessary financial resources. Benoit says this inflation pulls "into economic use, unused or underutilized resources which contribute to real growth."[47] Benoit cites as an example India after the brief Chinese-Indian war of the early 1960s: "I observed, however, that in India, the mainland Chinese attack of 1962-1963 resulted in rapid increases in defense spending, a liberalization of monetary fiscal policies, a considerable rise in prices, and a substantial speeding in the rate of real increase in civilian goods and services."[48]

It is difficult to establish, however, to what extent the inflationary aspect of arms imports has a valuable expansionary spinoff since the financial resources leave the country instead of increasing demand. Even if a correlation could be established, many economists deny that inflation is beneficial to developing economies. Saadet Deger and Ron Smith of London University write that evidence of a positive effect of inflation "is so contradictory that it is difficult to pass a clear-cut judgment."[49] According to them, inflation could just as easily lead to conspicuous consumption or capital flight. Similarly, the financial demands of arms imports may divert existing resources from other sources, rather than stimulating the production of new ones.

The diversion of resources from social spending and development: Critics of arms sales contend that even if the import of arms does provide an impetus for the development of infrastructure and the training of large quantities of civilians, it is an inefficient way to accomplish those ends. They maintain that such benefits could be more effectively achieved by channeling the resources consumed by the arms imports directly into development. Thus, the funds used to purchase weapon systems and the people employed to operate and maintain them instead would be used to build roads, dams and airports for civilian use, to train civilians in engineering, driving and languages, and to create welfare systems, health and sanitation projects, and industrial and agricultural development programs.

The most crucial of the diverted resources, according to arms sales critics, are the funds. Developing nations spend approximately $25 to $30 billion a year on arms imports, which does not even include the billions of dollars spent each year on operation and maintenance work performed by the recipient country. Most advanced military aircraft require more than 50 man hours of maintenance per sortie.[50] This creates large expenses not just for salaries, but for fuel and spare parts as well. As John T. Tyler, deputy planning director of the Defense Security Assistance Agency, told *The New York Times*, "you end up spending five times the original cost on parts and modifications over a 10 to 20-year life span" of a typical helicopter.[51]

This financial burden is carried not only by the comparatively wealthy oil-exporting nations, but also by other Third World countries much less able to afford the expenditure. (See Table 7–4.) In 1983 oil-importing nations accounted for 40 percent of Third World arms imports, and 16 of these countries spent more money on arms in than they received in development assistance.[52] The very poorest countries of the world, whose average annual GNP per capita was $260, imported more than $3.5 billion worth of arms in 1983, accounting for more than 12 percent of total Third World arms imports.[53] These countries, arms transfer critics contend, must sacrifice social expenditures and other development needs in order to fund their arms imports. Ruth Leger Sivard's *World Military and Social Expenditures* reports that in 1982, 24 developing nations spent more government funds on arms imports than on health services, and 13 of these nations spent more on arms imports than on education.[54]

Arms transfer critics assert that human resources, too, are diverted from development needs to operate and maintain the imported weapons. Gavin Kennedy in *The Military in the Third World* calculated that in 1970, 10 Third World countries required at least 3,000 full-time employees each in order to maintain their sophisticated weapon systems.[55] Critics of arms transfers maintain that these are often the nation's most talented technical and administrative personnel.[56] Although the number of skilled laborers employed to service the weapon systems is not significant in terms of

Table 7–4

Leading Third World Recipients of U.S. Military Deliveries Fiscal Years 1985 and 1986
(in thousands of current dollars)

Fiscal 1985		*Fiscal 1986*	
1. Saudi Arabia	$2,991,830	1. Saudi Arabia	$2,407,447
2. Israel	$ 717,385	2. Egypt	$ 661,753
3. Egypt	$ 669,437	3. South Korea	$ 489,011
4. Taiwan	$ 475,733	4. Taiwan	$ 481,699
5. Pakistan	$ 379,609	5. Israel	$ 422,818
6. South Korea	$ 303,196	6. Singapore	$ 186,593
7. Venezuela	$ 257,508	7. Pakistan	$ 156,215
8. Tunisia	$ 160,978	8. Thailand	$ 132,498
9. Jordan	$ 151,377	9. El Salvador	$ 109,103
10. Thailand	$ 144,113	10. Kuwait	$ 91,940
11. El Salvador	$ 117,378	11. Venezuela	$ 84,669
12. Morocco	$ 55,423	12. Jordan	$ 71,473

Source: Department of Defense Security Assistance Agency (DSAA), *Foreign Military Sales, Foreign Military Construction Sales and Military Assistance Facts* 1986 edition, (Washington: DSAA, 1987).

Offsets Play an Increasingly Large Role in U.S. Military Exports . . .

"Offset" is the most commonly used term for a variety of sale arrangements whereby the seller of military equipment agrees to compensate the buyer by making reciprocal purchases. Direct off-sets occur when the seller purchases from the recipient country components or raw materials that are used in the weapon system that is being sold. Indirect offsets involve the reciprocal purchase of goods unrelated to the weapons acquisition. In the latter case, the supplier must then itself use or market the goods that it has purchased as part of the offset agreement.

Offset agreements come in a variety of guises. Some are strict barter agreements or exchanges of goods, as in some of the more publicized arms-for-oil arrangements. They may involve technology transfer, such as in co-production (government-recipient) agreements or licensed production (company-recipient) agreements, which stipulate that the supplier furnishes the technology needed to produce all or part of the weapon system in the recipient country. The supplier might also invest overseas or form subsidiaries or joint ventures in the recipient country as part of an offset package.

According to the most recent figures available, a majority of U.S. arms exports involve offset arrangements. A study by the Office of Management and Budget (OMB) found that between 1980 and 1984, U.S. military export sales totaled more than $22 billion and offsets equalled $12.3 billion. Although most analysts believe that the number of offset agreements will grow, this is not a unanimous forecast. Many observers contend that if worldwide economic conditions improve, the arms trade will again become a seller's market, reducing the leverage the recipient countries have to demand offsets. Some also believe international pressures to dismantle trade barriers might lead to the reduced use of offsets.

The majority of offset agreements are made with industrialized countries. A 1984 Treasury Department study found that Canada accounts for almost half of U.S. offset agreements and Japan almost 13 percent. Great Britain and France will have a large share of American offset agreements in the future because of their decision to buy Boeing's airborne early warning aircraft (Awacs). Boeing has agreed to provide offset packages worth 130 percent of the value of the sale. Third World countries constitute less than 4 percent of all American offsets, with one country, Israel, accounting for 85 percent of this total. Since 1982, Indonesia has required 100 percent in offset purchases for contracts worth more than $750,000, with a penalty of 50 percent of the contract price should the firm fail to make good on its agreement. The Malaysian government's Ministry of Trade now maintains a division specific ally to encourage offsets, and South Korea, Egypt and Saudi Arabia also are increasingly demanding offset arrangements.

Before 1978, the Department of Defense itself arranged offset agreements in connection with foreign military sales. The Duncan Memorandum of 1978, however, reversed this policy, mandating that "(1) DoD will not become directly involved in offsets either as a participant or a guarantor; and (2) Foreign Military Sales (FMS) credits will not be used to directly finance coproduction or licensed production abroad." Thus, the companies making the sales became solely responsible for negotiating and executing the the terms of offset agreements. Coproduction agreements, which are government-arranged, are an

. . .Despite Questions About Effects on U.S. Economy, National Security

exception to this rule, although Department of Defense officials contend that these do not violate the Duncan Memorandum since "the sale of the production licenses is neither administered nor guaranteed by the U.S. government, nor are there any 'buy backs' involved." The U.S. government is also involved in offsets in so far as these agreements must comply with laws governing arms exports and the transfer of technology as a whole.

As offsets have grown considerably in the last decade, some members of Congress have become increasingly critical of their effects on the U.S. eonomy and have sought more extensive regulation of them. In 1984, Rep. Bruce Vento (D-Minn.) sponsored an amendment to the Defense Production Act of 1950 that required the Executive Branch to "study and report annually on the effect of offsets associated with military export sales." Critics complain that foreign firms use offsets to gain access to American technology and develop industries that will eventually compete with Amer ican firms. In this respect, Japan's coproduction of the McDonnell Douglas F-15 fighter was particularly controversial. Critics also contend that while offsets may help large defense firms win foreign contracts, they hurt smaller defense contractors and non-defense businesses by bringing foreign goods into the American market. In these ways, offsets are said to eliminate American jobs and contribute to trade deficits.

Supporters of offsets, however, argue that without them, American businesses would lose valuable contracts. This line of argument reasons that the inability of U.S. firms to enter into offset agreements would put them at a disadvantage when competing with other supplier-nations able to extend offset offers in what increasingly has become a buyers market. Because the net effect of foreign contracts tied to offsets on the American trade balance and domestic employment is positive, they argue that offsets on the whole are beneficial to the economy. Supporters also con tend that the foreign goods purchased through offsets are often re-sold in foreign markets rather than at home, and that even when they are sold at home, it is often other imported goods that they displace rather than domestically manufactured items. They cite the OMB study that says that "the positive effects of sales on employment exceed by far the adverse effects of offsets" and that "available evidence suggests the profitability of defense-related industries has not been damaged by offsets." The General Accounting Office found considerable problems with this study, however, contending that it underrepresented subcontractors—the group likely to be hurt the most by offsets—and neglected to examine the impact of offsets on nondefense industries.

Critics of offsets also are concerned about their effects on national security. Many worry that offsets will lead the United States to become dependent on foreign subcontractors, jeopardizing U.S. military readiness and undermining the U.S. military industrial base. They fear that technology transfers involved in many offset arrangements increase the risk that the Soviets will gain access to the technology. Offset supporters counter that they make military and economic modernization affordable for many allies, which is in the U.S. national interest. They also say that offsets increase the commonality of military equipment of the arsenals of the allies of the United State, which would be crucial in event of a coordinated war effort.

the total labor force of these countries, it is a severe drain on the skilled labor pool. These engineers and technicians, the critics argue, could make valuable contributions toward development if employed in the civilian economy instead.

Critics contend that arms imports also divert industries from development-oriented functions. This point is made by Helene Tuomi and Raimo Vayrynen of the Tampere Peace Research Institute in Finland, who claim that instead of manufacturing the products and supplying the raw materials that are needed by Third World nations, developing countries adapt their industrial and mining sectors to suit their military priorities: "Thus the industrial sector may be directed to supply parts and components for arms suppliers."[57] Because of offset agreements, the mining sector, too, "may be modified to supply raw materials for foreign military production."[58] Nicole Ball concurs that attempts to supply spare parts for the imported weapons or to create a domestic arms industry lead to "the establishment of industries which do not have much relevance to the population."[59] She suggests, furthermore, that following such a path means that the developing nation's "industrialization program is likely to be influenced in the direction of capital intensity."[60] Such a course is undesirable, she asserts, because it eliminates jobs in nations already struggling with high levels of under-employment.

There is considerable disagreement, however, on how much of the resources consumed by arms imports would in fact be used for development if sales of weapons ceased or were vastly reduced. In many nations the military sponsors the most challenging, innovative and independent technological research that the country has to offer. Arms sales supporters contend that many of the skilled engineers and technicians now employed in arms imports-related work would leave developing countries in search of challenging employment elsewhere if sophisticated military hardware ceased to be imported. Similarly, they argue that much of the financial resources saved by ending arms sales would also evaporate. Benoit suggests that most of the saved funds would be consumed in other, no more productive, ways: "In the normal case this will consist of a mix of consumption and civilian investment, with by far the larger part going into consumption (including civilian government consumption) with only slight growth effects, and with a substantial part even of the civilian investments going into housing, imports of consumer durables, or other uses with a relatively small impact on growth."[61]

At a glance, it appears that many of the claims of arms sales critics regarding the diversion of resources from development are valid. The imported arms themselves do not create infrastructure, nor do they manufacture consumer goods or in any way finance the employment of host country nationals. It therefore would be far more efficient for developing nations to invest their financial resources in ways specifically designed to create infrastructure, improve health care and education, or feed, clothe and shelter their population. Supporters of arms sales are correct, however, in saying that there is no guarantee that this would be done with any resources freed up by reduced arms imports. Developing nations are faced with many competing demands for their limited funds and many bureaucratic and logistic impediments to allocating the funds as the leaders see fit.

Regardless of the amount of additional resources that would be devoted to development if arms imports were reduced, they would be far from sufficient to change drastically the economic situation in the developing countries. Supporters of arms sales are accurate in dismissing as overly simplistic the disarmament-development equation that the United Nations promotes. Although an arms sales critic, Nicole Ball recognizes the fallacy of such an easy solution: "Those who argue that the military diverts scarce resources from developmental activities fail to see that the real issue for very many

Third World countries is inequitable political and socio-economic structures rather than the simple misallocation of resources."[62]

On the whole, the impact of arms imports on Third World economies does not seem positive. The spinoff benefits gained by such purchases are too meager to merit the severe foreign exchange burden imposed on the developing nations. While ample studies do laud the beneficial economic impact of domestic military spending by Third World countries, few of them will make the same appraisal of arms imports. Although his findings are cited by arms sales supporters to bolster their position, Benoit himself has sharp reservations about some types of military spending:

> Programs that absorb large amounts of foreign exchange for weapons purchases, or which utilize large amounts of domestic resources for indigenous weapons procurement—particularly if the weapons are advanced and sophisticated types—absorb financial or physical resources particularly strategic for development and thus heavily burden growth.[63]

The question remains, however, whether the alternative use of these resources would yield significantly better results.

Footnotes

1. Roger P. Labrie, John G. Hutchins and Edwin Peura, *U.S. Arms Sales Policy: Background and Issues* (Washington: American Enterprise Institute, 1982), p. 15.
2. Congressional Research Service, *Changing Perspectives on U.S. Arms Transfer Policy*, Sept. 25, 1981, p. 122.
3. *Ibid.*, p. 122.
4. Labrie et al., *op. cit.*, p. 51.
5. Testimony of Leslie Gelb before the Senate Committee on Foreign Relations, March 4, 1980, U.S. Senate, *The Conventional Arms Transfer Policy of the United States* (Washington: U.S. GPO, 1980), p. 6.
6. *Ibid.*, p. 6.
7. Testimony of Joseph A. Karth before the Senate Committee on Foreign Relations, March 6, 1980, U.S. Senate, *The Conventional Arms Transfer Policy of the United States*, (Washington: U.S. GPO, 1980), p 113.
8. *Ibid.*, p. 113.
9. *Ibid.*, p. 114.
10. Max Holland, "The 'Arms Embargo' to Southern Africa," *International Policy Report* May 1979, p. 13.
11. Center for International Policy, *Human Rights and the U.S Foreign Assistance Program, Fiscal Year 1978* (Washington: Center for International Policy, 1977) p. 3.
12. *Ibid.*, p. 3.
13. *Ibid.*, p. 3.
14. Lars Schoultz, *Human Rights and United States Policy toward Latin America* (Princeton, N.J.: Princeton University Press, 1981), p. 113.
15. *Ibid.*, p. 114.
16. Paul Hammond, David Louscher, Michael D. Salomone and Norman A. Graham, *The Reluctant Supplier: U.S. Decisionmaking for Arms Sales* (Cambridge, Mass.: Oelgeschlager, Gunn & Hain, Inc., 1983), p. 53.
17. Hammond et al., *op. cit.*, p. 95; and Michael Klare, *American Arms Supermarket* (Austin, Tex.: University of Texas Press, 1984), p. 190.
18. Congressional Research Service, *U.S. Military Sales and Assistance Programs: Laws, Regulations, and Procedures* (Washington: GPO, 1985), p. 45.
19. Klare, *op. cit.*, p. 191.
20. *Ibid.*, p. 191.
21. *Ibid.*, p. 191.
22. Michael Klare, and Cynthia Arnson, *Supplying Repression: U.S. Support for Authoritarian Regimes Abroad* (Washington: Institute for Policy Studies, 1981), p. 68.
23. *Ibid.*, p. 68.
24. Klare, *Supplying Repression*, p. 56 and Klare, *American Arms Supermarket*, p. 184.
25. Klare, *American Arms Supermarket*, p. 186.
26. Amnesty International, *Amnesty International Report 1984* (London: Amnesty International Publications, 1984), p. 148.
27. David Carleton and Michael Stohl, "The Foreign Policy of Human Rights: Rhetoric and Reality from Jimmy Carter to Ronald Reagan," *Human Rights Quarterly*, pp. 227–229.
28. Labrie et al., *op. cit.*, p. 55.
29. Gary Clyde Hufbauer and Jeffrey J. Schott, *Economic Sanctions Reconsidered*, (Washington: Institute for International Economics, 1985).
30. Schoultz, *op. cit.*, p. 363.
31. Stockholm International Peace Research Institute (SIPRI), *World Armaments and Disarmament Yearbook* 1986 edition (New York: Oxford University Press, 1986), p. 344.

32. U.S. Department of State, Arms Control and Disarmament Agency (ACDA), *World Military Expenditures and Arms Transfers*, 1984 edition.

33. SIPRI, *op. cit.*, p. 97.

34. Stephanie Neuman, "Offsets in the International Arms Market," in ACDA, *op. cit.*, 1985 edition, p. 35.

35. *Ibid.*, p. 36.

36. Emile Benoit, *Defense and Economic Growth in Developing Countries* (Lexington, Mass.: Lexington Books, 1973), p. 275.

37. Stephanie Neumann and Robert G. Harkavy, eds., *Arms Transfers in the Modern World* (New York: Praeger Books, 1979), p. 227.

38. *Ibid.*, p. 227.

39. *Ibid.*, p. 227.

40. Benoit, *op. cit.*, p. 277.

41. Steve Chan, "The Impact of Defense Spending on Economic Performance: A Survey of Evidence and Problems," *Orbis* Summer 1985, p. 403.

42. Nicole Ball, *The Military in the Development Process* (Claremont: Regina Books, 1981), p. 7.

43. Report of the Secretary-General of the United Nations, Department for Disarmament Affairs, *Economic and Social Consequences of the Arms Race and of Military Expenditures* (New York: United Nations, 1983), p. 40.

44. Neuman, *op. cit.*, p. 226.

45. Peter Lock and Herbert Wulf, "Consequences of the Transfer of Military-Oriented Technology on the Development Process" in Pradip K. Ghosh ed., *Disarmament and Development* (Westport, Conn.: Greenwood Press, 1984), pp. 110–113.

46. Michael Brzoska and Thomas Ohlson, *Arms Production in the Third World* (Philadelphia: Taylor & Francis, 1986), pp. 16–17.

47. Benoit, *op. cit.*, p. 278.

48. *Ibid.*, p. 278.

49. Saadet Deger and Ron Smith, "Military Expenditure and Growth in Less Developed Countries," *Journal of Conflict Resolution*, June 1983, p. 338.

50. James Fallows, *National Defense* (New York: Vintage Books, 1981), p. 41.

51. *The New York Times*, 9-29-85, p. E5.

52. ACDA, *op. cit.* 1985 edition; and World Bank, *World Development Report* 1986 edition (New York: Oxford University Press, 1986), p. 220–21.

53. *Ibid.*

54. Ruth Leger Sivard, *World Military and Social Expenditures* 1985 edition (Washington: World Priorities, 1985), pp. 35–36.

55. Gavin Kennedy, *The Military in the Third World* (London: Duckworth Press, 1974), p. 248.

56. John H. Hoagland and John B. Teeple, "The Economics of Regional Arms Races" in Emile Benoit ed., *Disarmament and World Economic Interdependence* (New York: Columbia University Press, 1967), p. 139.

57. Helena Tuomi and Raimo Vayrynen, *Transnational Corporations, Armaments and Development* (New York: St. Martin's Press, 1982), p. 226.

58. *Ibid.*, p. 226.

59. Ball, *The Military in the Development Process*, p. 12.

60. *Ibid.*, p. 12.

61. Benoit, *op. cit.*, p. 141.

62. Ball, *The Military in the Development Process*, p. 13.

63. Benoit, *op. cit.*, p. 279.

Chapter 8
Arms Exports and the Middle East

Conflicts in the Middle East

Conflicts in the Middle East* are numerous, in part because they run in many directions. Although every region of the world experiences a multitude of tensions and disputes that are unique and removed from the superpower dynamic, perhaps none is as fractionalized as the Middle East, where nations that are allied over one conflict frequently oppose each other in another. The most pronounced of these conflicts involves the Arab nations (excluding Egypt) loosely allied against Israel. A separate one pits the fundamentalist Islamic government of Iran, allied with Syria and one Arab state outside the region, Libya, against the majority of the Arab states. A third source of tension—although it is currently the least pronounced—conforms to the division of countries between those allied with the United States and those linked to the Soviet Union, and pits the radical Arab states such as Iraq, Syria and South Yemen against the more conservative states of the Arabian peninsula, plus Jordan and Egypt. Additional hostilities also exist entirely independently from any bloc of alliances or ideologies, the most important of which is the bitter rivalry between the Ba'ath party governments in Iraq and Syria. (See Table 8–2 at the end of the chapter for a list of recent conflicts in the Middle East.)

The levels of hostility between the nations within the opposing blocs vary. Relations between Kuwait and Iraq, for example, have been considerably more strained than North Yemen's relations with Iraq, and the hostility between Israel and Syria is much more pointed than that between Oman and Israel.

The Arab-Israeli conflict is the most prominent of the Middle Eastern confrontations. Since 1948, Israel has fought five wars with its Arab neighbors—the 1947–49 war, out of which Israel emerged as a nation, the 1956 Suez campaign, the Six Day War of 1967, the October 1973 war and the 1982 war in Lebanon. Not surprisingly, those nations directly involved in these wars imported vast amounts of arms. Between 1964 and 1973, the "confrontation states"—Israel, Egypt, Syria and Jordan—imported more than $5.6 billion worth of military equipment, which accounted for 60 percent of all arms imported into the Middle East.[1] In the late 1970s, though, arms imports by many of the confrontation states declined or were re-directed away from the Arab-Israeli conflict.

---

*For the purposes of this report, the Middle East includes all of the nations of the Arabian peninsula, plus Iran, Iraq, Syria, Lebanon, Jordan, Egypt, Israel and the Occupied Territories.

Israel reduced its arms purchases in the late 1970s and early 1980s as it began to satisfy many of its military needs through domestic arms production. Although Egypt has increased its arms imports since the signing of the Camp David peace accord with Israel in 1979, they are now ostensibly unrelated to the threat of armed conflict with Israel. Jordan's recent acquisition of advanced military equipment is, by most accounts, geared as much toward fending off an attack from Syria as one from Israel. Only Syria's increased arms imports are principally a result of hostilities between it and Israel, and even in that case, its involvement in the Lebanese civil war and the tremendous military buildup by another neighbor and rival, Iraq, are contributing factors.

The volume of arms transfers to the confrontation states was surpassed during the first half of the 1980s by transfers to the nations of the Persian Gulf. Teheran embarked on an enormous weapons buildup in the late 1970s as the Shah pursued dreams of regional hegemony. Despite a temporary resolution of differences between Iraq and Iran codified in the Algiers Declaration of 1975, Iraq was reluctant to allow Iran to gain a decisive military advantage, and therefore kept pace with Teheran's burgeoning arms imports at every turn. Since 1980 and the outbreak of war between the two Gulf nations, Iran and Iraq have imported massive amounts of weaponry to sustain their war efforts. Iraq has imported considerably larger quantities than Iran, primarily because it has had less trouble finding suppliers.

The bulk of the weapons used in the war have been of Soviet and American design and manufacture. Iran has drawn on the arsenal of American weapons amassed by the Shah during the 1970s. Although the United States formally prohibited transfers to Iran and Iraq at the war's start, weapons of American origin have been transferred to both countries through private international dealers and third countries such as Israel, Taiwan and South Korea. (See box, pp. 172–173.) In recent years, the United States has sold dual civilian/military use helicopters to Baghdad, and has covertly shipped arms to Iran. The Soviet Union, on the other hand, has directly supplied Iraq with arms throughout the war, while Soviet allies such as North Korea, Syria and Libya have shipped Soviet-made weapons to Iran. France also has supplied Iraq with large quantities of arms, and the People's Republic of China has transferred weapons to both sides. The London-based International Institute for Strategic Studies estimates that China alone entered into $1.6 billion worth of arms agreements with Iran in 1986. The Reagan administration in 1987 identified 41 nations other than the United States which had sold weapons, or from which weapons had been shipped, to Iran since the start of the war. U.S. intelligence sources put Iranian arms purchases for the first seven months of 1987 at approximately $1 billion. According to these sources, China led the way with $400 million in sales, followed by North Korea ($250 million), Warsaw Pact nations ($200 million) and Portugal and Spain ($150 million).[2]

The Iran-Iraq war has led the nations of the Gulf Cooperation Council (GCC)—Saudi Arabia, Kuwait, Bahrain, Qatar, the United Arab Emirates and Oman—to increase their arms imports. Iran, angry at the Council's financial support of Iraq, has bombed harbors and other targets in the GCC states and, like Iraq, has attacked oil-bearing ships in the Persian Gulf. According to SIPRI, "since late 1980, all of the six GCC members have purchased major warships or missile-armed fast attack craft, sophisticated jet fighters, helicopters, main battle tanks or other modern armoured vehicles, and a wide range of anti-air, anti-ship and anti-tank missiles."[3] In addition, the smaller nations have looked to Saudi Arabia to protect their security. Saudi Arabia has responded with a massive arms buildup: The Arms Control and Disarmament Agency reports that from 1979 to 1983 its arms imports increased 200 percent, from $1.2 billion to $3.6 billion before stabilizing at the $2.5 billion level over the next two years. Saudi purchases have included a vast air defense system that includes five Boeing Awacs aircraft, a radar network being built under the Department of Defense's Peace Shield project, a variety of anti-aircraft missiles and 72 British-built Tornado fighter aircraft to supplement the Saudi Air Force's 48 McDonnell Douglas F-15s.

Other sources of tension have contributed to the Saudis' arms buildup. Saudi Arabia often has felt apprehensive because it is geographically large but thinly populated and oil-rich. Before the outbreak of the Iran-Iraq war, Saudi Arabia had imported arms partly out of concern over its rocky relations with Iraq, which was considered one of the principal threats to Saudi security. The Saudis also have viewed Syria, South Yemen and the Soviet Union with concern. The Saudi government, in addition, has imported arms to be used to stifle internal opposition or insurgency, both of which the radical Arab states and Iran have encouraged periodically. Although Saudi Arabia has avoided military conflict with Israel, its arms imports also are intended to balance Israeli military power, and to reassure the Arab states and its citizens that it remains at the forefront of the Arab-Israeli confrontation.

Although the Arab-Israeli and the Iranian-Arab confrontations have had the largest effect on arms imports in recent years, other conflicts have played a part. Tensions between Syria and neighboring Jordan and Iraq have promoted arms imports by these countries, and Iraqi threats to annex Kuwait once led Kuwait to upgrade its armed forces. Tensions between Egypt and Libya have also been high at times, and have fueled arms imports. Cairo frequently has accused Tripoli of organizing subversive activities in Egypt, and in 1977 fighting broke out along the Libya-Egypt border. Another major source of friction in the region is trouble between North and South Yemen. Since South Yemen's independence in 1967, forces from North and South Yemen have skirmished at the border and have backed insurgents in the other's territory. In 1979, mounting hostilities between North and South Yemen led President Carter to invoke the special waiver provision in the Arms Export Control Act of 1976, which permits emergency arms transfers without congressional approval, to order an immediate arms shipment to North Yemen. Under Saudi pressure, the shipment was canceled after Arab mediation led to the temporary resolution of the conflict—a move that prompted North Yemen to purchase arms from the Soviet Union.

Episodes of direct confrontation are only one reason for large imports of arms by Middle Eastern nations. The pursuit of regional hegemony was the principal cause of Iran's arms imports under the Shah, and it has been an important factor in the weapon imports of Saudi Arabia, Iraq and Syria as well. An ingredient in some instances has been oil wealth. The dramatic rise in the price of oil in 1973 gave Iran, Iraq, Saudi Arabia and some of the other GCC states the funds to increase their arms imports considerably, as the increased value of these nations' assets heightened the perceived threats to their security. Arms imports by Iran, Iraq and the GCC nations climbed from $1.2 billion in 1973 to $5.7 billion in 1978 (a 194 percent increase above inflation).[4] Nevertheless, without the intense regional conflicts even wealthy nations would not see the need to import arms in large quantities. Although Saudi Arabia was wealthier in the late 1970s than it is in the 1980s, its level of arms imports has more than doubled since 1978 because of the increased instability in the Persian Gulf. On the whole, oil wealth has facilitated arms imports, but regional tensions and conflicts have caused them. Indeed, many of the largest arms-importing nations in the Middle East, including Israel, Egypt, Syria and Jordan, produce comparatively little oil for export and are not otherwise wealthy.

The Arms Market in the Middle East

The Middle East is by far the largest arms-importing region; its nations purchase approximately half of the weapons sold to the Third World.[5] Five Middle East nations ranked among the seven largest importers of major weapons between 1981 and 1985, and they alone accounted for approximately 40 percent of total Third World purchases during this period.[6] Even the smaller nations of the Arabian peninsula, such as North and South Yemen and Kuwait, import a considerable quantity of weapons in relation to their size. By 1982 arms imports had helped supply the Middle Eastern countries with almost as much conventional weaponry as NATO had, and more tanks and tactical aircraft. (See Table 8–1.)[7] These imports include some of the most advanced weapon systems in the world today.

The Middle East's share of the world arms market has risen considerably since the 1960s. According to the Arms Control and Disarmament Agency, the Middle East purchased only 26 percent of the arms sold to developing countries between 1969 and 1972, but the purchases skyrocketed to 42 percent between 1973 and 1976, and then increased to 44 percent for the period 1977 to 1980 and to 52 percent between 1981 and 1984. SIPRI shows a less dramatic increase.

Table 8–1

Weapon Systems Delivered to the Middle East, 1981–85
(in units)

Weapons System	U.S.	Other NATO	U.S.S.R.	Other Warsaw Pact	China
Land Armaments					
Tanks	1,228	375	1,790	860	2,000
Anti-Air Artillery	74	10	340	405	1,310
Field Artillery	1,317	4,825	825	460	645
Armored Personnel Carriers	3,270	1,175	3,210	510	995
Naval Craft					
Major Surface Combatants	0	12	4	0	2
Other Surface Combatants	17	43	17	0	12
Submarines	0	0	2	0	4
Missile Attack Boats	0	19	9	0	6
Aircraft					
Supersonic combat aircraft	208	165	625	25	95
Subsonic combat aircraft	0	40	85	0	0
Other Aircraft	8	40	35	80	0
Helicopters	16	120	340	10	0
Missiles					
Surface-to-air missiles	1,437	695	5,385	5,000	30

Source: U.S. Arms Control and Disarmament Agency.

According to its figures, the Middle East accounted for 42 percent of the Third World's arms market between 1969 and 1973, 54 percent between 1973 and 1976, 43 percent between 1977 and 1980, and 49 percent for the period 1981–1984.[8] Mostly because the Iran-Iraq war shows no sign of ending, the large Middle East share is not likely to decrease significantly in the near future.

Arms transfers to the Persian Gulf region surpassed those to the confrontation states in the late 1970s. By that time Iran and Saudi Arabia accounted for more weapons deliveries than Israel and its neighbors combined. The Iran-Iraq war has led to a further concentration of arms transfers in the Gulf. Iran has had difficulty acquiring arms since the fall of the Shah, however, and has been replaced by Iraq as the leading importer of arms in the Middle East. According to ACDA figures for 1981–85—the most recent years available—the largest Middle Eastern arms importers, in descending order, were Iraq, Saudi Arabia, Syria, Egypt, Iran, Israel and Jordan. SIPRI figures for this period differ considerably from those provided by the ACDA. SIPRI records the leading Middle East arms recipient as Iraq, followed by Egypt, Syria, Saudi Arabia, Israel and Jordan.[9]

The nations of the Middle East acquire military equipment from a diverse array of suppliers. (See Figure 8–1.)[10] Jordan imports approximately 30 percent of its arms from Great Britain, 30 percent from France, 30 percent from the United States and the remaining 10 percent mainly from

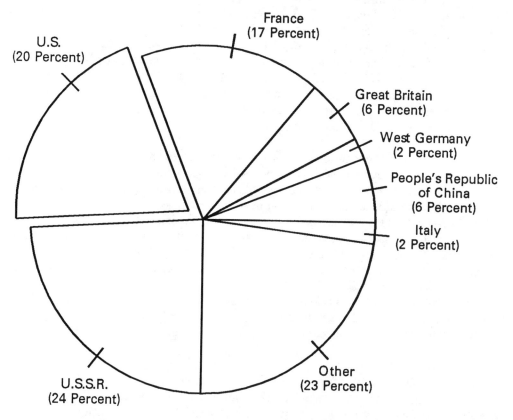

Source: U.S. Arms Control and Disarmament Agency, *World Military Expenditures and Arms Transfers, 1986*

Figure 8–1. Suppliers' Shares of Arms Deliveries to the Middle East 1981–1985

the Soviet Union. Western European nations, in particular France, Great Britain, West Germany and Italy, are currently the leading suppliers to all of the GCC nations except Saudi Arabia. Intense competition among multiple suppliers is a recent development. France accounted for only 6 percent of all arms exports to the Middle East between 1974 and 1978, but from 1981 to 1985 its share rose to 17.6 percent. The People's Republic of China similarly increased its portion of the Middle East arms market on the strength of its burgeoning sales to Iraq and Iran. While China had only $40 million worth of sales to the Middle East between 1974 and 1978, it registered more than $4.3 billion worth of sales between 1981 and 1985. Although Great Britain's share of the market did not increase appreciably during this period, Britain recently concluded an $8 billion sale of Tornado aircraft to Saudi Arabia that will give it a large share of the Middle East arms market through the remainder of the 1980s.

The United States and the Soviet Union nevertheless control more than half of the Middle East arms market. The superpowers have cornered the bulk of the market because of strong ties with their customers in the region, and they have been willing, as they are nowhere else in the Third World, to transfer their most sophisticated equipment. Recent reluctance on the part of Congress to ship arms to the moderate Arab states in the absence of tangible progress toward peace accords with Israel explains in part the shrinking U.S. slice of the market. The superpowers' share is also decreasing because of events beyond their control. Western European suppliers, as the British-Saudi Arabian Tornado sale and French shipments of the Mirage 2000 fighters to the United Arab Emirates illustrate, have become more aggressive in their pursuit of the Middle East market and more willing to transfer top-of-the-line equipment to the region. At the same time, many Middle Eastern nations are trying to extricate themselves from the constraints and stigma wrought by excessively close relations with the superpowers. Saudi Arabia, Egypt and Jordan have sought to reduce their dependence on Washington by diversifying their arms purchases. Similarly, Iraq has sought to reduce Soviet interference in its affairs by decreasing its military dependence on Moscow, and there is evidence that Syria would like to do the same.

Some Middle Eastern nations also have sought to decrease their dependence on the superpowers by developing domestic arms industries. During the 1970s, Israel rapidly built up its defense industry to become more self-sufficient in the production of fighters, tanks, missiles, bombs and small arms. One source estimates that Israel was manufacturing 40 percent of its own weapons by 1980.[11] At the heart of Israel's drive for self-sufficiency rests a desire to minimize its dependence on outside suppliers and to forge an autonomous military-political strategy. In some instances, however, notably the case of the Lavi fighter, Israel's arms production has not reduced its dependence on the United States, because it has continued to rely on the United States for key components and funding.

Israel has been able to gain precious foreign exchange by exporting domestically produced weapons—more than $1.3 billion worth between 1981 and 1985.[12] Its arms exports have been controversial, however, because its customers include pariah regimes such as South Africa and Chile.

Israel's arms sales to South Africa were the subject of heated debate in early 1987 following the release of a congressionally mandated State Department study on violations of the international arms embargo on South Africa. The study stated that Israel has sold "military systems and sub-systems, and provided technical assistance on a regular basis" to the South African government, and that "the Israeli government was fully aware of most or all of the trade." Although many sources had long been aware of Israel's extensive arms sales to South Africa, estimated at $400 to $800 million in 1986, the report represented the first official U.S. government confirmation of the trade.

In an effort to head off any punitive action, the Israeli government announced in March 1987 that it would not renew any existing military contracts with South Africa.[13]

Although Washington has veto power over sales of Israeli weapons that contain American-made components, at times Israel has circumvented these regulations with illegal sales to countries such as Iran. Critics assert that Washington has turned a blind eye to these transgressions or even encouraged them. According to this argument, Israel in effect has served as a proxy for the U.S. administration by selling arms to nations—such as Guatemala and Iran—that the U.S. Congress had prohibited from purchasing American weapons.

Egypt is the only other Middle Eastern country with a significant domestic arms industry. Egypt tried to develop a supersonic fighter in the 1960s, but because it lacked the manufacturing base and technological know-how, it was forced to settle for more modest coproduction ventures. Egypt established a joint domestic arms production venture in 1975 with Saudi Arabia, Qatar and the United Arab Emirates designed to serve Arab states and match Israeli arms production. The organization foundered, however, when the Gulf states terminated their financing in 1979 as part of their rejection of the Camp David accords between Egypt and Israel. Nevertheless, Egyptian arms production rebounded, partly because of new licensing arrangements and joint ventures with foreign companies.[14] Egypt's arms industry also has received a boost from the Iran-Iraq war, as the majority of Egyptian arms sales go to Iraq. Between 1981 and 1985, Egypt exported $650 million in arms.[15]

The Egyptian arms industry will be aided considerably if it goes ahead with plans to assemble, and eventually build, the United States' leading battle tank, the M-1A1 Abrams. Egypt already produces AN/TPS-63 radar and 105mm tank ammunition under license, and it has established a facility to repair and rebuild M60 main battle tanks. Egypt plans to use the M-1 production agreement to foster feeder defense industries, and hopes eventually to export the tanks. The proposed arrangement has met some opposition in Congress, however, because of concern over the potential threat to Israel that the tank poses, and because of skepticism about Egypt's ability to finance and successfully produce the advanced weapon system.

U.S. Arms Sales Policy and Practices: The Middle East

While American concern about stability in the Middle East has risen in recent years and formal U.S. policy toward the region has changed periodically, U.S. objectives have remained constant. American interests call for the military defense of Israel, for the protection of oil fields and the flow of oil to the West and for continued equilibrium in the balance of power with the Soviet Union. Through arms sales to its principal regional allies—Israel, the moderate Arab states and, at one stage, Iran—the United States has hoped to attain these objectives.

American arms sales to the Middle East have increased in direct proportion to concern over regional stability. (See Figure 8–2.) The Soviet invasion of Afghanistan and the fall of the Shah of Iran were the pivotal events that ushered in an era of heightened American apprehension. The occupation of Afghanistan in 1979 made the United States more wary of Soviet intentions in the region because the move placed Soviet troops even closer to the oil fields of the Middle East. The overthrow of the Shah in the same year further destabilized the region and cost the United States one of its principal regional allies. Washington responded by increasing arms transfers to the moderate Arab states in order to strengthen its relationship with them and enhance their defense capabilities.

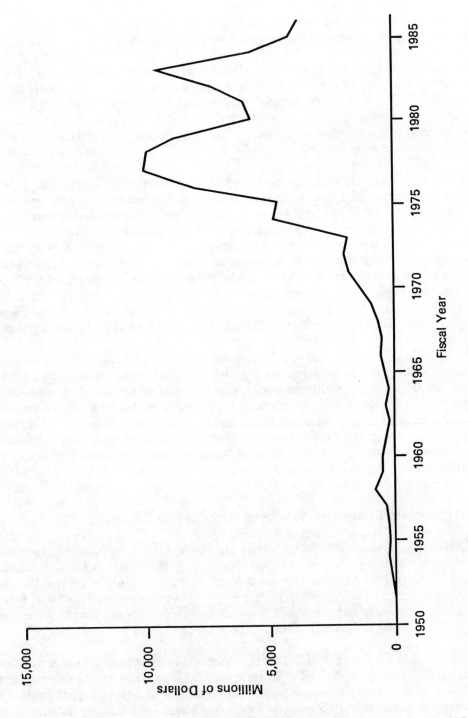

Source: Defense Security Assistance Agency (DSAA), "Fiscal Year Series," 1987

Figure 8–2.   U.S. Military Deliveries to the Middle East
(millions of constant 1986 dollars)

The United States and Israel: Paramount among American objectives in the Middle East is the defense of Israel, which has long occupied a special place within American foreign policy. Israel's preferential position is built in part upon the cultural ties between the influential American Jewish community and the state of Israel. Jewish Americans donate almost $1 billion a year to Israel, principally through the purchase of Israeli bonds and contributions to the United Jewish Appeal.[16] The American Jewish community also has banded together to form one of the most powerful lobbies in Washington. The largest pro-Israel lobbying organization, the American Israel Public Affairs Committee (AIPAC), has a staff of 80 spread out in five cities, a budget of $6 million and 50,000 members nationwide. Massive electoral campaign contributions by pro-Israel PACs—$3.6 million in 1984—help to retain the bloc of more than 50 senators who consistently back Israel in Congress.[17] Private individuals also contribute extensively to political campaigns to ensure congressional support for Israel. One American businessman from California, Michael Goland, spent more than $1 million of his own money in 1984 to help defeat Sen. Charles Percy (R-Ill.), who Goland thought had not been supportive enough of Israel as chairman of the Senate Foreign Relations Committee.

In addition to obtaining economic and military assistance for Israel, the agenda of pro-Israel PACs and individuals includes blocking arms sales to Arab nations. One example of intense pro-Israel lobbying to block an Arab arms sale occurred during 1981 when President Reagan proposed the sale of Awacs surveillance aircraft to Saudi Arabia. Despite extensive administration efforts to appease the pro-Israel community, AIPAC and other pro-Israel groups denounced the sale, prompting 54 senators, including 20 Republicans, to send President Reagan a letter asking him to "refrain from sending [the arms sale] proposal to Congress."[18] The $8.5 billion sale, which included five Awacs aircraft, eight KC-707 tanker refueling aircraft, 101 sets of conformal fuel tanks for Saudi F-15 fighters and 1,177 AIM-9L Sidewinder air-to-air missiles, was upheld on a 52–48 vote, but only after an intense personal lobbying effort by the President prompted eight of the original sponsors of the anti-Awacs resolution to switch their votes. The battle created bitterness on both sides. Reagan complained at one point that Sen. Robert Packwood (R-Ore.) was adamantly opposed to the Awacs sale principally because of his concerns about Republican fund-raising in the Jewish community, while Hyman Bookbinder, Washington representative for the American Jewish Committee, asserted that the administration "probably lost half of the new Jewish support they picked up in 1980."[19]

Compelling factors apart from the American-Israeli lobby also have contributed to the preferred treatment of Israel in U.S. foreign policy. In the first instance, foreign policy makers increasingly have come to view Israel as the most dependable and internally stable U.S. ally in the Middle East. Moreover, because many of the Arab states and organizations in the forefront of the conflict with Israel—including Syria, Iraq, the Palestine Liberation Organization and Egypt (until the mid 1970s)—have close ties with Moscow, American strategists have viewed the confrontation through an East-West lens. Washington has come to perceive military support for Israel as essential not only for the survival of the Jewish nation, but for the containment of Soviet influence in the region.

The special relationship of Israel with the United States has made it the principal recipient of American military and economic assistance. In 1987, it received one-third of U.S. military and economic assistance worldwide, or some $3 billion. Although military assistance to Israel comes in the form of foreign military sales loans, all loans in recent years and about half of Israel's FMS loans since 1973 have been forgiven. The United States also has rushed massive emergency shipments of arms to Israel when deemed necessary; during and after the 1973 war the United States sacrificed the military readiness of its own forces in order to replenish Israel's depleted arsenal.

Despite the special nature of the American-Israeli relationship, differences surface from time to time. In the early 1980s, strains arose because of Israel's invasion of Lebanon and its bombing of an Iraqi nuclear reactor—actions that the United States protested. Israel's use of American weapons in these two military strikes made them particularly controversial. In the case of Lebanon, additional tensions were created by Israel's use of American-made cluster bombs against civilian targets, a practice that the United States had expressly prohibited. The cluster bomb controversy surfaced again in 1986 when Israel was accused of trying to smuggle the technology for manufacturing them out of the United States. Other problems have arisen from attempts by Israel to smuggle nuclear technology, to export American arms illegally and, recently, to spy on the United States.

For the most part, staunch congressional support for Israel and recognition of its unique and tenuous geostrategic situation have left the U.S. administration powerless to take significant punitive measures, such as reducing its aid allotment, against the Jewish nation. While he was Secretary of State, Henry Kissinger once betrayed his exasperation at the paradox of Israel's independent dependence this way: "When I ask [Prime Minister] Rabin to make concessions, he says he can't because Israel is weak. So I give him more arms, and then he says he doesn't need to make concessions because Israel is strong."[20]

Israel's determination to remain independent despite its overwhelming dependence on the United States is illustrated by the case of the Lavi fighter/attack aircraft. Israel embarked on a program to build 300 of the aircraft from the ground up in order to sustain its domestic defense industries and reduce its military dependence on others. The United States, however, paid for 90 percent of the Lavi's $1.5 billion development costs. Washington, concerned in part that the Lavi might compete with American fighters for the international export market, argued that Israel had grossly underestimated the actual cost of the program, and that the acquisition of a comparable aircraft—such as the General Dynamics F-16—would cost much less. As early as May 1986, Secretary of State George Shultz and Secretary of Defense Caspar Weinberger urged Israeli Prime Minister Shimon Peres to cancel the program.[21] Their recommendation was echoed in 1987 by top Israeli officials of the ministries of Defense and Finance, who suggested that Israel purchase 75 to 100 General Dynamics F-16C fighters instead. The Israeli Cabinet finally heeded the recommendations for cancellation, in a close and contentious decision. The United States will help cover the cancellation cost of the Lavi and promised to continue to extend Foreign Military Sales credits to Israel at existing levels.

The close American-Israeli military relationship has frustrated some American policymakers for other reasons as well. To a certain extent, the U.S. support of Israel has alienated moderate Arab states. These moderate Arab states possess most of the world's untapped oil reserves and have already once made the United States feel the effects of an oil embargo. Their geographic location astride the Persian Gulf and the Red Sea also gives them the potential to grant the United States tremendous access to strategic facilities, but they have refrained from doing so because of U.S. support for Israel. Some critics also complain that unquestioning American support has removed pressure on Israel to leave the West Bank or otherwise settle its disputes with the Palestinians, and that this, in turn, has generated instability, terrorism and strong anti-American sentiments throughout the Middle East.

The United States and Iran: For many decades, America's other chief Middle Eastern ally was Iran. The close U.S. relationship with Iran dated back to 1953, when the Central Intelligence

Agency engineered a coup that overthrew Prime Minister Mossadeq—who had angered Washington by nationalizing American oil assets—and reinstated the Shah as leader of Iran. Under the Shah, Iran became a key American ally, and arms transfers to Iran mounted as the United States sought to gain influence in the region and to aid the Shah in his struggles against internal opposition.

The British withdrawal of military forces from the Persian Gulf during the late 1960s increased the importance of Iran to American strategists, who saw Iran as the new guardian of Western interests in the Gulf.[22] The Shah moved into this role willingly, supporting Kurdish insurgents in Soviet-backed Iraq and helping to crush an insurgency in Western-allied Oman. In return for the Shah's assistance, President Nixon and Secretary of State Kissinger offered to sell the Shah virtually any conventional weapon system he wanted.

The Nixon administration's liberal policy on arms transfers to Iran led to a 155 percent real term increase in U.S. arms exports to Iran between 1967 and 1972. (See Figure 8–3.) It was not until 1973, however, when the Arab oil embargo caused the price of oil to skyrocket, that arms transfers to Iran truly accelerated. With its newfound wealth, Iran became the world's leading arms recipient, acquiring almost $2 billion worth of American equipment and services in 1976 alone. During this period Iran ordered 160 F-16 fighters, 80 F-14 fighters, 209 F-4 fighter-bombers, 169 other fighters, 528 helicopters, four missile destroyers and numerous missiles.[23] Iranian arms purchases did not taper off after President Carter assumed office in January 1977. Indeed, the Carter administration's first major arms transfer agreement was the sale of seven highly sophisticated Awacs aircraft to Iran for $1.2 billion—a sale that was voided after the Shah was overthrown in 1979. After the Shah's fall, Carter issued an executive order imposing a U.S. arms embargo against Iran, which the Reagan administration renewed.

Many analysts believe that the Shah's unrestrained weapons-buying served to undermine the Iranian economy and his regime. One problem often cited as an important source of the Shah's downfall was his failure to increase the standard of living of the majority of the Iranian population at the same rate that the country's military expenditure and overall wealth were growing. Because military spending rather than social spending absorbed much of the increased government funds, the gap between rich and poor grew, causing widespread resentment. At the same time, the presence of a great number of Western military or defense industry personnel in Iran also created tensions. The values and mode of behavior of the Western personnel often clashed with traditional Iranian beliefs and customs. As a result, many critics argue, U.S. arms transfer policy toward Iran fed anti-Shah fervor and helped bring about a virulently anti-American government that has worked against U.S. interests in the region.

The large purchases of American arms and the influx of Americans into Iran, however, were only one element of the increased westernization and stratification of Iranian society that occurred under the Shah's rule. Certainly, U.S. arms transfers to Iran contributed to the Shah's difficulties, but it was his internal policies as a whole that were responsible for his overthrow in 1979.

The United States and the moderate Arab states: The other U.S. allies in the region—the moderate Arab states—have not received the same unequivocal support that the United States granted to Israel and to Iran under the Shah. On the one hand, the United States recognizes the strategic value of these nations' assets and staunch anti-Soviet attitude and, therefore, has tried to strengthen its relationship with them. On the other hand, Washington has chosen their avowed enemy, Israel, as its principal Middle Eastern ally and usually has subordinated their desires to those

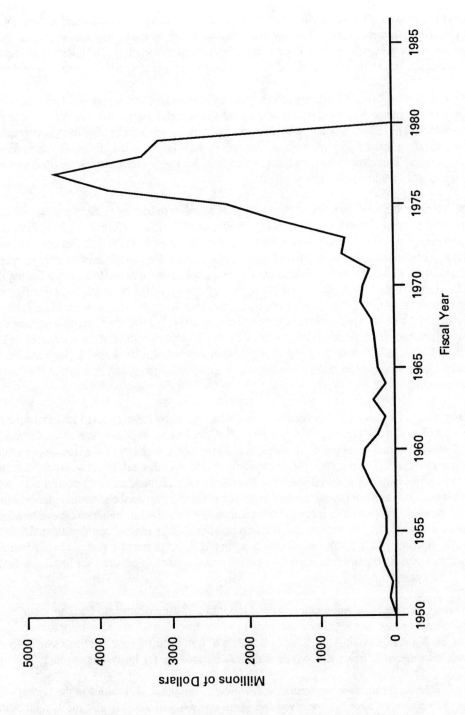

Source   Defense Security Assistance Agency, "Fiscal Year Series," 1986.

Figure 8–3.   U.S. Military Deliveries to Iran
(in millions of constant 1986 dollars)

of Israel. The wavering American policy toward the moderate Arab nations is reflected in the struggles between the executive and legislative branches of government. While successive administrations frequently have proposed arms sales to the moderate Arab nations as strategically wise and diplomatically necessary, Congress often has opposed them on the grounds that they pose a danger to Israel. The inconsistencies in American policy have angered moderate Arabs who have sought equal status with Israel. While the long-term significance of this may be minimal, on a few occasions Washington's refusal to sell certain weapons to the moderate Arab nations has caused breaches in its relationships with those states.

Arms sales to the moderate Arab nations were once less controversial. Throughout the 1950s and 1960s, the U.S. arms transfer programs to Jordan and Saudi Arabia created little dissent. The Eisenhower administration initiated the arms transfer programs to the pro-Western monarchies in these countries because it recognized the importance of maintaining alliances with friendly governments in the Middle East at a time of declining British influence in the region.[24] The arms that were sold to these countries throughout the 1950s and 1960s were not technologically advanced enough to provoke significant protests from supporters of Israel. Arab requests for more sophisticated American weapons that were lodged in the 1970s, though, aroused considerable opposition. Congress firmly opposed Jordan's 1976 attempt to purchase an air defense system. King Hussein of Jordan obtained the American Hawk anti-aircraft missiles he wanted only after he traveled to Moscow to discuss purchasing Soviet weapons instead. In 1979, Hussein returned to the Soviet Union and also discussed the possibility of purchasing tanks from Great Britain before the United States reversed its position and agreed to transfer 100 M60 tanks to Jordan.

Arms sales to Saudi Arabia historically have provoked the most opposition. Saudi purchases of U.S. arms grew in the early 1970s for many of the same reasons that Iranian purchases did. (See Figure 8–4.) The British withdrawal from the Persian Gulf at a time of heightened American interest in the strategic importance of the region increased U.S. willingness to strengthen the defense capabilities of friendly governments there. At the same time, the oil price rise enabled Saudi Arabia to pay for more American weapons. The expansion of arms sales to Saudi Arabia was much more vigorously contested than the growth in sales to Iran. During President Ford's tenure, Congress forced a 60 percent reduction in the number of air-to-ground missiles sold to Saudi Arabia. The Ford administration's decision to sell F-15 fighters to the Saudis was opposed by both Congress and the Carter administration, which inherited the uncompleted sale. President Carter eventually decided that he could not cancel the sale without seriously damaging Saudi-American relations. Nevertheless, he was forced to go to great lengths to obtain congressional approval of the sale, including removing the equipment needed for in-flight refueling, bomb racks and air-to-air missiles from the arms package; balancing the transfer with sales of similar fighters to Israel; and securing Saudi Arabia's promise that it would not base the fighters near Israel.

Congressional opposition to Saudi arms sales has also dogged the Reagan administration. Early in President Reagan's first term, senatorial opponents of a transfer that sent five E-3A Awacs to Saudi Arabia came within three votes of blocking the sale. In 1987, overwhelming congressional opposition forced President Reagan to withdraw a proposed sale of 1,600 Hughes Aircraft Maverick air-to-surface missiles.

The United States and Egypt: Egypt, the other principal U.S. Arab ally in the Middle East, only recently become a recipient of American arms. Following its defeat in the Palestine Wars of 1947–49, Egypt tried to purchase large quantities of military equipment from the United States, but

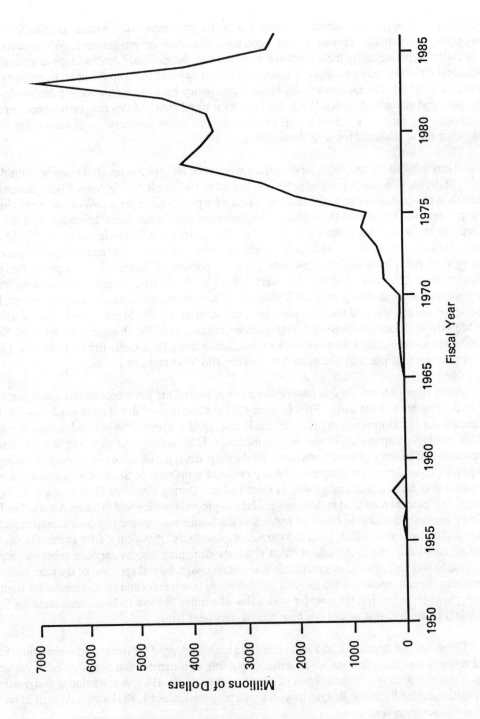

Source   Defense Security Assistance Agency (DSAA), "Fiscal Year Series," 1987.

Figure 8–4. U.S. Military Deliveries to Saudi Arabia
(millions of constant 1986 dollars)

Washington deferred to British concerns for maintaining the existing regional balance of power and fears that Egypt might use the arms to try to gain control of the Suez Canal, and turned down Egypt's requests. When Gamal Abdal Nasser came to power in 1952, the United States was no more receptive to Egyptian requests, a stance that became a factor in Nasser's turn toward the Soviet Union. In 1955 Egypt signed a Treaty of Friendship and Cooperation with Moscow and became the Soviets' premier Third World arms client. Soviet arms and technical support amounted to more than $2.3 billion between 1964 and 1973 alone, and included restocking Egypt's arsenals after its wars with Israel.[25] Many Egyptians, however, resented the Soviet presence and interference in their affairs, and Egyptian President Anwar Sadat, who succeeded Nasser in 1970, became increasingly disappointed with the quality of weapons provided by Moscow. In 1972, Sadat expelled most of the Soviet advisers from Egypt, and four years later he severed nearly all ties with the Soviet Union by abrogating the Treaty of Friendship and Cooperation.

Because of expected opposition in Congress to major arms sales to Egypt and because of its historically hostile relationship with Israel, the United States was slow to step into the void left by the Soviets' departure. Instead, Western European countries became Egypt's main suppliers between 1976 and 1979. Sadat's trip to Jerusalem in 1977, however, cleared the way for the sale of 50 F-5 aircraft to Egypt in 1978, and the signing of the Camp David accord in March 1979 opened the way for greater American arms sales to Cairo. As part of the Camp David agreement, Egypt was granted $1.5 billion in military credits, and over the course of the next six years it purchased more than $6.5 billion worth of American military equipment.

In trying to retain Egypt as a close ally, the United States has sought to strike a precarious balance between Egypt and Israel. (See Figure 8–5.) The result has been enormous aid allotments for Egypt, but even larger ones for Israel. In recent years, Egypt and Israel have consistently accounted for more than half of total U.S. foreign aid; in 1987 Egypt received $2.3 billion and Israel $3.0 billion. Since 1979, Egypt has received $8 billion in loans to purchase military equipment through the Foreign Military Sales program, of which $3.5 billion worth were converted into outright grants. Israel received a total of $13.5 billion in FMS loans in this period, of which repayment of $6.8 billion was forgiven.[26] While Egypt has obtained sophisticated American weapon systems, it has not done so as easily as Israel because of lingering congressional concern that these weapons might one day be used against the Jewish nation. In 1980, for example, the U.S. administration discouraged Egypt from asking for the McDonnell Douglas F-15 at the same time it was acquiring the General Dynamics F-16 for fear that it might have some difficulty in pushing the sale through Congress.

U.S. arms transfer policy to the Middle East in the 1980s: The United States has increased its arms shipments to the moderate Arab nations considerably in the 1980s—a change that has been prompted by several events. During the last years of the Carter administration, the perceived danger to Persian Gulf security rose precipitously because of the Soviet invasion of Afghanistan, the coming to power of an Islamic fundamentalist, anti-Western regime in Iran and the onset of the Iran-Iraq war with its potential and actual spillover into the Peninsular states. The American response to the increased danger to Western interests has been two-pronged. First, the United States moved to improve its ability to intervene militarily in the region by creating the the Central Command (formerly the Rapid Deployment Force). At the same time, Washington moved to enhance its allies' abilities to respond to military threats by increasing its arms transfers to the region. The Reagan administration's ascent to power reinforced this trend because it proved to be more willing than its predecessor to sell high quality weapons to friendly countries—including the moderate Arab states.

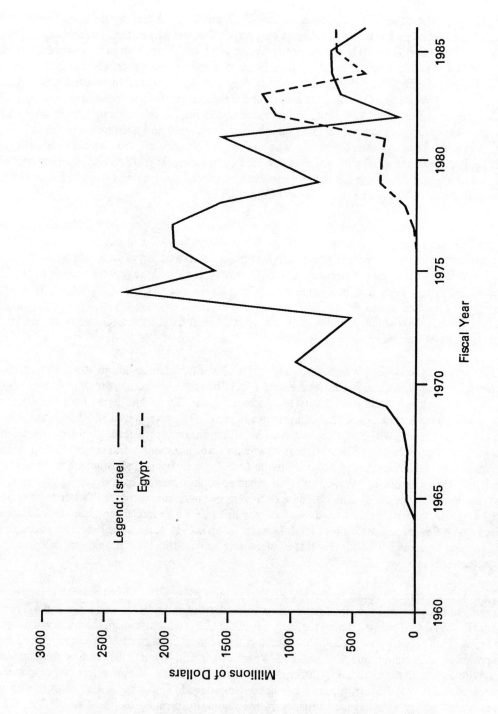

Source: Defense Security Assistance Agency, "Fiscal Year Series," 1987.

Figure 8–5.   U.S. Military Deliveries to Israel and Egypt
(millions of constant 1986 dollars)

Thus, the United States signed new arms agreements with North Yemen and Oman, and made major arms sales to the United Arab Emirates and Bahrain.

The bulk of the American effort to upgrade security in the region, however, was made via Egypt and Saudi Arabia, both of which received more top-of-the-line weapons systems than ever before. Between 1980 and 1986, the United States delivered more than $4.1 billion worth of military equipment to Egypt and $14.6 billion worth to Saudi Arabia. Saudi Arabia's purchases during this period included five Boeing E-3A Awacs aircraft and the enormous Peace Shield program, which together will constitute an air defense system equivalent in its capabilities to that of NATO. The Peace Shield system, which consists of a number of ground-based radar and command centers to detect intruders and coordinate defenses against them, alone will cost an estimated $1.2 billion.

Despite incentives for the United States to solidify its ties with the moderate Arab states and bolster their defense capabilities, the Reagan administration has encountered difficulties in persuading Congress to agree to expanded arms sales. Of the two principal Arab clients in the region, Saudi Arabia has had more problems than Egypt, because it has not entered into a peace accord with Israel and because it purchased more advanced weapon systems. The 1981 Awacs sale to Saudi Arabia was voted down by the House, 301–111, before the Senate upheld it on a 52–48 vote. In 1985, an F-15 sale to Saudi Arabia was scuttled altogether when it became clear that obtaining congressional approval would be extremely difficult even though the Saudis had purchased F-15s during the Carter administration. The Reagan administration therefore gave the Saudis the go-ahead to purchase Tornado aircraft from Britain instead. (See box, p. 21.) Another proposed Saudi arms deal was rebuffed in May 1986, when both houses of Congress voted against a $354 million missile sale. President Reagon vetoed the resolution rejecting the transfer and managed to gain approval the second time around by removing 600 mobile ground-to-air Stinger missiles and 200 launchers from the package, and by lobbying intensively. Congressional qualms forced the administration in June 1987 to withdraw a proposed $360 million package destined for Saudi Arabia that included 1,600 Maverick air-to-ground anti-tank missiles. A proposed sale of $2 billion worth of air defense-related arms to another moderate Arab country, Jordan, also was stymied by Congress. This sale, which had been promised to Jordan in return for its help in furthering the Palestinian peace process, was postponed indefinitely in February 1986.

If nothing else, Congress's mood forced the president to proceed with arms sales to the moderate Arab nations with great care. The Reagan administration in 1987 signaled its desire to conclude $1 billion worth of agreements with the Saudis. It would like to resubmit for Congress's approval the 1,600 Mavericks it withdrew earlier in the year, as well as electronic equipment for upgrading the Saudi fleet of McDonnell Douglas F-15 fighter aircraft, computers and gunbarrels for modernizing M60 main battle tanks, Bradley Infantry Fighting Vehicles, artillery ammunition carriers and between 12 and 14 F-15s that the administration says would be stored in the United States and turned over to the Saudi air force only as they are needed to replace existing Saudi F-15s that might be lost to attrition in the near term. The President embarked on a cautious and deliberate course of consultations with congressional leaders, though, before he took formal action.

The foreign policy implications of these rebuffs are difficult to assess. Jordan's recent overtures to Syria may be related to declining American influence in Jordan, and Saudi Arabia's recent diversification of its arms purchases may mean that the United States will have even less leverage over Saudi foreign policy in the future. Nevertheless, these nations still lie firmly within the Western camp and are likely to remain so as long as their current leaders are in power.

Reagan Weapons Export Practices in Crisis: The Iran-Contra Connection

The Reagan administration's Middle East foreign and arms export policies made front page headlines late in 1986 when it was revealed that the United States had secretly supplied the government of Iran with weapons. The revelations created a major crisis for the Reagan administration at home and abroad, and has revived the enduring debate over the efficacy of arms sales as an instrument of foreign policy. News of these transactions first surfaced in early November 1986 when a pro-Syrian Lebanese newspaper published a preliminary account of the dealings. President Reagan, amid growing speculation, on Nov. 12, 1986, admitted to having initiated the covert arms transfers. Subsequent Justice Department investigations led Reagan to announce several days later that, without his knowledge, profits from the sale had been transferred to the contras, the Nicaraguan rebels fighting the Sandinista government.

Reports regarding the U.S. administration's motives for the arms transfers conflict. President Reagan declared that the overriding reason for supplying arms to Iran was to establish a relationship with and strengthen the position of moderates in Teheran. Many analysts, members of Congress and the Israeli government disputed this claim, contending that the administration initiated the arms transfers principally in order to free American hostages held by pro-Iranian militias in Lebanon.

By all accounts, Israel played a crucial role in the American arms transfers to Iran, although the precise nature of its involvement remains murky. Israel's own arms shipments to Iran continued almost uninterrupted after the fall of the Shah. Reports conflicted, however, as to whether these shipments were conducted with American approval, and whether they involved American-made equipment or strictly Israeli-manufactured items. One source maintained that in 1981, then-Secretary of State Alexander Haig gave permission for Israel to ship American fighter aircraft tires and spare parts to Iran—an approval he withdrew after the first shipment.[27] Some press sources indicated that Israel had sold American-manufactured military equipment to Iran in an attempt to establish contact with anti-Khomeni factions within the Iranian military establishment in 1981 and 1982 but stopped at the request of Secretary of State Shultz. Private Israeli arms dealers were reported to have continued arms sales to Iran, albeit of Israeli-made equipment only, after Shultz's request had been honored.[28] Israeli sources, however, said that before 1985 their shipments did not involve American equipment.[29] Israeli officials maintained that Washington had been notified of the arms transfers, which were conducted covertly because the United States had called publicly on its friends and allies to embargo all arms transfers to Iran.

Sources agree that any reluctance on Washington's part to approve arms transfers to Iran began to wane during the summer and fall of 1985. Israeli officials, notably David Kimche, then the director general of Israel's Foreign Ministry, met with top administration officials frequently during this period, and counseled that moderate elements in Iran were ready to establish contact with the United States and that these Iranians believed that the United States could best signal its interest in renewed contact by releasing weapons that were purchased by the Shah but never delivered to Iran. Kimche reportedly also suggested that Israel could serve as a conduit through which weapons and military equipment could be funneled to the moderate Iranians, and offered to supply Iran with military equipment out of the Israeli arsenal on the condition that it be replenished by the United States.

According to Robert McFarlane, then the U.S. National Security Adviser, the President instructed him in August 1985 to tell the Israelis that Washington would "condone" any Israeli shipments to Iran and would replace the transferred equipment. Other U.S. government officials, however, maintained that McFarlane told Kimche that although the United States could not give its formal approval to any arms transfers to Iran, it would replenish Israeli supplies if Israel made such shipments. These officials later claimed that Kimche misconstrued McFarlane's statements as formal American authorization to proceed. In any case, Israel shortly thereafter sent two planeloads of American military equipment to Iran—including TOW anti-tank missiles and spare parts for Hawk anti-aircraft missile batteries—which coincided with the release of one American hostage. Another shipment made in November 1986 was reported to have angered the Iranians. Instead of sending parts for the Improved-Hawk (or I-Hawk) system, Israel sent equipment for an older, less sophisticated version of the anti-aircraft system which the Iranians refused to accept. Independent sources estimated that the arms sold by the Israelis during late 1985 and early 1986 were worth between $150 and $250 million, but Israeli officials close to the transactions said they were only worth between $25 and $30 million.

An interlude followed these transfers, during which administration officials vigorously debated the Iranian issue while further exploring the possibility of establishing contacts with Iran. Various government sources said that the United States decided to assume direct control of the operation early in 1986, and that the President formalized this decision in an executive "finding" in mid-January. The first shipment of American arms directly from U.S. supplies occurred in February 1986. It reportedly involved 500 TOW missiles that were routed through Israel and was said to have been prompted in part by the ill feelings created by Israel's shipment of obsolete Hawk parts three months earlier. Although McFarlane had resigned in December 1985, he continued to be a key player in the incipient arms relationship, and on May 28, 1986, he traveled to Iran in a transport aircraft laden with I-Hawk replacement parts to open a political dialogue. McFarlane reportedly believed that his trip would result in the release of all of the American hostages. No hostages were released immediately, however, and McFarlane returned expressing little hope of improvement of the situation in Iran. Nevertheless, the United States made two more arms shipments to Iran in August and October 1986, bringing the total number of weapons exported by the United States to Iran to 2,008 TOW anti-tank missiles and an undisclosed number of parts for 235 Hawk anti-aircraft batteries. Shortly after McFarlane's return from Iran a second hostage was freed, and a third was released in early November after the final arms shipment.

The contra connection: The profits from the arms sales to Iran were transferred to the contras through a complex network of intermediaries. The four U.S. shipments, which administration officials valued at $12 million, were handled by middlemen who helped finance the transaction and who reportedly included private Saudi arms dealer and billionaire Adnan Khashoggi. The weapons were sold at an inflated price to Iranians representing Ayatollah Khomeini's government. After the various intermediaries received their fees, between $10 and $30 million in profits from the sales found their way into a CIA-arranged Swiss bank account to which the contras had access. The Reagan administration claimed that Israeli representatives ultimately received the profits from the sales that they deposited into the Swiss bank account. The Israeli government denied this, however, contending that the Iranians deposited the money into the account directly. In any event, the profits from the Iranian arms sales were then mixed with $500 million in funds contributed to the Afghan rebels by the United States and Saudi Arabia—a fact that led to further criticism of the Central Intelligence Agency, which managed the account.[30] Press reports indicated that monies for "humanitarian" contra aid that were solicited by the State Department from the government of the oil rich nation of Brunei were also deposited in the account.

Reaction to the covert transfer and diversion of funds: Disclosure of the Iranian arms transfers and the diversion of funds to the contras presented President Reagan with the first major crisis of his tenure and led to a barrage of criticism from those concerned with the domestic and foreign policy implications of his administration's actions. One major concern was that the arms transfers undermined the official U.S. policy of not negotiating with terrorists—a policy the vast majority of Congress supports. Then-Speaker of the House Thomas P. O'Neill Jr. (D-Mass.) complained, "You let a half-dozen (hostages) out today because you send 5,000 tons of replacement arms to them, then the next time they need replacements all they have to do is swoop in and grab half a dozen more Americans."[31] The arms transfers also undermined U.S. credibility with its allies, whom Washington had pressured to halt all arms sales to Iran. In the spring of 1983, the United States launched Operation Staunch, a program designed to stem if not stop the flow of weapons into Iran from international arms suppliers. Officials close to the effort indicated that the initiative was "moderately successful," and said that the United States was able to persuade Argentina, Italy, Portugal, South Korea and Spain to cancel planned exports to Iran but failed to halt certain sales by Great Britain, Israel, Switzerland and West Germany.[32]

Much of the congressional criticism of the Iranian arms transfers and the diversion of funds to the contras centered around the legality of concealing the dealings from Congress. Leaders of both parties expressed concern that the President violated at least the spirit if not the letter of the law. Senate Foreign Relations Committee Chairman Richard G. Lugar (R-Ind.) said he suspected that "the President does not understand the law on informing Congress on these things."[33] The administration, however, claimed that the President exercised his right to defer telling Congress about the transfers. Many members of Congress also believed that Executive Branch involvement in the diversion of monies to the contras of Nicaragua might have illegally circumvented congressional limits on the levels of and rules governing U.S. funding of the insurgents. Moreover, the term "diversion" was used because, by law, funds earned from covert CIA operations must be deposited in the U.S. Treasury.

Congressional response to the unearthing of the covert transfers of weapons and monies was swift. Within a matter of weeks, five committees initiated investigations into the administration's actions. The Senate Select Committee on Intelligence, the House Permanent Select Committee on Intelligence and the House Foreign Affairs Committee all convened and held hearings even though Congress was in recess. Both chambers created their own special select committees patterned after the congressional committees that investigated the Watergate affair. The Justice Department also launched a full criminal investigation and appointed an independent counsel to examine allegations of misconduct by administration officials.

The investigating bodies were to determine whether any one of a series of laws that involve executive-legislative consultations was broken by the covert shipment of arms to Iran and funds to the Nicaraguan contras. These laws included: legislation passed in 1974 and amended in 1980 and 1985 that governs congressional notification of covert operations including covert arms shipments; provisions of the Arms Export Control Act, passed in 1968 and amended many times since then; the Export Administration Act, which was enacted in 1979 and strengthened in the summer of 1986, and which originally established the requirement for the Executive Branch to report exports to nations judged by the United States to "have repeatedly provided support for acts of international terrorism" and later banned outright the export of military equipment to such states; and an Executive Order signed by President Carter that prohibited all military exports to Iran.[34]

Although numerous laws pertain to the Reagan administration's Iran-contra dealings, the legal issues were clouded because the laws contain loopholes and other provisions that circumscribe their applicability. The law that on the face of it was perhaps the most clearly violated is the provision of the Arms Export Control Act of 1968 that required the President to report to Congress on a quarterly basis every "letter of offer" to sell major military equipment valued at $1 million or more. Congressional experts cautioned, however, that arms transfer law in particular "is so Byzantine that it could take months" to sort out legal answers.[35] Section 501 of the 1947 National Security Act also would seem to apply since it requires that the President tell the House and Senate intelligence committees "in a timely fashion" about covert operations by the CIA and other intelligence agencies.[36] However, a possible loophole in this law is the preamble, which states that the requirements were imposed "to the extent consistent with all applicable authorities and duties, including those conferred by the Constitution upon the executive and legislative branches of the government."[37] Some claimed that the president can invoke this clause and justify not informing Congress of the covert arms sales on the grounds that such actions were necessary in order for him to fulfill his duties as the nation's commander-in-chief.

Other laws pertaining to the case may also contain loopholes. Reagan's secret executive finding of January 1986 that reportedly authorized the shipment of military equipment from government stock may create an exception to the Executive Order promulgated by his predecessor in 1979. The quantity and type of arms shipped to Iran may not be significant enough to violate the Export Administration Act of 1979 and the fiscal 1987 intelligence authorization law. Although violation of the law seems more clear cut in the diversion of funds to the contras, administration officials contend that the diversion took place without the knowledge of President Reagan and other top officials. On this issue the Justice Department took a stronger stand, indicating that it would proceed with prosecution if it decided laws were, in fact, violated.

Regardless of the legal implications for the administration, disclosure of the covert funneling of monies to the contras seemed certain to make it more difficult for the Reagan administration to obtain military assistance for the contras in the future. The Iran-contra episode also added fuel to the push within Congress and among the wider public to strengthen the laws that govern executive-congressional consultation and legislative oversight over U.S. arms export policy and practice.

U.S. Arms Sales Policy to the Middle East: After the Crisis

News of the arms transfers damaged American foreign policy in the Middle East. Many of the moderate Arab allies—particularly Egypt and Jordan—harshly criticized the arms sales. Jordan's King Hussein called the Reagan administration's actions "an insult to all Arabs," and Egypt's Hosni Mubarak publicly warned the United States "to do something so as not to lose its credibility in the Arab world because of such an act."[38] The moderate Arabs' fear is that an Iranian victory in the seven year old war might destabilize the moderate Arab states in the region. Although the military value of the weapons transferred may or may not be significant, analysts say their symbolic value is considerable. Analysts say that, by giving the impression that it expects or would condone an Iranian victory, the United States supplied a "new impetus" to forces seeking the overthrow of Iraqi President Saddam Hussein and indirectly encouraged other Western countries to sell arms to Iran.[39] Egypt and Jordan were also dismayed by what they perceived to be inconsistency in U.S. arms export policy and practice toward the region. The Jordanians, whose 1986 request for an American arms package that included Hawk anti-aircraft missiles had been turned down, were reported to be bitter that Hawk replacement parts were sent to Iran. Similarly, the Egyptians, who were in the midst of

Preventing Illegal Arms Transfers Becomes a Top Priority. . . . . . .

Preventing the illegal transfer of military equipment and related technologies has become a top priority among American foreign policy and military leaders. Illegal transactions are principally the result of U.S. inability to enforce the "end-use" provision of arms sales, which requires that the equipment not be transferred to any country other than the one specified without the permission of the U.S. government. The recipient sometimes ignores the end-use regulation. Israel, for example, has admitted transferring American military equipment to Iran in order to bolster it in the continuing war with Iraq. Preventing this type of illegal arms transaction is difficult even when the United States discovers the transgression. In most cases, the United States generally is limited to admonishing the offending party and invoking threats in order to prevent future illegal transfers; its only other recourse is to cut off arms sales to the offending country.

Perhaps more common are the illegal sales arranged by private arms dealers. In some cases, dealers use fraudulent documents to obtain arms from manufacturers purportedly for transfer to a friendly country, whereupon the weapons are immediately shipped to a third country. Private dealers also obtain arms through theft rings, and U.S. military officials report that the theft of military equipment is now commonplace. Poor record-keeping, according to General Accounting Office audits, prevents the armed forces from even recognizing that the equipment was stolen. In 1984, soldiers stationed in Europe who were offered an amnesty in exchange for returning pilfered equipment handed over approximately 200 tons of ammunition. Because of the overwhelming response to this program, domestic supply centers have offered similar amnesty programs. Nonetheless, the majority of arms that are illegally transferred by private dealers are initially obtained through legal methods. Usually, individuals and embargoed governments will use fronts to purchase the arms in the United States, purportedly for domestic use, and then will smuggle the equipment out of the country. Illegal arms transfers using these three methods generally involve less sophisticated weapons, weapon parts and components, or dual civilian/military use equipment, which is less strictly regulated. There are no diplomatic impediments to preventing these types of illegal arms transfers, and the increasingly sophisticated techniques used by arms dealers as well as the relatively loose supervision of many types of arms sales have enabled illegal arms transfers to flourish.

A recent prominent illegal arms transfer involves the sale of two Lockheed L100-30 Hercules transport planes—the commercial version of the military C-130 aircraft—with spare parts to the Libyan government in 1985 for $57.4 million. The aircraft were part of a planned package worth $160 million, which was to include two additional planes as well as kits to convert the aircraft into tanker aircraft for in-flight refueling. American businessmen used several small firms in California to purchase the planes and had Lockheed fly them to the West African country of Benin, where the Libyans collected them. Libya, on its part, had set up two dummy firms in West Germany to coordinate the purchases. Because these aircraft have civilian as well as military applications, the sale was not closely regulated by the U.S. government, nor was Lockheed required to investigate into the

. . . . . .But Cracking Down on Private Dealers Has Proved Difficult

backgrounds of the purchasers. This was not the first time an L-100 aircraft has been diverted to Libya, while the stricter regulations governing the sale of the similar C-130 have prevented it from ever being transferred illegally to any country. The obvious military value, however, is illustrated by the uproar the 1985 sale caused in Washington. Lockheed says it was unaware that the aircraft might be illegally diverted, pointing out that the company "complied with all U.S. government regulations in the original sale of the aircraft," an assertion the Justice Department does not dispute.

The vast majority of recent illegal transfers of American military equipment have been to Iran. Since the fall of the Shah and the outbreak of the Iran-Iraq war, the principal arms-manufacturing countries have embargoed arms sales to Teheran for the most part, forcing Iran to purchase weapons on the black market, through independent middlemen or third countries. Iran has sought American military equipment in particular, because it has needed spare parts for the many American weapon systems it bought during the Shah's reign, and because most Iranians were trained to use American weapons and would require additional training to learn how to use equipment from other countries. U.S. authorities in 1985 broke up a ring of at least eight people who have since pleaded guilty to charges of having stolen $7 million worth of F-14 fighter parts from the Navy and of having smuggled roughly half of them to Iran between 1981 and 1985. Also in 1986, the United States brought charges against 17 people—including a former Israeli general—involved in five conspiracies to sell Iran more than $2 billion worth of American arms illegally.

The resort to illegal methods of obtaining American equipment has often forced Teheran to pay exorbitant prices for the goods it is able to acquire. In some instances, Iran itself has been defrauded by international arms dealers. Many experts believe that the recent $2 billion-plus attempted sale of McDonnell Douglas A-4 and F-4 and Northrop F-5 fighters along with Lockheed C-130 transports, Hughes TOW, Raytheon Sparrow and Hawk and Ford Aerospace Chaparral missiles was actually an elaborate hoax. Some international arms dealers say that a transaction of such magnitude is beyond the capabilities of even the most skillful and well-connected arms merchants.

The November 1986 disclosure of the U.S. administration's covert arms transfers to Iran might well put a damper on its attempts to stop the flow of arms to Iran. Several of the defendants in arms smuggling cases have claimed that they were operating with the tacit approval of the U.S. government, and others maintain that they expected arms transfers to Iran to be legalized at any moment. This revelation might also make it more difficult for the United States to stop third-country transfers. State Department officials intimate that news of the covert Iranian operations has left the department unsure of how to persuade U.S. allies to subscribe to Operation Staunch, an initiative that was launched in 1983 and that was designed to dissuade those nations aligned with the U.S. from supplying weapons to Iran.

an economic crisis, were said to be angry over Washington's willingness to make exceptions and deal with Iran while resisting Cairo's pleas for relaxed interest rates, payment schedules and penalty fees associated with Egypt's outstanding $4.5 billion worth of U.S. military sales loans.

Saudi Arabia, on the other hand, was conspicuously silent, which led some analysts to question Saudi involvement in the arms transfers via Adnan Khashoggi. Although Saudi Arabia ostensibly would be one of the states most threatened by an Iranian victory in the war, analysts contended that traditional Saudi foreign policy, which has sought to minimize risks by preparing for all possible outcomes, might lead Riyadh to endorse arms sales to Iran. By gaining a diplomatic foothold in Teheran through arms sales, the Saudis might protect themselves from future problems should Iran emerge victorious in the war. While refusing to condemn the arms transfers, Saudi Arabia strongly denied that Khashoggi in any way represented the Saudi government. If Saudi Arabia did prove to be involved, however, analysts claim the psychological blow to Iraq would be devastating.[40]

The Reagan administration made a number of efforts to regain the confidence of the moderate Arab nations. The most prominent effort involved its decision to reflag Kuwaiti oil tankers as American ships, and to deploy the U.S. Navy to the Persian Gulf to protect them. The administration took this step both to bolster its own image in the region and to counter what it viewed as expanding Soviet influence in Kuwait. The Soviets had signed an agreement with Kuwait to escort three Kuwaiti tankers through the Persian Gulf with Soviet warships, and reportedly were prepared to escort additional ships if the United States declined to perform the task. The administration's decision was roundly criticized by both Democratic and Republican members of Congress. Critics feared that in reflagging the tankers the United States would be perceived to be taking sides in the Gulf war and would risk military confrontation with Iran. The fear was intensified when Iran acquired advanced Chinese Silkworm anti-ship missiles, and when an Iraqi aircraft attacked an American warship and killed 37 sailors.

The reflagging policy was well received by the moderate Arab nations. Several of them responded by granting the United States access to their military facilities, treatment that previously they had been unwilling to extend. Kuwait began allowing regular port visits by U.S escort warships, and Bahrain expanded one of its harbor facilities to accommodate additional American warships, while the United Arab Emirates granted overflight rights to American aircraft for the first time. U.S. military officials hoped that these temporary arrangements would become permanent and that one of the Gulf nations might go so far as to grant the United States a site for the headquarters of the U.S. Central Command.

Table 8–2

Major Conflicts and Arms Transfers in the Middle East

Participants*	Dates of conflict	Principal arms suppliers	Type of conflict
Israel vs. Egypt, Syria and Jordan (Iraq)	1967 (border fighting in 1969 and 1970)	US, France USSR, US, Iraq	inter-state war
Israel vs. Egypt and Syria	1973	US USSR	inter-state war
Iran vs. Iraq	1980–present	N. Korea, Syria, Libya, Israel, PRC USSR, France, PRC	inter-state war
Iranian government vs. Partisan, leftist and separatist rebels	1979–present	N. Korea, Syria, Libya, Israel, PRC Iraq	insurgency
Iranian government vs. Islamic fundamentalist and leftist forces	1978–1979	US, Britain, W. Germany Iraq, Syria, USSR	revolution
Iraqi government vs. Separatist and sectarian rebels	1958–70, 1974–75, 1979–present	USSR Iran, Syria	insurgency
Omani government (Iran) vs. Leftist rebels (S. Yemen)	1962–75	Saudi Arabia, Britain, Iran South Yemen, USSR, PRC	insurgency
Jordanian government vs. the PLO (Syria)	1970	US, Britain USSR, Arab states, PRC	civil war
North Yemenese Monarchist forces vs. North Yemenese Republican forces and Egypt	1962–70	Britain, Saudi Arabia Egypt, USSR	civil war

Participants*	Dates of conflict	Principal arms suppliers	Type of conflict
North Yemen vs. South Yemen	1970–80	Saudi Arabia, US, USSR USSR, East Europe	border fighting
Syrian government vs. Sunni Moslem rebels	1976–present	USSR Jordan	insurgency
Israel vs. Palestinian guerrillas	1948–present	US, France, Britain USSR, Arab states, PRC	insurgency
Israel vs. Lebanese Moslem forces	1982–present	US Arab nations, Iran	guerrilla war against occupier
Syria vs. Lebanese forces and the PLO	1975–present	USSR, France	guerrilla war against occupier
Lebanese sectarian and partisan conflict (PLO, Israel, Syria)	1975–present	PLO, Israel, Iran, US, France, Arab states	civil war

*   Parentheses indicate the participation of additional troops in the conflicts.

Sources: Center for Defense Information; Ruth Leger Sivard, *World Military and Social Expenditures 1985*; ACDA, *World Military Expenditures and Arms Transfers*.

Footnotes

1. U.S. Department of State, Arms Control and Disarmament Agency (ACDA), *World Military Expenditures and Arms Transfers* 1975 edition (Washington: ACDA, 1975).
2. "List of 41 Nations with Iran Sales," *The New York Times*, April 11, 1987, p. 2; "1987 Arms Buying by Iran is Put at $1 Billion," *Baltimore Sun*, Aug. 8, 1987, p. 4 (based on an Associated Press story).
3. Stockholm International Peace Research Institute (SIPRI), *World Armaments and Disarmament Yearbook 1984* (Philadelphia: Taylor & Francis, 1984), p. 200.
4. ACDA, *op. cit.* 1985 edition, pp. 94–130.
5. ACDA, *op. cit.* 1986 edition, pp. 143–146, and SIPRI, *op. cit.* 1986 edition, p. 325.
6. ACDA, *op. cit.* 1986 edition, pp. 143–146 and SIPRI, *op. cit.* 1986 edition, pp. 354–55.
7. Leslie Gelb, *The New York Times*, Jan. 24, 1982, cited in Michael Klare, *American Arms Supermarket* (Austin, Texas: University of Texas Press, 1984), p. 130.
8. ACDA, *op. cit.* 1976 and 1985 editions, and SIPRI *op. cit.* 1986 edition, pp. 354–55.
9. ACDA, *op. cit.* 1986 edition, pp. 143–146 and SIPRI, *op. cit.* 1986 edition, p. 334.
10. All figures that appear in the following paragraphs are from ACDA, *op. cit.* 1986 edition, pp. 143–146.
11. Andrew Pierre, *The Global Politics of Arms Sales* (Princeton, N.J.: Princeton University Press, 1982), p. 161.
12. ACDA, *op. cit.* 1986 edition, p. 121.
13. U.S. Department of State, *Report to Congress Pursuant to Section 508 of the Comprehensive Anti–Apartheid Act of 1986: Compliance with the U.N. Arms Embargo* (Washington, D.C.: U.S. Department of State, April 1, 1987); "Congress Gets Report on Israeli Military Aid to South Africa," *The New York Times*, April 3, 1987, p. 3; "Israel Pledges to Reduce Military Ties to South Africa," *The Washington Post*, March 20, 1987, p. 1; and Brzoska, Michael, *Shades of Grey: Ten Years of South African Arms Procurement in the Shadow of the Mandatory Arms Embargo* (Hamburg, FRG: University of Hamburg, Centre for the Study of Wars, Armaments and Development, 1987).
14. Jim Paul, "The Egyptian Arms Industry," *Merip Reports*, February 1983, pp. 26–28.
15. ACDA, *op. cit.*, p. 115.
16. *The Washington Post*, Aug. 8, 1986, p. 1.
17. *The Washington Post*, Oct. 5, 1986, p. 12.
18. *Congressional Quarterly Almanac 1981* (Washington: Congressional Quarterly Inc., 1982), p. 131.
19. *Ibid.*, p. 135.
20. Chris Smith, "Arms for the Middle East: Open Season for the Superpowers," *The Middle East*, September 1982, p. 18.
21. *Aerospace Daily*, June 11, 1986, p. 403.
22. Pierre, *op. cit.*, p. 145.
23. U.S. Senate, Committee on Foreign Relations, *Arms Transfer Policy*, (Washington: U.S. Government Printing Office, July 1977).
24. Pierre, *op. cit.*, p. 173.
25. ACDA, *op. cit.* 1975 edition, p. 70.
26. U.S. Department of Defense, Defense Security Assistance Agency, *Foreign Military Sales, Foreign Military Construction Sales and Military Assistance Facts 1985*, p. 24–25.
27. *The Washington Post*, Nov. 29, 1986, p. A9.
28. *The Wall Street Journal*, Dec. 3, 1986.
29. *The Washington Post*, Nov. 24, 1986.
30. *The Washington Post*, Dec. 4, 1986, p. A42.
31. *Congressional Quarterly Weekly Report*, Nov. 15, 1986, p. 2884.
32. *The Washington Post*, Dec. 10, 1986, p. A22.
33. *Congressional Quarterly Weekly Report*, Nov. 22, 1986, p. 2929.
34. *Congressional Quarterly Weekly Report*, Nov. 22, 1986, pp. 2930–2931.
35. *Ibid.*, p. 2931.
36. *Ibid.*, p. 2929.

37. *Ibid.*, p. 2930.
38. *The Washington Post*, Nov. 23, 1986, p. A17; *The Washington Post*, Nov. 24, 1986, p. A1.
39. *The Washington Post*, Dec. 5, 1986, p. A23.
40. *Ibid.*

Chapter 9
U.S. Arms Exports and Asia

Conflicts in Asia

The large quantity of weapons imported by the nations of Asia* results primarily from the many inter-state and intra-state conflicts that have erupted in the region. Territorial disputes, hegemonic desires and ideological differences have contributed to the outbreak of wars. Many Asian nations must also contend with deep political, ethnic and cultural divisions within their own borders, which—along with, in some cases, poverty and repressive internal policies—have given birth to domestic insurgency. (See Table 9-2 for a chart of recent conflicts in Asia.)

Intense Soviet and American jockeying for influence in Asia has also fed conflict in the region and served as an impetus for a brisk arms trade. Since the end of World War II, American troops have spent four years fighting in Korea and roughly a decade in Indochina, and since 1979 Soviet troops have occupied and engaged in a guerrilla war in Afghanistan. These developments contrast with those of the other Third World regions where Washington and Moscow generally have shied away from direct participation in armed conflicts. Nevertheless, the superpowers' favored approach to influencing events in Asia has assumed the form of support for insurgent movements or the governments facing them, rather than direct involvement. The United States and the Soviet Union have transferred a great deal of weaponry to Asia in efforts to bolster their regional allies or to undermine governments friendly to the other—a tactic also employed by the larger Asian nations.

Korea and Vietnam: The two largest post-war Asian conflicts—the Korean war and the Vietnam war—directly involved the superpowers and led to large-scale infusions of arms into the region from these giants as well as from China. The limited geographic scope of the Korean conflict meant that arms transfers were relatively focused. The U.S.-led United Nations contingent provided South Korea with its weapons, while the Soviet Union and China were North Korea's chief suppliers of arms and, in the case of China, of combat troops. Conversely, the Vietnam war eventually involved or posed a threat to the Indochinese nations adjacent to North and South Vietnam, and

---

*In referring to Asia we include the nations of South Asia, comprising Afghanistan, Pakistan, India, Nepal, Sri Lanka, Bhutan and Bangladesh, and the nations of East Asia, comprising Burma, Cambodia, the People's Republic of China, North Korea, South Korea, Laos, Mongolia, Taiwan, Vietnam, and the ASEAN nations (Indonesia, Malaysia, the Philippines, Singapore, Thailand and Brunei). We do not include Japan, the Soviet Union, any nations west of Afghanistan or any island nations other than the ones mentioned.

therefore arms transfers resulting from this conflict were more diffuse. The United States shipped arms to Laos, Cambodia and Thailand as well as to South Vietnam.

Although arms transfers to the nations involved in the Korean and Vietnamese wars decreased when the wars ended, they have remained sizable, largely because of continued regional tensions. On the Korean peninsula, the hostility is overt: Both the North and the South ostensibly desire the reunificaiton of Korea, but on their own terms. The proximity of the South Korean capital to the North Korean border along with North Korea's hostile attitude and occasional acts of violence, such as the 1983 bombing that killed four South Korean cabinet members in Burma, have fueled insecurity in the south. South Korea views an American military presence and arms shipments as vital to its survival, and it has been one of the largest arms-importing countries in Asia throughout the last three decades. Conversely, North Korea has felt uneasy because of the presence of American troops and nuclear weapons in South Korea, as well as by Seoul's modern and well-equipped military and its economic might.

Similarly, tensions have remained high in Southeast Asia. Soon after the fall of Saigon to North Vietnam and the Viet Cong, Cambodia and Laos also succumbed to communist forces. In December 1978 Vietnam invaded and occupied Cambodia, displacing the brutal, Chinese-backed Khmer Rouge regime. China responded by launching a brief punitive invasion of Vietnam. Since then, Cambodian rebels grouped at the Thai border have fought a guerrilla war against the occupying Vietnamese force of 160,000 armed troops and their Cambodian allies, while shellings and skirmishes occur spora dically at the Sino-Vietnamese border. Because of these conflicts, the Vietnamese army of more than 1 million remains highly mobilized and continues to import large quantities of arms. The peak years of the Vietnamese arms buildup were 1979 to 1980, at the outset of these two conflicts, when Vietnam imported $3.2 billion worth of arms and became the world's fifth largest arms importer. Since then Vietnam's arms imports have dropped to between $600 and $800 million per year, which is approximately 10 times the level recorded in the years immediately following the fall of the south.

The ASEAN nations: Thailand and, to a lesser extent, Singapore and Malaysia feel threatened by Vietnam. On many occasions, the Vietnamese army has entered Thailand in pursuit of Cambodian rebels and has skirmished with Thai forces. Thailand, Malaysia and Singapore also continue to be wary of the People's Republic of China, although these fears have dissipated in the last decade, partly because of China's support of Thailand in opposing the Vietnamese invasion of Cambodia. An increased Soviet presence in the Pacific and the Soviets' extensive use of former American bases at Cam Ranh Bay and Da Nang in Vietnam also have created a certain feeling of unease in Thailand, Malaysia and Singapore, as well as in the Philippines and Indonesia. The Philippines and Indonesia have little to fear from China and Vietnam, which lack the air and naval power to threaten them. The same cannot be said about the Soviet Union, however, because of its formidable Pacific fleet.

Three of the ASEAN nations, Thailand, Malaysia and the Philippines, also face domestic insurgency movements. In the case of the Philippines, the potential threat is particularly pointed: Some estimates of the size of the communist rebel force approach 20,000 soldiers in control of 20 percent of the nation's territory. These threats and fears, along with the increased prosperity of some of these newly industrialized countries, have contributed to the dramatic increase in the dollar value of the ASEAN nations' arms imports. (See Figure 9–1.) Between 1976 and 1978 the ASEAN nations imported an average of $550 million worth of arms each year (in constant 1983 dollars). This figure

Source: U.S. Arms Control and Disarmament Agency, *World Military Expenditures and Arms Transfers*, 1986

Figure 9–1.   Arms Deliveries to ASEAN Nations and Vietnam, 1975–1985
(millions of constant 1983 dollars)

roughly doubled to $1 billion between 1979 and 1981, and then leveled off at about $900 million for the period 1982–85.[2]

China and Taiwan: Another significant tension in the region is that between the People's Republic of China and Taiwan. Although this long-simmering conflict has not led to a full-pitched war since the flight of Chiang Kaishek's army to the island of Formosa and the establishment of two separate republics in 1948, each nation publicly embraces the goal of regaining the other's territory. Taiwan, like South Korea, views American arms transfers as essential to its survival, and through them has assembled an impressive military force for a nation of its size. Since the end of the Vietnam war, it has been the region's second largest importer of American arms, after South Korea. Though numerical superiority prevents the People's Republic of China from fearing an attack from Taiwan, the PRC is concerned with its smaller neighbor's activities, as is evidenced by its vigorous protest when weapons it deems to have significant offensive capabilities—such as Israeli missiles and Dutch submarines—have been sold to Taiwan.

India and Pakistan: The one regional conflict that has existed relatively removed from the superpower rivalry is that between India and Pakistan. Although both superpowers have acted as major arms suppliers to both countries, neither can be said to have fomented the conflict. Since India's independence and the creation of Pakistan in 1948, India and Pakistan have been unable to settle their border disputes, the most important of which involves conflicting claims to the Himalayan province of Jammu and Kashmir. These disputes are magnified by both nations' pursuit of regional hegemony and by deep historical grievances between Hindus and Moslems of the two nations that have been compounded with each succeeding war. In addition to the wars fought in 1948, 1965 and 1971, India and Pakistan have each supported numerous insurgencies in the other. India backed the successful rebellion in East Pakistan that led to the creation of the independent country of Bangladesh and has supported uprisings in Baluchistan, while Pakistan has encouraged insurgency in the Punjab and Assam. Intense distrust of the other nation has led both India and Pakistan to import large quantities of arms, Pakistan mainly from the United States, France and China, and India from the USSR and Britain. (See Figure 9–2.) India's appetite for armaments, however, is also a product of its lukewarm relations with the People's Republic of China, with whom it fought a losing mountain war in 1962 over a border dispute that has yet to be resolved. India, in fact, deploys 10 divisions on its border with China and 16 divisions on its border with Pakistan.[3] In 1987, many sources reported increased tensions along the Sino-Indian border.

The introduction of Soviet troops into Afghanistan has led to a further increase in the level of arms transferred to South Asia. Since it intervened in December 1979, the USSR has shipped large quantities of arms to Afghanistan for use by its soldiers and what remains of the Afghan army. The United States, meanwhile, has supplied arms to the resistance via Pakistan and has sought to strengthen the Pakistani military's ability to fend off any Soviet incursion. The influx of military hardware into Pakistan, in turn, has worried New Delhi, which has responded with increased arms imports of its own. As a result, arms transfers to South Asia skyrocketed from an annual average of $1 billion (in 1983 constant dollars) in the late 1970s to an annual average of more than $2 billion in the 1980s.[4]

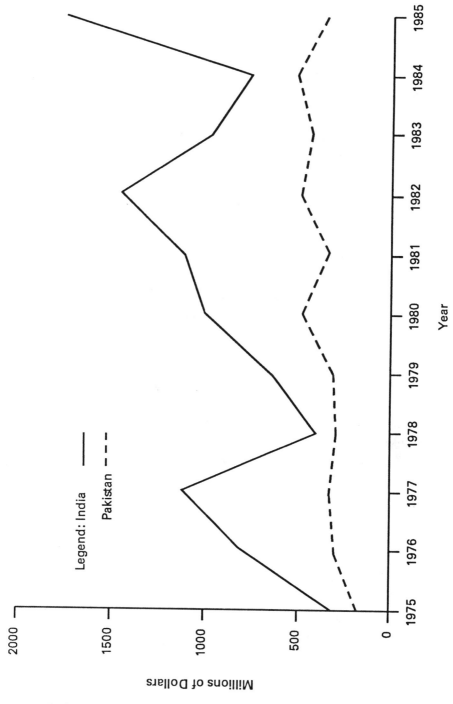

Source: U.S. Arms Control and Disarmament Agency, *World Military Expenditures and Arms Transfers,* 1986.

Figure 9–2.   Arms Deliveries to India and Pakistan
(millions of constant 1983 dollars)

The Arms Market in Asia

Once the Vietnam war ended, Asia, which once had been the largest arms-importing region in the world, fell behind the Middle East, Europe and Africa in terms of the value and quantity of arms imported annually.[5] ACDA figures show the level of Asian arms imports dropping 56 percent in real terms between 1973 and 1983 to an annual average of around $5 billion. This decrease occurred almost entirely in Southeast Asia; the value of arms imported into Southwest Asia, in contrast, rose by more than 70 percent. While Stockholm International Peace Research Institute figures also show Asian arms imports falling slightly behind those of Africa in the late 1970s and early 1980s, SIPRI attributes this change in position to dramatically increasing African arms imports rather than to declining Asian imports. Both sources note a recent upswing in Asian imports, owing to increased arms purchases in South Asia. According to SIPRI, Asian arms imports once again eclipsed those of African nations beginning in 1983, while ACDA does not record this occurrence until 1985. In recent years, the numbers of major weapon systems imported by Asian nations are roughly equivalent to those purchased by African nations. (See Table 9–1.)

Table 9–1

Weapon Systems Delivered to Asia, 1981–85
(in units)

Weapons System	U.S.	Other NATO	U.S.S.R.	Other Warsaw Pact	China
Land Armaments					
Tanks	293	70	1,090	270	40
Anti-Air Artillery	45	10	310	0	30
Field Artillery	894	360	750	0	55
Armored Personnel Carriers	530	520	1,450	0	0
Naval Craft					
Major Surface Combatants	15	7	6	2	0
Other Surface Combatants	3	24	37	0	10
Submarines	0	2	0	0	0
Missile Attack Boats	0	0	2	0	16
Aircraft					
Supersonic combat aircraft	115	80	360	0	80
Subsonic combat aircraft	206	25	0	0	0
Other aircraft	9	75	200	50	95
Helicopters	52	80	190	80	0
Missiles					
Surface-to-air missiles	1,511	340	840	0	70

Source: U.S. Arms Control and Disarmament Agency.

Both sources concur for the most part on the leading arms-importing countries in this region. Between 1981 and 1985—the last years for which figures are available—ACDA records the major recipient of arms in the region as India, which was followed by Vietnam, Taiwan, Pakistan, South Korea and Afghanistan. Recent attempts by Indonesia, Malaysia and Thailand to upgrade their forces led them to import a considerable quantity of arms during this period as well, according to ACDA figures. SIPRI's list of the leading arms importers during this period begins with India, Taiwan and Pakistan.[6]

According to the ACDA, the majority of arms transfers to this region are made by the Soviet Union and the United States, with the USSR accounting for approximately 40 percent of the 1981–85 total, and the United States approximately 30 percent. (Figure 9–3 illustrates the nature of the suppliers' market shares.) The Soviets' principal clients in South Asia are India and Afghanistan (in the latter case, most of the weapons go to the occupying Soviet troops), and their principal client in East Asia is Vietnam. Afghanistan, Vietnam, Mongolia, Laos and the Vietnamese or pro-Vietnamese forces in Cambodia now receive almost all of their arms from the Soviets. Vietnam

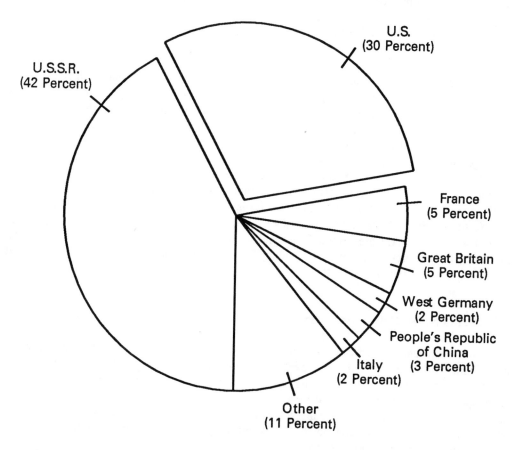

Source: U.S. Arms Control and Disarmament Agency, *World Military Expenditures and Arms Transfer,* 1986.

Figure 9–3. Suppliers' Shares of Arms Deliveries to Asia 1981–1985

also possesses a considerable stockpile of American weapons that formerly belonged to South Vietnamese forces. The Soviet Union is also one of several major arms suppliers to North Korea and the People's Republic of China. The principal U.S. clients in the region are South Korea, Thailand, Taiwan and Pakistan, although all except South Korea also purchase large quantities of arms from other sources. The Philippines and Singapore also depend primarily on the United States for the weapons they purchase abroad.[7]

Great Britain, because of its colonial ties to many Asian countries, traditionally has been a major arms supplier. India, Singapore and Malaysia imported arms principally from Britain in the first years of their independence. The British share of the Asian arms market has declined considerably, however, so that Britain now accounts for only 5 percent of arms sales to the region. It is, nevertheless, the region's third largest arms supplier after the Soviet Union and the United States, largely on the strength of renewed sales to India. France, which also accounts for approximately 5 percent of Asian arms sales in the region, is a major supplier of arms to Pakistan, Malaysia and Indonesia. Indonesia also has a large stockpile of Soviet weapons dating from the late 1950s and early 1960s when its relations with Moscow were close. China's role in the Asian arms market also is significant because it is the chief supplier of weapons to Bangladesh, and also supplies large quantities of arms to North Korea and Pakistan. Lesser suppliers to the region include West Germany, Italy, Czechoslovakia and Romania.[8]

Unlike the other parts of the Third World, Asia includes newly industrialized nations, many of which are able to produce weapons themselves. Arms imports, therefore, are not an accurate indicator of the overall militarization of the region. China and North Korea are nearly self-sufficient in arms production, and India, China and North and South Korea have established significant indigenous arms industries. Taiwan, the Philippines, Indonesia, Pakistan and Singapore manufacture major weapons systems, and even Burma, Malaysia and Thailand engage in some arms production. Several of the countries with domestic arms industries, notably China and North and South Korea, export their indigenously produced weapons. China, for example, had more than $5.4 billion in arms exports between 1981 and 1985, as opposed to only $385 million in imports, while both North and South Korea made more than $2 billion in arms exports during this period.[9] According to the ACDA, China, South Korea and North Korea are the Third World's leading arms exporters. SIPRI figures list China as the leading Third World exporter, but rank North Korea and South Korea as the sixth and seventh largest.

U.S. Arms Sales Policy and Practices: Asia

Until quite recently, American strategists generally have regarded Asia more than any other part of the Third World as a target of Soviet expansionism—a perspective supported by the success the Soviets have achieved in gaining an enduring presence in Southeast Asia, North Korea and India, and temporary influence in China and Indonesia. Alarmed by the pro spect of widespread Soviet influence in Asia, a region of increasing economic importance to the United States, Washington has gone to great lengths to contain it. Not surprisingly, Asia has been an arena of frequent confrontation between the superpowers.

The evolution of U.S. policy toward Asia: In the 1950s and 1960s, the United States used American troops to try to check what it perceived to be Soviet and Chinese expansionism in the region. Americans fought in Indochina and Korea, and guarded Taiwan and South Korea against outside attack. The death toll in Vietnam, the unpopularity of the war at home and the economic costs of the effort forced a reevaluation of this policy, however. In a 1969 briefing in Guam, President Nixon outlined the fundamentals of a new policy governing the use of American troops overseas. The President elaborated on the new policy seven months later in his State of the World address:

> First, the United States will keep all of its treaty commitments. Second, we shall provide a shield if a nuclear power threatens the freedom of a nation allied with us, or of a nation whose survival we consider vital to our security. Third, in cases involving other types of aggression we shall furnish military and economic assistance when requested in accordance with our treaty commitments. But we shall look to the nation directly threatened to assume the primary responsibility of providing the manpower for its defense.[10]

The Nixon Doctrine reestablished the Military Assistance Program (the primary conduit through which arms transfers were conducted at the time) in particular and arms exports in general as the cornerstone of American military assistance policy. The then-Secretary of Defense, Melvin Laird, emphasized:

> The Military Assistance Program is the key to this approach. It is the essential ingredient of our policy if we are to honor our obligations, support our allies, and yet reduce the likelihood of having to commit American ground combat units. When looked at in these terms, a MAP dollar is of far greater value than a dollar spent directly on U.S. forces.[11]

Although the American exodus from Vietnam took four more years, the number of U.S. troops stationed in Asia declined. By the mid–1970s, 20,000 troops had been withdrawn from South Korea, 12,000 from Japan, 5,000 from Okinawa, 9,000 from the Philippines, and 16,000 from Thailand— although the last Americans left Thailand only upon formal request by the Thai government in 1976. (See Figure 9–4.) As American troops marched out of Southeast Asia, American arms poured in. American arms transfers to South Vietnam, Laos and Cambodia and the ASEAN nations increased 150 percent (above inflation) between 1969 and 1973.[12] After the fall of South Vietnam, Cambodia and Laos, the United States encouraged the ASEAN nations in particualr to upgrade their defense capabilities. Growing unease among those nations themselves, coupled with expanded economic prosperity that provided increased resources for arms purchases, has led to stepped-up weapons imports. Singapore, for example, purchased 21 Nothrop F-5E fighters from the United States in 1976, and Indonesia purchased 16 F-5Es one year later.

The U.S. military relationship with Taiwan and South Korea has steered a steadier course than that with the ASEAN nations. American military support for Taiwan and South Korea pre-dates U.S. involvement in the Vietnam war and is more firmly wedded to the specific political predicament faced by these two countries than to regional instability. The United States has viewed its support for these nations as essential to their survival, and has rebuilt their armies from their tattered post-war condition. Since 1953, the United States has provided the South Korean army with more military assistance than any non-European nation except for South Vietnam. U.S. economic and technical assistance helped develop many of South Korea's successful industries, which have given it the base to produce sophisticated weapons. Taiwan, which has received the third largest portion of American military assistance to the Third World, similarly owes much of its current militaary and economic strength to American support. The United States, in return, has received base rights and other

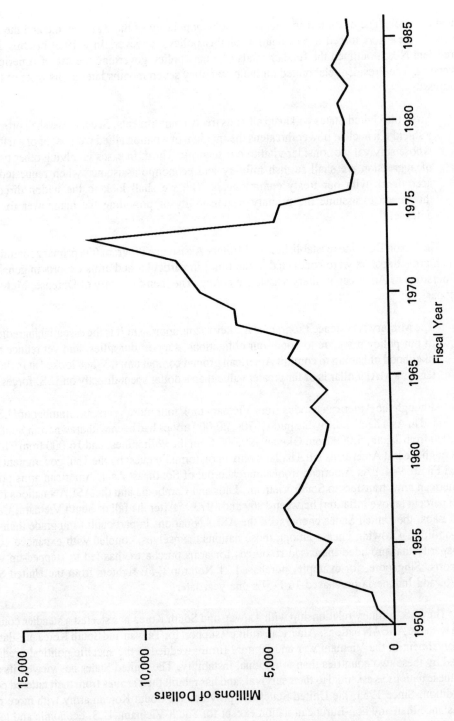

Source: Defense Security Assistance Agency, "Fiscal Year Services." 1987.

Figure 9–4. U.S. Military Deliveries to Asia
(millions of constant 1986 dollars)

privileges in both nations. Because of the extreme dependence of Taiwan and South Korea on American military support, the United States has also acquired a great deal of influence over the military policies of both nations.

The U.S. military relationship with these countries did change somewhat in the 1970s, however. In South Korea, developments have paralleled those elsewhere in Asia in that the Nixon Doctrine gradually led to reduced troop levels and increased arms transfers. Because of the peculiar geo-political predicament of South Korea, however, this evolution has not been nearly as complete as in other Asian nations. In the early 1970s, President Nixon withdrew approximately 20,000 of the 50,000 troops stationed in South Korea, but because of the large numbers of remaining troops, arms transfers to South Korea did not increase appreciably. The upsurge in arms transfers to South Korea did not occur until 1977, when President Carter, acting on a campaign promise, began to withdraw the remaining troops. Continued American concern about the security of South Korea, however, led to the suspension of the withdrawal in 1979 after 4,000 of the 33,000 ground troops had been removed, and arms transfers have since dropped to pre–1977 levels. (See Figure 9–5.) The total number of U.S. service personel from all branches of the armed forces that are stationed in South Korea currently exceeds 40,000.

The Philippines, a former American colony, also has had a long military relationship with the United States and has provided strategic bases and other privileges for American forces. The Philippines has not depended on the presence of American troops for its own security because external threats have been minimal during the postwar era. Instead, it has provided the United States with rights to the use of bases that successive U.S. governments have considered crucial—the Subic Bay naval installation and Clark air base—in exchange for military and economic assistance.

Dilemmas in U.S. Arms Sales Policy toward Asia

U.S. arms transfer policy toward Asia has not been without its detractors, both inside and outside the policymaking community. Broad criticism of U.S. arms transfer policy to Asia arose in the wake of the Vietnam war and the wish of many Americans to be extricated from the region. Recent debates have been more focused, centering on such issues as the desirability and effectiveness of covert military assistance to the Afghan rebels, and the desirability of supporting Cambodian rebel groups that are operating in a coalition with the Khmer Rouge. These have been comparatively minor issues in U.S. arms transfer policy toward Asia, however. More important criticisms are directed at broader themes: American military support of Pakistan in light of Islamabad's bitter rivalry with India and its pursuit of a nuclear weapons capability; American military support for both Taiwan and the People's Republic of China in light of their antagonistic relationship with each other; and American military support for governments that violate human rights. These last issues havc been the subject of extensive debate, and have given birth to a surprisingly diverse body of opinion within the last two administrations.

U.S. arms transfers to Pakistan: Unlike the Northeast and Southeast Asian nations that have imported American arms, until recently Pakistan had not faced serious internal or external Communist threats. U.S. arms exports to Pakistan were initially intended more to obtain a strategically situated ally willing to allow the placement of military installations and intelligence facilities on the periphery of the Soviet Union than to ward off insurgency or invasion. The United States found Pakistan willing to become dependent and fully integrated into western defense

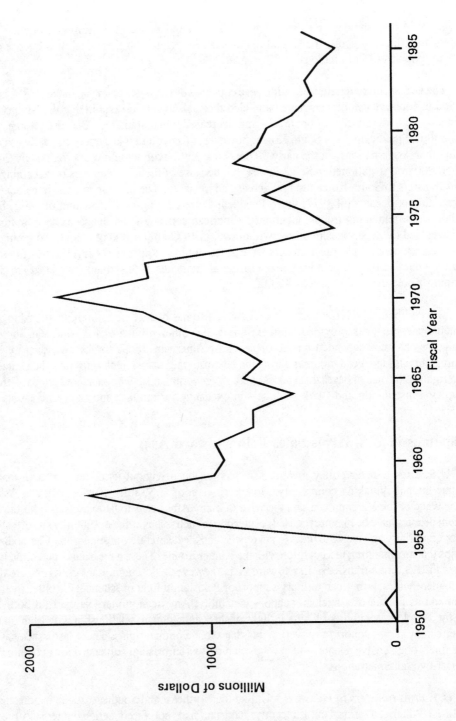

Source: Defense Security Assistance Agency, "Fiscal Year Services," 1987.

Figure 9–5.   U.S. Military Deliveries to South Korea
(millions of constant 1986 dollars)

planning in a way that the other South Asian power, India, was not. Thus, the United States and Pakistan signed one mutual security agreement in 1954 and another in 1959, and Pakistan became a member of two Western-instigated alliances, the South East Asia Treaty Organization (SEATO) and the Central Treaty Organization (CENTO). At the same time, the United States stepped up arms transfers to Pakistan.

The cost of close ties with Pakistan has been a tenuous Americn relationship with India. India's determination to remain non-aligned and to pursue an independent foreign policy kept it at a distance from the United States from the beginning, but the marked U.S. tilt toward Pakistan alienated India even further. Relations between India and the United States improved somewhat during the Kennedy administration, especially after the Sino-Indian border war of 1962, when the U.S. supplied India with support planes, light equipment and infantry weapons. Washington, however, refused a subsequent Indian request for heavier defense equipment. The relationship quickly deteriorated in 1965 when Pakistan invaded Kashmir. The United States refused to take sides in the conflict and, along with Britain—which to that point had supplied India with most of its weapons—cut off arms shipments to both nations. The Soviets, meanwhile, backed India and supplied it with steadily increasing quantities of military and economic assistance. As a result of the American embargo, Indian relations with the Soviets grew stronger, and by 1971 the Soviets had supplied India with $1.1 billion in military equipment.[13] Also by 1971, the Indian-supported rebellion in East Pakistan (now Bangladesh) had drawn India to the brink of war with Pakistan yet again. Fearing a two-pronged war with Pakistan and Pakistan's ally, China, India moved to consolidate its relationship with the Soviet Union by signing a 20-year Treaty of Friendship and Cooperation with Moscow.

Relations between Washington and Islamabad have not always been ideal, either. The embargo the United States imposed on both nations at the outbreak of the 1965 war hurt Pakistan more than India because Pakistan relied more heavily on the United States for arms. The embargo lasted until 1975, but because its terms varied considerably during this period it seriously strained the special relationship the United States had developed with Pakistan. Partly as a result of the embargo, Pakistan did not renew the lease on an American radar base and listening outpost in northern Pakistan and ceased to allow U-2 reconnaissance planes to take off from Pakistani airfields.

Pakistan's continued pursuit of membership in the nuclear weapons club has also caused cracks in the special relationship. In the early 1970s, U.S. policy hinged on trying to dissuade Pakistan from developing nuclear weapons by supplying it with enough conventional weapons to fulfill its legitimate defense needs. The Carter administration reversed this policy and attempted to discourage Pakistan's efforts at building nuclear weapons by imposing sanctions. Thus, most U.S. economic assistance—including military sales financing—was suspended in late 1977 after Pakistan agreed to purchase a nuclear fuel reprocessing plant from France. Although the suspension of aid was lifted one year later when the French canceled the sale, a similar ban was instituted in April 1979 in accordance with the 1976 Symington Amendment to the Foreign Assistance Act, which prohibited U.S. assistance to any country that "receives or supplies nuclear enrichment equipment, materials or technology without placing it under multilateral management and the safeguard system of the International Atomic Energy Agency."[14]

The fall of the Shah in Iran and the Soviet invasion of Afghanistan have brought Washington and Islamabad closer. These two events heightened American policymakers' feeling of unease vis-a-vis the Persian Gulf and left Pakistan as America's sole reliable regional ally. Since the Soviet invasion, the United States has poured arms into Pakistan in order to upgrade its conventional defense capabilities and funnel arms to Afghan rebels resisting the occupation—objectives that eclipsed concern for checking Pakistan's march toward obtaining a nuclear weapons capability. The Carter administration adopted what eventually became an open-ended exemption from the Symington Amendment, which bars aid to Pakistan because of its uranium enrichment activities, and transfers to Pakistan soared. The only stipulation attached to the policy about-face was that aid would be terminated if Pakistan were to test a nuclear weapon. American arms transfers to Pakistan increased from $53 million in 1978, the year before the Soviet intervention, to $380 million in 1985.[15] (See Figure 9–6.) In 1981, President Reagan crafted a $3.2 billion, six-year economic and military aid package for Pakistan, successfully lobbied against repeated congressional attempts to cut the size of the program and persuaded Congress to exempt Pakistan from the provisions of the Symington Amendment for the six-year period. Congress, though, retained the right to terminate U.S. assistance in the event of a Pakistani nuclear test. With these funds, Pakistan has purchased advanced weaponry such as F-16 fighters and TOW anti-tank missiles. Pakistan also has tried to purchase or lease Boeing Awacs aircraft, but the Reagan administration has so far rebuffed these attempts. The administration has offered instead to lease the less-sophisticated Grumman E-2C Hawkeye surveillance aircraft to Pakistan, and Islamabad is considering this offer.

The Reagan Administration in 1987 put before Congress a second six-year, $4 billion military and economic aid package for Pakistan, and again asked that Pakistan's adherence to the Symington Amendment be waived. The issue of Pakistan's apparent pursuit of a nuclear weapons capability, though, once again percolated to the surface and brought into question the viability of the administration's proposed aid plan. Although Pakistan President Mohammed Zia-ul Haq reassured Washington in 1984 that his country was not producing weapons-grade enriched uranium, reports regarding Pakistan's efforts at manufacturing nuclear weapons persist, and they include allegations that the People's Republic of China has helped Pakistan secure nuclear weapons material and design actual weapons. The Reagan administration's second six-year assistance package was jeopardized when a Pakistani native who allegedly received instructions from a retired Pakistani brigadier general was arrested in the United States for allegedly attempting illegally to export 25 tons of extremely high-strength alloy, whose export is tightly controlled because it is commonly used to construct uranium enrichment machinery. Some members of Congress asked that the 1985 Solarz Amendment, which requires that all U.S. aid to a non-nuclear nation be terminated if it seeks to obtain illegally nuclear-related materials from the United States, be invoked.

Although both Pakistan and the United States have insisted that the modernization of Pakistan's armed forces is directed at Afghanistan and the Soviet Union, and not India, New Delhi has objected strongly to the military buildup. The Indian government has charged that 90 percent of the weapons that Pakistan has purchased from the U.S. have been deployed on the Indian border, rather than on Pakistan's border with Afghanistan. India initially responded to the American-Pakistani rapprochement by tightening its military relationship with Moscow, despite Indian objections to the Soviet occupation of Afghanistan. In 1985, however, India and the United States held talks regarding opening up arms sales to India, and subsequently the United States agreed to sell India a supercomputer as well as General Electric engines and other components for an indigenously developed light combat aircraft. The agreement is on hold, however, because of U.S. concerns about India's ability to protect the sensitive technology, and because of the chill in U.S.-Indian relations caused by continued American weapon sales to Pakistan.

Critics of U.S. policy in the region contend that alienating the largest and most powerful country in South Asia is not in the best interests of the United States over the long term. Critics also point

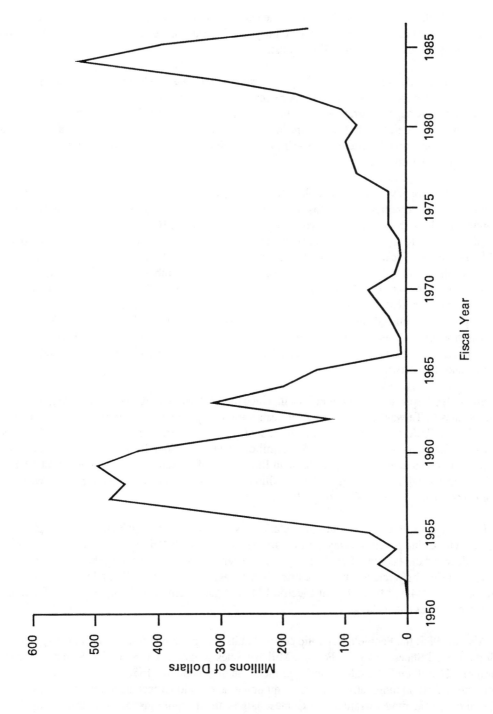

Source: Defense Security Assistance Agency, "Fiscal Year Series," 1987.

Figure 9–6.   U.S. Military Deliveries to Pakistan
(millions of constant 1986 dollars)

out that despite the U.S. tilt toward Pakistan, the United States has not been able to obtain Pakistan's consent to build military bases within the country, nor has Pakistan supported the United States on foreign policy issues such as the Middle East.

Arms transfers to Taiwan and the People's Republic of China: The gradual opening up of ties with China has also created a dilemma for American arms transfer policy. Although the United States has recognized the superior strategic and diplomatic value to the United States of the world's most populous nation, its ties with Taiwan are long-lived and its desire to ensure the island nation's security is deeply rooted. Attempts to achieve both objectives, while partially successful, have aroused substantial criticism.

Pesident Nixon's visit to the People's Republic of China in 1972 initiated the United States' two-pronged China policy. Partly as a result of this trip and the signing of the Shanghai Communique, U.S. troops in Taiwan were gradually reduced from 10,000 to 750. The United States refused, however, to agree to China's demands that it cut all official ties with Taiwan and abrogate the Mutual Defense Treaty of 1954 in return for the establishment of official relations with the PRC. Relations with Taiwan, therefore, remained unchanged until December 1978 when President Carter announced that he was establishing full relations with the People's Republic and terminating the formal defense pact with Taiwan. Most of the critics' cries that the United States was abandoning Taiwan proved unfounded, however. While the United States halted all arms sales to Taiwan for one year in accordance with the treaty, the Taiwan Relations Act enacted in 1979 specifically stated that "Taiwan shall be provided with arms," albeit "of a defensive character," and sales were resumed shortly afterward.[17]

Similarly, despite a 1982 communique in which the United States agreed to "reduce gradually" its arms sales to Taiwan, the level of American military equipment sold to Taiwan has remained steady. Indeed, U.S. arms sales to Taiwan have not fluctuated severely either up or down since 1978: The United States delivered on average $433 million (constant 1986 dollars) worth of military goods and entered into an annual average of $582 million worth of agreements during the period 1978 to 1982, compared with an average of $493 million worth of deliveries and $672 million worth of agreements for the years 1983 through 1986.

In addition to its effect on military relations with Taiwan, the establishment of diplomatic relations with China paved the way for military transactions with Beijing. In June 1984, President Reagan declared the People's Republic eligible to receive U.S. arms, clearing the way for an arms sale relationship between the two countries. China agreed to buy 24 Sikorsky S70C2 civilian helicopters in 1984 and five General Electric LM2500 gas turbine naval engines in 1985 through direct commercial channels.

Also in 1985, the People's Republic concluded its first government-to-government agreement with the United States under the Foreign Military Sales program. On Sept. 30, Reagan unveiled a proposed $6 million FMS sale of fuzes, primers and detonators for 155mm artillery ammunition, along with plans, administrative services, equipment and optional technical data packages worth $98 million for the modernization of a Chinese large-caliber munitions factory. Reagan stipulated that the sale would be an equipment-for-cash transaction that would not involve U.S. credits. Congress chose not to disapprove the export, although some members opposed it.

The munitions plant modernization sale was the first and least controversial of a series of transactions. The administration notified Congress in May 1986 of a proposed sale of 55 advanced avionics kits for China's F-8 fighter aircraft. The $550 million government-to-government sale is the largest deal with mainland China to date: It involves the upgrading of aging Chinese warplanes with modern radar, navigational and computer equipment. The Department of Defense awarded two contracts to the Grumman Corp. in 1987 worth $245 million in the first phase of the program. Some 25 civilian technicians and five Air Force personnel will be assigned to train the Chinese in the use and maintenance of the equipment, once the aircraft have been modified.

Despite the administration's favorable attitude toward future arms sales and China's interest in such items as anti-tank missiles, military helicopters and advanced jet engines, many observers believe the fabled "China Market" may prove to be at least partially illusory. Although most American aerospace companies are enthusiastic about selling to the PRC, the industry recognizes that it is a high risk proposition that requires patience. Few immediate sales are possible; the PRC's protracted bureaucratic review process makes for lengthy negotiations, it is relatively inexperienced with Western business practices, and it is hesitatant to part with scarce capital. China also has expressed interest in the wares of other weapons suppliers, most recently Israel and Brazil. Moreover, the PRC maintains ties with their former Soviet patrons: If relations between the two states improve, China may well resume buying arms from the Soviets.

Most analysts agree that, on the whole, prospects for defense trade with China remain positive in the near future. NATO and Japan have agreed recently to loosen trade restrictions on advanced technology and munitions for export to China. Chinese officials at the highest levels have expressed a desire to develop their own industry further, both for internal growth and as a deterrent to the sizable Soviet military presence to the north. Future U.S. business ventures in China might include cooperative development ventures, and coproduction and licensing agreements.

Some congressional sources and Far Eastern defense officials have opposed the slow opening of an arms relationship with China, particualrly in light of the U.S. failure to secure a guarantee from China that it will not use force against Taiwan. Conservatives in Congress are concerned that arms sales to China may tip the balance of power in the Taiwan Straits heavily in favor of China, and some Southeast Asian officials reportedly are worried by the prospect of resurgent Chinese military power. Administration officials and the majority in Congress have argued in turn that arms sales to China are meant solely for defense against the Soviet Union and would not disturb the equilibrium in the China-Taiwan relationship. Many observers believe the relationship between the two Chinese nations is moving away from confrontation and toward peaceful rapprochement, as evidenced by growing bilateral trade and recent tacit Mainland recognition of the legality of the Taipei regime. They argue that Taiwan's powerful armed forces and continued arms purchases from the United States will be sufficient to discourage any possible Mainland aggression.

Arms transfers and human rights in Asia: Another dilemma that arms transfer policymakers have encountered in determining policy in the region has been the poor human rights record of some of the Asian governments that are recipients of U.S. arms. The consistent human rights violations by the South Korean police and the security agencies, as well as South Korea's attempt to bribe American congressmen in the 1970s, led to much criticism of American support for this nation. Similarly, U.S. economic and military assistance to the Philippines were the subject of much protest because of human rights abuses under the Marcos regime. For the most part, however, the United States has been more reluctant in Asia than elsewhere to impose sanctions against governments that violate human rights. This reluctance can be attributred to the policymakers' perception of the importance of U.S. interests in this region and the seriousness of the Soviet (or Chinese) threat to these interests, and the fact that those nations that are criticized the most—South Korea, the

Philippines, Pakistan and Indonesia—either are the most geo-strategically important in the region or face tangible security threats.

Current U.S. arms transfer policy in Asia: U.S. arms transfer policy toward Asia under the Reagan administration has varied somewhat, although not dramatically, from the policies of previous administrations. Although the Reagan administration has downplayed the issue of human rights when formulating its military assistance policy, this has had little effect on the level of arms transfers to Asia, unlike other Third World regions. The quantity of U.S. arms transfers to the region has been roughly the same during the Reagan and Carter administrations, except for arms transfers to Pakistan, which have increased considerably in recent years because of increased concern over stability in the Persian Gulf and the suspending of the restraints imposed because of Pakistan's development of nuclear weapons. President Reagan has returned to the reasoning of pre-Carter administrations and argues that Pakistan can be deterred from pursuing the nuclear option only by satisfying its conventional weaponry needs.

Recent evidence, however, suggests that this policy has been no more effective than the previous one. In early 1987, Pakistani President Mohammed Zia ul-Haq said that "Pakistan has the capability of building the bomb. You can write today that Pakistan can build a bomb whenever it wishes.Once you have acquired the technology which Pakistan has, you can do whatever you like." Despite this admission, Zia, referring to the Soviet occupation of Afghanistan, said he was confident that the United States would look "to the higher national interest rather than to Pakistan's tiddly-widdly nuclear program."[18] This statement, coupled with the arrest of the Pakistani native charged with attempting illegally to export materials used in uranium enrichment facilities out of the United States, has refocused concern in congressional and executive circles over the possibility of Pakistan developing nuclear weapons. Congressional leaders responded by considering efforts to cut off Pakistan's aid, should evidence show that the Pakistan government was involved in the illegal export attempt or that it has proceded with the production of nuclear weapons. The Reagan administration, in an effort to defuse the controversy, asked Pakistan to reduce the efficiency of its uranium enrichment plant to a level applicable only to non-military nuclear activities, to permit outside inspection of the facilities, and otherwise to offer concrete evidence that it is not engaged in nuclear weapons production.

While the quantity of arms transfers to Asia has remained steady, the quality of the weapon systems the United States is willing to export to the region has changed considerably. Under the Carter administration and before, the United States for the most part had refused to sell top-of-the-line weapons to Asian nations. This reluctance was tempered under the Reagan administration. In 1981 Reagan approved the sale of General Dynamics F-16 fighters to South Korea, which Carter previously had blocked because he felt the fighters' long-range penetration capabilities would provoke the North. The Reagan administration has since sold F-16 aircraft to Pakistan, Singapore, Thailand and Indonesia. The Reagan administration also has transferred portable Stinger anti-aircraft missiles to rebel groups in Afghanistan. These missiles along with less-advanced Redeye anti-aircraft missiles reportedly have enabled the insurgents to fend off Soviet air attacks with increasing effectiveness, which has altered the pace and the character of the war.

Reagan arms transfer policy toward Taiwan has not differed from Carter administration policy, however. Despite strident denunciations of Carter policy for "abandoning" Taiwan, the Reagan administration, in order not to alienate China, has refrained from raising the quality and quantity of arms transfers to Taiwan. Indeed, the United States has refused to sell Taiwan any fighter that is more advanced than the Northrop F-5. In 1982 the Reagan administration went so far as to pledge in the Second Shanghai Communique that arms sales to Taiwan "will not exceed either in qualitative or quantitative terms" the level supplied in the first two years of the Reagan administration. At the same time, the Reagan administration initiated an arms transfer program to the People's Republic of China.

Finally, the Reagan Administration initiated changes in relations with South Korea that largely reflect that nation's growing economic power and independence. South Korea's improved economic performance led the United States in 1987 to terminate military grants and credits, which effectively gave the Koreans more flexibility in choosing its arms suppliers because recipients of American military assistance in all but a few cases are required to spend the grants on American-produced military equipment. The Reagan administration also launched an exploratory initiative to study the possibility of entering into a broad agreement, or Memorandum of Understanding, to cover increased defense industrial cooperation and the reciprocal procurement of military goods. A Memorandum of Understanding would facilitate the transfer of technology to South Korea, which in turn would allow the Koreans to develop more fully their own defense industrial base and capabilities. From South Korea's vantage point, the agreement is desirable because it would reduce its dependence on the United States, and introduce a dimension of greater equality in the U.S.-Korean defense trade relationship, elevating Korea to a status closer to that of Western Europe and Japan. Precisely how far the United States will go in restructuring U.S.-Korean relations in this regard remains to be seen, for the proposition involves many thorny dilemmas. Signing a Memorandum of Agreement would commit the United States to importing Korean military goods—a requirement that might be opposed by those concerned with the American trade deficit with Korea, which hit $7 billion in 1986. Many observers are concerned that a Korea with a strong defense industrial base, coupled with access to cheaper materials and lower labor costs and a proclivity to market goods aggressively, will create a fierce international competitor.

Table 9–2

Major Conflicts and Arms Transfers in Asia

Participants*	Dates of conflict	Principal arms suppliers	Type of conflict
Pakistani government vs. Bangladeshi rebels (India)	1971	PRC, France, US India	war for independence
Vietnam vs. Cambodia	1978	USSR PR	inter-state war
Cambodian government and Vietnam vs. Cambodian rebels	1979–present	USSR PRC, US, Thailand	guerrilla war against occupier
Vietnam vs. China	1979 (Border fighting continues)	USSR Britain	inter-state war
India vs. Pakistan	1965	USSR, Britain US, PRC, France	inter-state war
India vs. Pakistan	1971	USSR PRC, France, US	inter-state war
South Vietnam and US (Australia, S. Korea) vs. Viet Cong and North Vietnam	1954–75	US USSR, PRC	civil war
Cambodian government (US) vs. Khmer Rouge (N. Vietnam)	1970–75	US PRC, North Vietnam	civil war

Participants*	Dates of conflict	Principal arms suppliers	Type of conflict
Laotian government (US) vs. Communist rebels (N. Vietnam)	1945–75	US North Vietnam, USSR, PRC	civil war
Laotian government (Vietnam) vs. Laotian insurgents	1975–present	USSR, Vietnam PRC, Khmer Rouge	insurgency
Burmese government vs. Leftist and separatist rebels	1948–present	US, Western Europe PRC	insurgency
Indonesia vs. East Timor rebels	1975–present	US, Western Europe	guerrilla war against occupier
Indian government vs. Separatist rebels	1948–present	USSR, Britain Pakistan, PRC	insurgency
Philippines government vs. Moslem and leftist rebels	1972–present	US Libya	insurgency
Thai government vs. Leftist & separatist rebels and drug rings	1965–present	US, W. Germany PRC, Vietnam	insurgency
Malaysian government vs. Communist rebels	1945–present	US, Western Europe PRC	insurgency
Pakistani government vs. Separatist and partisan rebels	1972–present	US, France, PRC India	insurgency
USSR and Afghan government vs. Afghan rebels	1979–present	USSR US, PRC, Pakistan, Arab nations	guerrilla war against occupier

Particpants*	Dates of conflict	Principal arms suppliers	Types of conflict
North Korea vs. South Korea (US)	1954–present US	USSR, China	limited border fighting
Sri Lankan government (India) vs. Tamil insurgents	1983–present	Britain, PRC, India	insurgency
Indonesian military and anti-communists vs. communists	1965–66	USSR, US PRC	uprising followed by massacres

* Parentheses indicate the participation of additinal troops in the conflicts.

Sources: Center for Defense Information; Ruth Leger Sivard, *World Military and Social Expenditures*; Arms Control and Disarmament Agency, *World Military Expenditures and Arms Transfers*.

Footnotes

1. All figures from U.S. Department of State, Arms Control and Disarmament Agency (ACDA), *World Military Expenditures and Arms Transfers*, 1986 edition (Washington: ACDA, 1986).

2. ACDA, *op. cit.*, 1986 edition.

3. Zalmay Khalilzed et al., *Security in Southern Asia* (New York: St. Martin's Press, 1984), p. 105.

4. ACDA, *op. cit.*, 1986 edition.

5. ACDA, *op. cit.*, 1985 edition, pp. 89–92, and Stockholm International Peace Research Institute (SIPRI), World Armaments and Disarmament Yearbook 1986 edition (New York: Oxford University Press, 1986), pp. 354–55.

6. ACDA, *op. cit.*, 1986 edition, and SIPRI, 1984 and 1986 editions.

7. All figures from ACDA, *op. cit.*, 1985 edition, pp. 132–34.

8. *Ibid.*, pp. 132–34.

9. *Ibid*, pp. 100, 111.

10. President Richard M. Nixon, *State of the World Address*, Feb. 18, 1970.

11. Cited in Virginia Brodie, *Open Secret: The Kissinger-Nixon Doctrine in Asia* (New York: Harper Books, 1972), p. 132.

12. Calculated from constant 1985 dollar data from the Department of Defense, Defense Security Assistance Agency.

13. Francine Frankel, "Play the India Card," *Foreign Policy*, No. 62, Spring 1986, p. 157.

14. Congressional Research Service, *Changing Perspectives on U.S. Arms Transfer Policy* (Washington: U.S. Government Printing Office, Sept. 25, 1981), p. 73.

15. Calculated from constant 1985 dollar data from the Department of Defense, Defense Security Assistance Agency.

16. Frankel, *op. cit.*, p. 160.

17. Downen, Robert L., *The Tattered China Card: Reality or Illusion in United States Strategy* (Washington: Council for Social and Economic Studies, 1984), p. 19.

18. *Time*, March 30, 1987.

Chapter 10
Arms Exports and Africa

With several exceptions, the countries of Africa* possess fewer and less sophisticated armaments than nations in other developing regions of the world. Post-colonial African governments, though, have been obtaining weaponry at a rapid pace. A renewed appreciation of the strategic value of the region has made the major suppliers of military goods increasingly willing to supply military equipment or to finance arms transfers to Africa. In part because African nations on the whole possess less modern military equipment relative to the rest of the Third World, arms exports to the region rose enormously during the 1970s; the Arms Control and Disarmament Agency reports that arms transfers to Africa escalated at an 18.1 percent real annual rate for the years 1973 to 1983.[1]

The United States historically has transferred fewer arms to Africa than to any other region of the world, largely because much of the continent remained under the colonial control or tutelage of European powers well into the post-war era. The European colonial powers provided their colonies with arms and in most cases retained the role of weapons suppliers after the colonies gained their independence. America's relative inactivity in the African arms trade also reflects a lack of U.S. concern about Africa in comparison with other regions. In Africa, the United States has often allowed the former colonial powers—France, Great Britain, Belgium and Portugal—along with South Africa to guard western interests. While the role of Belgium and Portugal in African affairs declined considerably after decolonization, Great Britain, South Africa and, especially, France, continue to have substantial influence in the region. The United States rarely has taken the lead role in relations with the former French colonies, and instead has allowed France to determine how to respond to threats to Western interests—a policy that has been noticeable most recently in the Chadian civil war. Great Britain has played a more limited role in its former colonies, but here again the United States has at times deferred to British policy. Since the decolonization of the formerly Portuguese colonies, the United States to a certain extent has relied upon South Africa to protect Western interests in southern Africa and at the same time has tried to distance itself from the apartheid state. The United States, though, is becoming increasingly more involved in this sub-region of Africa.

---

*The Middle East section, which includes Egypt, discusses a number of issues that are particularly relevant to the Arab nations of North Africa. In referring to North Africa we include Libya, Algeria, Tunisia and Morocco, but not Egypt. Sub-Saharan Africa comprises all the other African nations.

Conflicts in Africa

Dozens of armed conflicts have been fought in Africa in recent years, as Table 10–2 at the end of the chapter illustrates. These conflicts range from large-scale civil wars to guerrilla attacks and counter-raids, and from struggles for independence against colonial powers to interstate clashes. In two colonies, Namibia and Western Sahara, insurgents are still fighting for independence. Nations outside the continent have provided most of the weapons used in these wars, and also frequently have intervened militarily in the conflicts.

Most of the recent fighting has taken place in southern or eastern Africa. West Africa's 16 countries have been spared major armed conflict for the last decade, although they account for more than half of the continent's nearly 60 coups during that period.[2]

From the perspective of the arms trade, the focal point of recent conflict is the strategic Horn of Africa. Somalia has fought neighboring Ethiopia, and internal fighting has continued for more than 20 years in Ethiopia and Sudan. What is notable about the arms competition in this area is the remarkable lack of stability in the relationships among weapons suppliers and recipients. During the first half of the 1970s, Somalia was the major sub-Saharan recipient of Soviet arms and military aid, and Ethiopia was the major sub-Saharan recipient of U.S. arms and military aid. With the 1977 Somali invasion of the Ethiopian province of Ogaden, the three-year old revolutionary regime in Ethiopia switched from buying all Western arms to buying only from the communist bloc. Conversely, after Somalia terminated Soviet base rights in 1977, communist sales to Somalia stopped, and by 1982 the United States had become Somalia's major supplier. A 1985 SIPRI analysis argues that "the end result of [this] regional arms race was to lock all the countries of the region more tightly into the respective security frameworks of the two superpowers—at the same time committing the latter to defend narrowly based and increasingly threatened regimes."[3]

The other focal point for conflict from an arms transfer perspective has been in southern Africa. Three states—Zimbabwe (formerly Rhodesia) and the former Portuguese colonies of Angola and Mozambique—gained their independence in the last 10 years after protracted military struggles, but all of them still must contend with guerrilla movements. In South Africa-controlled Namibia, for more than 15 years the South West African People's Organization (SWAPO) has waged a guerrilla campaign aimed at winning independence for the territory. South Africa also has been wracked by internal strife as the principal South African liberation movement—the African National Congress—has stepped up its insurgency campaign to bring an end to the system of apartheid. The South African government has responded harshly, imposing a state of emergency and attacking ANC sites in neighboring countries. Although South Africa is the only one of the four states facing growing insurgency movements that does not import a significant quantity of arms, it supports a mature indigenous defense industry and spends considerably more on its military than all of the subregion's other states combined.[4]

Of the various insurgencies in the region, the one in Angola has been the most severe. The insurgency has continued unabated since a Soviet-backed group, the Popular Movement for the Liberation of Angola (MPLA), emerged victorious from the struggle for power at the time of Angola's independence in 1975. The main insurgent group now operating in Angola is the National Union for the Total Independence of Angola (UNITA), led by Jonas Savimbi, which receives its arms principally from South Africa. South African military forces also have made numerous incursions into Angolan territory in support of the insurgents, including a large-scale invasion in

1975. The Reagan administration recently renewed American support of the UNITA rebels as well, and has supplied them with shoulder-fired Stinger anti-aircraft missiles.

The Angolan government, on the other hand, relies on large-scale Soviet and Cuban military assistance in its battle against the UNITA insurgents. According to U.S. government figures, Angola received more than $2.9 billion in arms transfers between 1981 and 1985.[5] Angola also depends on the presence of 25,000 to 37,000 Cuban troops to guard its oil fields from the insurgents.

Mozambique also has been beset by internal insurgency since 1978, which has been a factor in its large-scale arms imports—$825 million between 1981 and 1985.[6] This conflict, unlike that in Angola, to a large degree was conceived externally. The former white-dominated government of Rhodesia (now Zimbabwe) organized the insurgent group in order to harass the Mozambican government, which was then aiding Rhodesian insurgents. After the change of government in Rhodesia in 1980, South Africa assumed the role of assisting the insurgents. Although the insurgent group, Renamo, remained small, when its ability to disrupt the Mozambican economy was added to Mozambique's other economic problems, Mozambique was prompted to sign the Nkomati accord with South Africa in 1984. This agreement specified among other things that South Africa would cease to aid Renamo in exchange for Mozambique's termination of aid to black nationalist groups in South Africa. Since the accord, however, Renamo has grown stronger. Mozambique has frequently complained that South African aid to the insurgents has continued in large quantities, an allegation verified by documents gathered during a Mozambican raid on a guerrilla base. South Africa, which claimed that the documents proved only "technical" violations of the accord, has complained in return that Mozambican aid to black nationalists has continued.[7] Despite pressure by conservatives in Congress, the Reagan administration has refrained so far from aiding the Mozambican insurgents.

Although insurgencies are numerous, they have not played as large a role as rivalries among nations in encouraging arms transfers to Africa in recent years. Although there have been few actual inter-state wars, the end of the colonial period ushered in an era in which "the threats that seem to be driving the increases in military expenditures," according to one scholar, Bruce Arlinghaus, became mostly "fears of neighboring African states, in particular the emerging regional powers such as Nigeria, Libya, Ethiopia and South Africa."[8]

Each government's demand for arms is also closely tied to its available economic resources; some African countries, despite active separatist movements, are simply too poor to be large importers of military goods. In North and West Africa, though, oil wealth has provided the funds for increased military spending by Libya, Algeria and Nigeria, while Morocco has financed its growing arms purchases from its phosphate exports and U.S. military assistance. Both ACDA and SIPRI data show that these four nations received roughly 60 percent of Africa's arms transfers in the period 1981–85.[9]

The Arms Market in Africa

During the late 1970s, the arms trade to Africa increased at a faster pace than to any other region. According to the ACDA, arms buying by African countries grew by roughly 580 percent in constant dollars from 1973 to 1980. Similarly, data compiled by SIPRI using a different method of accounting reveal that the volume of major arms imports by African countries increased by 700 percent in real terms during this period. SIPRI data also show that Africa's percentage share of major weapons imported into the Third World more than doubled, from 9 percent for 1970–74, to 22 percent for 1975–79. ACDA figures show a similar jump from 5 percent in 1973 to 22 percent in 1980. In recent years, Africa's imports of major weapons have been comparable to those of Asia. (See Table 10–1.) Much of this rapid arms build-up can be attributed to the five oil exporting countries: Algeria, Congo, Gabon, Libya and Nigeria. They account for half of the continent's imported major weapons during the two "oil shocks" of the 1970s, according to SIPRI data for 1975–76 and 1978–80.[10]

ACDA data for the most recent period for which data are available, 1981–85, show that during the first half of the decade Libya was easily the largest African arms-importing nation, with $10.5 billion in imports, followed by Algeria ($3.9 billion), Angola ($3.0 billion), Ethiopia ($2.1 billion), Nigeria ($1.8 billion) and Morocco ($1.3 billion). Other important arms importers include Somalia and Sudan in the east, Mozambique in the south and Tunisia in the north. SIPRI also ranks Libya as the leading arms importer during this period, followed by Nigeria, Algeria, Morocco and Angola. In part because of its oil wealth, North Africa accounts for an enormous share of the African arms market. Its share rose from 47 percent between 1964 and 1973 to 59 percent for the period 1981–85,

Table 10–1

Weapon Systems Delivered to Africa, 1981–85
(in units)

Weapons System	U.S.	Other NATO	U.S.S.R.	Other Warsaw Pact	China
Land Armaments					
Tanks	80	420	1,070	5	140
Anti-Air Artillery	3	15	1,095	5	115
Field Artillery	173	495	1,750	120	80
Armored Personnel Carriers	209	1,080	1,915	40	5
Naval Craft					
Major Surface Combatants	0	24	19	0	0
Other Surface Combatants	0	105	17	3	0
Submarines	0	0	5	0	0
Missile Attack Boats	0	10	9	0	0
Aircraft					
Supersonic Combat Aircraft	38	30	535	0	25
Subsonic Combat Aircraft	6	70	15	15	0
Other Aircraft	2	180	110	145	10
Helicopters	0	115	255	55	0
Missiles					
Surface-to-air missiles	311	265	4,745	0	0

Source: U.S. Arms Control and Disarmament Agency.

according to the ACDA. SIPRI similarly records arms transfers to North Africa in the 1980s as accounting for slightly under 60 percent of all African arms transfers.[11]

During the 1980s, worldwide arms transfers to both north and sub-Saharan Africa on average leveled off from the late 1970s and then declined. During the five years ending in 1984, Africa accounted for only 19 percent of the weapons transferred to the Third World. Nevertheless, the value of arms imported by Africa by the mid–1980s has stabilized on a plateau that is still three to four times higher than the levels of the mid–1970s.[12]

Competition among suppliers: The nature of the arms trade in Africa has changed substantially since the 1960s, when imports were relatively low, and France and Great Britain—by dint of their status as former colonial rulers—controlled much of the market. Competition among suppliers increased during the 1970s, although most sources contend that the Soviets now have come to dominate the market. Figure 10–1 illustrates the division of the African market share between 1981 and 1985, as seen by the Arms Control and Disarmament Agency. In sub-Saharan Africa, the ACDA and the Congressional Research Service say that the Soviets now control more than 50 percent of the arms market, while SIPRI has the Soviets accounting for only 30 percent of the market in the 1980s, down from more than 50 percent in the late 1970s.[13] By all accounts, however, the Soviet Union is now Africa's principal arms supplier, whereas in the 1960s and early 1970s its arms exports to the region approximately equaled those of France. U.S. government figures show that between 1981 and 1985 the Soviets directed about 30 percent of their Third World arms transfers to Africa. Many of the Soviets' military relationships in the region were established when the U.S.S.R. supplied arms to insurgent groups fighting colonial rule. Later, when the insurgent groups came to power, the arms transfers and Soviet influence continued.

The Soviet Union and other nations aligned with or sympathetic to the Eastern bloc have supplied weapons and advisers to about two dozen countries in sub-Saharan Africa. In the mid–1970s, the Soviets demonstrated a new capability to move substantial arms and personnel rapidly to African battlegrounds with their Angola and Ethiopia campaigns. The USSR transported approximately $200 million in arms and flew 16,000 Cuban troops to support the MPLA national liberation forces in Angola in 1975.[14] Other recipients of Soviet aid include Equatorial Guinea, Guinea, Guinea-Bissau, Mali, Mozambique and Uganda. In return for arms, the Soviets often have sought overflight rights and the use of staging facilities for military operations on and near the continent.

Although the People's Republic of China, like the USSR, supplied arms to many of the insurgency movements in colonial Africa, it has not become a significant military factor in Africa. According to the ACDA, its share of the arms market in Africa actually dropped from 3 percent between 1964 and 1973 to its current level of less than 2 percent.[15] One explanation is the limited resources and quality of arms that China, in comparison with the other major powers, has been able to offer the African states. Furthermore, in some instances the insurgent groups backed by the PRC lost out to the Soviet-supported groups in independence struggles. Robert Mugabe's ZANU movement in Zimbabwe is the notable exception.

France's share of the African arms market also dropped from about 30 percent in the 1960s and early 1970s to between 10 and 15 percent in the late 1970s and early 1980s, according to both SIPRI and the ACDA. In sub-Saharan Africa, CRS and the ACDA report that France controlled approximately 9 percent of the market in the late 1970s and early 1980s, whereas SIPRI puts France's

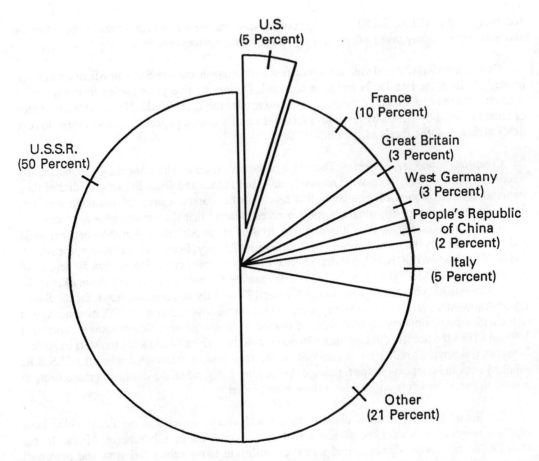

U.S.
(5 Percent)

France
(10 Percent)

Great Britain
(3 Percent)

West Germany
(3 Percent)

People's Republic
of China
(2 Percent)

Italy
(5 Percent)

U.S.S.R.
(50 Percent)

Other
(21 Percent)

Source: U.S. Arms Control and Disarmament Agency, *World Military Expenditures and Arms Transfers*, 1986.

Figure 10–1. Suppliers' Shares of Arms Deliveries to Africa, 1981–1985

share slightly higher at 13 percent. While its percentage share of the African arms market may have decreased, France has maintained close relations with many of its former colonies, and is the principal arms supplier to a majority of them. France also has military assistance agreements with 23 African countries—most of them former colonies—and has approximately 5,000 military advisers in Africa. That Great Britain has not been able to retain the same influence as France in the post-colonial period in Africa is evident in Britain's share of the African arms market. According to the ACDA, Great Britain now accounts for approximately 3 percent of the African arms market, as opposed to more than 10 percent in the late 1960s and early 1970s. Both CRS and ACDA figures show that Great Britain has about a 6 percent share of the sub-Saharan arms market.[16]

Annual U.S. arms transfers to Africa started to grow in the late 1970s and now hover at two or three times the level of the 1960s. Sources vary considerably, however, as to what portion they represent of the African arms market. SIPRI says that the United States has controlled approximately 15 percent of the African arms market thus far in the 1980s, and about 8 percent of it in the 1970s. The ACDA, on the other hand, reports that the United States has accounted for less than 5 percent of the African arms market throughout the 1970s and 1980s. Most of the discrepancy seems to lie in estimates of exports to sub-Saharan Africa, where both the ACDA and CRS record arms transfers during the late 1970s and early 1980s as constituting between 3 and 4 percent of the total arms market. SIPRI, on the other hand, lists much higher figures for the American share of the sub-Saharan African arms market, 9 percent in the late 1970s and 21 percent in the early 1980s.[17]

Other smaller suppliers, including Czechoslovakia, Brazil, India and Israel, have also broken into the African market. Some of the Third World arms exporters, such as Brazil, have found the market easy to enter, partly because they produce low-cost, easily maintained systems and partly because they are able to capitalize on some African nations' desire to avoid over-reliance on former colonial rulers or on the superpowers.[18]

South Africa is the only African country that produces a meaningful volume of weapons, although indigenous production is also germinating in a few black African states, such as Kenya, Nigeria, Algeria, Zimbabwe and Zaire.[19] South Africa designs and manufactures guided missiles, small fighting ships, artillery, light tanks, armored vehicles and small arms; it also manufactures jet fighters and major attack vessels, and it recently fielded a prototype of an armed helicopter that it expects to produce. South Africa developed its indigenous arms industry in reaction to a voluntary arms embargo that the United Nations passed in 1963 and that became mandatory in 1977. Despite the embargo, technical assistance and military goods have continued to flow into South Africa. The U.S. State Department, in response to a congressional request mandated by the Anti-Apartheid Act of 1986, issued an unclassified report in 1987 that stated: "We believe companies in France, Italy and Israel have continued to be involved in the maintenance and upgrade of major systems provided [to South Africa] before the 1977 embargo." The report continued: "Companies in Germany, the United Kingdom, the Netherlands and Switzerland have on occasion exported articles covered by the embargo without government permission or have engaged in sales to South Africa in the gray area between civilian and military applications."[20]

Israel has cooperated most closely in the development and transfer of arms to South Africa. Israel, though, did not admit to the existence of an arms relationship until March 1987, when it succumbed to American pressure and pledged to phase out its involvement with South Africa gradually by not entering into new arms agreements. Existing pacts, though, were left untouched and will run their course. One Israeli official reportedly estimated that four years might pass before these agreements expire, but a U.S. congressman says some of the contracts that are in place contain automatic renewal clauses. Although reliable data regarding the level of Israeli military sales to South Africa do not exist, unofficial estimates vary widely, from between $50 million to $125 million and $400 million to $800 million annually for the first half of the 1980s.[21] South Africa exports some of its indigenously produced weapons, mostly to South American countries, but its export efforts are hampered by a worldwide reluctance to do business with the apartheid state.

Recipient instability and supplier leverage: African governments have been prone to frequent and sudden shifts in regime and political orientation and have exhibited a willingness to purchase weapons regardless of allegiance, undermining the use of arms transfers by suppliers as a source of political leverage. Suppliers—particularly the United States and the Soviet Union—also have changed direction in mid-stream and supplied arms to nations or guerrilla movements that they had originally opposed. As discussed earlier, Ethiopia and Somalia are prominent examples of countries in which both the Americans and the Soviets poured money into arms transfers and military facilities but ultimately severed all ties. In a different kind of switch, Zambia moved in the early 1970s to a nonaligned policy of acquiring arms from both the Eastern and the Western blocs. More than one-third of the African countries currently spread their arms buying among a variety of suppliers, purchasing no more than half of their arms from any single source.[22]

The volatility of supplier-recipient relationships may lessen as African countries begin receiving more sophisticated weaponry. Initially, weak economies and reluctance on the part of suppliers to transfer top-of-the-line systems forced African nations to accept equipment that was outdated and relatively lacking in technical sophistication. Since the mid–1970s, however, more advanced weapons have been transferred to a growing number of African states, mainly because of renewed interest in the states' geostrategic value or their ability to pay with revenues derived from the sale of oil or other natural riches. Only seven nations in all of Africa had missile systems during the quarter century ending in 1974, whereas 14 new countries acquired missile systems in the following five years, and an additional 11 countries obtained them by 1984.[23]

Some analysts see this development as a harbinger of more stable relations with customers in the region. As the Iranians discovered after the ouster of the Shah, once a nation—particularly a Third World nation that lacks significant weapons-related industries and adequate training and maintenance for keeping sophisticated weapons in working order—purchases large quantities of advanced weaponry, it becomes more dependent on the original supplier for spare parts and servicing. Typical are the comments before Congress in 1979 of Chester Crocker, who at the time was the director of African Studies at the Center for Strategic and International Studies and now is the Assistant Secretary of State for African Affairs: "As weapons proliferate in Africa and more states acquire more advanced weapons systems, African dependence on outsiders *increases* not decreases: Dependence [is] a function of training and technology."[24]

Although advanced weapons have been transferred to Africa at an increasing rate, they have not been distributed evenly; instead, regional focal points of military power have emerged. The 1985 SIPRI study comments that Ethiopia, Nigeria and South Africa are the only three sub-Saharan countries that "can be said to possess an all-round conventional military capability comparable to states outside the region."[25] It also categorizes the north African countries of Libya, Algeria and Morocco as having advanced militaries. These six countries accounted for more than 70 percent of the African arms trade, according to ACDA figures for the period 1981 to 1985.[26] An additional seven to nine nations, according to SIPRI, are "in principle well enough equipped to fight a conventional military campaign outside their own boundaries."[27]

U.S. Arms Sales Policy and Practices: Africa

Historically, Africa has held a less important strategic role in U.S. foreign policy interests than the Middle East, Latin America or Asia. As a result, U.S. arms transfers to Africa have been smaller than those to other regions of the Third World, and the United States participated only marginally in the continent's arms trade until the late 1970s. U.S. arms transfers to Africa seldom exceeded 1 percent of total U.S. transfers worldwide before 1976.

Africa's strategic relevance to the United States is rooted in its proximity to the Persian Gulf, its key shipping lanes and its vast deposits of minerals that are crucial to American commercial and military industries. For the most part, however, U.S. policymakers view African affairs as marginal to the core of key U.S. interests. Economically, Africa is the weakest of the four Third World regions, and American economic ties to the continent are relatively weak. African countries, for example, receive just 7.5 percent of total U.S. exports to nonindustrial nations.[28] Most analysts would agree that the increased U.S. interest in African affairs that marked the late 1970s and 1980s had more to do with developments nearby than with the African countries themselves.[29]

U.S. ventures into the African market also seem to be driven in many instances by the desire to prevent nations there from becoming clients of the Soviet Union or otherwise allowing the Soviets influence in the region. The anti-Communist rationale for arms sales persists today in U.S. efforts to support insurgents in Angola or "to defend against Soviet expansionism" in the Horn of Africa, as Chester Crocker has noted.[30]

U.S. military deliveries to Africa during the 1950s were small—as Figure 10–2 indicates, averaging $16 million (in constant 1986 dollars) per year throughout the decade—and concentrated among only a few of the countries on the vast continent. Nearly all U.S. military assistance for sub-Saharan Africa during the 1950s went to Ethiopia; even during the next decade, the only other significant U.S. weapons recipient was Zaire.

U.S. arms deliveries increased considerably during the 1960s, and average annual deliveries reached $100 million in constant 1985 dollars (roughly $35 million annually in current dollars). In 1963, Congress limited annual U.S. arms sales and military aid to sub-Saharan Africa to $25 million. In doing so, Congress followed the recommendation of a bipartisan committee, appointed by President Kennedy, to reduce economic and military aid to Africa and leave more of the responsibility for providing aid to Western Europe. The committee expressed the belief that "the problems created by military assistance programs in African countries generally would be greater than those they would forestall or resolve." It singled out the Congo, where, it said, "we believe that the United States . . . has contributed proportionately more than its share of the task assumed."[31]

The sales restriction was superseded by the Foreign Military Sales Act of 1968, which set a $40 million ceiling on annual military grants, credits and sales to Africa. Cash sales, however, were exempted in 1973, and beginning in 1974 the limit could be waived in the interests of national security. According to one scholar, Joseph P. Smaldone, now chief of the Licensing Division of the State Department's Office of Munitions Control, "The president exercised this waiver authority every year until 1979, when the ceiling was repealed and replaced by the mild 'sense of the Congress' injunction."[32] Instead, Congress asked the President, in the foreign military aid authorization bill, to "exercise restraint" in selling weapons, on grounds that "the problems of sub-Saharan Africa are primarily those of economic development and that U.S. policy should assist in limiting the development of costly military conflict in that region."[33]

Although concern in U.S. policymaking circles with promotion of economic development remained high throughout the 1970s, it increasingly began to compete with two policy objectives: countering what was perceived as growing Soviet influence on the continent and securing military facilities close to the Middle East. These conflicting imperatives came to a head during the late 1970s. As elsewhere around the globe, the Carter administration initially viewed prospective arms transfers to Africa with an eye to their effects on regional stability rather than to the role the continent played in larger global strategic competition. However, posturing with the Soviets in Africa and securing the use of territories close to the Persian Gulf—particularly after the fall of the Shah—quickly grew to be an important determinant of U.S. policy. Many decisionmakers came to espouse

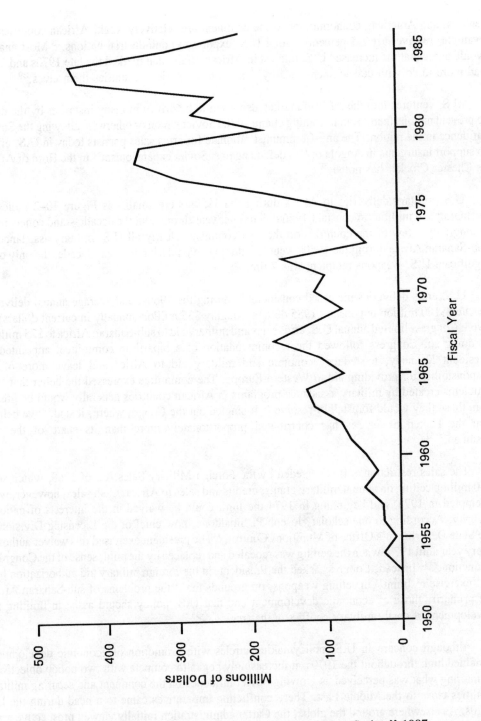

Source: Defense Security Assistance Agency, "Fiscal Year Series," 1987.

Figure 10–2. U.S. Military Deliveries to Africa
(in millions of constant 1986 dollars)

the view that extending arms to strategically placed African nations was an effective way of securing basing rights and overflight privileges.[34] Nowhere was this new policy played out with more intensity than in East Africa.

In the late 1970s, East Africa was buffeted by military conflict and political turbulence. Insurgents toppled the long-lived regime of Emperor Haile Selassie of Ethiopia in 1974. Shortly after it came to power, the new Dergue government began a slow drift toward the Soviet Union that eventually resulted in the loss of the closest U.S. ally in the region. In the process, the United States lost numerous military facilities, including one of the world's largest communication complexes.[35] Ethopia's drift to the Soviets coincided with a deterioration in Somalian-Ethiopian relations, which resulted principally from Somalian claims to Ethiopian territory. Somalia aided rebels in the Ogaden area of Ethiopia and in 1977 invaded Ethiopia. The invasion touched off a war that lasted through 1978, and intermittent fighting continues to this day.

Tensions in East Africa combined with an increased appreciation on the part of U.S. policymakers of the region's strategic proximity to the Middle East to stimulate American arms transfers to the region. Whereas military deliveries to sub-Saharan Africa averaged $50 million annually (constant 1986 dollars) in the years 1970 to 1975, the figures for 1976 to 1978 jumped to an annual average of $162 million. The initial increase in deliveries was caused mainly by stepped-up deliveries to Ethiopia as the United States sought to bolster its principal regional ally in the face of Somalian aggression. After Ethiopia drifted toward the Soviet Union, American arms deliveries to Sudan, Kenya and later Somalia increased dramatically.

When U.S.-Ethiopian arms ties were severed, the United States intimated that it would entertain arms requests from affected nations in the area. One of the first nations to respond was Sudan, the continent's largest country, which had been gradually moving away from the Soviet Union. Sudan became a valuable new ally for the United States because it is located between pro-Soviet Libya and Ethiopia, south of new ally Egypt, and across the Red Sea from Saudi Arabia. Sudan was cleared for delivery of $32 million in U.S. arms in 1978—the first time the country had received American weapons. Congress subsequently authorized $160 million in FMS loans to Sudan between 1979 and 1982, and waived payment of $50 million worth of these loans, preferential treatment that has been extended only to Egypt and Israel. Saudi Arabia also strengthened its relationship with Sudan, to the extent that it financed the Sudanese purchase of 12 Northrop F-5 fighters.[36]

At the same time, the United States improved its military relationship with Kenya. In 1975, the U.S. began to provide Kenya with military assistance via FMS loans and the International Military Education Training (IMET) program. As regional tensions grew and American strategists became increasingly convinced of the geo-strategic importance of East Africa, U.S. arms transfers to Kenya were increased. Kenya received more than $92 million worth of FMS deliveries between 1977 and 1979, including F-5 fighter aircraft, whereas previously the country had purchased only a small quantity of arms through commercial sales channels. In exchange for the military sales and assistance, the United States was granted overflight and landing rights for its military aircraft, and port visits by its navy.

The United States was slowest to open an arms relationship with Somalia. The Soviets had long possessed close and valued ties with Somalia, supplying the country with more than $300 million in arms between 1963 and 1976—more than any other sub-Saharan African nation.[37] In return, Somalia allowed the Soviets to build a major air and naval base in Berbeira, near the southern entrance to the Red Sea. Beginning in 1976, however, Soviet-Somalian relations grew strained, largely because Somalia would not relent on claims to territories held by Ethiopia at a time when the Soviets were seeking closer ties there. After Somalia invaded the Ogaden, the Somalian-Soviet military relationship came to an abrupt end, and the Soviets initiated large-scale military assistance to Ethiopia. U.S. policymakers at this time considered substantial arms sales to Somalia, but the Carter administration backed away from the idea out of concern that the weaponry would be used to support the Somali invasion of Ethiopia. American reluctance to supply Somalia with military equipment, though, faded in the face of the Soviet invasion of Afghanistan and the fall of the Shah in Iran, which heightened U.S. interest in the potential usefulness of Somalia's geostrategic location. After considerable negotiation, the United States agreed to provide military aid to Somalia in return for the use of bases, and Somalia agreed not to intervene directly in Ethiopia again.[38] The United States provided Somalia with $20 million in FMS loans in 1980, and since 1982 it has supplied comparable amounts of MAP grant aid. Somalia, in turn, has granted the United States use of the former Soviet base at Berbeira.

The desire to gain base rights and gain influence in the Middle East also affected U.S. arms export policy in North Africa in recent years. Morocco and Tunisia, the two Arab allies of the United States in the region, have received military assistance since the 1960s, but until the late 1970s American policymakers had minimized their strategic importance. At this time, American efforts to obtain docking privileges, overflight rights and staging bases for the Rapid Deployment Force (which has been renamed the Central Command) created a new strategic relevance for these countries. This rethinking led to stepped-up American arms transfers to Morocco and Tunisia in the late 1970s and early 1980s. Military deliveries to Morocco, which had averaged $17.6 million (constant 1986 dollars) annually from 1970 to 1976, jumped to an annual average of $146 million between 1977 and 1981, and then leveled off at about $64 million a year between 1982 and 1986. Similarly, delivery of American weapons to Tunisia trebled, from a $9 million annual average (constant 1986 dollars) in the early and mid–1970s to a $26 million annual average for the period 1977 to 1981, and then trebled again, to a $76 million annual level between 1982 and 1986.

Morocco, especially, came to be viewed as an important ally, because of "its strategic location at the mouth of the Strait of Gibraltar and its deep water harbors."[39] American strategists theorized that in the event that Spain and Portugal might deny Mediterranean transit rights to U.S. military aircraft, they could obtain rights from Morocco. Despite its recognition of these strategic assets, the Carter administration exhibited a certain ambivalence toward Morocco, largely because Morocco has been attempting to annex the Western Sahara, doing battle with the Polisario insurgent group, which opposes the annexation, and the administration was unable to resolve its own stance vis-a-vis the Western Sahara. While this did not prevent U.S.-Moroccan arms transfers as a whole from skyrocketing, it did inhibit American sales of certain types of military equipment. Until October 1979, when it finally acceded to Morocco's persistent demands, the Carter administration refused to sell Morocco Cobra helicopter gunships, OV-10 Bronco counterinsurgency aircraft and electronic sensors for its counterinsurgency campaign.[40]

The Reagan administration has felt no such ambivalence toward Morocco. The administration reinstituted the military assistance grant program to Morocco and has supplied it with equipment such as Maverick missiles and M60 tanks. In 1987, the Reagan administration sold 100 M48 tanks to Morocco, which elicited a strong condemnation by the Polisario. In exchange for U.S. military assistance, Morocco has "agreed to access and transit for U.S. forces on a case-by-case basis; it participates in numerous joint military exercises; and it provides training areas for U.S. forces in

Europe as well as facilities for Voice of America broadcasts."[41] The increased American willingness to expand formal military ties with Morocco was fostered by its assistance in furthering U.S. foreign policy interests by exhibiting an increased proclivity to act the part of a moderate Arab force in Mideast politics. Morocco was instrumental in arranging initial contacts between Israel and Egypt—contacts that opened the way for the Camp David Accords—and in 1986 Morocco's King Hassan met with Israeli Prime Minister Shimon Peres to discuss Arab-Israeli relations.

The Reagan administration has gone only so far, though, in its arms relationship with Morocco. It cited concern for the long-term political stability of the country as the reason for signaling its unwillingness to accept a reported 1987 offer from Morocco to allow the United States to establish bases on its soil. According to press accounts, Morocco made the offer in anticipation of increased American economic and military aid after it became apparent that the renewal of U.S. basing rights in Spain, which are set to expire in 1988, was far from certain.[42]

The United States has formulated and achieved more modest goals in Tunisia. While the U.S. has supplied Tunisia with sophisticated military equipment such as F-5 fighters and numerous combat vehicles such as M60 tanks and M109 self-propelled howitzers, Tunisia has pursued an independent foreign policy and has not allowed the U.S. military more than occasional port visits. The principal motives of the United States in transferring arms to Tunisia have been to contain Soviet influence and to deter an attack by Libya, which at times has directly threatened or fomented insurgency in Tunisia. According to American officials, "The U.S. has contributed to the modernization of Tunisia's military forces with the prime objective of strengthening deterrence to potential Libyan aggression."[43]

Although interest in Africa, because of its geostrategic implications for security interests in the Middle East, has loomed large, it has not dominated U.S policy across the board. Much of the congressional debate on Africa during the mid–1970s focused on details of the arms trade with the southern portions of the continent. Congress, scarred by the Vietnam war experience, resisted successive administrations' plans for military assistance to African nations because it might signal increasing U.S. involvement in the region. In this atmosphere, both conservatives and liberals in Congress were able to mobilize more moderate members of Congress to oppose military assistance where they saw fit. Although in 1976 Congress supported the Ford administration's new Africa policy by approving security assistance to Zaire and to those countries, including Mozambique, that had closed their borders to white-ruled Rhodesia, the following year Congress resisted that policy. The result was a foreign aid bill stipulating that $80 million in a military aid fund for southern Africa could not go to Mozambique, Angola, Tanzania or Zambia—nations with ties to the Soviet bloc—unless President Carter determined that such aid would further U.S. foreign policy objectives. Instead, Congress allocated specific sums to Botswana, Lesotho and Swaziland.

In 1976 Congress also prohibited military assistance to any groups or persons in Angola, where a Soviet-allied regime backed by Cuban troops continues to fight an insurgency. Supporters of the ban, which was codified in the Clark Amendment, argued that U.S. involvement would serve to entrench Cuban involvement, disturb black African leaders and detract from negotiations over South Africa-occupied Namibia. The Reagan administration's call for a repeal of the ban, with an eye toward supporting the anti-communist rebels, was finally accepted by Congress in 1985. Subsequently, the United States began to supply covert military assistance to the insurgent group, UNITA, and it has supplied the insurgents with, among other things, automatic weapons, ammunition and 50 Stinger shoulder-fired anti-aircraft missile systems. The Reagan administration has stated that it supplied UNITA with $15 million in assistance in 1986 and an additional $15 million in 1987 in discretionary funding drawn from the coffers of the Central Intelligence Agency which do not have to be approved by Congress before they are disbursed.[44]

Congress also resisted the Carter and Reagan administrations' proposed military assistance programs to Zaire. In 1979, it cut from $10.5 million to $8 million the FMS credits granted to Zaire with the proviso that military aid "not be used corruptly or to violate the human rights of Zairian citizens."[45] Zaire again came under criticism in 1981 when Congress authorized only $6 million in FMS loans, and opposition to Reagan's proposed increases in military transfers to Zaire continued in 1982 and 1983. Successive administrations have viewed Zaire as an important ally, however, because of the country's size and mineral wealth, and have managed to maintain military aid to the country at a relatively stable level. The Reagan administration has particularly valued Zaire's help in serving as a conduit for U.S. military aid to the UNITA rebels in Angola.

Data compiled by the Defense Department's Defense Security Assistance Agency show that, in real terms, U.S. arms deliveries to both North Africa and sub-Saharan Africa have grown by only 5 percent in real terms from the Carter to the Reagan administrations. (See Figure 10–2.) This is a small jump in comparison with the dramatic increase that occurred between the Nixon/Ford and Carter administrations, when military deliveries to Sub-Saharan Africa doubled and military deliveries to North Africa quadrupled.

The number of African recipients of American arms has increased significantly under President Reagan's leadership, however. Since 1980, Algeria, Botswana, Chad, Cote-D'Ivoire, Djibouti, Equatorial Guinea, Guinea, Guinea-Bissau, Madagascar, Malawi, Mauritania, Niger, Rwanda, Senegal, Sierra Leone and Togo all received official American arms transfers and military assistance for the first time. Of these new arms transfer programs, the most significant are the ones to Chad and Algeria. A large area of northern Chad has been occupied by Libya, which, until a recent falling out, had aided a large Chadian rebel army. France has been supplying extensive military assistance— including a sizable French military presence—to the Chadian government and at times has used its air force to bomb Libyan and Chadian rebel positions. According to the Defense Security Assistance Agency, U.S. military assistance is meant to "complement French assistance . . . to deter Libyan aggression and to keep Libyan influence and expansionism in check."[46] To this end, the United States has transferred Redeye portable surface-to-air missiles and combat vehicles to Chad. Arms transfers to Chad might well decline in the immediate future because of a string of resounding Chadian military victories that began in the spring of 1987 and pushed the occupying Libyan forces across the border. The Chadians are reported to have captured between $500 million and $1 billion worth of usable military equipment in the process of routing the Libyan army, equipment that is said to include at least 130 tanks, 170 armoured vehicles, 150 artillery pieces, 40 rocket launchers, 600 trucks and jeeps, shoulder-launched anti-aircraft missiles and several advanced airplanes and helicopters, all of Soviet or Eastern bloc design. Although Chad undoubtedly will sell a portion of the captured material, it will incorporate much of it into its arsenal.

While arms sales to Algeria remain limited, its size and oil wealth make the budding arms transfer relationship between it and the United States significant. The DSAA notes that U.S.-Algerian relations "have improved dramatically in recent years," and believes that a closer military relationship "opens doors to wider commercial cooperation, provides potential economic benefits to U.S. companies, and encourages Algeria's move toward closer contacts with the West."[47] In 1986, the U.S. delivered C-130 Hercules transport aircraft to Algeria.[48]

Many of the smaller African nations have entered into an arms transfer relationship with the United States partly as a result of the Reagan administration's move back to grant military assistance. The administration switched to an increasing emphasis on MAP in part because of the poor rate of repayment by African countries. According to Noel Koch, formerly the principal deputy assistant secretary of defense for international affairs, "none of the African FMS debtors meet their payments on time."[49] Koch stated that Sudan, Somalia and Kenya, which together account for more than 50 percent of the FMS credits extended to African nations in the last two administrations, "miss repayments regularly and do not make these payments at a later date."[50]

The Reagan administration's plan to substitute MAP grants for FMS credits may have hit a stumbling block, however. Budgetary constraints in the wake of Gramm-Rudman have turned congressional sentiment against foreign assistance, leading to decreased MAP allocations for Africa. MAP grants to African countries fell from $147 million in fiscal year 1985 to $93 million in 1986, and then to $42 million in 1987, a trend that is likely to persist in the near future.

Table 10–2

Major Conflicts and Arms Transfers in Africa

Participants*	Dates of conflict	Principal arms suppliers during conflict	Type of conflict
Angolan government (Cuba) vs. Insurgents (South Africa, Zaire)	1975–present	USSR South Africa, US	civil war
Chadian government (Libya) vs. Insurgents	1980–82	Libya, France US	civil war
Chadian government (France) vs. Insurgents (Libya)	1965–80 1982–present	France Libya	civil war
Ethiopian government (Cuba) vs. Separatist rebels	1961–present	USSR, Cuba, GDR (pre–1977, US) Arab states	civil war
Ethiopian government (Cuba) vs. Somalia and ethnic Somali rebels	1977–78 (some fighting continues)	USSR Western Europe	inter-state war
Mozambican government (Zimbabwe, Tanzania) vs. Mozambican insurgents	1977–present	USSR South Africa (pre–1980 Rhodesia)	insurgency
South Africa vs. Namibian guerrillas	1966–present	France, Israel USSR, Angola	war for independence
South African government vs. Black nationalist rebels	1970s–present	France, Israel Black African nations	insurgency

Participants*	Dates of conflict	Principal arms suppliers during conflict	Type of conflict
Ugandan government (Libya) vs. Insurgents	1972	USSR, Arab states Tanzania	insurgency
Tanzania vs. Uganda (Libya)	1978–79	USSR, China USSR, Libya	inter-state war
Ugandan government (Tanzania) vs. Insurgents	1981–86	Tanzania, Western Europe Libya	civil war
Spain vs. Western Saharan rebels	1973–75	US Algeria, Mauritania	war for independence
Morocco & Mauritania (France) vs. Western Saharan rebels	1975–present	France, US (Mauritania until 1979) Algeria, Libya	war for independence
Zimbabwean government vs. Insurgents	1980–present	Britain, N. Korea, PRC South Africa	insurgency
Sudanese government vs. Non-Moslem insurgents	1956–72 1980–present	US, W. Europe (USSR pre–1977) Ethiopia	civil war
France and right-wing groups vs. Algerian rebels	1954–62	Egypt, PRC, USSR	war for independence
Portugal vs. Angolan rebels	1961–74	France, US USSR, PRC	war for independence
Portugal vs. Guinea-Bissau rebels	1963–74	France, US USSR	war for independence

Participants*	Dates of conflict	Principal arms suppliers during conflict	Type of conflict
Malawi government vs. Malawi rebels	1964–67	Western Europe PRC	insurgency
Nigeria vs. Separatist rebels	1967–70	Britain, USSR, US France, Tanzania	insurgency
Zairean government (UN, Belgium France, Morocco) vs. Separatist rebels	1960–67 1977–78	US, France USSR, Cuba, PRC	insurgency
Burundi government (Zaire) vs. Hutu rebels	1972	PRC	insurgency
Rwandan government vs. Tutsi rebels	1956–65	Western nations PRC	insurgency
Portugal vs. Mozambican rebels	1962–74	France, US USSR, PRC	war for independence
France vs. Cameroonian rebels	1955–62	Czechoslavakia	war for independence
Rhodesian government vs. Zimbabwean rebels	1966–80	South Africa, Israel USSR, PRC	war for independence
Somalia vs. Kenya and Ethiopia	1962–68	USSR Britain, US	inter-state war

*   Parenthesis indicate the participation of additional troops in the conflicts.

Sources: Center for Defense Information; Ruth Leger Sivard, *World Military and Social Expenditures*; ACDA, *World Military Expenditures and Arms Transfers*; Robin Luckham, *SIPRI Yearbook 1985*.

Footnotes

1. U.S. Department of State, Arms Control and Disarmament Agency (ACDA), *World Military Expenditures and Arms Transfers* 1985 edition, p. 89.
2. Robin Luckham, "Militarization in Africa," in Stockholm International Peace Research Institute (SIPRI), *World Armaments and Disarmament Yearbook*, 1985 edition (Cambridge, Mass.: Oelgeschlager, Gunn & Hain Inc., 1983), pp. 325–28.
3. *Ibid.*, p. 314.
4. ACDA, *op. cit.* 1985 edition, and Luckham, *op. cit.*, p. 320.
5. ACDA, *op. cit.* 1985 edition, p. 131.
6. ACDA, *op. cit.* 1986 edition, SIPRI figures from SIPRI database.
7. Europa Publications, *Africa South of the Sahara* 1987 edition, (London: Europa Publications, 1986), p. 708.
8. Bruce E. Arlinghaus, *Military Development in Africa: The Political and Economic Risks of Arms Transfers* (Boulder, Colo.: Westview Press, 1984), p. 59.
9. ACDA, *op. cit.* 1985 edition, p. 131.
10. ACDA, *op. cit.* 1985 edition, and SIPRI *op. cit.* 1985 and 1986 editions.
11. ACDA, *op. cit.* 1975 and 1985 editions, and SIPRI *op. cit.* 1985 edition.
12. ACDA, *op. cit.* 1985 edition, and SIPRI *op. cit.* 1986 edition.
13. ACDA, *op. cit.* 1975, 1980 and 1985 editions, SIPRI, *op. cit.* 1985 edition, and Richard Grimmett, *Trends in Conventional Arms Transfers to the Third World by Major Supplier* 1985 edition (Washington: Congressional Research Service, April 19, 1985).
14. Andrew Pierre, *The Global Politics of Arms Sales* (Princeton, N.J.: Princeton University Press, 1982), p. 257.
15. ACDA, *op. cit.* 1975 and 1985 editions.
16. ACDA, *op. cit.* 1975, 1980 and 1985 editions, SIPRI, *op. cit.* 1985 edition, and Grimmett, *op. cit.* 1985 edition.
17. *Ibid.*
18. Cynthia A. Cannizzo, "Western Approaches to Military Assistance to Sub-Saharan Africa: An Overview," in Arlinghaus, Bruce, ed., *Arms for Africa* (Lexington, Mass.: Lexington Books, 1983), p. 122.
19. Herbert Wulf, "Arms Production in the Third World," in SIPRI, *op. cit.* 1985 edition, p. 340, and Cannizzo, *op. cit.*, p. 122.
20. U.S. Department of State, *Report to Congress Pursuant to Section 508 of the Comprehensive Anti-Apartheid Act of 1986: Compliance with the U.N. Arms Embargo* (Washington, D.C.: U.S. Department of State, April 1, 1987).
21. "Congress Gets Report on Israeli Military Aid to South Africa," *The New York Times*, April 3, 1987, p. 3, "Israel Pledges to Reduce Military Ties to South Africa," *The Washington Post*, March 20, 1987, p. 1, and Brzoska, Michael, *Shades of Grey: Ten Years of South African Arms Procurement in the Shadow of the Mandatory Arms Embargo* (Hamburg, FRG: University of Hamburg, Centre for the Study of Wars, Armaments and Development, 1987).
22. ACDA, *op. cit.* 1985 edition.
23. Luckham, *op. cit.*, p. 304.
24. Chester Crocker, in Hearings of the House Committee on Foreign Affairs "U.S. Interests in Africa" 1979.
25. Luckham, *op. cit.*, p. 304.
26. ACDA, *op. cit.* 1986 edition.
27. Luckham, *op. cit.*, p. 304.
28. U.S. Department of Commerce, *Survey of Current Business*, June 1986, p. 48.
29. Bruce Arlinghaus, "Linkage and Leverage in African Arms Transfers" in *Arms For Africa*, p. 10.
30. Chester Crocker, *Department of State Bulletin*, Nov. 13, 1985.
31. Congressional Quarterly, *Congressional Quarterly Almanac* 1963 edition (Washington, 1963), p. 264.

32. Joseph P. Smaldone, "U.S. Arms Transfers and Security Assistance Programs in Africa: A Review and Policy Perspective" in *Arms for Africa*, p. 186.
33. Cited in Smaldone, *op. cit.*, p. 186.
34. Michael Klare, *American Arms Supermarket* (Austin, Texas: University of Texas Press, 1984), p. 31.
35. Smaldone, *op. cit.*, p. 192.
36. Pierre, *op. cit.*, p. 260.
37. ACDA, *op. cit.*, 1974 and 1979 editions.
38. Pierre, *op. cit.*, p. 261.
39. Stephanie Neuman, *Military Assistance in Recent Wars: The Dominance of the Superpowers* (New York: Praeger Publishers, 1986), p. 36.
40. Neuman, *Ibid.*, p. 84.
41. Defense Security Assistance Agency, *Congressional Presentation for Security Assistance Programs, Fiscal Year 1987* vol. I, p. 35.
42. "Morocco Angling for U.S. Bases," *Atlanta Journal and Constitution*, Aug. 16, 1987, p. 19.
43. Defense Security Assistance Agency, *op. cit.*, p. 41.
44. "U.S. Arms Airlift to Angola Rebels Is Said to Go On," *The New York Times*, July 27, 1987, p. 1.
45. Cited in Congressional Quarterly, *op. cit.* 1979 edition, p. 125.
46. Defense Security Assistance Agency, *op. cit.*, p. 40.
47. DSAA, *op. cit.*, p. 51.
48. SIPRI, *op. cit.*, 1987 edition.
49. Noel Koch, "U.S. Assistance to the Third World: Time for a Reappraisal," *Journal of International Affairs*, Summer 1986 (vol. 40/no. 1), p. 54.
50. Koch, *Ibid.*, p. 55.

Chapter 11
The Arms Trade and Latin America

Conflicts in Latin America

Unlike much of the rest of the Third World, full-fledged inter-state warfare in Latin America*
in the modern age has been the exception rather than the rule. (See Table 11–3 at the end of the
chapter for a list of recent conflicts in the region.) Nevertheless, inter-state tensions and rivalries—
born largely out of territories lost and wars fought well in the past—contribute to the militarization
of the region and arms transfers to it. Many of the Andean and Central American nations have
engaged in a number of longstanding border disputes. Other governments have contended with
internal armed opposition movements in recent decades that—with the notable exceptions of Cuba
and Nicaragua—have failed on the battlefield.

Fighting today ranges from relatively small insurgencies, as in Peru, to the large-scale civil war
in El Salvador. The best publicized of the continuing conflicts is the war between the Nicaraguan
government and its U.S.-backed opposition, known as the "contras," which has served as an
impetus for arms transfers to Central American countries.

The 'Andean arms race': Hostilities between Peru and Chile, and to a lesser extent between
Ecuador and Bolivia, have led to what foreign policy analysts have labeled an "Andean arms race."
Border tensions in the Andes can be traced to historical animosities that have flared periodically since
World War II. By most accounts, Peru's decision to embark on a military buildup after the 1968
coup that brought the military to power prompted both Chile and Ecuador to increase their defense
expenditures and to acquire more advanced weaponry abroad. According to the U.S. government,
in the early 1980s Peru spent about one-fourth of its national budget, accounting for roughly 5
percent of GNP, on its military.[1] Other sources, most notably the International Institute for Strategic
Studies, place the GNP figure in the 2.5 to 3.5 percent range.[2]

The Andean nations acknowledged their arms competition in the 1974 Declaration of Ayacucho
and subsequent consultations aimed at restraining the regional military competition and the arms
trade in the area. Six Andean nations—Bolivia, Chile, Colombia, Ecuador, Peru and Venezuela—
along with Panama and Argentina agreed in the Declaration to "create conditions which permit
effective limitations of armaments and put an end to their acquisition for offensive warlike purposes

---

*For the purposes of this study, Latin America includes the countries of South America, the Caribbean and Central America.

in order to dedicate all possible resources to economic and social development."[3] According to Andrew Pierre, the participants sought "to freeze existing ratios of weapons-to-manpower and levels of military expenditures in relation to gross national product."[4] The talks, however, reached an impasse, as did later consultations among Peru, Chile and Bolivia. Peru, Chile and Ecuador again engaged in a series of high level talks in 1985 at the suggestion of the newly elected Peruvian president, Alan Garcia. Nevertheless, the Declaration of Ayacucho has yet to evolve beyond the form of a statement of principles.

Arms competition among neighbors appears to be a relatively important component of Latin American demand for weapons. This view, however, is not universally accepted. A 1973 study by the Rand Corp. maintained that "selective efforts at regional balancing have some influence on arms demands among neighbors, but no arms races exist today or seem likely to exist in the future."[5] According to the Rand study, during the 1960s Latin American militaries demanded weapons to upgrade "the generational obsolescence or aging of local inventories," to meet external and internal defense requirements, and to support independent foreign policies. The Rand report's emphasis on intrinsic military needs rather than "arms races" remains valid today if only because countries try to keep pace with the ever-changing technology of advanced weaponry.

The Falklands/Malvinas war: The one recent full-fledged inter-state war in Latin America pitted Great Britain against Argentina in a 74-day war in 1982 over the disputed Falklands/Malvinas Islands of the South Atlantic. Many observers were concerned that the war would trigger a South American arms race. The Stockholm International Peace Research Institute wrote in a 1983 analysis of the conflict that the impetus for an arms build-up would be the replacement of the equipment that Argentina lost during the war—which included a cruiser and 75 aircraft—and the upgrading of Argentina's navy and air defense systems, which the war with Britain proved lacking in certain respects. Estimates of the amount the Argentines would eventually spend on rearmament ranged from $1 to $3 billion.[6]

SIPRI wrote that, "Having demonstrated the insufficient degree of military preparedness of Latin American countries, Argentina's defeat may stimulate an escalation of the arms build-up in the region. . . . Argentina's immediate neighbors cannot remain indifferent to the rapid Argentine rearmament."[7] Brazil and Chile, in particular, were considered likely to respond with arms purchases to maintain the perceived military balance. After the war, for instance, Britain sold Chile three Canberra bombers of a type never before sold overseas. Brazil acted "clearly in response" to the Falkland/Malvinas Island war, reported SIPRI, by initiating plans for an air and naval base on an island 750 miles off its coast.

The evidence, however, does not bear out early concerns of an arms buildup spawned by the Falklands/Malvinas war. Argentina's rearmament program resulted in sizable immediate weapons imports. The U.S. government has estimated that the value of Argentina's arms imports more than tripled, from $290 million in 1982 to $975 million the following year, but has since declined considerably. In fact, Argentina's total military expenditures have dropped steadily since 1982.[8] Chile's arms imports also have decreased, from $280 million in 1982 to an annual average of $90 million since then, while Brazil's have largely remained the same.[9] Most of Brazil's military requirements are filled by domestic production, however.

Argentina's rearmament program appears to have slowed considerably, largely because the civilian government headed by Raul Alfonsin that replaced the military dictatorship in 1983 was forced to come to grips immediately with an astronomical rate of inflation and external debt:

Argentina's Central Bank in 1983 estimated that the country had incurred roughly $5 billion in foreign debt just from the purchase of arms abroad from 1978 to 1982. The new civilian government quickly opted for a reduction in military expenditures, including money spent on imported arms, as a necessary first move: SIPRI reports that "very few orders for new weapons were signed in 1984–85."[10] Argentina's most extreme measure involves the proposed sale of two of its newest diesel-powered submarines. In June 1986, West Germany granted the Alfonsin government permission to sell the submarines, which Bonn had delivered in 1984 and 1985, so that the proceeds might be used against outstanding Argentine debts, which include $215 million owed to German military firms for work on various projects.

Analysts also attribute the dampening of a potential arms buildup in the post-Falklands/Malvinas South America to a lessening of tension between Argentina and neighboring Chile. Late in 1984, negotiations between the two nations, aided by mediation from the Vatican, produced a treaty settling a century-long dispute involving sovereignty over three islands in the Beagle Channel at the southern tip of South America.

In addition to these intra-state conflicts, many nations of Latin America have faced insurgent movements—some of which have been large enough in scale to be considered civil wars—which have to varying degrees influenced the amount and types of weapons that they import. Since 1960, the goverments of Cuba, the Dominican Republic, Guatemala, Uruguay, Argentina, El Salvador, Nicaragua, Colombia and Peru have experienced armed challenges from insurgents. The most heated internal conflicts currently involve El Salvador, which has been locked in battle with leftist rebels since the late 1970s, and Nicaragua, which is fighting a war with conservative forces that were toppled from power by the Sandinista revolution in 1979.

The Arms Market in Latin America

By all accounts Latin America imports fewer armaments than any other region. According to the Arms Control and Disarmament Agency and the Congressional Research Service, during the period 1977–85 Latin America accounted for between 8 and 9 percent of all arms imported by developing nations. While SIPRI records a slightly higher 11 percent share for Latin America during this period, this is still substantially less than the other regions.[11] The nations of Latin America spend less on imported military weapons than other areas of the Third World because of their unusually large debt burdens and relatively small military budgets. Some analysts also attribute the below-average weapons buying in Latin America to the fact that the various conflicts, described in the previous section, have not led to all-out wars on the scale of those in the Middle East, Africa or Asia. Nevertheless, as Table 11–1 illustrates, Latin American countries still import a considerable quantity of military equipment. Moreover, some observers expect an above average growth rate for the region in the future because of widespread territorial tensions, especially in Central America; a rising need for counterinsurgency weapons in countries such as Chile; and the influence wielded by military elites, even in the emerging democracies.[12]

According to both SIPRI and ACDA data, during the five year period ending in 1985, the leading arms importers in Latin America were Cuba, Argentina, Venezuela and Peru. Together these nations accounted for more than 65 percent of arms deliveries to Latin America during this period, according to the ACDA. If the next largest arms importers in Latin America, Chile, Ecuador and Colombia, are included, they account for almost 85 percent of Latin America's arms market.[13]

Table 11–1

Weapon Systems Delivered to Latin America, 1981–85
(in units)

Weapons System	U.S.	Other NATO	U.S.S.R.	Other Warsaw Pact	China
Land Armaments					
Tanks	23	40	445	115	0
Anti-Air Artillery	0	5	220	55	0
Field Artillery	388	0	555	110	0
Armored Personnel Carriers	0	445	185	165	0
Naval Craft					
Major Surface Combatants	2	43	4	0	0
Other Surface Combatants	6	23	36	2	0
Submarines	0	8	1	0	0
Missile Attack Boats	0	0	6	0	0
Aircraft					
Supersonic Combat Aircraft	33	0	100	0	0
Subsonic Combat Aircraft	60	25	0	0	0
Other Aircraft	18	145	40	30	0
Helicopters	113	75	85	5	0
Missiles					
Surface-to-air missiles	0	530	1,295	0	0

Source: U.S. Arms Control and Disarmament Agency

Local arms production: Brazil and Argentina maintain significant domestic arms manufacturing industries, and several other countries are working toward weapons production capability. In the course of the last decade, Brazil's indigenous weapons industry has become the largest of all Third World nations. (For more on the Brazilian arms industry, see Chapter 1.) Regional producers have competed most effectively against foreign imports with small arms, munitions and counterinsurgency weapons. Moreover, coproduction agreements and technology transfers are rapidly broadening the manufacturing bases of many Latin America nations. SIPRI in 1985 ranked Argentina and Brazil with Israel and India as the most diversified and sizable arms producers among 27 Third World nations.[14] Both Latin American countries design and produce their own combat aircraft, guided missiles and small fighting ships. They also produce under license a wide range of weapons systems that require some imported parts. SIPRI also cites Chile and Peru as countries with "production in several categories," including fighter components, small fighting ships, and indigenous design and manufacturing of small arms, and it lists Colombia and Mexico as capable of more limited weapons production.[15]

Competition among suppliers: The arms market of Latin America is characterized by a high degree of competition among suppliers. Figure 11–1, drawn from data compiled by the ACDA, shows that the major Western European suppliers accounted for 37 percent of the arms delivered to Latin America between 1981 and 1985, the Soviet Union for 31 percent, and the United States for 10 percent. Israel, Czechoslovakia, Poland, South Africa and Taiwan also supply Latin America with military equipment. The People's Republic of China has expressed interest in breaking into the Latin American arms market, and is reported to have offered 110 of its F-7 fighters to Brazil on very favorable terms.

Data from the Congressional Research Service, presented in Table 11–2, which were compiled by a different method and examine different periods of time, illustrate how competition makes for significant shifts in the market share of the major arms suppliers from year to year. The rise in U.S. arms transfers to Latin America from 3.9 to 9.7 percent during the periods tabulated by the CRS results mainly from the sale of F-16s to Venezuela and a reformulation of U.S. policy in Central America.

Some observers believe that in commercial terms the Latin American region is the most competitive area in the world.[16] Only Cuba and a couple of countries in Central America are aligned with a single weapons supplier. Most Latin American nations buy principally from Western European and smaller Third World suppliers.[17]

In 1973, Peru became the only Latin American country other than Cuba to acquire arms from the Soviet Union when it bought Soviet-made tanks. Peru has since obtained Soviet fighter-bombers, helicopters and artillery, but a concomitant closer political alignment between the two nations has not accompanied the sizable purchases. Andrew Pierre comments, "It is a rare example, in the global politics of arms sales, of a recipient state buying weapons from both East and West fairly openly and without a resulting political impact of realignment."[18] From 1981 to 1985, Peru acquired half of its imported arms from Western Europe, one-third from the Soviet Union, and one-tenth from the United States.[19]

While the money involved in the Latin American arms trade is less than in other regions, a great deal of weaponry is transferred because it consists mostly of lower cost, less advanced arms well-suited for maintaining internal security, such as small arms, armored vehicles, artillery, patrol boats, small cargo planes, and reconnaissance aircraft and helicopters. The demand for goods at the lower end of the military technology spectrum, and the reluctance of the United States to make available its most advanced armaments, has given Western European and other suppliers an edge over the superpowers. ACDA data show that both the major European sellers and the world's minor arms exporting countries have a larger share of the Latin American market than any other Third World regions.

U.S. Arms Sales Policy and Practices: Latin America

Although U.S. dominance over the Latin America arms market slipped during the 1960s, during the last five years it has moved to regain its competitive position among arms suppliers to the region. The Reagan administration has expanded arms sales, in particular, by increasing the sophistication of weaponry through an F-16 fighter sale to Venezuela and stepping up the quantity of arms and military assistance provided to government forces in Central America. Depending on their financial

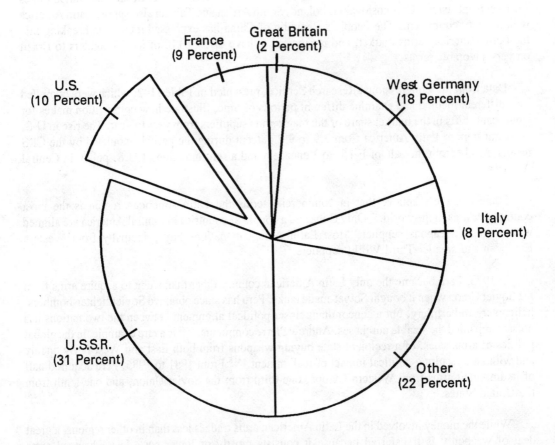

Source: U.S. Arms Control and Disarmament Agency, *World Military Expenditures and Arms Transfers*, 1986

Figure 11–1.   Suppliers' Shares of Arms Deliveries to Latin America, 1981–1985

Table 11–2

Market Share of Arms Suppliers to Latin America

Supplier	1979–1982	1983–1986
United States	3.9%	9.7%
France	16.1	2.7
United Kingdom	5.1	0.7
West Germany	3.3	17.0
Italy	8.7	3.0
Other Non-Communist	19.9	7.0
USSR	42.0	48.1
Other Communist	1.0	11.9
Total	100.0%	100.0%

Source: Grimmet, Richard F. "Trends in Conventional Arms Transfers to the Third World by Major Supplier, 1978–1985" Congressional Research Service, 1986.

resources, the trends among Latin American countries are to accumulate weapons both to advance territorial interests and for counterinsurgency, to aim for the best weapons from competing suppliers, and to develop domestic arms industries.

Latin America is strategically important to the United States for economic reasons that transcend geographical proximity and political alliance or influence. U.S. business has a vital stake in Latin America, which accounts for about three-quarters of all U.S. Third World investments and two-fifths of the nonindustrial world's imports of U.S. merchandise.[20] The Latin American countries also provide critical raw materials to U.S. industry, including about two-fifths of its imported oil. Access to sea lanes and the Panama Canal are also essential to U.S. commerce.

In 1951, Congress passed the Mutual Security Act to channel funds for Latin American forces as part of the Cold War effort to contain communism. During the 1950s, the United States sold arms left over from World War II and the Korean War through mutual defense assistance agreements with Chile, Colombia, Cuba, Ecuador and Peru (1952), Brazil, the Dominican Republic and Uruguay (1953), Honduras and Nicaragua (1954), Guatemala and Haiti (1955) and Bolivia (1958). Concerned with potential external threats to Latin American nations, the United States concentrated on providing maritime arms for coastal defense and, by the late 1950s, anti-submarine warfare. The 1950s agreements also designated the United States as sole provider of military advisory missions.[21]

However, Fidel Castro's successful revolution in Cuba, as well as guerrilla insurgencies in Southeast Asia, Algeria, Colombia and Venezuela, caused U.S. policymakers to rethink their focus on an outward looking hemispheric defense. President Kennedy, who had sought as a congressman to curb military assistance to Latin America, called for new tactics and policies to counter Communist-inspired rebellions. While he stepped up U.S. anti-guerrilla military readiness, he believed that economic aid, information programs and intelligence operations would allow the development of Third World countries to proceed free from Communist subversion. An influential

State Department counterinsurgency expert argued in 1961 that Third World countries must couple tighter internal security measures with reforms to "at least ameliorate those grievances and causes of discontent which the Communists exploit."[22] Also in 1961, Congress placed limits on weapons grants to Latin America in an effort to ensure that available resources be used mainly for socio-economic development.

President Kennedy set up a special sub-cabinet level interagency group for counterinsurgency in 1962 and revised arms export programs, and counterinsurgency concerns soon shaped Military Assistance Program grants and credit sales to Latin America and Southeast Asia. As a 1969 Senate study noted, "The basis for military aid to Latin America abruptly shifted from hemispheric defense to internal security, from the protection of coastlines and antisubmarine warfare to defense against Castro-communist guerrilla warfare."[23] This shift was accompanied by an emphasis on efforts of economic development that were in part conducted by the recipients' military establishments. Civic actions by armed forces to improve roads, water supplies, public health and education accounted for about one-seventh of U.S. military assistance to Latin America during the mid-1960s. One scholar, Douglas F. Blaufarb, concluded that "the military facet of counterinsurgency was subordinate in theory and doctrine to the civilian facets."[24]

In practice, though, American transfers of military equipment and supplies to Latin America fluctuated, and on the whole did not abate, in the 1960s. (See Figure 11–2.) Many of the weapons used for counterinsurgency were identical to those relevant to conventional warfare; the most noticeable shift was in the type of advice and training provided for the use of the imported weaponry.

The Johnson administration followed Kennedy's lead and linked counterinsurgency to social development and economic aid. Secretary of Defense Robert McNamara posited in 1968 that "without internal development of at least a minimal degree, order and stability are impossible . . . because human nature cannot be frustrated indefinitely."[25] The United States hoped to prevent the diversion of scarce resources to weapons purchases by limiting the sales of the more expensive state-of-the-art systems, such as supersonic jet fighters.

Latin American governments did not accept wholeheartedly the U.S. proclivity for providing only counterinsurgency weaponry. The predicted wave of Communist-backed rebellions did not materialize, and those movements that did—such as Che Guevara's challenge to the government of Bolivia—were suppressed. Thus, the nations of South America, in particular, pressed for more advanced arms for territorial security, and a rift soon developed between the United States and its Latin American customers.

During the mid-1960s, the United States tried to keep advanced jet fighters out of the region and rejected requests by Peru, Chile and Venezuela to buy the supersonic Northrop F-5 Freedom Fighter. U.S. critics saw the F-5, according to the 1973 Rand study on Latin America, "as a prime example of wasteful military expenditures for unnecessarily sophisticated equipment at a time when generous U.S. credits were being extended for economic development."[26] Venezuela and Chile responded by purchasing subsonic aircraft, including some from Great Britain, and Chile considered buying a British made supersonic fighter.

Peru, however, broke both the Latin America "sound barrier" and the U.S. stranglehold on the regional arms market by purchasing, on credit, Mirage-V fighters from France. As a result, other Latin American countries began buying Mirage fighters to balance their rival's new-found air combat

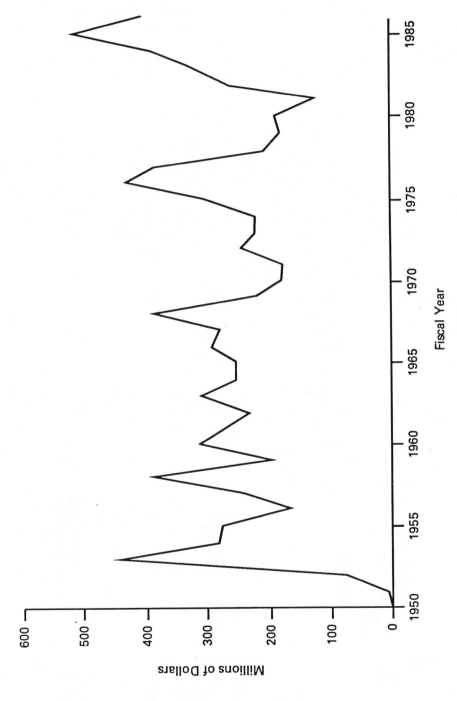

Source: Defense Security Assistance Agency, "Fiscal Year Series," 1987.

Figure 11–2. U.S. Military Deliveries to Latin America
(in millions of constant 1986 dollars)

capabilities. The United States reacted by threatening to suspend economic aid to Peru, which in turn prompted the other nations of Latin America to diversify their arms purchases even further so as not to be completely dependent on Washington and thereby locked into its foreign policy objectives. Within a few years, Argentina, Brazil, Colombia and Venezuela also bought squadrons of Mirage fighters—bringing sales of the French jet to a quarter of a billion dollars by 1973.[27]

The momentum toward diversification continued into the 1970s. Venezuela purchased French tanks, Italian frigates, submarines from West Germany, machine guns from Belgium and British aircraft.[28] "While the United States unilaterally maintained restrictions on sales and credits for several years," wrote Andrew Pierre, "the West Europeans sold $1.3 billion of arms between 1968 and 1972. This represented 84 percent of Latin American arms purchases (excluding Cuba)."[29] European suppliers of aircraft and ships dominated sales to the region while, according to the Rand report, "about 60 percent of U.S. foreign military sales volume went for parts, services, and rehabilitation costs, rather than end-items." The report found that the six top South American buyers "contracted to spend about five times more on European than on U.S. equipment during the period from 1968 to 1972."[30] It was during this period that Argentina and Brazil started expanding their manufacturing capability as well.

The Nixon administration opposed the sales limitations and development approach taken by Presidents Kennedy and Johnson. The Nixon approach to weapons transfers to Latin America perhaps was best summarized by Nelson Rockefeller—then the governor of New York—whom Nixon sent to Latin America on a presidential mission during his second year in office. When Rockefeller returned, he wrote:

> The United States must face more forthrightly the fact that while the militaries in the other American nations are alert to the problems of internal security, they do not feel this is their only role and responsibility. They are conscious of the more traditional role of the military establishment to defend the nation's territory, and they possess understandable professional pride which creates equally understandable desires for modern arms.[31]

Congress, however, resisted new proposed weapons transfers to Latin America for two reasons: lingering anger over Latin America's drive for diversification and advanced arms, and concern with the Vietnam war and its implications for American military involvement elsewhere in the Third World. The Foreign Military Sales Act of 1968 restricted sales of sophisticated arms, such as missile systems and jet fighters, to most Third World countries and set a $75 million credit ceiling on annual military aid to Latin America. The bill further asked that sales "not be approved where they would have the effect of arming military dictators who are denying social progress to their own people."[32] Congress also amended the Foreign Assistance Act to cut aid to governments that used surplus funds to buy advanced weaponry.

Unable to alter congressional opinion, Nixon invoked a waiver provided in the act that allowed him to circumvent congressional limits on the sale of advanced weapons if he determined that the transfer was "important to the national security of the United States" in order to sell F-5E supersonic fighters to five South American nations (Brazil bought 42 and Chile bought 18) and, later, other advanced weapons such as air-to-air missiles. Under Nixon, FMS sale agreements between the United States and Latin American countries quadrupled from $24 million in 1970 to a record $212 million in 1974, and the United States staged a comeback as a supplier to Latin America.[33] For the 10 years ending in 1976, according to one analysis of ACDA figures, the United States was the major supplier to Bolivia, Guatemala, Nicaragua, Paraguay and Uruguay, and the supplier of more than 30 percent of the weapons transferred to Argentina, Brazil and Colombia.[34]

Congressional opposition to liberal arms sales to Latin America increased with the military takeovers of the governments of Chile and Uruguay in 1973 and Argentina in 1976 and with the greater frequency of reporting of human rights abuses. During the Carter administration, Congress banned all military sales and assistance to Chile, took similar action against Argentina and Uruguay, and made Brazil, El Salvador and Guatemala ineligible for FMS credits.[35] Although many of the nations barred from receiving American arms found alternative suppliers easily enough, those that had purchased U.S. manufactured major weapon systems encountered difficulties because of the embargoes. Chile, for example, is able to keep only two or three of its fleet of 14 remaining F-5s in flying condition because the United States refuses to sell it spare parts.

President Carter's revision of arms sales policy, and the congressionally mandated strictures for certain countries, caused a sharp drop in U.S. weapons exports to Latin America, as Figure 11-2 illustrates. By fiscal year 1981, U.S. weapons deliveries to Latin America fell to the lowest level—taking inflation into account—since 1952. In following the new policy's ban on sophisticated weapons sales, the administration prevented the sale of F-5Es to Ecuador and Guatemala. Sales of internal security weapons were also blocked during this period on the basis of human rights concerns.

By 1979, nonetheless, the Carter administration began to make exceptions for certain Latin American countries, as it had done frequently in the Middle East. The Carter administration sold sophisticated surface-to-air missiles and antiaircraft guns to Ecuador in 1979 and F-5E fighters to Mexico in 1980. FMS agreements with El Salvador increased from less than $500 in 1979 to $10 million in fiscal year 1981, and commercial exports licensed under the Arms Export Control Act similarly increased from $151,000 to $1.4 million as the civil war there escalated.[36] These exceptions were made largely because the successful Nicaraguan revolution, the insurgency in El Salvador and the increased level of European arms sales to the region came to eclipse the importance of consideration of human rights as a driver of policy.

Current U.S. arms transfer policy in Latin America: The Reagan administration quickly dismantled Carter's guidelines on arms sales restrictions. While stating that it was also concerned with human rights, it abandoned the Carter approach of withholding arms and assistance in the hopes of coercing violators to change their ways and instead chose a policy of extending equipment and aid as rewards for improved human rights records. Thus, in March 1981, Secretary of State Alexander Haig called for a resumption of arms sales to Argentina and soon loosened the policy toward Guatemala by allowing the sale of army vehicles. When episodes of political violence decreased following the 1982 Guatemalan coup, the Reagan administration approved a $6 million FMS cash sale of aircraft spare parts, and agreed to a more restricted package when Guatemala was unable to come up with the funds. The Reagan administration in 1987 certified that the police forces of El Salvador had improved their human rights record and notified Congress that it intended to supply them with $9.1 million in military supplies, including shotguns, pistols, M-16 rifles, vehicles and communications equipment. Late in 1981, the administration announced the sale of 18 General Dynamics F-16A fighters and six F-16B trainers to Venezuela, a crucial oil-exporting country with a pro-U.S. government. FMS agreements skyrocketed from $26 million in 1980 to a record $684 million in 1982 because of the F-16 sale to Venezuela.

The potential efficacy of withholding military assistance and curtailing arms transfers as a diplomatic tool for signaling discontent or trying to effect a change in a recipient's behavior, though, has not been entirely lost on the Reagan administration. In 1987, the administration quietly suspended military and economic aid to Panama when its leader, Gen. Manuel Antonio Noriega, came under a broad based attack from domestic protesters who charged corruption and misrule. As an extension of its support for Britain in its conflict with Argentina over the Falkland/Malvinas islands, the United States also rebuffed an Argentine request for additional A-4 attack aircraft. Argentina's existing fleet of A-4s is reported to be seriously hobbled by Washington's unwillingness to supply spare parts needed to keep the aircraft flying. U.S. arms deliveries to Argentina have not exceeded $10 million (constant 1986 dollars) in any of the years since the Falklands war. Nevertheless, as a result of the less restrictive Reagan policy in general, aggregate U.S. arms exports to Latin America rose from an annual average of roughly $200 million during President Carter's tenure to an annual average of almost $400 million (in constant 1986 dollars) under the Reagan administration.

Most observers do not expect that the resurgence of U.S. arms sales to the region will replace either the large share held by European suppliers or the growing self-sufficiency of Argentina and Brazil. Michael Klare's assertion is typical: "While the Reagan policy will undoubtedly improve America's overall competitive position, it will not alter the basic structure of the Latin American arms market."[37]

Central America: While the easing of sales restrictions permitted a rise in arms exports to the major South American buyers, U.S. arms transfers to Latin America also have grown dramatically because of the Reagan administration's Central America policy. Actual deliveries to Central America have grown steadily and rapidly from $18 million to $168 million between 1981 and 1985. As Figure 11–3 illustrates, recent FMS agreements with Central American governments comprised 80 percent of all 1985 FMS agreements to Latin America, compared with less than 10 percent during the Carter presidency. (Figure 11–3 excludes commercial sales.) In real terms, FMS agreements increased 1,640 percent in the five year period ending in fiscal year 1985.

Besides growing in absolute terms, U.S. military aid to Central America has grown relative to other forms of assistance. (In addition to arms transfer and training programs, security assistance includes Economic Support Funds for specific projects as well as cash transfers.) A 1986 SIPRI study found that, "in 1979, U.S. security assistance was less than 3 percent of total U.S. aid to Costa Rica, El Salvador, Guatemala and Honduras. Six years later, it accounted for more than two-thirds of the total." By SIPRI's calculations, total U.S. aid to these four countries rose from $85.4 million in 1979 to $947 million in 1985.[38] The dramatic increase in weapon transfers is consistent with the 1984 report of the National Bipartisan Commission on Central America—called the "Kissinger Commission" after its chairman, former Secretary of State Henry Kissinger—which recommended a five-year, $8 billion regional aid program, one-fourth of which was to assume the form of military assistance.[39]

Conflicting human rights and anticommunist priorities, as well as debate over intervention, make for an erratic and hotly contested U.S. policy toward Central America. Moreover, reliable estimates of the magnitude of the arms influx are difficult to come by because of the covert nature of operations there. Irregularities in the flow of arms to Central America are common because of congressional restrictions on government-financed arms transactions, and administration efforts to work around them compound the difficulties involved in formulating a precise picture of weapons transfers to the region. For example, Pierre asserts that despite legislation limiting arms sales to Guatemala because of its inadequate human rights record, "the Reagan administration chose to

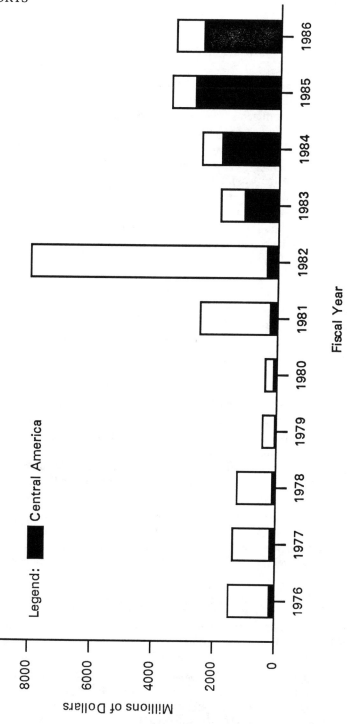

Source: Defense Security Assistance Agency, "Fiscal Year Series," 1987.

Figure 11–3. U.S. Arms Exports Agreements with Latin America
(in millions of constant 1986 dollars)

circumvent the legislation by having large military trucks and jeeps taken off the 'crime control' list,'' so that they could be exported to Guatemala.[40]

U.S. policy quickly came to involve stepped up efforts at funneling arms to the governments of El Salvador and Honduras, and clandestinely to the Nicaraguan "contra" forces challenging the rule of the Sandinista government. (Figure 11–4 illustrates the increase in U.S. military deliveries to El Salvador and Honduras.) The administration contends that U.S. arms transfers to Central America will contain the threat that Nicaragua and Cuba will export Communist revolution elsewhere, particularly through the civil war in El Salvador. In 1981, the administration issued a White Paper stating that the Communists were sending a large, steady flow of weapons to the Salvadoran armed opposition. The report on El Salvador did not find much support among European governments, and Pierre maintains that it was "revealed to be inaccurate in many of its details, thereby increasing the credibility problem."[41] Nonetheless, the United States followed up the report with $35 million in military and $100 million in economic aid for El Salvador, a package that included helicopters, light arms and training.

The Reagan administration also began to provide military assistance to the Nicaraguan exiles who oppose the rule of the Sandinista regime that came to power in 1979. Congress, which was notified of the covert aid program in December 1981, sought early on to place limitations on the size and nature of the operation. As part of its fiscal 1983 defense appropriations legislation it passed the Boland Amendment, which prohibited the use of covert funds for the purpose of overthrowing the Sandinista regime or for instigating a military confrontation between Nicaragua and Honduras. Estimates of the funding for the contras that was taken from the coffers of the Central Intelligence Agency during fiscal 1982 and 1983 range from $45 to $55 million. Congress then imposed a $24 million limit on aid to the contras for fiscal 1984. It rebuffed the President's attempts at securing an additional $21 million in assistance, and the funds were depleted partway through the year. The President's request for funds for military assistance to the contras was denied again in 1985, and instead Congress approved $27 million in "humanitarian" non-lethal aid to the Nicaraguan exiles. Administration officials indicated in December 1985 that the aid could include transport equipment, such as aircraft and helicopters, that would not be designed for combat but could be used in militarily useful ways, such as for moving weapons and ammunition. In 1986, the administration was able to reverse earlier votes and win congressional approval of a $100 million aid package for the contras, including $70 million in arms and military assistance. President Reagan requested $270 million for the contras for an 18-month period starting on Oct. 1, 1987, the beginning of the 1988 fiscal year.

Meanwhile, more and more sophisticated weaponry has been introduced to Central American counterinsurgency (El Salvador) and insurgency (Nicaragua) efforts. The United States supplied remotely powered surveillance vehicles to guard Honduras and assist the contras in Nicaragua.[42] U.S.-made helicopter gunships are used in El Salvador to detect and destroy guerrilla forces. Most recently, the Reagan administration cited the delivery of six to eight advanced Soviet helicopter gunships as a reason for considering the sale to Honduras of eight Northrop F-5A and F-5B fighter aircraft. The White House reportedly had turned down a July 1986 Honduran request for more advanced F-5Es and made a counter-offer for the less sophisticated version of the fighter instead. The administration has also considered the alternate option of allowing Honduras to purchase equally capable Israeli Kfir fighters with U.S. military assistance funds. The administration's decision to supply F-5s to Honduras generated considerable controversy. The Pentagon maintained that the aircraft are simply replacements for obsolete French Super Mysterie jets and are needed by Honduras to counter Nicaragua's advanced Soviet-made helicopters. Critics, though, contended that

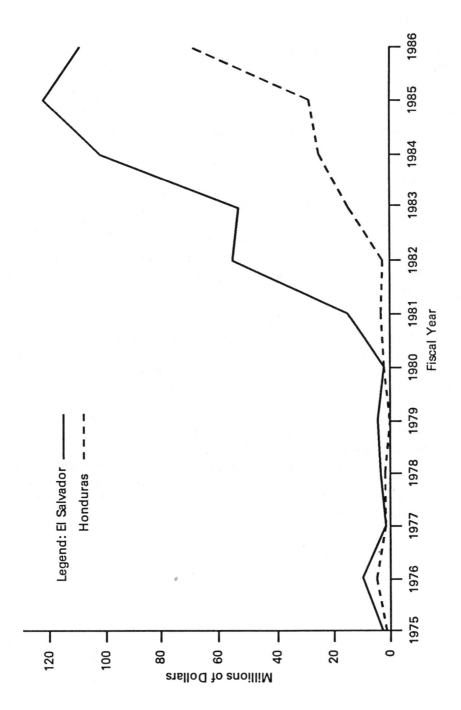

Source: Defense Security Assistance Agency, "Fiscal Year Series," 1987.

Figure 11–4.   U.S. Military Deliveries to Honduras and El Salvador
(millions of constant 1986 dollars)

transferring the supersonic F-5s to Honduras is tantamount to introducing a new and higher level of weapons technology into the region, and warned that the move would lead other Central American militaries to try to acquire similar supersonic aircraft. Indeed, after Washington announced its plans, Nicaraguan Defense Minister Gen. Humberto Ortega, speaking about the Sandinistas' plans to purchase Soviet MiG fighters, said: "To the degree that the U.S. continues to arm Honduras with weapons like the F-5, it undoubtedly makes it more possible and justified for Nicaragua to obtain the interceptor jets we need."[43] Washington's decision to provide F-5s to Honduras also angered Brazil, which earlier had asked for 25 of the aircraft, but had been told that none were available.

In its request for 1987 arms sales to El Salvador and Honduras, the administration told Congress that security assistance would help El Salvador "defend itself against a Marxist insurgency supported by Nicaragua, Cuba and the Soviet bloc," and enable the Salvadoran armed forces to "promote professionalism, respect for human rights, self-defense capabilities, discipline under elected civilian leaders, and concern for civilians caught up in the conflict." It said that U.S. military transfers to Honduras would modernize and give confidence to the armed forces. For 1987, the administration proposed $222 million in MAP grants and $240 million in FMS credits for El Salvador and Honduras, compared with $69 million in MAP grants and $140 million in FMS credits for all other Latin American countries.

Despite the rapid growth in recent years, the prognosis for arms exports to Central America is uncertain. An unexpected spin was put on the future debate over aid to the contras when late in 1986 revelations of the potentially illegal diversion of $10 to $30 million to the Nicaraguan insurgents in profits garnered from the covert sale of American weapons to Iran came to the fore. Members of Congress and contra leaders speculated in the wake of the disclosure that congressional approval of military assistance for the anti-Sandinista movement would be more difficult to secure in the near term. Immediate uncertainties aside, U.S. weapons transfers are geared to the supply of war materiel for the extensive fighting underway in Nicaragua and El Salvador. A settlement of either conflict would logically reduce the need for arms. There are also signs that the mounting U.S. federal deficit might result in prolonged annual budget cuts that could adversely affect Washington's ability to sustain high levels of foreign military assistance to the region and to the world in general. Nevertheless, even if these two civil wars ended, border tensions and the influx of weaponry in recent years might sustain the Central American arms buildup for years to come.

Table 11–3

Major Conflicts and Arms Transfers in Latin America

Participants*	Dates of conflict	Principal arms suppliers	Type of conflict
El Salvador vs. Honduras	1969	US US	inter-state war
Ecuador vs. Peru	1981	France, Italy, W. Germany USSR, Western Europe	border fighting
Argentina vs. Great Britain	1982	W. Germany, France, Israel	inter-state war
Argentine government vs. Leftist guerrillas	1969–76	W. Germany, France, Israel	insurgency
Colombian government vs. Drug rings & leftist guerrillas	1978–present	US, Western Europe, Israel Cuba	insurgency
El Salvador government and right-wing forces vs. Leftist rebels	1977–present	US, France, Israel Nicaragua, Cuba	civil war
Guatemalan government and right-wing forces vs. Leftist and Mayan rebels	1967–present	US, Israel, France Cuba	insurgency
Peruvian government vs. Maoist guerrillas	1980–present	USSR, France, W. Germany	insurgency
Nicaraguan government vs. Right-wing and Miskito rebels	1981–present	Cuba, USSR, France US	insurgency

Participants*	Dates of conflict	Principal arms suppliers	Type of conflict
Uruguayan government vs. Leftist rebels	1968–73	US	insurgency
Nicaraguan government vs. Sandinista rebels	1978–79	US, Israel Cuba	revolution
United States vs. Grenada (Cuba)	1983	 Cuba, USSR	inter-state war
Dominican government and United States vs. Leftist groups	1965	US	civil war
Cuban government vs. Cuban exiles	1961	USSR US	insurgency

* Parentheses indicate the participation of additional troops in the conflicts.

Sources: Center for Defense Information; Ruth Leger Sivard, *World Military and Social Expenditures*; ACDA, *World Military Expenditures and Arms Transfers*.

Footnotes

1. U.S. Department of State, Arms Control and Disarmament Agency (ACDA), *World Military Expenditures and Arms Transfers 1986* (*WMEAT*) (Washington: ACDA, 1986).
2. International Institute for Strategic Studies (IISS), *The Military Balance 1982–1983* (London: IISS, 1982), p. 125.
3. Andrew Pierre, *The Global Politics of Arms Sales* (Princeton: Princeton University Press, 1982), p. 283.
4. *Ibid.*, p. 284.
5. Luigi Einaudi, Hans Heymann, Jr., David Ronfeldt, and Caesar Sereseres, *Arms Transfers to Latin America* (Santa Monica, Calif.: Rand Corp., 1973), p. vi.
6. Stockholm International Peace Research Institute (SIPRI), *World Armaments and Disarmament Yearbook 1983* (Philadelphia: Taylor & Francis, 1983) and Michael Klare, *American Arms Supermarket* (Austin, Texas: University of Texas Press, 1984), p. 81.
7. SIPRI, *Ibid.*, p. 487.
8. ACDA, *op. cit.* 1986 edition.
9. *Ibid.*
10. SIPRI, *Yearbook 1986* (New York: Oxford University Press, 1986), p. 342.
11. ACDA, *op. cit.*, p. 131, SIPRI, *Yearbook 1984* and Richard Grimmett, *Trends in Conventional Arms Transfers to the Third World By Major Supplier, 1978–1985* (Washington: Congressional Research Service, May 9, 1986), p. 40.
12. Klare, *op. cit.*, Chapter 5, and Pierre, *op. cit.*, Part 3.
13. SIPRI, *op. cit.*, 1986 edition; ACDA, *op. cit.*, 1986 edition.
14. Wulf, Herbert, "Arms Production in the Third World," in SIPRI *Yearbook 1985*, pp. 332, 340.
15. *Ibid.*, p. 340.
16. Pierre, *op. cit.*, p. 233.
17. ACDA, *op. cit.* 1986 edition.
18. Pierre, *op. cit.*, p. 241.
19. ACDA, *op. cit.*, p. 133.
20. U.S. Department of Commerce, *Survey of Current Business*, June 1986, p. 48, and SIPRI, *Yearbook 1982*.
21. Klare, *op. cit.*, pp. 85–86.
22. U. Alexis Johnson, cited in Douglas S. Blaufarb, *The Counterinsurgency Era: U.S. Doctrine and Performance* (New York: Macmillan Publishing Co., 1977), p. 63.
23. Edwin Lieuwin, "The Latin American Military," p. 115, cited in Klare, *op. cit.*, p. 87.
24. Blaufarb, *op. cit.*, p. 65.
25. Robert S. McNamara, *The Essence of Security*, p. 149, cited in Klare, *op. cit.*, p. 88.
26. Einaudi et al., *op. cit.*, p. 2.
27. *Ibid.*, pp. 2–4.
28. Pierre, *op. cit.*, p. 245.
29. *Ibid.*, p. 234.
30. Einaudi et al., p. 7.
31. Nelson Rockefeller, "Quality of Life in the Americas: Report on a Presidential Mission for the Western Hemisphere," *Department of State Bulletin*, Dec. 8, 1969, pp. 516–518.
32. Congressional Research Service, *Changing Perspectives on U.S. Arms Transfer Policy*, Sept. 25, 1981, p. 5.
33. Department of Defense, Defense Security Assistance Agency, *Foreign Military Sales, Foreign Military Construction Sales and Military Assistance Facts 1982*, p. 2.
34. Michael Mihalka, "Supplier-Client Patterns in Arms Transfers: The Developing Countries, 1967–76," in Stephanie Neuman and Robert Harkavy (eds.), *Arms Transfers in the Modern World* (New York: Praeger Publishers, 1979), Table 4.3, p. 61.
35. Klare, *op cit.*, p. 92.

36. Department of Defense, Defense Security Assistance Agency, *Foreign Military Sales, Foreign Military Construction Sales and Military Assistance Facts 1985*, pp. 6–7, 42–43.

37. Klare, *op. cit.*, p. 98.

38. Rita Tullberg, and Victor Millan, "Security Assistance: The Case of Central America," SIPRI, *Yearbook 1986*, p. 310.

39. *Report of the National Bipartisan Commission on Central America* (Washington: Government Printing Office, 1984).

40. Pierre, *op. cit.*, p. 248.

41. *Ibid.*, p. 247.

42. *Jane's Defense Weekly*, Aug. 24, 1985.

43. "Nicaragua Says it Will Proceed with Plans to Get MIGs," *The Washington Post*, Aug. 3, 1987, p. 17.

Part II
Company Profiles

Part II
Note on Methodology

Part II contains 27 profiles that describe the weapons export activities of the 19 publicly held American corporations and their major subsidiaries that historically have been ranked among the largest U.S. arms exporters. Table II–1 provides a broader listing of the 50 U.S. companies that received the most Foreign Military Sales contract dollars for each of the fiscal years 1985 and 1986. The profiles look principally at arms exports made through the Department of Defense's Foreign Military Sales program, although sections II and III of each profile include some data on military-related sales made through the Commerce Department and the State Department Office of Munitions Control's Commercial Sales channel. A few of the companies have made especially large arms exports through commercial sales channels. The General Accounting Office's list of the top arms exporters through this program for fiscal years 1977–81 (the last years for which data are available) is reproduced as Table 7–1.

Each profile is divided into four sections. Section I—titled "Summary Data"—contains basic summary data on the company and its foreign military sales. The terms "DoD prime contract awards" and "FMS program awards" are used to signify awards issued by the Department of Defense to a particular firm or consortium in support of a contract. Reliance on this type of data has certain limitations. One is that much of the actual work is passed on to other companies under subcontract. A second is that awards in any given year are for work performed over periods ranging from less than a year to almost a decade. Thus the amounts awarded are not equivalent to actual sales for a given year. Finally, the dollar figures presented here are for the U.S. government fiscal year ending Sept. 30, except for the total sales figures, which correspond to the individual company's fiscal year. (Most companies use the calendar year ending Dec. 31.)

Data for section I were compiled from the companies' annual reports, the Department of Defense's publication *100 Companies Receiving the Largest Dollar Volume of Prime Contract Awards* for each fiscal year, and the General Accounting Office's list of the top Foreign Military Sales (FMS) contractors for fisal years 1982 through 1984. Fiscal years 1985 and 1986 FMS data for all companies, and total DoD and FMS contract awards for companies not listed in the above publications, were compiled by IRRC from Department of Defense records of all contract awards above $25,000 ($10,000 for fiscal year 1982). The symbol "NA" in this and all other sections means not available, while the symbol "n/a" denotes not applicable.

Section II—titled "Arms Export Business at a Glance"—contains a brief description of the company's arms export business. Data for this section comes from a variety of sources, including

Table II–1

U.S. Companies Receiving the Most Department of Defense
Foreign Military Sales Prime Contract Awards
(thousands of current dollars)

Fiscal Year 1985		Fiscal Year 1986	
1. McDonnell Douglas	$1,621,604	1. General Dynamics	$1,369,492
2. Boeing	1,293,654	2. General Electric	630,382
3. General Dynamics	1,230,867	3. Raytheon	602,288
4. General Electric	503,046	4. McDonnell Douglas	573,592
5. Northrop	295,831	5. Texas Instruments	217,867
6. Lockheed	295,473	5. United Technologies	213,609
7. United Technologies	294,835	7. General Motors	207,423
8. Raytheon	234,021	8. Boeing	206,044
9. Grumman	182,315	9. Westinghouse	203,567
10. Teledyne	123,869	10. Grumman	125,197
11. Ford Motor	100,795	11. Ford	105,194
12. Hughes Aircraft[1]	94,269	12. Northrop	104,159
13. General Motors	86,917	13. Honeywell	91,293
14. Westinghouse	82,721	14. Burroughs[2]	81,677
15. Rockwell International	75,089	15. Vinnell Corp.	81,381
16. Sperry[2]	73,967	16. Textron	80,652
17. Science Applications	65,012	17. Allied Signal	73,798
18. CFM International[3]	50,887	18. Hospital Corp. of America	61,672
19. Litton	47,195	19. Harsco	52,764
20. LTV	45,026	20. Lockheed	51,643
21. CRS Sirrine Metcalf Eddy[4]	40,376	21. Science Applications	48,488
22. Honeywell	37,543	22. Litton	42,836
23. IBM	36,677	23. Lear Siegler[5]	40,794
24. FMC	36,672	24. IBM	39,383
25. RCA[6]	36,008	25. CFM International[3]	35,267
26. Allied Signal	31,323	26. Teledyne	33,053
27. AT&T	30,601	27. FMC	32,108
28. Sanders Associates[7]	28,260	28. LTV	30,615
29. Gould	27,346	29. Joint Venture of MDTT[8]	27,236
30. Textron	26,693	30. Singer	25,579
31. IRT Inc.	24,959	31. 3D-International	24,564
32. Goodyear[9]	24,925	32. Gould	24,317
33. Texas Instruments	21,666	33. Martin Marietta	24,292
34. Martin Marietta	17,614	34. Motorola	18,399
35. Singer	17,426	35. Computer Tech. Associates	17,721
36. EG&G	15,082	36. Swiftships	17,200
37. Mitre	15,051	37. Mitre	16,960
38. Todd Shipyards	14,642	38. Central Power Engineering	15,874
39. BDM	14,283	39. National Airmotive Corp.	15,828

Table II–1. Continued

Fiscal Year 1985		*Fiscal Year 1986*	
40. Advanced Technologies	$ 14,104	40. Rockwell	$ 15,307
41. Emerson Electric	13,398	41. Sanders Associates[7]	14,586
42. Ex-Cell-O[10]	12,778	42. Hercules	10,122
43. Control Data	11,044	43. Lantana Boatyard	9,521
44. White Cons. Industries	10,802	44. Kay & Associates	9,030
45. Hercules	10,556	45. Exxon	8,711
46. CACI	10,438	46. Metric Systems	8,637
47. Booz, Allen & Hamilton	10,201	47. ITT	8,100
48. Kay and Associates	8,144	48. Penn Central Corp.	8,081
49. National Airmotive Corp.	7,569	49. Contel Page Inc.	7,128
50. Penn Central Corp.	7,195	50. EG&G	7,082
All contractors	$8,692,271	All contractors	$6,320,968

1. Hughes Aircraft, formerly a part of the privately held Howard Hughes Medical Institute, was purchased by General Motors in 1985. The fiscal 1986 total for General Motors incorporates awards to Hughes Aircraft.
2. In 1986, Sperry merged with Burroughs to form Unisys, which then sold Sperry's aerospace division to Honeywell. Because the transactions were not completed until after the end of fiscal 1986, each company stands on its own in these tables.
3. CFM International is a joint venture between General Electric and SNECMA of France.
4. This is a joint venture involving CRS Sirrine and Metcalf Eddy.
5. In 1987, Forstmann Little & Co. acquired Lear Siegler and subsequently broke up the company, selling its divisions to a variety of other companies.
6. RCA was acquired by General Electric in 1986. The fiscal 1986 total for General Electric incorporates awards to RCA.
7. Sanders Associates was acquired by Lockheed in 1987.
8. This is a joint venture involving an American and several European companies.
9. Goodyear Aerospace Corp. was acquired by Loral Corp. in 1987.
10. In 1986, Textron acquired Ex-Cell-O Corp. The fiscal 1986 total for Textron incorporates awards to Ex-Cell-O.

government documents and the companies' annual reports. Orders for "dual use"systems—those that have civilian applications but are frequently used to fulfill military roles—are listed in a number of profiles and mention of them is made in section II.

Section III—titled "Military Orders, 1982–1986"—lists orders made by foreign countries for weapon systems manufactured by the company in question. Some of the weapons ordered were delivered almost immediately, but other orders take years to fill. IRRC has tried to identify and delete from these listings any orders that were placed but subsequently canceled. These orders were compiled from open sources. The sources are identified by the letter or letters that follow the description of the weapon system being ordered. The source code is as follows:

a.   Department of Defense, *Prime Contract Awards by Contractor, Unclassified*

b.   *News Release*, Office of the Assistant Secretary of Defense for Public Affairs

c.   Defense Security Assistance Agency, quarterly reports to Congress

d.   Stockholm International Peace Research Institute, *World Armaments and Disarmament Yearbook* series

e.   International Institute for Strategic Studies, *Military Balance* series

f.   *International Defense Review*

g.   *Defense and Foreign Affairs*

h.   *Aviation Week & Space Technology*

i.   *Jane's Weapon Systems*

j.   *Defense Electronics*

k.   *The Washington Post*

l.   *The Wall Street Journal*

m.   *The New York Times*

n.   *Defense News*

r.   Company's annual report

These open sources were used because no comprehensive government listing of arms sales is available. IRRC attempted to verify all of the orders listed, but in some instances the companies were unable to offer confirmation. Parentheses have been placed around those dates or numbers of weapon systems ordered where uncertainty about the accuracy of the data exists.

Section III does not present a complete picture of each company's foreign arms orders. Many weapon sales of relatively low dollar value and most of those exported through commercial sales channels went unreported in the sources used for this study. Moreover, this section of some of the profiles excludes work conducted under subcontracts from other U.S. arms exporters because the information was not readily available.

The price given for each order represents the total cost of the transaction. In most cases, a substantial portion of the purchase price goes to companies that perform subcontract work on the system. The prices are usually taken from formal notices to Congress or are estimated by knowledgeable sources. These figures sometimes are preliminary, and vary from the final costs of the sales. The symbol "NA" indicates that reliable estimates were not available. Footnotes often follow either the price listing or the description of the deal. These provide important additional information, and should be consulted at the back of each profile.

In several instances, comparatively few orders for the contractor in question could be identified for the years 1982 through 1986, generally because the company performs subcontract work on larger weapon systems. In these cases, additional funding in the form of contract awards for orders placed before 1982 have been included in order to give a fuller picture of the company's arms export business, and mention of them is made in an explanatory paragraph that precedes section III of the profiles. As explained below, these contract awards do not represent complete orders and should not be regarded as such. The value given for the contract award represents only a portion of the total purchase price of the system.

Section IV of the profiles—titled "FMS Program Contract Awards, FY 1983–1986"—records all Department of Defense Foreign Military Sales prime contract awards greater than $25,000, arranged by weapon system and the U.S. government fiscal year in which they were awarded. Contract awards represent Department of Defense allocations of funds to contractors in support of orders, but do not constitute orders. Often the orders are placed several years before the contract award, which represents only an increment of the total purchase price. Contract awards, unlike orders, do represent the total amount of funds received by the company for all of the company's military equipment that was exported through the Foreign Military Sales program for the given years. This section, unlike section III, therefore includes all prime contract awards the company has received for components or services provided on larger weapon systems for which other companies are the prime contractor. Sections III and IV stand independent of one another and in no way should be construed to be cumulative; the figures in section IV will not add up to the total cost figures cited in section III. All data for section IV were derived from IRRC analysis of Department of Defense records of all contract awards of more than $25,000 for government fiscal years 1983–86.

AVCO CORP.

(a subsidiary of Textron Inc.)

I. SUMMARY DATA

Data, except for the total sales figures, are for U.S. government fiscal years, ending Sept. 30. FMS program award totals were calculated by IRRC from Department of Defense contract data.

	1982	1983	1984	1985	1986
Total sales (millions)	$1,223	$1,514	$1,528	NA	NA
DoD contract awards (millions)	$ 668	$ 676	$ 873	$1,198	$813
DoD contractor rank	28	29	27	n/a	n/a
DoD awards/total sales	.27	.24	.30	NA	NA
FMS contract awards (millions)	$ 36	$ 12	$ 9	$ 8	$ 8
FMS contractor rank	n/a	n/a	n/a	n/a	n/a
FMS/total DoD awards	.05	.02	.01	.01	.01
FMS/total sales	.029	.008	.006	NA	NA

II. ARMS EXPORT BUSINESS AT A GLANCE

Avco was purchased by Textron in 1984. Unlike Textron, Avco has not been ranked among the top U.S. FMS exporters during the 1970s or 1980s. Its FMS-related Department of Defense contract awards ranged from $8 million to $36 million for the period from fiscal 1982 to 1986, and averaged $14.6 million annually for the five years.

Avco Lycoming helicopter engines are the most widely exported of the company's military products. Bell Helicopter Textron makes extensive use of Avco turbine engines: Its UH-1 Iroquois transport and AH-1 Cobra Attack helicopters are powered by the Avco Lycoming T-53 engine. Boeing uses the company's T-55 engine in its CH-47 Chinook transport helicopter series as well. Awards for work related to the T-53 accounted for nearly all of Avco's FMS awards in each of the fiscal years 1982 through 1986.

In addition to helicopter turbine engines, Avco manufactures the turbine engine that propells the General Dynamics M-1 main battle tank. The U.S. government has not yet exported the M-1, although the prospect of allowing coproduction of the tank by Egypt was raised in 1987. It is not clear, though, that Avco's weapons exports would increase appreciably if the Egyptians are allowed to produce the M-1; Egyptian officials have suggested that the Avco turbine might not be well suited for sustained action in desert climates.

Avco engines also power one of the Navy's newest military crafts, the Bell Aerospace Landing Craft Air Cushion, an amphibious assault hovercraft. Avco's 1983 annual report said that orders for the craft by foreign governments "are possible."

III. MILITARY ORDERS, 1982–1986 (includes first quarter of 1987)

The relative dearth of information on Avco's arms exports is due less to the size of the company's military export business than to the fact that Avco makes components for larger systems, such as turbine engines for helicopters and tanks. Sources of FMS data usually list the major weapon system, and not lesser components. The profiles that discuss Textron's and Boeing's FMS business help to explain more fully the scope of Avco's arms export activities.

Country	Date of Agreement	Description of Order	Price (in millions)
– EUROPE AND MAJOR ALLIES –			
Turkey	1986	15 T-55-L-13B engine kits/g	$7.3
– ASIA AND PACIFIC –			
South Korea	1985	T-53 turbine engines for 21 Bell Textron AH-1s Cobra attack helicopters/m	NA
	1986	60 T-53 turbine engines for 50 Bell Textron UH-1H transport helicopters/c,d	NA[1]
Thailand	1986	T-53 turbine engines for Bell Textron AH-1 Cobra TOW helicopters/c,d,f,g	NA[2]
– MIDDLE EAST –			
Egypt	1985	10 T-55 turbine engines for Boeing Model 414 Chinook heavy lift helicopters/g	NA

IV. FMS PROGRAM CONTRACT AWARDS, FY 1983-1986
(millions of dollars)

Item	Fiscal Year	Award Total
T-53 turbine engine for helicopters	1983	$11.54
	1984	9.32
	1985	8.23
	1986	6.92
T-55 turbine engine for helicopters	1983	.12
	1984	−.79
	1985	.06
Unidentified awards	1986	.59

Negative figure results from downward contract adjustment.

_____

NOTES

1. This is part of a $155 million package, whose price covers both the 60 Avco engines and the 50 Bell Textron helicopters.

2. This is part of a $45 million package, whose price covers four Bell Textron AH-1 helicopters and Avco spare engines.

BEECH AIRCRAFT CO.

(a subsidiary of Raytheon Co.)

I. SUMMARY DATA

Data, except for the total sales figures, are for U.S. government fiscal years, ending Sept. 30. FMS program award totals were calculated by IRRC from Department of Defense contract data.

	1982	1983	1984	1985	1986
Total sales (millions)*	$568	$642	$723	$743	$ 686
DoD contract awards (millions)	$167	$156	$116	$245	$ 245
DoD contractor rank	n/a	n/a	n/a	n/a	n/a
DoD awards/total sales	.29	.24	.16	.33	.28
FMS contract awards (millions)	$ 2	$ 8	$ 1	$ .5	$ .2
FMS contractor rank	n/a	n/a	n/a	n/a	n/a
FMS/total DoD awards	.01	.05	.01	.002	.001
FMS/total sales	.004	.012	.001	.001	.0002

*   Listed in Raytheon publications as "Sales to unaffiliated customers for Raytheon's Aircraft Products Division."

II. ARMS EXPORT BUSINESS AT A GLANCE

The sale of military systems abroad currently accounts for a small portion of Beech Aircraft's total annual sales. Contracts issued to Beech under the foreign military sales program, however, are not an accurate measure of the company's total arms export business because many of its products are those that are frequently exported through direct, company-to-government commercial channels. The company, which was acquired by Raytheon early in 1980, manufactures a wide array of small turboprop aircraft and guided missile drones that are used by armed forces as targets for weapons tests and training. Most of Beech's aircraft are designed for civilian markets and are widely used by commuter and business concerns. Many governments, however, employ Beech aircraft for specialized—including military—missions. Military forces have used Beech airplanes for light troop transport, reconnaissance and surveillance, counter-insurgency and forward air control, and as trainers. The Japanese Maritime Safety Agency took delivery on 13 King Air aircraft during the early 1980s, and will use the planes to conduct maritime patrols. Various versions of King or Super King Airs have also been delivered to the governments of Ecuador, Uruguay and Morocco since 1980.

Beech's most popular export item is the T-34 trainer aircraft. Records compiled by the Department of Defense's Security Assistance Agency indicate that 53 T-34s had been exported through the FMS program and 71 through the Military Assistance Program as of September 1986. The DSAA's records do not include those T-34s that have been exported through the direct commercial channel. The armed forces of Algeria, Argentina, Ecuador, Gabon, Indonesia,

Morocco, Peru, Uruguay and Venezuela have purchased the most modern version of the aircraft—the T-34C Turbo Mentor—and some have used it in attack and counterinsurgency modes. The Beech T-34 has been produced under license in Argentina, Canada and Japan.

Beech also manufactures target drones like the MQM-107, now used by the armed forces of Sweden, Jordan, Taiwan, South Korea, the United Arab Emirates and Egypt. The company reports that it received an $11.9 million contract in 1981 for target systems (most likely the MQM-107) destined for Taiwan and says it delivered target drones to six foreign customers in 1984 in accordance with contracts worth $18.8 million. Another Beech target system—the AQM-37—was delivered to France, Great Britain and Italy during the late 1960s and early 1970s. Great Britain and France still use the AQM-37. According to the company, export sales of Beech target systems totaled $80 million as of 1986.

III. MILITARY ORDERS, 1982–1986 (includes first quarter of 1987)

The sources used for this study do not indicate in all cases whether the Beech aircraft ordered by the following countries during 1983 to 1985 are configured for military or civilian missions. The following orders are listed in the sources used for this study and in this profile because they were placed by foreign governments (as opposed to foreign commercial concerns), which may use the aircraft for military roles if they so choose.

Country	Date of Agreement	Description of Order	Price (in millions)
– ASIA AND PACIFIC –			
Indonesia	1983	9 T-34C Turbo Mentor trainer aircraft/d,g	$12.4
Malaysia	1982	1 Super King Air transport aircraft/e	NA
Taiwan	1984	42 T-34C Turbo Mentor trainer aircraft/ d,e,g	NA
Thailand	(1983)	1 Super King Air transport aircraft/d	NA
– MIDDLE EAST –			
Egypt	1985	6 model 1900C utility aircraft modified for special missions/f,r	$73
Saudi Arabia	1987	1 C-12 Huron transport aircraft/f	NA[1]
– AFRICA –			
Gabon	1985	4 T-34 Turbo Mentor trainer aircraft/e	NA
Morocco	(1983)	1 Super King Air transport aircraft/d	NA

Country	Date of Agreement	Description of Order	Price (in millions)
– LATIN AMERICA –			
Chile	(1984)	1 C-90 King Air transport aircraft/d	NA
Ecuador	1985	25 T-33A Bonanza jet trainers/d	NA[2]
Haiti	(1983)	1 A-36 Bonanza utility aircraft/d	NA
Mexico	(1984)	4 F-33C Bonanza utility aircraft/d	NA
	1986	21 F33C Bonanza utility aircraft/e,g	$4.9
Venezuela	(1982)	2 Super King Air transport aircraft/d	NA

IV. FMS PROGRAM CONTRACT AWARDS, FY 1983–1986
(millions of dollars)

Item	Fiscal Year	Award Total
MQM-107 guided missile target systems	1983	$4.54
	1984	.97
	1986	−.10
Technical services for unidentified guided missile systems*	1983	2.54
	1985	.58+
	1986	.27
Maintenance and repair of unidentified aircraft	1983	.54#

Negative figure results from downward contract adjustments.

*	IRRC analysis of DoD contract data suggests that these awards most likely involve the MQM-107 guided missile target system.
+	These awards are for work conducted in Jordan.
#	These awards are for work conducted in Saudi Arabia.

NOTES

1. This is part of a $400 million package that includes 13 United Technologies UH-60 helicopters and 15 Bell-Textron model 406 helicopters.

2. These are ex-U.S. reserve aircraft, which were refurbished to AT-33 specifications before being transferred to Ecuador.

THE BOEING CO.

I. SUMMARY DATA

Data, except for the total sales figures, are for U.S. government fiscal years, ending Sept. 30. FMS program award totals for 1982 to 1984 were calculated by the General Accounting Office; the 1985 and 1986 totals were calculated by IRRC from Department of Defense contract data.

	1982	1983	1984	1985	1986
Total sales (millions)	$9,035	$11,129	$10,354	$13,636	$16,341
DoD contract awards (millions)	$3,239	$ 4,423	$ 4,564	$ 5,485	$ 3,556
DoD contractor rank	6	5	5	5	8
DoD awards/total sales	.35	.39	.44	.40	.22
FMS contract awards (millions)	$ 395	$ 899	$ 461	$ 1,294	$ 206
FMS contractor rank	5	1	3	2	8
FMS/total DoD awards	.12	.20	.10	.24	.06
FMS/total sales	.043	.081	.045	.095	.012

II. ARMS EXPORT BUSINESS AT A GLANCE

Boeing, long a leader in aircraft production, is also one of the nation's largest exporters of military goods. According to the General Accounting Office, the company was the largest supplier of military equipment, construction and services exported through the Foreign Military Sales program during fiscal 1983, and it was among the top five from 1982 through 1984. From 1977 to 1981, more of Boeing's arms exports were routed through commercial channels than through the FMS program. The company was not ranked among the nation's top 20 FMS contractors for those years, but the GAO did place it among the top 12 suppliers of weapon systems provided through commercial sales for each of the years, and listed Boeing as the third largest in 1977 and second in 1979. Boeing was ranked among the top 20 FMS contractors from 1972 to 1975, when its FMS prime contract awards ranged from $18 million (fiscal 1972) to $192 million (1975).

Boeing's best selling export item—which in recent years has also been its largest overall military program—is the E-3A Airborne Warning and Control System (Awacs). The company received $1.52 billion in identifiable prime contract awards in fiscal years 1983 through 1986—out of a total of $3.25 billion—for work on exported Awacs aircraft. (The actual ratio of Awacs awards to Boeing's total FMS awards for the period, however, is probably much higher: The bulk of $1.2 billion in unidentified fiscal 1985 FMS-related awards are most probably for the export of Awacs, and $21 million in unidentified 1986 awards also appear to have been earmarked for Awacs-related work.) To date, Boeing has delivered 34 Awacs to the U.S. Air Force and 18 to NATO. A request from Iran for seven E-3As was shelved when the Shah fell from power.

In 1987, the company completed the delivery of five Awacs aircraft that were ordered by Saudi Arabia in 1981 as part of an $8.5 billion arms package. The sale was approved by Congress only after a prolonged and acrimonious domestic debate, and the first Awacs was delivered in 1986. The

Saudis initially asked for five E-3As and six KE-3A aerial refueling tankers—both of which are built around the airframe of the Boeing 707 commercial transport—but later increased the number of refueling tankers to eight. The magnitude of the venture is reflected by the fact that, during the Awacs debate of the early 1980s, Alexander Haig, then Secretary of State, said that about 480 civilian contractor representatives and 30 U.S. Air Force personnel would be stationed in Saudi Arabia in support of the system "well into the 1990s."

Boeing has found new markets for the E-3A in Europe. After laborious and protracted decision-making processes, France and Great Britain committed themselves to E-3A purchases in 1987, which prevented the company from having to close its production line. The French air force studied its options for four years and recommended late in 1984 that the E-3A be purchased, but the government ordered a review of the air force's recommendation in December 1985. France finally agreed to procure three of the Boeing aircraft in February 1987 for the price of $550 million and soon afterwards upped the order to four. The contract includes an option for additional E-3As and three years worth of airframe spare parts, ground support equipment and technical assistance. Estimates of the total cost of the sale to France range from $800 million to $1 billion. The difference between the price set by Boeing and the higher, actual cost will cover the procurement of additional equipment that is essential to the Awacs' operation but that is not manufactured by Boeing, the modification of France's existing command and control system, training personnel, and operating and maintaining the aircraft and their base.

France's decision was influenced in part by an earlier British decision to purchase the Boeing aircraft. In 1977, Britain withdrew from the multinational NATO Awacs program—thereby forfeiting the right to use the alliance's early warning aircraft—and committed itself to producing one indigenously. The British airborne early warning aircraft (AEWC), named the Nimrod, was plagued with development cost overruns and technical problems. The British government decided in 1986, after it had spent close to $1.5 billion on developing the Nimrod, to solicit bids from other AEWC manufacturers and to arrange an open competition. Boeing—along with Grumman (maker of the E-2C AEWC aircraft), Lockheed (manufacturer of the P-3 AEWC plane, which has not yet been orderd by any defense establishments) and four British firms—responded to the British Defense Ministry's request for bids. The field was subsequently narrowed to Boeing and GEC Avionics, the British company that had been developing the Nimrod, and Britain decided at the end of 1986 to cancel the Nimrod program and purchase six Boeing Awacs for $1.2 billion. Like France, Britain took out an option on an two additional Awacs, which, if purchased, would raise the cost of the acquisition to $1.47 billion. Boeing will begin delivering E-3As to the two European nations by 1991.

Boeing offered both countries an offset package worth 130 percent of the value of the Awacs purchases—a commitment of $2.4 billion in all. France's offset agreement is reported to be set at $715 million, and stipulates that the United States will purchase military equipment almost exclusively over the next eight years. According to most reports, between 60 and 80 percent of the offset dollars will be earmarked for the purchase of aircraft engines from CFM International, a joint venture between General Electric and France's SNECMA. CFM International engines power some versions of the Boeing E-2As, the aerial refueling tankers that Saudi Arabia purchased with its Awacs, and the U.S. Air Force's KC-135 aerial tanker/cargo aircraft. The terms of the British offset package, by comparison, are looser. Any new business awarded to British firms by Boeing or any of its Awacs subcontractors will be counted as part of the offset, whether the business is military or civilian. Boeing maintains that the British offset package will create 50,000 man-years of employment.

Awacs contracts will continue to be an important part of Boeing's military business, and the sale to Britain and France might have opened the way for new orders. The company has formally briefed Italian defense officials, who are said to see the need for six Awacs to patrol the Mediterranean peninsula, on the E-3A's capabilities. Italy, though, will not decide whether to procure AEWC aircraft until the end of the 1980s. Boeing has also held exploratory talks on possible Awacs aircraft sales with Australia and Japan. Pakistan has approached the U.S. government about the possibility of buying or leasing three Boeing Awacs for use along its border with Afghanistan, but this request is highly controversial because of concerns about Pakistan's nuclear program and the possibility that the planes could be used against India. Even if additional orders are not forthcoming, the existing aircraft will be maintained and improved for years to come and will provide Boeing with a continuing source of income. The company is also reported to be casting about for international partners for the joint development and production of a new low-cost, easily maintained airborne early warning and control aircraft for marketing in the developing world.

Boeing's experience with the E-3A led it to bid for the DoD's Saudi Arabian Peace Shield program. Boeing beat out Hughes Aircraft Co. and Litton Systems Inc. and was appointed prime contractor for the project in February 1985. Peace Shield has as its goal the construction in Saudi Arabia of a ground-based air defense command, control and communications complex that will consist of local and centralized underground command centers and 17 modified General Electric AN/FPS-117 long-range surveillance radars that will work with the Saudi Awacs to detect air attacks and coordinate defenses against them.

The ground-based air defense network will be operational by 1992, and most sources—including the company—put the cost of the Peace Shield project at $1.2 billion. (*The New York Times*, however, has estimated that the cost to the Saudis will be $4 billion.) The largest portion of the $1.2 billion—$848 million—is for the acquisition, installation and testing of equipment. An additional $331 million has been earmarked for logistics, maintenance and support services, and the remaining $3 million for training. Boeing says that approximately 75 percent of the award dollars for the program will be subcontracted out to other companies. *The New York Times* reported in May 1986 that the air defense project would be supported by a permanent staff of approximately 400 contractor personnel and a small number of American military advisers.

Before Boeing was selected as prime contractor, Saudi Arabia and the United States agreed to tether the Peace Shield sale to an economic package designed to help Saudi Arabia develop high-technology industries of its own. As part of the arms deal, Boeing is required to orchestrate an offset package equal to an investment of 35 percent of the military program's technical content, or roughly $600 million. Boeing and its subcontractors have proposed nine joint ventures, which include a maintenance facility for commercial and military aircraft, and a helicopter factory. The Saudi Arabian government and commercial banks will provide 75 percent of the required financing. The remaining 25 percent will be divided between the Boeing team and its Saudi partners, and observers speculate that Boeing's share will amount to about $20 million. As part of the offset agreement, Boeing announced in January 1986 that it had agreed to assist three Persian Gulf companies in building a $250 million aircraft overhauling plant in Saudi Arabia.

Boeing might well break into a new export market in the near future: the maritime patrol and anti-submarine aircraft area. The Department of Defense awarded Boeing a $244 million contract for upgrading the Navy's Lockheed P-3 submarine trackers. A Boeing program manager for the P-3 work stated at a press conference when the company announced the contract that its work for the Navy might lead to contracts for similar programs overseas. Boeing has already upgraded New Zealand's P-3s, and Greece, Japan, Spain, Australia and the Gulf Cooperative States all fly the anti-submarine aircraft. Independent of the P-3 contract, Boeing is considering whether it will enter the competition for the right to produce the next generation submarine tracker. The company is considering entering an anti-submarine aircraft that would be based on its commercial B-757 airframe. Boeing also says it is studying the viability of manufacturing a low cost maritime patrol and anti-submarine aircraft by modifying its de Havilland DHC-8 aircraft.

III. MILITARY ORDERS, 1982–1986 (includes first quarter of 1987)

Country	Date of Agreement	Description of Order	Price (in millions)
– EUROPE AND MAJOR ALLIES –			
Australia	1982	2 KC-135 refueling tankers/d,g	NA
France	1982	Re-engine kits and modification of 11 KC/C-135F aerial refueling tankers/b,g,r[1]	$275
	1986	4 re-engining kits for KC-135R aircraft/f	NA[2]
	1987	4 E-3A AWACS surveillance aircraft with ground installations, training and support/d,f,g,n	$550[3]
Great Britain	1982	3 Chinook Model 414 heavy lift transport helicopters/d,r	NA
	1983	5 Chinook Model 414 heavy lift transport helicopters/d,f,r[4]	$55
	1986	6 E-3A Awacs aircraft/d[5]	$1,200
Greece	1982	2 Chinook Model 414 heavy lift transport helicopters/e	NA
Japan	1984	3 Chinook Model 414 heavy lift transport helicopters/d,e,f,r[6]	NA
Spain	1985	6 Chinook Model 414 heavy lift transport helicopters/d,e,f,r[7]	$80
	1985	2 converted B-707 aerial refueling tankers/r	NA
– ASIA AND PACIFIC –			
Indonesia	1983	4 Jetfoil (hydrofoil) patrol ships/d,e,r[8]	$150

Country	Date of Agreement	Description of Order	Price (in millions)
– MIDDLE EAST –			
Saudi Arabia	1981	5 E-3A Awacs, 6 KE-3A aerial refueling tankers, trainers, spares, and support services and equipment/b,d,e,f,g,h,r[9]	$8,500
	1983	111 rotary rudder servo actuators for F-15 fighter/b	$3
	1984	2 KE-3A aerial refueling tankers/b,r	NA
	1985	Command, control and communications equipment, support services and training for Project Peace Shield/b,f,g,h,r[10]	$1,200
	1986	Maintenance of E-3A Awacs and KE-3A aerial refueling tankers/f	$207
– AFRICA –			
Nigeria	1983	5 Chinook Model 414 heavy lift transport helicopters/d,r[11]	$74
– LATIN AMERICA –			
Brazil	1985	Conversion of 4 B-707 transports to aerial refueling tankers/r[12]	NA

IV. FMS PROGRAM CONTRACT AWARDS, FY 1983-1986
(millions of dollars)

Item	Fiscal Year	Award Total
E-3A Awacs for Saudi Arabia (includes awards for Saudi KE-3A tankers)	1983	$870.81
	1984	450.90
	1985	45.69
	1986	152.84
KC-135 aircraft and re-engine program	1983	21.31
	1984	24.08
	1985	20.21
	1986	16.03

Item	Fiscal Year	Award Total
411L air weapons control systems	1983	4.29
	1984	−19.43
	1985	9.11
	1986	−5.10
Chinook Model 414 heavy lift helicopters	1983	.10
	1984	.92
	1985	.14
	1986	.03
Peace Shield	1985	1.00
	1986	.13
Unidentified awards	1983	1.27*
	1984	3.33#
	1985	1,217.32+
	1986	42.02**

Negative figures result from downward contract adjustments.

*	IRRC analysis of DoD contract data suggests that the bulk of this sum is most likely for the Saudi Awacs program.
#	IRRC analysis of DoD contract data suggests that approximately $2 million of this sum is for the KC-135 re-engine program and the rest for the Saudi Awacs program.
+	IRRC analysis of DoD contract data suggests that the bulk of this sum is for the Saudi Awacs program, with perhaps $300,000 earmarked for the KC-135 re-engine program.
**	IRRC analysis of DoD contract data suggests that $20.89 million of this figure is for the Saudi Peace Shield program and that the remaining $20.79 million is for the Saudi Awacs program.

NOTES

1. The 11 French air force KC-135s are being re-engined at Boeing's Wichita, Kan., plant. The original Pratt & Whitney powerplants are being replaced with CFM-56-2 engines, which are produced jointly by General Electric and SNECMA of France. The replacement program reportedly will be completed by 1987-88.

2. This is part of a $151.7 million contract that includes 43 re-engining kits for the U.S. Air Force KC-135R aircraft.

3. This contract includes an option on two more E-3A aircraft. The negotiated price of the first 3 Awacs sale is $550 million, but analysts predict that France will ultimately spend between $800 million and $1 billion on its airborne early warning aircraft system. France plans to spend an additional $212 million on communications, electronic warfare, and electronic counter-countermeasure systems that are not included as standard equipment on the basic Awacs. A value-added tax of 18.6 percent and a customs duty fee of 6.4 percent reportedly will increase the cost of the importation of the three aircraft by $191 million. Finally, the French air force will refurbish the airfield where its Awacs will eventually be based, and will create a logistics-maintenance center there.

4. By the end of 1986, the British Royal Air Force had taken delivery of 38 Chinooks.

5. This sale includes an option on two additional Awacs. If the option is exercised, the total cost of the sale will increase to $1.47 billion.

6. In 1984, a licensing agreement was signed with Kawasaki Heavy Industries of Japan for the coproduction of the Model 414 Chinook. The Japanese Defense Agency plans to purchase an additional 51 Chinooks that will be produced jointly by Kawasaki and Boeing. Two Chinooks were delivered in 1986.

7. By the end of 1986, the Spanish Army had taken delivery of 18 Chinooks.

8. SIPRI reports that Indonesia has an option for six hydrofoil patrol boats and a license production run of 36. The company's annual report confirms only the option for six Jetfoils.

9. The Saudi Awacs sale is listed in this study because of its size and scope, even though it was concluded in 1981. The Saudi KE-3As and E-3A Awacs, like the French KC-135s, are being re-engined with the CFM-56 powerplant.

10. Project Peace Shield was originally agreed upon by the governments of the United States and Saudi Arabia in 1981, and therefore technically is a 1981 order. A prime contractor was not selected, however, until February 1985. *The New York Times* puts the total cost of Project Peace Shield to the Saudi Arabian government at $4 billion.

11. SIPRI reports that delivery of these vehicles was halted because of funding problems. However, the sale was reactivated in 1987.

12. Boeing delivered the first converted 707 to Brazil in 1986.

CESSNA

(a subsidiary of General Dynamics Corp.)

I. SUMMARY DATA

Data, except for the total sales figures, are for U.S. government fiscal years, ending Sept. 30. FMS program award totals were calculated by IRRC from Department of Defense contract data.

	1982	1983	1984	1985	1986
Total sales (millions)	$832	$524	$694	NA	NA
DoD contract awards (millions)	$ 7	$ 2	$ 8	NA	$25
DoD contractor rank	n/a	n/a	n/a	n/a	n/a
DoD awards/total sales	.01	.004	.01	NA	NA
FMS contract awards (millions)	$ 4	$ .4	$ 6	$ −.4*	$ .7
FMS contractor rank	n/a	n/a	n/a	n/a	n/a
FMS/total DoD awards	.58	.19	.77	NA	.03
FMS/total sales	.005	.001	.009	NA	NA

> *   A downward contract adjustment of $427 thousand led to a negative total of Cessna's FMS program awards in 1985.

II. ARMS EXPORT BUSINESS AT A GLANCE

Cessna, a leading producer of general aviation aircraft, was acquired by General Dynamics in 1985. Its planes are used widely as business and utility aircraft and as transports.

Cessna's FMS-related contract awards for the last four years have been small, ranging from a negative total of awards in 1985 to slightly less than $6 million in 1984. Nevertheless, foreign military sales from time to time have accounted for a substantial portion of the company's defense work. For two of the last five years—1982 and 1984—the ratio of Cessna's FMS awards to its total DoD prime contract awards has exceeded .50. FMS contracts, however, are not the best measure of Cessna's export business because many of the company's products are exported through direct commercial channels, rather than through the FMS program.

Some of the company's civilian planes are purchased by foreign governments which then modify and assign them to their armed forces. Cessna aircraft are used worldwide to fulfill reconnaissance and observation, military transportation, training and counter-insurgency roles. Other Cessna aircraft are specially configured for military missions from the start. The company's most widely distributed military export is the A-37 Dragonfly attack aircraft. The A-37, which is based on the T-37 Dragonfly trainer, is especially well suited for counter-insurgency operations and is popular with Third World countries, especially those of Latin America. Brazil, Chile, Colombia, Ecuador, El Salvador, Guatemala, Honduras, Panama, Peru and Uruguay either possess or have ordered Dragonflys. The air forces of Burma, Greece, Jordan, Pakistan, Portugal, Thailand, Turkey and West Germany also fly either trainer or attack Dragonflys. Data compiled by the Pentagon's Defense Security Assistance Agency indicate that 494 A-37s and 428 T-37s had been exported through FMS channels and the Military Assistance Program as of September 1986. DSAA's records, which do not include those Cessna aircraft that have been exported through direct, commercial sales channels, also show that two additional A-37s and eight T-37s had been ordered, but not yet delivered as of that date.

III. MILITARY ORDERS, 1982–1986 (includes first quarter of 1987)

Country	Date of Agreement	Description of Order	Price (in millions)
– EUROPE AND MAJOR ALLIES –			
Turkey	1983	2 Citation II utility aircraft/d,g	$6
– ASIA AND PACIFIC –			
Burma	1982	1 Citation II utility aircraft/d	NA
Thailand	(1984)	4 0-2 Super Skymaster spotter/forward air control aircraft/d	NA
	1985	10 model 208 Caravan I lightplanes/d	NA
– LATIN AMERICA –			
Colombia	1982	12 A-37B Dragonfly attack aircraft/c,d,g	$11.7
Costa Rica	(1984)	2 model 206 Stationair 6 utility aircraft/g	NA
	1985	2 A-37 Dragonfly attack aircraft/g	NA
	1985	2 T-41 Mescalaro trainer aircraft/e,g	NA
Dominican Republic	1984	12 A-37 Dragonfly attack aircraft/g	$2.5
Ecuador	1982	A-37B Dragonfly attack aircraft/d	NA
El Salvador	1982	6 A-37 Dragonfly attack aircraft 4 0-2 Super Skymaster spotter/forward air control aircraft/d,e,g	NA[1]
	1984	12 A-37 Dragonfly attack aircraft/e	$2.5
	1985	3 A-37 Dragonfly attack aircraft/e,g	NA
	1986	1 A-37 Dragonfly attack aircraft/g[2]	NA
Honduras	1984	6 A-37B Dragonfly attack aircraft/d	NA
Panama	(1984)	(5) A-37B Dragonfly attack aircraft/d	NA

IV. FMS PROGRAM CONTRACT AWARDS, FY 1983–1986
(millions of dollars)

Item	Fiscal Year	Award Total
A-37 Dragonfly attack aircraft	1983	$ .17
	1984	.10
	1985	.03
T-37 Dragonfly trainer aircraft	1983	.35
Unidentified aircraft and aircraft components*	1984	6.07
	1986	.69
Maintenance and repair of unidentified aircraft	1985	−.43

Negative figures result from downward contract adjustments.

* IRRC analysis of DoD contract data indicates that these awards are for work on either the A-37 or T-37 Dragonfly aircraft. Of the awards issued in 1986, $58,000 was earmarked for training services that were conducted in Bolivia.

NOTES

1. This is part of a $25 million package that includes 6 A-37s, 4 O-2s, 3 Lockheed C-123 transport aircraft, and 6 Bell/Textron UH-1H helicopters.

2. Part of a package that includes 6 UH-1H Iroquois and 12 UH-1N Twin Huey attack helicopters.

EX-CELL-O CORP.

(a subsidiary of Textron Inc.)

I. SUMMARY DATA

Data, except for the total sales figures, are for U.S. government fiscal years, ending Sept. 30. FMS program award totals for 1982 to 1985 were calculated by IRRC from Department of Defense contract data.

	1982	1983	1984	1985	1986
Total sales (millions)	$1,027	$954	$1,141	$1,140	NA
DoD contract awards (millions)	$ 60	$ 36	$ 44	$ 53	$82*
DoD contractor rank	n/a	n/a	n/a	n/a	n/a
DoD awards/total sales	.06	.04	.04	.05	NA
FMS contract awards (millions)	$ 28	$ 3	$ 18	$ 13	$34
FMS contractor rank	n/a	n/a	n/a	n/a	n/a
FMS/total DoD awards	.46	.08	.39	.25	.41
FMS/total sales	.027	.003	.016	.012	NA

*   The figure includes awards issued by the Department of Defense to Ex-Cell-O, Cadillac-Gage, Babco Industries and Norwood Precision Products.

II. ARMS EXPORT BUSINESS AT A GLANCE

Textron Inc. acquired Ex-Cell-O Corp. in the fall of 1986 for $1.05 billion. (Textron's arms export business is described in a separate profile.) While Ex-Cell-O usually is not ranked among the Department of Defense's top 100 contractors, its defense and aerospace divisions have been consistently profitable and now contribute significantly to Textron's military business. In 1985, Ex-Cell-O acquired Babco Industries, which manufactures jet engine cases and frames, and Norwood Precision Products, which the company believes will play an important role in its effort to enter the aircraft gearing field.

Ex-Cell-O's aerospace division manufactures a variety of engine components, including fan blades, fuel nozzles and airfoils. It is the sole supplier of several components for Pratt & Whitney's F100 engine, which is used on some General Dynamics F-16 fighter aircraft. (For information on F100 sales abroad, see the United Technologies profile.) Ex-Cell-O's Cadillac Gage subsidiary produces armored vehicles and has a major contract to supply the stabilization system and turret control for the U.S. Army's M1A1 Abrams main battle tank. Cadillac-Gage also produces components for the widely exported FMC M113 armored personnel carrier and M48 tank and manufactures the Commando armored car series. More than 4,500 Commando series vehicles have been exported under commercial license to more than 15 nations.

Foreign military sales constitute an important part of Ex-Cell-O's defense business. They reached a high of $122 million in 1981 when Ex-Cell-O was ranked 12th among American FMS arms exporters, but have since declined. This is not a true measure of the company's arms export business, though, for an unidentified but significant portion of its goods are exported through direct, commercial sales channels. Ex-Cell-O's Cadillac Gage subsidiary does most of the exporting, and in most recent years foreign military sales have comprised a substantial portion of its Department of Defense contract awards. Of Cadillac-Gage's total fiscal 1986 DoD awards, for example, 61 percent was earmarked for foreign military sales. For Ex-Cell-O as a whole, FMS exports accounted for 46 percent of its defense business in fiscal 1982, 39 percent in 1984, and 41 percent in 1986.

Ex-Cell-O is basing much of its hopes for future arms exports on the lightweight Commando Stingray tank. The company cooperated with Royal Ordnance Factories of Great Britain for the development of the vehicle's turret. According to Ex-Cell-O's annual report, exports "of light-weight, simple, low-cost vehicles, which form the backbone of an expanding Cadillac Gage product line, are likely to expand as Third World nations seek to make shrinking U.S. military support dollars go further."

III. MILITARY ORDERS, 1982–1986 (includes first quarter of 1987)

Country	Date of Agreement	Description of Order	Price (in millions)
– EUROPE AND MAJOR ALLIES –			
Turkey	1985	760 M48A5 main battle tank conversion kits/c	NA[1]
– ASIA AND PACIFIC –			
Indonesia	(1983)	28 Commando Scout armored reconnaissance cars/d	NA
	(1983)	22 Commando Ranger armored cars/d	NA
Philippines	1982	10 V150 Commando armored cars/d	NA
	1984	100 V150 Commando armored cars/c,e,g	$30
– MIDDLE EAST –			
Egypt	(1986)	Commando Scout reconnaissance armored cars/d	$22.8
Kuwait	1984	20 V150 Commando armored cars/d 62 V300 Commando armored cars/d,e	$40
– AFRICA–			
Botswana	1986	'12) V150 Commando armored cars/d	NA
Cameroon	1982	2 V150 Commando armored cars/d	NA
Chad	1985	6 V150 Commando armored cars/d	NA

Country	Date of Agreement	Description of Order	Price (in millions)
Gabon	(1985)	(15) V150 Commando armored personnel carriers/d	NA
Sudan	1982	2 V150 Commando armored cars/d	NA
	1984	36 V150 Commando armored cars/d,e,g	$10.7
	1984	V150 Commando armored cars/e,g	NA
	(1986)	24 V150 Commando armored cars/d	NA
		– LATIN AMERICA –	
Panama	1982	12 V300 Commando armored cars/d	NA
	1984	12 V300 Commando armored cars/e	NA

IV. FMS PROGRAM CONTRACT AWARDS, FY 1983–1986
(millions of dollars)

Item	Fiscal Year	Award Total
Commando series armored cars	1985	$ 1.42
	1986	18.89
Turret control components for M-113 armored personnel carriers	1983	.05
	1984	10.68
	1985	.07
Turret control components for M-48 tanks	1983	.06
	1984	.31
	1985	6.12
Turret control components for M-60 tanks	1983	1.30
Components for F-100 turbofan engines	1983	.25
	1984	.22
	1985	.67
	1986	.16
Unidentified guns, 75 to 125mm	1986	14.85

Item	Fiscal Year	Award Total
Miscellaneous vehicular components for unidentified vehicles	1983	1.14
	1984	6.25
	1985	1.07
	1986	.21
Tires and tire tubes for unidentified vehicles	1985	3.43

NOTES

1. Ex-Cell-O is one of three principal contractors for this $206 million program.

FMC CORP.

I. SUMMARY DATA

Data, except for the total sales figures, are for U.S. government fiscal years, ending Sept. 30. FMS program award totals for 1982 to 1984 were calculated by the General Accounting Office; the 1985 and 1986 totals were calculated by IRRC from Department of Defense contract data.

	1982	1983	1984	1985	1986
Total sales (millions)	$3,187	$3,247	$3,338	$3,261	$3,003
DoD contract awards (millions)	$1,371	$1,236	$1,157	$ 831	$ 836
DoD contractor rank	14	17	18	32	27
DoD awards/total sales	.39	.35	.35	.25	.29
FMS contract awards (millions)	$ 133	$ 165	$ 167	$ 37	$ 32
FMS contractor rank	19	12	12	23	n/a
FMS/total DoD awards	.10	.13	.14	.05	.04
FMS/total sales	.042	.051	.050	.011	.011

II. ARMS EXPORT BUSINESS AT A GLANCE

FMC manufactures chemicals, petroleum equipment, agricultural machinery and weapon systems. Despite its varied product line, the company derives between 30 and 40 percent of its sales from the production of military equipment. FMC's Defense Systems Division produces armored vehicles, missile launching systems and gun mounts for ships.

The General Accounting Office ranked FMC among the top 25 FMS contractors for every year but one between 1972 and 1984. According to the GAO, the level of FMC's recent foreign military sales peaked in fiscal 1980, when the company received $233 million in FMS prime contract awards. In 1985, however, the company's awards for foreign military sales—along with its contracts for military work in general—plummeted. Most of the company's recent weapons exports have gone to the Middle East and Asia.

FMC's chief military export item is the M113 armored personnel carrier. The armies of nearly 40 nations use the M113—which was introduced in 1959—as troop transports, command posts, ambulances and heavy weapons carriers. Approximately 1,250 were delivered in 1985 alone, and most went to overseas customers. FMC received at least $219 million in foreign military sales contract awards during fiscal years 1983 through 1986 for various versions of the M113s. Deliveries of M113s to the U.S. and foreign governments declined by 20 percent in 1986, largely because of lower foreign sales. FMC stated in its 1986 annual report that "foreign sales will continue to decrease, resulting in lower production" levels. The Pentagon, though, has indicated that it intends to procure an improved line of M113s, suggesting that production and exportation of the armored vehicle will continue in the near future, even if at reduced levels.

FMC also makes the Bradley M2 Infantry Fighting Vehicle, which critics have alleged is overpriced and poorly designed. The company received its first inquiries from Allied governments interested in purchasing the Bradley in 1984, and made its first sale of the vehicle to Saudi Arabia in 1987.

Awards received by FMC for fiscal years 1983 through 1985 for ship-borne gun mounts and missile launching systems bound for foreign customers were worth at least $114 million.

III. MILITARY ORDERS, 1982–1986 (includes first quarter of 1987)

Country	Date of Agreement	Description of Order	Price (in millions)
\- EUROPE AND MAJOR ALLIES –			
Australia	1984	3 Mk 13 guided missile launching systems/b[1]	$39
France	1985	Upgrade of fire control system on 2 Tartar air defense missile systems/c,f	NA[2]
Greece	1982	110 M113-A2 armored personnel carriers/d	NA
	1983	51 M113-A2 armored personnel carriers/d	NA
Italy	1984	Upgrade of 2 Tartar shipborne air defense missile systems/c	NA[3]
Japan	1983	Mk 13 guided missile launching systems/b[4]	$26
Norway	1986	16 M113 armored personnel carriers/d,e	NA
Spain	1983	11 LVTP7-A1 amphibious landing vehicles, 2 LVTC7-A1 amphibious command vehicles/d,g	$16
\- ASIA AND PACIFIC –			
Pakistan	1985	110 M113-A2 armored personnel carriers/c,e,f,g	$25
Philippines	1982	55 LVT7-A1 amphibious landing vehicles & support/d,f,g	$64
South Korea	1982	42 LVT7-A1 amphibious landing vehicles/d,g	$59
Taiwan	1983	100 M113-A2 armored personnel carriers	$97
		90 M106-A2 mortar carriers	
		72 M125-A2 mortar carriers	

Country	Date of Agreement	Description of Order	Price (in millions)
		31 command post vehicles	
		24 M113-A2 armored ambulances/d,g	
Thailand	1982	148 M113-A2 armored personnel carriers/d,g	NA
	1984	21 LVT71-A1 amphibious landing vehicles/e	NA
		– MIDDLE EAST –	
Egypt	1984	354 M113-A2 armored personnel carriers	$157[5]
		13 M577-A2 command post vehicles	
		19 M125-A2 mortar carriers	
		23 M113-A2 armored ambulances	
		43 M806-E1 armored recovery vehicles/ d,f,g	
	1987	90 M113 armored personnel carriers with communications equipment, armament, spares and tools/d,f,g	$27
Kuwait	1982	16 M113-A2 armored personnel carriers/d,e,g	NA[6]
	1982	188 M113-A2 armored personnel carriers/d,e	NA
Lebanon	1982	24 M113-A2 armored personnel carriers/g (part of a package)	NA
	1983	102 M113-A2 armored personnel carriers	$57
		25 M577-A2 command vehicles	
		93 M125-A2 mortar carriers/d,g[7]	
Saudi Arabia	1983	176 M113-A2 armored personnel carriers	NA[8]
		24 M106-A2 mortar carriers	
		80 M577-A2 command vehicles	
		62 M125-A2 mortar carriers/d,g	
	1987	200 M2 Bradley infantry fighting vehicles/g	NA[9]

Country	Date of Agreement	Description of Order	Price (in millions)
		– LATIN AMERICA –	
Brazil	1983	12 to 16 LVTP7-A1 amphibious landing craft/d,e,g	NA
Costa Rica	(1984)	(3) M113-A2 armored personnel carriers/d	NA

IV. FMS PROGRAM CONTRACT AWARDS, FY 1983–1986
(millions of dollars)

Item	Fiscal Year	Award Total
M113 armored personnel carrier	1983	$100.06
	1984	57.29
	1985	23.76
	1986	36.98
Mk-45 Mod-0 5.54 in gun mount	1983	43.39
	1985	6.08
	1986	−6.67
Mk 13 guided missile launcher	1983	14.44
	1984	10.68
	1985	.66
	1986	1.89
LVTP7 amphibious landing vehicle	1985	2.94
Mk-26 missile launcher	1985	1.33
20 ton, 3/4 cubic yard crane	1983	.33
	1984	.60
	1985	.05
Mk-75 76mm gun mount	1984	−.45
	1985	−1.50
	1986	−.11
Unidentified vehicles	1983	3.31
	1984	52.18
Unidentified missile launching systems, guns and gun mounts	1983	2.39
	1984	42.25

Item	Fiscal Year	Award Total
Other unidentified awards	1983	1.52
	1984	4.98
	1985	3.36
	1986	.03

Negative figures result from downward contract adjustments.

NOTES

1. This $39 million transaction is a continuation of an agreement concluded earlier with the government of Australia.

2. FMC shares this $58 million contract with GE, Raytheon and Sperry.

3. FMC is one of four principal contractors on this $94 million program, along with General Electric, Raytheon and Vitro Corp.

4. This $26 million transaction is a continuation of an agreement concluded earlier with the government of Japan.

5. The price of this package includes the cost of 40 additional trucks.

6. These are part of a $97 million package including Hughes Aircraft anti-tank missiles and Kollman Instrument Co. night sight equipment.

7. According to some sources, the number of M113s involved in this transaction is 135 and the price $61 million. The package also includes M2 .50 caliber machine guns. Its status is unclear.

8. These FMC-manufactured systems are reported to be part of a $271 million package that also includes 33 M578 armored recovery vehicles (initially made by FMC, but now made by the Bowen-McLaughlin-York (BMY) division of Harsco), 19 BMY-manufactured M88 armored recovery vehicles, 111 M992 field artillery ammunition support vehicles and 18 M109-A2 self-propelled howitzers. SIPRI does not list the 18 howitzers as part of the package.

9. This transaction was initially approved as a direct, company-to-government sale. The Saudis, however, later decided that they preferred to purchase the vehicles directly from U.S. government stocks, necessitating a resubmission of the sale for congressional approval late in 1987.

FORD MOTOR CO.

I. SUMMARY DATA

Data, except for the total sales figures, are for U.S. government fiscal years, ending Sept. 30. FMS program award totals were calculated by IRRC from Department of Defense contract data.

	1982	1983	1984	1985	1986
Total sales (millions)	$37,067	$44,455	$52,366	$52,774	$67,716
DoD contract awards (millions)	$ 897	$ 1,072	$ 1,124	$ 1,019	$ 752
DoD contractor rank	20	22	20	28	30
DoD awards/total sales	.02	.02	.02	.02	.01
FMS contract awards (millions)	$ 34	$ 5	$ 7	$ 101	$ 105
FMS contractor rank	n/a	n/a	n/a	11	11
FMS/total DoD awards	.04	.005	.007	.09	.14
FMS/total sales	.0009	.0001	.0001	.0019	.0017

II. ARMS EXPORT BUSINESS AT A GLANCE

Most of Ford Motor Co.'s defense work is conducted by a wholly owned consolidated subsidiary, Ford Aerospace and Communications Corp., which manufactures tactical missiles; command, control and communications systems; ammunition and ordnance; and satellite systems.

Ford was listed among the top 25 U.S. FMS contractors for five of the 13 years preceding 1985, but it has never been ranked higher than 11th. FMS-related prime contract awards issued to the company since 1972 have ranged from a low of $5 million in fiscal 1983 to a high of $105 million in 1986. The company was not ranked among the top 25 commercial arms exporters for the years 1977 to 1981 (the most recent years for which government figures are available), suggesting that its commercial sales were less than an average of $50 million annually for that period.

Ford's most widely exported weapon systems are the AIM-9 Sidewinder air-to-air missile and the MIM-72 Chaparral, a surface-to-air missile system that is used for low altitude air defense and employs modified Sidewinder missiles. More than 20 nations have equipped military aircraft with Sidewinders. Numerous versions of the missile have been produced since it was introduced into the U.S. arsenal in the mid-1950s, some of which have been manufactured by Raytheon rather than Ford. The Sidewinder at one point was produced under license by a West German firm in association with companies in Denmark, Greece, the Netherlands, Norway, Portugal and Turkey. Data compiled by the Pentagon's Defense Security Assistance Agency indicate that 44,640 Sidewinders and 3,904 Chaparrals had been exported through the FMS and Military Assistance programs as of September 1986.

In 1986, the United States agreed to sell Saudi Arabia 1,666 AIM-9L and AIM-9P Sidewinders as part of an arms package. Congress approved the transaction only after General Dynamics Stinger shoulder-fired anti-aircraft missiles were dropped from the package. Earlier in the year, congressional intransigence forced the Reagan administration to postpone indefinitely an arms sale to Jordan that included 300 AIM-9P4 Sidewinders. Indonesia ordered this version of the Sidewinder in 1986 as part of a $432 million package that includes eight General Dynamics F-16 fighters.

Many fewer countries have purchased the Chaparral. Nevertheless, awards for the Chaparral system accounted for 95 percent of the total FMS-related contract awards that Ford received in fiscal 1985.

III. MILITARY ORDERS, 1982–1986 (includes first quarter of 1987)

Raytheon Co. was selected by the Department of Defense to produce Sidewinder air-to-air missiles as a second source to Ford Aerospace. In most cases, IRRC was not able to determine which foreign military sales of Sidewinders are being handled by Raytheon and which by Ford. (The nature of Defense Department contract reporting makes it difficult even for the companies themselves, without spending enormous amounts of time, to separate the sales.) Therefore, most Sidewinder orders have been listed in both companies' profiles.

Country	Date of Agreement	Description of Order	Price (in millions)
– EUROPE AND MAJOR ALLIES –			
Australia	1982	1 AN/AVO-26 Pave Tack designator pod for General Dynamics F-111 fighter aircraft/g[1]	NA
	1983	AIM-9 Sidewinder training missiles/c	$4.6
	1984	Additional funding for WGU-4A/B guidance and control components for AIM-9M Sidewinder air-to-air missiles/b	NA[2]
	1984	AIM-9 Sidewinder air-to-air missiles/d,f	NA[3]
Belgium	1983	200 AIM-9P3 Sidewinder air-to-air missiles/d	NA
Canada	1984	AIM-9M Sidewinder air-to-air missiles/c,e,g	NA[4]
Denmark	1983	200 AIM-9L Sidewinder air-to-air missiles/c,d	NA
Greece	1984	AIM-9L Sidewinder air-to-air missiles/c,d,f,g	NA[5]
Netherlands	1983	900 AIM-9L Sidewinder air-to-air missiles/d	$78
Portugal	1986	5 Chaparral surface-to-air missile systems with 66 missiles/d,g	$45[6]

Country	Date of Agreement	Description of Order	Price (in millions)
Sweden	1984	(960) AIM-9L Sidewinder air-to-air missiles/d	($75)
	1986	25mm cartridges for M791, M792 and M793 guns/g	$25.4
Turkey	1982	750 AIM-9P3 Sidewinder air-to-air missiles/c,d,g	$50

– ASIA AND PACIFIC –

Country	Date of Agreement	Description of Order	Price (in millions)
Indonesia	(1986)	(72) AIM-9P Sidewinder air-to-air missiles/c,d,e,g	NA[7]
Malaysia	(1983)	(84) AIM-9L Sidewinder air-to-air missiles/d	NA
Pakistan	1985	AIM-9L Sidewinder air-to-air missiles/c,e,f,g	NA[8]
People's Republic of China	1985	Training and spares for 5 General Electric LM-2500 naval engines/g	NA
South Korea	1983	8 AN/AVO-26 Pave Tack designator pods, training and support/g	$50
Taiwan	1983	384 MIM-72F Improved Chaparral surface-to-air missiles/c,d,g	$291
		120 Sea Chaparral surface-to-air missiles for mounting on ships/d,g	
	1985	262 MIM-72F Chaparral surface-to-air missiles with 16 launch vehicles/e,g,h	$94
	1986	Guidance control sections and support for AIM-9-P-4 Sidewinder air to air missiles/b	NA
	1986	262 Chaparral surface-to-air missiles with support/g	$13.2
Thailand	1983	AIM-9P3 Sidewinder air-to-air missiles/c	$4.7

– MIDDLE EAST –

Country	Date of Agreement	Description of Order	Price (in millions)
Bahrain	1985	60 AIM-9P3 Sidewinder air-to-air missiles/e	NA[9]
	1987	AIM-9 Sidewinder air-to-air missiles/g	NA[10]

Country	Date of Agreement	Description of Order	Price (in millions)
Egypt	1984	450 MIM-72F Chaparral surface-to-air 0 missiles with 26 towed launchers/d,e,g	$16
	1986	AIM-9 Sidewinder air-to-air missiles/d,e,g	NA[11]
Israel	1983	200 AIM-9L Sidewinder air-to-air missiles/d,g	$16
Jordan	1986	Guidance control sections and support for AIM-9-P-4 Sidewinder air-to-air missiles/b	NA
Oman	1985	300 AIM-9P4 Sidewinder air-to-air missiles/c,f,g,l	$22
Saudi Arabia	1986	995 AIM-9L and 671 AIM-9P4 Sidewinder air-to-air missiles/c,d,g	NA[12]
– LATIN AMERICA –			
Venezuela	1983	AIM-9P3 Sidewinder air-to-air missiles/c	$2.9

IV. FMS PROGRAM CONTRACT AWARDS, FY 1983–1986
(millions of dollars)

Item	Fiscal Year	Award Total
AIM-9 Sidewinder air-to-air missile	1983	$ 1.92
	1984	2.99
	1985	1.74
	1986	81.35
MIM-72 Chaparral surface-to-air missiles	1984	.63
	1985	96.45
	1986	8.87
Unidentified missiles, including components	1986	14.26
Unidentified electronic testing and measuring equipment	1983	2.43
	1984	2.43
	1986	.89
Other unidentified awards	1983	.48
	1984	.44
	1985	2.55

NOTES

1. Pave Tack is an improved tactical bombing system that incorporates the Ford Forward Looking Infrared Radar system and laser designator pods. The Pave Tack system is designed for use on McDonnell Douglas F-4 and General Dynamics F-111 aircraft.

2. This $60.7 million award includes 2,603 of the guidance systems to be divided among the U.S. Navy, the U.S. Air Force and Australia.

3. The reported cost of this transaction is 5 million Australian dollars.

4. Ford and Raytheon share this $41 million contract to provide 416 Sidewinder missiles and 56 training missiles to Canada.

5. Ford and Raytheon share this $30 million contract to provide 300 Sidewinder missiles to Greece.

6. This sale consists of 5 Chaparral M48A2 aerial intercept fire unit launcher stations, 66 MIM-72 Chaparral missiles, 2 AN/MPQ-54 FAAR radar systems, spares and support.

7. This is part of a $432 million package including 8 General Dynamics F-16 aircraft, Westinghouse AN/APG-66 radar, Litton AN/ALR-69 radar warning receivers, and Loral AN/ALQ-131 electronic countermeasure instruments.

8. Ford and Raytheon share this $50 million contract to provide 500 Sidewinder missiles to Pakistan.

9. This is part of a $114 million package that includes 6 Northrop F-5 fighters.

10. It is unclear whether these Sidewinder missiles were supplied by Ford, Raytheon or both companies. The missiles are part of a $400 million package that includes 12 General Dynamics F-16 fighter aircraft, Westinghouse AN/ALQ-131 electronic countermeasure pods, radar warning receivers, chaff/flare dispensers, Hughes Aircraft AGM-65 air-to-surface missiles and General Dynamics and/or Raytheon Sparrow missiles.

11. Ford and Raytheon share this $42 million contract to provide 560 Sidewinder missiles to Egypt.

12. This is part of a $285 million package that includes 100 McDonnell Douglas Harpoon missiles. Because of intense congressional opposition, the Reagan administration deleted 200 Stinger missile launchers with 600 missiles from this package. An unknown number of the 995 AIM-9L Sidewinder missiles were supplied by Raytheon instead of Ford.

GENERAL DYNAMICS CORP.

I. SUMMARY DATA

Data, except for the total sales figures, are for U.S. government fiscal years, ending Sept. 30. FMS program award totals for 1982 to 1984 were calculated by the General Accounting Office; the 1985 and 1986 totals were calculated by IRRC from Department of Defense contract data.

	1982	1983	1984	1985	1986
Total sales (millions)	$5,890	$6,799	$7,291	$7,952	$8,892*
DoD contract awards (millions)	$5,891	$6,818	$5,951	$7,440	$8,013*
DoD contractor rank	1	1	3	2	1
DoD awards/total sales	1.00	1.00	.82	.94	.90
FMS contract awards (millions)	$ 761	$ 450	$ 967	$1,231	$1,369*
FMS contractor rank	3	3	2	2	1
FMS/total DoD awards	.13	.07	.16	.17	.17
FMS/total sales	.129	.066	.133	.155	.154

* These figures include sales by and awards to Cessna Aircraft. Cessna's arms export business is covered in detail in a separate profile.

II. ARMS EXPORT BUSINESS AT A GLANCE

Over the last 10 years, General Dynamics has emerged as one of the top U.S. foreign military sales contractors. In the early 1970s the company was never ranked higher than 14th in volume of FMS sales; since 1977 it has not fallen out of the top five. Some of this success has been a result of General Dynamics' aggressive international marketing techniques and some has stemmed from the company's enormous military program. General Dynamics consistently receives more Department of Defense contract awards than all but one or two other corporations, and in 1982, 1983 and 1986 it was the nation's largest defense contractor. The vast majority of General Dynamics' arms exports are routed through the Foreign Military Sales program. General Dynamics is usually not one of the leading commercial sales exporters, though this may change with the increased industry-wide push toward direct company-to-government sales. Greece, for example, is purchasing its F-16s via commercial sales channels.

General Dynamics produces a broad array of military equipment. Its Forth Worth division manufactures electronic equipment and aircraft such as the F-16 fighter and is also working on an advanced tactical fighter that employs Stealth technology. General Dynamics' Convair, Pomona and Valley Systems divisions produce tactical missile and gun systems. Convair is one of two sources for Tomahawk sea-launched and ground-launched cruise missiles. The Pomona unit manufactures the shipborne Standard missiles and Phalanx guns that have proved popular with foreign militaries. It also produces Sparrow air-to-air missiles and has been competing with a second source— Raytheon—for the large foreign market for this missile. The Valley Systems division's principal product is the Stinger hand-held anti-aircraft missile. General Dynamics' Electric Boat division, which is the Department of Defense's prime contractor for the Trident submarine, is assisting Great Britain with its Trident submarine-launched ballistic missile program. The company's Land Systems division is the main contractor for the new M-1 Abrams main battle tank, and the older M-48 and M-60 tanks, which the U.S. government continues to export to a variety of nations. The Land Systems division is assisting Taiwan with a hybrid M-48 battle tank and is assisting South Korea with another specially designed tank. General Dynamics added to its already vast product line when it acquired Cessna Aircraft Co. in 1985. (Cessna's foreign military sales business is discussed in a separate profile.)

General Dynamics' largest export program involves its F-16, the top-of-the-line fighter aircraft. Fifteen foreign countries have agreed to purchase more than 1,000 F-16s. Awards for F-16s accounted for 66 percent of the company's total FMS-related prime contract awards in fiscal 1983, 83 percent in 1984, 68 percent in 1985 and 86 percent in 1986. In 1986, more FMS contract awards were issued for export of the F-16 than for any other system. The most recent sales have been to Indonesia, which ordered 12 F-16s, and Bahrain, which ordered 12. In 1986 South Korea received 12 of the 36 F-16s it has on order. This arms agreement involves a $200 million offset program that requires General Dynamics to purchase goods from South Korea and establish manufacturing ventures there, including facilities for producing F-16 spare parts. South Korea also would like to undertake licensed production of additional fighter aircraft in the near future, but has not yet indicated which American aircraft it prefers. Japan had also considered a variation of the F-16 as an alternative to its fighter support experimental (FSX) program until the company formally withdrew its offer in 1987, citing the high cost of producing the variant. An F-16 buy is likely in Switzerland, which is also considering McDonnell Douglas's F-18 and the French Dassault-Breguet Mirage 2000 for an 80 aircraft purchase. Denmark, which already has 70 F-16s either in hand or on order, is reported to be choosing between the F-16 and the French Mirage 2000 for a 44 fighter buy to replace two wings of its aging Saab fleet. Finally, Israel signaled its interest in purchasing 75 to 100 F-16s after it canceled its indigenous Lavi fighter program in 1987. Information from General Dynamics on all the countries that have ordered F-16s is shown in the chart below.

General Dynamics also exports modification kits for upgrading the aircraft's operational capabilities. Belgium, the Netherlands, Norway and Denmark have purchased these kits for retrofitting aircraft already delivered or for incorporating into fighters still being assembled by the company, an upgrade that involves 770 F-16s in all. The Netherlands government plans to spend $70 million and four years to modify its 213 F-16s. General Dynamics also has proposed an aircraft production partnership with these four NATO nations to develop an advanced version of the F-16C fighter. One purpose of this move is to compete against two European consortiums (the French team led by Dassault-Breguet that is building the Rafale fighter, and the British-German-Italian-Spanish team that is designing the Eurofighter) that are developing fighters for the 1990s.

The company said in a recent annual report that its hand-held Stinger anti-aircraft missile "has the greatest international sales potential of any system yet produced by Pomona." The relatively low level of technological know-how needed to operate the Stinger and its versatility in many types of warfare make it attractive to many Third World countries. This weapon has already been sold to 10 foreign nations, and has been supplied to rebel groups in Angola and Afghanistan. Records compiled by the Defense Security Assistance Agency indicate that 2,402 Stingers had been ordered through the FMS program, and 1,546 delivered as of September 1986. This, however, does not provide a complete picture of the total number of Stingers that have been transferred because many of the exported missiles have come from U.S. government stock and have been transferred through unconventional channels. The administration in 1987 planned to transfer 600 additional Stingers to the Afghan resistance because of the success they have had with the weapon.

Country	Number delivered in 1986	Number delivered through 1986	Number contracted to date	Current acquisition plans
Bahrain	0	0	12	12
Belgium	0	116	160	188
Denmark	0	58	70	110
Egypt	13	54	80	120
Greece	0	0	40	60
Indonesia	0	0	0	12
Israel	6	81	150	150
Netherlands	18	150	214	238
Norway	0	72	72	98
Pakistan	0	40	40	46
Singapore	0	0	8	20
South Korea	12	12	36	156
Thailand	0	0	18	20
Turkey	0	0	160	160
Venezuela	0	24	24	36
Total:	49	607	1,084	1,426

The sale of Stingers to foreign customers is especially controversial. Citing concern that Stingers could fall into the hands of terrorists, in the spring of 1986 Congress forced the administration to delete 200 Singer missile launchers and 600 reload missiles from an arms package destined for Saudi Arabia, although the Saudis had already received 200 Stingers in a 1984 arms transfer that was arranged through the Special Defense Acquisition Fund. The transfer of 150 Stingers to the Afghan rebels and 50 Stingers to Angolan rebels met with opposition for similar reasons, but the transfers were not canceled. The administration's decision to send 600 additional Stingers to Afghan resistance groups exacerbated the controversy surrounding these transfers since all Afghan rebel groups will receive the weapon, and some of the Stingers will be the advanced Stinger-POST version.

General Dynamics' other widely exported military goods include the M60 main battle tank and its forebear, the M48. The company also reports that its Land Systems division, which it acquired from Chrysler Corp. in 1982, delivered 379 M60 tanks to Egypt and Jordan in 1982 and "delivered 226 M60 hulls and 112 M60 chassis to allied nations in 1986." The company completed the delivery of a final 94 M60 tanks to Egypt in 1987. According to the company, the last deliveries of M60 tanks, chassis and hulls are planned for 1987, but the chassis line will be kept open to produce an improved hybrid of the M48. General Dynamics is also providing South Korea with technical assistance and parts for a tank, the XK-1, that the country is developing, and it expects South Korean industry to produce 700 of the vehicles.

General Dynamics also has held preliminary discussions with Egypt regarding the possibility of its coassembling—and perhaps eventually coproducing—part of the U.S. Army's top-of-the-line M-1 Abrams main battle tank, a system that has not yet been exported. The Reagan administration has agreed in principle to transfer some technology for the tank. Egypt plans to use the M-1 production arrangement to foster feeder defense industries, and eventually hopes to export the tanks. The proposed arrangement met some opposition in Congress, because of the possibility of the technology being diverted to the Soviet bloc and because of concern that the tank might one day be used against Israel. Critics also expressed skepticism about Egypt's ability to finance and successfully produce the advanced weapon system. Nevertheless, the proposed transfer appears to have cleared the initial hurdles. General Dynamics has already signed a contract to design and help construct and maintain a tank repair facility in Egypt. The plant initially will service Egypt's inventory of tanks—which include 600 M60s—as well as those of friendly nations in the region. The tank overhaul facility would be used as an assembly plant if Congress allows Egypt to proceed with the M-1 program.

Widely exported General Dynamics missile and gun systems include the air-to-air AIM-7 Sparrow missiles—although Raytheon appears to have captured the bulk of the export market—and for foreign navies the RIM-66 Standard (SM-1) shipborne anti-aircraft missile and the Phalanx Close-in Weapon System air defense gun. The company reports that eight Allied navies use Standard missiles and that the Phalanx system has been mounted on 70 ships of at least six foreign navies. Data compiled by the Department of Defense's Security Assistance Agency indicate that 2,193 Standard missiles had been ordered—and 1,523 actually delivered—through the FMS program as of September 1986. In 1986, Japan was offered six of the Close-in Weapon Systems for $70 million and Taiwan four. General Dynamics has also gained substantial export earnings from its various technical services, which include support services and maintenance and repair of F-16s in Egypt, Pakistan and Venezuela.

A number of new weapon systems should help General Dynamics maintain its strong export market. The M-1 tank and RIM-67 Standard II missile should pick up considerable orders as they become available for export to more nations. Reports emerged in 1986 indicating that the Pentagon was considering the sale of M-1s to Pakistan. General Dynamics is also teaming up with foreign firms to develop missiles that would have immediate access to foreign markets. The Convair division is working with companies in Great Britain and West Germany to submit proposals for the development of a Modular Standoff Weapon for NATO. The Valley Systems division is developing a Rolling Airframe Missile (RAM) with West Germany and Denmark, and is planning a commercial joint venture with Danish and German firms to develop a lightweight RAM missile that would be "adaptable to a wide variety of ships of allied countries," according to the company.

III. MILITARY ORDERS, 1982–1986 (includes first quarter of 1987)

The Department of Defense selected General Dynamics to produce Sparrow and Seasparrow missiles as a second source to Raytheon. In most cases, IRRC was able to determine which exports of Sparrows and Seasparrows were being handled by General Dynamics and which by Raytheon. In the instances where IRRC was unable to determine which contractor was responsible for a certain Sparrow or Seasparrow order, IRRC has listed the order in both profiles.

Country	Date of Agreement	Description of Order	Price (in millions)
– EUROPE AND MAJOR ALLIES –			
Australia	1984	AIM-7M Sparrow air-to-air missiles/c,d,f	NA[1]
	1986	Materials for Standard (SM-1) surface-to-air missiles/b	$2.7
	1986	Additional funding for Phalanx Close-in Weapon Systems/f	NA[2]
Belgium	1983	44 F-16 fighter aircraft/c,e,g	$944
Canada	1984	AIM-7M Sparrow air-to-air missiles/c,e,g	NA[3]
	1984	RIM 7-H-2 Seasparrow surface-to-air missiles/e,f	NA[4]
	1985	AIM-7M Sparrow air-to-air missiles/c,e	NA[5]
	1986	4 Standard surface-to-air missile systems for naval destroyers/g	NA
	1986	4 Seasparrow surface-to-air missile systems with (80) missiles/d[6]	NA
	1987	Sparrow air-to-air missiles/c	NA[7]
Denmark	1984	12 F-16 fighter and trainer aircraft with spares and support/c,d,e,f,g	$210
	1986	336 Stinger-Post portable surface to air missile launchers with 504 missiles/c,d,e,f,g[8]	$65
France	1986	Materials for Standard (SM-1) surface-to-air missiles/b	$1.4
Great Britain	1982	FIM-92A Stinger portable surface-to-air missiles/d	NA
	1982	3 shipborne Phalanx Mk 15 Close-in Weapon Systems with ammunition and support/c,g	$48
	1983	Design for Trident II nuclear missile submarines/g	$63.8
	1984	12 shipborne Phalanx Mk 15 Close-in Weapon Systems with support and training/c,e,g	$151

Country	Date of Agreement	Description of Order	Price (in millions)
	1985	3 shipborne Phalanx Mk 15 Close-in Weapon Systems with ammunition, spares and support/c,e,f,g	$46
	1985	4 shipborne Phalanx Mk 15 Close-in Weapons Systems with support/c,e,f,g	$56
	1986	2 Phalanx shipborne Close-in Weapon Systems with support/c,g	$22
Greece	1982	280 AIM-7M Sparrow air-to-air missiles/d,f,g	$98
	1983	110 M60A3 main battle tanks/d,g	$186
	1984	2 shipborne Mk 15 Phalanx Close-in Weapon Systems /c,f,g	$40
	1984	40 F-16G/D fighter aircraft/d,k,r	NA
	1986	2 Phalanx shipborne Close-in Weapon Systems/c,d	$26
	1986	200 M48A1 tanks and 300 M48A5 tanks without communications equipment, machine guns or other support/d,g	$138
	1987	4 Phalanx shipborne Close-in Weapon Systems with spare parts and engineering support/d,f,g	$56
	1987	34 F-16C and 6 F-16D fighter aircraft/f,g[9]	$940
Italy	1983	150 FIM-92A Stinger portable surface-to-air missile launchers with 450 missiles/c,d,e,g	$51
	1986	Materials for Standard (SM-1) surface-to-air missiles/b	$.6
Japan	1982	20 FIM-92A Stinger portable surface-to-air missile launchers with 100 missiles/d,g	NA
	1982	3 shipborne Mk 15 Phalanx Close-in Weapon Systems/g	NA[10]
	1983	Phalanx Close-in Weapon Systems/g	NA[11]
	1983	FIM-92A Stinger portable surface- to-air missile systems/c	$5.6

Country	Date of Agreement	Description of Order	Price (in millions)
	1985	3 shipborne Phalanx Mk 15 Close-in Weapon Systems/c,e,f,g,j	$41
	1986	6 Phalanx shipborne Close-in Weapon Systems with spares and support/c,d,f,g	$70
	1986	Stinger portable surface-to-air missiles/c	$11.9
	1986	Standard (SM-1) surface-to-air missiles/c	$9.7
	1986	Materials for Standard (SM-1) surface-to-air missiles/b	$1
NATO	1984	1,845 guidance and control sets for AIM-7 Sparrow air-to-air missiles/f[12]	$250
Netherlands	1982	646 FIM-92A Stinger portable surface-to-air missiles/d	NA
	1982	57 F-16 fighter aircraft/d,e,r	NA[13]
	(1983)	(48) RIM-24 Tartar shipborne surface-to-air missiles/d	NA
	1985	78 Standard (SM-1) RIM-66 shipborne surface-to-air missiles/e,f,g	$32
	1986	AN/ASA-70 tactical data display groups for P-3 Orion aircraft/b	NA
Norway	1986	2 F-16 aircraft to replace those lost by attrition/c[14]	$30
Portugal	1986	3 Phalanx shipborne Close-in Weapon Systems/d	NA
Spain	1982	(72) Standard (SM-2) RIM-67 shipborne surface-to-air missiles/d	NA
	(1983)	AIM-7F Sparrow air-to-air missiles/d	NA
Turkey	(1983)	FIM-92A Stinger portable surface-to-air missiles/c,d	NA
	1983	160 F-16 fighter aircraft/d,e,g	$4,000[15]
	(1983)	(320) AIM-7M Sparrow air-to-air missiles/d[16]	NA
	(1986)	(4) Seasparrow surface-to-air, shipborne missiles systems/d[17]	NA
	1986	590 conversion kits for M48A1 tanks/g	$71

Country	Date of Agreement	Description of Order	Price (in millions)
	1986	760 conversion kits for M48A1 tanks/e,g	$206
	1987	24 guidance and control sections for AIM/RIM-7M Sparrow air-to-air missiles/b	$3
West Germany	1983	75,000 FIM-92A Stinger and advanced Stinger-POST portable surface-to- air missiles/g[18]	$200
	1985	110 Standard (SM-1) RIM-66 shipborne surface-to-air missiles with 70 Mk 372 containers, 55 training missiles, spares and support/d,e,f	$44
	1986	(2) Seasparrow surface-to-air missile systems with (48) missiles/d[19]	NA

–ASIA AND PACIFIC –

Country	Date of Agreement	Description of Order	Price (in millions)
Indonesia	1986	8 F-16A/B fighter aircraft/c,d,e,g	$432[20]
Pakistan	1982	100 M48A5 tanks/d,g	NA[21]
	1983	4 Phalanx Mk 15 Close-in Weapon Systems/g	$38
	1984	100 M48A5 tanks/e	$42.1
	1985	100 FIM-92 Stinger portable surface-to-air missiles/e,g	$8.5
Singapore	1985	8 F-16A/B fighter and trainer aircraft with F100 engines, spares and training/c,d,g,h	$330
	(1986)	6 Phalanx shipborne Close-in Weapon Systems/d	NA
South Korea	1982	36 F-16 fighter aircraft/d,g	($240)
	1985	113 Stinger portable surface-to-air missiles systems with 599 reload rounds/c,d	$57
	1986	Standard (SM-1) missiles/c	NA
Taiwan	1983	170 Standard (SM-1) RIM-66A ship-borne surface-to-air missiles with 10 launchers/d,g	NA[22]
	1983	100 AIM-7M Sparrow air-to-air missile/d,g	$105
	1984	50 to 75 M60 main battle tank hulls/e	$12.2

Country	Date of Agreement	Description of Order	Price (in millions)
Thailand	1983	20 MIM-43A Redeye portable surface-to-air missiles/d	NA
	1984	(1) Phalanx Close-in Weapon System/d	NA
	1985	8 F-16A fighter and 4 F-16B trainer aircraft with training and spare parts/d,e,f,k,l,r	$360
	1987	6 F-16A/B fighter aircraft/h,n	$115

–MIDDLE EAST–

Country	Date of Agreement	Description of Order	Price (in millions)
Bahrain	1986	54 M60A3 tanks with communications equipment, spares, and support/c,d,e,f,g	$90
	1987	12 F-16C/D fighters with AIM-9 Sparrow air-to-air missiles/f,g	NA[23]
Egypt	1982	34 F-16C fighter and 6 F-16D trainer aircraft/d,e,g,r[24]	$1,460
	1982	220 M60A3 main battle tanks/d,g	NA[25]
	1984	Design, construction and management of a main battle tank repair depot/r	NA
	1985	36 M60A3 main battle tanks with thermal sights and .50 caliber machine guns/c	$68
	1985	94 M60A3 main battle tanks/c,d,e,g,r	$165
	1986	Additional funding for an Avionics Intermediate Shop (AIS) to test F-16 radar and electronic countermeasure systems/b	NA
	1986	Contract for operation and maintenance of 5 air force bases/g	$12.9
	1986	One year extension to a contract for F-16 oriented training and support services for the Egyptian Air Force/b	$4.2
	1986	Missile parts and base support/f	$21
	1987	40 additional F-16C/D fighters with an avionics shop, spares support and training/f,g	$1300[26]
	1987	Sparrow AIM-7 air-to-air missiles/c	NA[27]

Country	Date of Agreement	Description of Order	Price (in millions)
Israel	1983	75 F-16C fighter aircraft/c,d,e,f,g,r	$2,500[28]
	1984	150 AIM-7M Sparrow air-to-air missiles/c,d,g	$52
Lebanon	1983	68 M48 main battle tanks/d,e[29]	NA
	1984	35 M60A3 main battle tanks/c,d,f	$28
Saudi Arabia	1983	100 M60A3 main battle tanks/d,f,g	$176
	1984	200 FIM-92A Stinger portable surface-to-air missiles launchers with 400 missiles/c,d,e,g	$40[30]

–AFRICA–

Country	Date of Agreement	Description of Order	Price (in millions)
Morocco	(1982)	108 M60A3 main battle tanks/d	NA
Tunisia	1982	54 M60A3 main battle tanks/d	NA

–LATIN AMERICA–

Country	Date of Agreement	Description of Order	Price (in millions)
Venezuela	1982	24 F-16 fighter aircraft/d,e,g,r	$616
	1983	Radio installation in F-16 aircraft/g	$5

IV. FMS PROGRAM CONTRACT AWARDS, FY 1983–1986
(millions of dollars)

Item	Fiscal Year	Award Total
F-16 fighter aircraft	1983	$ 295.54*
	1984	801.26#
	1985	836.08
	1986	1,182.93+
M60 main battle tanks	1983	39.40
	1984	66.38
	1985	202.77
	1986	33.76
Mk-15 Phalanx Close-in Weapon Systems	1983	60.23
	1984	3.49
	1985	51.51
	1986	68.26

Item	Fiscal Year	Award Total
RIM-66 Standard (SM-1) shipborne surface-to-air missiles	1983	11.83
	1984	14.29
	1985	63.67
	1986	12.70
AIM-7 Sparrow air-to-air missiles	1983	5.43
	1984	2.56
	1985	45.27
	1986	38.21
FIM-92A Stinger portable surface-to-air missiles	1983	3.33
	1984	8.98
	1985	1.19
	1986	24.96
Components for F-86 Sabre fighter aircraft	1985	20.90
Architectural, engineering and training services on Trident submarine	1984	19.92
	1986	.13
F-111 fighter/bomber aircraft	1983	5.19
	1984	.21
	1985	3.23
	1986	2.78
Electronic countermeasure system for P-3 Orion aircraft	1986	1.13
Miscellaneous communication equipment for E-2 Hawkeye surveillance aircraft	1984	1.69
M48 main battle tanks	1983	-.07
	1984	.58
	1985	.67
Components for AIM-9 Sidewinder missiles	1984	-.88
	1985	.55
AN/FPS-100 radar set	1985	-.68
Unidentified technical training services	1983	5.19
	1984	-1.79**
	1985	.60
	1986	2.72

Item	Fiscal Year	Award Total
Unidentified guns through 30 mm	1983	11.11
Unidentified troop housing facilities in Egypt	1984	6.80
Research and development of unidentified missile systems	1983	6.21
	1984	1.52
	1985	.82
Unidentified advanced production engineering	1983	1.80
Modification of unidentified equipment	1983	1.39
Unidentified optical sighting and ranging equipment	1983	1.24
Unidentified aircraft bombing fire control	1983	.89
Other unidentified awards	1983	1.86
	1984	1.63
	1985	4.10
	1986	1.32x

Negative figures result from downward contract adjustments.

*	Includes awards for work performed in Belgium, Denmark, Israel, Norway and Pakistan.
#	Includes awards for work performed in Belgium, Israel, Norway, Pakistan and Venezuela.
+	Includes awards for work performed in Egypt, South Korea, Pakistan and Venezuela.
**	Includes awards for work performed in Pakistan.
x	Includes awards for work performed in France.

NOTES

1. General Dynamics and Raytheon share this contract, which is valued at 21 million Australian dollars.

2. This is part of a funding increase of $57.3 million for 57 Phalanx systems to be divided among Australia, Japan and the U.S. Navy.

3. General Dynamics and Raytheon share this $113 million contract to provide 408 Sparrow missiles to Canada.

4. This is part of a $16 million package including AN/SPS-49 shipboard air search radar.

5. General Dynamics and Raytheon share this $42 million contract to provide 184 Sparrow missiles to Canada.

6. It is unclear whether these Seasparrow missiles were supplied by Raytheon, General Dynamics or both companies. These are in addition to the six Seasparrow missile systems with (168) missiles ordered by Canada in 1984.

7. General Dynamics and Raytheon share this $17 million contract to supply Canada with 88 Sparrow missiles.

8. SIPRI reports that a final decision on this order was postponed until 1987.

9. Included in this sale is an option on 20 additional F-16s. This is a commercial sale.

10. This is part of a $50 million package that includes three McDonnell Douglas Harpoon anti-ship missiles.

11. This is part of a $105 million package that includes 100 Raytheon AIM-7F Sparrow missiles.

12. Some of these sets are destined for the U.S Navy and Air Force and four non-NATO countries: Australia, Egypt, Israel and Taiwan.

13. Government sources indicate that the Netherlands took delivery on 12 F-16s in December 1982 in a $222 million transaction.

14. These are in addition to the 72 F-16s Norway purchased earlier.

15. Eight F-16B two-seat trainers were manufactured in the United States and delivered to Turkey in 1984. Thirty-two F-16s will be assembled in Turkey from kits shipped from the United States during 1985 and 1986. The licensed coproduction of the remaining 24 F-16 trainers and 96 fighters will begin in 1988, and the Turkish government will own 51 percent of the coproduction facility and General Dynamics the rest. General Dynamics said in its 1983 annual report that the transaction "should result in sales of more than $3 billion."

16. It is unclear whether these Sparrow missiles were supplied by General Dynamics, Raytheon or both companies.

17. It is unclear whether these Seasparrow missiles were supplied by General Dynamics, Raytheon or both companies.

18. This transaction encompasses a coproduction agreement between the United States and West Germany. The Stinger-POST is an advanced version of the basic Stinger with a more sophisticated and capable guidance system.

19. It is unclear whether these Seasparrow missiles were supplied by General Dynamics, Raytheon or both companies.

20. The purchase price includes an estimated 72 Ford AIM-9P Sidewinder missiles, Westinghouse AN/APG-66 radar, Litton AN/ALR-69 radar warning receivers, and Loral AN/ALQ-131 electronic countermeasure instruments. Two U.S. government personnel and 40 contractor representatives will spend one year in Indonesia providing services and training in support of this sale. Indonesia has an option on four more F-16s.

21. This $117 million package includes 35 Harsco M88A1 recovery vehicles.

22. This is part of a $103 million package including Hughes Aircraft AN/SPS-52C air surveillance radar systems, and a guided missile fire control and launching system.

23. It is unclear whether these Sparrow missiles were supplied by Raytheon, General Dynamics or both companies. This is a $400 million package including Westinghouse AN/ALQ-131 electronic countermeasure pods, radar warning receivers, chaff/flare dispensers, Hughes Aircraft AGM-65 Maverick air-to-surface missiles, and Ford and/or Raytheon AIM-9 Sidewinder air-to-air missiles.

24. The Egyptian F-16s will carry Westinghouse AN/ALQ-131 electronic countermeasure pods.

25. This is part of a $426 million package including 23 Harsco M88A1 armored recovery vehicles and an unspecified number of Harsco M109A2 self-propelled howitzers.

26. The F-16s will be equipped with Tracor AN/ALE-40 countermeasure dispenser systems, Westinghouse AN/APG-68 radar systems, and Litton AN/ALR-69 radar warning receivers.

27. General Dynamics and Raytheon share this $190 million sale for 282 air-to-air and 514 ground-to-air Sparrow missiles.

28. Half of the purchase price is a U.S. government grant; the other half is covered by U.S. government credit that includes an offset agreement whereby $300 million of F-16 components are to be purchased in Israel. Reports of the total cost of the package vary. The International Institute for Strategic Studies reports the cost as $2.5 billion, the Defense Security Assistance Agency puts it at $2.2 billion, and SIPRI at $2.7 billion.

29. The status of these orders is unclear.

30. Because of congressional opposition, the Reagan administration withdrew a larger Stinger sale to Saudi Arabia. The administration instead shipped these 200 Stinger launchers to Saudi Arabia under "emergency" authority, which enabled it to bypass congressional approval. The President cited the pressing need to protect shipping lanes in the Persian Gulf that were threatened by the Iran-Iraq war.

GENERAL ELECTRIC CO.

I. SUMMARY DATA

Data, except for the total sales figures, are for U.S. government fiscal years, ending Sept. 30. FMS program award totals for 1982 to 1984 were calculated by the General Accounting Office; the 1985 and 1986 totals were calculated by IRRC from Department of Defense contract data.

	1982	1983	1984	1985	1986
Total sales (millions)	$26,500	$26,797	$27,947	$28,285	$36,725*
DoD contract awards (millions)	$ 3,654	$ 4,518	$ 4,514	$ 5,891	$6,847*
DoD contractor rank	4	4	6	4	2
DoD awards/total sales	.14	.17	.20	.21	.19
FMS contract awards (millions)	$ 25	$ 164	$ 297	$ 503	$630*
FMS contractor rank	10	13	4	4	2
FMS/total DoD awards	.07	.04	.07	.08	.09
FMS/total sales	.009	.006	.011	.018	.017

*   These figures include sales by, and awards issued to, RCA Corp. RCA, a GE subsidiary, is covered in a separate profile.

II. ARMS EXPORT BUSINESS AT A GLANCE

General Electric has been one of the 10 largest FMS contractors since fiscal 1972 except during 1979, 1980 and 1983. Prime contract awards of $630 million made 1986 a peak foreign military sales year for GE.

GE's most widely exported systems are aircraft engines, notably the F404, which powers the McDonnell Douglas F/A-18 fighter, and the J85 series engines, which power the Northrop F-5 fighter, the Northrop T-38 trainer and the Cessna A-37 attack aircraft. Sweden has selected a variant of the F404—designated the RM12—for its new JAS 39 Grippen fighter, and will assemble the engines and manufacture some of the parts starting in 1989. The governments of Japan, India and Yugoslavia are also considering the F404 for fighters that they are developing. GE also exports the J79 engine, which is used in the McDonnell Douglas F-4 fighter. The J79 is also the powerplant around which the General Dynamics F-16/79 fighter is built. The F-16/79 was designed and offered as an export aircraft in response to the Carter administration's call for specially configured fighters for export, but it has not been ordered by overseas buyers. Singapore is considering the J79 for the eight F-16s that it has ordered from General Dynamics, but reportedly would rather purchase a more powerful engine.

The U.S. Air Force's selection of GE's newer F110 engine for part of its fleet of F-16s appears to have had a positive effect on GE's military exports: Israel, Egypt, Greece, Turkey and Bahrain subsequently requested the same engine for their F-16s. These sales are sizable. The Greek order, which is a direct, company-to-government commercial sale and was announced in July 1986, is reported to be worth $200 million and to involve an offset agreement under which GE will create a joint venture company with Hellenic Aerospace Industry of Greece. Prime contract awards for exported jet engines accounted for 66 percent of GE's total FMS awards for 1983, 74 percent for 1984, 82 percent for 1985 and 59 percent for 1986.

General Electric also markets its wares abroad through CFM International, a joint venture with SNECMA of France. CFM International, which registered foreign military sales awards of $35 million in both 1985 and 1986, manufactures aircraft engines for military and commercial aircraft. CFM powerplants are used on some versions of the Boeing Awacs aircraft and on all of the Boeing KC-135 aeriel refueling tankers that overseas customers and the U.S. Air Force use to keep the Awacs and other aircraft airborne for extended periods of time.

General Electric also exports and services helicopter engines, aircraft-mounted and anti-aircraft guns, naval engines, ground-based and airborne radar systems and gun and missile fire control systems. It is supplying, for example, modified AN/FPS-117 landbased, long-range surveillance radar systems for the Saudi Arabian Peace Shield program, which is designed to provide the Persian Gulf nation with an advanced air defense system. The company also produces fire control systems for the British Trident ballistic missile submarine program and LM 2500 turbine engines—which the company says has both naval and industrial applications—to various countries, including the People's Republic of China.

GE's acquisition of RCA in 1986 will increase the company's volume of weapons systems exports. RCA's military export business—which netted the company $84 million during the period 1982 to 1986—is outlined in a separate profile.

III. MILITARY ORDERS, 1982–1986 (includes first quarter of 1987)

The non-government sources used for this study do not list many military orders placed with General Electric for the period 1982 through 1986. Therefore, some of the data in this section refer to additional funding for orders placed earlier than 1982. Although these awards are not orders per se for the period indicated, they are used here to give a fuller picture of the work the company performs under the Foreign Military Sales program.

In addition to the transactions listed below, GE received a $7.6 million award in 1986 for a component improvement program in support of J85 engines for Northrop T-38 trainer aircraft. This contract combines purchases for the U.S. Air Force, Austria, Bahrain, Brazil, Canada, Dominican Republic, Greece, Honduras, Indonesia, Jordan, Kenya, Korea, Malaysia, Mexico, Morocco, Norway, Peru, Philippines, Thailand, Taiwan and Tunisia.

Country	Date of Agreement	Description of Order	Price (in millions)
– EUROPE AND MAJOR ALLIES –			
Australia	1983	F404-GE-400 engines for F/A-18 aircraft/c	$4.7[1]
	1986	32 F404-GE-400 engines for F/A-18 aircraft/g	$36
	1987	37 T700 turboshaft engines/g	NA
Canada	1984	Additional funding for F404-GE-400 engines for F/A-18 aircraft/b	$6.1[2]
France	1985	Tartar surface-to-air missile fire control upgrade/c,f	NA[3]
Great Britain	1984	Additional funding for development of Trident II submarine-launched ballistic missile fire control system/b,f	$36.5
	1985	Additional funding for development of Trident II submarine-launched ballistic missile fire control system/b,f	$4.4
	1987	Additional funding for 20mm automatic guns/b	NA[4]
Greece	1987	Additional funding for 20mm automatic guns/b	NA[4]
Italy	1982	4 LM 2500 gas turbine engines for naval cruisers/f	NA
	1984	Upgrade of 2 Tartar shipborne missile defense missile systems/c	NA[5]
Portugal	1987	10 M163A1 Vulcan 20 mm self-propelled air defense guns with support and spares/g	$18
	1986	6 LM 2500 gas turbine engines for 3 guided missile frigates/c,d,g	NA[6]
Spain	1983	12 F404-GE-400 engines for F/A-18 aircraft/g	NA[7]
	1984	Funding for 39 AV-8 Harrier fighter 25 mm Armaments (gun) System/b	$9.3
	1986	37 F-404-GE-400 engines for F/A-18 aircraft/g	$35.7
	1987	200 Bushmaster 25 mm automatic cannons/g	$9

Country	Date of Agreement	Description of Order	Price (in millions)
Turkey	1985	Funding for 14 F110-GE-100 engines for F-16 fighter aircraft/b	NA
	1986	F110-GE-100 aircraft engines for F-16 fighter aircraft/f,n	$6.3
	1986	Additional funding for F110 alternate fighter engine coproduction support/b	$38.3
	1987	32 F110 aircraft engines for F-16 fighter aircraft/f	NA[8]
West Germany	1983	3 CF-34 engines/c	$4
		– ASIA AND PACIFIC –	
India	1987	11 F404 aircraft engines/g[9]	$22
Indonesia	1987	Additional funding for 20mm automatic guns/b	NA[4]
People's Republic of China	1985	5 LM-2500 gas turbine engines for naval destroyers/f,g	NA
Philippines	1984	24 M-167 A1 20mm Vulcan towed air defense systems/c,e,f,g	$30
	1985	F404 engines for McDonnell Douglas A-4 attack aircraft upgrade program/h	NA
Singapore	1987	Additional funding for 20mm automatic guns/b	NA[4]
South Korea	1982	4 LM 2500 turbine engines for naval corvettes/f	NA
Taiwan	1982	150 J85-21 engines/g	NA[10]
Thailand	1982	24 M-167 A1 20 mm Vulcan towed air defense systems with radar, communications equipment, and spares/f,g	$23
	1983	J85 engines/c	$1.8
	(1986)	AN/MPQ-4 mortar-locating radar/d	NA
		– MIDDLE EAST –	
Bahrain	1985	15 J85 engines/f,g	NA[11]

Country	Date of Agreement	Description of Order	Price (in millions)
	1987	F110-GE-100 engines for General Dynamics F-16 fighter aircraft/h	NA
Egypt	1984	4 AN/TPS-59 land-based air search radars/e,c	NA[12]
	1986	1 AN/TPS-59 3-D tactical radar/d	NA
	1987	F110-GE-100 engines for F-16 fighter aircraft/h,n	NA
Israel	1985	35 F110-GE-100 engines for F-16 fighter aircraft/f	NA[13]
Saudi Arabia	1985	Funding for 1 AN/FPS-117(v) 3 long-range air defense radar/b,f[14]	$31.4
	1986	16 AN/FPS-117(V)3 long range radar systems for the Saudi Peace Shield program/b	$88

IV. FMS PROGRAM CONTRACT AWARDS, FY 1983–1986
(millions of dollars)

Item	Fiscal Year	Award Total
F404 engines for F/A-18 fighter aircraft	1983	$ 60.35
	1984	143.38
	1985	209.02
	1986	130.25
J85 engines for F-5 fighter aircraft	1983	47.19
	1984	69.23
	1985	42.36
	1986	26.01*
F100 engines for fighter aircraft	1986	344.48
F110 engines for F-16 fighter aircraft	1986	.35
Engine instruments, training devices, gun systems and services for F-16 aircraft	1983	22.21
	1984	2.88
	1985	1.14
	1986	−.20

Item	Fiscal Year	Award Total
Radio equipment for E-2 Hawkeye surveillance aircraft	1984	22.46
	1985	2.93
	1986	-4.50
AN/SQR-19 tactical towed array sonar tracking system	1983	4.39
	1984	4.08
Fire control for Trident submarine-launched ballistic missile	1984	.80
	1985	5.85
	1986	11.35
Gunnery fire control and maintenance and repair on F-5 aircraft	1983	2.55
	1984	.73
	1985	.26
	1986	.45
J79 engines for F-4 fighter aircraft	1983	1.17
	1984	1.88
	1985	.34
	1986	.95
AV-8 Harrier fighter 25 mm Armament (gun) System	1984	3.84
	1985	.50
	1986	.29
AN/TPS-59 land-based tactical radar system	1985	3.22
Fire control for Polaris submarine-launched ballistic missile	1984	1.52
	1985	1.81
	1986	1.06
Electronic equipment for E-3A Awacs	1983	1.11
	1984	.13
	1985	.15
Engineering development for electrical and communications systems for the Patriot air defense system	1986	1.65
2500 LM gas turbines	1986	1.55
Radar equipment for P-3 Orion reconnaissance aircraft	1983	1.51
7.62 mm M 134 minigun	1983	.81

Item	Fiscal Year	Award Total
	1984	.14
LAU-68 rocket launchers	1985	.50
Auto-pilot mechanisms for F-15 fighter aircraft	1986	.44
Unidentified gas turbines and jet engines	1983	.12
	1984	6.36
	1985	179.92
	1986	.17
Unidentified ground based radar equipment	1983	4.23
	1984	35.41
	1985	31.90
	1986	91.87
Unidentified guns, 30 mm or smaller	1983	6.48
	1984	-9.83
	1985	10.16
	1986	3.09#
Unidentified fire control equipment, including maintenance and repair	1983	7.86
	1984	8.37
Unidentified electrical control equipment, including maintenance and repair	1983	.09
	1984	.10
	1985	1.20
	1986	.38
Unidentified non-aircraft turbines	1986	.68
Other unidentified awards	1983	2.53
	1984	2.86
	1985	6.15
	1986	4.72

Negative figures result from downward contract adjustments.

* Of this total, $168,000 worth of work was performed in South Korea, $140,000 in Mexico and $737,000 in the Philippines.

\# DoD contract data suggest that $1.24 million of this total was earmarked for work on gun systems for the AH-1S Cobra TOW helicopter.

NOTES

1. GE is supplying F-404 engines foɪ the 75 F/A-18 fighters that Australia agreed to purchase in 1981.

2. GE is supplying F-404 engines for the 138 F/A-18 fighters that Canada agreed to purchase in 1980.

3. GE is one of several contractors for this $58 million program.

4. This $9.3 million contract award increase is for 328 guns to be divided among Indonesia, Singapore, Greece and Great Britain.

5. GE shares this $94 million contract with Raytheon, FMC and Vitro Corp.

6. This is part of a $216 million package that includes 3 McDonnell Douglas Harpoon missile systems with 24 missiles, 3 Raytheon Seasparrow missile systems with 24 missiles, 6 U.S. government-manufactured Mk 32 torpedo tubes and 3 Aerojet General AN/SLQ-25 torpedo countermeasure sets.

7. GE is supplying F-404 engines for the 84 F/A-18 fighters that Spain agreed to purchase in 1982.

8. This is part of a $475 million contract that includes 172 F-110 engines for the U.S. Air Force.

9. This is part of a package that includes gas turbine engines of unknown manufacture, which are valued at $38 million. These engines will be employed on Indian frigates.

10. This is part of a $240 million package that includes 60 AN/ALR-46(v)3 radar warning receivers and 60 AN/ALE-40(v)7 chaff/flare dispensers.

11. This is part of a $92 million package that includes 6 F-5 aircraft.

12. This is part of a $154 million package that includes 8 AN/TPS-65 radars.

13. This is part of a $564 million package that includes 126 F110 engines for the United States.

14. This is one of 17 modified GE AN/FPS-117 long-range surveillance radars that are part of the DoD's Saudi Arabian Peace Shield program.

GENERAL MOTORS CORP.

I. SUMMARY DATA

Data, except for the total sales figures, are for U.S. government fiscal years, ending Sept. 30. The FMS program award total for 1983 was calculated by the General Accounting Office; the 1982, 1984, 1985 and 1986 totals were calculated by IRRC from Department of Defense contract data.

	1982	1983	1984	1985	1986
Total sales (millions)	$60,026	$74,582	$83,890	$96,372	$102,813
DoD contract awards (millions)	$ 689	$ 893	$ 1,019	$ 1,614	$5,069*
DoD contractor rank	26	23	23	17	5
DoD awards/total sales	.01	.01	.01	.02	.05
FMS contract awards (millions)	$ 51	$ 51	$ 28	$ 86	$207*
FMS contractor rank	n/a	24	n/a	n/a	7
FMS/total DoD awards	.07	.06	.03	.05	.04
FMS/total sales	.0008	.0006	.0003	.0009	.0020

> *   Figures include awards issued to Hughes Aircraft and the Santa Barbara Research Center.

II. ARMS EXPORT BUSINESS AT A GLANCE

General Motors has placed increasing emphasis on its defense business in recent years. In 1983, the company organized a new Power Products and Defense Operations Group and in 1984 established within this group a new Military Vehicles Operation. More significantly, in late 1985 GM won a bidding war and acquired Hughes Aircraft Co., which had been the nation's seventh largest military contractor. (Hughes Aircraft's arms export business is detailed in a separate profile.) GM incorporated Hughes as a separate subsidiary, combining it with the auto company's former Delco Electronics division to create GM Hughes Electronics.

Even before it acquired Hughes, GM registered substantial annual sales of military equipment to foreign governments. The General Accounting Office has ranked GM among the top 25 foreign military sales contractors for five of the eight years before 1985. The company's annual prime contract FMS awards have fluctuated considerably since 1978, ranging from a low of $28 million in fiscal 1984 to a high of $109 million in fiscal 1980, and accounted for less than one-tenth of 1 percent of the company's total sales for the period 1982-1985. General Motors' acquisition of Hughes Aircraft, though, will guarantee the company a more prominent position among the nation's largest arms exporters.

GM's leading military export products are engines and transmissions, used in aircraft, ships and armored vehicles. The company's Allison Gas Turbine Division exports the T56 turboprop engine, used in the Grumman E-2C electronic warfare aircraft, the Lockheed C-130 transport aircraft and the Lockheed P-3 antisubmarine/maritime patrol aircraft. Allison also exports components for the TF41 turbofan engine, which is no longer produced but powers the Vought A-7 attack aircraft. At least 20 foreign countries have purchased the T56. In fiscal years 1985 and 1986, for example, GM received FMS prime contracts for T-56 parts and related services purchased by Australia, Belgium, Brazil, Canada, Egypt, Great Britain, Greece, Honduras, Indonesia, Israel, Japan, the Netherlands, New Zealand, Norway, Oman, Pakistan, Singapore, Spain, Sudan, Thailand, Turkey and Zaire. Greece is the largest overseas customer for the TF41. Allison Gas Turbine Division also received an order in 1984 from the Canadian Navy for engines to power destroyers and frigates. Through other divisions, GM also supplies engines and transmissions for a variety of armored ground vehicles. As recently as fiscal year 1982, GM received $37 million in FMS awards for transmission kits for M48 tank modernization programs.

III. MILITARY ORDERS, 1982–1986 (includes first quarter of 1987)

The non-government sources used for this study did not list many military orders placed with General Motors for the period 1982 through 1985. Therefore, the data in this section refer largely to additional funding for orders placed earlier than 1982. Although these awards are not orders per se, they are used here to give a fuller picture of the work the company performs under the Foreign Military Sales program. The relative dearth of information on General Motors' arms exports is due less to the size of the company's military export business than to the fact that GM makes components for larger systems, such as engines and transmissions. Sources of FMS data usually list the major weapon system, and not lesser components.

Country	Date of Agreement	Description of Order	Price (in millions)
– EUROPE AND MAJOR ALLIES –			
Australia	1982	7 T56-A14 engines for P-3 maritime patrol aircraft/b	$3.8
Belgium	1983	Inertial navigation units for E-3A Awacs/b[1]	$4.0
Canada	1984	Engines for destroyers and frigates/r	NA
Great Britain	1984	T56 engines as spares for C-130 cargo aircraft/b[2]	NA
Greece	1983	TF41 engine component improvement program/b,g	$5.4
	1983	6 TF41 engines for A-7 aircraft/b	$14.0
Japan	1983	8 T56 engines apiece for E-2, P-3 and C-130 aircraft/b	$9.2
	1985	T56 engines for installation and spares/b[3]	NA
	1986	Additional funding for T56-A-15 engines for C-130 aircraft/b	NA

Country	Date of Agreement	Description of Order	Price (in millions)
Sweden	1982	570-K turbine engines for 3 fast patrol boats/f	NA
		– ASIA AND PACIFIC –	
Taiwan	1986	Additional funding for T56A turboprop engines/b	NA
		– MIDDLE EAST –	
Egypt	1985	T56 engines for various aircraft/b	NA
	1986	Additional funding for T56A turboprop engines/b	NA
Saudi Arabia	1983	Inertial navigation units for E-3A Awacs/b[3]	$4.0

IV. FMS PROGRAM CONTRACT AWARDS, FY 1983–1986
(millions of dollars)

Item	Fiscal Year	Award Total
M60 main battle tank transmissions	1984	$17.19
	1985	30.50
	1986	.66
T56 engines	1983	10.81
	1984	1.14
	1985	41.74
	1986	4.37
TF41 engines and parts	1983	14.05
	1984	1.00
	1985	.73
	1986	.08
M113 armored personnel carrier diesel engines, transmissions and components	1983	9.03
	1984	2.81
	1985	4.18
	1986	8.60
M88 medium recovery vehicle transmissions	1984	4.51
	1985	8.37
	1986	4.91

Item	Fiscal Year	Award Total
M48 main battle tank transmissions	1983	7.78
M109 self-propelled howitzer diesel engines and transmissions	1983	3.83
	1985	.37
	1986	11.28
E-3A Awacs navigational instruments	1983	2.15
F-16 fighter fire control system	1984	1.34
	1985	.76
	1986	.34
Unidentified diesel engines, transmissions and components	1983	1.17
	1986	8.05
Other unidentified awards	1984	1.23
	1985	.08
	1986	1.17

NOTES

1. This is a sale divided between Saudi Arabia and Belgium.

2. This is under a $6.6 million contract award that combines purchases for Britain and the U.S. Air Force.

3. This is under a contract award of $21.6 million that also includes purchases for Japan, Egypt and the U.S. Air Force and Navy.

GRUMMAN CORP.

I. SUMMARY DATA

Data, except for the total sales figures, are for U.S. government fiscal years, ending Sept. 30. FMS program award totals for 1983 and 1984 were calculated by the General Accounting Office; the 1982, 1985 and 1986 totals were calculated by IRRC from Department of Defense contract data.

	1982	1983	1984	1985	1986
Total sales (millions)	$2,057	$2,255	$2,604	$3,099	$3,502
DoD contract awards (millions)	$1,900	$2,298	$2,419	$2,733	$2,967
DoD contractor rank	11	11	11	10	10
DoD awards/total sales	.92	1.02	.93	.88	.85
FMS contract awards (millions)	$ −31*	$ 111	$ 235	$ 182	$ 125
FMS contractor rank	n/a	15	7	9	10
FMS/total DoD awards	n/a	.05	.10	.07	.04
FMS/total sales	−.015	.049	.090	.059	.035

*   A downward contract adjustment of $72 million led to a negative total for Grumman's FMS program awards in 1982.

II. ARMS EXPORT BUSINESS AT A GLANCE

Grumman is a major aerospace firm that is heavily dependent on defense and government business and is best known for the fighter, attack and electronic warfare aircraft that it manufactures for the U.S. Navy. The level of Grumman's awards under the FMS program has fluctuated substantially from year to year. The company fell from the ranks of the top 25 FMS contractor list for fiscal years 1979, 1980 and 1982, but for the other years since 1977 has been ranked among the top 15. Fiscal 1984 represented Grumman's highest total since 1977, when it received FMS prime contract awards worth $253 million.

Grumman's chief military export in recent years has been the E-2C Hawkeye, an airborne early warning and control (AEWC) aircraft. So far, Israel, Egypt, Japan and Singapore have purchased the E-2C, under agreements that will have generated more than $1 billion in revenues by the end of 1988. The popularity of the E-2C increased dramatically after Israel employed the planes with great success in its invasion of Lebanon in 1982. The company reports that other countries that are considering E-2 purchases include Australia, Malaysia, Pakistan, South Korea, Spain, Turkey and the United Arab Emirates. An E-2C sale to the United Arab Emirates appears unlikely, however, since the Gulf Cooperation Council states decided to purchase jointly either the Lockheed P-3 Orion or the French or Dutch AEWC systems.

Pakistan's interest in the E-2C, and in airborne early warning and control aircraft aircraft in general, has provoked concern in some quarters. The country first expressed interest in obtaining AEWC capabilities from the United States in 1984, and it approached the United States again in

1987. The Pakistani government says it needs the aircraft to defend against Afghan government combat aircraft that have been entering Pakistan's airspace to strike at Afghan rebel strongholds there and, in the process, to signal Afghanistan's disapproval of Pakistan's support of the Afghani resistance. Critics of the transfer of such capabilities are concerned that such a move would anger the Indian government, which fears that any AEWC aircraft possessed by Pakistan might be used offensively at some point against India. Moreover, some congressional critics oppose any transfer of American arms to Pakistan because of that nation's pursuit of the ability to manufacture nuclear weapons. The controversy could benefit Grumman, even though the Pakistani government prefers the more advanced Boeing Awacs aircraft. Some within U.S. government circles have suggested that either transferring or leasing the less capable and expensive E-2C might prove to be the most workable compromise.

Records compiled by the DoD's Security Assistance Agency indicate that 23 E-2Cs had been ordered through the FMS program and 15 delivered as of September 1986. Grumman received at least $610 million in FMS-related prime contract awards for fiscal years 1983 through 1986 for work on the E-2C. The E-2C sale to Singapore is tied to a $14 million offset agreement that requires Grumman to assist in the creation of a computer-aided design and computer-aided manufacturing (CAD/CAM) center. Grumman will supply technical expertise and some computer equipment and software to the five year joint venture.

Grumman expects that programs to refurbish older planes also will generate significant foreign sales in the near future. The company signed an agreement with Malaysia in 1984 to refurbish 40 A-4 attack aircraft, originally built by McDonnell Douglas, and it was hired in 1985 as an engineering consultant to Singapore Aircraft Industries for a similar project. Grumman also has received contracts from Turkey and Taiwan to modernize their S-2 Tracker submarine hunting planes, which were first built in the 1950s by Grumman, and South Korea and Thailand have expressed interest in a similar upgrade program. The Taiwanese program—which drew a protest from the People's Republic of China—reportedly will cost $260 million and involve the modernization of two of the aircraft, the development of two additional prototypes of the more advanced version and the sale of kits and engineering services for upgrading 30 more S-2s. Pakistan has commissioned the company to study the cost and feasibility of refurbishing 150 unidentified aircraft for its Air Force. Grumman says a production contract could net it approximately $500 million in business. The U.S. Air Force selected Grumman over Rockwell and Boeing for a unique foreign upgrade order in 1987 when it awarded $245 million to the company to provide modern aircraft avionics and fire control equipment to the People's Republic of China. The sale involves refurbishing 55 Chinese F-8 fighter aircraft, and is part of a larger, $550 million upgrade package, the largest made to date between the U.S. and the PRC.

Grumman was also involved in Israel's Lavi fighter program. Israel conceived of the Lavi when it decided during the late 1970s to produce an indigenous fighter aircraft to fill its air defense and ground attack needs and to serve as an aircraft for export. Two prototypes were made before the program was canceled by the Israeli cabinet in 1987. More than 90 percent of the Lavi's development costs—which have passed the $1.5 billion mark—came from U.S. aid to Israel. The decision to scrap the project was divisive for Israel domestically and internationally. The Reagan Administration had long pressed for the aircraft's cancellation on the grounds that Israel could not afford the cost of building the 300 aircraft that it envisioned. The United States claim was eventually supported by the Israeli Finance Ministry and the Defense Ministry, which feared that production of the Lavi would drain scarce financial resources from other vital defense programs. Israeli supporters of the

Lavi countered that at issue was national pride and the need to provide employment for Israel's high-technology work force. Instead of the Lavi, Israel most likely will purchase additional General Dynamics F-16s, and seek to increase its involvement in the production of the current model and next generation Agile Falcon F-16.

Grumman's participation in the Lavi program was relatively limited: It was contracted to provide Israel with 22 wing and vertical tail sets for the reported price of $120 million, although one source put Grumman's stake in the Lavi as of December 1986 at $150 million.[4]

III. MILITARY ORDERS, 1982–1986 (includes first quarter of 1987)

Country	Date of Agreement	Description of Order	Price (in millions)
– EUROPE AND MAJOR ALLIES –			
Japan	1983	Additional funding for 4 E-2C Hawkeye early warning aircraft/b[1]	$102
Turkey	(1985)	18 S-2E Tracker anti-submarine warfare aircraft/d	NA[2]
– ASIA AND PACIFIC –			
Malaysia	1984	Refurbish 40 A-4 attack aircraft/h,r	$125
	1985	2 refurbished HU-16B Albatross maritime patrol aircraft/d	NA
Pakistan	1986	Program definition for refurbishing unidentified aircraft/r[3]	$1.5
People's Republic of China	1987	Avionics and fire control systems for 55 F-8 fighter aircraft/h,l,n	$245
Singapore	1984	4 E-2C Hawkeye early warning aircraft/e,g,h,r	$410
Taiwan	1986	32 upgrade kits for S-2 anti-submarine aircraft/h	$260
– MIDDLE EAST –			
Egypt	1982	4 E-2C Hawkeye early warning aircraft/c,d,e,g	$465
	1984	1 additional E-2C Hawkeye early warning aircraft/c,g	$50

Country	Date of Agreement	Description of Order	Price (in millions)
	1986	Data for Identification Friend or Foe electronic surveillance systems/f	$9.2
Israel	1983	22 wing and vertical tail shipsets for Lavi fighters/h,r	$120
– LATIN AMERICA –			
Uruguay	1982	5 S-2G Tracker antisubmarine warfare aircraft/d	NA

IV. FMS PROGRAM CONTRACT AWARDS, FY 1983–1986
(millions of dollars)

Item	Fiscal Year	Award Total
E-2C Hawkeye, including spare parts and technical services	1983	$111.17*
	1984	229.51#
	1985	171.31 +
	1986	97.87
Systems engineering for F-111 fighter-bomber aircraft	1986	.30
Unidentified awards	1984	5.41##
	1985	2.91
	1986	27.03

*	Of this total, $101.58 million was awarded for hardware and/or services purchased by Japan.
#	Of this total, $86.31 million was awarded for hardware and/or services purchased by Singapore and $41.32 million by Egypt.
+	Of this total, $90.40 million was awarded for hardware and/or services purchased by Egypt, $36.37 million by Singapore and $3.65 million by Israel.
##	IRRC analysis of DoD contract data suggests these awards are most likely for hardware and/or services related to the export of E-2C Hawkeyes.

NOTES

1. Japan ordered 4 E-2Cs in 1979, which Grumman finished assembling in 1983.

2. These aircraft were purchased through the Military Assistance Program (MAP).

3. Under this exploratory contract, Grumman proposes to install a new nose section, engines and avionics systems on unidentified aircraft. The company says full production would entail modifying 150 aircraft and an award worth approximately $500 million.

4. Data compiled by the Washington Analysis Corp. and reported in *Defense News*, August 24, 1987, p. 40.

HARSCO CORP.

I. SUMMARY DATA

Data, except for the total sales figures, are for U.S. government fiscal years, ending Sept. 30. The FMS program award total for 1984 was calculated by the General Accounting Office; the 1982, 1983, 1985 and 1986 totals were compiled by IRRC from Department of Defense contract data.

	1982	1983	1984	1985	1986
Total sales (millions)	$979	$839	$1,101	$1,261	$1,130
DoD contract awards (millions)	$102	$139	$ 233	$ 106	$ 707
DoD contractor rank	n/a	95	75	n/a	32
DoD awards/total sales	.10	.16	.21	.08	.63
FMS contract awards (millions)	$ 16	$ 10	$ 48	$ 1	$ 53
FMS contractor rank	n/a	n/a	25	n/a	19
FMS/total DoD awards	.02	.07	.21	.51	.07
FMS/total sales	.016	.012	.044	.0004	.047

II. ARMS EXPORT BUSINESS AT A GLANCE

Harsco's defense division, BMY, produces wheeled and tracked land combat systems. The types of weapons that Harsco makes are standard stock in all modern land armies and, therefore, are popular with overseas customers. Harsco's most widely exported military products are the M109A2 155 mm self-propelled howitzer and the M88A1 armored recovery vehicle, which is designed to evacuate damaged combat vehicles from the battlefield and currently is used by 14 nations. Increasingly popular is the Harsco Command Post Vehicle, which is designed for battlefield use as a command and control center. In 1985, a banner year for the company in terms of deliveries of weapons systems to foreign customers, Harsco delivered 385 vehicles—most of which were howitzers—to Belgium, Canada, Greece, South Korea and Israel through direct, commercial sales channels. Egypt and Pakistan have been large Harsco customers in recent years: Both have purchased howitzers and recovery vehicles, and Egypt has also ordered the company's Command Post Vehicle.

Harsco has been ranked among the top 25 FMS contractors in eight of the last 14 years. During these eight years, the company's FMS-related prime contract awards ranged from $21 million in fiscal 1973 to $64 million in 1978. Harsco's sales of defense vehicles were almost equally divided between the U.S. government and foreign nations in 1984 and 1985.

As is the case with all defense contractors, the true extent of Harsco's arms export business cannot be appreciated without taking into account the sales that it makes through direct, commercial channels. Reliable data regarding the company's commercial exports, however, are not available. Harsco has indicated its preference for company-to-government transactions in its annual reports. In 1986, the company wrote that it "will continue its international marketing efforts for direct sales of new vehicles....Direct sales, as well as other international opportunities, provide the company with an expanded backlog and with potential for a higher level of profitability because of customer-design flexibility, the offer of expedited delivery, sales on a firm, fixed price basis and a product warranty, among others."

Harsco expects to export its newest vehicles, primarily the M992 Field Artillery Ammunition Support Vehicle (FAASV), which is used to resupply self-propelled howitzers in the field, the M9 Armored Combat Earthmover and the Counter Obstacle Vehicle, a prototype of which has been evaluated by a Middle Eastern nation. The company also hopes that its early participation in the DoD's Howitzer Improvement Program (HIP) will lead to continued arms exports. Harsco is upgrading 11 howitzers as prototypes for the United States and Israel, and it expects that being selected as the HIP prime contractor for full scale production might mean an income of $800 million over a five year period for upgrading more than 1,700 howitzers at home and abroad. In anticipation of requests from abroad for howitzer upgrade services, the company has teamed up with a British firm—Royal Ordnance—as well as other foreign contractors to develop improved howitzer prototypes designed for the international market.

Harsco has also displayed interest in the Pentagon's "Bear Spares" program. The Department of Defense decided in the mid-1980s that refurbishing weapons originally provided by the Soviets to Third World nations that are no longer aligned with Moscow might be more feasible economically and politically than supplying them with new American weapons. The DoD therefore began encouraging U.S. firms to develop modification and conversion kits for Soviet-built systems. Harsco is one of the U.S. companies that has heeded the call: It is competing with Britain's Royal Ordnance to provide a chassis for a Soviet-made 122 mm howitzer for the Egyptian army.

III. MILITARY ORDERS, 1982–1986 (includes first quarter of 1987)

Country	Date of Agreement	Description of Order	Price (in millions)
		– EUROPE AND MAJOR ALLIES –	
Austria	1982	24 M109A2 155mm self-propelled howitzers/d,f,g	$22
Belgium	1983	124 M109A2 155mm self-propelled howitzers/d,g,r	$110
Canada	1983	26 M109A2 155mm self-propelled howitzers/d,r	NA
Greece	1982	48 M109A2 155mm self-propelled howitzers/d,f,g,r[1]	$47
	1987	23 Command Post Vehicles/n[2]	$30.5
Japan	1984	12 M110A2 203mm self-propelled howitzers/d[3]	NA
West Germany	1986	(80) M109A2 155mm self-propelled howitzers/d	NA

Country	Date of Agreement	Description of Order	Price (in millions)
		– ASIA AND PACIFIC –	
Pakistan	1982	40 M110A2 203mm self-propelled howitzers	NA[4]
		64 M109A2 155mm self-propelled howitzers/d,g	
	1982	35 M88A1 armored recovery vehicles/d,g[5]	NA
	1982	36 M109A2 155mm self-propelled howitzers with guns, spares and support/d,e,f,g	$30
	1985	88 M109A2 155mm self-propelled howitzers	$78
		M2 50-caliber machine guns/c,f,g	
South Korea	1982	M109A2 155mm self-propelled howitzers/r[6]	NA
Taiwan	1983	33 M88A1 armored recovery vehicles/c,d,g	$35.4
		–MIDDLE EAST–	
Egypt	1982	100 M109A2 155mm self-propelled howitzers/d,g,r	NA[7]
	1983	23 M88A1 armored recovery vehicles/d,g	NA[8]
	1983	Command post vehicles/r	NA
	1984	56 M88A1 armored recovery vehicles/c,d,f,g	$63
	1985	48 M109A2 155 mm self-propelled howitzers/d[9]	NA
Israel	1985	Upgraded, M109A5 155 mm self-propelled howitzers/r[10]	NA
Kuwait	1983	M88A1 armored recovery vehicles/c	$9
Lebanon	1982	4 M578 armored recovery vehicles/g[11]	$3
	1982	12 M109A2 155mm self-propelled howitzers/g	NA
Saudi Arabia	1983	18 M109A2 155mm self-propelled howitzers/d	NA
	(1985)	(214) M88A1 armored recovery vehicles/d	NA

Country	Date of Agreement	Description of Order	Price (in millions)
		–AFRICA–	
Tunisia	1983–84	19 M109A2 155mm self-propelled howitzers/d,e[5]	NA

IV. FMS PROGRAM CONTRACT AWARDS, FY 1983–1986
(millions of dollars)

Harsco received relatively few FMS-related prime contract awards during fiscal years 1983 through 1986, mostly because a large portion of its arms exports involve direct commercial sales, which are not included in the DoD contracting data from which the following table was calculated.

Item	Fiscal Year	Award Total
M88 armored recovery vehicles	1983	$16.94
	1984	49.15
	1986	15.72
M109 155mm self-propelled howitzer	1983	–5.97
	1984	–1.39
	1986	36.72
M114A2 155mm towed howitzer	1986	.32
M110 A2 self-propelled howitzer	1983	–.08
	1984	.03
7.62 mm M60 machine guns	1983	.50
Unidentified tank and auto services and technology	1985	.78

Negative figures result from downward contract adjustments.

NOTES

1. SIPRI and *Defense & Foreign Affairs* list this order as having been initiated in 1981. In its 1985 annual report, however, the company mentions an order for self-propelled howitzers placed by the government of Greece in 1982.

2. Greece has already taken delivery on 12 Command Post Vehicles.

3. This order might be increased, and might eventually lead to a coproduction agreement.

4. This is a $176 million package that includes 75 M-198 155mm medium-towed howitzers. SIPRI reports this sale as having been initiated in 1981.

5. SIPRI reports this sale as having been initiated in 1981.

6. This sale was expanded into a coproduction agreement in 1984.

7. This is part of a $140 million package including a small quantity of other vehicles.

8. This is part of a $426 million package.

9. These are in addition to the 100 M109s supplied in 1984.

10. Under the Howitzer Improvement Program, Harsco was awarded a development contract to upgrade 11 prototype M109A2 howitzers to the M109A5 configuration for the U.S. Army and the Israeli Defense Forces. Harsco is leading a team that includes Honeywell, Emerson and RCA.

11. Some sources indicate this order may have been placed in 1981.

HONEYWELL INC.

I. SUMMARY DATA

Data, except for the total sales figures, are for U.S. government fiscal years, ending Sept. 30. FMS program award totals for 1982 to 1984 were calculated by the General Accounting Office; the 1985 and 1986 totals were calculated by IRRC from Department of Defense contract data.

	1982	1983	1984	1985	1986
Total sales (millions)	$5,387	$5,667	$6,073	$6,625	$5,378
DoD contract awards (millions)	$1,217	$1,114	$1,354	$1,886	$1,846
DoD contractor rank	16	21	17	14	12
DoD awards/total sales	.23	.20	.22	.29	.34
FMS contract awards (millions)	$ 20	$ 8	$ 29	$ 16	$ 91
FMS contractor rank	n/a	n/a	n/a	n/a	13
FMS/total DoD awards	.02	.01	.02	.01	.05
FMS/total sales	.004	.001	.005	.002	.017

II. ARMS EXPORT BUSINESS AT A GLANCE

Honeywell Inc. produces ordnance such as torpedoes, bomb components and ammunition, and a variety of computers and related equipment that have military applications. The company also produces navigation, testing and sighting equipment for military aircraft, and stabilizing and sighting systems for armored vehicles. Although Honeywell is consistently one of the top 20 U.S. defense contractors, historically it has not been one of the nation's larger weapons exporters.

Honeywell's most widely exported military item is the Mk 46 torpedo, which is used by more than 20 nations. The Mk 46 can be launched from surface ships, helicopters and fixed wing aircraft, and is also employed on the Mk 60 Captor mine system. Honeywell did not manufacture the early models of the Mk 46, but has been the weapon's prime contractor since 1965 and has produced more than 9,000 torpedoes for the U.S. and foreign governments. FMS-related prime contract awards for the Mk 46 torpedo accounted for 47 percent of the company's total FMS awards in fiscal 1984, 35 percent in 1985 and 77 percent in 1986. Honeywell is also the prime contractor for Neartip (Near-term Improvement Program) conversion kits that are used to upgrade early models of the Mk 46. Honeywell is now working on a five year contract to develop the Mk 50, a replacement for the Mk 46.

Honeywell's RUR-5A Asroc ship-launched anti-submarine rocket system was once another popular export item and is still used by more than 10 foreign navies. Honeywell has also exported optical sighting and ranging systems and the fire control stabilization system it provides for the widely used M-60 tank.

Honeywell is engaged in the sale of various industrial and commercial products and services in Saudi Arabia. One of these was a joint venture with a Saudi company conducted under the auspices of the U.S. Army Corps of Engineers. The venture—called Honeywell Turki-Arabia—involved the purchase and installation of a Delta 5600 energy management control system at King Khalid Military City, for which Honeywell received $30 million in FMS prime contract awards in fiscal 1982, $3.9 million in 1983, $1.7 million in 1984 and $22 million in 1985. (These figures have not been included in Honeywell's FMS totals that appear in Section I of this profile because Turki-Arabia is a joint venture.)

Honeywell has a number of other foreign subsidiaries, mainly in Europe, and also engages in other cooperative ventures abroad. It has been cooperating with Mitsubishi Heavy Industries, which is producing the Mk 46 under license for Japan, and its German affiliate Sondertechnik has been working on a number of programs for the German government. In 1983 Honeywell acquired Leefield's Engineering Ltd. in Britain, which it believes will enhance its "ability to serve that country's Ministry of Defense."

Honeywell's Foreign Military Sales earnings should increase considerably as a result of its November 1986 acquisition of the Sperry aerospace division of Unisys Corp. for $1.03 billion. Sperry's aerospace division became available when Burroughs Corp. acquired Sperry Corp. for $4.8 billion and formed Unisys. The sale of Sperry's aerospace division was necessary in part to finance the larger acquisition. According to analysts, Sperry's aerospace group's product line of flight controls and instrumentation systems is the perfect complement to Honeywell's gyroscopes and guidance and navigational equipment. Sperry as a whole registered more than $73 million in arms export earnings in 1985, making it one of the top 20 FMS contractors for the year. (See Sperry profile for details.) Much of these earnings, however, came from sales of radar and submarine navigation systems by Sperry's defense systems unit, which Unisys will retain.

III. MILITARY ORDERS, 1982–1986 (includes first quarter of 1987)

Country	Date of Agreement	Description of Order	Price (in millions)
		– EUROPE AND MAJOR ALLIES –	
Australia	1987	Upgrade of shore-based tactical naval trainer/f	NA[1]
Canada	1984	220 Mk 46 mod 5 torpedoes with support equipment/e,f,c	$57
	1985	1 DPS-8/70C computer system	NA[2]
	1985	129 Mk 46 mod 5 torpedoes with support/c,e,g	$30
Japan	1984	Additional funding for 1 Mk 540 model 3 torpedo system test set with ancillary services and supplies/b	$4.8
Netherlands	1986	99 MK46 torpedos in containers with spares and support/c,g	$26

Country	Date of Agreement	Description of Order	Price (in millions)
New Zealand	1986	Mk46-2 torpedoes/c	$2.4
Turkey	1986	Mk 46 mod 5 Neartip torpedoes/b	NA
West Germany	1986	Airborne reconnaissance linescanner systems/n[3]	$60
		–ASIA AND PACIFIC–	
Indonesia	1982	48 Mk 46 model 2 torpedoes/c,g	$13
Pakistan	1983	Bomb fuses for laser guided bombs/b	NA[4]
Thailand	1983	Bomb fuses for laser guided bombs/b	NA[4]

IV. FMS PROGRAM CONTRACT AWARDS, FY 1983–1986
(millions of dollars)

Item	Fiscal Year	Award Total
Mk 46 torpedoes	1984	$13.68
	1985	5.66
	1986	70.37
Mk 48 torpedoes	1986	5.20
Optical sighting, ranging and fire control	1983	–1.58
stabilization systems for M60 tanks	1984	3.73
RUR-5A Asroc anti-submarine rockets	1984	.95
Radar equipment and electrical components	1984	.59
for P-3 Orion maritime patrol aircraft	1985	.09
	1986	.14
Electronic measuring instruments and radar	1984	.04
equipment for E-2 Hawkeye aircraft	1985	.57
Equipment for F-15 fighter aircraft	1983	.49
	1985	.15
	1986	.03
Unidentified training devices for systems used in F-16 fighter aircraft	1986	2.96

Item	Fiscal Year	Award Total
Construction of unidentified utilities*	1983	3.91
	1984	1.72
	1985	21.98
Miscellaneous communication equipment	1984	6.35
	1986	1.52
Unidentified automated data processing equipment	1983	3.25
and software, including maintenance and repair	1984	2.83
	1986	8.61
Unidentified bombs	1983	3.09
	1984	.56
Unidentified communication security equipment	1983	.33
and components	1984	.41
	1985	2.21
Leasing of advanced data processing equipment	1983	1.35
	1984	.04
Unidentified fire control systems	1985	1.17
Unidentified utilities	1984	1.71
Maintenance and repair of unidentified	1985	1.01
communication and detection equipment		
Unidentified still picture cameras, sound	1986	1.35
recording and reproducing equipment		
Unidentified airborne radar equipment	1984	.88
	1986	−.02
Unidentified torpedo components	1983	.72
Other unidentified awards	1986	.96

Negative figures result from downward contract adjustments.

* These awards are for work conducted by Honeywell Turki-Arabia in Saudi Arabia.

NOTES

1. Honeywell of Australia received this contract valued at 1.8 million Australian dollars.

2. This contract with the Canadian Defense Research Establishment is estimated to be worth $6 million (Canadian dollars).

3. Honeywell's German subsidiary, Sondertechnik, will execute approximately two-thirds of this five year contract.

4. This contract award of $3.9 million is divided between Pakistan and Thailand.

HUGHES AIRCRAFT CO.

(a subsidiary of General Motors Corp.)

I. SUMMARY DATA

Data, except for the total sales figure, are for U.S. government fiscal years, ending Sept. 30. FMS program award totals for 1982 to 1984 were calculated by the General Accounting Office; the 1985 and 1986 totals were calculated by IRRC from Department of Defense contract data.

	1982	1983	1984	1985	1986
Total sales (millions)	$4,386	$4,938	$4,925	$5,900#	NA
DoD contract awards (millions)	$3,141	$3,240	$3,231	$3,551	$3,749
DoD contractor rank	7	9	7	8	n/a
DoD awards/total sales	.69	.64	.65	.60#	NA
FMS contract awards (millions)+	$ 304	$ 172	$ 176	$94	$ 158
FMS contractor rank	8	10	10	n/a	n/a
FMS/total DoD awards	.10	.05	.05	.03	NA
FMS/total sales	.069	.035	.035	.016#	NA

#	Based on an estimate.
+	Hughes Aircraft's records of FMS program awards differ from the totals derived by the GAO and IRRC from DoD contract data. According to the company, it received FMS awards of $374 million in 1982, $257 million in 1983, $249 million in 1984, $162 million in 1985, and $166 million in 1986. The discrepancies in the two sets of figures might stem from the fact that Hughes's fiscal year differs from that of the government.

II. ARMS EXPORT BUSINESS AT A GLANCE

Hughes Aircraft Co. and its major subsidiaries—Hughes Communications Inc. and the Santa Barbara Research Center—produce missiles, radar, and sighting and communications systems. From 1953 until 1985 Hughes Aircraft was a private company, owned solely by the Howard Hughes Medical Institute, a not-for-profit medical research center that was established by the industrialist Howard Hughes. In December 1985, General Motors purchased Hughes Aircraft for more than $5 billion.

Hughes Aircraft is made up of seven divisions: Electro-Optical & Data Systems Group, Ground Systems Group, Industrial Electronics Group, Missile Systems Group, Radar Systems Group, Space & Communications Group and Support Systems. These divisions, along with Hughes's subsidiaries, work on many small and medium-sized Department of Defense programs, rather than on a few extremely large ones. In 1983, for example, no defense program accounted for more than 6 percent of Hughes's total DoD contract awards. Some analysts see this large and varied product line as the key to Hughes's consistently high level of earnings and its steady position among the top 10 U.S. defense contractors.

Hughes was among the top 25 foreign military sales exporters from 1972 to 1984. Its FMS prime contract awards ranged from $22.1 million in 1973 to $304 million in 1982, when it was the eighth largest FMS contractor, according to the General Accounting Office. (The company's own figures differ; it says it received $103 million in 1973 and $374 million in 1982.) Hughes Aircraft has also registered sizable arms exports sold through direct, company-to-government sales channels. From 1977 to 1981, the last year for which government data are available, its annual commercial arms exports were one-quarter to one-half the size of its government-to-government foreign military sales. Hughes's commercial sales during the period ranged from $24 million in fiscal 1979, when the company was the 11th largest commercial arms exporter, to $121 million in 1981, when it was the second largest.

Documents filed by General Motors with the Securities and Exchange Commission late in 1985 reveal that 24.7 percent of Hughes's 1984 sales were to foreign government and military customers—including 5 percent that were routed through the FMS program and 10.7 percent through direct, commercial channels. The documents also state that "Hughes has . . . attempted to increase sales to foreign governments, largely in order to realize economies of scale from the sale of similar systems to more than one customer."

Hughes launched a joint venture in 1978 with Bendix and Holmes & Narver Inc.—called HBH Co.—to provide logistical support and operation and maintenance services for the Saudi Naval Expansion Program. HBH—whose FMS awards are not included in the parent companies' contract figures—received FMS awards of $176 million in fiscal 1982, $251 million in 1983 and $20 million in 1984, for a total of $447 million, according to the GAO. (The company's figures, again, differ: It calculates it received a total of $823 million between 1980 and 1986. These awards made HBH the 13th largest U.S. FMS contractor in fiscal 1982 and the fifth largest in 1983.

Hughes Aircraft's most widely exported item is the TOW (Tube-launched, Optically tracked, Wire-guided) anti-tank missile. Three basic versions of the missile—the TOW, I-(Improved) TOW and TOW 2—are used by the armed forces of more than 30 nations. Contract awards for TOW missiles accounted for 28 percent of the company's total FMS awards in 1983, 12 percent in 1984 and 57 percent in 1985. (The company's own calculations are 30 percent for 1983, 20 percent for 1984 and 22 percent for 1985.) Data compiled by the Pentagon indicate that 255,494 TOW missiles have been exported, and all but 27,563 had been delivered as of September 1986. A consortium of European nations led by Italy and including Belgium, Denmark, West Germany, the Netherlands and Turkey is considering a joint Maverick purchase, which Hughes forecasts might involve 4,000 missiles. The consortium, which is reported to be considering coproduction of the Maverick, will not reach a decision until 1988. Other leading exports are Hughes's Maverick air-to-surface missiles—12,029 of which had been delivered to foreign customers or were on order as of September 1986—and its AN/TPQ-36 and AN/TPQ-37 weapon locating radar systems. Hughes Aircraft is also a leader in air defense radar, such as the shipborne AN/SPS-52. More than 23 nations now use Hughes air defense radar systems.

The company exports some of its wares as subcontract items for larger systems. It produces an airborne radar system—the AN/APG-65—that is used on the McDonnell Douglas F/A-18 fighter/attack aircraft, which has been sold to Canada, Australia and Spain. West Germany is also using the system as part of its McDonnell Douglas Phantom F-4 fighter upgrade program. Hughes also manufactures the bomber fire control system for the McDonnell Douglas AV-8 Harrier aircraft and proximity fuses for Ford Aerospace/Raytheon Sidewinder air-to-air missiles. A future source of FMS awards may come from the company's AIM-120 advanced medium range air-to-air missile (AMRAAM). Many of the NATO allies have taken an active interest in the missile, which is still in the development stage.

III. MILITARY ORDERS, 1982–1986 (Includes first quarter of 1987)

Country	Date of Agreement	Description of Order	Price (in millions)
– EUROPE AND MAJOR ALLIES –			
Australia	1982	7 AN/TPQ-36 mortar locating radar systems and 1 AN/TPQ simulator/g	$46
	1984	AN/APG-65 radar systems/f	NA[1]
	1987	8 AN/APG-65/g	$3.6
Canada	1986	360 TOW-2 anti-tank missile launchers with 1,800 TOW-2 missiles/d,e,f	NA
Finland	(1985)	BGM-71C I-TOW anti-tank missiles/d	NA
Great Britain	1983	23 angle-rate bombing sets for AV-8 Harrier aircraft/b,f	NA
	1984	40 angle-rate bombing sets for AV-8 Harrier aircraft/c	NA
	1985	29 angle-rate bombing sets for AV-8 Harrier aircraft/c	NA
	1986	34 angle-rate bombing sets for AV-8 Harrier aircraft/c	NA
Greece	(1982)	579 BGM-71 TOW anti-tank missiles/d	NA
	1984	1,097 BGM-71 I-TOW anti-tank missiles with 54 launchers/c,d,f,g	$19
Italy	1984	1,421 BGM-71 I-TOW anti-tank missiles/c,d,f	$57
Japan	1983	AN/SPS-52C air surveillance radar systems/g	NA[2]
	1983	9 BGM-71A TOW anti-tank missile system/d	NA[3]
	1986	BGM-71A TOW anti-tank missiles/c	$2.5
	1986	1 AN/SPS-52C shipborne radar/g	$8.7

Country	Date of Agreement	Description of Order	Price (in millions)
Netherlands	(1984)	AN/TPQ-37 Firefinder artillery locating radar systems/r	NA
	1985	2,477 BGM-71D TOW-2 anti-tank missiles/g,l	$32
	1987	1,878 BGM-71 TOW-2 anti-tank missiles/d,g	$22
	1986	4 AN/TPQ-37 weapon-locating radar sets with spares and support/c,d,f,g	$45
Norway	1984	Low Altitude Surveillance Radar Systems/f,r	$18
Portugal	1982	AGM-65 Maverick air-to-surface missiles/c	$2.6
Spain	1984	Additional funding for AN/APG-65 radar systems for F/A-18 fighters/b	$3.9
	1984	Angle-rate bombing sets/c	NA
	1986	Additional funding for spares and support for AN/ASB-19(v)2 angle bombing sets/b	$1.7
Sweden	1984	508 BGM-71D TOW-2 anti-tank missiles/d	NA
Switzerland	1982	381 AGM-65A Maverick air-to-surface missiles/c,d	$31.8
	1985	BGM-71 TOW-2 anti-tank missiles/f,g	NA[4]
Turkey	(1983)	(48) BGM-71A TOW anti-tank missiles/c,d	NA
	1986	6 AN/TPQ-36 radar sets with communications equipment and support/d,f,g	$27
West Germany	1982	455 AGM-65B Maverick air-to-surface missiles/d,f,g	$50
	1985	310 AGM-65B Maverick air-to-surface missiles/c,e,g	$25
Yugoslavia	1982	(40) AGM-65B Maverick air-to-surface missiles/d	NA

– ASIA AND PACIFIC –

Country	Date of Agreement	Description of Order	Price (in millions)
Pakistan	1982	10 AN/TPQ-36 mortar locating radar systems with spares and support/g	$40

Country	Date of Agreement	Description of Order	Price (in millions)
	1985	15 AN/TPQ-36 mortar locating radar systems/c,f,g	$65
	1985	4 AN/TPQ-37 Firefinder artillery locating radar systems/c,f,g	$41
	1986	F-16 logistics support/f	$3.6
	1986	2,030 BGM-71C I-TOW anti-tank missiles/c,f,g,e,h	$20
	1987	2,386 TOW-2 anti-tank missiles/g,h,n	$78
Peoples Republic of China	1984	Agreed in principle to the sale of BGM-71A TOW anti-tank missiles/d	NA
	1986	2 AN/TPQ-37 weapon locating radar systems/d,f,g	NA[5]
	1987	2 AN/TPQ-37 weapon locating radar systems/c	NA
Singapore	1982	6 AN/TPQ-36 mortar locating radar systems/g	$30
South Korea	1983	BGM-71 TOW anti-tank missiles/c	$3.2
	1984	Laser rangefinder and thermal imaging systems/r	NA
	1986	1,410 AGM-65 Maverick air-to-surface missiles/c	NA
	1986	(504) BGM-71C I-TOW anti-tank missiles for 21 AH-1S helicopters/c,d	$6.5
Taiwan	1986	(1) AN/TPQ-37 mortar locating radar/d	NA
Thailand	1982	3 AN/TPQ-36 mortar locating radar systems/f,g	$26

– MIDDLE EAST –

Country	Date of Agreement	Description of Order	Price (in millions)
Bahrain	1987	AGM-65 Maverick air-to-surface missiles/g	NA[6]
Egypt	1984	First phase of a national air defense system/f,r	$210
	1985	2 AN/TPQ-37 Firefinder artillery locating radar systems with support equipment/c,d,e,g	$24

Country	Date of Agreement	Description of Order	Price (in millions)
Israel	1987	2 AN/TPQ-37 Firefinder artillery locating radar systems/c	$87[7]
Jordan	1982	(192) BGM-71A TOW anti-tank missiles for 24 AH-1S helicopters/d	NA
	1982	4 AN/TPQ-36 mortar locating radar systems/c	NA
	(1983)	(60) AGM-65C Maverick air-to-surface missiles/d	NA
	1984	AN/TPQ-37 Firefinder artillery locating radar systems/r	NA
Kuwait	1982	4,010 BGM-71 I-TOW anti-tank missiles with 56 M901 I-TOW missile launchers/d,e,g	NA[8]
Saudi Arabia	1982	2,010 BGM-71 I-TOW anti-tank missiles/d,f,g	$22
	1983	2,538 BGM-71 I-TOW anti-tank missiles/c,d,f,g[10]	$26
	1984	AN/TPQ-37 Firefinder artillery locating radar systems/r	NA
	1984	BGM-71 I-TOW anti-tank missiles/c	NA
	1987	BGM-71 TOW anti-tank missiles for 15 Bell-Textron model 406 Kiowa helicopters/f,g	NA[9]
–AFRICA–			
Morocco	1982	381 AGM-65B Maverick air-to-surface missiles/d,g	$29
	1983	BGM-71 TOW anti-tank missiles/c	$15
	(1985)	BGM-71C I-TOW anti-tank missiles/d	NA
–LATIN AMERICA–			
Brazil	1984	12 BGM-71 TOW anti-tank missiles/e,g	NA

IV. FMS PROGRAM CONTRACT AWARDS, FY 1983–1986
(millions of dollars)

Item	Fiscal Year	Award Total
BGM-71 TOW anti-tank missiles	1983	$48.17
	1984	21.86*
	1985	53.24
	1986	1.87
AGM-65 Maverick air-to-ground missiles	1983	48.28#
	1984	2.52+
	1985	−1.41
	1986	3.45
AN/TPQ-36 mortar-locating radar systems	1983	45.59
	1984	12.82
	1985	−1.16
	1986	7.69
AN/SPS-52 air surveillance radar systems	1983	6.08
	1984	38.49
	1985	.04
	1986	6.73
Components, including warheads, for AIM-9 Sidewinder air-to-air missiles	1983	7.06
	1984	5.97
	1985	15.98
	1986	6.96
Radar equipment for F-15 fighter aircraft	1983	13.37x
	1984	13.34
	1985	−.05
	1986	2.83
Bomber fire control for AV-8 Harrier aircraft	1984	19.83
	1985	5.22
	1986	39.32
Intercom systems for E-3A Awacs aircraft	1984	5.28
	1985	2.00
	1986	−.87
MAN/UYQ-21 shipborne weapon control display systems	1983	2.15
	1984	4.51
	1986	1.40

Item	Fiscal Year	Award Total
Guided missile remote control and other components for F/A-18 fighter/attack aircraft	1984	4.12
	1985	.70
	1986	13.73
AN/UYA-4 naval fire control radar systems	1984	4.35
	1985	.32
	1986	−.05
AN/TPQ-37 artillery locating radar systems	1985	3.22
	1986	27.10
Optical ranging and sighting system for M-60 tank	1985	2.32
	1986	.62
Peace Hawk Saudi Air Force modernization program	1985	1.50
	1986	1.37
AN/TVQ-2 laser designator fire control systems	1983	.92
	1984	.14
	1985	.08
Technical services for MIM-23 Hawk missile	1984	.87
	1985	.21
	1986	.14
Unidentified guided missile remote control systems	1983	−2.49
	1984	15.19
	1986	3.47
Unidentified ground-based radar equipment	1983	5.20
	1984	−.15
	1985	5.48
	1986	.41
Unidentified guided missiles	1983	4.20
	1986	40.86
Unidentified electronic countermeasure systems	1983	1.09
Unidentified miscellaneous electrical and electronic equipment	1983	.98
	1985	.64
	1986	.23
Unidentified ground-based fire control radar systems	1983	.59

Negative figures result from downward contract adjustments.

*	These awards include funds for hardware and/or services purchased by South Korea.
#	These awards include funds for hardware and/or services purchased by Morocco, Pakistan and Yugoslavia.
+	These awards include funds for hardware and/or services purchased by Morocco and Pakistan.
x	These awards include funds for hardware and/or services purchased by Israel.

NOTES

1. This is part of a $4.75 million package that includes spares for McDonnell Douglas F/A-18 aircraft.

2. This is part of a $103 million package that includes General Dynamics Phalanx Close-in Weapon Systems.

3. The licensed production of TOW missiles began in 1985.

4. The $209 million purchase price includes 400 AN/TAS-4A night sight systems.

5. This is a $62 million package that includes 8 AN/VRC-46 radio sets that are manufactured by various contractors, ancillary and support equipment, spare parts and maintenance.

6 This is a $400 million package that includes 12 General Dynamics F-16 fighter aircraft, Westinghouse AN/ALQ-131 electronic countermeasure pods, radar warning receivers, chaff/flare dispensers, Ford and/or Raytheon AIM-9 Sidewinder air-to-air missiles, and General Dynamics and/or Raytheon AIM-7 Sparrow air-to-air missiles.

7. This sale was arranged under a Special Defense Acquisition Fund production contract.

8. This is part of a $97 million package that includes FMC M-113 armored personnel carriers and 56 Kollman Instrument Co. AN/UAS-12 night sight systems. Production of the 1986 and 1987 AN/TPQ-37 systems was arranged through the Special Defense Acquisition Fund.

9. This is part of a $400 million package that includes 13 United Technologies UH-60 helicopters and 1 Beech C-12 transport aircraft.

LOCKHEED CO.

I. SUMMARY DATA

Data, except for the total sales figures, are for U.S. government fiscal years, ending Sept. 30. FMS program award totals for 1982 to 1984 were calculated by the General Accounting Office; the 1985 and 1986 totals were calculated by IRRC from Department of Defense contract data.

	1982	1983	1984	1985	1986
Total sales (millions)	$5,613	$6,490	$8,113	$9,535	$10,273
DoD contract awards (millions)	$3,499	$4,006	$4,967	$5,082	$ 4,896
DoD contractor rank	5	6	4	6	6
DoD awards/total sales	.62	.62	.61	.53	.48
FMS contract awards (millions)	$ 348	$ 171	$ 225	$ 295	$ 52
FMS contractor rank	7	11	8	6	20
FMS/total DoD awards	.09	.04	.05	.06	.01
FMS/total sales	.062	.026	.028	.031	.005

II. ARMS EXPORT BUSINESS AT A GLANCE

The export of weapons systems currently figures less prominently in Lockheed's defense business than it did in the early 1980s: Total sales to foreign governments—including FMS program transactions and direct, company-to-government sales—accounted for 15.3 percent of the company's sales in 1982 and remained unchanged over the next four years. The fact that the ratio of sales to foreign governments to the company's total sales slipped to between 6 and 7 percent in 1985 and 1986 is attributable to increased domestic sales. The vast majority of Lockheed's foreign sales, like the company's domestic sales, involve defense equipment.

Lockheed's defense exports increasingly involve missile, space and electronic systems, a trend that should continue because of the company's acquisition of Sanders Associates, a major defense electronics manufacturer. Seventy-five percent of Lockheed's 1986 foreign sales were of aeronautical systems, with sales of missiles, space and electronic systems representing 24 percent of the total, and information systems approximately 1 percent. However, in 1985, missiles, space and electronic systems accounted for only 21 percent of the company's foreign sales, as opposed to 68 percent for aeronautical systems, and in 1984 the shares were 15.3 percent for the missiles, space and electronics division and 84 percent for the aeronautical segment. Foreign sales of aeronautical systems have actually declined sharply in dollar value since 1984, while exports of missiles, space and electronic systems have risen somewhat.

Lockheed, more than most defense contractors, exports its defense equipment through the direct, company-to-government sales program, rather than through government-arranged FMS channels. Of the 15.3 percent of sales to foreign governments in 1982, 12.2 percent involved direct sales and 3.1 percent FMS program transactions. The breakdown for 1983 was 8.6 percent direct sales and 3.6 percent FMS; and for 1984, 7 percent direct sales and 2.8 percent FMS. The General

Accounting Office found that Lockheed exported more weapons via the commercial sales route than any other contractor in fiscal years 1977, 1978, 1980 and 1981.

The General Accounting Office and the Department of Defense also ranked Lockheed among the top 10 FMS contractors every year between 1972 and 1984 except for 1974 (when it was ranked 11th), 1980 (13th), 1981 (11th) and 1983 (11th). The company was the third largest FMS contractor in 1977, with prime contract awards of $305 million.

Lockheed's arms exports were at one point a source of controversy. In the mid-1970s, an investigation by the Senate Subcommittee on Multinational Corporations led to the disclosure by Lockheed that it had paid $38 million to political organizations and government officials in foreign nations to facilitate arms exports, including a $1 million donation in the early 1960s to the Inspector General of the Netherlands Armed Forces, Prince Bernhard. This last revelation led to the resignation of Prince Bernhard from his post with the armed forces.

Lockheed's principal exports continue to be military aircraft. Fifty-six nations fly the Lockheed C-130 Hercules transport aircraft and its commercial version, the L-100.[1] Records compiled by the Department of Defense's Security Assistance Agency indicate that as of Sept. 30, 1986, 237 C-130s had been exported through the FMS program and 56 through the Military Assistance Program. This does not include the large number of C-130s that have been acquired through direct, company-to-government sales channels. IRRC was able to identify $290 million in FMS-related prime contract awards allocated to the company during fiscal years 1983 through 1985 for work on C-130s for foreign governments. In addition to the recent C-130 exports listed in Part III of this profile, the following transactions appear to have been arranged directly by the U.S. government (involving aircraft taken from U.S. Air Force inventory or surplus stock) without the participation of Lockheed: two C-130s sold to Canada in 1986, two sold to Japan in 1986 for $55 million, one to Oman in 1986, two to Chad in 1986, four to Colombia in 1982 and one configured as a KC-130 tanker/transport to Morocco in 1985.

Although the L-100 is classified as a commercial aircraft, it is often used by foreign governments to fulfill military roles. The L-100 has been the subject of some controversy, because it has been illegally transferred on a number of occasions, through no fault of the company's, including most recently to Libya. According to analysts, the looser regulations governing the sale of this aircraft, as opposed to the military C-130, has enabled these diversions to occur.

Eight foreign nations use the P-3 Orion antisubmarine/maritime patrol aircraft, another popular Lockheed export item. Sixty-three P-3s had been exported through the FMS program as of September 1986, with two more on order. In addition, 28 have been sold directly to foreign governments, including 10 P-3Cs to Australia and 18 CP140 aircraft to Canada. The company completed delivery of 13 P-3s to the Netherlands in 1984, and in 1986 it completed delivery of 10 to Australia. Kawasaki Heavy Industries of Japan is co-producing 105 P-3 Orions under license, and has already delivered some to the Japanese defense forces. The Japanese Defense Agency had initially agreed to produce 75 of the aircraft, but in November 1985 it signed a commitment to purchase an additional 30 aircraft. Six of the aircraft appear to have been transferred directly by the U.S. government out of its inventory to New Zealand in 1985.

Formerly, Lockheed's principal export was the F-104 Starfighter aircraft, and Lockheed continues to perform support work on these aircraft for foreign nations. As of September 1986, 418

Starfighters had been exported through the MAP program, and 271 had been ordered through the FMS program. Additional Starfighters have been produced under license by West Germany, which alone procured a total of 1,128 of the aircraft, and other countries. Thirteen other foreign nations— including, Taiwan, Jordan, Pakistan, and most of NATO—fly the F-104. The aircraft was a source of some controversy, partly because of the political commissions paid to further its sales in such countries as the Netherlands and West Germany, and partly because more than 500 Starfighters were lost in crashes. According to analysts, most of these crashes occurred because the aircraft was used to perform a variety of roles for which it was poorly suited.

Lockheed is involved in this country's most unusual foreign military sales: the export of strategic sea-launched ballistic missiles (SLBMs) to Britain. The United States has sold 133 Lockheed-manufactured Polaris SLBMs to Britain since the mid-1960s, and the company has received contracts ever since for maintaining and upgrading the missiles. The British government announced in July 1980 that it would replace its aging Polaris arsenal with a newer American system. Britain initially chose the Trident I (C-4) SLBM, but reversed its decision and opted for the more advanced and expensive Trident II (D-5). (Both systems are manufactured by Lockheed.) As was the case with the Polaris program, only the missiles will be purchased from the United States; the British will manufacture the nuclear warheads and the four submarines on which the Tridents will be deployed.

Firm estimates of the size of the British Trident purchase are hard to come by. Current plans call for the construction of four submarines, each capable of carrying 16 Trident IIs, for a total of 64 missiles. Reliable sources estimated in 1982 that the total cost of the procurement program will be $14 billion, roughly $3 billion of which will be earmarked for the procurement of 72 Trident II missiles. IRRC identified $354 million in FMS-related prime contract awards issued to Lockheed during fiscal years 1983 through 1986 for work related to the British Polaris and Trident programs.

Lockheed is trying to break into the international airborne early warning and command (AEWC) market, which thus far Boeing and Grumman have dominated. The company said in its 1984 annual report that it had "applied for export licenses to offer a C-130 Hercules-based airborne early warning version to more than 25 countries around the world."

The company has also produced a modified P-3 Orion that is configured as an airborne early warning aircraft. According to a Lockheed executive, the most promising prospects for sales of the modified P-3 aircraft, which Lockheed now calls the Sentinel, are Canada, Australia and Japan.

These sales are far from certain, however. Canada decided to improve its ground-based radar systems before considering an AEWC purchase, and Australia postponed temporarily any AEWC purchase because of a funding shortage. While Japan is still determining its AEWC needs, Lockheed may have an edge on its competitors; Japan is already familiar with the P-3, since it is producing the maritime patrol version of it under license. Moreover, Japan has decided against purchasing additional Grumman E-2 Hawkeye airborne early warning and control aircraft to complement its existing fleet of E-2s, because the plane's range is too short. Lockheed's prime American competitor for the Japanese AEWC buy is Boeing's E-3A Awacs, which is considerably more expensive than the P-3 AEWC aircraft. The early warning and control version of the P-3 is expected to cost $70 million, which is more than Grumman's E-2 Hawkeye if cheaper than the Awacs.

Additional markets for Lockheed's AEWC system may lie in the developing world. Because Lockheed's P-3 Orion is less advanced than Boeing's Awacs, the U.S. government is willing to export it to a larger number of Third World countries. Moreover, the P-3 Orion's price tag compared with that of Boeing's Awacs makes the P-3 a more attractive option for many developing nations. The six-country Gulf Cooperation Council has narrowed the competition to Lockheed's P-3 Orion and systems made by French and Dutch companies for its planned $1 billion purchase of an airborne early warning and control system. Lockheed also has submit a bid for Pakistan's AEWC purchase, although the Pakistanis have voiced a strong preference for either buying or leasing Boeing's AWACS.

Lockheed's P-3 Sentinel AEWC aircraft received an additional boost when the U.S. Customs Service decided to buy one for detecting drug smugglers. Officials from the North American Air Defense (NORAD) organization will fly along with customs officials for a brief period to test the AEWC aircraft's performance. Lockheed executives hope that a positive assessment by NORAD, along with the endorsement already gained from the U.S. Customs Service, will enhance the aircraft's standing in the eyes of foreign governments.

Lockheed also provides technical and support services to the armed forces of a variety of nations. Under a five year contract signed in 1982, Lockheed provides training and maintenance support for Kawasaki helicopters purchased by the Saudis. Lockheed also maintains a presence in Saudi Arabia to service the Saudis' fleet of C-130 cargo aircraft and support the country's air defense and navigational aids system.

Lockheed's foreign military sales should rise in the coming years as a result of its recent $1.18 billion acquisition of Sanders Associates. Sanders, which manufactures electronic countermeasure systems, radar, automated test systems and computer simulation systems, will give Lockheed a major entree into the defense electronics business. Sanders was awarded $28.2 million in foreign military sales contracts in 1985 and ranked 27th among U.S. FMS exporters. It received $14.6 million in FMS awards in 1986. Sanders's most important military exports are the ALQ-126B electronic countermeasure system, which is used on F-18 fighters, and the Low Altitude Aircraft Detection System (LAADS) air defense radar, for which Thailand placed a $17.5 million order in 1985.

Another source of future arms exports by Lockheed is the company's Altair remotely piloted vehicle. Lockheed is conducting an aggressive marketing effort in support of foreign sales of this unmanned aircraft, and has contacted 36 of the 44 countries reportedly interested in purchasing unmanned aircraft. The international drone market is already crowded, however, and foreign sales may depend on whether NATO decides to employ unmanned aircraft. The future of the Altair also depends heavily on whether the U.S. Army procures the Aquila drone on which the Altair is based. The Pentagon has not yet made a firm decision on the Aquila, and the aircraft has met some stiff opposition in Congress because of problems Lockheed has experienced developing the vehicle.

III. MILITARY ORDERS, 1982–1986 (includes first quarter of 1987)

Country	Date of Agreement	Description of Order	Price (in millions)
– EUROPE AND MAJOR ALLIES –			
Australia	1982	10 P-3C Orion antisubmarine maritime patrol aircraft/d,r	NA
Canada	1984	2 C-130 Hercules transport aircraft/d,e,f,g[3]	$35.1[2]
Great Britain	1984	4 L-1011 Tri-Star tanker aircraft modification support/d,e	NA
	1982	72 Trident II sea-launched ballistic missiles/d,g	$3,200
Japan[4]	1982	2 C-130 Hercules transport aircraft/d,f,g	$26.0
	1984	2 C-130 Hercules transport aircraft/d	$26.6
	1985	2 C-130 Hercules transport aircraft/c,e,f	$51
	1985	Co-production of 30 additional P-3C Orion maritime patrol aircraft/g	NA
NATO	1983	Flight data recorders and data playback units for Awacs aircraft/r	NA
New Zealand	1985	1 P-3B Orion antisubmarine maritime patrol aircraft/d,g	NA
Norway	1986	2 P-3C Orion surveillance aircraft/d,n	$42
Portugal	1985	6 P-3B Orion antisubmarine maritime patrol aircraft/e	NA
Spain	1986	1 C-130 Hercules transport aircraft/c	$19.7
– ASIA AND PACIFIC –			
Taiwan	1984	12 C-130 Hercules transport aircraft/c,e,f,g	$325
Thailand	1982	1 C-130 Hercules transport aircraft/b	$15.4
– MIDDLE EAST –			
Egypt	1986	Additional funding for depot maintenance for 4 C-130H aircraft/b,f	$3.9
Jordan	1982	2 C-130 Hercules transport aircraft/d[3]	$28.1[2]
Oman	1982	1 C-130 Hercules transport aircraft/r	$13

Country	Date of Agreement	Description of Order	Price (in millions)
United Arab Emirates	1982	2 C-130 Hercules transport aircraft/d[3]	$22.9[2,5]
– AFRICA –			
Algeria	1982	8 C-130 Hercules transport aircraft/d[3]	$152.3[2]
	1984	3 C-130 Hercules transport aircraft/d[3]	$92.5
Cameroon	1982	1 C-130 Hercules transport aircraft/d	$19.0[2]
Nigeria	1983	3 C-130 Hercules transport aircraft/d[3]	$71.3[2]
Sudan	1985	Maintenance of 6 C-130 Hercules transport aircraft/f	$.5
	1986	Overhaul of 3 DHC-5D Buffalo aircraft/g	$6.2
Tunisia	1984	2 C-130 Hercules transport aircraft/d,e,f[3]	$48[2]
– LATIN AMERICA –			
Brazil	1986	3 C-130 Hercules transport aircraft/c	$49.6
Colombia	1984	2 C-130 Hercules transport aircraft/d,e,g[3]	$39.5[2]

IV. FMS PROGRAM CONTRACT AWARDS, FY 1983–1986
(millions of dollars)

Item	Fiscal Year	Award Total
C-130 Hercules transport aircraft	1983	$ 48.42
	1984*	3.67
	1985	238.09
	1986#	-2.53
Polaris A-3 submarine-launched ballistic missiles	1983	51.56
	1984	166.43
	1985	49.67
	1986	32.75
P-3 Orion maritime patrol aircraft	1983	$ 43.32
	1984	3.18
	1985	1.35
	1986	.08

Item	Fiscal Year	Award Total
Trident II (D-5) submarine-launched ballistic missiles	1983	6.10
	1984	23.84
	1985	3.19
	1986	19.76
Support of F-104 Starfighter fighter aircraft	1983	8.05
	1984	.18
	1985	1.10
F-4 Phantom fighter structural components	1983	.56
Technical representative services for unidentified aircraft	1986 +	1.18
Unidentified awards	1983**	12.41
	1984	3.39
	1985	.52
	1986	.36

Negative figure results from downward contract adjustments.

* DoD contracting records show that awards totaling $0.84 million were issued for work to be performed in Egypt, $0.74 million for work in Sudan, and $0.74 million in Zaire.

This includes work performed in Egypt, the Philippines, Sudan, Taiwan and Zaire.

+ IRRC analysis of DoD contracting data suggests that these awards are most likely for C-130 aircraft, with $1.05 million of the awards for work conducted in Egypt.

** IRRC analysis of DoD contracting data suggests that $11.4 million of these unidentified awards may well be for the British Polaris and Trident sea-launched ballistic missiles, and $.25 million for C-130 work.

NOTES

1. Some sources list transactions involving the L-100 Hercules as foreign military sales, largely because the deals were concluded with foreign governments and because it is difficult to know what function the aircraft will serve. SIPRI, for example, reports the sale of six L-100s to Iraq, one to Gabon, one to Ecuador and four to Argentina during 1982 and 1983, and three to Peru during 1985. *Defense & Foreign Affairs* also reports a $90 million agreement in 1982 for the sale of four L-100s to Kuwait.

2. Spares, training and miscellaneous items were included in the contract price.

3. These sales are direct company-to-government sales.

4. SIPRI reports that the government of Japan is purchasing a total of 18 C-130 Hercules transport aircraft. All of these sales were conducted through the Foreign Military Sales program.

5. The contract price includes credit for two used C-130 trade-ins.

THE LTV CORP.

I. SUMMARY DATA

Data, except for the total sales figures, are for U.S. government fiscal years, ending Sept. 30. FMS program award totals for 1983 and 1984 were calculated by the General Accounting Office; the 1982, 1985 and 1986 totals were calculated by IRRC from Department of Defense contract data.

	1982	1983	1984	1985	1986
Total sales (millions)	$4,777	$4,578	$7,046	$8,199	$7,271
DoD contract awards (millions)	$ 548	$1,343	$1,655	$1,585	$1,445
DoD contractor rank	37	16	14	18	17
DoD awards/total sales	.11	.29	.23	.19	.20
FMS contract awards (millions)	$ 15	$ 85	$ 91	$ 45	$ 31
FMS contractor rank	n/a	17	17	20	20
FMS/total DoD awards	.03	.06	.05	.03	.02
FMS/total sales	.003	.019	.013	.005	.004

II. ARMS EXPORT BUSINESS AT A GLANCE

LTV's aerospace and defense division, formerly known as Vought, manufactures missiles, rocket launchers and fighter aircraft. LTV's largest military program involves supplying the aft and aft-intermediate fuselage sections for the B-1B bomber. In September 1983, LTV's defense segment was greatly expanded when the company acquired AM General—the world's largest supplier of tactical wheeled vehicles—and the Sierra Research Center. Sierra Research, which posts annual Department of Defense contract awards of more than $50 million, produces stationkeeping devices used by aircraft for low visibility formation flying and communication equipment. AM General accounts for roughly one-third of LTV's defense business.

LTV has encountered some serious difficulties. In July 1986, the company filed for bankruptcy in the midst of its fifth straight year of operating in the red, and plans to reorganize by selling its energy products unit, scaling back its steel division and emphasizing its profitable aerospace and defense line. LTV recently reorganized its defense operations into two segments: LTV Missiles and Electronics Group and LTV Aircraft Products Group. LTV Missiles and Electronics Group includes AM General, and accounts for the majority of the company's military exports.

LTV, which exports arms principally through the Foreign Military Sales program, was ranked among the top 25 U.S. FMS exporters for six years between 1972 and 1984. Sales of $91 million made LTV the ninth largest FMS exporter in fiscal 1974 and the 12th largest in 1984. The acquisition of AM General returned the company to ranks of the top 25 after a six year absence.

LTV's principal export has beem the A-7 Corsair attack aircraft. Introduced into the U.S. arsenal in 1966, this jet fighter has since been bought by Greece, Indonesia, Pakistan and, most recently, Portugal. Records compiled by the Department of Defense's Security Assistance Agency indicate that 90 A-7s had been ordered through the FMS program and 62 through the Military Assistance program as of September 1986. The DSAA reports, however, that 42 of the A-7s ordered through the MAP program, and three of the A-7s ordered through the FMS program, had not yet been delivered as of this date. Corsair-related awards accounted for 46 percent of the company's total FMS contracts in fiscal 1983, 65 percent in 1984 and 12 percent in 1985.

LTV also exports AM General 5 ton M39, 5 ton M939, 2 1/2 ton M44-A2 and 1/4 ton M151 trucks, for which the company received $122 million in prime contract awards from 1983 through 1986. AM General recently received a major order for 5-ton and 2 1/2 ton trucks from Saudi Arabia, which is purchasing 2,263 5-ton, 2 1/2-ton, and 1 1/4-ton trucks. Nonetheless, in its 1986 annual report the company states that a decrease in operating income for its missiles and electronics division was partly the result of lower sales of lower foreign sales of 5-ton trucks and spare parts. The company states that it has "reduced prospects for foreign sales" of its M939 5-ton truck for the future, particularly in light of LTV's loss of a continued production contract from the Army for this vehicle.

The Pentagon selected LTV to provide it with its newest tactical vehicle, the High Mobility Multipurpose Wheeled Vehicle (Hummer), for which the company received the largest wheeled-vehicle contract ever awarded by the Army for the production of a minimum of 60,000 vehicles. The Hummer is replacing a range of light military vehicles, including the venerable Jeep, and it became an export item in 1986 when Luxembourg placed the first foreign order for the vehicle. The company has since received orders from Djibouti, Thailand and the United Arab Emirates for this vehicle.

Also popular overseas are LTV's Multiple Launch Rocket System (MLRS) and its MGM-52 Lance battlefield support missile. The MLRS has been adopted by NATO and will be deployed in Great Britain, France, Italy, West Germany and the Netherlands—the original partners in the MLRS development program. The Netherlands became the most recent country to adopt the system when it agreed to purchase 21 MLRS launchers with rockets and spare parts for $190 million. Delivery will begin in 1989. LTV reportedly projects exports worth $4 billion for the MLRS. According to one source, Egypt, Thailand and Saudi Arabia are all seriously negotiating for the purchase of the system.

Belgium, West Germany, Italy, Israel, the Netherlands and Great Britain have purchased the Lance, which can carry either a nuclear or a conventional warhead. As of September 1986, 902 Lance missiles had been ordered through the FMS program, of which 816 had been delivered.

The company is developing a long-range missile (dubbed the ATACMS) designed to be used with the MLRS, and a kinetic energy Hypervelocity Missile that would be used against armored vehicles. Both should also be exported in the future if the Department of Defense decides to move them into full production. LTV is also developing components for the C-17 Airlifter transport aircraft, which would be a source of large export earnings should the aircraft be sold abroad.

III. MILITARY ORDERS, 1982–1986 (includes first quarter of 1987)

Country	Date of Agreement	Description of Order	Price (in millions)
– EUROPE AND MAJOR ALLIES –			
France	1983	55 Multiple Launch Rocket Systems/e	NA
Great Britain	1983	4 Multiple Launch Rocket System launchers with 108 practice rockets and training equipment/i	$5.2
Italy	1983	Multiple Launch Rocket Systems/i	NA
Japan	1986	Stationkeeping equipment for C-1 transport aircraft/g	$2.2
Luxembourg	1986	22 M998 Hummer multi-purpose wheeled vehicles/g	NA
Netherlands	1986	21 multiple launch rocket systems with 2,700 M77 rocket pods, 31 practice pods and 34 rocket pod trainers, plus support/c,d,f,g,n	$192
Portugal	1983	24 modernized A-7P Corsair-2 attack and 6 TA-7P trainer aircraft/c,d,r	$143.6
West Germany	1983	2 Multiple Launch Rocket System launchers with training equipment/c,i	$6.5
– ASIA AND PACIFIC –			
Djibouti	1986	83 M939A1 five-ton trucks/g	$3.7
	1986	10 M998 Hummer multi-purpose wheeled vehicles/g	NA
Pakistan	1987	140 M809 5-ton trucks and 40 M44-A2 2 1/2 ton trucks/g,n	$18.5
Thailand	1986	150 M998 Hummer multi-purpose wheeled vehicles/g	NA
Kuwait	1986	685 5-ton trucks plus diagnostic test equipment and spares/c,f,g	$70
– MIDDLE EAST –			
Saudi Arabia	1986	2,263 5-ton and 2 1/2 ton trucks/c,g	NA[1]
United Arab Emirates	1986	3 M998 Hummer multi-purpose wheeled vehicles/g	NA

Country	Date of Agreement	Description of Order	Price (in millions)
		– AFRICA –	
Tunisia	1986	70 5-ton trucks and 3 5-ton wreckers/c,g	NA[2]

IV. FMS PROGRAM CONTRACT AWARDS, FY 1983–1986
(millions of dollars)

Item	Fiscal Year	Award Total
A-7 Corsair attack aircraft	1983	$38.86
	1984	58.80
	1985	5.24
	1986	.47
5 ton M39 cargo trucks	1983	31.37*
	1984	4.63
	1985	36.25
	1986	22.65
1/4 ton M151 utility trucks	1983	5.06*
	1984	16.10
	1985	.05
Multiple Launch Rocket System (MLRS)	1983	3.67
	1984	3.61
	1985	-.84
	1986	.03
MGM-52 Lance battlefield support missiles	1983	2.35#
	1984	3.57
	1985	2.84
	1986	3.04
5 ton M939 trucks	1984	4.51
	1985	.11
	1986	.69
Ground servicing equipment for FA-18 aircraft	1986	.10
Unidentified trucks and truck tractors	1983	3.70*
	1986	3.81

Item	Fiscal Year	Award Total
Unidentified miscellaneous communication equipment	1984	2.86
Technical representative services	1986	-.17

Negative figures result from downward contract adjustments

    *   Because LTV acquired AM General and Sierra Research Center in September 1983, the 1983 awards for these divisions are not entirely attributable to LTV.

    #   These awards include work performed in West Germany.

NOTES

1. This is a $202 million package that includes 1,389 trailers, and 129 ambulances plus spare parts and support. Some portion of the 2,263 trucks will be 1 1/4 ton trucks, which may not be manufactured by LTV.

2. This is part of a $60 million package including 57 U.S. government manufactured M198 howitzers and ammunition.

MCDONNELL DOUGLAS CORP.

I. SUMMARY DATA

Data, except for the total sales figures, are for U.S. government fiscal years, ending Sept. 30. FMS program award totals for 1982 to 1984 were calculated by the General Accounting Office; the 1985 and 1986 totals were calculated by IRRC from Department of Defense contract data.

	1982	1983	1984	1985	1986
Total sales (millions)	$7,331	$8,111	$9,663*	$11,478*	$12,661*
DoD contract awards (millions)	$5,630	$6,143	$7,684*	$8,857*	$6,586*
DoD contractor rank	2	2	1	1	3
DoD awards/total sales	.77	.76	.80	.77	.52
FMS contract awards (millions)	$1,032	$500	$993*	$1,616*	$574*
FMS contractor rank	1	2	1	1	3
FMS/total DoD awards	.18	.08	.13	.18	.09
FMS/total sales	.141	.062	.103	.141	.045

*   These figures include sales by and awards to McDonnell Douglas Helicopter. McDonnell Douglas Helicopter's arms export business is covered in detail in a separate profile.

II. ARMS EXPORT BUSINESS AT A GLANCE

McDonnell Douglas has been the first or second largest American arms exporter for 11 of the last 15 years, and in five of those years—1972, 1981, 1982, 1984 and 1985—its FMS-related prime contract awards exceeded $800 million. Foreign military sales accounted for nearly one-fifth of MDC's defense business in 1982 and 1985. The company's preeminence among exporters of military goods is due, in part, to the fact that historically it has been one of the largest American military contractors. MDC strengthened its position as a national leader when it acquired the Hughes Helicopters Co. (and renamed it McDonnell Douglas Helicopter) in 1984. (McDonnell Douglas Helicopter's foreign military sales are discussed in a separate profile.)

McDonnell Douglas produces major weapon systems rather than components for larger systems or otherwise less expensive equipment, and nearly all of its sales go through the Foreign Military Sales program instead of commercial channels. The bulk of McDonnell Douglas's exports go to the closest allies of the United States because they are more readily cleared to accept the sophisticated technologies used in many of MDC's modern military wares and more often possess the technological base and experience needed to absorb the equipment. Sizable markets exist in the Third World, however, for many of the company's older weapons, such as its F-4 Phantom fighter and A-4 Skyhawk attack aircraft. The Harpoon anti-ship missile, although a weapon of comparatively recent vintage, also has begun to be exported to numerous Third World nations.

McDonnell Douglas's major export items are the F/A-18 Hornet and F-15 Eagle fighters, the Harpoon anti-ship missile and, to a lesser extent, the AV-8 Harrier vertical or short take-off and landing (V/STOL) jet. MDC has entered into agreements to export a total of 297 F/A-18s, of which 138 are destined for Canada, 84 for Spain and 75 for Australia. In 1985, more FMS contract awards were issued for the F-18 than any other weapon system. FMS-related DoD prime contract awards received by the company for F/A-18 production—which accounted for 32 percent of MDC's overall FMS awards in 1983 and 43 percent in 1984—ballooned to 81 percent of its total FMS awards in 1985. McDonnell Douglas is aggressively pursuing further F/A-18 sales to Japan, South Korea and Switzerland.

Japan is considering a variation of the F/A-18 as well as the F-15 for its Support Fighter Experimental (FSX) program through which it will procure between 100 and 170 planes. Japanese officials, however, prefer building their own fighter from the ground up in order to develop further Japan's indigenous defense industry. This predisposition has provoked much protest from U.S. congressmen and defense industry officials who are already concerned with the imbalance in the U.S.-Japan trade relationship. They contend that either purchasing an American aircraft off-the-shelf or opting for licensed production would be considerably cheaper propositions, and that Japan's insistence on developing its own aircraft would constitute another example of unfair Japanese trade practices. Japan, on the other hand, denies that building its own aircraft would be a protectionist act and maintains that there would not be a significant price difference between the aircraft. In an effort to assuage American concerns, however, the Japanese have proposed American collaboration during a research and development phase of the FSX, at the end of which Japan will accept proposals for both the purchase of American aircraft and domestic development of the planes. Some American industry and defense officials, however, view this plan as inevitably leading toward domestic development of the aircraft, and fear that the Japanese might use it to scavenge American technology.

South Korea is also considering licensed production of the F/A-18, but might opt for additional purchases of General Dynamics F-16s (Seoul purchased 36 of the fighters in 1982). McDonnell Douglas's has offered a co-production package with extensive South Korean industrial involvement, and has opened an office in Seoul to assist its efforts to sell the F/A-18 to the South Koreans as well as to support its other sales there. One potential problem is that South Korea wants to purchase the planes through direct, commercial sales channels, while the U.S. government prefers to go through the FMS program with the Defense Department acting as an intermediary. U.S. officials state that unless South Korea operates through the Pentagon, it might not gain access to all the necessary technology and might experience problems procuring items from the thousands of subcontractors.

Switzerland might also make a large F/A-18 purchase. The Swiss are planning to buy 80 planes, in two lots of 40 aircraft each, and have narrowed the competition to the F/A-18, the General Dynamics F-16 and the French Dassault-Breguet Mirage 2000. Switzerland will choose between the F/A-18 and the F-16, and hold a flyoff between the chosen American plane and the Mirage 2000, indicating a preference on the part of the Swiss that a European aircraft participate in the final round of competition. Switzerland also has indicated that any purchase must involve 100 percent direct and indirect offsets. The U.S. Department of Commerce, however, in light of the $3 billion American trade deficit with Switzerland, opposes any offset arrangements except some "direct offsets . . . made under extraordinary circumstances on a case-by-case basis with the agreement of both signatories." The U.S. Department of Defense has temporarily postponed any decision in the matter.

McDonnell Douglas also has received several large F-15 export orders: Saudi Arabia ordered 60 in 1978 (at a cost of $2.5 billion) and Israel has ordered 55. Japan is building 141 F-15s under license and has purchased 14 outright. According to *Aviation Week and Space Technology*, a variation of the F-15 also has emerged as the leading contender for the Japanese FSX project. Japanese officials reportedly regard the F-15 as superior to the F/A-18 and the F-16, and the F-15's cause was given an added boost by the recent devaluation of the American dollar relative to the Yen, which made the aircraft more affordable. In 1985, Congress blocked the sale of 48 F-15s to Saudi Arabia, which then opted for British-made Toronado fighters. MDC estimates the total contract for these additional Saudi fighters would have exceeded $3 billion. In 1987, the administration floated the idea of selling 12 to 15 more F-15s to Saudi Arabia as replacement aircraft to compensate for those that have been or might in the near future be lost because of accidents.

Harpoon anti-ship missiles have also proved popular with foreign militaries: More than 20 nations have ordered them. According to the Pentagon's Defense Security Assistance Agency, 1,869 Harpoons had been ordered by overseas customers through the FMS program as of September 1986. In 1985 and 1986, more FMS awards were issued to contractors in support of Harpoon exports than for any other missile.

McDonnell Douglas co-produces the AV-8 Harrier V/STOL with British Aerospace. Spain possesses 11 of the "jump jets" and has ordered 12 more. In addition, MDC is manufacturing shipsets for 62 of the aircraft that will be assembled in Great Britain and used by the Royal Air Force. Some sources suggest that the total number of AV-8s ordered by Britain could eventually increase to 102. The future of the AV-8 Harrier was jeopardized in 1987 when the U.S. House of Representatives voted to cut off all funds for the Marine Corps's planned $5 billion purchase of 248 Harriers. The British government responded by saying that it might not have enough funds on hand to purchase two Boeing Awacs aircraft that it has an option on unless the Pentagon continues to help subsidize production costs of the Harrier by purchasing more of the jump jets.

McDonnell Douglas also receives foreign military sales awards for its F-4 Phantom II and A-4 Skyhawk fighters, both 1960s vintage aircraft still in service in the United States and abroad. Records compiled by the Department of Defense's Security Assistance Agency indicate that 1,191 F-4s and 789 A-4s had been exported through the FMS program and 22 F-4s had been transferred via the MAP program, as of September 1986. Countries that use F-4s include West Germany, Greece, Israel, Japan, Saudi Arabia, South Korea, Spain, Turkey and Great Britain. A-4s are still in service with the armed forces of Argentina, Australia, Indonesia, Israel, Kuwait, Malaysia, New Zealand and Singapore. MDC held preliminary discussions with the government of Argentina during early 1986 regarding the possibility of establishing an A-4 production line there. MDC and Argentine officials are reported to have talked about joint production of the A-4, of spare parts for the aircraft and of the McDonnell Douglas model 500 helicopter.

As the company notes in a recent annual report, "Opportunities for overseas sales of combat aircraft are limited at present." MDC, however, should register high foreign military sales awards over the long haul because of its current backlog of fighter aircraft and missile orders. The company states in its 1985 annual report that "The F/A-18, the AV-8B and the Apache helicopter are all likely to be strong competitors when allies turn to the U.S. government for combat aircraft in the years ahead." If the Pentagon opts for full scale production of the McDonnell Douglas C-17 transport aircraft, it might become a popular export item because the aircraft's design makes it particularly well suited for use on short and undeveloped runways. McDonnell Douglas also has developed a mobile, land-based version of its Harpoon missile in order to capture a part of the large international market for coastal defense weapons, which has long been dominated by European suppliers.

MDC's annual report also states its interest in international collaboration—as is the case with the AV-8B Harrier and the T45TS undergraduate pilot training system—in order to boost sales. MDC currently is embarked on an evaluation and coproduction venture with Switzerland that is designed to improve the Dragon anti-tank system for export.

III. MILITARY ORDERS, 1982–1986 (includes first quarter of 1987)

Country	Date of Agreement	Description of Order	Price (in millions)
– EUROPE AND MAJOR ALLIES –			
Australia	1982	(30) AGM-84A Harpoon air-to-surface missiles/d	NA
	1984	Spares for F/A-18 aircraft/f[1]	NA[2]
	1984	35 F/A-18 fighter aircraft/g	$754
	1986	28 Harpoon anti-ship missiles plus 6 missile bodies without warheads, 2 training missiles and spares/ c,d,f,g	$47
	1987	15 weapon systems for F/A-18A aircraft and 2 weapon systems for TF/A-18A aircraft/g	$63.9
Canada	1984	34 RGM-84D-4 Harpoon ship-to-surface missiles with 2 training missiles/c,d,e,g	$47
	1986	Harpoon anti-ship missiles/f	NA[3]
Denmark	1983	33 RGM-84A Harpoon ship-to-surface missiles/c,d,g	$37
Great Britain	1982	20 AGM-84A Harpoon air-to-surface missiles/c	$18.7
	1983	15 F-4J fighter aircraft for conversion to F-4S/d,g	$51
	1983	60 AGM-84A Harpoon air-to-surface missiles/c	$67.8
	1983	Support for F-4S fighter aircraft/c,g	$58.6
	1984	300 RGM-84A Harpoon ship-to-surface missiles/d,f	NA[4]

Country	Date of Agreement	Description of Order	Price (in millions)
	1985	31 UGM-84D Harpoon submarine-to-surface missiles with spares and engineering support/e,f,g	$33
	1986	Harpoon anti-ship missiles/f	NA[3]
Greece	1982	32 RGM-84A-3 Harpoon ship-to-surface missiles/e,g	$32
	1986	32 Harpoon anti-ship missiles with containers and spares/c,d,f,g	$43
Japan	1982	3 Harpoon missiles and training equipment/g	NA[5]
	1982	6 AGM-84A Harpoon air-to-surface missiles/c	$6.6
	1983	24 AGM-84A Harpoon air-to-surface missiles with spare parts/c,g	$25
	1984	14 F-15J fighter aircraft with a license agreement to produce an additional 86 F-16Js in Japan/r	NA
	1985	License granted for the production of an additional 55 F-15J fighter aircraft/g,r[6]	NA
	1986	38 Harpoon missiles with containers, spares and support/c,d,g	$47
Netherlands	1986	8 Harpoon missile systems including 25 Harpoon anti-ship missiles with containers, 1 exercise section, and spares/c,d,f,g	$37
Portugal	1986	3 Harpoon anti-ship missile systems with 24 Harpoon missiles/c,d,g	NA[7]
Spain	1982	15 AGM-84A Harpoon air-to-surface missiles/d,g	$18
	1982	12 AV-8 Harrier V/STOL fighter aircraft with spares and support/c,d,f,g	$379
	(1983)	Computer software and cockpits for AV-8 Harrier fighter aircraft simulators/f,i	$5.1
	1987	20 Harpoon anti-ship missiles with 2 ATM-84 Harpoon ballistic air test vehicles, plus containers, spares, support and training/d,g	$26

Country	Date of Agreement	Description of Order	Price (in millions)
	1987	17 EF-18A and 4 EF-18B weapon systems/g	$90.6
	1983	(24) RGM-84A Harpoon ship-to-surface missiles/d	NA
	1983	12 Harpoon shipboard equipment sets and spares/g	$29
	1983	84 F/A-18 fighter aircraft and 3 maintenance trainer aircraft/c,d,g,h	$2,700[8]
	1985	25 RGM-84 Harpoon ship-to-surface missiles/f,g,h	$27
	1985	50 RGM-84 Harpoon ship-to-surface missiles/e	$47
	1985	Spares for 33 F/A-18 aircraft/c	$82
Turkey	1983	(48) RGM-84 Harpoon ship-to-surface missiles/c,d	NA
	1986	Harpoon anti-ship missiles/f	NA[3]
West Germany	1986	(4) RGM-84A Harpoon anti-ship missile systems with (48) missiles/d	NA
		– ASIA & PACIFIC –	
Indonesia	1987	8 Harpoon missiles/g	$6.5
Pakistan	1984	2 RGM-84 Harpoon ship-to-surface missile systems with 16 missiles/d,e	$28.4
	1985	Harpoon anti-ship missiles/c	NA
	1986	Harpoon anti-ship missiles/f	NA[3]
Singapore	1984	Classified equipment/c	NA
	1985	16 to 20 RGM-84A Harpoon ship-to-surface missiles/j,r	NA
	1985	31 AGM-84A Harpoon anti-ship missiles for aircraft/d	NA
	(1986)	6 RGM-84A Harpoon anti-ship missile systems with (72) missiles for 6 corvettes/d	NA
South Korea	1982	6 F-4D Phantom fighter aircraft/ c,d,f,g	$16.8

Country	Date of Agreement	Description of Order	Price (in millions)
	1984	3 RGM-84A Harpoon ship-to-surface missile systems with (64) missiles/d	NA
	1985	4 F-4E modified fighter aircraft/e,f,g	$22
	1986	Harpoon anti-ship missiles/f	$20
Thailand	1983	2 RGM-84A Harpoon ship-to-surface missile systems with 24 missiles/c,d	$11.5
	1986	Harpoon anti-ship missiles/f	NA[3]
– MIDDLE EAST –			
Bahrain	1984	2 Harpoon anti-ship missile systems with (24) missiles/d	NA
Egypt	1982	F-4 Phantom fighter aircraft/c[9]	$7
	1983	16 RGM-84D Harpoon surface-to-ship missiles/d,g	$40
Israel	1986	Additional funding for logistics support for Harpoon anti-ship missiles/b	NA
Kuwait	1987	Establishment of a flight training center/f	$9.9
Saudi Arabia	1983	Contractor technical services for F-15 fighter aircraft/g	$1,500
	1983	Conformal fuel tanks for F-16 fighter aircraft/g	$3.8
	1984	111 Rudder servo actuators for F-15 fighter aircraft/f,g	$3.0
	1984	Support for F-15 fighter aircraft/f	$167
	1984	1 KC-10A tanker aircraft/d	NA
	1986	100 aircraft fuel tanks/f	$30.9
	1986	100 Harpoon anti-ship missiles/c,d,g	NA[10]
	1986	Contractor technical services for F-15 aircraft/g	$500
– LATIN AMERICA –			
El Salvador	1984	1 converted DC-3 transport aircraft/g[11]	$1.5

IV. FMS PROGRAM CONTRACT AWARDS, FY 1983–1986
(millions of dollars)

Item	Fiscal Year	Award Total
F/A-18 Hornet fighter aircraft	1983	$ 161.79
	1984	429.24
	1985	1,307.00
	1986	364.03
F-15 Eagle fighter aircraft	1983	170.93
	1984	317.12
	1985	114.60
	1986	50.67
AGM-84 Harpoon anti-ship missiles	1983	145.09
	1984	149.07
	1985	132.36
	1986	96.08
AV-8 Harrier vertical or short take-off and landing (V/STOL) aircraft	1984	30.24
	1985	35.09
	1986	74.11
F-4 Phantom fighter aircraft	1983	1.07*
	1984	3.80
	1985	1.39
	1986	−23.22
Miscellaneous accessories and electronic countermeasure equipment for F-16 aircraft	1983	8.05
	1984	.60
	1985	.05
	1986	4.51
Fire control systems for P-3 Orion aircraft	1983	2.87
	1984	.12
	1985	−.03
	1986	−.07
Technical representative services for C-3 transport aircraft	1983	2.60#
	1984	.20
Hush House engine noise muffling facility	1985	1.20
	1986	−.52
Launchers for AIM-9 Sidewinder missile	1983	1.01
	1984	.49

Item	Fiscal Year	Award Total
Launchers for AIM-7 Sparrow missile	1983	.90
	1986	−.24
A-4 Skyhawk attack aircraft	1983	−3.57
	1984	.74
	1985	−3.61
Unidentified miscellaneous aircraft accessories	1984	6.74
	1985	17.82
Unidentified guided missile launchers and remote control equipment	1983	8.30
	1984	.19
Unidentified gunnery fire control equipment	1985	6.76
Unidentified technical services	1983	.27
	1984	2.13
	1985	2.29
Unidentified electronic countermeasure equipment	1985	1.00
Unidentified maintenance and repair services	1984	.16
	1985	.85
Technical representative services for unidentified aircraft and airframe structural components	1986 +	1.19
Unidentified fire control systems	1986	.74
Components for unidentified guided missiles	1986	.62
Other unidentified awards	1986	2.44

Negative figures result from downward contract adjustments.

* These awards include funds for work performed in Turkey.
\# These awards include funds for work performed in Kuwait.
+ This award is for work performed in Kuwait.

NOTES

1. Australia ordered a total of 75 F/A-18 fighter aircraft in 1981 at a reported price of $2.4 billion.

2. This is part of a $4.75 million package that includes Hughes AN/APG-65 radar systems.

3. This is part of a contract worth $285 million for 435 Harpoon anti-ship missiles and 24 inert training missiles to be divided among the U.S. Navy, Great Britain, Pakistan, Japan, Canada, Australia, the Netherlands, Thailand and Turkey.

4. The reported price of this agreement is 130 million British pounds.

5. This is part of a $50 million package that includes 3 General Dynamics Phalanx Close-In weapon systems.

6. Japan will produce a total of 141 F-15Js in addition to the 14 it initially purchased from McDonnell Douglas.

7. This is part of a $216 million package deal including 6 General Electric LM2500 engines, 3 Raytheon Seasparrow missile systems, 6 U.S. government manufactured Mk 32 torpedo tubes, and 3 Aerojet General AN/SLQ-25 torpedo countermeasure sets.

8. Some sources list the total price of this agreement at $3 billion, and state that the Spanish government has agreed to buy 72 F/A-18s and has an option for the purchase of an additional 12.

9. SIPRI reports that Egypt ordered 35 F-4s during the early 1980s.

10. This is part of a $265 million package that includes 995 Raytheon and Ford AIM-9L Sidewinder missiles and 671 Ford AIM-9P4 Sidewinder missiles. Because of intense congressional opposition, the Reagan administration deleted 200 Stinger missile launchers with 600 missiles from this package.

11. This aircraft might have come out of U.S. government surplus stock.

MCDONNELL DOUGLAS HELICOPTER CO.

(a subsidiary of McDonnell Douglas Corp.)

I. SUMMARY DATA

Data, except for the total sales figures, are for U.S. government fiscal years, ending Sept. 30. FMS program award totals for 1982 to 1986 were calculated by IRRC from Department of Defense contract data.

	1982	1983	1984	1985	1986
Total sales (millions)	NA	$575	NA	NA	NA
DoD contract awards (millions)	$ 310	$615	$1,005	$1,082	$ 231
DoD contractor rank	42	34	n/a	n/a	n/a
DoD awards/total sales	NA	1.07	NA	NA	NA
FMS contract awards (millions)	$ .04	$ .84	$6.34	$ 3.78	$3.39
FMS contractor rank	n/a	n/a	n/a	n/a	n/a
FMS/total DoD awards	.0001	.001	.006	.003	.001
FMS/total sales	NA	.001	NA	NA	NA

II. ARMS EXPORT BUSINESS AT A GLANCE

In January 1984, McDonnell Douglas purchased Hughes Helicopters from Summa Corp.—a holding company that has been administered by the Hughes estate since the death of industrialist Howard Hughes in 1976—and renamed it McDonnell Douglas Helicopter. The purchase price of $470 million included approximately $280 million for the company's assets and $190 million to cover its debts. The company's FMS contract awards historically have been small, but they do not give a true measure of McDonnell Douglas Helicopter's military export business because many of its products are sold abroad through direct, company-to-government commercial sales.

McDonnell Douglas Helicopter produces commercial and military helicopters and guns, including the Bushmaster 25mm automatic cannon, which is used on the Bradley infantry fighting vehicle. In early 1987, 200 Bushmasters were purchased by Spain, marking the first foreign export of this weapon system. The bulk of McDonnell Douglas Helicopter's current business comes from sales of its AH-64 Apache attack helicopter. The U.S. government has already appropriated more than $3 billion for the Apache, and the company says it should become available for export in the future. The company also hopes to win major contract awards for work on the LHX, a family of new light helicopters that will eventually replace much of the Army's aging fleet. This helicopter, too, may eventually become available for export.

McDonnell Helicopter currently exports the military versions of its model 500 and 530 light helicopters to a variety of nations and maintains licensing agreements with Argentina, Italy, Japan and South Korea. Italy recently selected the MD500E as its future helicopter trainer, and may order as many as 50 of the aircraft from an Italian company, Breda Nardi Costruzioni Aeronautiche, which builds the helicopters under license from McDonnell Douglas. Records compiled by the Pentagon's Defense Security Assistance Agency indicate that 23 of the company's OH-6 Cayuse scout helicopters—which are derived from the Model 500 helicopter—had been exported under the Military Assistance Program by September 1986. Another popular MDC Helicopter export is the model 300C utility helicopter. This helicopter, which is built under license by Schweizer Aircraft Co., is generally sold through commercial sales channels and is used to fulfill both military and civilian roles. McDonnell Douglas received $2.59 million in FMS awards in 1986 for the model 300C helicopter, and Schweizer Aircraft received $5.54 million.

The exportation of military helicopters should continue to be a significant part of the company's business. In June 1986, Defense Security Assistance Agency director Lt. Gen. Philip C. Gast told the Helicopter Society of America that military helicopter exports were expected to grow through the mid-1990s. *Aviation Week & Space Technology* has quoted an official of the Sikorsky subsidiary of United Technologies Corp. as saying that the People's Republic of China is in need of new trainer/attack helicopters. The trade journal identified the McDonnell Douglas model 500 series as one of three well-placed candidates and indicated that demand for a new light helicopter could reach 4,000 to 5,000 aircraft.

III. MILITARY ORDERS, 1982–1986 (includes first quarter of 1987)

Country	Date of Agreement	Description of Order	Price (in millions)
\- EUROPE AND MAJOR ALLIES -			
Finland	1982	2 model 500D utility helicopters/d	NA
Spain	1987	200 25mm Bushmaster automatic cannons/n	$9
Sweden	1982	10 model 300C utility helicopters/d,g	NA
	1985	16 model 300C training helicopters/d	NA[1]
Switzerland	(1985)	30 model 300C utility helicopter/d	NA
Turkey	(1982)	10 model 300C utility helicopters/d	NA
\- ASIA AND PACIFIC -			
Indonesia	1982	9 model 300C utility helicopters/d,g	$2
South Korea	1983	26 model 500MD Defender TOW missile armed scout helicopters/c,e	$12.5
Thailand	(1986)	(24) model 300C utility helicopters/d	NA
\- MIDDLE EAST -			
Iraq[2]	1983	30 model 500D utility helicopters and 30 model 300C utility helicopters/h	$25

Country	Date of Agreement	Description of Order	Price (in millions)
	1985	24 model 530F helicopters/g,h	NA
Israel	1983	6 model 500MD Defender scout helicopters/c	$5.4
– AFRICA –			
Kenya	1985	8 model 500MD Defender scout helicopters/e	NA
– LATIN AMERICA –			
Colombia	(1983)	8 model 300C utility helicopters/d	NA
	1986	6 500MG Defender scout helicopters and 2 500E trainer helicopters/d,e,g	$9.46
Costa Rica	1985	4 model 500E utility helicopters/e,g	NA
El Salvador	1985	4 model 500MD Defender scout helicopters/e,g	NA
	1985	10 model 500E utility helicopters/g	NA
	(1986)	(6) model 300C utility helicopters/d	NA

IV. FMS PROGRAM CONTRACT AWARDS, FY 1983–1986
(millions of dollars)

Item	Fiscal Year	Award Total
OH-6 Cayuse scout helicopter*	1984	$5.84
	1985	3.18
	1986	−.15
Model 300C helicopters	1986	2.59
Miscellaneous accessories for OH-58 Kiowas scout helicopter#	1985	1.06
Unidentified airframe structural components	1986	.75
Unidentified awards +	1983	.84
	1984	.50
	1985	.60
	1986	.20

*   The OH-6 Cayuse is a variant of the Model 500 series helicopter.

\#   Bell Helicopter Textron manufactures the OH-58, which is based on its
          model 206 helicopter.

\+   These awards are for work performed in Kenya.

The negative figure results from downward contract adjustments.

NOTES

1. The total cost of this transaction is 20 million Swedish krone.

2. All of the MDC/Hughes helicopters sold to Iraq are civilian versions and, therefore, fall under the Export Administration Act and require approval of the Commerce Deparment, but not of the Departments of State and Defense or Congress. The Commerce Department requires a special license for the export of all MDC/Hughes model 500 and 530 series helicopters to prevent exports to illegal recipients. The $25 million price tag of the 1983 sale includes training, ground equipment and spare parts.

NORTHROP CORP.

I. SUMMARY DATA

Data, except for the total sales figures, are for U.S. government fiscal years, ending Sept. 30. FMS program award totals for 1982 to 1984 were calculated by the General Accounting Office; the 1985 and 1986 totals were calculated by IRRC from Department of Defense contract data.

	1982	1983	1984	1985	1986
Total sales (millions)	$2,473	$3,261	$3,688	$5,057	$5,608
DoD contract awards (millions)	$1,598	$ 847	$ 882	$1,195	$ 742
DoD contractor rank	12	26	26	25	31
DoD awards/total sales	.65	.26	.24	.24	.13
FMS contract awards (millions)	$ 894	$ 181	$ 162	$ 296	$ 104
FMS contractor rank	2	9	13	5	12
FMS/total DoD awards	.56	.21	.18	.25	.14
FMS/total sales	.362	.056	.044	.059	.018

II. ARMS EXPORT BUSINESS AT A GLANCE

Northrop is one of the nation's largest arms exporters. Unlike McDonnell Douglas or General Dynamics, however, the high level of Northrop's foreign military sales is not attributable to economies of scale. Perhaps more than any other contractor, Northrop has consciously cultivated overseas markets, and it is the only contractor that on its own has developed weapons designed exclusively for sale abroad—like the F-5 and F-20 fighters. Although the level of its arms exports has declined, as recently as 1980 Northrop registered a ratio of foreign military sales to total defense awards of .70. The company's annual average FMS/total DoD awards ratio between 1978 and 1985 was .40. The company states that as of December 1986, overseas customers accounted for 16 percent of its backlog.

Northrop was among the General Accounting Office's top 10 FMS exporters from 1977 through 1983 and during four of those years was ranked among the nation's three largest. The GAO and the Department of Defense listed the company as the nation's largest FMS exporter in fiscal 1977 and 1976, when it received $1.29 billion in FMS-related prime contract awards. The company registered FMS awards of $296 million in 1985, down from $895 million in 1982, a peak year.

Between 1982 and 1985, Saudi Arabia received between 50 and 70 percent of the company's FMS program sales, according to the company's annual report. In calendar year 1986, however, Saudi Arabia accounted for less than 30 percent of Northrop's foreign military sales, because of a sharp drop in the amount of military-related services the company provided to the Saudis. Military-related services had previously accounted for at least 70 percent of sales to the Saudi government, and aircraft equipment sales accounted for most of the remainder.

Although most of Northrop's military exports go through FMS channels, the company's commercial exports of military equipment are also substantial: Between 1977 and 1979, Northrop was ranked among the top 10 U.S. firms in this category as well. According to the company's annual report, direct foreign sales (the majority of which are military-related) in calendar year 1986 totaled $215.4 million. This was a sharp drop from calendar year 1985 when direct foreign sales reached $463.2 million. Between 1982 and 1984, direct foreign sales hovered between $370 and $380 million per year. Unlike Northrop's FMS program sales, less than 20 percent of Northrop's direct foreign sales are to the Middle East.

Northrop's leading export item until recently was the F-5 fighter aircraft, which the company says "is the most widely used U.S.-built supersonic fighter in the world," and which is highly regarded because of its relative simplicity and durability. Northrop received at least $646 million in FMS prime contract awards during fiscal years 1983 through 1986 for F-5s, related services and hardware. Northrop says in its 1985 annual report that "sales for the 60 F-5s delivered in 1985, and various spare parts and other items, totaled $393 million, compared to 57 deliveries and $369 million in 1984." Only 15 F-5s were delivered in 1986, while 10 were ordered that year. Since 1964, the company has delivered more than 2,600 F-5s to more than 30 nations, and 20 nations currently fly the most advanced F-5s: the F-5E and F-5F fighters. Production of F-5s ceased in late 1987.

The administration's 1987 decision to sell 10 F-5E and 2 F-5F aircraft taken from U.S. government stock to Honduras has provoked considerable protest. Despite concerted efforts, however, congressional critics were unable to gather enough votes to block the sale. Critics viewed the sale as unnecessary since Honduras already holds a significant air power advantage over other countries in the region. They contended that such a sale would be viewed as provocative by other countries in the region, particularly El Salvador, which fought a brief war with Honduras in 1969, and Nicaragua, which has had poor relations with Honduras for the past several years. Critics fear that this sale could lead Nicaragua to import Soviet Mig-21 fighter aircraft—an event the United States has said it will not permit. The administration, however, maintains that the Hondurans' French Super Mystere fighters needed to be replaced and that Honduras must maintain its air superiority in order to counter the superior size of Nicaragua's armed forces.

Northrop's F-5 sales were also the subject of controversy in the mid-1970s. The Senate Subcommittee on Multinational Corporations uncovered payments of $450,000 by Northrop to two Saudi generals to encourage the purchase of F-5s by Saudi Arabia. Northrop also was embroiled in a mini-scandal in connection with payments of $2 million to sales representatives in Iran for their work in support of the sale of F-5s to Iran. The Iranian government protested that this had raised the purchase price by $2 million. Northrop then refunded $2 million to Iran, but denied any wrongdoing in the payment of the commissions.

In addition to the F-5, Northrop has exported the T-38 Talon trainer aircraft—88 of which had been transferred through the FMS Program and Military Assistance Program as of September 1986— and continues to export the Chukar target drone aircraft and the AN/ALQ-135 electronic radar jamming device for F-15 aircraft. Northrop delivered 88 Chukars to foreign customers in 1985 and 94 in 1984. A reconnaissance version of the Chukar has been developed and is being marketed actively overseas. In a joint venture with a Greek company, Northrop is developing an update to the Chukar, the Telamon, with the intention of marketing it worldwide. The government of Switzerland is underwriting the cost of development and pre-production of another new Northrop system, the AN/ALQ-171 electronic counter-measure (ECM) system. The company believes that "the overseas market potential [for the AN/ALQ-171] could exceed $500 million."

Perhaps Northrop's most succesful electronic countermeasure system has been the AN/ALQ-162 reprogrammable radar jammer. This system will be installed on a larger variety of aircraft than any other ECM system being produced, including the Canadian and Spanish McDonnell Douglas F/A-18s, and the Danish General Dynamics F-16 and J-35 aircraft. Northrop is also working with a British firm on a new ECM system for the Royal Air Force's fleet of Harrier attack aircraft.

Northrop receives foreign military sales income for sub-system work that it does on exported weapon systems such as the E-3A Awacs, the F/A-18 fighter, Hawk surface-to-air missiles, and Poseidon and Trident II submarine-launched ballistic missiles. Much of this work is sizable. The company, for example, builds the center and aft fuselage sections and vertical stabilizers for the McDonnell Douglas F/A-18, 258 of which have been ordered by Australia, Canada and Spain.

Repair, maintenance and support services also contribute to Northrop's foreign military sales. The company recently phased out a project that began in 1972—initially called the Royal Saudi Air Force Peace Hawk but later changed to the F-5 Advanced Technical Training Support Program— for support and maintenance of F-5 aircraft. In fiscal year 1983, $56 million of the $167 million in identifiable F-5 FMS prime contract awards was allocated for the Saudi program. Tunisia and Bahrain recently signed agreements for similar services.

One major failure for Northrop has been its inability to sell the F-20 Tigershark fighter, which was created as part of the Carter administration's fighter export (FX) program. (See box, p. 51.) Northrop's inability to match its record 1970s FMS levels in recent years can be attributed in part to the lack of F-20 sales, since Northrop had hoped to gain export earnings by selling the new fighter as a replacement for aging F-5s. Although a few countries such as Jordan expressed interest in the aircraft, Northrop was unable to obtain enough orders to open a production line, and the company's subsequent effort to sell the aircraft to the U.S. Air Force failed. In November 1986, Northrop announced that it was stopping work on the plane, which it had developed with its own money.

It is unclear what the future of Northrop's arms export business will be. Northrop is developing Tacit Rainbow, a tactical antiradiation missile system which the company says is "intended for use by all three armed services and foreign nations." The U.S. Air Force is expected to begin procuring the missile in quantity in 1988. However, much of the company's work is on the Advanced Technology (Stealth) Bomber, which will not in all likelihood be exported. Another major Northrop project, the Advanced Technology Fighter, also is not likely to be exported in the foreseeable future. Nevertheless, the company's continued work on sub-systems should be a steady source of export earnings.

III. MILITARY ORDERS, 1982–1986 (includes first quarter of 1987)

Country	Date of Agreement	Description of Order	Price (in millions)
– EUROPE AND MAJOR ALLIES –			
Great Britain	1983	15 Chukar II target drones/c	$2.4
	(1984)	Checking equipment for Trident II (D-5) submarine-launched ballistic missiles/f	$96
Portugal	(1983)	(20) F-5E Tiger II fighter aircraft/d	NA
Spain	1986	Electro-optical tracking equipment for Hawk surface-to-air missile systems/f	NA[1]
Turkey	(1985)	(6) F-5B fighter aircraft/d	NA[2]
– ASIA AND PACIFIC –			
India	1986	5 Chukar III target drones and related equipment/g	$6.6
Malaysia	1985	14 F-5E and 2 F-5F Tiger II fighter aircraft/d[3]	$260
Singapore	1984	6 F-5 Tiger II fighter aircraft/r	NA
South Korea	1985	Spares for F-5 Tiger II aircraft/f	NA[4]
Taiwan	1982	30 F-5E and 30 F-5F Tiger II fighter aircraft/f,g	$622
Thailand	1984	2 RF-5E Tiger Eye reconnaissance aircraft and 8 F-5E Tiger II fighter aircraft/d,e	NA
	1987	Upgrade of Thai F-5 aircraft including installation of a weapons aiming computer/h	$42
– MIDDLE EAST –			
Bahrain	1985	4 F-5E and 2 F-5F Tiger II fighter aircraft/c,e,f,g	NA[5]
	1985	6 F-5E/F aircraft/c,d	NA[6]
Egypt	1984	Hawk air defense missile system upgrade/c,f	NA[7]
	1986	Electro-optical tracking equipment for Hawk surface-to-air missile systems/f	NA[1]

Country	Date of Agreement	Description of Order	Price (in millions)
Jordan	1984	Hawk air defense missile system upgrade/c,f	NA[8]
	1986	Electro-optical tracking equipment for Hawk surface-to-air missile systems/f	NA[1]
Kuwait	1984	Hawk air defense missile system upgrade/c	NA[9]
	1986	Electro-optical tracking equipment for Hawk surface-to-air missile systems/f	NA[1]
Saudi Arabia	1982	4 F-5F Tiger II trainer aircraft, 1 F-5F trainer aircraft, and 10 RF-5E Tiger Eye reconnaissance aircraft/d,e,g	$350
	1984	Support follow-on for F-5 aircraft and F-15 aircraft bases/c,g[10]	$330
	1987	95 AN/ALQ-171 electronic counter-measure systems to upgrade Saudi F-5 and F-15 aircraft/f	$325
		– AFRICA –	
Sudan	1984	2 F-5E Tiger II fighter aircraft/d	NA
Tunisia	1982	8 F-5E and 4 F-5F Tiger II fighter aircraft/d,e,g	$200
		– LATIN AMERICA –	
Honduras	1987	10 F-5E fighter aircraft and 2 F-5F trainer aircraft/n	$72

IV. FMS PROGRAM CONTRACT AWARDS FY 1983–1986
(millions of dollars)

Item	Fiscal Year	Award Total
F-5 fighter and reconnaissance aircraft	1983	$167.19*
	1984	123.26#
	1985	287.96
	1986	67.07+
Tracking system for MIM-23 Hawk surface-to-air missiles	1983	–.77
	1984	35.15
	1986	21.91

Item	Fiscal Year	Award Total
Unidentified airborne radio navigation equipment for Boeing E-3A Awacs	1985	3.42
	1986	.30
Electronic countermeasures and communications equipment for A/EA-3 Skywarrior aircraft	1985	2.19
	1986	12.30
AN/ALQ-135 electronic countermeasure system	1983	.47
	1984	.49
	1985	.54
	1986	.67
Maintenance and repair of F-15 equipment and aircraft	1983	.50
	1984	.55
	1985	.36
Management services and program review for AN/ALR-46 radar warning system	1983	1.40
Airframe structural components for F/A-18 aircraft	1986	.47
Unidentified training services	1983	11.30
Unidentified surface-based radio navigation equipment	1986	.57
Other unidentified awards	1983	.50
	1984	2.89
	1985	1.04
	1986	.88x

Negative figure results from a downward contract adjustment.

* Of this total, $56 million is earmarked for Saudi Arabia, $5 million for South Korea, and the rest for Indonesia, Kenya, Morocco, Mexico, the Philippines, Singapore, Sudan, Thailand and South Yemen.

These awards include work conducted in Indonesia, Kenya, Morocco, Mexico, Saudi Arabia, Sudan, Thailand, Tunisia, Taiwan and South Yemen.

+ These awards include work conducted in Bahrain, Indonesia, Kenya, South Korea, Morocco, Mexico, the Philippines, Saudi Arabia, Sudan, Tunisia and South Yemen.

x These awards include $147,000 in awards for work performed in Tunisia.

NOTES

1. This is part of a $24 million contract for equipment to be divided among Egypt, Kuwait, Jordan and Spain.

2. These aircraft were purchased through the military assistance program (MAP).

3. This sale was initiated in 1982, postponed, and resurrected in 1985.

4. This is part of an $88 million package that includes spare parts for Lockheed F-100 and F-104 fighters.

5. This is part of a package worth $114 million that includes spares, support equipment, and 60 Ford AIM-9P3 Sidewinder air-to-air missiles.

6. This $92 million package deal includes 15 General Electric J-85 engines. Bahrain has purchased a total of 12 F-5 aircraft to date.

7. Northrop shares this $63 million contract with Raytheon.

8. Northrop shares this $70 million contract with Raytheon.

9. This $82 million contract is shared among Northrop, Raytheon, Litton and ITT, and includes work performed on Litton's AN/TSQ-73 Missile Minder radar.

10. Saudi Arabia has purchased 114 F-5 aircraft through the Peace Hawk program, and 62 F-15 aircraft through the Peace Sun program.

RAYTHEON CO.

I. SUMMARY DATA

Data, except for the total sales figures, are for U.S. government fiscal years, ending Sept. 30. FMS program award totals for 1982 to 1984 were calculated by the General Accounting Office; the 1985 and 1986 totals were calculated by IRRC from Department of Defense contract data.

	1982	1983	1984	1985	1986
Total sales (millions)	$5,217	$5,631	$5,996	$6,409	$7,308
DoD contract awards (millions)	$2,262	$2,728	$3,093	$2,999	$4,052
DoD contractor rank	9	10	9	9	7
DoD awards/total sales	.41	.46	.52	.47	.55
FMS contract awards (millions)	$ 172	$ 221	$ 262	$ 234	$ 602
FMS contractor rank	15	7	5	8	3
FMS/total DoD awards	.08	.08	.08	.08	.15
FMS/total sales	.033	.081	.085	.037	.086

These figures include Beech Aircraft, a subsidiary of Raytheon. Beech Aircraft's arms export business is discussed in detail in a separate profile.

II. ARMS EXPORT BUSINESS AT A GLANCE

Raytheon has long been one of the largest American arms exporting firms. It has received more than $100 million in FMS contract awards every year since 1975, and it has dropped from the list of top 10 foreign military sales contractors only once since 1972. Although Raytheon conducts most of its arms exports through the Foreign Military Sales program, it also sells a substantial quantity of arms through direct, company-to-government channels, and between 1978 and 1981 (the last years for which figures are available) ranked among the top 10 firms in this category as well.

Raytheon's defense electronics divisions produce missiles, radar, sonar, electronic counter-measure devices and communication systems, and its Beech Aircraft subsidiary manufactures a variety of general purpose aircraft, some of which are configured for military use by foreign governments. (Beech's FMS business is discussed in the separate Beech Aircraft profile.) All told, Raytheon is involved in more than 150 DoD pro-grams. Its defense business is the largest of the company segments, and it helps to make Raytheon one of the top 100 industrial companies in the country.

Raytheon's largest export program is the Hawk surface-to-air missile, which is deployed in 20 foreign nations. Records compiled by the Department of Defense's Security Assistance Agency indicate that 7,847 Hawks had been exported through the FMS program and Military Assistance Program as of September 1986, and that 691 more Hawks are on order. Belgium, Denmark, France, Germany, Greece, Italy and the Netherlands coproduce the Hawk under license. Over the years, Raytheon has made a number of improvements in this air defense system, which have led to continued sales of the system itself and brought in revenue from the sale of modification kits. The most modern Hawk missile is referred to as the Improved or I-Hawk. Raytheon narrowly missed out on a major follow-up Hawk sale in 1986 when the Reagan administration shelved a proposed arms sale to Jordan because of congressional resistance. The proposed package included 14 I-Hawk command posts and radar, 12 I-Hawk launch units, and 222 I-Hawk missiles, along with two Litton AN-TSQ-73 Missile Minder radar systems. Contract awards for the Hawk system accounted for 69 percent of Raytheon's total FMS-related awards in fiscal 1983, 59 percent in 1984, 13 percent in 1985 and 39 percent in 1986.

Next to the Hawk missile, Raytheon's most widely exported items have been Sidewinder and Sparrow air-to-air missiles and a variant of the Sparrow, the RIM-7H-2 NATO Seasparrow surface-to-air missile. Raytheon is one of two manufacturers of these missiles, but it received all of the Defense Department's contract awards for the Sparrow in 1984 and a majority of the awards for both weapon systems in 1985. Australia, Canada, Colombia, Egypt, Great Britain, Greece, the Netherlands, Pakistan, Spain and Taiwan are among the nations that have purchased Sparrows. The company received $147 million in FMS contract awards from 1983 to 1986 for exported Sparrows. Sidewinders also have been extremely widely exported, although most exports have been made by the original prime contractor, Ford Aerospace. A consortium of European countries led by West Germany, and including Italy, Norway and Great Britain, will manufacture Sidewinders for their own use.

Raytheon also exports its AN/SPG-51 fire control radar, MK-74 fire control system, AN/SPS-49 shipboard air search radar, and AN/SQS-56/DE 1160, DE 1164 and DE 1167 sonar systems. The DE 1160 system has been sold to Australia, Egypt, Italy, Morocco, Saudi Arabia, Spain and Turkey. Ten DE 1164 sonar systems have been deployed by the Italian navy.

The weapon system likely to be Raytheon's most popular export in the near future is the Patriot air defense missile system. The Patriot is currently Raytheon's largest defense program, and it already has been sold to West Germany, the Netherlands and Japan. According to Raytheon's 1986 annual report, several other nations also have expressed interest in the Patriot. In 1985, the company received contract awards for the Patriot worth $107 million, 46 percent of its total FMS-related awards for the year. In 1986 the Patriot brought in $279 million in awards, which again represented 46 percent of Raytheon's total FMS awards.

Possible future exports might include Raytheon's version of the Imaging Infrared Maverick air-to-surface missile, the Standard II surface-to-air missile, the AN/TRC-170 tactical troposcatter radio system and the Hughes AMRAAM air-to-air missile, for which Raytheon is a second source producer.

Raytheon should be assured of some easy access to foreign markets through its work with several foreign companies. Raytheon's British subsidiary already has won a contract from the British government to work with the Plessey Co. on the definition of the next generation of NATO Identification Friend or Foe electronic surveillance systems. Should Raytheon develop this system, it would guarantee the company numerous foreign orders. Raytheon is also working with a French company, Thomson-Sintra, to develop an advanced mine-hunting sonar system.

III. MILITARY ORDERS, 1982–1986 (includes first quarter of 1987)

The Department of Defense selected Raytheon to produce Sidewinder air-to-air missiles as a second source to Ford Aerospace. In most cases, IRRC was able to determine which foreign military sales of Sidewinders were being handled by Raytheon and which by Ford. In the instances where IRRC was unable to determine which contractor was responsible for a certain Sidewinder order, IRRC has listed the order in both profiles. Since General Dynamics was selected to produce Sparrow and Seasparrow missiles as a second source to Raytheon, the same methodology was used for orders of these missiles.

Country	Date of Agreement	Description of Order	Price (in millions)
– EUROPE AND MAJOR ALLIES –			
Australia	1983	AIM-9 Sidewinder training missiles/c	$4.6
	1984	AIM-7M Sparrow air-to-air missiles/c,d,f	NA[1]
	1984	AIM-9 Sidewinder air-to-air missiles/d,f	NA
	1985	Equipment for a Sidewinder depot/r	NA
	1985	Additional funding for AN/SLQ-32 (v) electronic countermeasure system/b	$2.0
	1986	Engineering services for the MK-74 guided missile fire control system/b	$.8
Canada	1984	AN/SPS-49 shipboard air search radar and RIM 7-H-2 NATO Sea Sparrow surface-to-air missiles/e	$16
	1984	AIM-7 Sparrow air-to-air missiles/e	NA[2]
	1984	AIM-9M Sidewinder air-to-air missiles/c	NA[3]
	1985	AIM-7M Sparrow air-to-air missiles/c,e,f	NA[4]
	1985	4 AN/DSM-156A guided missile test set for AIM/RIM-7 Sparrow air-to-air/ surface-to-air missiles/b	2.1
	1986	Guidance control sections for AIM-9M Sidewinder air-to-air missiles/b	NA
	1986	4 Seasparrow surface-to-air missile systems with (80) missiles/d[5]	NA
	1987	Sparrow air-to-air missiles/c	NA[6]
Denmark	1986	Optical target detectors for Sidewinder air-to-air missiles/b	NA

Country	Date of Agreement	Description of Order	Price (in millions)
France	1986	Engineering services for the MK-74 guided missile fire control system/b	$.2
Great Britain	1985	AIM-9 Sidewinder air-to-air missiles/r	NA
	1985	Optical target detectors for Sidewinder air-to-air missiles/b	$5.2
	1985	Equipment for a Sidewinder depot/r	NA
Greece	1982	280 AIM-7E Sparrow air-to-air missiles/d	NA
	1984	50 AIM-7E Sparrow air-to-air missiles/b	$12.8
	1984	AIM-9L Sidewinder air-to-air missiles/c,d,f,g	NA[7]
Italy	1984	4 DE 1164 and DE 1167 LF shipboard sonar systems/f	$6.1
	1984	Upgrade of 2 Tartar shipborne air defense missile systems/c	NA[8]
	1986	Engineering services for the MK-74 guided missile fire control system/b	$1.2
Japan	1983	100 AIM-7F Sparrow air-to-air missiles/g	NA[9]
	1984	MIM-104 Patriot air defense system comprising 24 batteries with 130 missile launchers plus 2 training units/d,e,g,h,r	NA[10]
	1986	Engineering services for the MK-74 guided missile fire control system/b	$.2
	1986	Optical target detectors for Sidewinder air-to-air missiles/b	NA
NATO	1984	190 AIM-7M Sparrow air-to-air missiles/b	$44.1
	1984	1,845 guidance and control sets for AIM-7 Sparrow air-to-air missiles/f	$250[11]
Netherlands	1983	900 AIM-9L Sidewinder air-to-air missiles/d	$78
	1984	Patriot air defense system comprising 160 MIM-104 Patriot surface-to-air missiles and 20 missile launchers plus 4 AN/MPQ-53 radar sets/d,e,g,r	$333
	1985	RIM-7H-2 NATO Seasparrow surface-to-air missiles/r	NA

Country	Date of Agreement	Description of Order	Price (in millions)
	1985	Optical target detectors for Sidewinder air-to-air missiles/b	$2.1
Norway	1983	30 MIM-23 I-Hawk surface-to-air missiles with support and overhaul equipment/c,d,f,g	NA[12]
	1986	2 additional Hawk surface-to-air missile batteries/g	$28.2
Portugal	1986	3 RIM-7M Seasparrow surface-to-air missile systems with 24 missiles/c,d,g	NA[13]
Spain	(1983)	AIM-7F Sparrow air-to-air missiles/d	NA
	1985	Additional funding for AN/SPS-49 radar system/b	$2.6
Sweden	(1984)	(960) AIM-9L Sidewinder air-to-air missiles/d	($75)
	1985	Active optical target detectors for Sidewinder air-to-air missiles/b	$2.6
Turkey	(1983)	(320) AIM-7M Sparrow air-to-air missiles/d[14]	NA
	1986	Optical target detectors for Sidewinder air-to-air missiles/b	NA
	(1986)	(4) Seasparrow surface-to-air, shipborne missile systems/d[15]	NA
West Germany	1985	MIM-104 Patriot air defense system composed of 14 batteries with 100 launcher stations and 779 missiles/c,d,e[16]	$1,149
	1986	Spare parts for Patriot air defense missile systems/f	$67
	1986	(2) Seasparrow surface-to-air missile systems with (48) missiles/d[17]	NA
–ASIA AND PACIFIC–			
Pakistan	1985	AIM-9L Sidewinder air-to-air missiles/e,f,g	NA[18]
	1985	Modernization of 2 solid-state transmitters in AN/SQS-23 shipboard sonar systems/f,j	$1.6
Singapore	(1982)	(162) MIM-23B Hawk surface-to-air missiles/d	NA[19]

Country	Date of Agreement	Description of Order	Price (in millions)
South Korea	1982	28 modification kits for I-Hawk surface-to-air missiles/g	NA[20]
	1982	170 MIM-23B Hawk surface-to-air missiles including 720 rocket motors/c,d,f,g	$68
	(1983)	(298) MIM-23B Hawk surface-to-air missiles/d	NA
	1985	28 modification kits for I-Hawk surface-to-air missile system with spares, training and services/c,f,g	$61
	1985	28 modification kits for I-Hawk surface-to-air missile system/c	$53
	1985	AIM-9 Sidewinder air-to-air missiles/c	NA[21]
	1987	Upgrade of 28 Hawk surface-to-air missile systems/f,g	$84
Taiwan	(1983)	100 AIM-7F Sparrow air-to-air missiles/d,g,r	$105
	1986	Engineering services for the MK-74 guided missile fire control system/b	$.4

– MIDDLE EAST –

Country	Date of Agreement	Description of Order	Price (in millions)
Bahrain	1987	AIM-9 Sidewinder air-to-air missiles and AIM-7 Sparrow air-to-air missiles/g	NA[22]
Egypt	1982	I-Hawk air defense system equipment/c	$11
	1982	4 Hawk air defense batteries comprised of 24 missile launchers and 72 MIM-23B Hawk surface-to-air missiles/d	$20
	1983	300 AIM-9L Sidewinder air-to-air missiles/d,g	NA
	1983	2 AN-SQS-56 (DE 1167) sonar systems/f,g	$9
	1984	Product improvement program for I-Hawk surface-to-air missiles/f,g	$63[23]
	1984	402 AIM-7F Sparrow air-to-air missiles with 22 training missiles/c,f,g	$96
	(1985)	(10) I-Hawk mobile surface-to-air missile systems with (120) missiles/d	NA

Country	Date of Agreement	Description of Order	Price (in millions)
	1986	AIM-9 Sidewinder air-to-air missiles/d,e,f,g	NA[24]
	1987	Sparrow AIM-7 air-to-air missiles/c,h	NA[25]
Israel	1982	200 MIM-23B Hawk surface-to-air missiles/d,g	$47
	1983	200 AIM-9L Sidewinder air-to-air missiles/d	$16
	1984	150 AIM-7M Sparrow air-to-air missiles/d,e	$52
Jordan	1984	Product improvement program for I-Hawk surface-to-air missiles/f,g	$70[26]
Kuwait	1984	Improvement kits for 200 Hawk surface-to-air missiles/c,f	NA[27]
	1985	Technical assistance and engineering for Hawk surface-to-air missiles/b,f	$5
Saudi Arabia	1986	Services, training and technology for Hawk anti-aircraft missile systems/f,g	$518
	1986	AIM-9L Sidewinder air-to-air missiles with 30 training missiles/c,d,g	NA[28]
United Arab Emirates	1984	5 batteries of Hawk air defense system/r	$114
	1985	45 MIM-23B Hawk surface-to-air missiles/c,f,g	$21
	1986	Engineering support of Hawk surface-to-air missile systems/f	$3.6
	1986	8 AN/TRC-170 digital troposcatter radio systems with spares, support and testing equipment/c,f,g[29]	$40
– AFRICA –			
Chad	1986	(1) Hawk mobile surface-to-air missile system with 27 missiles/d	NA

IV. FMS PROGRAM CONTRACT AWARDS, FY 1983–1986
(millions of dollars)

Item	Fiscal Year	Award Total
MIM-23 Hawk surface-to-air missiles	1983	$151.37*
	1984	154.23#
	1985	31.86
	1986	234.52+
Patriot air defense missile systems	1984	27.91
	1985	107.01
	1986	279.51
AIM-7 Sparrow air-to-air missiles	1983	10.34x
	1984	42.15
	1985	57.41
	1986	37.47
AIM-9 Sidewinder air-to-air missiles	1983	5.93
	1984	4.11
	1985	18.18
	1986	12.73
AN/SPG-51 shipboard fire control radar systems	1983	8.49
	1984	26.54
MK-74 fire control systems	1984	1.58
	1985	4.13
	1986	19.44
RIM 7H-2 NATO Seasparrow surface-to-air missiles	1983	15.19
	1984	.03
	1985	.28
	1986	.20
AN/SQS-56/DE 1160 shipboard sonar systems	1983	16.30
AN/SPS-49 shipboard air search radar systems	1984	4.53
	1985	2.40
	1986	−.16
Guided missile remote controls for F-4 Phantom II aircraft	1983	.50
	1984	.24
OU/BQH-5 signal convertors	1986	.27

Item	Fiscal Year	Award Total
Electronic countermeasure systems for SH-60 Seahawk helicopters	1986	.41
Technical services for unidentified guided missiles	1985	2.72
	1986	9.74y
Unidentified advanced engineering services	1983	2.35
	1984	.29
Unidentified research and development	1986	2.35
Components for unidentified guided missiles	1983	1.01
	1984	.13
	1985	.91
	1986	.10
Maintenance and repair of unidentified communications or detection equipment	1983	.68
	1984	.10
	1986	1.88
Unidentified electronic countermeasure equipment	1983	.84
	1984	.14
	1985	.62
Miscellaneous fire control equipment	1986	1.70
Maintenance equipment for unidentified guided missiles	1986	.98
Unidentified fire control radar systems	1983	.62
	1984	.03
Unidentified underwater sound equipment	1983	.58
	1984	.04
	1986	.08
Other unidentified awards	1983	1.89
	1984	1.63
	1985	.56
	1986	.91

Negative figure results from downward contract adjustments.

*   Includes awards for work performed in Spain, South Korea, Taiwan, Egypt, Israel, Jordan, Kuwait and Saudi Arabia.

#	Includes awards for work performed in Great Britain, South Korea, Egypt, Jordan and Kuwait.
+	Includes awards for work performed in Israel, Egypt and Jordan.
x	Includes awards for work performed in Greece and Turkey.
y	Includes awards for work performed in Kuwait.

NOTES

1. Raytheon and General Dynamics share this contract, which is reported to be worth 21 million Australian dollars.

2. Raytheon and General Dynamics share this $113 million contract to provide 408 Sparrow missiles to Canada.

3. Raytheon and Ford share this $41 million contract to provide Canada with 416 Sidewinder missiles and 56 training missiles.

4. Raytheon and General Dynamics share this $42 million contract to provide 184 Sparrow missiles to Canada.

5. It is unclear whether these Seasparrow missiles were supplied by General Dynamics or Raytheon or both companies. These are in addition to the 6 Seasparrow missile systems with (168) missiles ordered by Canada in 1984.

6. General Dynamics and Raytheon share this $17 million contract to supply Canada with 88 Sparrow missiles. This is Canada's third order of Sparrow missiles.

7. Raytheon and Ford share this $30 million contract to provide 300 Sidewinder missiles to Greece.

8. Raytheon, General Electric, FMC and Vitro share this $94 million contract.

9. This $105 million package includes Phalanx air defense guns.

10. All but the first installment of Patriots will be produced under license by Mitsubishi Heavy Industries of Japan. The first order—worth $132 million for 20 launchers and 40 missiles—has been placed. Japan will procure 20 launchers and 80 missiles annually from 1986 through 1991, and the total program is estimated to cost $4 billion.

11. Some of these sets are for the U.S. Navy and Air Force, and for four non-NATO countries, Australia, Egypt, Israel and Taiwan.

12. Estimates of the price of this transaction vary. U.S. government documents put the price at $48.6 million, *International Defense Review* at $80 million and *Defense and Foreign Affairs* at $61 million.

13. This is part of a $216 million package including 3 McDonnell Douglas Harpoon missile systems with 24 missiles, 6 General Electric LM 2500 engines, 6 U.S. government-manufactured Mk 32 torpedo tubes, and 3 Aerojet General AN/SLQ-25 torpedo counter-measure sets.

14. It is unclear whether these Sparrow missiles were supplied by General Dynamics, Raytheon or both companies.

15. It is unclear whether these Seasparrow missiles were supplied by General Dynamics, Raytheon or both companies.

16. West Germany will reportedly receive additional Patriot batteries in exchange for the Roland 2 air defense systems that protect American air bases in Germany.

17. It is unclear whether these Seasparrow missiles were supplied by General Dynamics, Raytheon or both companies.

18. Raytheon and Ford share this $50 million contract to provide 500 Sidewinder missiles to Pakistan.

19. Additional missiles and launchers reportedly are on order.

20. This $72 million package includes 6 Applied Devices AN/TPQ-29 simulators.

21. Raytheon and Ford share this contract to provide Sidewinder missiles to South Korea.

22. It is unclear whether these Sidewinder missiles were supplied by Raytheon, Ford or both companies, and whether these Sparrow missiles were supplied by Raytheon, General Dynamics or both companies. This is a $400 million package including 12 General Dynamics F-16 fighter aircraft, Westinghouse AN/ALQ-131 electronic countermeasure pods, radar warning receivers, chaff/flare dispensers, and Hughes Aircraft AGM-65 air-to-surface missiles.

23. This $63 million contract is divided between Raytheon and Northrop.

24. Ford and Raytheon share this $42 million contract to provide 560 Sidewinder missiles to Egypt.

25. General Dynamics and Raytheon share this $190 million contract for 282 air-to-air and 514 ground-to-air Sparrow missiles.

26. This $70 million contract is divided between Raytheon and Northrop.

27. This $82 million contract is shared between Raytheon, Northrop, Litton & ITT.

28. This is part of a $265 million package deal that includes 995 Ford and Raytheon AIM-9L Sidewinder missiles, 671 Ford AIM-9P4 Sidewinder missiles, and 100 McDonnell Douglas Harpoon missiles. Because of intense congressional opposition, the Reagan administration

deleted 200 Stinger missile launchers with 600 missiles from this package. It is unclear how many of the AIM-9L Sidewinder missiles were manufactured by Raytheon, and how many were manufactured by Ford.

29. Two contractor representatives will be stationed in the United Arab Emirates for three years to perform work in support of this sale.

RCA CORP.

(a subsidiary of General Electric)

I. SUMMARY DATA

Data, except for the total sales figures, are for U.S. government fiscal years, ending Sept. 30. FMS program award totals were calculated by IRRC from Department of Defense contract data.

	1982	1983	1984	1985	1986
Total sales (millions)	$8,016	$8,977	$10,112	$8,972	NA
DoD contract awards (millions)	$ 996	$1,181	$ 1,116	$1,315	$1,246
DoD contractor rank	19	18	22	23	n/a
DoD awards/total sales	.12	.13	.11	.15	NA
FMS contract awards (millions)	$ 12	$ 10	$ 10	$ 36	$ 16
FMS contractor rank	n/a	n/a	n/a	25	n/a
FMS/total DoD awards	.01	.01	.01	.03	.01
FMS/total sales	.002	.001	.001	.004	NA

II. ARMS EXPORT BUSINESS AT A GLANCE

A $6.3 billion merger agreement brought together two defense electronics giants—General Electric and RCA—in 1986. GE's acquisition of RCA will increase GE's foreign military sales, but only marginally, given the relatively small size of RCA's FMS prime contract awards.

The segments of RCA involved in military production specialize in communications and radar systems. The company's largest defense program is the sophisticated Aegis air defense system for the U.S. Navy's Ticonderoga class of guided missile cruisers.

III. MILITARY ORDERS, 1982–1986

The sources used for this study did not list many military orders placed with RCA for the period 1982 through 1986. From Department of Defense press releases, however, IRRC was able to identify four FMS awards that were issued to the company for additional funding of contracts that predate 1982.

RCA provides engineering services and logistical support work on instrumentation radars for the governments of Great Britain, West Germany, South Korea and Taiwan. The company received a $3.3 million award in September 1983, a $3.5 million award in March 1984 and a $4.5 million award in April 1985 for these services. The Department of Defense also issued a $3.8 million award to RCA in June 1984 for engineering services related to a Japanese guided missile destroyer.

RCA's largest foreign military sales order is for an Aegis air defense system that the company will be supplying to the Japanese Navy. This system will be installed aboard a DDG-class destroyer. The total cost of the Aegis-equipped ship is estimated to be between $1.1 and $1.4 billion. The purchase of a second Aegis-class vessel is likely to be funded by Japan in 1990. According to the company, NATO is also considering equipping new ships with the Aegis system.

IV. FMS PROGRAM CONTRACT AWARDS, FY 1983–1986
(millions of dollars)

Item	Fiscal Year	Award Total
Modifications of ships for the Mk-15	1985	$ 1.07
Close in Weapon System	1986	2.35
Radio and TV equipment for the P-3 Orion anti-submarine maritime patrol aircraft	1985	.51
Components for E-2 Hawkeye aircraft	1986	.53
Aegis air defense system	1986	.11
Unidentified communications equipment, including maintenance and repair	1983	4.17
	1984	2.71
	1985	31.38
	1986	.13
Unidentified engineering services	1983	3.97
	1984	5.76
	1985	1.90
	1986	13.10
Unidentified intelligence studies*	1983	.43
	1984	.96
	1985	.47
	1986	.67
Unidentified logistics support services	1984	.74#
Other unidentified awards	1983	1.69
	1984	.17
	1985	.68
	1986	.24

*   DoD contract data indicate that these awards are for work performed in West Germany.

\#   DoD contract data indicate that one-third of these awards are for work related to the Mk-75 76mm gun mount.

ROCKWELL INTERNATIONAL CORP.

I. SUMMARY DATA

Data, except for the total sales figures, are for U.S. government fiscal years, ending Sept. 30. FMS program award total for fiscal year 1984 was calculated by the General Accounting Office; the 1982, 1983, 1985 and 1986 totals were calculated by IRRC from Department of Defense contract data.

	1982	1983	1984	1985	1986
Total sales (millions)	$7,395	$8,098	$9,322	$11,338	$12,296
DoD contract awards (millions)	$2,691	$4,545	$6,219	$ 6,264	$ 5,590
DoD contractor rank	8	3	2	3	4
DoD awards/total sales	.35	.55	.64	.55	.46
FMS contract awards (millions)	$ 19	$ 33	$ 91	$ 75	$ 15
FMS contractor rank	n/a	n/a	16	15	n/a
FMS/total DoD awards	.01	.01	.01	.01	.01
FMS/total sales	.003	.004	.010	.007	.001

II. ARMS EXPORT BUSINESS AT A GLANCE

Although Rockwell is probably best known as the manufacturer of the space shuttle and the B-1 bomber, the company has significant exports of military equipment of a smaller variety. Rockwell's foreign military sales include communications and navigation equipment used on an array of military aircraft, tactical weapons, and counter-insurgency and training aircraft.

Rockwell's most widely distributed military product is the AN/ARN-118 tactical air communications and navigation (Tacan) system, which the company has sold to more than two dozen foreign nations. Countries that the Defense Department has listed as participants in foreign military sales of the AN/ARN-118 and its spare parts include Australia, Belgium, Britain, Denmark, Ecuador, Egypt, El Salvador, Germany, Greece, Honduras, Israel, Japan, Jordan, Korea, the Netherlands, Norway, Pakistan, Portugal, Saudi Arabia, Singapore, Spain, Sudan, Taiwan, Thailand, Turkey, Venezuela and Yemen. According to *Aviation Week & Space Technology*, China also has purchased ARN-118 Tacan sets. The company exports several other radio systems used on various military aircraft, including systems that enable the Awacs aircraft and other planes to communicate with the Air Force Satellite Communications System (Afsatcom). Perhaps the company's most lucrative military export contract in the last few years has been its sale of Very Low Frequency (VLF) communication systems for use on French C-160 aircraft. These systems include kits for hardening the planes against ElectroMagnetic Pulse (EMP).

In 1987, the Australian government chose Rockwell to head a team that will furnish combat systems for six new diesel-electric submarines. This contract is worth more than $500 million, and includes an option for two additional submarine combat systems. Singer and several foreign companies will participate in the program.

In the field of tactical weapons, Rockwell registered its first international sale of a Hellfire-derived shore defense anti-armor missile in 1987. The $65 million contract is for the sale of 700 Hellfires, including launchers and spare parts. Bofors Co. of Sweden will manufacture the Hellfire's launcher, warhead and missile container, and will conduct the final assembly of the weapon. Rockwell had received an $8 million contract from Sweden in 1985 for development and initial production of Hellfires adapted for coastal defense. The company reports that Greece, Norway and South Korea all have expressed interest in purchasing the missile system. Another tactical weapon exported by Rockwell is the GBU-15 modular glide bomb, which can be guided toward its target after it is released.

Rockwell also proposed reopening its production line for the OV-10 Bronco counterinsurgency aircraft after a 1984 Letter of Offer request from South Korea for 24 gunship configured aircraft capable of day or night air-to-ground and air-to-air operations. The OV-10 was originally developed in the early 1960s and was widely used in Vietnam. Records compiled by the Defense Department's Security Assistance Agency indicate that 88 OV-10s had been exported through the FMS program as of September 1986. In its current configuration, the OV-10D has a Forward Looking Infrared (FLIR) sensor and laser target designator/ranger and can carry a wide variety of ordnance. Older versions of the OV-10 are in service in Indonesia, Morocco, Thailand, Venezuela and West Germany.

III. MILITARY ORDERS, 1982–1986 (includes first quarter of 1987)

The non-government sources used for this study did not list many military orders placed with Rockwell for the period 1982 through 1986. Therefore, much of the data in this section refer in large part to additional funding for orders placed earlier than 1982. Although these awards are not orders per se, they are used here to give a fuller picture of the company's arms exports.

Country	Date of Agreement	Description of Order	Price (in millions)
– EUROPE AND MAJOR ALLIES –			
Australia	1986	8 avionics suites for Sikorsky S-70B-2 Seahawk helicopters/f	$53
	1987	Combat systems for 6 submarines/j	$500
	1987	User equipment for the Navistar Global Positioning System/n[1]	$4
Canada	1984	High-frequency radio equip./f,r	$11
	1987	User equipment for the Navistar Global Positioning System/n[1]	$NA
France	1985	Additional funding for 4 electromagnetic pulse hardened VLF transmission sub systems for C-160 aircraft/b	$37

Country	Date of Agreement	Description of Order	Price (in millions)
Great Britain	1984	UHF transceivers and components/b	NA[1]
Japan	1984	Radio, antennas and engineering services/b (in millions)	$10.3
NATO	1983-84	Radio systems and spares for E-3A Awacs and Air Force Satellite Communications System/b	NA[2]
Spain	1986	Additional funding for spare parts for the ARN-118 tactical airborne communications system/b	NA
West Germany	1987	User equipment for the Navistar Global Positioning System/n	NA[1]
Sweden	1985	Development of portable, shore-defense version of the Hellfire missile/h,r	$8
	1987	700 Hellfire missiles adapted for shore defense/n	$65
– ASIA AND PACIFIC –			
Indonesia	1982	Communications, navigation and pulse equipment/g	NA
Pakistan	1983	Communication Electronic Warfare System (CEWS)/c	$21.4
Singapore	1984	Additional funding for radio and TV equipment for E-2C Hawkeye airborne early warning and control aircraft/b	$2.21
South Korea	1985	Classified equipment/c	NA
Thailand	1984	UHF and VHF radios and transceivers/b	$5.9[4]
– MIDDLE EAST –			
Egypt	1985	Additional funding for radio and TV equipment for E-2C Hawkeye airborne early warning and control aircraft/b	$2.6
	1986	Additional funding for GBU-15 glide bombs/c	$6
Israel	1983-85	Additional funding for GBU-15 guided weapon system/b,c	$28[5]

Country	Date of Agreement	Description of Order	Price (in millions)
	1985	Spares and support for installation of AN/ARC-190 radios/b	$1.2
Saudi Arabia	1984	Contract awards for items for AN/ARC-165, -166, and -167 radios/b	NA[6]
	1984	Air Force Satellite Communications System equipment for E-3A Awacs/b	NA
	1984	Contract award for spares for AN/AYC-1 system on E-3A Awacs/b	NA
	1983-85	Contract awards for line items for AN/ARC-171 radios/b[8] (several awards)	$11.5[7]
	1983-84	Voice privacy equipment for radios/b	$8.7[9]
– AFRICA –			
Nigeria	1983	Radio system for use with Air Force Satellite Communications System/b	NA[10]
Somalia	1983	Radio system for use with Air Force Satellite Communications System/b	NA[10]
– LATIN AMERICA –			
Dominican Rep.	1984	Additional funding for items for AN/ARC-165, -166, and -167 radios/b	NA
El Salvador	1984	PRC 515 high frequency radio packsets/b	$1.1

IV. FMS PROGRAM CONTRACT AWARDS, FY 1983–1986
(millions of dollars)

Item	Fiscal Year	Award Total
French C-160 aircraft avionics*	1983	$6.92
	1984	22.60
	1985	43.78
	1986	.28
Modification of C-130 aircraft structural components	1986	5.62
AN/ARN-118 Tacan systems#	1983	1.89
	1984	3.63

Item	Fiscal Year	Award Total
	1985	5.79
	1986	.64
AN/ARC-186 radios +	1983	1.21
	1984	1.03
	1985	1.40
	1986	1.24
GBU-15 modular glide bombs**	1983	3.35
	1984	14.51
	1985	1.65
	1986	1.24
Mk30 mobile targets	1985	8.60
	1986	5.44
Air Force Satellite Communications System (Afsatcom) communications equip.	1983	4.72
	1984	2.94
	1985	.75
	1986	-.78
Unidentified radio and TV equipment for E-2 Hawkeye early warning and control aircraft	1984##	2.21
	1985+ +	2.55
	1986	.77
Radio and TV equipment for E-3A Awacs aircraft	1984	7.43
	1986	−2.21
Radio navigation equipment for F-16 fighters***	1984	1.26
Radio and TV equipment for H-46 Sea Knight helicopter	1984	2.13
	1986	.46
Flight instruments for F-15 fighters	1984	.73
	1986	.04
Maintenance and repair of floating docks used for Poseidon submarine launched ballistic missiles	1984	1.70
Structural components for T-33 trainer aircraft	1985	4.47
Unidentified electrical and electronic components and instruments	1984	20.19
Unidentified communications security equipment	1983	2.63

Item	Fiscal Year	Award Total
Radio, navigation and TV equipment for	1983	6.98
unidentified aircraft	1984	6.90
	1985	2.57
	1986	.90
Unidentified logistic support services	1986	1.43
Awards for modification of unidentified equipment	1984	1.5
Awards for spare components for aircraft	1984	1.4

Negative figures result from downward contract adjustments.

*	DoD press releases indicate that these awards are most probably for EMP hardened VLF communications equipment destined for France.
#	Rockwell's records differ from IRRC's analysis of DoD contract data. According to the company, it received $3.6 million in 1983, $5.5 million in 1984 and $5.1 million in 1985.
+	Rockwell's records differ from IRRC's analysis of DoD contract data. According to the company, it received $0.9 million in 1983 and $0.3 million in 1984.
**	Rockwell's records differ from IRRC's analysis of DoD contract data. According to the company, it received $1.0 million in 1983, $19.2 million in 1984 and $2.7 million in 1985.
##	These awards are for hardware and/or services purchased by Egypt.
++	These awards are for hardware and/or services purchased by Singapore.
***	Rockwell's records differ from IRRC's analysis of DoD contract data. According to the company, it received $0.4 million in 1983, none in 1984 and $0.6 million in 1985.

NOTES

1. The Navistar Global Positioning System is a space-based radio navigation network now being developed and deployed. It allows ships, aircraft and infantry soldiers to determine instantaneously their position on the globe within tens of feet and their speed within fractions of a mile per hour.

2. Part of this contract award of $11.8 million was for the U.S. Navy.

3. These involve three contract awards split among NATO, the U.S. Air Force, and other countries. The awards totaled $13.6 million.

4. Rockwell's records differ from IRRC's analysis of DoD contract data. According to the company, it received $1.6 million in this award.

5. Rockwell's records differ from IRRC's analysis of DoD contract data. According to the company, it received $20.0 million in this award: $18.0 million in 1984 and $1.0 million each in 1983 and 1985.

6. Purchases for Saudi Arabia, the Dominican Republic and the U.S. Air Force have been combined under a $17.1 million contract award. The ARC-167 is a high frequency radio used on the Awacs.

7. Of this total, $8 million was issued in 1983, $2.5 million in 1984 and $1.0 million in 1985. The total value of the contract awards is $33 million.

8. The AN/ARC-171 enables various types of aircraft to communicate with Afsatcom and Awacs on ultra-high frequencies.

9. Of this total, $4.4 million was issued in 1983 and $4.3 million in 1984.

10. Purchases by Nigeria, Somalia and NATO were combined under a single $4.5 million contract award.

SPERRY CORP.

(a subsidiary of Unisys)

I. SUMMARY DATA

Data, except for the total sales figures, are for U.S. government fiscal years, ending Sept. 30. FMS program award totals for fiscal 1983 and 1984 were calculated by the General Accounting Office; the totals for 1982, 1985 and 1986 were calculated by IRRC from Department of Defense contract data.

	1982	1983	1984	1985	1986
Total sales (millions)	$5,096	$4,729	$4,950	$5,695	NA
DoD contract awards (millions)	$1,149	$1,133	$1,615	$1,628	$1,557
DoD contractor rank	18	20	15	16	16
DoD awards/total sales	.24	.23	.22	.29	NA
FMS contract awards (millions)	$ 91	$ 52	$ 108	$ 74	$ 6
FMS contractor rank	n/a	23	15	16	n/a
FMS/total DoD awards	.08	.05	.07	.05	.01
FMS/total sales	.018	.011	.022	.013	NA

II. ARMS EXPORT BUSINESS AT A GLANCE

The bulk of Sperry's business is related to high technology electronics, especially information processing equipment, and systems integration services. In May 1986, Sperry agreed to be acquired by Burroughs Corp. in a $4.8 billion merger that created Unisys Corp., the nation's second largest computer manufacturer after IBM. To finance the merger, Unisys sold Sperry's aerospace division to Honeywell for $1.03 billion. Unisys will retain the defense systems unit of Sperry, which makes radar and submarine navigation systems, and the loss of the aerospace division should be easily offset by Burroughs's defense business. Although traditionally Burroughs has not been a major arms exporter, in 1986 the company logged $81.7 million in foreign military sales awards. This unusually high total stemmed from $80.4 million worth of awards the company received for work on an air defense system for Thailand that will be completed in 1988. Usually, the majority of Burroughs's FMS awards, like its domestic defense awards, are for automated data processing equipment. Burroughs also engages in engineering support and research and development of other air defense and tactical missile systems.

Sperry was listed among the top 25 U.S. FMS arms exporters during eight years between 1972 and 1985, but was ranked no higher than 15th. The company's largest year for exports was 1984, when it received $108.4 million in FMS-related prime contract awards. Sperry also has ranked among the 25 leading arms exporters of arms through the commercial sales program, registering sales worth $13.4 million in fiscal 1980 and $19.9 million in 1981, the last two years for which government figures are available.

Sperry's primary exports to foreign militaries are shipboard computers and fire control systems, aircraft flight and navigation instruments, simulated flight trainers, and various technical and engineering services. One of the company's largest defense contracts is from a foreign government. In June 1983, Sperry received a subcontract for electronic and combat systems for the Canadian Patrol Frigate program that will be worth $1.25 billion over a nine year period. Canada also awarded Sperry a contract to define the capabilities of a follow-on group of frigates. Sperry is also working on combat systems for the Spanish, Australian and Japanese navies.

In terms of contract awards through DoD's FMS program, the MK 92 fire control system has been Sperry's largest source of revenue in recent years. Department of Defense prime contract awards for the exportation of the MK 92, which is used on a variety of ships, accounted for 22 percent of the company's total FMS-related awards in fiscal 1984 and 45 percent in 1985. Other Sperry arms exports include central air data computers for the General Dynamics F-16 fighter, technical assistance for the British Trident and Polaris nuclear missile submarine programs, sonars and electronic warfare training for the British armed forces and F/A-18 fighter trainers for Australia.

III. MILITARY ORDERS, 1982–1986 (includes first quarter of 1987)

The non-government sources used for this study did not list many military orders placed with Sperry for the period 1982 through 1986. Therefore, the data in this section refer largely to additional funding for orders placed earlier than 1982. Although these awards are not orders per se, they are used here to give a fuller picture of the work the company performs under the Foreign Military Sales program.

Country	Date of Agreement	Description of Order	Price (in millions)
– EUROPE AND MAJOR ALLIES –			
Australia	1982	Additional funding for data exchange auxiliary consoles for use with UYK series computers/b	NA[1]
	1983	Mk 92 missile fire control system/r	NA
	1983	2 F/A-18 flight trainers/r	$23
	1984	Additional funding for software for Navy destroyer modernization program/b	$11.5
	1985	Additional funding for data exchange auxiliary consoles/b	NA[2]
	1986	Engineering support for the MK-92 fire control system/b	NA
Canada	1983	Electronics and weapons systems for Patrol Frigate program/r	$1,100

Country	Date of Agreement	Description of Order	Price (in millions)
Denmark	1983	Additional funding for F-16 central air data computers/b	NA[3]
France	1985	Upgrade of 2 Tartar fire control systems/c	NA[4]
Great Britain	1983	Color displays for Navy intelligence system/r	NA
	1985	Additional funding for technical assistance in support of Polaris and Trident submarines/b	$3.3
Japan	1982	Additonal funding for data exchange auxiliary consoles used with UYK series computers/b	NA[1]
	1982	8 AN/ASQ-114 avionics computers for P-3 patrol aircraft/b	NA[5]
	1983	Computer software for destroyer combat direction system/b	$4.8
Netherlands	1982	3 AN/ASQ-114 avionics computers for P-3 patrol aircraft/b	NA[5]
	1984	Additional funding for F-16 central air data computers/b	NA[6]
	1984	Additional funding for F-16 central air data computers/b	NA[7]
Spain	1982	Additional funding for data exchange auxiliary consoles used with UYK series computers/b	NA[1]
	1984	Management services for Navy carrier and frigate combat system development/b	$39.1
	1985	Additional funding for data exchange auxiliary control consoles/b	NA[2]
	1986	100 PC-IT microprocessors/f	NA[8]
	1986	Engineering support for the MK-92 fire control system/b	NA
Turkey	1984	Additional funding for F-16 central air data computers/b	NA[7]
West Germany	1986	Additional funding for automated data processing equipment/b	$15.4

Country	Date of Agreement	Description of Order	Price (in millions)
– ASIA AND PACIFIC –			
South Korea	1984	Additional funding for F-16 central air data computers/b	NA[6]
– MIDDLE EAST –			
Egypt	1983	Additional funding for F-16 central air data computers/b	NA[3]
Saudi Arabia	1982	Operation and maintenance of land-based test site for combat systems used on patrol gunboats/b	$14.2
	1983	Flight instruments and spares for weapons systems used on various aircraft/b	$5.6
	1986	Engineering support for the MK-92 fire control system/b	NA
– AFRICA –			
Tunisia	1984	Precision measurement equipment lab for Air Force repair work/b	$6.5
– LATIN AMERICA –			
Venezuela	1983	Additional funding for F-16 central air data computers/b	NA[3]

IV. FMS PROGRAM CONTRACT AWARDS, FY 1983–1986
(millions of dollars)

Item	Fiscal Year	Award Total
MK 92 fire control systems	1984	$ 23.26
	1985	33.13
	1986	–12.65
Management services for naval carrier and frigate combat system development for Spain	1984	39.15
Patrol gunboat management services	1983	13.67
	1984	1.94
	1985	.84

Item	Fiscal Year	Award Total
Software for combat data systems for Australian Navy destroyers	1984	11.48
Electronic countermeasure system for naval frigates	1985	8.17
Precision measurement equipment laboratory for the Tunisian Air Force	1984	6.51
Computer software for Japanese destroyers	1983	4.78
P-3 ASW aircraft communication equipment	1983 1985	3.97 .12
AN/UYK-7 shipboard computers	1983 1984 1985 1986	2.87 1.76 1.04 3.48
Trident submarine management services and training	1983 1984 1985 1986	2.59 .47 .84 5.57
Training services for UGM-96 Trident missiles	1986	.87
Flight instruments for F-16 fighter aircraft	1983 1985 1986	.41 3.63 1.7
Architecture and engineering services for Submarine Chaser patrol craft	1986	4.44
AN/USQ-20 naval tactical data systems	1986	1.43
AN/TPS-32 ground-based, long-range radar systems	1983	1.20
AN/APN-59 weather radar systems	1986	.93
AN/WSN-1 inertial navigation systems	1984	.63
Flight instruments for F-15 fighter aircraft	1983 1984 1985 1986	.32 .62 .52 .04

Item	Fiscal Year	Award Total
Miscellaneous technical services and maintenance and repair of unidentified shipboard equipment	1983	1.03
	1984	10.57
	1985	4.24
	1986	.11
Unidentified electronic modules	1983	7.52
Unidentified automatic data processing equipment and services	1983	2.54
	1984	.95
	1985	9.52
	1986	.57
Unidentified fire control equipment	1983	1.98
	1984	.93
	1985	3.86
	1986	.20
Unidentified electronic countermeasure systems	1983	.24
	1985	2.06
Unidentified engineering services	1983	3.42
	1985	2.25
Unidentified communications equipment	1983	.72
Unidentified electronics and electrical devices	1983	1.51
	1985	1.88
Unidentified architecture and engineering services	1986	.81
Other unidentified awards	1986	1.6

Negative figure results from downward contract adjustments

NOTES

1. This $7.8 million award covers the cost of 45 consoles for Australia, Japan, Spain and the U.S. Navy. Twenty percent of the funds—$1.56 million—is earmarked for the Australian, Japanese and Spanish systems.

2. This $3.2 million award covers the cost of 25 consoles to Australia, Spain and the U.S. Navy.

Four percent of the funds—$128,000—is earmarked for the Australian systems and 8 percent—$256,000—for the Spanish systems.

3. This $3.5 million award covers the cost of 163 computers to be divided among Denmark, Egypt and Venezuela.

4. Sperry is one of several contractors on this $58 million program.

5. This $3.7 million award covers the cost of eight computers for Japan, three for the Netherlands and seven for the U.S. Navy.

6. This $3.5 million award covers the cost of 202 computers to be divided between the Netherlands and South Korea.

7. This $10.8 million award is earmarked for division among the Netherlands, Turkey and the U.S. Air Force.

8. This sale is valued at 150 million Spanish pesetas.

TELEDYNE INC.

I. SUMMARY DATA

Data, except for the total sales figures, are for U.S. government fiscal years, ending Sept. 30. FMS program award totals for 1982 to 1984 were calculated by the General Accounting Office; the 1985 and 1986 totals were calculated by IRRC from Department of Defense contract data.

	1982	1983	1984	1985	1986
Total sales (millions)	$2,864	$2,979	$3,494	$3,256	$3,241
DoD contract awards (millions)	$ 590	$ 589	$ 426	$ 694	$ 488
DoD contractor rank	33	38	44	35	41
DoD awards/total sales	.21	.20	.09	.21	.15
FMS contract awards (millions)	$ 111	$ 91	$ 50	$ 122	$ 33
FMS contractor rank	23	16	24	10	26
FMS/total DoD awards	.19	.15	.12	.18	.07
FMS/total sales	.039	.031	.014	.037	.010

II. ARMS EXPORT BUSINESS AT A GLANCE

Although not as well known as most other major defense contractors, Teledyne has consistently been a significant arms exporter over the last several years. The company was ranked among the top 25 FMS contractors every year from 1976 to 1984—the last year for which the U.S. government made rankings available—but has never risen above the 16th slot. Teledyne also owns 27 percent of Litton Corp., an electronics corporation that has consistently ranked among the top 25 FMS contractors.

Teledyne comprises several dozen consolidated subsidiaries, which the company groups into four business segments: aviation and electronics, industrial, specialty metals and consumer products. The company reported commercial and military sales to foreign customers of $278 billion in 1986, $282 million in 1985, $288 million in 1984 and $263 million in 1983, accounting for about 8.5 percent of total sales over that period.

Among Teledyne's military product lines are a wide range of electronic components and systems, including navigation and communication systems for aircraft; engines for aircraft, missiles and tanks; specialty metals and composite materials used in airframe and engine construction; and systems engineering and computer support services for programs such as the U.S. Army Ballistic Missile Defense Program, now a part of the Strategic Defense Initiative.

The military export item for which Teledyne has received the most money in recent years is the engine for the M60 main battle tank. FMS awards for M60 engines accounted for 83 percent of the company's total FMS-related prime contract awards in fiscal 1983, 44 percent in 1984, 69 percent in 1985 and 42 percent in 1986. Recent recipients of the tank include Egypt, Saudi Arabia, Greece, Morocco, Tunisia and Israel. Production of the M60A3 series was extended after the U.S.

Army had fulfilled its own needs in order to continued support foreign military sales. The company has also had significant sales of its J69 turbine engine, which powers remotely piloted vehicles and military training aircraft, and of aircraft Identification Friend or Foe (IFF) systems, including a $250 million sale to Saudi Arabia in 1985.

III. MILITARY ORDERS, 1982–1986 (includes first quarter of 1987)

The non-government sources used for this study did not list many military orders placed with Teledyne for the period 1982 through 1985. The dearth of information on Teledyne's arms exports springs less from the size of the company's arms export business than from the fact that Teledyne manufactures components that are used in larger systems: Sources of weapon export data generally list the major weapon systems, and not lesser components. Therefore, the data in this section refer largely to additional funding for orders placed earlier than 1982. Although these awards are not orders per se, they are used here to give a fuller picture of the work the company performs under the Foreign Military Sales program.

Country	Date of Agreement	Description of Order	Price (in millions)
– EUROPE AND MAJOR ALLIES –			
Denmark	1984	Additional funding for aircraft radar system components/b	NA[1]
Great Britain	1983	Additional funding for J402-CA-400 engines for the Harpoon anti-ship missile/b	NA[2]
Greece	1983	Additional funding for J402-CA-400 engines for the Harpoon anti-ship missile/b	NA[2]
	1984	Additional funding for overhaul of J69 engines/b	NA[3]
Japan	1983	Additional funding for J402-CA-400 engines for the Harpoon anti-ship missile/b	NA[2]
NATO	1983–84	Additional funding for AN/APN-230 Doppler radar navigation systems and AN/APN-213 systems/b	NA[4]
Spain	1983	Additional funding for J402-CA-400 engines for the Harpoon anti-ship missile/b	NA[2]
Turkey	1983	Additional funding for J402-CA-400 engines for the Harpoon anti-ship missile/b	NA[2]
	1984	Additional funding for the overhaul of J69 engines/b	NA[3]
West Germany	1984	Additional funding for the overhaul of J69 engines/b	NA[3]

Country	Date of Agreement	Description of Order	Price (in millions)
\multicolumn{4}{c}{– ASIA AND PACIFIC –}			
South Korea	1985	Electronic countermeasure equipment/f	$3
Thailand	1984	Additional funding for aircraft radar system components/b	NA[1]
	1984	Additional funding for the overhaul of J69 engines/b	NA[3]
\multicolumn{4}{c}{– MIDDLE EAST –}			
Egypt	1983	Additional funding for unidentified spares for various fighter aircraft/b	$4.7
	1984	Retrofit kits for Soviet T-54 tanks including 105mm guns, transmissions, periscopes and fire control systems/n	NA
	1984	Additional funding for aircraft radar system components/b	NA[1]
	1985	Additional funding for components for AN/ALQ-110 electronic counter-measures pods/b	NA[5]
Israel	1984	Additional funding for aircraft radar system components/b	NA[1]
	1985	Receiver transmitters for the APX 101 Identification Friend or Foe system for F-16 fighter aircraft/b	NA
Saudi Arabia	1983	629 Mk 12 mode 4 Peace Query Identification Friend or Foe electronic surveillance systems/b,c,f	$250
	1983–84	Additional funding for AN/APN-230 Doppler radar navigation systems and AN/APN-213 systems/b	NA[4]
	1984	Additional funding for aircraft radar system components/b	NA[1]
\multicolumn{4}{c}{– AFRICA –}			
Morocco	1985	Receiver transmitters for the APX 101 Identification Friend or Foe system for aircraft/b	NA[6]

Country	Date of Agreement	Description of Order	Price (in millions)
Sudan	1984	Additional funding for aircraft radar system components/b	NA[1]

IV. FMS PROGRAM CONTRACT AWARDS, FY 1983–1986
(millions of dollars)

Item	Fiscal Year	Award Total
Engines for the M60 main battle tank	1983	$75.51
	1984	21.84
	1985	84.62
	1986	13.46
Engines for Harpoon anti-ship missile	1983	10.22
	1985	-.44
	1986	-.18
J69 engines	1983	9.00
	1984	.76
	1985	7.33
	1986	.19
Saudi Arabian Peace Query IFF Program	1983	6.20
Communications equipment and flight instruments for F-16 aircraft	1983	-.38
	1984	1.28
	1985	4.36
	1986	-.19
Communications equipment for Stinger surface-to-air missiles	1983	1.86
	1984	2.30
	1985	.47
	1986	1.10
Equipment for and maintenance and repair of F100 turbofan engine	1983	1.03
	1985	.24
	1986	.06
Cryptological equipment	1983	1.60
Management and engineering services for 2 1/2 ton trucks	1983	1.26

Item	Fiscal Year	Award Total
Miscellaneous components and equipment for F-5 fighter aircraft	1984	.45
	1985	1.11
	1986	.14
Fire control system for AH-1S Cobra TOW helicopter	1983	.50
Electrical rotating convertors for F-4 aircraft	1986	.47
Radar equipment for E-3A Awacs aircraft	1986	.31
AN/APQ-218 Doppler radar systems	1986	.21
Airframe structural components for E-2 Hawkeye aircraft	1986	.12
R-3350 gas reciprocating engines	1986	.05
Miscellaneous components for and maintenance and repair of unidentified guided missiles*	1983	18.11
	1984	19.73
	1985	21.95
Miscellaneous items	1986	17.24

Negative figures result from downward contract adjustments.

*   IRRC analysis of DoD contract data suggests that these awards are most probably for Harpoon-related work.

NOTES

1. This $9.9 million award provides radar system components to Denmark, Egypt, Israel, Saudi Arabia, Sudan and Thailand.

2. This $23.4 million award is earmarked for the purchase of 389 engines to be divided among the U.S. Navy, Great Britain, Greece, Japan, Spain and Turkey.

3. This $10.6 million award provides overhaul work for Greece, Thailand, Turkey and West Germany.

4. These awards are for the purchase of 18 AN/APN-230 and 10 AN/APN-213 systems to be divided between NATO and Saudi Arabia. Awards of $4.2 million were issued in fiscal 1983 and $8.2 million in 1984.

5. This $4.4 million award is for components to be divided between the U.S. Air Force and Egypt.

6. This $11.4 million award will be divided between the U.S. Air Force and Morocco.

TEXTRON INC.

I. SUMMARY DATA

Data, except for the total sales figures, are for U.S. government fiscal years, ending Sept. 30. The FMS program award total for 1982 was calculated by the General Accounting Office; the totals for the remaining years were calculated by IRRC from Department of Defense contract data.

	1982	1983	1984	1985	1986
Total sales (millions)	$2,936	$2,980	$3,221	$5,721#	$6,951#
DoD contract awards (millions)	$ 584	$ 671	$ 805	$1,920*	$1,671*
DoD contractor rank	34	31	28	13	14
DoD awards/total sales	.20	.23	.25	.34	.32
FMS contract awards (millions)	$ 128	$ 43	$ 7	$ 27*	$ 81*
FMS contractor rank	22	n/a	n/a	29	16
FMS/total DoD awards	.22	.06	.01	.01	.05
FMS/total sales	.044	.014	.002	.005	.012

| # | Textron's sales figures include sales made by Avco for 1985 and 1986, and Ex-Cell-O's 1986 fourth quarter sales. |
| * | These figures include awards issued by the Department of Defense to Avco Corp., a Textron subsidiary, which is covered in a separate profile. The 1986 figures also include awards issued to Ex-Cell-O, another Textron subsidiary, which is also covered in a separate profile. |

II. ARMS EXPORT BUSINESS AT A GLANCE

Textron, a highly diversified corporation, conducts its business through divisions that are separated into three sectors and seven segments. The segment that produces military goods, the company's aerospace and electronics group—which includes Bell Helicopter Textron, Bell Aerospace Textron, HR Textron Inc. and Basic Microelectronics—accounted for 35 percent of Textron's total sales in 1984 and one-quarter of its total sales for each of the three years before that. Bell Helicopter alone registered sales of $766 million in 1983, $672 million in 1984, $855 million in 1985 and $1.1 billion in 1986.

In 1984, Textron acquired Avco Corp.—a company with sizable defense work of its own— and shortly thereafter placed Bell Helicopter, which it had acquired in 1960, on the selling block, in part to finance the acquisition of Avco. (Avco's foreign military sales business is discussed in a separate profile.) Four months later, the company terminated its search for a buyer in the midst of a Justice Department investigation into the helicopter manufacturer's accounting practices. Later in 1986, Textron bought Ex-Cell-O Corp. for $1.05 billion. (Ex-Cell-O's foreign military sales business also is discussed in a separate profile.)

Textron's most widely exported military items are Bell helicopters. In 1986, Bell Helicopter Textron's international sales of military and commercial helicopters totaled more than $300 million, more than one-quarter of the company's total sales. The company reports that sales of its military helicopters were down in 1986, due to the completion of deliveries to Israel and Turkey. Bell also has "large after-market sales of technical training and logistics support," according to the company's annual report.

Bell manufactures no fewer than 20 versions of commercial and military light and medium helicopters. Its line of AH-1 Cobra attack and UH-1 Iroquois (also known as Huey) transport helicopters are particularly popular: More than 40 nations fly the Iroquois. In many instances, however, these helicopters are not purchased directly from Bell, but come from existing U.S. government stock. In 1982, 12 U.S. government surplus UH-1s were transferred to Pakistan, 12 to Thailand, 12 to Colombia and 12 to El Salvador; three were transferred to Switzerland, one to Japan and 20 to Brazil in 1984; and 15 more to El Salvador in 1985. The Philippines has 10 U.S. Government-surplus UH-1 helicopters on order.

Textron received a total of $29.3 million in identifiable prime contract awards from the DoD for export UH-1s and $19.1 million in awards for work related to the AH-1 during fiscal years 1983 through 1986. Some of the Cobra helicopters that Bell exports are armed with TOW (Tube-launched, Optically tracked, Wire-guided) anti-tank missiles. Older Bell systems, such as the OH-58 Kiowa observation helicopter, also remain in service overseas. The Pentagon's Defense Security Assistance Agency reports that 2,354 UH-1 Iroquois, 262 AH-1 Cobras and 107 OH-58 Kiowas had been transferred overseas as of September 1986. This does not include those Bell Helicopters manufactured under license in foreign countries or those exported through direct company-to-government commercial channels.

Bell's commercial helicopters are also widely used by foreign governments. Norway, for example, agreed in 1986 to a $30 million purchase of 12 Bell model 412SP (Special Performance) transport helicopters to replace aging Iroquois used by the Norwegian air force in support of army operations. At least eight foreign governments ordered Bell model 214ST Super Transport helicopters from 1982 to 1985.

Bell Helicopter arranges coproduction agreements for some of its systems. Agusta-Bell of Italy built upwards of 350 Iroquois, and Dornier of Germany assembled that many more. Textron established Korea Bell Helicopter Co. with Samsung Precision Industries of South Korea early in 1986 and is building a 120,000 square foot factory where Korea Bell will produce light and medium helicopter components and assemble helicopters under license. Indonesia, Turkey and Japan also have coproduction programs for Bell helicopters. Brazil is currently studying proposals from foreign helicopter companies for the construction of a helicopter factory, in which Bell could become involved. This factory reportedly would be two-thirds Brazilian-owned, and one-third foreign-owned.

One of Bell's largest programs, the V-22 Osprey tilt-rotor aircraft, may soon become available for export, according to the Osprey's government program manager. Several nations have expressed interest in the helicopter-airplane hybrid, and there is pressure to export it before other nations develop competing aircraft. France, for example, is reported to be designing a tilt-rotor plane. Bell produces the Osprey in a joint venture with Boeing, but the two firms will compete for production contracts in the 1990s. Bell is also competing in a team with McDonnell Douglas Helicopter Co. for contracts to develop the Army's new LHX light helicopter, which might also be exported some time in the distant future.

Before 1986, Textron also exported Dalmo-Victor electronic countermeasure systems for aircraft. Its AN/ALR-46, -62 and -69 systems are used on F-111, F-16 and F-4 fighters and A-10 attack aircraft. Textron sold its Dalmo-Victor division to Singer in March 1986.

III. MILITARY ORDERS, 1982–1986 (includes first quarter of 1987)

Country	Date of Agreement	Description of Order	Price (in millions)
		– EUROPE AND MAJOR ALLIES –	
Japan	1983	5 Head-up displays and 2 test sets for AH-1S Cobra attack helicopters/c	$1
Norway	1986	12 Bell 412SP helicopters/d,e,g[1]	$30
	1986	6 Bell 412SP helicopters/f,g	NA[2]
Turkey	1982	15 UH-1H Iroquois transport helicopters/b,c,d,e,f	$34
	1983	6 AH-1S Cobra TOW attack helicopters/c,d,e,g	$50
	1983	Components for UH-1H Iroquois transport helicopters/c,d,g	$27
	1985	Components and sub-assemblies for 15 UH-1H helicopters to be assembled in Turkey/c,d	$33
		– ASIA AND PACIFIC –	
Indonesia	1983	8 model 412ST Super Transport helicopters/d	NA
Pakistan	1983	10 AH-1S TOW Cobra attack helicopters/c,d,f,g	$74
South Korea	1985	21 AH-1S Cobra TOW attack helicopters/c,f,h,m[3]	$178
	1986	AH-1 Cobra attack helicopters/g	$127.5[4]
	1986	50 model 205 UH-1H Iroquois transport helicopters/c,d,f	$155[5]
Sri Lanka	1985	4 model 212 helicopters/d[6]	NA
Thailand	1984	2 model 214ST Super Transport helicopters/d,e,g	NA

Country	Date of Agreement	Description of Order	Price (in millions)
	1986	4 AH-1 Cobra TOW helicopters with Avco spare engines and support/d,f,g	$45
	(1986)	(5) model 214ST transport helicopters/d	NA
– MIDDLE EAST –			
Bahrain	1982	2 model 412ST Super Transport helicopters/e	NA
Iraq	1985	45 model 214ST Super Transport helicopters/e,l,m[7]	$275
Israel	1986	25 AH-1 Cobra attack helicopters/d,g	Free lease
Jordan	1982	24 AH-1S Cobra attack helicopters armed with TOW missiles/d	NA
Oman	1983	4 214ST Super Transport helicopters/d	NA
Saudi Arabia	1987	15 model 406 Kiowa helicopters/f,g	NA[8]
– LATIN AMERICA –			
Bolivia	1986	6 UH-1 Iroquois helicopters/d,g	Grant
Brazil	1985	16 Bell model 206 JetRanger 3 trainer helicopters/e,g	NA
	(1985)	1 model 412 helicopter/d	NA
El Salvador	1986	6 UH-1H Iroquois and 12 UH-1N Twin Huey attack helicopters/d,g[9]	NA
Honduras	1985	5 model 412 helicopters/d	NA
	1986	5 Bell 412 helicopters/d,e,f,g[10]	$13.4
Peru[11]	1983	6 model 214ST Super Transport helicopters/c,d,f	$65
	1984	25 model 212 helicopters/j	NA
– AFRICA –			
Botswana	(1986)	6 model 206B JetRanger helicopters/d	NA

IV. FMS PROGRAM CONTRACT AWARDS, FY 1983–1986
(millions of dollars)

Item	Fiscal Year	Award Total
UH-1 Iroquois transport helicopters	1983	$ 6.82
	1984	.38
	1985	16.10
	1986	6.03
AH-1 Cobra attack helicopters	1983	26.08
	1984	-5.13
	1985	-1.26
	1986	-.24
AH-1S Cobra TOW attack helicopters	1986	-.21
AN/ALR-46 electronic countermeasure systems	1982	2.07
	1983	.30
	1985	.41
AN/ALR-69 electronic countermeasure systems	1983	5.38
	1984	.22
	1985	-.03
AN/DLQ-3B electronic countermeasure systems	1984	1.98
Unidentified helicopters	1983	-3.44
	1984	1.11
	1985	2.81
	1986	31.90
Technical representative services for unidentified aircraft	1986	.44*
Unidentified awards	1983	5.46
	1984	1.00
	1986	1.12

Negative figures result from downward contract adjustments.

*   This award is for work performed in Honduras.

NOTES

1. This transaction includes an option for six additional helicopters. All but the first one will be assembled in Norway.

2. The value of this contract is reported to be 180 million Norwegian Krones.

3. This sale includes Avco spare engines. *Aviation Week & Space Technology* reports that seven representatives of Bell Helicopter and Avco will spend a year in South Korea to perform support work on the helicopters as part of the transaction.

4. This contract is most likely in support of the South Korean AH-1 coproduction program.

5. This $155 million contract includes 60 Avco T53-L-13B engines.

6. These helicopters were transferred to Sri Lanka via Singapore.

7. These commercially configured helicopters were ordered by the Iraqi Ministry of Transport. *The Wall Street Journal* reports, however, that Iraqi defense officials were involved in the negotiations that led to the order.

8. This is part of a $400 million package that includes 13 United Technologies UH-60 helicopters and 1 Beech C-12 transport aircraft. The Kiowa helicopters will be armed with Hughes Aircraft TOW missiles.

9. This is part of a package that includes 1 A-37 Dragonfly attack aircraft.

10. These are in addition to the five helicopters ordered in November 1985.

11. Peru financed these purchases partly through a $35 million countertrade arrangement, whereby Peru will supply Bell-Textron with silver products.

UNITED TECHNOLOGIES CORP.

I. SUMMARY DATA

Data, except for the total sales figures, are for U.S. government fiscal years, ending Sept. 30. FMS program award totals for 1982 to 1984 were calculated by the General Accounting Office; the 1985 and 1986 totals were calculated by IRRC from Department of Defense contract data.

	1982	1983	1984	1985	1986
Total sales (millions)	$12,510	$13,327	$14,826	$14,992	$15,669
DoD contract awards (millions)	$ 4,208	$ 3,867	$ 3,206	$ 3,906	$ 3,527
DoD contractor rank	3	7	8	7	9
DoD awards/total sales	.31	.26	.20	.25	.00
FMS contract awards (millions)	$ 673	$ 321	$ 171	$ 295	$ 214
FMS contractor rank	4	4	11	7	6
FMS/total DoD awards	.16	.08	.05	.08	.08
FMS/total sales	.054	.021	.012	.020	.014

II. ARMS EXPORT BUSINESS AT A GLANCE

United Technologies Corp., a highly diversified company, exports a wide variety of military equipment. Its Sikorsky division is the leading American manufacturer of medium and heavy military helicopters, and the Pratt & Whitney subsidiary is one of the two largest American suppliers of military aircraft engines. UTC's Norden Systems division manufactures radar and display systems for military aircraft, and the Hamilton Standard division produces propellers and engine controls.

UTC broke into the ranks of the 25 largest U.S. foreign military sales exporters in 1975, and since then has been among the top 12. The company's FMS exports peaked in the early 1980s—exceeding $600 million each year from 1980 through 1982—but have declined since. Although the bulk of its exports are routed through the U.S. government's Foreign Military Sales program, United Technologies sells a significant amount of weapons through commercial channels as well. The GAO calculates the company's commercial sales were $86 million in fiscal 1980—making UTC the second largest commercial sales exporter for the year—and $17 million in 1981.

UTC's most widely exported military systems are Sikorsky helicopters and Pratt & Whitney jet engines. Sikorsky's Black Hawk army transport helicopter and its Seahawk and less sophisticated Sea King helicopters—both used as antisubmarine warfare platforms—were sold to a dozen countries between 1982 and 1985. UTC also exports the CH-53 Super Stallion helicopter. United Technologies' most popular export item in recent years, however, has been the Pratt & Whitney F100 engine. Before 1984, F-16 aircraft were fitted with Pratt & Whitney F100 engines, which generated extensive export sales for UTC. However, following an intense competition—which was appropriately dubbed "The Great Engine War"—between Pratt & Whitney and General Electric, the U.S. Air Force announced in 1984 that it would switch to the General Electric F110 engine for the F-16, a move that prompted Israel and Turkey to request GE engines for the F-16s they had ordered. In January 1985, the U.S. Air Force partially reversed itself, announcing that it would purchase the P&W F100 engine for 20 percent of its new F-16s. Some observers speculate that this action may have influenced subsequent decisions by the governments of Egypt, South Korea, Thailand, Indonesia and Singapore to ask for P&W F100 engines for their F-16s. Pratt & Whitney's F100 engine also powers McDonnell Douglas F-15 fighters, which have been sold to Saudi Arabia, Israel and Japan. If Congress had not blocked the sale of 48 more F-15s to Saudi Arabia in 1985, UTC would have had an additional order for 96 F100 engines worth approximately $300 million. FMS-related prime contract awards for the F100 accounted for at least 88 percent of UTC's FMS award total for each of the last three years. The company attributes declining Pratt & Whitney sales in calendar year 1986 to the second-sourcing of F100 engines and the "phasing-down of European fighter purchases."

UTC's plans for providing the engine for the Lavi, Israel's indigeniously produced fighter/ground attack aircraft, fell through when the Israeli cabinet canceled the 300 aircraft program in 1987. United Technologies will still sell the engine that was to power the Lavi—the PW1120—to Israel, though, because the Israeli Defense Industry is using the engine as part of a McDonnell Douglas F-4 Phantom fighter upgrade program. Israel has not divulged how many of its F-4s it will re-engine with the PW1120 powerplant, nor how much the program will cost.

UTC has shown the proclivity, in recent years, to compete in the international market by engaging in joint ventures, offering industrial offset arrangements and creating new companies or consortia abroad. The company offered in 1986 to build a factory in Belgium as part of its strategy for winning a Belgian defense contract for 46 transport and anti-tank helicopters that is valued at $250 to $300 million. UTC's proposal involves the coproduction of an additional 120 military versions of its S-76 helicopter at the Belgian plant for sale in Europe. United Technologies also has signed agreements with companies in Japan, Spain, Great Britain and Australia, and is a prime competitor to help construct a helicopter factory in Brazil that would be one-third foreign-owned and two-thirds Brazilian owned. Brazil has set its long-term helicopter requirements at 500 aircraft, but most analysts think that France's Aerospatiale has the inside track in the competition. Aerospatiale already owns 45 percent of Brazil's only helicopter supplier, Helibras. Pratt & Whitney also has agreed to purchase a 25 percent share of the jet engine division of Kongsberg Vaapenfabrikk, a state-owned Norwegian arms manufacturer. Kongsberg produces components for Pratt & Whitney commercial and military aircraft engines.

UTC rescued a major British defense manufacturer—Westland Helicopters—in 1986 from impending bankruptcy when Sikorsky teamed up with Fiat of Italy and purchased 21 percent of Westland's outstanding stock. The deal was fraught with controversy: A consortium of defense firms from Britain, France, West Germany and Italy sought to keep Westland out of American hands by offering counterbids, but failed. Michael Heseltine, the outspoken British minister of defense, resigned in protest over the Thatcher government's handling of the affair, claiming that the prime minister had manipulated policy so as to favor the UTC-Fiat initiative. Some analysts say Sikorsky was motivated by what the company has referred to as "commercial logic," because it viewed Westland as an appropriate conduit for sales to European allies. They point out that Westland has built and marketed under license four Sikorsky helicopters over the course of more than 30 years and speculate that UTC's partial ownership of Westland and the resulting access to the European market may ease the way for increased exports of Sikorsky helicopters. Indeed, India recently ordered 25 Westland/Sikorsky Advanced Sea King transport aircraft.

III. MILITARY ORDERS, 1982–1986 (includes first quarter of 1987)

Country	Date of Agreement	Description of Order	Price (in millions)
– EUROPE AND MAJOR ALLIES –			
Australia	1985	8 S-70B-2 Seahawk anti-submarine warfare helicopters with weapons and sensors/d,e,f,g,h,r	$159[1]
	1986	14 UH-60 Black Hawk helicopters and 8 additional S-70B-2 Seahawk anti-submarine warfare helicopters/f,g,h	$235
	1987	25 S-70A Black Hawk helicopters/n	$200[2]
	1986	40 modification kits for the TF30 P3 aircraft engine/b	NA
Belgium	(1983)	SH-3D Sea King anti-submarine warfare helicopters/d	NA
Japan[3]	1983	2 SH-60B Seahawk anti-submarine warfare helicopters/d	NA
	1984	1 UH-60A Black Hawk helicopter/d	NA
	(1985)	4 S-65 minesweeping helicopters/d	NA
	1987	45 HH-60A Night Hawk helicopters/h	NA
NATO	1984	Additional funding for TF33-PW-100A engines for E-3A Awacs operations/b	$12.2
Netherlands	1984	Additional funding for F100 engine retrofit kits/b,f	NA[4]
	1985	F100 engines for F-15 and F-16 fighter aircraft/f	NA[5]
New Zealand	1986	Component improvement program for TF-30 and J-52 engines/b	$.2
Spain	1984	6 SH-60B Seahawk LAMPS MK III anti-submarine warfare helicopters/d,e,g	NA[6]
Switzerland	(1983)	3 UH-60A Black Hawk utility helicopters/d	NA
– ASIA AND PACIFIC –			
Brunei	1986	2 S-70C commercial versions of Black Hawk helicopter/d	NA

Country	Date of Agreement	Description of Order	Price (in millions)
Indonesia	1986	12 F100-PW-220 engines for F-16 aircraft/h	$60
	1986	Component improvement program for TF-30 and J-52 engines/b	$.1
People's Republic of China	1984	24 S-70C Black Hawk utility helicopters (commercial version)/d,g	$150
Pakistan	1984	Additional funding for F100 engine retrofit kits/f	NA[4]
	1985	F100 engines for F-16 fighter aircraft/b,f	NA[5]
Philippines	1983	2 UH-60A Black Hawk and 17 S-76 Spirit utility helicopters/d,g	$60
	(1985)	2 S-70C commercial versions of Black Hawk helicopter/d	NA
Singapore	1985	F100 engines for 8 F-16 aircraft/c	$50
South Korea	1985	F100-PW-220 engines for 36 F-16 fighters/f,k	$250
Taiwan	1986	14 S-70C Black Hawk helicopters/d,e	NA[7]
Thailand	1983	4 UH-60 Black Hawk helicopters/d,g	$38
	1986	Additional funding for the component improvement program for the F100 aircraft engine/b	NA

– MIDDLE EAST –

Country	Date of Agreement	Description of Order	Price (in millions)
Egypt	1984	45 F100 engines for F-16 fighter aircraft/b,f,k	NA[5]
Israel	1984	Additional funding for F100 engine retrofit kits/b,f	NA[4]
	1985	Radar systems for F-4 fighter aircraft upgrade/j	NA[8]
Jordan	(1986)	3 S-70A Black Hawk helicopters/h	NA
Kuwait	1986	Component improvement program for TF-30 and J-52 engines/b	$.3
Saudi Arabia	1983	65 TF-33-PW-100A engines/g	$10.9

Country	Date of Agreement	Description of Order	Price (in millions)
	1987	12 UH-60 Black Hawk helicopters and 1 VIP-configured Black Hawk/f	NA[9]
		– AFRICA –	
Cameroon	(1986)	(6) UH-60 Black Hawk helicopters/d	NA
		– LATIN AMERICA –	
Brazil	1984	4 SH-3D Sea King anti-submarine warfare helicopters/e	NA
Peru	1983	8 UH-60A Black Hawk helicopters/e	$110.5
Venezuela	1984	Additional funding for F-100 engine retrofit kits/b,f	NA[4]
	1984	4 SH-3D Sea King anti-submarine warfare helicopters/e	NA
	1985	F100 engines for F-16 aircraft/f	NA[5]

IV. FMS PROGRAM CONTRACT AWARDS, FY 1983–1986
(millions of dollars)

Item	Fiscal Year	Award Total
F100 turbofan engines*	1983	$288.28
	1984	153.44
	1985	286.23
	1986	188.94
TF33 turbofan engines#	1983	11.11
	1984	2.64
	1985	.26
	1986	–9.41
TF30 turbofan engines	1983	6.21
	1984	3.42
	1985	1.61
	1986	5.19
SH-60 Seahawk helicopters	1985	4.50
	1986	23.38

Item	Fiscal Year	Award Total
CH-53 Sea Stallion helicopters	1983	.03
	1984	.70
	1985	-.17
	1986	.17
Maintenance and repair of F-15 fighter aircraft	1983	3.01
	1986	.03
AN/SPS-40 radar systems	1986	2.45
Propellers for C-130 Hercules transport aircraft	1983	.03
	1984	2.88
	1986	-.03
Propellers, structural components and research and development for C-2 transport aircraft	1983	1.34
	1984	.56
	1985	-.37
	1986	1.35
Air conditioning and heating equipment for F-5 fighter aircraft	1983	.07
	1984	1.02
	1985	-.05
	1986	.29
AN/SYS-1 integrated automatic detection and tracking (IADT) data processing systems	1986	.13
SH-3D Sea King helicopters	1986	.05
Air conditioning and heating equipment for E-3A Awacs aircraft	1984	.63
	1985	.09
Research and development, propellers and hand tools for E-2 Hawkeye aircraft	1986	.14
Components and services for F-16 aircraft	1986	.37
Miscellaneous fire control equipment	1984	1.05
Unidentified radar equipment	1985	1.02
Unidentified aircraft engine fuel systems components	1984	.90
	1986	-.45

Item	Fiscal Year	Award Total
Unidentified management services and logistic support	1985	.71
Unidentified aircraft air conditioning and heating equipment	1983 1984	.29 .70
Unidentified guided missile remote control systems	1983 1985	.50 .29+
Technical services for unidentified aircraft engines	1986	.21
Unidentified airframe structural components	1986	.72

Negative figures result from downward contract adjustments.

*   These awards include funds for work conducted in Belgium, the Netherlands, Norway, South Korea, Israel and Venezuela.

These awards include funds for work conducted in Greece.

+   DoD contract data suggest these awards are probably for the MIM-14 Nike Hercules missile.

NOTES

1. All but the first two Seahawks will be assembled from kits in Australia, and Australian industry will produce certain components as part of an offset package worth 30 percent of the import value of the aircraft. This is a commercial sale.

2. Australia has ordered a total of 55 Black Hawk and Seahawk helicopters at a total cost of $600 million.

3. Mitsubishi Heavy Industries of Japan currently is developing a variant of Sikorsky's Seahawk—designated SH-60J—of which Japan plans to procure 36 starting in 1988.

4. Additional funds totaling $10.4 million for 273 F100 engine retrofit kits that were ordered in 1980 will be divided among the Netherlands, Pakistan, Israel and Venezuela.

5. The $404 million package includes 86 F100 engines sold to the U.S. Air Force, the Netherlands, Pakistan, South Korea, Egypt and Venezuela.

6. These helicopters are being assembled in Spain, and Spanish companies are manufacturing some components. SIPRI estimates the cost of this sale is $275 million.

7. This contract includes an option on 10 additional S-70C helicopters.

8. Norden Systems is developing a new radar system for the Israeli F-4 upgrade program. The reported cost of developing and integrating it is close to $500 million, including about $200 million in nonrecurring design and development costs.

9. This is part of a $400 million package deal that includes 15 Bell-Textron model 406 helicopters and 1 Beech C-12 transport aircraft.

WESTINGHOUSE CORP.

I. SUMMARY DATA

Data, except for the total sales figures, are for U.S. government fiscal years, ending Sept. 30. FMS program award totals for 1982 to 1984 were calculated by the General Accounting Office; the 1985 and 1986 totals were calculated by IRRC from Department of Defense contract data.

	1982	1983	1984	1985	1986
Total sales (millions)	$9,745	$9,533	$10,265	$10,700	$10,731
DoD contract awards (millions)	$1,492	$1,778	$ 1,943	$ 1,941	$ 1,713
DoD contractor rank	13	14	13	12	13
DoD awards/total sales	.15	.19	.20	.18	.15
FMS contract awards (millions)	$ 147	$ 194	$ 240	$ 83	$ 204
FMS contractor rank	17	8	6	14	9
FMS/total DoD awards	.10	.11	.12	.04	.12
FMS/total sales	.015	.020	.023	.008	.019

II. ARMS EXPORT BUSINESS AT A GLANCE

Westinghouse's sales of advanced electronic systems—particularly radar equipment—have secured it a position among the nation's top 20 FMS suppliers since 1972. The company's FMS-related DoD prime contract awards dipped to $83 million in fiscal 1985, but quickly rose again to $204 million in fiscal 1986. The 1985 figure, which was 65 percent below the 1984 record of $240 million, represented the first time that Westinghouse's FMS awards had fallen below the $100 million mark since 1980. The company has exported relatively little through direct, company-to-government sales channels.

Westinghouse's most widely exported military systems in recent years have been ground-based air defense radars and an airborne radar and gunnery fire control system that is used in the General Dynamics F-16 aircraft. These fighters are being sold to Bahrain, Belgium, Denmark, the Netherlands, Norway, Israel, Egypt, Pakistan, Venezuela, Korea, Turkey, Greece, Indonesia and Singapore. Awards for F-16 fire control systems accounted for 35 percent of Westinghouse's fiscal 1983 FMS awards, 64 percent of its 1984 awards, 52 percent of its 1985 awards, and 83 percent of its 1986 awards.

Westinghouse also produces the air surveillance radar system used in the NATO and Saudi Arabian Awacs. Its AN/TPS-43 ground-based air defense radar rests at the heart of the Tactical Air Control System (TACS) and the Tactical Air Defense System (TADS)—both of which are popular with overseas customers. Argentina, Australia, Egypt, Greece, Israel, Morocco, Singapore, South Korea, Spain, Taiwan, Thailand and Venezuela have ordered the TADS or related Westinghouse systems. The company entered into a seven year, $190 million agreement with Egypt in September 1985 for the coproduction of its AN/TPS-63 air defense radar system, which already has been delivered to six international customers.

Westinghouse also manufactures systems designed to counter adversaries' radar equipment. It supplies the U.S. and allied nations' armed forces with the AN/ALQ-131 radar jamming device, which is carried by a variety of aircraft. The company received $65.5 million in contract awards in fiscal 1983 through 1985 for AN/ALQ-131 systems. In 1986, Westinghouse entered into a $23 million agreement with Israel for 20 of the radar jamming devices.

III. MILITARY ORDERS, 1982–1986 (includes first quarter of 1987)

Country	Date of Agreement	Description of Order	Price (in millions)
– EUROPE AND MAJOR ALLIES –			
Denmark	1985	Additional funding for AN/APG-66 fire control systems for F-16 fighter aircraft/b	NA[1]
Netherlands	1983	13 AN/ALQ-131 radar-jamming electronic counter measure pods/b,c	$40.8
Spain	1983	2 AN/TPS-43E ground-based air defense radar systems/c	$6.8
Switzerland	1982	1 AN/TPS-70(v)2 mobile ground-based air defense radar system/g,i	NA
Yugoslavia	1983	Funding for 6 AN/TPS-70 mobile ground-based tactical radar systems and spares/b	$39.1
– ASIA AND PACIFIC –			
India	1984	5 transducer arrays for sonar (via Fathom Co. of Canada)/f	$2.8
Indonesia	1986	AN/APG-66 radars for F-16 aircraft/c	NA[2]
South Korea	1986	Additional funding for AN/APG-68 fire control radar systems for F-16 aircraft/b	NA
Thailand	1985	1 AN/TPS-70 mobile ground-based tactical radar system/g	$10
	1986	AN/APG-66 radar systems for F-16 aircraft/f,g	$8.03
– MIDDLE EAST –			
Bahrain	1987	AN/ALQ-131 electronic countermeasure pods for 12 F-16 aircraft/g	NA[3]
Egypt	1985	8 AN/TPS-65 ground-based air search radars/c,e	NA[4]

Country	Date of Agreement	Description of Order	Price (in millions)
	1985	Coproduction of 34 AN/TPS-63 ground-based air defense radar systems/f,g,r	$190
	1987	AN/APG-68 radar systems for 40 F-16 aircraft/g	NA[5]
Israel	1986	20 AN/ALQ-131 airborne electronic countermeasure systems with spares, training and support/f,g,n	$23
	1986	Additional funding for AN/APG-68 fire control radar systems for F-16 aircraft/b	NA
Jordan	1984	Automated air defense system/f,g	NA
Kuwait	1984	Air defense command, control and communication system/g	NA
Saudi Arabia	1983	Additional funding for spare parts for AN/APY-1 radar systems for E-3A Awacs/b	NA[6]
	1985	Additional funding for 1 AN/TPS-43 radar system/b	$9.3
	1985	AN/TPS-43 tactical 3-D radar/d	NA

IV. FMS PROGRAM CONTRACT AWARDS, FY 1983–1986
(millions of dollars)

Item	Fiscal Year	Award Total
AN/APG-66 and -68 gunnery fire control and radar system for F-16 fighter aircraft	1983	$ 52.92
	1984	153.89
	1985	43.60
	1986	169.88
AN/TPS-43 radar system for 407L Tactical Air Control Systems	1983	47.81
	1984	7.18
	1985	22.32
	1986	10.28
AN/ALQ-131 radar jamming systems	1983	35.55
	1984	30.28
	1986	4.13*

Item	Fiscal Year	Award Total
Components, including APY-1 radar systems for E-3A Awacs	1983	20.44
	1984	2.70
	1985	2.53
	1986	2.05
Launchers for, and development, maintenance and repair of Trident II submarine launched ballistic missiles	1984	3.78
	1985	2.08
	1986	6.13
Maintenance and repair of Polaris submarine launched ballistic missiles	1986	2.60
Gunnery fire control equipment for F-111 aircraft	1983	.08
	1984	6.62
Guided missile remote control and maintenance and repair services for F-4 Phantom II fighter aircraft	1983	3.85
	1984	1.18
	1985	.05
	1986	.84
Guided missile remote control system for MIM-23 Hawk surface-to-air missiles	1984	1.73
	1985	.13
	1986	.52
Generators for F-5 fighter aircraft	1983	.56
	1984	.10
	1985	.56
	1986	.30
AN/ALQ-119 radar systems	1986	.76#
AN/TPS-63 radar systems	1986	.17
Unidentified surface-based radar equipment	1983	20.32
	1984	25.18
	1986	2.24
Unidentified generators and generator sets	1983	16.72
Unidentified technical services on electrical systems	1983	.95
	1984	2.65
	1986	1.32x

Item	Fiscal Year	Award Total
Unidentified technical training	1983	1.13
	1984	1.76
	1985	1.58
Unidentified electronic countermeasure equipment	1983	1.91
Unidentified steam turbines and components	1986	.76
Other unidentified awards	1983	1.87
	1984	2.36
	1985	8.91
	1986	1.61

*	These awards include funds for work performed in Pakistan.
#	These awards include funds for work performed in Egypt.
x	These awards include funds for work performed in West Germany, Honduras, the Netherlands, Somalia and Thailand

NOTES

1. This award for $9.0 million is funding for 96 AN/APG-66 fire control systems to be shared with the Netherlands.

2. This is part of a $432 million package including 8 General Dynamics F-16 aircraft, an estimated 72 Ford Sidewinder missiles, Litton AN/ALR-69 radar warning receivers, and Loral AN/ALQ-131 electronic countermeasure instruments.

3. This is a $400 million package including 12 General Dynamics F-16 fighter aircraft, radar warning receivers, chaff/flare dispensers, Hughes Aircraft AGM-65 Maverick air-to-surface missiles, Ford and/or Raytheon AIM-9 Sidewinder air-to-air missiles, and General Dynamics and/or Raytheon AIM-7 Sparrow air-to-air missiles.

4. This is part of a $154 million package that includes four General Electric AN/TPS-59 radar systems.

5. The AN/APG-68 radars are part of a $1.3 billion package for 40 General Dynamics F-16 aircraft, an avionics shop, spares, support and training.

6. This $26.9 million award includes parts to be used by NATO on its Awacs.

Table II-2

Foreign Military Sales: Company Totals
FY 1972–1986

(in millions of current dollars)

Company	1972	1973	1974	1975	1976	1977	1978	1979	1980	1981	1982	1983	1984	1985	1986
Boeing	$18	$95	$31	$129	NA	NA	NA	NA	NA	NA	$395	$899	$461	$1,291	$206
Ex-Cell-O	NA	NA	NA	$31	NA	NA	NA	NA	NA	$122	$28	$3	$18	$13	$34
FMC	$24	$27	$272	$69	$201	NA	$71	$65	$233	$106	$133	$165	$167	$37	$32
Ford	$6	NA	NA	$59	NA	$42	$66	NA	NA	$79	$34	$5	$7	$101	$105
General Electric	$99	$165	$169	$209	$248	$221	$176	$101	$176	$175	$251	$164	$297	$503	$630
General Dynamics	$17	$14	$13	$73	$46	$303	$1,476	$518	$993	$377	$761	$450	$967	$1,231	$1,369
General Motors	$11	$19	$43	$89	$45	NA	$32	$51	$109	$64	$51	$51	$28	$87	$207
Grumman	NA	NA	$42	$298	$304	$253	$70	NA	NA	$116	$–31	$111	$235	$182	$125
Harsco	NA	$21	$30	$33	$61	$40	$64	NA	NA	NA	$16	$10	$48	$1	$53
Honeywell	$49	$12	$20	NA	$55	NA	$33	NA	NA	NA	$20	$8	$29	$16	$91
Hughes Aircraft	$32	$22	$122	$156	$174	$156	$156	$86	$96	$260	$304	$172	$176	$94	$151
Lockheed	$29	$51	$60	$172	$139	$305	$297	$142	$149	$135	$348	$171	$225	$295	$52
LTV	NA	$13	$91	$90	$83	NA	NA	NA	NA	NA	$15	$85	$91	$45	$31
Northrop	$110	$171	$221	$293	$1,293	$853	$267	$639	$471	$1,211	$1,032	$501	$993	$1,616	$574
McDonnell Douglas	$802	$224	$120	$419	$480	$446	$274	$472	$859	$164	$894	$181	$162	$296	$104
Raytheon	$12	$191	$34	$172	$219	$149	$271	$132	$435	$185	$172	$221	$262	$234	$602
Rockwell	$19	$11	$17	$50	$56	NA	NA	NA	NA	NA	$19	$33	$91	$75	$15
Sperry	$6	$10	NA	NA	NA	NA	NA	$75	$73	$84	$91	$52	$108	$74	$6
Teledyne	NA	NA	$33	NA	$27	$21	$27	$53	$109	$86	$111	$91	$50	$124	$33
Textron	NA	$508	$60	$249	$115	$74	$441	NA	NA	NA	$128	$43	$7	$27	$81
United Technologies	NA	NA	NA	$192	$104	$87	$115	$249	$749	$632	$673	$321	$170	$295	$214
Westinghouse	$33	$33	$40	NA	$44	$71	$56	$85	$140	$188	$147	$194	$240	$83	$204

Sources: General Accounting Office; Defense Security Assistance Agency; Investor Responsibility Research Center

Part III
Orders for U.S. Arms by
Region and Country

Part III
Note on Methodology

Part III contains a country by country listing of weapon orders that were placed between 1982 and the first quarter of 1987. With the exception of some of the additional funding awards—which are not orders per se and therefore have been deleted from this section—this listing is a reformulation of the Military Orders sections of the company profiles contained in Part II of this volume.

As noted in the introduction to Part II, the transactions listed represent *orders*, not deliveries. Some of the weapons ordered were delivered almost immediately, but other orders take years to fill. IRRC has tried to identify and delete from this listing any orders that were placed but subsequently canceled.

This listing was compiled from open sources, which are identified by letters that follow the description of the weapon system being ordered. The source code is as follows:

a. Department of Defense, *Prime Contract Awards by Contractor, Unclassified*

b. *News Release*, Office of the Assistant Secretary of Defense for Public Affairs

c. Defense Security Assistance Agency, reports to Congress

d. Stockholm International Peace Research Institute, *World Armaments and Disarmament Yearbook* series

e. International Institute for Strategic Studies, *Military Balance* series

f. *International Defense Review*

g. *Defense and Foreign Affairs*

h. *Aviation Week & Space Technology*

i. *Jane's Weapon Systems*

j. *Defense Electronics*

k. *The Washington Post*

l. *The Wall Street Journal*

m. *The New York Times*

n.   *Defense News*

r.   Company's annual report

These sources were used because no comprehensive government listing of arms sales is available. IRRC attempted to verify all of the orders listed here, but in some instances the companies themselves were unable to confirm—but did not disclaim—the orders. Parentheses have been placed around those dates or numbers of weapon systems ordered where a degree of uncertainty about the accuracy of the data exists.

This compilation is not a complete listing of worldwide orders of American weapons. Many American weapon sales of relatively low dollar value and many of those exported through the direct commercial sales channels were not reported in the sources used for this study. Furthermore, this study includes only those weapon systems manufactured by contractors judged by IRRC to be historically among the top 25 arms-exporting companies. Nevertheless, the vast majority of major arms transfer agreements made between 1982 and the first quarter of 1987 are included herein.

The price given for each order represents the total cost of the transaction. The prices are usually taken from formal notifications to Congress or are estimates by knowledgeable sources. They do not necessarily represent the amount of money that the respective U.S. defense contractors receive for the sale. IRRC has used the symbol "NA" to indicate that reliable estimates were not available. Footnotes often follow either the price listing or the description of the order. These provide important additional information, and should be consulted at the back of each regional section.

Some of the listed sales are package deals that involve several different weapons systems and sometimes multiple contractors. They are listed under the heading of a single year and a single price because breakouts of the prices of the individual components are not available.

The last column of each page provides the name of the prime contractor of the exported equipment. In some cases, abbreviations were used, and the legend reads as follows:

GD	General Dynamics Corp.
GE	General Electric Corp.
GM	General Motors Corp.
Hughes	Hughes Aircraft Co. (now owned by General Motors)
MDC	McDonnell Douglas Corp.
Rayth.	Raytheon Corp.
UTC	United Technologies Corp.

It should be remembered that when weapon systems are exported, a substantial portion of the purchase price goes to subcontractors. Where a particular weapon system is manufactured by two sources and IRRC was unable to determine which company supplied the system in any particular sale, both contractors are listed and divided by a slash mark. In most instances, the name of the contractor given is also the name of the parent firm. Where this is not the case, the name of the parent firm follows in brackets. A symbol "#" that follows the name of the contractor indicates that the weapon systems in question were delivered from U.S. government stock, and that the prime contractor received no money from the sale unless it was contracted to refurbish the weapons in some manner. In many instances, however, the purchasing country will later employ the prime contractor to provide support services for the weapon systems. An asterisk "*" that follows the name of the contractor indicates that the weapon systems were *probably* delivered from U.S. government stock.

– EUROPE AND MAJOR ALLIES –

Date of Order	Description of Order	Price	Contractor
	– Australia –		
1982	2 KC-135 refueling tankers/d,g	NA	Boeing
1984	3 MK 13 guided missile launching systems/b[1]	$39	FMC
1982	1 AN/AVO-26 Pave Tack designator pod for General Dynamics F-111 fighter aircraft/g	NA	Ford
1983	AIM-9 Sidewinder training missiles/c	$4.6	Ford/Raytheon
1984	AIM-9 Sidewinder air-to-air missiles/d,f	NA[2]	Ford/Raytheon
1983	F404-GE-400 engines for McDonnell Douglas F/A-18 fighter aircraft/c[3]	NA	GE
1986	32 F404-GE-400 engines for F/A-18 aircraft/g	$36	GE
1987	37 T700 turboshaft engines/g	NA	GE
1982	7 T56-A14 engines for P-3 maritime patrol aircraft/b	$3.8	GM
1987	Upgrade of shore-based tactical naval trainer/f	NA[4]	Honeywell
1982	7 AN/TPQ-36 mortar locating radar systems and 1 AN/TPQ-36 simulator/c,g	$46	Hughes [GM]
1987	8 AN/APG-65 radars/g	$3.6	Hughes [GM]
1982	10 P-3C Orion antisubmarine/maritime patrol aircraft/d,r	NA	Lockheed
1982	(30) AGM-84A Harpoon air-to-surface missiles/d	NA	MDC
1984	Spares for F/A-18 aircraft	$4.75	MDC
	AN/APG-65 radar systems/f		Hughes [GM]
1986	28 Harpoon anti-ship missiles plus 6 missile bodies without warheads, 2 training missiles and spares/c,d,f,g	$47	MDC

Date of Order	Description of Order	Price	Contractor
1987	15 weapon systems for F/A-18A aircraft and 2 weapon systems for TF/A-18A aircraft/g	$63.9	MDC
1984	AIM-7M Sparrow air-to-air missiles/c,d,f	NA[5]	Raytheon & GD
1985	Equipment for a Sidewinder depot/r	NA	Raytheon
1986	8 avionics suites for Sikorsky S-70B-2 Seahawk helicopters/f	$53	Rockwell
1987	Combat systems for 6 submarines/j	$500	Rockwell
1983	Mk 92 missile fire control system/r	NA	Sperry
1983	2 F/A-18 flight trainers/r	$23	Sperry
1984	Software for Navy destroyer modernization program/b	$11.5	Sperry
1985	8 S-70B-2 Seahawk anti-submarine warfare helicopters with weapons and sensors/d,e,f,g,h,r[6,7]	NA	UTC
1986	14 UH-60 Black Hawk helicopters and 8 additional S-70B-2 Seahawk anti-submarine warfare helicopters/f,g,h	$235	UTC
1986	40 modification kits for the TF30 P3 aircraft engine/b	NA	UTC
1987	25 S-70A Black Hawk helicopters/n	$200	UTC

Austria

1982	24 M109A2 155mm self-propelled howitzers/d,f,g	$22	Harsco

Belgium

1983	200 AIM-9P3 Sidewinder air-to-air missiles/d	NA	Ford
1983	44 F-16 fighter aircraft/c,e,g	$944	General Dynamics
1983	Inertial navigation units for E-3A Awacs/b	NA	GM
1983	124 M109A2 155mm self-propelled howitzers/d,g,r	$110	Harsco
(1983)	SH-3D Sea King anti-submarine warfare helicopters/d	NA	UTC

Date of Order	Description of Order	Price	Contractor
Canada			
1984	416 AIM-9M Sidewinder air-to-air missiles with 56 training missiles/c,e,g	$41	Ford & Raytheon
1984	408 AIM-7 Sparrow air-to-air missiles/c,e,g	$113	GD & Raytheon
1986	4 Standard surface-to-air missile systems for naval destroyers/g	NA	GD
1986	4 Seasparrow surface-to-air missile systems with (80) missiles/d	NA	GD/Raytheon
1987	88 Sparrow air-to-air missiles/c	$17	GD & Raytheon
1984	F404-GE-400 engines for F/A-18 fighter aircraft/b[8]	NA	GE
1984	Engines for destroyers and frigates/r	NA	GM
1983	26 M109A2 155mm self-propelled howitzers/d,r	NA	Harsco
1984	220 Mk 46 mod 5 torpedoes with support equipment/c,e,f	$57	Honeywell
1985	1 DPS-8/70C computer system/g	NA[9]	Honeywell
1985	129 Mk 46 mod 5 torpedoes with support/c,e,g	$30	Honeywell
1986	360 TOW-2 anti-tank missile launchers with 1,800 TOW-2 missiles/d,e,f	NA	Hughes [GM]
1984	2 C-130 Hercules transport aircraft/d,e,f,g[7]	$35.1[10]	Lockheed
1984	34 RGM-84D-4 Harpoon ship-to-surface missiles with 2 training missiles/c,d,e,g	$47	MDC
1984	AN/SPS-49 shipboard air search radar RIM 7-H-2 NATO Sea Sparrow air-to-air missiles/e	$16	Raytheon Raytheon/GD
1985	184 AIM-7M Sparrow air-to-air missiles/e,f	$42	Raytheon & GD
1985	4 AN/DSM-156A guided missile test set for AIM/RIM-7 Sparrow air-to-air and surface-to-air missiles/b	$2.1	Raytheon
1984	High-frequency radio equip./f,r	$11	Rockwell

Date of Order	Description of Order	Price	Contractor
1983	Electronics and weapons systems for Patrol Frigate program/r	$1,100	Sperry
Denmark			
1983	200 AIM-9L Sidewinder air-to-air missiles/c,d	NA	Ford
1984	12 F-16 fighter and trainer aircraft with spares and support/c,d,e,f,g	$210	General Dynamics
1986	336 Stinger-Post portable surface to air missile launchers with 504 missiles/c,d,e,f,g[11]	$65	General Dynamics
1983	33 RGM-84A Harpoon ship-to-surface missiles/c,d,g	$37	MDC
Finland			
(1985)	BGM-71C I-TOW anti-tank missiles/d	NA	Hughes [GM]
1982	2 model 500D utility helicopters/d[12]	NA	MDC Helicopter
France			
1982	Re-engine kits and modification of 11 KC/C-135F aerial refueling tankers/b,g,r[13]	$275	Boeing
1986	4 re-engining kits for KC-135R aircraft/f	NA[14]	Boeing
1987	4 E-3A AWACS surveillance aircraft with ground installations, training and support/d,f,g,n	$550[15]	Boeing
1985	Upgrade of 2 Tartar surface-to-air missile fire control systems/c,f	$58	GE, Raytheon, FMC & Sperry
1983	55 Multiple Launch Rocket Systems/e,j	NA	LTV
Great Britain			
1982	3 Chinook Model 414 heavy lift helicopters/d,r	NA	Boeing
1983	5 Chinook Model 414 heavy lift helicopters/d,f,r	$55	Boeing
1986	6 E-3A Awacs aircraft/d[16]	$1,200	Boeing

Date of Order	Description of Order	Price	Contractor
1982	FIM-92A Stinger portable surface-to-air missiles/d	NA	General Dynamics
1982	3 shipborne Phalanx Mk 15 Close-in Weapon Systems with ammunition and support/c,g	$48	General Dynamics
1983	Design for Trident II nuclear missile submarines/g	$63.8	General Dynamics
1984	12 shipborne Phalanx Mk 15 Close-in Weapon Systems with support and training/e,g	$151	General Dynamics
1985	3 shipborne Phalanx Mk 15 Close-in Weapon Systems with ammunition, spare parts and support/c,e,f,g	$46	General Dynamics
1985	4 shipborne Phalanx Mk 15 Close-in Weapon Systems with support/c,e,f,g	$56	General Dynamics
1986	2 shipborne Phalanx Mk 15 Close-in Weapon Systems with support/c,g	$22	General Dynamics
1984-5	Development fire control system for Trident II submarine-launched ballistic missile/b,f	$40.9	GE
1984	T56 engines as spares for C-130 cargo aircraft/b	NA[17]	GM
1983	23 angle-rate bombing sets for AV-8 Harrier aircraft/b,f	NA[18]	Hughes [GM]
1984	40 angle-rate bombing sets for AV-8 Harrier aircraft/c	NA	Hughes [GM]
1985	29 angle-rate bombing sets for AV-8 Harrier aircraft/c	NA	Hughes [GM]
1986	34 angle-rate bombing sets for AV-8 Harrier aircraft/c	NA	Hughes [GM]
1984	4 L-1011 Tri-Star tanker aircraft/d,e	NA	Lockheed
1982	72 Trident II sea-launched ballistic missiles/d,g	$3,200	Lockheed
1983	4 Multiple Launch Rocket System launchers with 108 practice rockets and training equipment/j	$5.2	LTV

Date of Order	Description of Order	Price	Contractor
1982	20 AGM-84A Harpoon air-to-surface missiles/c	$18.7	MDC
1983	15 F-4J fighter aircraft for conversion to F-4S/d,g	$51	MDC*
1983	60 AGM-84A Harpoon air-to-surface missiles/c	$67.8	MDC
1983	Support for F-4S fighter aircraft/c,g	$58.6	MDC
1984	300 RGM-84A Harpoon ship-to-surface missiles/d,f	NA[19]	MDC
1985	31 UGM-84D Harpoon submarine-to-surface missiles with spares and engineering support/e,f,g	$33	MDC
1983	15 Chukar II target drones/c	$2.4	Northrop
(1984)	Checking equipment for Trident II submarine-launched ballistic missiles/f	$96	Northrop
1985	AIM-9 Sidewinder air-to-air missiles/r	NA	Raytheon
1985	Active optical target detectors for Sidewinder air-to-air missiles/b	$5.2	Raytheon
1985	Equipment for a Sidewinder depot/r	NA	Raytheon
1984	UHF transceivers and components/b	NA	Rockwell
1983	Color displays for Navy intelligence system/r	NA	Sperry
1985	Technical assistance in support of Polaris and Trident submarines/b	$3.3	Sperry
Greece			
1982	2 Chinook Model 414 heavy lift helicopters/e	NA	Boeing
1982	110 M113A2 armored personnel carriers/d	NA	FMC
1983	51 M113A2 armored personnel carriers/d	NA	FMC
1984	300 AIM-9L Sidewinder air-to-air missiles/c,d,f,g	$30	Ford & Raytheon
1982	280 AIM-7M Sparrow air-to-air missiles/d,f,g	$98	GD/Raytheon

Date of Order	Description of Order	Price	Contractor
1983	110 M60A3 main battle tanks/d,g	$186	General Dynamics
1984	2 shipborne Mk 15 Phalanx Close-in Weapon Systems/c,f,g	$40	General Dynamics
1986	2 Phalanx shipborne Close-in Weapon Systems/c,d	$26	General Dynamics
1986	200 M48A1 tanks and 300 M48A5 tanks without communications equipment, machine guns or other support/d,g	$138	General Dynamics
1987	4 Phalanx shipborne Close-in Weapon Systems with spare parts and engineering support/d,f,g ·	$56	General Dynamics
1987	34 F-16C and 6 F-16D fighter aircraft/f,g[20]	$940	General Dynamics
1983	TF41 engine component improvement program/b,g	$5.4	GM
1983	6 TF41 engines for A-7 aircraft/b	$14.0	GM
1982	48 M109A2 155mm self-propelled howitzers/d,f,g,r	$47	Harsco
1987	23 Command Post Vehicles/n[2]	$30.5	Harsco
(1982)	579 BGM-71 TOW anti-tank missiles/c,e	NA	Hughes [GM]
1984	1,097 BGM-71 I-TOW anti-tank missiles with 54 launchers/c,d,f,g	$19	Hughes [GM]
1982	32 RGM-84A-3 Harpoon ship-to-surface missiles/e,g	$32	MDC
1986	32 Harpoon anti-ship missiles with containers and spares/c,d,f,g	$43	MDC
1982	280 AIM-7E Sparrow air-to-air missiles/d	NA	Raytheon
1984	50 AIM-7E Sparrow air-to-air missiles/b	$12.8	Raytheon
Italy			
1983	150 FIM-92A Stinger portable surface-to-air missile launchers with 450 missiles/c,d,e,g	$51	General Dynamics
1982	4 LM 2500 gas turbine engines for naval cruisers/f	NA	GE

Date of Order	Description of Order	Price	Contractor
1984	Upgrade of 2 Tartar shipborne weapon systems/c	$94[21]	GE, FMC, & Raytheon
1984	1,421 BGM-71 I-TOW anti-tank missiles/c,d,f	$57	Hughes [GM]
1983	Multiple Launch Rocket Systems/j	NA	LTV
1984	4 DE 1164 and DE 1167 LF shipboard sonar systems/f	$6.1	Raytheon

Japan

Date of Order	Description of Order	Price	Contractor
1984	3 Chinook Model 414 heavy lift helicopters/d,e,f,r[22]	NA	Boeing
1983	Mk 13 guided missile launching systems/b[23]	$26	FMC
1982	20 FIM-92A Stinger portable surface-to-air missile launchers with 100 missiles/d,g	NA	General Dynamics
1982	3 shipborne Mk 15 Phalanx Close-in Weapon Systems	$50	General Dynamics
	3 Harpoon anti-ship missiles/g		MDC
1983	FIM-92A Stinger portable surface-to-air missile systems/c	$5.6	General Dynamics
1985	3 shipborne Phalanx Mk 15 Close-in Weapon Systems/c,e,f,g,j	$41	General Dynamics
1986	6 Phalanx shipborne Close-in Weapon Systems with spares and support/c,d,f,g	$70	General Dynamics
1986	Stinger portable surface-to-air missiles/c	$11.9	General Dynamics
1986	Standard (SM-1) surface-to-air missiles/c	$9.7	General Dynamics
1983	8 T56 engines apiece for E-2, P-3 and C-130 aircraft/b	$9.2	GM
1983	Final assembly of 4 E-2C early warning aircraft/b[24]	$102	Grumman
1984	12 M110A2 203mm self-propelled howitzers/d[25]	NA	Harsco
1984	1 Mk 540 model 3 torpedo system test set with ancillary services and supplies/b	NA	Honeywell

Date of Order	Description of Order	Price	Contractor
1983	AN/SPS-52C air surveillance radar systems/g	$103	Hughes [GM]
	Phalanx Close-in Weapon systems		General Dynamics
	100 AIM-7F Sparrow air-to-air missiles/c,g		Raytheon
1983	9 BGM-71A TOW anti-tank missile systems/d[26]	NA	Hughes [GM]
1986	BGM-71A TOW anti-tank missiles/c	$2.5	Hughes [GM]
1986	1 AN/SPS-52C shipborne radar/g	$8.7	Hughes [GM]
1982	2 C-130 Hercules transport aircraft/d,f,g[27]	$26	Lockheed
1982	4 C-130 Hercules transport aircraft/d	$26.6	Lockheed
1984	2 C-130 Hercules transport aircraft/c,e,f	$51	Lockheed
1985	Co-production of 30 P-3C Orion maritime patrol aircraft/g	NA	Lockheed
1986	2 C-130H Hercules transport aircraft with spares and data/c,d,g	$55	Lockheed#
1986	Stationkeeping equipment for C-1 transport aircraft/g	$2.2	LTV
1982	6 AGM-84A Harpoon air-to-surface missiles/c	$6.6	MDC
1983	24 AGM-84A Harpoon air-to-surface missiles with spare parts/c,g	$25	MDC
1984	14 F-15J fighter aircraft with a license agreement to produce an additional 86 F-15Js in Japan/r	NA	MDC
1985	License granted for the production of an additional 55 F-15J fighters/g,r[28]	NA	MDC
1986	38 Harpoon missiles with containers, spares and support/c,d,g	$47	MDC
1984	MIM-104 Patriot air defense system comprising 24 batteries with 130 missile launchers plus 2 training units/d,e,g,h,r	NA[29]	Raytheon
1986	Aegis air defense system for naval destroyer/n,r	NA	RCA [GE]
1984	Radio, antennas and engineering services/b	$10.3	Rockwell

Date of Order	Description of Order	Price	Contractor
1982	8 AN/ASQ-114 avionics computers for P-3 patrol aircraft/b	NA	Sperry
1983	Computer software for destroyer combat direction system/b	$4.8	Sperry
1983	5 Head-up displays and 2 test sets for AH-1S Cobra attack helicopters/c	$1	Textron
1984	1 UH-1H Iroquois transport helicopter/d	NA	Textron#
1983	2 SH-60B Seahawk anti-submarine warfare helicopters/d[30]	NA	UTC
1984	1 UH-60A Black Hawk helicopter/d	NA	UTC
(1985)	4 S-65 minesweeping helicopters/d	NA	UTC
1987	45 HH-60A Night Hawk helicopters/h	NA	UTC

Luxembourg

1986	22 M998 Hummer multi-purpose wheeled vehicles/g	NA	LTV

NATO

1983	Flight data recorders and data playback units for Awacs aircraft/r	NA	Lockheed
1984	190 AIM-7M Sparrow air-to-air missiles/b	NA	Raytheon
1984	1,845 guidance and control sets for AIM-7 Sparrow air-to-air missiles/f	$250[31]	Raytheon/GD
1983-4	Radio systems and spares for E-3A Awacs and Air Force Satellite Communications System/b	NA[32]	Rockwell
1984	TF33-PW-100A engines for E-3A Awacs operations/b	NA	UTC

The Netherlands

1983	900 AIM-9L Sidewinder air-to-air missiles/d	$78	Ford/Raytheon
1982	646 FIM-92A Stinger portable surface-to-air missiles/d	NA	General Dynamics
1982	57 F-16 fighter aircraft/d,e,r	NA[33]	General Dynamics

Date of Order	Description of Order	Price	Contractor
(1983)	(48) RIM-24 Tartar shipborne surface-to-air missiles/d	NA	General Dynamics
1985	78 Standard (SM-1) RIM-66 shipborne surface-to-air missiles/e,f,g	$32	General Dynamics
1986	AN/ASA-70 tactical data display groups for P-3 Orion aircraft/b	NA	General Dynamics
1986	99 MK46 torpedoes in containers with spares and support/c,g	$26	Honeywell
(1984)	AN/TPQ-37 Firefinder artillery locating radar systems/r	NA	Hughes [GM]
1985	2,477 BGM-71D TOW-2 anti-tank missiles/g,l	$32	Hughes [GM]
1987	1,878 BGM-71 TOW-2 anti-tank missiles/d,g	$22	Hughes [GM]
1986	4 AN/TPQ-37 weapon-locating radar sets with spares and support/c,d,f,g	$45	Hughes [GM]
1986	21 multiple launch rocket systems with 2,700 M77 rocket pods, 31 practice pods and 34 rocket pod trainers, plus support/c,d,f,g,n	$192	LTV
1986	8 Harpoon missile systems including 25 Harpoon anti-ship missiles with containers, 1 exercise section, and spares/c,d,f,g	$37	MDC
1984	Patriot air defense system comprising 160 MIM-104 Patriot surface-to-air missiles and 20 missile launchers plus 4 AN/MPQ-53 radar sets/d,e,g,r	$333	Raytheon
1985	RIM-7H-2 NATO Seasparrow surface-to-air missiles/r	NA	Raytheon
1985	Active optical target detectors for Sidewinder air-to-air missiles/b	$2.1	Raytheon
1982	3 AN/ASQ-114 avionics computers for P-3 patrol aircraft/b	NA	Sperry
1985	F100 engines for F-16 fighter aircraft/f	NA	UTC
1983	13 AN/ALQ-131 radar-jamming electronic counter measure pods/b,c	$40.8	Westinghouse

Date of Order	Description of Order	Price	Contractor
	New Zealand		
1986	Mk46-2 torpedoes/c	$2.4	Honeywell
1983	1 P-3B Orion anti-submarine maritime patrol aircraft/d,g	NA	Lockheed
1985	6 P-3C Orion anti-submarine maritime patrol aircraft/d,g	NA	Lockheed#
	Norway		
1986	16 M113 armored personnel carriers/d,e	NA	FMC
1986	2 F-16 aircraft to replace those lost by attrition/c	$30	General Dynamics
1984	Low Altitude Surveillance Radar Systems/f,r	$18	Hughes [GM]
1986	2 P-3C Orion surveillance aircraft/d,n	$42	Lockheed
1983	30 MIM-23 I-Hawk surface-to-air missiles with support and overhaul equipment/c,d,f,g	NA[34]	Raytheon
1986	2 Hawk surface-to-air missile batteries/g	$28.2	Raytheon
	Portugal		
1986	5 Chaparral surface-to-air missile systems with 66 missiles/d,g	$45[35]	Ford
1986	3 Phalanx shipborne Close-in Weapon Systems/d	NA	General Dynamics
1986	6 LM 2500 gas turbine engines for 3 guided missile frigates	$216	GE
	3 Harpoon anti-ship missile systems with 24 missiles		McDonnell Douglas
	3 Seasparrow surface-to-air missile systems with 24 missiles		Raytheon
	6 Mk 32 torpedo tubes		U.S.G
	3 AN/SLQ-25 torpedo countermeasure sets/c,d,g		Aerojet
1987	10 M163A1 Vulcan 20 mm self-propelled air defense guns with support and spares/g	$18	GE

Date of Order	Description of Order	Price	Contractor
1982	AGM-65 Maverick air-to-surface missiles/c	$2.6	Hughes [GM]
1985	6 P-3B Orion antisubmarine/maritime patrol aircraft/e	NA	Lockheed
1983	24 modernized A-7P Corsair-2 attack and 6 TA-7P trainer aircraft/c,d,r	$143.6	LTV
(1983)	(20) F-5E Tiger II fighter aircraft/d	NA	Northrop
Spain			
1985	6 Chinook Model 414 heavy lift helicopters/d,e,f,r	$80	Boeing
1985	2 converted B-707 aerial refueling tankers/r	NA	Boeing
1983	11 LVTP-7-A1 amphibious landing vehicles and 2 LVTC-7-A1 amphibious command vehicles/d,g	$16	FMC
1983	12 F404-GE-400 engines for McDonnell Douglas F/A-18 fighter aircraft/g[36]	NA	GE
1984	39 25 mm gun systems for McDonnell Douglas AV-8 Harrier fighters/b	NA	GE
1986	37 F404-GE-400 engines for F/A-18 aircraft/g	$35.7	GE
1987	200 Bushmaster 25 mm automatic cannons/g	$9	GE
1982	(72) Standard (SM-2) RIM-67 shipborne surface-to-air missiles/d	NA	General Dynamics
(1983)	AIM-7F Sparrow air-to-air missiles/d	NA	GD/Raytheon
1984	Angle-rate bombing sets/c	NA	Hughes [GM]
1983	4 P-3A Orion antisubmarine/maritime patrol aircraft/d,g	NA	Lockheed
1986	1 C-130 Hercules transport aircraft/c	$19.7	Lockheed
1982	15 AGM-84A Harpoon air-to-surface missiles/d,g	$18	MDC
1982	12 AV-8 Harrier V/STOL fighter aircraft with spares and support/c,d,f,g	$379	MDC

Date of Order	Description of Order	Price	Contractor
(1983)	Computer software and cockpits for AV-8 Harrier fighter aircraft simulators/f,j	$5.1	MDC
1983	(24) RGM-84A Harpoon ship-to-surface missiles/d	NA	MDC
1983	12 Harpoon shipboard equipment sets and spares/g	$29	MDC
1983	73 F/A-18A and 8 F/A-18B fighter aircraft and 3 maintenance trainer aircraft/c,d,g,h	$2,700[37]	MDC
1985	25 RGM-84 Harpoon ship-to-surface missiles/c,f,g,h	$27	MDC
1985	50 RGM-84 Harpoon ship-to-surface missiles/e	$47	MDC
1985	Spares for 33 F/A-18 fighter aircraft/c	$82	MDC
1987	20 Harpoon anti-ship missiles with 2 ATM-84 Harpoon ballistic air test vehicles, plus containers, spares, support and training/d,g	$26	MDC
1987	17 EF-18A and 4 EF-18B weapon systems/g	$90.6	MDC
1987	200 25mm Bushmaster automatic cannons/n	$9	MDC Helicopter
1986	Electro-optical tracking equipment for Hawk surface-to-air missile systems/f	NA	Northrop
1985	AN/SPS-49 radar system/b	NA	Raytheon
1984	Management services for Navy carrier and frigate combat system development/b	$39.1	Sperry
1986	100 PC-IT microprocessors/f	NA[38]	Sperry
1984	6 SH-60B Seahawk LAMPS MK II anti-submarine warfare helicopters/d,e,g	NA[39]	UTC
1983	2 AN/TPS-43E ground-based air defense radar systems/c	$6.8	Westinghouse

Sweden

1984	(960) AIM-9L Sidewinder air-to-air missiles/d	($75)	Ford/Raytheon

Date of Order	Description of Order	Price	Contractor
1986	25mm cartridges for M791, M792 and M793 guns/g	$25.4	Ford
1982	570-K diesel engines for 3 fast patrol boats/f	NA	GM
1984	508 BGM-71D TOW-2 anti-tank missiles/d	NA	Hughes [GM]
1982	10 model 300C utility helicopters/d,g[12,40]	NA	MDC Helicopter
1985	16 model 300C training helicopters/d	NA[41]	MDC Helicopter
1985	Active optical target detectors for Sidewinder air-to-air missiles/b	$2.6	Raytheon
1985	Development of portable, shore-defense version of the Hellfire missile/h,r	$8	Rockwell
1987	700 Hellfire missiles adapted for shore defense/n	$65	Rockwell

Switzerland

Date of Order	Description of Order	Price	Contractor
1982	381 AGM-65A Maverick air-to-surface missiles/c,d	$31.8	Hughes [GM]
1985	BGM-71 TOW-2 anti-tank missiles/c,e,f,g	NA[42]	Hughes [GM]
(1985)	30 model 300C utility helicopter/d	NA	MDC Helicopter
1984	3 UH-1H Iroquois transport helicopters/d	NA	Textron#
(1983)	3 UH-60A Black Hawk utility helicopters/d	NA	UTC
1982	1 AN/TPS-70(v)2 mobile ground-based air defense radar system/g,i	NA	Westinghouse

Turkey

Date of Order	Description of Order	Price	Contractor
1986	15 T-55-L-13B engine kits/g	$7.3	Avco
1983	2 Citation II utility aircraft/d,g[12]	$6	Cessna [GD]
1985	760 M48A5 conversion kits/c	$206[43]	Ex-Cell-O
1982	750 AIM-9P3 Sidewinder air-to-air missiles/c,d,g	$50	Ford
(1983)	FIM-92A Stinger portable surface-to-air missiles/d	NA	General Dynamics
1983	160 F-16 fighter aircraft/d,e,g	$4,000[44]	General Dynamics

Date of Order	Description of Order	Price	Contractor
(1983)	(320) AIM-7M Sparrow air-to-air missiles/d	NA	GD/Raytheon
(1986)	(4) Seasparrow surface-to-air, shipborne missile systems/d	NA	GD/Raytheon
1986	590 conversion kits for M48A1 tanks/g	$71	General Dynamics
1986	760 conversion kits for M48A1 tanks/e,g	$206	General Dynamics
(1985)	18 S-2E Tracker anti-submarine warfare aircraft/d	NA	Grumman
1986	Mk 46 mod 5 Neartip torpedoes/b	NA	Honeywell
(1983)	(48) BGM-71A TOW anti-tank missiles/d	NA	Hughes [GM]
1986	6 AN/TPQ-36 radar sets with communications equipment and support/d,f,g	$27	Hughes [GM]
1983	(48) RGM-84 Harpoon ship-to-surface missiles/d	NA	MDC
1984	15 F-4E Phantom fighter aircraft/c,d,f	$70	MDC#
(1982)	10 model 300C utility helicopters/d[12]	NA	MDC Helicopter
(1985)	(6) F-5B fighter aircraft/d	NA	Northrop
1982	15 UH-1H Iroquois transport helicopters/b,d,e,f	$34	Textron
1983	6 AH-1S Cobra TOW attack helicopters/d,e,g	$50	Textron#
1983	Components for UH-1H Iroquois transport helicopters/d,g	$27	Textron
1985	Components and sub-assemblies for 15 UH-1H helicopters/c	$33	Textron

West Germany

1983	3 CF-34 engines/c	$4	GE
1983	75,000 FIM-92A Stinger and advanced Stinger-POST portable surface-to-air missiles/g[45]	$200	General Dynamics
1985	110 Standard (SM-1) RIM-66 shipborne surface-to-air missiles/c,d,e,f	$44	General Dynamics

Date of Order	Description of Order	Price	Contractor
1986	(2) Seasparrow surface-to-air missile systems with (48) missiles/d	NA	GD/Raytheon
1986	(80) M109A2 155mm self-propelled howitzers/d	NA	Harsco
1986	Airborne reconnaissance linescanner systems/n	$60	Honeywell
1982	455 AGM-65B Maverick air-to-surface missiles/d,f,g	$50	Hughes [GM]
1985	310 AGM-65B Maverick air-to-surface missiles/c,e,g	$25	Hughes [GM]
1983	2 Multiple Launch Rocket System launchers with training equipment/c,j	$6.5	LTV
1986	(4) RGM-84A Harpoon anti-ship missile systems with (48) missiles/d	NA	MDC
1985	MIM-104 Patriot air defense system composed of 14 batteries of 100 surface-to-air missile launcher stations 779 missiles and support/c,d,e	$1,149	Raytheon
1986	Spare parts for Patriot air defense missile systems/f	$67	Raytheon

Yugoslavia

1983	6 AN/TPS-70 mobile ground-based tactical radar systems and spares/b	NA	Westinghouse

NOTES

1. This $39 million transaction is a continuation of an agreement concluded earlier with the government of Australia.

2. The reported cost of this transaction is 5 million Australian dollars.

3. Australia ordered a total of 75 F/A-18 fighter aircraft in 1981 at a reported price of $2.4 billion.

1. Honeywell of Australia received this contract valued at 1.8 million Australian dollars.

5. The reported price of this transaction is 21 million Australian dollars.

6. Reports of the cost of these helicopters conflict. *Aviation Week & Space Technology* and *International Defense Review* put the price of the eight Seahawks ordered in 1985 at $159 million. The remaining sources report the price as $219 million. All but the first two Seahawks will be assembled from kits in Australia, and Australian industry will produce certain components as part of an offset package worth 30 percent of the import value of the aircraft. When Australia ordered these helicopters, it was presented with an option for an additional 24, and *Aviation Week & Space Technology* reports that Australia placed a $235 million order in the spring of 1986 for eight additional S-70B-2 Seahawks and 14 UH-60 Black Hawk helicopters.

7. This is a direct company-to-government commercial sale.

8. Canada ordered 138 McDonnell Douglas F/A-18 fighters in 1980.

9. This contract with the Canadian Defense Research Establishment is estimated to be worth 6 million Canadian dollars.

10. Spares, training and miscellaneous items were included in the contract price.

11. SIPRI reports that a final decision on this order was postponed until 1987.

12. These are commercially configured systems that frequently fulfill military roles.

13. The 11 French air force KC-135s are being re-engined at Boeing's Wichita, Kansas, plant. The original Pratt & Whitney powerplants are being replaced with CFM-56-2 engines, which are produced jointly by General Electric and SNECMA of France. The replacement program reportedly will be completed by 1987-88.

14. This is part of a $151.7 million contract that includes 43 re-engining kits for the U.S. Air Force KC-135R aircraft.

15. This contract includes an option on two more E-3A aircraft. The negotiated price of the first three Awacs sale is $550 million, but analysts predict that France will ultimately spend between $800 million and $1 billion on its airborne early warning aircraft system. France plans to spend an additional $212 million on communications, electronic warfare, and electronic counter-countermeasure systems that are not included as standard equipment on the basic Awacs. A value-added tax of 18.6 percent and a customs duty fee of 6.4 percent reportedly will increase the cost of the importation of the three aircraft by $191 million. Finally, the French air force will refurbish the airfield where its Awacs will eventually be based, and will create a logistics-maintenance center there.

16. This sale includes an option on two additional Awacs. If the option is exercised, the total cost of the sale will increase to $1.47 billion.

17. This is under a $6.6 million contract award that combines purchases for Great Britain and the U.S. Air Force.

18. This $15.7 million award was divided equally between Great Britain and the U.S. Marine Corps.

19. The reported price of this agreement is 130 million British pounds.

20. Included in this sale is an option on 20 additional F-16s.

21. Vitro Corp. is also a contractor on this $94 million program.

22. In 1984, a licesning agreement was signed with **Kawasaki Heavy Industries of Japan** for the coproduction of the Model 414 Chinook. The Japanese Defense Agency plans to purchase an additional 51 Chinooks that will be produced jointly by **Kawasaki and Boeing.**

23. This $26 million transaction is a continuation of an agreement concluded earlier with the government of Japan.

24. Japan ordered 4 E-2Cs in 1979 which Grumman finished assembling in 1983.

25. This order might be increased, and might eventually lead to a coproduction agreement.

26. The licensed production of TOW missiles began in 1985.

27. SIPRI reports that the government of Japan is purchasing a total of 18 C-130 Hercules transport aircraft.

28. Japan will produce a total of 141 F-15Js in addition to the 14 it initially purchased from McDonnell Douglas.

29. All but the first installment of Patriots will be produced under license by Mitsubishi Heavy Industries of Japan. The first order—worth $132 million for 20 launchers and 40 missiles—has been placed. Japan will procure 20 launchers and 80 missiles annually from 1986 through 1991, and the total program is estimated to cost $4 billion.

30. Mitsubishi Heavy Industries of Japan currently is developing a variant of Sikorsky's Seahawk—designated SH-60J—of which Japan plans to procure 36 starting in 1988.

31. Some of these sets are destined for the U.S. Navy and Air Force and for four non-NATO countries: Australia, Egypt, Israel and Taiwan.

32. These involve three contract awards split among NATO, the U.S. Air Force and other countries. The awards totaled $13.6 million.

33. The Netherlands has purchased a total of 213 F-16s.

34. Estimates of the price of this transaction vary. U.S. government documents put the price at $48.6 million, *International Defense Review* at $80 million and *Defense and Foreign Affairs* at $61 million.

35. This sale consists of 5 Chaparral M48A2 aerial intercept fire unit launcher stations, 66 MIM-72 Chaparral missiles, 2 AN/MPQ-54 FAAR radar systems, spares and support.

36. GE is supplying F-404 engines for the 84 F/A-18 fighters Spain agreed to purchase in 1982.

37. Some sources list the total price of this agreement at a minimum of $3 billion.

38. This sale is valued at 150 million Spanish pesetas.

39. These helicopters are being assembled in Spain, and Spanish companies are manufacturing some components. SIPRI estimates the cost of this sale is $275 million.

40. Schweizer Aircraft Co. of Elmira, N.Y., manufactures the piston powered 300C under a license issued by Hughes/McDonnell Douglas Helicopter in 1983.

41. The total cost of this transaction is $20 million Swedish krone.

42. The $209 million purchase price includes 400 AN/TAS-4A night sight systems.

43. Ex-Cell-O is one of three prime contractors working on this $206 million contract.

44. Eight U.S. manufactured F-16B two-seat trainers were delivered to Turkey in 1984. Thirty-two F-16s will be assembled in Turkey from kits shipped from the United States during 1985 and 1986. The licensed coproduction of the remaining 24 F-16 trainers and 96 fighters will begin in 1988, with the Turkish government owning 51 percent of the coproduction facilities and General Dynamics owning the rest. General Dynamics said in its 1983 annual report that the transaction "should result in sales of more than $3 billion."

45. This transaction encompasses a coproduction agreement between the United States and West Germany. The Stinger-POST is an advanced version of the basic Stinger with a more sophisticated guidance system.

– MIDDLE EAST –

Date of Order	Description of Order	Price	Contractor
	Bahrain		
1986	54 M60A3 tanks with communications equipment, spares, and support/c,d,e,f,g	$90	General Dynamics
1987	12 F-16C/D fighters	$400	GD
	AIM-9 Sparrow air-to-air missiles		GD/Raytheon
	AIM-9 Sidewinder air-to-air missiles		Ford/Raytheon
	AGM-65 Maverick air-to-surface missiles		Hughes [GM]
	AN/ALQ-131 electronic countermeasure systems/c,f,g		Westinghouse
1987	F110-GE-100 engines for F-16 fighter aircraft/h	NA	GE
1984	2 Harpoon anti-ship missile systems with (24) missiles/d	NA	McDonnell Douglas
1985	4 F-5E and 2 F-5F Tiger II fighter aircraft/c,e,f,g	$114	Northrop
	60 AIM-9P3 Sidewinder air-to-air missiles		Ford
1985	6 F-5E/F fighter aircraft	$92	Northrop
	15 J-85 jet engines/c,f,g		GE
1982	2 model 412ST Super Transport helicopters/e[1]		Textron
	Egypt		
1985	10 T-55 turbine engines for Boeing Model 414 Chinook heavy lift helicopters/g	NA	Avco [Textron]
1985	6 model 1900C utility aircraft modified for special missions/f,r	$73	Beech [Raytheon]
(1986)	Commando Scout reconnaissance armored cars/d	$22.8	Ex-Cell-O [Textron]

Date of Order	Description of Order	Price	Contractor
1984	354 M113A2 armored personnel carriers 13 M577A2 command post vehicles 19 M125A2 mortar carriers 23 M113A2 armored ambulances 43 M806E1 armored recovery vehicles/d,f,g	$157[2]	FMC
1987	90 M113 armored personnel carriers with communications equipment, armament, spares and tools/d,f,g	$27	FMC
1984	450 MIM-72F Chaparral surface-to-air missiles/d,e,g	$160	Ford
1986	560 AIM-9 Sidewinder air-to-air missiles/d,e,g	$42	Ford & Raytheon
1982	220 M60A3 main battle tanks	$426	General Dynamics
	23 M88A1 armored recovery vehicles/d,g,r		Harsco
1982	34 F-16C fighter and 6 F-16D trainer aircraft/d,e,g,r[3]	$1,460	General Dynamics
1984	Design, construction and management of a main battle tank repair depot/r	NA	General Dynamics
1985	94 M60A3 main battle tanks with thermal sights and machine guns/c,d,e,g,r	$165	General Dynamics
1985	36 M60A3 main battle tanks with thermal sights and machine guns/c	$68	General Dynamics
1986	Additional funding for an Avionics Intermediate Shop (AIS) to test F-16 radar and electronic countermeasure systems/b	NA	General Dynamics
1986	Contract for operation and maintenance of 5 air force bases/g	$12.9	General Dynamics
1986	One year extension to a contract for F-16 oriented training and support services for the Egyptian Air Force/b	$4.2	General Dynamics
1986	Missile parts and base support/f	$21	General Dynamics
1987	40 F-16C/D fighters with an avionics shop and support	$1300	General Dynamics
	AN/APG-68 radar systems/f,g		Westinghouse

Date of Order	Description of Order	Price	Contractor
1987	282 Sparrow AIM-7 air-to-air missiles and 514 Sparrow ground-to-air missiles/c,h	$190	GD & Raytheon
1986	1 AN/TPS-59 3-D tactical radar/d	NA	GE
1987	F110-GE-100 engines for F-16 fighter aircraft/h,n	NA	GE
1985	T56 engines for various aircraft/b	NA	GM
1982	4 E-2C Hawkeye early warning aircraft/c,d,e,g	$465	Grumman
1984	1 E-2C Hawkeye early warning aircraft/c,g	$50	Grumman
1986	Data for Identification Friend or Foe electronic surveillance systems/f	$9.2	Grumman
1982	M109A2 155mm self-propelled howitzers	NA[4]	Harsco
1983	Command post vehicles/r	NA	Harsco
1984	56 M88A1 armored recovery vehicles/c,d,f,g	$63	Harsco
1985	48 M109A2 155 mm self-propelled howitzers/d	NA	Harsco
1984	First phase of a national air defense system/f,r	$210	Hughes [GM]
1985	2 AN/TPQ-37 Firefinder artillery locating radar systems with support equipment/e	$24	Hughes [GM]
1982	F-4 Phantom fighter aircraft/c[5]	$7	McDonnell Douglas
1983	16 RGM-84D Harpoon surface-to-ship missiles/d,g	$40	McDonnell Douglas
1984	Hawk air defense missile system upgrade/c,f,g	$63	Northrop & Raytheon
1982	I-Hawk air defense system equipment/c	$11	Raytheon
1982	4 Hawk air defense batteries comprised of 24 missile launchers and 72 MIM-23B Hawk surface-to-air missiles/d	$20	Raytheon
1983	300 AIM-9L Sidewinder air-to-air missiles/d,g	NA	Raytheon
1983	2 AN-SQS-56 (DE 1167) sonar systems/f,g	$9	Raytheon

Date of Order	Description of Order	Price	Contractor
1984	424 AIM-7F Sparrow air-to-air missiles plus 22 training missiles, spares and support/c,d,f,g	$96	Raytheon
1986	GBU-15 glide bombs/b	NA	Rockwell
1984	45 F100 engines for F-16 fighter aircraft/b,f,k	NA[6]	UTC
1985	8 AN/TPS-65 ground-based air search radars	$154	Westinghouse
	4 AN/TPS-59 radars/c,e		GE
1985	Co-production of 34 AN/TPS-63 ground-based air defense radar systems/f,g,r	$190	Westinghouse

Iraq

Date of Order	Description of Order	Price	Contractor
1983	30 model 500D utility helicopters and 30 model 300C utility helicopters/h[1,7]	$25	MDC Helicopter
1985	24 model 530F helicopters/g,h[1,7]	NA	MDC Helicopter
1985	45 model 214ST Super Transport helicopters/e,l[1]	$275	Textron

Israel

Date of Order	Description of Order	Price	Contractor
1983	200 AIM-9L Sidewinder air-to-air missiles/d,g	$16	Ford/Raytheon
1983	75 F-16C fighter aircraft/c,d,e,f,g,r	$2,500[8]	General Dynamics
1984	150 AIM-7M Sparrow air-to-air missiles/c,d,g	$52	GD/Raytheon
1983	22 wing and vertical tail shipsets for Lavi fighters/h,r	$120	Grumman
1985	Upgraded, M109A5 155 mm self-propelled howitzers/r[9]	NA	Harsco
1987	7 AN/TPQ-37 Firefinder artillery locating radar systems/c	NA[10]	Hughes [GM]
1983	6 model 500MD Defender scout helicopters/c	$5.4	MDC helicopter

Date of Order	Description of Order	Price	Contractor
1982	200 MIM-23B Hawk surface-to-air missiles/d,g	$47	Raytheon
1983–5	GBU-15 guided weapon system/b,c	NA[11]	Rockwell
6/85	Spares and support for installation of AN/ARC-190 radio/b	$1.2	Rockwell
1985	Receiver transmitters for the APX 101 Identification Friend or Foe system for F-16 fighter aircraft/b	NA	Teledyne
1986	25 AH-1 Cobra attack helicopters/d,g	Free lease	Textron
1985	Radar systems for F-4 fighter aircraft upgrade/j	NA[12]	UTC
1986	20 ANL/ALQ-131 airborne electronic countermeasure systems with spares, training and support/f,g,n	$23	Westinghouse

Jordan

Date of Order	Description of Order	Price	Contractor
1982	(192) BGM-71A TOW anti-tank missiles for 24 AH-1S helicopters/d	NA	Hughes [GM]
1982	4 AN/TPQ-36 mortar locating radar systems/c	NA	Hughes [GM]
(1983)	(60) AGM-65C Maverick air-to-surface missiles/d	NA	Hughes [GM]
1984	AN/TPQ-37 Firefinder artillery locating radar systems/r	NA	Hughes [GM]
1982	2 C-130 Hercules transport aircraft/d[14]	$28.1[13]	Lockheed
1984	Hawk air defense missile system upgrade/c,f,g	$70	Northrop & Raytheon
1982	24 AH-15 Cobra attack helicopters/d	NA	Textron
(1986)	3 S-70A Black Hawk helicopters/h	NA	UTC
1984	Automated air defense system/f,g	NA	Westinghouse

Kuwait

Date of Order	Description of Order	Price	Contractor
1984	20 V-150 Commando armored cars	$40	Ex-Cell-O
	62 V-300 Commando armored cars/d,e		[Textron]

Date of Order	Description of Order	Price	Contractor
1982	188 M113A2 armored personnel carriers/d,e	NA	FMC
1982	16 M113A2 armored personnel carriers/d,e,g	$97	FMC
	4,010 BGM-71 I-TOW anti-tank missiles with 56 M901 I-TOW launchers		Hughes [GM]
	56 AN/UAS-12 passive night sights/d,e,g		Kollman Instrument
1983	M88A1 armored recovery vehicles/c	$9	Harsco
1986	685 5-ton trucks plus diagnostic test equipment and spares/c,f,g	$70	LTV
1987	Establishment of a flight training center/f	$9.9	McDonnell Douglas
1984	Improvement kits for 200 Hawk surface-to-air missiles/c,f	$82	Northrop & Raytheon
	1 AN/TSQ-73 Missile Minder radar/f		Litton
1985	Technical assistance and engineering for Hawk surface-to-air missiles/b,f	$5	Raytheon
1984	Air defense command, control and communication system/g	NA	Westinghouse
Lebanon			
1982	24 M113A2 armored personnel carriers/g	NA	FMC
1983	102 M113A2 armored personnel carriers	$57	FMC
	25 M577A2 command vehicles		
	93 M125A2 mortar carriers/d,g[15]		
1983	68 M48 main battle tanks/d,e[16]	NA	General Dynamics*
1984	35 M48A5 main battle tanks/d,e[16]	$64	General Dynamics*
1984	35 M60A3 main battle tanks/c,d,f	$28	General Dynamics
1982	4 M578 armored recovery vehicles/g[17]	$3	Harsco
1982	12 M109A2 155mm self-propelled howitzers/g	NA	Harsco

Date of Order	Description of Order	Price	Contractor
	Oman		
1985	300 AIM-9P4 Sidewinder air-to-air missiles/c,f,g,l	$22	Ford
1982	1C-130 Hercules transport aircraft/r	$13	Lockheed
1983	4 214ST Super Transport helicopters/d[1]	NA	Textron
	Saudi Arabia		
1987	1 C-12 Huron transport aircraft	$400	Beech
	15 model 406 Kiowa helicopters		Textron
	BGM-71 TOW anti-tank missiles for Kiowa helicopters		Hughes [GM]
	12 UH-60 Black Hawk helicopters and 1 VIP-configured Black Hawk/f		UTC
1981	5 E-3A Awacs, 6 KE-3A aerial refueling tankers, trainers, spares, and support services and equipment/b,d,e,f,g,h,r[18]	$8,500	Boeing
1983	111 rotary rudder servo actuators for F-15 fighter/b	$3	Boeing
1984	2 additional KE-3A aerial refueling tankers/b,r	NA	Boeing
1985	Command, control and communications equipment, support services and training for Project Peace Shield/b,f,g,h,r[19]	$1,200	Boeing
1986	Maintenance of E-3A Awacs and KE-3A aerial refueling tankers/f	$207	Boeing
1983	176 M113A2 armored personnel carriers 24 M106A2 mortar carriers 80 M577A2 command vehicles 62 M125A2 mortar carriers	$271[20]	FMC
	33 M578 armored recovery vehicles 111 M992 field artillery ammunition support vehicles 19 M88A1 armored recovery vehicles 18 M109A2 self-propelled howitzers/d,g		Harsco
1987	200 M2 Bradley infantry fighting vehicles/g	NA	FMC

Date of Order	Description of Order	Price	Contractor
1986	995 AIM-9L Sidewinder air-to-air missiles	$285[21]	Ford/Raytheon
	671 AIM-9P4 Sidewinder air-to-air missiles		Ford
	100 Harpoon anti-ship missiles/c,d,g		MDC
1983	100 M60A3 main battle tanks/d,f,g	$176	General Dynamics
1984	200 FIM-92A Stinger portable surface-to-air missile launchers with 400 missiles/d,e,g	$40[22]	General Dynamics
1986	16 AN/FPS-117(V) 3 long range radar systems for the Saudi Peace Shield program/b	$88	GE
1983	Inertial navigation units for E-3A Awacs/b[23]	$4.0	GM
1983	42 M198 155mm self-propelled howitzers/g	$42	Harsco
1983	18 M109A2 155mm self-propelled howitzers/d	NA	Harsco
(1985)	(214) M88A1 armored recovery vehicles/d	NA	Harsco
1982	2,010 BGM-71 I-TOW anti-tank missiles/d,f,g	$22	Hughes [GM]
1983	2,538 BGM-71 I-TOW anti-tank missiles/c,d,f,g	$26	Hughes [GM]
1984	2,538 additional BGM-71 I-TOW anti-tank missiles/c	$26	Hughes [GM]
1984	AN/TPQ-37 Firefinder artillery locating radar systems/r	NA	Hughes [GM]
1984	BGM-71 I-TOW anti-tank missiles/c	NA	Hughes [GM]
1986	2,263 5-ton and 2 1/2 ton trucks/c,g	NA[24]	LTV
1983	Contractor technical services for F-15 fighter aircraft/g[25]	$1,500	McDonnell Douglas
1983	Conformal fuel tanks for F-16 fighter aircraft/g	$3.8	McDonnell Douglas
1984	111 rudder servo actuators for F-15 fighter aircraft/f,g	$3.0	McDonnell Douglas
1984	Support for F-15 fighter aircraft/f	$167	McDonnell Douglas

Date of Order	Description of Order	Price	Contractor
1984	1 KC-10A tanker aircraft/d	NA	McDonnell Douglas
1986	100 aircraft fuel tanks/f	$30.9	McDonnell Douglas
1986	Contractor technical services for F-15 aircraft/g	$500	McDonnell Douglas
1982	4 F-5F Tiger II trainer aircraft,1 F-5F trainer aircraft, and 10 RF-5E Tiger Eye reconnaissance aircraft/d,e,g	NA[26]	Northrop
1984	Support follow-on for F-5 aircraft and F-15 aircraft bases/g	$330	Northrop
1987	95 AN/ALQ-171 electronic counter-measure systems to upgrade Saudi F-5 and F-15 aircraft/f	$325	Northrop
1986	Services, training and technology for Hawk anti-aircraft missile systems/f,g	$518	Raytheon
1984	Air Force Satellite Communications System equipment for E-3A Awacs/b	NA	Rockwell
1982	Operation and maintenance of land-based test site for combat systems used on patrol gunboats/b	14.2	Sperry
1983	Flight instruments and spares for weapons systems used on various aircraft/b	$5.6	Sperry
1983	629 Mk 12 Mode 4 Identification Friend or Foe electronic surveillance systems/b,c,g	$250	Teledyne
1983	65 TF-33-PW-100A engines/g	$10.9	UTC
1983	Additional funding for spare parts for AN/APY-1 radar systems for E-3A Awacs/b	NA[27]	Westinghouse
1985	AN/TPS-43 tactical 3-D radar/d	NA	Westinghouse

United Arab Emirates

Date of Order	Description of Order	Price	Contractor
1986	3 M998 Hummer multi-purpose wheeled vehicles/g	NA	LTV
1982	2 C-130 Hercules transport aircraft/d[13]	$22.9[14,28]	Lockheed
1984	5 batteries of Hawk air defense system/r	$114	Raytheon

Date of Order	Description of Order	Price	Contractor
1985	45 MIM-23B Hawk surface-to-air missiles/c,f,g	$21	Raytheon
1986	Engineering support of Hawk surface-to-air missile systems/f	$3.6	Raytheon
1986	8 AN/TRC-170 digital troposcatter radio systems with spares, support and testing equipment/c,f,g	$40	Raytheon

NOTES

1. These are commercially configured systems that frequently fulfill military roles.

2. This is part of a $140 million package that includes a small quantity of other vehicles.

3. These 40 F-16s are in addition to the 40 F-16s that Egypt purchased earlier.

4. The price of this package includes the cost of 40 additional trucks.

5. SIPRI reports that Egypt ordered 35 F-4s during the early 1980s.

6. The $404 million package includes 86 F100 engines sold to the U.S. Air Force, the Netherlands, Pakistan, South Korea, Egypt and Venezuela.

7. All of the MDC/Hughes helicopters sold to Iraq are civilian versions and therefore fall under the Export Administration Act and require approval of the Commerce Department, but not of the Departments of State and Defense or of Congress. The Commerce Department requires a special license for the export of all MDC/Hughes model 500 and 530 series helicopters to prevent exports to illegal recipients. The $25 million price tag of the 1983 sale includes training, ground equipment and spare parts.

8. Half of the purchase price is a U.S. government grant, with the other half covered by U.S. government credit that includes an offset agreement whereby $300 million of F-16 components are to be purchased in Israel. Reports of the total cost of the package vary. The International Institute for Strategic Studies reports the cost as $2.5 billion, the Defense Security Assistance Agency puts it at $2.2 billion, and SIPRI at $2.7 billion.

9. Under the Howitzer Improvement Program, Harsco was awarded a development contract to upgrade 11 prototype M109A2 howitzers to the M109A5 configuration for the U.S. Army and the Israeli Defense Forces. Harsco is leading a team that includes Honeywell, Emerson and RCA.

10. This sale was arranged under a Special Defense Acquisition Fund production contract.

11. Rockwell's records differ from IRRC's analysis of DoD contract data. According to the company, it received $20.0 million in this award: $18.0 million in 1984 and $1.0 million each in 1983 and 1985.

12. United Technologies' Norden Systems is developing a new radar system for the Israeli F-4 upgrade program. The reported cost of developing and integrating it is close to $500 million, including about $200 million in nonrecurring design and development costs.

13. These sales are direct company-to-government commercial sales.

14. Spares, training and miscellaneous items were included in the contract price.

15. According to some sources, the number of M113s involved in this transaction is 135 and the price $61 million. The package also includes M2 .50 caliber machine guns. Its status is unclear.

16. The status of these orders is unclear.

17. Some sources indicate that this order might have been placed in 1981.

18. The Saudi Awacs deal is listed in this study because of its size and scope, even though it was concluded in 1981. The Saudi KE-3A and E-3A Awacs aircraft are being re-engined with the CFM-56 powerplant.

19. Project Peace Shield was originally agreed upon by the governments of the United States and Saudi Arabia in 1981, and therefore technically is a 1981 order. A prime contractor was not selected, however, until February 1985.

20. SIPRI does not include the M109A2 self-propelled howitzers in the package.

21. Because of intense congressional opposition, the Reagan administration deleted 200 Stinger missile launchers with 600 missiles from this package.

22. Reports of the total price of this transaction vary. SIPRI and *Defense & Foreign Affairs* put the price at $30 million.

23. This is under a contract award of $21.6 million that also includes purchases for Japan, Egypt and the U.S. Air Force and Navy.

24. This is a $202 million package that includes 1,389 trailers and 129 ambulances plus spare parts and support. Some portion of the 2,263 trucks will be 1 1/4 ton trucks, which may not be manufactured by LTV.

25. Saudi Arabia purchased 60 F-15s in 1978, but was blocked by the U.S. Congress from purchasing 48 more of them in 1985.

26. This is part of a $350 million package.

27. This $26.9 million award includes parts to be used by NATO on its Awacs.

28. The contract price includes credit for two used C-130 trade-ins.

– ASIA AND PACIFIC –

Date of Order	Description of Order	Price	Contractor
	Brunei		
1986	2 S-70C commercial versions of Black Hawk helicopter/d	NA	UTC
	Burma		
1982	1 Citation II utility aircraft/d[1]	NA	Cessna [GD]
	India		
1987	11 F404 aircraft engines/g[2]	$22	GE
1986	5 Chukar III target drones and related equipment/g	$6.6	Northrop
1984	5 transducer arrays for sonar (via Fathom Co. of Canada)/f	$2.8	Westinghouse
	Indonesia		
1983	9 T-34C Turbo Mentor trainer aircraft/d,g	$12.4	Beech [Raytheon]
1983	4 Jetfoil (hydrofoil) patrol ships/d,e,r[3]	$150	Boeing
(1983)	28 Commando Scout armored reconnaissance cars/d	NA	Ex-Cell-O [Textron]
(1983)	22 Commando Ranger armored cars/d	NA	Ex-Cell-O [Textron]
1986	8 F-16A/B fighter aircraft	$432	GD
	72 AIM-9P Sidewinder air-to-air missiles		Ford
	AN/APG-66 radars		Westinghouse
	AN/ALR-69 radar warning receivers		Litton
	AN/ALQ-131 electronic countermeasure sets/c,d,e,g		Westinghouse
1982	48 Mk 46 model 2 torpedoes/c,g	$13	Honeywell
1987	8 Harpoon missiles/g	$6.5	MDC
1982	9 model 300C utility helicopters/d,g[1]	$2	MDC Helicopter
1982	Communications, navigation and pulse equipment/g	NA	Rockwell

Date of Order	Description of Order	Price	Contractor
1983	8 model 412ST Super Transport helicopters/d[1]	NA	Textron
1986	12 F100-PW-220 engines for F-16 aircraft/h	$60	UTC

Malaysia

1982	1 Super King Air transport aircraft/e[1]	NA	Beech [Raytheon]
(1983)	(84) AIM-9L Sidewinder air-to-air missiles/d	NA	Ford
1984	Refurbish 40 A-4 attack aircraft/h,r	$125	Grumman
1985	2 refurbished HU-16B Albatross maritime patrol aircraft/d	NA	Grumman
1985	14 F-5E and 2 F-5F Tiger II fighter aircraft/d[4]	$260	Northrop

Pakistan

1985	110 M113A2 armored personnel carrier/c,e,f,g	$25	FMC
1985	500 AIM-9L Sidewinder air-to-air missiles/c,e,f,g	$50	Ford & Raytheon
1982	100 M48A5 tanks	$117	General Dynamics*
	35 M88A1 recovery vehicles/d,g		Harsco
1983	4 Phalanx Mk 15 Close-in Weapon Systems/g	$38	General Dynamics
1984	100 M48A5 tanks/e	$42.1	General Dynamics*
1985	100 FIM-92 Stinger portable surface-to-air missiles/e,g	$8.5	General Dynamics
1986	Program definition for refurbishing unidentified aircraft/r[5]	$1.5	Grumman
1982	40 M110A2 203mm self-propelled howitzers/d,g	$176	Harsco
	64 M109A2 155 mm self-propelled howitzers		
	75 M198 155 mm self-propelled howitzers/d,g		USG

Date of Order	Description of Order	Price	Contractor
1982	36 M109A2 155mm self-propelled howitzers with guns, spares and support/d,e,f,g	$30	Harsco
1985	88 M109A2 155mm self-propelled howitzers with M2 50-caliber machine guns/c,f,g	$78	Harsco
1983	Bomb fuses for laser guided bombs/b	NA[6]	Honeywell
1982	10 AN/TPQ-36 mortar locating radar systems with spares and support/g	$40	Hughes [GM]
1985	15 AN/TPQ-36 mortar locating radar systems/c,f,g	$65	Hughes [GM]
1985	2,030 BGM-71C I-TOW anti-tank missiles/c,f	$19	Hughes [GM]
1985	4 AN/TPQ-37 Firefinder artillery locating radar systems/c,f,g	$41	Hughes [GM]
1986	F-16 logistics support/f	$3.6	Hughes [GM]
1986	2,030 BGM-71C I-TOW anti-tank missiles/c,f,g,e,h	$20	Hughes [GM]
1987	2,386 TOW-2 anti-tank missiles/g,h,n	$78	Hughes [GM]
1987	140 M809 5-ton trucks and 40 M44A2 2 1/2 ton trucks/g,n	$18.5	LTV
1984	16 RGM-84 Harpoon ship-to-surface missiles/e	$28.4	McDonnell Douglas
1985	Harpoon anti-ship missiles/c	NA	McDonnell Douglas
1984	2 RGM-84 Harpoon ship-to-surface missile systems with 16 missiles/d,e	$28.4	MDC
1985	Harpoon anti-ship missiles/c	NA	MDC
1985	Modernization of 2 solid-state transmitters in AN/SQS-23 shipboard sonar systems/f,j	$1.6	Raytheon
1983	Communication Electronic Warfare System (CEWS)/c	$21.4	Rockwell
1982	12 UH-1H Iroquois transport helicopters/d	NA	Textron#
1983	10 AH-15 TOW Cobra attack helicopters/c,d,f,g	$74	Textron

Date of Order	Description of Order	Price	Contractor
1985	F100 engines for F-16 fighter aircraft/b,f	NA[7]	UTC
People's Republic of China			
1985	Training and spares for 5 General Electric LM-2500 naval engines/g	NA	Ford
1985	5 LM-2500 gas turbine engines for naval destroyers/f,g	NA	GE
1987	Avionics and fire control systems for 55 F-8 fighter aircraft/h,1,n	$245	Grumman
1986	2 AN/TPQ-37 weapon locating radar systems/d,f,g	NA[8]	Hughes [GM]
1987	2 AN/TPQ-37 weapon locating radar systems/c	NA	Hughes [GM]
1984	24 S-70C Black Hawk utility helicopters (commercial version)/d,g[1]	$150	UTC
Philippines			
1982	10 V-150 Commando armored cars/d	NA	Ex-Cell-O [Textron]
1984	100 V-150 Commando armored cars/c,e,g	$30	Ex-Cell-O [Textron]
1982	55 LVT-7-A1 amphibious landing vehicles & support/d,f,g	$64	FMC
1984	24 M167 A1 20mm Vulcan towed air defense systems/c,e,f,g	$30	GE
1983	2 UH-60A Black Hawk and 17 S-76 Spirit utility helicopters/d,g	$60	UTC
(1985)	2 S-70C commercial versions of Black Hawk helicopter/d	NA	UTC
Singapore			
1985	8 F-16A/B fighter and trainer aircraft with spares and training	$330	General Dynamics
	8 P&W F100 jet engines/c,d,g,h		UTC
(1986)	6 Phalanx shipborne Close-in Weapon Systems/d	NA	General Dynamics
1985	F404 engines for A-4 upgrade program/h	NA	GE

Date of Order	Description of Order	Price	Contractor
1984	4 E-2C Hawkeye early warning aircraft/e,g,h,r,	$410	Grumman
1982	6 AN/TPQ-36 mortar locating radar systems/g	$30	Hughes Aircraft
1985	16 to 20 RGM-84A Harpoon ship-to-surface missiles/j,r	NA	McDonnell Douglas
1984	Classified military equipment/c	NA	McDonnell Douglas
1985	31 AGM-84A Harpoon anti-ship missiles for aircraft/d	NA	McDonnell Douglas
(1986)	6 RGM-84A Harpoon anti-ship missile systems with (72) missiles for 6 corvettes/d	NA	McDonnell Douglas
1984	6 F-5 Tiger II fighter aircraft/r	NA	Northrop
(1982)	(162) MIM-23B Hawk surface-to-air missiles/d	NA[9]	Raytheon

South Korea

Date of Order	Description of Order	Price	Contractor
1982	42 LVT-7-A1 amphibious landing vehicles/d,g	$59	FMC
1983	8 AN/AVO-26 Pave Tack designator pods, training and support/g	$50	Ford
1985	AIM-9 Sidewinder air-to-air missiles/c	NA	Ford & Raytheon
1982	36 F-16 fighter aircraft/d,g	($240)	General Dynamics
1985	133 Stinger portable surface-to-air missile systems with 599 reload rounds/c,d	$57	General Dynamics
1986	Standard (SM-1) missiles/c	NA	General Dynamics
1982	4 LM 2500 turbine engines for naval corvettes/f	NA	GE
1982	Self-propelled howitzers/r[10]	NA	Harsco
1983	BGM-71 TOW anti-tank missiles/c	$3.2	Hughes [GM]
1984	Laser rangefinder and thermal imaging systems/r	NA	Hughes [GM]
1986	1,410 AGM-65 Maverick air-to-surface missiles/c	NA	Hughes [GM]

Date of Order	Description of Order	Price	Contractor
1986	(504) BGM-71C I-TOW anti-tank missiles for 21 AH-1S helicopters/c,d	$6.5	Hughes [GM]
1982	6 F-4D Phantom fighter aircraft/c,d,f,g	$16.8	McDonnell Douglas
1984	3 RGM-84A Harpoon ship-to-surface missile systems with (64) missiles/d	NA	McDonnell Douglas
1985	4 F-4E modified fighter aircraft/c,e,f,g	$22	McDonnell Douglas#
1986	Harpoon anti-ship missiles/f	$20	McDonnell Douglas
1983	26 model 500MD Defender TOW missile armed scout helicopters/c,e	$12.5	MDC Helicopter
1985	Spares for F-5 Tiger II aircraft	$88	Northrop
	Spares for F-100 and F-104 aircraft/f		Lockheed
1982	28 modification kits for I-Hawk surface-to-air missiles/g	$72	Raytheon
	6 AN/TPQ-29 simulators		Applied Devices
1982	170 MIM-23B Hawk surface-to-air missiles including 720 rocket motors/c,d,f,g	$68	Raytheon
(1983)	(298) MIM-23B Hawk surface-to-air missiles/d	NA	Raytheon
1985	28 modification kits for I-Hawk surface-to-air missile system with spares, training and services/c,f,g	$61	Raytheon
1985	28 modification kits for I-Hawk missile systems/c	$53	Raytheon
1987	Upgrade of 28 Hawk surface-to-air missile systems/f,g	$84	Raytheon
1985	Electronic countermeasure equipment/f	$3	Teledyne
1985	21 AH-15 Cobra TOW attack helicopters T-53 turbine engines/f,h,m	$178	Textron Avco [Textron]
1986	AH-1 Cobra attack helicopters/g	$127.5[11]	Textron
1986	50 model 205 UH-1H Iroquois transport helicopters/c,d,f	$155	Textron
	60 T-53 turbine engines		Avco [Textron]

Date of Order	Description of Order	Price	Contractor
1985	F100-PW-220 engines for 36 F-16 fighters/f,k	$250	UTC

Sri Lanka

Date of Order	Description of Order	Price	Contractor
1985	4 model 212 helicopters/d	NA	Textron

Taiwan

Date of Order	Description of Order	Price	Contractor
1984	42 T-34C Turbo Mentor trainer aircraft/d,e,g	NA	Beech
1983	100 M113A2 armored personnel carriers 90 M106A2 mortar carriers 72 M125A2 mortar carriers 31 command post vehicles 24 M113A2 armored ambulances/d,g	$97	FMC
1983	384 MIM-72F Improved Chaparral surface-to-air missiles/c,d,g	$291	Ford
	120 Sea Chaparral surface-to-air missiles for mounting on ships/d,g		
1985	262 MIM-72F Chaparral surface-to-air missiles with 16 launch vehicles/e,g,h	$94	Ford
1986	262 Chaparral surface-to-air missiles with support/g	$13.2	Ford
1983	170 Standard (SM-1) RIM-66A ship-borne surface-to-air missiles and	$105	General Dynamics
	100 AIM-7F Sparrow air-to-air missiles/d,g		Raytheon
1984	50 to 75 M60 main battle tank hulls/e	$12.2	General Dynamics
1982	150 J85 engines	$240	GE
	60 AN/ALR-46 radar warning receivers		Litton
	60 AN/ALE-40 (v7) chaff/flare dispensers/g		Tracor
1986	32 upgrade kits for S-2 anti-submarine aircraft/h	$260	Grumman
1983	33 M88A1 armored recovery vehicles/c,d,g	$35.4	Harsco
1986	(1) AN/TPQ-37 mortar locating radar/d	NA	Hughes [GM]
1984	12 C-130 Hercules transport aircraft/c,e,f,g	$325	Lockheed

Date of Order	Description of Order	Price	Contractor
1982	30 F-5E and 30 F-5F Tiger II fighter aircraft/f,g	$622	Northrop
1986	14 S-70C Black Hawk helicopters/d,e	NA	UTC

Thailand

Date of Order	Description of Order	Price	Contractor
1986	T-53 turbine engines for Bell Textron AH-1 Cobra TOW helicopters/c,d,f,g	NA	Avco [Textron]
(1983)	1 Super King Air transport aircraft/d[1]	NA	Beech (Raytheon)
(1984)	4 0-2 Super Skymaster spotter/forward air control aircraft/d	NA	Cessna [GD]*
1985	10 model 208 Caravan I lightplanes/d	NA	Cessna [GD]
1982	148 M113A2 armored personnel carriers/d,g	NA	FMC
1984	21 LVT-7-A1 amphibious landing vehicles/e	NA	FMC
1983	AIM-9P3 Sidewinder air-to-air missiles/c	$4.7	Ford
1983	20 MIM-43A Redeye portable surface-to-air missiles/d	NA	General Dynamics
1984	40 M48A5 tanks with ancillary equipment/c	$32	General Dynamics#
1984	(1) Phalanx Close-in Weapon System/d	NA	General Dynamics
1985	8 F-16A fighter and 4 F-16B trainer aircraft with training and spare parts/d, e,f,k,l,r	$360	General Dynamics
1987	6 F-16A/B fighter aircraft/h,n	$115	General Dynamics
1982	24 M167 A1 20 mm Vulcan towed air defense systems with radar, communications equipment, and spares/f,g	$23	GE
1983	J85 engines/c	$1.8	GE
(1986)	AN/MPQ-4 mortar-locating radar/d	NA	GE
1983	Bomb fuses for laser guided bombs/b	NA[6]	Honeywell
1982	3 AN/TPQ-36 mortar locating radar systems/f,g	$26	Hughes [GM]
1982	1 C-130 Hercules transport aircraft/b	$15.4	Lockheed

Date of Order	Description of Order	Price	Contractor
1986	150 M998 Hummer multi-purpose wheeled vehicles/g	NA	LTV
1983	2 RGM-84A Harpoon ship-to-surface missile systems with 24 missiles/c,d	$11.5	MDC
(1986)	(24) model 300C utility helicopters/d	NA	MDC Helicopter
1984	2 RF-5E Tiger Eye reconnaissance aircraft and 8 F-5E Tiger II fighter aircraft/d,e	NA	Northrop
1984	UHF and VHF radios and transceivers/b	$5.9[12]	Rockwell
1982	12 UH-1H Iroquois transport helicopters/d,g[1]	$30	Textron
1984	4 model 214ST Super Transport helicopters/e	NA	Textron
1984	2 model 214ST Super Transport helicopters/d,e,g	NA	Textron
1986	4 AH-1 Cobra TOW helicopers Spare engines/d,f,g	$45	Textron Avco [Textron]
(1986)	(5) model 214ST transport helicopters/d	NA	Textron
1983	4 UH-60 Black Hawk helicopters/d,g	$38	UTC
1985	1 AN/TPS-70 mobile ground-based tactical radar system/g	$10	Westinghouse
1986	AN/APG-66 radar systems for F-16 aircraft/f,g	$8.03	Westinghouse

NOTES

1. These are commercially configured systems that frequently fulfill military roles.

2. This is part of a package that includes gas turbine engines of unknown manufacture, which are valued at $38 million. These engines will be employed on Indian frigates.

3. SIPRI reports that Indonesia has an option for six hydrofoil patrol boats and a license production run of 36. The company's annual report confirms only the option for six Jetfoils.

4. This sale was initiated in 1982, postponed, and resurrected in 1985.

5. Under this exploratory contract, Grumman proposes to install a new nose section, engines and avionics systems on unidentified aircraft. The company says full production would entail modifying 150 aircraft and an award worth approximately $500 million.

6. This contract award of $3.9 million is divided between Pakistan and Thailand.

7. This $404 million package includes 86 F100 engines sold to the U.S. Air Force, the Netherlands, Pakistan, South Korea, Egypt and Venezuela.

8. This is a $62 million package that includes 8 AN/VRC-46 radio sets that are manufactured by various contractors, ancillary and support equipment, spare parts and maintenance.

9. Additional missiles and launchers are reportedly on order.

10. This sale was expanded into a coproduction agreement in 1981.

11. This contract is most likely in support of the South Korean AH-1 coproduction program.

12. Rockwell's records differ from IRRC's analysis of DoD contract data. According to the company, it received $1.6 million in this award.

– AFRICA –

Date of Order	Description of Order	Price	Contractor
	Algeria		
1982	8 C-130 Hercules transport aircraft/d[1]	$152.3[2]	Lockheed
1984	3 C-130 Hercules transport aircraft/d[1]	$92.5	Lockheed
	Botswana		
1986	(12) V-150 Commando armored cars/d	NA	Ex-Cell-O [Textron]
(1986)	6 model 206B JetRanger helicopters/d	NA	Textron
	Cameroon		
1982	2 V-150 Commando armored cars/d	NA	Ex-Cell-O [Textron]
1982	1 C-130 Hercules transport aircraft/d[1]	$19[2]	Lockheed
(1986)	(6) UH-60 Black Hawk helicopters/d	NA	UTC
	Chad		
1983	MIM-43A Redeye portable surface-to-air missiles/d,g	NA[3]	General Dynamics#
1985	6 V-150 Commando armored cars/d	NA	Ex-Cell-O [Textron]
1986	2 C-130B Hercules transport aircraft/d	Grant	Lockheed#
1986	(1) Hawk mobile surface-to-air missile system with 27 missiles/d	NA	Raytheon
	Djibouti		
1986	83 M939A1 five-ton trucks/g	$3.7	LTV
1986	10 M998 Hummer multi-purpose wheeled vehicles/g	NA	LTV
	Gabon		
1985	4 T-34 Turbo Mentor trainer aircraft/e	NA	Beech [Raytheon]
(1985)	(15) V-150 Commando armored personnel carriers/d	NA	Ex-Cell-O [Textron]

Date of Order	Description of Order	Price	Contractor
	Kenya		
1985	8 model 500MD Defender scout helicopters/e	NA	MDC Helicopter
	Morocco		
(1983)	1 Super King Air transport aircraft/d	NA	Beech [Raytheon]
(1982)	108 M60A3 main battle tanks/d	NA	General Dynamics
1982	381 AGM-65B Maverick air-to-surface missiles/d,g	$29	Hughes [GM]
1983	BGM-71 TOW anti-tank missiles/c	$15	Hughes [GM]
(1985)	BGM-71C I-TOW anti-tank missiles/d	NA	Hughes [GM]
(1985)	1 KC-130H tanker/transport aircraft/d	NA	Lockheed#
1985	Receiver transmitters for the APX 101 Identification Friend or Foe system for aircraft/b	NA[4]	Teledyne
	Nigeria		
1983	5 Chinook Model 414 heavy lift helicopters/d,r	$74	Boeing
1983	3 C-130 Hercules transport aircraft/d[1]	$71.3[2]	Lockheed
1983	Radio system for use with Air Force satellite/b	NA[5]	Rockwell
	Somalia		
1983	Radio system for use with Air Force satellite communication system/b	NA[5]	Rockwell
	Sudan		
1982	2 V-150 Commando armored cars/d	NA	Ex-Cell-O [Textron]
1984	36 V-150 Commando armored cars/d,e,g	$10.7	Ex-Cell-O [Textron]
1984	V-150 Commando armored cars/e,g	NA	Ex-Cell-O [Textron]
1985	Maintenance of 6 C-130 Hercules transport aircraft/f	$.5	Lockheed
1984	2 F-5E Tiger II fighter aircraft/d	NA	Northrop

Date of Order	Description of Order	Price	Contractor
(1986)	24 V-150 Commando armored cars/d	NA	Ex-Cell-O [Textron]

Tunisia

Date of Order	Description of Order	Price	Contractor
1982	54 M60A3 main battle tanks/d	NA	General Dynamics
1983/84	19 M109A2 155mm self-propelled howitzers/d,e[6]	NA	Harsco
1986	70 5-ton trucks and 3 5-ton wreckers/c,g	NA[7]	LTV
1984	2 C-130 Hercules transport aircraft/d,e,f[1]	$48[2]	Lockheed
1982	8 F-5E and 4 F-5F Tiger II fighter aircraft/d,e,g	$200	Northrop
1984	Precision measurement equipment lab for Air Force repair work/b	$6.5	Sperry

NOTES

1. These sales are direct company-to-government commercial sales.

2. Spares, training and miscellaneous items were included in the contract price.

3. The Redeyes are part of a $25 million package that includes jeeps, food and clothing.

4. This $11.4 million award will be divided between the U.S. Air Force and Morocco.

5. Purchases by Nigeria, Somalia and NATO were combined under a single $4.5 million award.

6. SIPRI reports this sale as having been initiated in 1981.

7. This is part of a $60 million package including 57 U.S. government-manufactured M198 howitzers and ammunition.

– LATIN AMERICA –

Date of Order	Description of Order	Price	Contractor
Bolivia			
1986	6 UH-1 Iroquois helicopters/d,g	Grant	Textron
Brazil			
1985	Conversion of 4 B-707 transports to aerial refueling tankers/r	NA	Boeing
1983	12 to 16 LVTP-7-A1 amphibious landing craft/d,e,g	NA	FMC
1984	12 BGM-71 TOW anti-tank missiles/e,g	NA	Hughes [GM]
1986	3 C-130 Hercules transport aircraft/c	$49.6	Lockheed
1985	16 model 206 JetRanger III trainer helicopters/e,g	NA	Textron
(1985)	1 model 412 helicopter/d	NA	Textron
1984	4 SH-3D Sea King anti-submarine warfare helicopters/e	NA	UTC
Chile			
(1984)	1 C-90 King Air transport aircraft/d[1]	NA	Beech [Raytheon]
Colombia			
1982	12 A-37B Dragonfly attack aircraft/c,d,g	$11.7	Cessna [GD]
1982	4 C-130 Hercules transport aircraft/d	NA	Lockheed#
1984	2 C-130 Hercules transport aircraft/d,e,g[2]	$39.5[3]	Lockheed
(1983)	8 model 300C utility helicopters/d[1]	NA	MDC Helicopter
Costa Rica			
(1984)	2 model 206 Stationair 6 utility aircraft/g[1]	NA	Cessna [GD]
1985	2 A-37 Dragonfly attack aircraft/g	NA	Cessna [GD]
1985	2 T-41 Mescalaro trainer aircraft/e,g	NA	Cessna [GD]
(1984)	(3) M113A2 armored personnel carriers/d	NA	FMC
1985	4 model 500E utility helicopters/e,g[1]	NA	MDC Helicopter

Date of Order	Description of Order	Price	Contractor
	Dominican Republic		
1984	12 A-37 Dragonfly attack aircraft/g	$2.5	Cessna [GD]
	Ecuador		
1985	25 T-33A Bonanza jet trainers/d	NA[4]	Beech
1982	A-37B Dragonfly attack aircraft/d	NA	Cessna [GD]
	El Salvador		
1982	6 A-37 Dragonfly attack aircraft/d,e	$25	Cessna [GD]*
	4 0-2 Super Skymaster spotter/forward air control aircraft/e,g		Cessna [GD]*
	3 C-123 transport aircraft/e		Fairchild*
	6 UH-1H helicopters		Textron*
1984	12 A-37 Dragonfly attack aircraft/e	$2.5	Cessna [GD]
1985	3 A-37 Dragonfly attack aircraft/e,g	NA	Cessna [GD]
1986	1 A-37 Dragonfly attack aircraft	NA	Cessna [GD]
	6 UH-1H Iroquois and 12 UH-1N Twin Huey attack helicopters/d,g		Textron
1984	1 converted DC-3 transport aircraft/g	$1.5	McDonnell Douglas
1985	4 model 500MD Defender scout helicopters/e,g	NA	MDC Helicopter
1985	10 model 500E utility helicopters/g[1]	NA	MDC Helicopter
(1986)	(6) model 300C utility helicopters/d	NA	MDC Helicopter
1984	PRC 515 high frequency radio packsets/b	$1.1	Rockwell
	Haiti		
(1983)	1 A-36 Bonanza utility aircraft/d[1]	NA	Beech [Raytheon]
	Honduras		
1984	6 A-37B Dragonfly attack aircraft/d	NA	Cessna [GD]
1987	10 F-5E fighter aircraft and 2 F-5F trainer aircraft/n	$72	Northrop
1985	5 model 412 helicopters/d	NA	Textron

Date of Order	Description of Order	Price	Contractor
1986	5 Bell 412 helicopters/d,e,f,g	$13.4	Textron
Mexico			
(1984)	4 F-33C Bonanza utility aircraft/d[1]	NA	Beech [Raytheon]
1986	21 F33C Bonanza utility aircraft/e,g	$4.9	Beech [Raytheon]
Panama			
(1984)	(5) A-37B Dragonfly attack aircraft/d	NA	Cessna [GD]
1982	12 V-300 Commando armored cars/d	NA	Ex-Cell-O [Textron]
1984	12 V-300 Commando armored cars/e	NA	Ex-Cell-O [Textron]
Peru			
1983	6 model 214ST Super Transport helicopters/c,d,f	$65	Textron
1984	25 model 212 helicopters/j	NA	Textron
1983	8 UH-60A Black Hawk helicopters/e	$110.5	UTC
Uruguay			
1982	5 S-2G Tracker antisubmarine warfare aircraft/d	NA	Grumman
Venezuela			
(1982)	2 Super King Air transport aircraft/d[1]	NA	Beech [Raytheon]
1983	AIM-9P3 Sidewinder air-to-air missiles/c	$2.9	Ford
1982	24 F-16 fighter aircraft/d,e,g,r	$616	General Dynamics
1983	Radio installation in F-16 aircraft/g	$5	General Dynamics
1984	4 SH-3D Sea King anti-submarine warfare helicopters/e	NA	UTC
1985	F100 engines for F-16 aircraft/f	NA[5]	UTC

NOTES

1. These are commercially configured systems that frequently fulfill military roles.

2. These sales are direct company-to-government commercial sales.

3. Spares, training and miscellaneous items were included in the contract price.

4. These are ex-U.S. reserve aircraft, which were refurbished to AT-33 specifications before being transferred to Ecuador.

5. This $404 million package includes 86 F100 engines that were sold to the U.S. Air Force, the Netherlands, Pakistan, South Korea, Egypt and Venezuela.

Bibliography

Arlinghaus, Bruce E., ed. *Arms for Africa*. Lexington, Mass.: Lexington Books, 1983.

Arlinghaus, Bruce E. *Military Development in Africa: The Political and Economic Risks of Arms Transfers*. Boulder, Colo.: Westview Press, 1984.

Ball, Nicole. *The Military in the Development Process*. Claremont, Calif.: Regina Books, 1981.

Benoit, Emile. *Defense and Economic Growth in Developing Countries*. Lexington, Mass.: Lexington Books, 1973.

Blaufarb, Douglas S. *The Counterinsurgency Era: U.S. Doctrine and Performance*. New York: Macmillan Publishing Co., 1977.

Brzoska, Michael, and Thomas Ohlson, eds. *Arms Production in the Third World*. Philadelphia: Taylor & Francis, 1986.

Brzoska, Michael. *Shades of Grey: Ten Years of South African Arms Procurement in the Shadow of the Mandatory Arms Embargo*. Hamburg, FRG: University of Hamburg, Centre for the Study of Wars, Armaments and Development, 1987.

Cahn, Anne Hessing; Joseph J. Kruzel; Peter M. Dawkins; and Jacques Huntzinger. *Controlling Future Arms Trade*. New York: McGraw-Hill Book Company, 1977.

Cannizo, Cindy. *The Gun Merchants: Politics and Policies of the Major Arms Suppliers*. New York: Pergamon Press, 1980. Center for International Policy. *Human Rights and the U.S Foreign Assistance Program, Fiscal Year 1978*. Washington: Center for International Policy, 1977.

Chan, Steve. "The Impact of Defense Spending on Economic Performance: A Survey of Evidence and Problems." *Orbis* (Summer 1985).

Congressional Budget Office (CBO). *Foreign Military Sales and U.S. Weapons Cost*. Washington: CBO, May 5, 1976.

Congressional Research Service (CRS). *Changing Perspectives on U.S. Arms Transfer Policy*. Washington: U.S. Government Printing Office, Sept. 25, 1981.

Congressional Research Service. *Executive-Legislative Consultation on U.S. Arms Sales*. Washington: U.S. Government Printing Office, 1982.

Congressional Research Service. *U.S. Military Sales and Assistance Programs: Laws, Regulations, and Procedures*. Washington: U.S. Government Printing Office, 1985.

Cornell, Alexander H. "Collaboration in Weapons and Equipment." *NATO Review* (October 1980).

Defense Agency of Japan. *Defense of Japan*. Tokyo: Japan Times Ltd., 1986.

Deger, Saadet, and Ron Smith. "Military Expenditure and Growth in Less Developed Countries." *Journal of Conflict Resolution* (June 1983).

Downen, Robert L. *The Tattered China Card: Reality or Illusion in United States Strategy*. Washington: Council for Social and Economic Studies, 1984.

Drifte, Reinhard. *Arms Production in Japan: The Military Applications of Civilian Technology*. Boulder, Colo.: Westview Press, 1986.

Edmonds, Martin, ed. *International Arms Procurement: New Directions*. New York: Pergamon Press, 1981.

Einaudi, Luigi; Hans Heymann, Jr.; David Ronfeldt; and Caesar Sereseres. *Arms Transfers to Latin America*. Santa Monica, Calif.: Rand Corp., 1973.

Farley, Philip J.; Stephen S. Kaplan; and William H. Lewis. *Arms Across the Sea*. Washington: The Brookings Institution, 1978.

Frankel, Francine. "Play the India Card," *Foreign Policy* 62 (Spring 1986).

Frost, Ellen. *For Richer, For Poorer: The New U.S.-Japan Relationship*. New York: Council on Foreign Relations, 1987.

Ghosh, Pradip K., ed. *Disarmament and Development*. Westport, Conn.: Greenwood Press, 1984.

Graves, Ernest, and Steven A. Hildreth, eds. *U.S. Security Assistance: The Political Process*. Lexington, Mass.: D.C. Heath and Co., 1985.

Grimmett, Richard. *Trends in Conventional Arms Transfers to the Third World By Major Supplier, 1979–1986*. Washington: Congressional Research Service, May 15, 1987, and earlier editions.

Hagan, Lawrence S. *Twisting Arms: Political, Military and Economic Aspects of Arms Cooperation in the Atlantic Alliance*. Kingston, Canada: Centre for International Relations, 1980.

Hammond, Paul; David J. Louscher; Michael D. Salomone; and Norman A. Graham. *The Reluctant Supplier: U.S. Decisionmaking for Arms Sales*. Cambridge, Mass.: Oelgeschlager, Gunn & Hain, Publishers Inc., 1983.

Harkavy, Robert. *The Arms Trade and International Systems*. Cambridge, Mass.: Ballinger Publishing Co., 1975.

Heritage Foundation. "New Directions in Security Assistance." Washington: High Frontier, May 1981.

International Institute for Strategic Studies (IISS). *The Military Balance 1985–1986*. London: IISS, 1986 and earlier editions.

International Institute for Strategic Studies (IISS). *Strategic Survey 1985–1986*. London: IISS, 1986 and earlier editions.

"The Arms Trade." *Journal of International Affairs*. vol. 40/no. 1 (Summer 1986).

Kelleher, Catherine M., and Gale A. Mattox, eds. *Evolving European Defense Policies*. Lexington, Mass.: Lexington Books, 1987.

Kennedy, Gavin. *The Military in the Third World*. London: Duckworth Press, 1974.

Klare, Michael. *American Arms Supermarket*. Austin, Tex.: University of Texas Press, 1984.

Klare, Michael, and Cynthia Arnson. *Supplying Repression: U.S. Support for Authoritarian Regimes Abroad*. Washington: Institute for Policy Studies, 1981.

Labrie, Roger P.; John G. Hutchins; and Edwin W.A. Peura. *U.S. Arms Sales Policy: Background and Issues*. Washington: American Enterprise Institute for Public Policy Research, 1982.

Louscher, David J., and Michael D. Salomone, eds. *Marketing Security Assistance: New Perspectives on Arms Sales*. Lexington, Mass.: Lexington Books, 1987.

Louscher, David J., and Michael D. Salomone. *Technology Transfer and U.S. Security Assistance: The Impact of Licensed Production*. Boulder, Colo.: Westview Press, 1987.

Nakada, Yasuhisa. "Japan's Security Perceptions and Military Needs." In O. Marwah and J.D. Pollack, eds., *Military Power and Policy in Asian States*. Boulder, Colo.: Westview Press, 1980.

Neuman, Stephanie. "The Arms Trade and American National Interests" in Vojtech Mastny, ed., *Power and Policy in Transition*. Westport, Conn.: Greenwood Press, 1984.

Neuman, Stephanie. *Military Assistance in Recent Wars: The Dominance of the Superpowers*. New York: Praeger Publishers, 1986.

Neumann, Stephanie, and Robert G. Harkavy, eds. *Arms Transfers in the Modern World*. New York: Praeger Books, 1979.

Newhouse, John. "Politics and Weapons Sales." *The New Yorker* (June 9, 1986).

Okazaki, Hisahiko. *A Grand Strategy for Japanese Defense*. Lanham, Md.: Abt Books, 1986.

Paul, Jim. "The Egyptian Arms Industry." *Merip Reports* (February 1983).

Pearson, Frederic S. "Of Leopards and Cheetahs: West Germany's Role as a Mid-Sized Arms Supplier." *Orbis* (Spring 1985).

Pierre, Andrew, ed. *Arms Transfers and American Foreign Policy*. New York: New York University Press, 1979.

Pierre, Andrew. *The Global Politics of Arms Sales*. Princeton, N.J.: Princeton University Press, 1982.

Ra'anan, Uri; Robert L. Pfaltzgraff Jr.; and Geoffrey Kemp. *Arms Transfers to the Third World: The Military Buildup in Less Industrial Countries*. Boulder, Colo.: Westview Press, 1978.

Sampson, Anthony. *The Arms Bazaar*. New York: The Viking Press, 1977.

Schoultz, Lars. *Human Rights and United States Policy toward Latin America*. Princeton, N.J.: Princeton University Press, 1981.

Secretary-General of the United Nations, Department for Disarmament Affairs. *Economic and Social Consequences of the Arms Race and of Military Expenditures*. New York: United Nations, 1983.

Sivard, Ruth Leger. *World Military and Social Expenditures*. 1986 edition. Washington: World Priorities, 1987 and earlier editions.

Smith, Chris. "Arms for the Middle East: Open Season for the Superpowers." *The Middle East* (September 1982).

Sorley, Lewis. *Arms Transfers Under Nixon*. Lexington, Ky.: University of Kentucky Press, 1983.

Stockholm International Peace Research Institute (SIPRI). *World Armaments and Disarmament Yearbook 1987*. New York: Oxford University Press, 1987 and earlier editions.

Tuomi, Helena, and Raimo Vayrynen. *Transnational Corporations, Armaments and Development*. New York: St. Martin's Press, 1982.

U.S. Department of Defense. *Congressional Presentation for Security Assistance Programs*. Fiscal Year 1988. Washington: U.S. Government Printing Office, 1987 and earlier editions.

U.S. Department of Defense, Defense Security Assistance Agency (DSAA). "1986 Fiscal Year Series." Washington: DSAA, 1987 and earlier editions.

U.S. Department of Defense, Defense Security Assistance Agency. *Foreign Military Sales, Foreign Military Construction Sales and Military Assistance Facts 1986*. Washington: DSAA, 1987 and earlier editions.

U.S. Department of Defense, Defense Security Assistance Agency. *Weapons Acquisition Report (WAR) 1986*. Washington: DSAA, 1987.

U.S. Department of Defense, Office of the Under Secretary of Defense for Research and Engineering. *Report of Defense Science Board Task Force on Industry-to-Industry International Armaments Cooperation Phase III-Japan*. Washington: Government Printing Office, June 1984.

U.S. Department of State. *Conventional Arms Transfers in the Third World, 1972–1981*, Special Report No. 102. Washington: U.S. Government Printing Office, August 1982.

U.S. Department of State. *Report to Congress Pursuant to Section 508 of the Comprehensive Anti-Apartheid Act of 1986: Compliance with the U.N. Arms Embargo*. Washington: U.S. Department of State, April 1987.

U.S. Department of State, Arms Control and Disarmament Agency (ACDA). *World Military Expenditures and Arms Transfers 1986*. Washington: ACDA, 1986 and earlier editions.

U.S. General Accounting Office. *Military Loans: Repayment Problems Mount as Debt Increases*. Washington: U.S. Government Printing Office, October 1985.

U.S. General Accounting Office. *Opportunities to Improve Decisionmaking and Oversight of Arms Sales*. Washington: U.S. Government Printing Office, May 1979.

U.S. General Accounting Office. *U.S. Security and Military Assistance: Programs and Related Activities*. Washington: General Accounting Office, 1982.

U.S. General Accounting Office. *U.S. Security and Military Assistance: Programs and Related Activities—An Update*. Washington: General Accounting Office, 1985.

U.S. Japan Advisory Commission. *Challenges and Opportunities in United States-Japan Relations*. Washington: U.S. Government Printing Office, September 1984.

U.S. Senate Committee on Foreign Relations. *Prospects for Multilateral Arms Export Restraint*. Washington: U.S. Government Printing Office, 1979.

U.S. Senate Democratic Policy Committee. *An Unconventional Arms Policy: Selling Ourselves Short, Promotion of Foreign Military Sales to the Developing World Under the Reagan Administration*. Washington: U.S. Government Printing Office, 1983.

Williams, Phil. *U.S. Troops in Europe*. London: Routledge & Kegan Paul, 1984.

Wulf, Herbert. "West European Cooperation and Competition in Arms Procurement: Experiments, Problems, Prospects." *Arms Control: Journal of Arms Control and Disarmament* (September 1986).